Birding
in Connecticut

A Driftless Connecticut Series Book

This book is a 2018 selection in the Driftless Connecticut Series, for an outstanding book in any field on a Connecticut topic or written by a Connecticut author.

Birding
in Connecticut

Frank Gallo

Wesleyan University Press
Middletown, Connecticut

Dedication

This book is dedicated to my mother, Eileen, who started me on my journey and has been there with me through it all. All my love.

And to the memory of my mentors and friends now gone, Ed Shove, fearless leader of the Lighthouse Hawk Watch; Noble Proctor; Sal Masotta; George and Millie Letis; Richard Haley; Mark Hoffman; and Lee Aimesbury. And to Marion Aimesbury, who, happily, is still with us. Thank you all.

Wesleyan University Press
Middletown CT 06459
www.wesleyan.edu/wespress
© 2018 Frank Gallo
All rights reserved
Manufactured in the United States of America
Designed by Nord Compo
Typeset in France by Nord Compo
All the photos are Frank Gallo's except where noted Mark S. Szantyr.

The Driftless Connecticut Series is funded by the
Beatrice Fox Auerbach Foundation Fund
at the Hartford Foundation for Public Giving

5 4 3 2

Library of Congress Cataloging-in-Publication Data
Names: Gallo, Frank (Naturalist), author.
Title: Birding in Connecticut / Frank Gallo.
Description: Middletown, Connecticut : Wesleyan University Press, [2018] |
Series: Garnet books | Includes bibliographical references and index. |
Identifiers: LCCN 2017046022 (print) | LCCN 2017050274 (ebook) | ISBN
9780819576361 (ebook) | ISBN 9780819576354 (pbk. : alk. paper)
Subjects: LCSH: Bird watching--Connecticut--Guidebooks. |
Birds--Connecticut--Identification.
Classification: LCC QL677.5 (ebook) | LCC QL677.5 .G3545 2018 (print) | DDC
598.072/34746--dc23
LC record available at https://lccn.loc.gov/2017046022

CONTENTS

THE NORTHWEST HIGHLANDS

THE CENTRAL INTERIOR

THE SOUTHEAST COAST

FOREWORD

In the early 1970s, a common question among fellow birders was, "Where can I go to see such and such species, and how can I get there?" In response to that often-asked question, I chose twenty-five sites in Connecticut that would take birders to easily accessible habitats and produce a wide selection of bird species. This was published over thirty years ago as *25 Birding Areas in Connecticut*. As might be expected, many of the sites have changed dramatically since then. Some have practically disappeared due to the encroachment of buildings; others have been sealed off by private lands. Only a few have remained stable. Birding itself also has changed significantly in Connecticut, with an incredible increase in the numbers of birders in the field.

Bird populations throughout the state have changed remarkably as well. Species that once were extremely rare, such as American Oystercatcher, are now breeding here. In the early 1960s, I can remember spending eight hours at a backyard feeder, hoping to glimpse a Red-bellied Woodpecker. Now, they are one of the most common woodpecker species in the area. Forty years ago, species such as Common Raven and Black Vulture would have been out of the question for Connecticut; we would have had to travel (either north or far to the south, respectively) to find them. Today, ravens nest throughout the state and Black Vultures can be seen in flocks of more than fifty individuals.

Yet another change has been the widespread loss of open fields. A decline in nesting grassland species has followed, to the point where only small pockets of breeders are left. In direct contrast, our woodlands have increased and woodland residents such as Cooper's Hawks have moved from rare to common. Given all of these changes, it is obviously time for an update of the guide I published for birders so many years ago.

In 1980, when Frank Gallo first walked into my ornithology class at Southern Connecticut State University, it was clear that he was dedicated to learning as much about birds as he could. This dedication has persisted over the years, and Frank now knows every key birding location in Connecticut. Although he has traveled widely, New England remains his favorite spot for birding ventures. He is, therefore, the ideal person to update and expand the approach of my earlier book.

Birding in Connecticut offers a trove of birding information. The records of past occurrences of rare species, information on their population changes over time, as well as updated material on when and where such species can be presently found makes this the best available guide to the top birding sites in Connecticut.

Take it with you every time you go afield: it will prove a constant resource and lead to many exciting days. By knowing the key times and places to find specific species, you will enhance not only your birding skills but also your success and enjoyment of birding in Connecticut.

Noble S. Proctor, PhD, Professor Emeritus,
Southern Connecticut State University

ACKNOWLEDGMENTS

Writing a book such as this takes the input of a village of birders. The task would have been insurmountable without the help and encouragement of so many. I thank you all: Marion Aimesbury, Michael Anderson, Joe Bear, Steve Bird, Andy Brand, Milan Bull, Jerry and Janet Connolly, Louise Crocco, Julio de la Torre, Buzz Devine, Angela Dimmitt, Patrick and Jim Dugan, Ken Elkins, Daniel Field, Eileen, John, Pam, and Paul Gallo, Sean Greasser, Tina Green, Andy Griswold, John Himmelman, Julian Hough, Jim Hunter, Denise Jernigan, Jay Kaplan, Scott Kruitbosch, Twan Leenders, Carol and Gary Lemmon, Michael Moccio, Frank Mantlik, Shai Mitra, Dan and Karen Mercurio, Don Morgan, Keith Mueller, Jacob Musser, Gina Nichol, Brian O'Toole, Noble Proctor, Parker Smathers, Suzanna Tamminen, Jesus Tirado, Luke Tiller, Joan Walsh, Sara Zagorski, Anthony Zemba, Marla Zubel, Amy Zvonar, Fran Zygmont, Kristof Zyskowski, all the CT Birders, the wonderful staff at WUP and UPNE, and, of course, the cats. If I've forgotten anyone, my humble apologies; feel free to chastise me. I'll correct my memory lapses in the future.

I'd like to thank dearest Vanessa Mickan, for all she did; without her, this book wouldn't exist. Mike Tucker and Hough Willoughby deserve special accolades; Rhode Island is coming. Nick Bonomo, Carolyn Cimino, Patrick Comins, Bob Dixon, Ken Elkins, Sarah Heminway, Stefan Martin, Brian O'Toole, James Purcell, Andy Rzeznikiewicz, Phil Rusch, Dave Tripp, Glenn Williams, and Jay Withgott all went above and beyond. Many, many, thanks.

I need to single out and thank my dear friends Margaret Rubega, Chris Elphick, and their sons, Owen and Adam, who adopted me while I wrote much of this book. Chris made the first edits on many of the chapters, making this a better book and me a better writer. (Any mistakes are mine).

Old friends Mark Szantyr and Pat Lynch came through when needed most, as they always do; you're the best. I thank my wise friend Greg Hanisek for his insights and for the use of his wonderful bar charts, and Russell Galen and David Sibley; they both know why.

Birding
in Connecticut

Introduction

This book is about the bird life of Connecticut and includes the best birding sites in the state. I have purposely included sites not found in earlier guides, adding some off-the-beaten-track hotspots, while retaining and updating information on essential sites well known to area birders.

Connecticut is located on the Atlantic Flyway, one of North America's four major migratory corridors used by birds moving to and from their wintering and breeding grounds. The state's ridgelines, rivers, and nearly 620 miles of coastline provide pathways for birds to follow, sometimes helping to funnel them to specific locations, particularly along the coast.

The state lies within an ecological and geographical transition zone for plants and animals, a region of overlap where, for example, Common Raven from the north meets Black Vulture from the south, as each species continues to expand its range. Several southern species near the northern limit of their range here, including White-eyed Vireo, Acadian Flycatcher, Yellow-throated and Prothonotary Warblers, Blue Grosbeak, and Chuck-wills-widow. Northern species include Olive-sided, Least, and Alder Flycatchers, Golden-crowned Kinglet, Hermit Thrush, Dark-eyed Junco, White-throated Sparrow, and Nashville, Magnolia, and Mourning Warblers. To Connecticut's breeding list can now be added Mississippi Kite, a southern visitor, and possibly Clay-colored Sparrow from the north and west. Periodically, additional species reach our area. Golden Eagle, Merlin, and Sandhill Crane now nest in New England. All three could conceivably breed in Connecticut, as suitable habitat exists. What species will be next?

The status of many species of birds in Connecticut has changed dramatically since the 1990s and the publication of previous site guides. Species that were once common, such as Ruffed Grouse and Northern Bobwhite, are now rare, or, in the case of bobwhite, considered extirpated from the state altogether. Others that were once rare, such as Black Vulture and Common Raven, are now widespread and increasing throughout New England.

Inevitably things change—at times, cyclically, at others, gradually, randomly, or even catastrophically. Storms periodically drive seabirds ashore and sometimes bring new species to the region. Such was the case when Boat-tailed Grackles arrived in the aftermath of Hurricane Gloria in 1985; they now nest here. At the same time, the wooly adelgid, a destructive aphid, also entered the state, decimating hemlock forests and the bird species dependent upon them. Change happens on both broad and small scales, and little is static about the system or process.

Connecticut is now more than 60 percent forested. As abandoned farmland reverts to forest, field-loving species decline, while forest edge and forest-dependent species increase. Shrub and field habitat continues to be lost to forest regeneration, industry, and development; breeding populations of scrub-loving species, such as Yellow-breasted Chat, now hang on by a thread.

In 1997, following the publication of a previous Connecticut site guide, the state's bird list featured 399 species; in 2017 it had 439. The Breeding Bird Atlas survey, conducted from 1982 to 1986, confirmed that there were 173 nesting species within the state. At least four species—Black Vulture, Mississippi Kite, Monk Parakeet, and Mourning Warbler—have been added to the list since then. Northern Bobwhite was removed as a breeding species in 2014.

State Bird Checklist

Birding through the Seasons

A Note about Migration

Although migration is considered seasonal, it is in reality almost a continuous event. For example, some shorebirds still heading north to their breeding grounds in June may overlap with those heading south, having already been to the Arctic and completed breeding. The busiest seasons for observing birds in the Connecticut region are spring and fall. Spring migration, particularly for hawks, tends to range across a broad front, whereas fall migration is often concentrated, especially along the coast and inland ridgelines.

During migration, weather patterns ultimately will determine where birds end up on a given day. In autumn, migrants take advantage of north winds to help propel them south. Strong winds out of the northwest tend to push birds to the coast; winds out of the northeast often move them inland. South winds in autumn can halt or slow migration, but in spring, south winds are the driving force pushing migrants north. When birds in migration meet the edge of a weather front, it can cause a "fall-out," literally forcing them to drop from the sky. Thunderstorms and other major weather events can also ground birds, causing them to abandon their journeys to seek shelter. A major thunderstorm can even force down birds that would normally pass unseen, high overhead, such as Red and Red-necked Phalaropes or Sabine's Gulls, much to the joy of birders.

Coastal parks such as Bluff Point, Hammonasset Beach, Lighthouse Point, Sandy Point, Milford Point, Sherwood Island, Cove Island, and Tod's Point see great numbers of migrants annually, especially in autumn. Bluff Point is known for its landbirds, and Milford and Sandy Points for their shorebirds, while Hammonasset Beach, Sherwood Island, Cove Island, and Tod's Point are considered good sites generally.

Sea watchers may encounter hundreds, or occasionally thousands, of Scoters, of all three species, passing along the horizon during peak migration periods in mid-May and late October. Careful observations have revealed large numbers of other ducks and geese, loons (especially Red-throated), and Red-necked and Horned Grebes moving through as well.

Quaker Ridge, West Rock Ridge, and the other traprock ridges throughout the state provide landmarks for raptors and landbirds to follow. In spring, sites such as East Rock and Edgewood Parks, green islands within an urban setting, act as migrant traps, sometimes concentrating landbirds in remarkable numbers. Other areas, such as the River Road (Kent), Mohawk Mountain, and Trout Brook Valley Preserve, are so large and have such diverse habitats that a broad array of bird species is naturally drawn to them.

Spring

The earliest of the spring passerine migrants are the blackbirds, which arrive in mid-February. March sees the influx of many species, especially ducks, geese, gulls, and several shorebirds, such as Piping Plover, both species of yellowlegs, American Woodcock, and Wilson's Snipe; their numbers build from mid-March to April, and for some, into early May. Flocks of Bonaparte's Gulls gather in coastal estuaries in March and April and occasionally attract Little and Black-headed Gulls.

More landbirds start appearing in March and early April as well, beginning with Tree Swallow, kinglets, Pine and Palm Warblers, and Field and Fox Sparrows, followed closely by species such as Louisiana Waterthrush, Black-and-white Warbler, and Black-throated Green Warbler. April is a good month for finding rarities, southern species that overshoot during migration, such as Blue Grosbeak, Summer Tanager, Yellow-throated Warbler, and Prothonotary Warbler. However, the majority of birds, including warblers, vireos, cuckoos, and thrushes do not begin to arrive until late April or May, with stragglers such as Eastern Wood-Pewee, Alder Flycatcher, and Mourning and Blackpoll Warblers appearing into June.

Summer

Summer is the breeding season for most birds; a few species, including members of the dove family, may nest year-round. Because Connecticut encompasses a narrow band of latitude, many species are widespread in suitable habitat. However, some species typical of more northern climes, such as White-throated Sparrow, Hermit Thrush, or Dark-eyed Junco, are restricted as breeders to the north, especially the northwest highlands. To find a rare breeding Mourning Warbler in Connecticut, it's the northern border or nothing. Given the limited highland habitat, many of these species have very local distributions.

Summer is when the majority of shorebirds depart the Arctic, with species such as Lesser Yellowlegs, Least Sandpiper, and Short-billed Dowitcher passing through Connecticut as early as late June. Peaks for many species are in July, August, or September; by late October, most are long gone.

Some landbirds, including many of the swallows, a few warblers (such as Cerulean, Golden-winged, and Yellow Warblers, along with Louisiana Waterthrush), and many *Empidonax* flycatchers (Alder, Willow, and Acadian) have mostly gone by July and August, the heart of summer.

Fall

Fall migration happens over an extended period, giving birders a broad window of opportunity for viewing migrants. The term "fall" is a bit misleading, however, with many warblers, swallows, shorebirds, and herons departing in midsummer, as early as July. Because the attention of most birders at that time is captured by the shorebird migration, few witness the early landbird exodus, unless the bird's departure takes it along the coast. Some species, such as Cerulean and Golden-winged Warblers, leave so early that they seem to vanish from their breeding grounds only to reappear in their Caribbean wintering sites, with birders along their route none the wiser.

Peak migration times for many species, including most landbirds and raptors, range from late August into October. Diurnal species such as Blue Jays, American Robins, Cedar Waxwings, Bobolinks, and other blackbirds gather in flocks before departing south, often becoming conspicuous, especially along the coast. Although Bobolinks depart Connecticut in August and September, most other blackbirds stage an exodus in October or November, when the sparrow migration is in full swing and most ducks and geese are arriving from the north, many to overwinter. During migration, Common Grackles and Red-winged Blackbirds may form roosts of thousands or even tens of thousands, occasionally lingering in the state into winter.

The fall hawk migration can be wonderful in the region. Many raptors, especially accipiters, harriers, Osprey, eagles, and falcons, move along the coast. Lighthouse Point Park in New Haven, in particular, sees thousands of hawks each autumn. Few realize that among Northeast coastal sites, Lighthouse Point is second only to Cape May, New Jersey, in annual hawk numbers. Inland, sites like Quaker Ridge, in Greenwich, also witness large hawk flights in fall, mostly Broad-winged Hawks and other buteos. The single-day mid-September record for Broad-wings at Quaker Ridge exceeds 30,000.

An annual autumn spectacle well worth viewing is the gathering of Tree Swallows along the lower Connecticut River in Essex. In September and early October, up to 500,000 Tree Swallows can congregate each evening in the reeds (*Phragmites*) on a river island. River Quest and The Connecticut Audubon Society take groups to witness the swirling masses of birds as they assemble to feed and bathe before coming to roost in the reeds. It is sometimes a protracted affair, with groups settling in, then rising and resettling, again and again. Birds of prey such as Peregrine Falcons and Merlins are often in attendance, attempting to secure a final meal for the day.

Another remarkable sight to behold is the daily staging, often along major highways and in cemeteries, of American and Fish Crows, which gather each evening in communal roosts that occasionally number in the tens of thousands. Large roosts exist in West Hartford, Waterbury, Norwalk, and West Haven.

Fall Vagrancy Phenomenon

Like the month of April, November is a transition time, an opportunity for finding rarities, western and southern overshoots, and other wanderers. Western and southern rarities, such as Ash-throated Flycatcher and Tropical and Gray Kingbirds, generally occur from mid-October into December, with the sightings of many species concentrated in November.

In the 1990s, an unprecedented November migration phenomenon began following periods of prolonged southwest winds, when Cave Swallows from the Southwest suddenly began to appear along the Connecticut and Rhode Island coasts. Astonishingly, this has become an annual occurrence, with reappearances ranging from late October into early December, but concentrated in November.

Winter

Although most warblers, flycatchers, vireos, and other predominantly insect-eating species have departed south, many seed- and fruit-eaters remain, joined by species from the north that will winter in our area. These include White-throated Sparrows, Dark-eyed Juncos, and other seed-eaters that are uncommon breeders within the state but in winter gather in flocks and become quite easy to view, especially as they often visit bird-feeding stations. American Robins, Cedar Waxwings, and Eastern Bluebirds eat mostly fruit in winter; where sufficient fruit is available, robins can mass in flocks of hundreds, or even thousands. Eastern Bluebirds, less widely distributed in winter, flock and roost communally in small groups.

Winter is a season for a changing of the guard; Double-crested Cormorants, for example, have mostly left for less-frozen climes, only to be replaced by Great Cormorants from the north. Chipping Sparrows are supplanted by American Tree Sparrows, and in some years Red-breasted Nuthatches invade from the boreal areas to far outnumber the local White-breasted Nuthatches. Winter is also the season when rarities such as Bohemian Waxwings and Hoary Redpolls, normally restricted to higher latitudes, occasionally shift south and infiltrate flocks of their more common cousins.

For many birders, the real winter fun in Connecticut comes from geese, ducks, and gulls. Among the flocks of Canada Geese that form on fields, agricultural land, and lawns throughout the state, a few rarities will turn up; Cackling, Greater White-fronted, and Barnacle Geese are sighted annually in small numbers. Ross's Goose, Pink-footed Goose, "Black" Brant, and the Greylag Goose (very rare in Connecticut), have all been teased out of flocks by careful observers.

Larger gulls gather in winter along the Housatonic River in Southbury, and along the coast at places such as Long and Russian Beaches in Stratford, Shippan Point, Stamford, and Southport and Burying Hill Beaches in Westport. Found among the Herring, Ring-billed, and Great Black-backed Gulls are some less common annual visitors such as Lesser Black-backed, Glaucous, and Iceland Gulls. Diligent searching has revealed rarities such as "Thayer's," Mew, and California Gulls. Numbers build into early spring when rafts of thousands of gulls gather all along the coast to feed on barnacle larvae.

Horned and, less frequently, Red-necked Grebes, Common and Red-throated Loons, and many species of sea ducks winter in the region. Impressive rafts of Greater Scaup can be found along the coast, especially from New Haven Harbor westward. Northern Gannets enter Long Island Sound in fall, their numbers taper off in midwinter, and they return in spring.

As northern lakes and rivers ice over in midwinter, Bald Eagles move south, following the ice line; by late winter, they are typically concentrated in the lower reaches of the state's major rivers. Numbers vary, but in cold years, seventy or more eagles may reside along the lower Connecticut River near Essex. Wonderful views are possible from shore or from boats that cruise the river (see chapter 37). In many years, a Golden Eagle or two and a few Red-shouldered and Rough-legged Hawks also winter on the river; together with resident Peregrine Falcons, they add flair to the winter raptor mix.

Mixed Species Flocks

In winter, songbird flocks form, comprising a mix of species that roam the woodlands together in search of food. These mixed feeding flocks contain a core group of species, usually Black-capped Chickadees, Tufted Titmice, and White-breasted Nuthatches, and may include Golden-crowned Kinglets and a woodpecker (often Downy). These are joined occasionally by other wintering songbirds, such as Brown Creepers or Yellow-rumped Warblers.

Irruptive Species

Common Redpoll and Pine Siskin, along with other "winter finches" such as Purple Finch, Pine Grosbeak, and Red and White-winged Crossbills, are irruptive visitors, ranging from absent to locally common in any given year. Other winter-flocking species, such as Horned Lark and Snow Bunting, gather in farm fields and on coastal dunes, lawns, and airport runways, often accompanied by a few Lapland Longspurs. Nomadic single-species flocks of American Goldfinch, Common Redpoll, and Pine Siskin also form in winter, when they visit birch groves, weed patches, and feeding stations.

Some predators are also irruptive winter visitors. Species such as Northern Shrike, Rough-legged Hawk, and Snowy Owl can be fairly common in some years and totally absent in others. Other raptors, including the elusive Northern Goshawk, the Red-shouldered Hawk, and the ubiquitous Red-tailed Hawk, sometimes establish winter territories in places such as Hammonasset Beach State Park. They are often more approachable at this time, frequently providing exceptional opportunities for viewing. (Birders take care to avoid spooking them, however, as excess stress, especially in winter, can be deadly to these species.)

A Quick Note on Weather

Connecticut generally lacks temperature extremes, but the weather can be quite variable, even during a single day. The local adage is "If you don't like the weather in Connecticut, stick around 20 minutes."

Weather by Season

Spring

Spring is generally mild. March temperatures are typically in the 30s (Fahrenheit), with individual days in the 40s and occasionally 50s. Temperatures may reach the low to mid-60s by May. March through April is mud season, when rubber boots can be handy. Late April and early May tend to be rainy; this is the time when the trees leaf out.

Summer

Although summer temperatures average in the 70s, there are usually week-long bouts in the 80s or 90s, with highs rarely exceeding 100. Humidity is often fairly high, making it feel muggy even when temperatures are in the 70s, but there is typically a cooling breeze along the coast. Hurricane season officially lasts from June 1 to November 30.

Fall

Fall is a glorious time, with little rain in October and average daytime temperatures decreasing from the 60s in September to the low 40s in November. The trees turn color and drop their leaves, with peak colors inland occurring in mid-October, later in the month along the coast.

Winter

Winter temperatures average in the mid to upper 20s from December through February, rarely dipping to the single digits. Expect cooler temperatures in the interior highlands and slightly higher temperatures along the coast, although these temperature gains are often offset by wind. Snowfall is generally light along the coast, but there may be snow cover throughout the winter in the highlands, where backroads can be impassable without—or even with—four-wheel-drive.

Weather Events

Nor'easters

Winter storms called nor'easters drive pelagic species toward the coast, providing an opportunity for spotting rarities. The windows of opportunity are brief—just before, during, and immediately after a storm—but the rewards can be spectacular. Black-legged Kittiwakes, Common and Thick-billed Murres, and even Dovekie—all species not normally found in Connecticut waters—are sometimes stranded in Long Island Sound or driven inland during these weather events.

Hurricanes

Summer and fall hurricanes can have a similar effect on birds as nor'easters. At these times of year, shearwaters, storm-petrels, jaegers, and southern breeding terns such as Sooty, Bridled, and Sandwich—species that feed in the warm offshore waters of the Gulf Stream—are the most likely culprits to appear. Even such "exotic" species as the White-tailed Tropicbird and Magnificent Frigatebird have been recorded, albeit rarely. Any peninsula or point of land jutting into Long Island Sound, such as Saybrook Point, Hammonasset Beach State Park, or Stratford Point could be rewarding. Large inland lakes and reservoirs should also be checked, as birds are often driven well inland.

Almost any species is possible during such a weather event, which is what makes hurricane birding so exciting and potentially rewarding. That said, there are potential dangers associated with such storms that must be kept in mind. As tempting as it may be to rush to the coast during a storm, it's never worth risking injury to see a bird.

Hazards

Among the prospective hazards for birders are poison ivy, the rare poison sumac (found very locally in swamps), stinging nettle, mosquitoes, biting flies, and especially ticks. Lyme disease and other potentially dangerous tick-borne illnesses exist throughout Connecticut. Special care should be taken to avoid ticks, especially the minuscule black-legged tick; tuck pants into socks and check for ticks upon returning home. Blackflies, no-see-ums (biting midges), and mosquitoes are plentiful from early spring well into summer, particularly at dawn and dusk. Green-headed, horse, and other biting flies can be common, especially in marshy areas late spring into fall. Repellent is recommended.

There are only two venomous snakes in Connecticut: the northern copperhead and the endangered timber rattlesnake, with the latter mainly restricted to traprock ridges, mostly in the northwestern corner of the state. Both are rarely encountered. Black bears are becoming increasingly common, especially in the northern half of the state. Although they tend to avoid people, they are attracted to food. Heed any posted warnings, especially when camping in these areas. In spring, be prepared for wet and mud.

How to Use This Book

Birding by Region

For ease of use, this book divides the state into six regions, mirroring somewhat the general topography and major habitat regions of the state. These are the northwest and northeast highlands, inland central, and southeast, central, and western coastlines. At least four chapters are included in each region, more along the coast.

Many chapters are set up as tours, either circuits or linear birding trails to be visited in a morning or over the course of a day. Addresses are listed for each site in the tour, so that specific sites can be visited as individual destinations. The rest of the chapters each focus on a specific site and may list nearby sites to visit if time is available.

Checklists

Near the bird list at the start of each site description, you will find a QR code that looks like this. When scanned with a smartphone, the code links to an eBird species checklist and bar chart, showing the relative abundance of each species at a specific site or tour area. If there are multiple sites within a tour, each site will be listed individually at the top of the bar chart; click on a specific site at the top, and you will see the bar chart for that site. You will need to download a free QR code reader, such as i-nigma, from your app store in order to read the codes.

Appendixes

The appendixes at the end of the book are intended as tools to help you determine when and where to look for species. The bar graphs in Appendix A, for example, provide an invaluable visual aid to understanding the status of a given species within the state.

Appendix B, the Annotated Species List, contains information on status and distribution for all but the most rare species. Knowing something of a bird's natural history, especially its habitat and food preferences, will greatly help your ability to locate it. Appendix C shows what species to expect when you are in any given habitat.

Appendix D is the state bird checklist. Appendix E is the Avian Records Committee of Connecticut's (ARCC) review list, comprising very rare species—

that is, those with five or fewer sightings annually. The number of sightings, months of occurrence, and first and last year of occurrence for each species are noted so that possible patterns or trends may be inferred.

Appendix F offers a list of resources for birders, including bird clubs and related organizations.

① Grass Island, Greenwich

- Grass Island
- Grass Island Natural Area
- Greenwich Harbor

Seasonal rating: Sp ** Su * F *** W ***
Best time to bird: Late October to April.
Habitats: Harbor, mudflats, marinas, open lawn, thickets, and second-growth forest.

SPECIALTY BIRDS

Resident – Mute Swan, American Black Duck, Killdeer, Fish Crow
Summer – Great and Snowy Egrets, Black-crowned Night-Heron, Laughing Gull, Ruby-throated Hummingbird (nest?), Warbling Vireo, Orchard Oriole (some years)
Winter – Canvasback and Redhead (both uncommon), Lesser Scaup, Ruddy Duck, American Coot, Bonaparte's Gull

OTHER KEY BIRDS

Resident – Ring-billed, Herring, and Great Black-backed Gulls; Double-crested Cormorant, Northern Flicker, Cedar Waxwing
Summer – Osprey; Northern Rough-winged, Tree, and Barn Swallows; House and Carolina Wrens, Yellow Warbler, Common Yellowthroat, Baltimore Oriole, American Goldfinch
Winter – Gadwall, Greater Scaup, Long-tailed Duck, Bufflehead; Hooded, Common, and Red-breasted Mergansers; Red-throated and Common Loons, Horned and Pied-billed Grebes

MIGRANTS

Red-necked Grebe (uncommon), Great Blue Heron, Little Gull (occasional)

Location: Grass Island Road, Greenwich.
Restrooms: Portable toilets in the first parking lot; bathrooms in the building by the point.

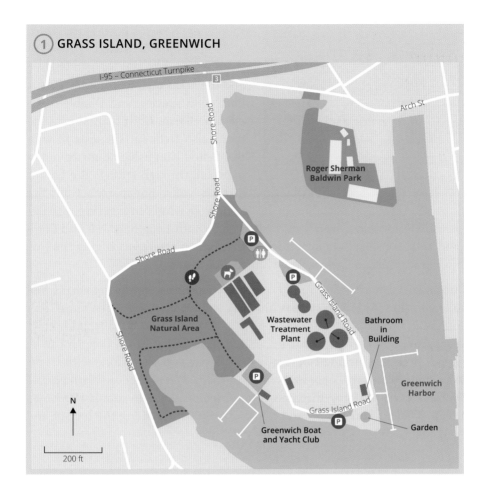

I-95 – Connecticut Turnpike

3

Shore Road

Shore Road

Shore Road

Arch St

Roger Sherman
Baldwin Park

Grass Island
Natural Area

Grass Island Road

Wastewater
Treatment
Plant

Bathroom
in
Building

Greenwich
Harbor

Shore Road

N

Grass Island Road

Greenwich Boat
and Yacht Club

Garden

200 ft

The Birding

Grass Island is not an island at all but a small peninsula jutting into the west side of Greenwich Harbor, nearly in downtown Greenwich. The Grass Island Natural Area is located on the north and west sides of the peninsula. The harbor lies to the east, there are marinas on the southern tip, and a deep cove lies on the southwest side. There is a wastewater treatment plant in the center of the peninsula.

The main draw of Grass Island is the view of Greenwich Harbor, which local birders have long recognized as a reliable place for finding a few Canvasback and Redhead among the Greater and, especially, Lesser Scaup wintering here. They are joined seasonally by all three merganser species; Gadwall, Long-tailed, and Ruddy Ducks; and other estuary-loving ducks. Rarities

Mixed flock of ducks: Redheads, Canvasbacks, and American Wigeon.

found here have included Tufted Duck and Pink-footed Goose. American Coot, Pied-billed and Horned Grebes, and the occasional Red-necked Grebe, both loon species, and Double-crested and Great Cormorants (uncommon) also frequent the area in winter. Belted Kingfishers hunt from the piers fall through spring. The harbor attracts gulls; Bonaparte's Gulls are seen from winter into spring, and Little Gulls (rare) have been found with them. Both Laughing Gull and Common Tern are seen here in summer. Occasionally the lawns edging the harbor attract Horned Lark or Snow Bunting in winter.

The Grass Island Natural Area is generally worth a visit during spring and fall migration. Although species diversity is limited, many of the more common migrant warblers filter through in small numbers. Usually, both kinglet species, a few vireos, thrushes, and occasionally a Brown Creeper can be found. Breeders include common urban nesting species, along with Cedar Waxwing, Warbling Vireo, House and Carolina Wrens, Yellow Warbler, and Baltimore Oriole. Ruby-throated Hummingbird occurs in summer and may breed. Killdeer is resident, and a few usually winter along the harbor and field edges.

How to Bird this Site

A spotting scope is highly recommended. As you enter Grass Island Road, the first parking lot on the right is for the Grass Island Natural Area. In winter, stop here, or at the second lot on the right; both lots overlook the upper harbor and the docks across the street. Be sure to check the far shore to the north, where waterfowl often gather. After scoping the upper harbor, continue south along Grass Island Road past the entry booth and treatment plant. The road veers right and circles counterclockwise around the marina, past the point, where there is roadside parking. At the first bend, the yacht club parking area is on the right. Although the yacht club and its docks are private, there are a few public parking spots on the lot's north side, providing access to the south end of the natural area. An old road, now a hiking path, skirts the natural area's western edge, allowing views of the cove and edge thickets, and is often productive for landbirds in winter. Once at the point, walk south across the lawn to scope the docks on the left and the cove on the right. Pay careful attention to the edges. Ducks tuck up along the shore to rest during the day.

If time permits, return to the yacht club lot or the first parking lot, then walk the trails at the natural area for landbirds, especially sparrows and lingering fruit-eaters, fall through spring. At the first lot, stairs lead up to a white-pine-covered knoll beside the dog park. The best area to explore includes the fields and thickets down the hill beyond the dog park. In fall, American Tree, Fox, Swamp, White-crowned, Lincoln's, and Savannah Sparrows can sometimes be found with the overwintering White-throated and Song Sparrows. With luck, a Winter Wren, Hermit Thrush, Eastern Towhee, or lingering Gray Catbird may turn up in the thickets, and perhaps a Yellow-bellied Sapsucker in the woods. Yellow-breasted Chat and Brown Thrasher have occurred in fall and may linger into winter. Also, watch for migrating Red-headed Woodpeckers (rare) in October. Mixed-species blackbird flocks also frequent the area in winter.

(2) Tod's Point (Greenwich Point), Greenwich

Seasonal rating: Sp *** Su ** F *** W ****
Best time to bird: September to May.
Habitats: Long Island Sound, coves, mudflats, small marsh, rocky and sandy shores, open lawns, thickets, second-growth forest, and nearshore islands.

Bird list for this site:

SPECIALTY BIRDS

Resident – Mute Swan, Killdeer, Great Horned Owl, Northern Flicker, Fish Crow, Cedar Waxwing (most years)
Summer – Great and Snowy Egrets, Black-crowned Night-Heron, American Oystercatcher, Ruby-throated Hummingbird, Willow Flycatcher, Brown Thrasher, Purple Martin, Cedar Waxwing, Warbling Vireo, Orchard Oriole (some years)
Winter – Greater and Lesser Scaup (uncommon), Long-tailed Duck, Ruddy Duck (uncommon), Black-bellied Plover, Ruddy Turnstone; Bonaparte's, Iceland, and Lesser Black-backed Gulls; Razorbill (almost annual), Horned Lark, Hermit Thrush, Snow Bunting, American Pipit

OTHER KEY BIRDS

Resident – Double-crested Cormorant, Carolina Wren
Summer – House Wren, Yellow Warbler, Common Yellowthroat, Baltimore Oriole
Winter – Bufflehead, Common Goldeneye, Hooded and Red-breasted Mergansers, Red-throated and Common Loons, Horned Grebe, American Robin

MIGRANTS

Red-necked Grebe (annual), Little Gull (occasional)

Location: Tod's Driftway, at the end of Shore Road, Greenwich.
Parking: Nonresidents must pay an entry fee from May 1 to December 1.
Restrooms: Main concession building (open year-round); summer seasonal bathrooms at clambake field.
Additional information: Free bird walks, organized by the Bruce Museum, meet at 9:00 a.m. at the second concession stand on the first Sunday of the month, and the first three Sundays in May and October.

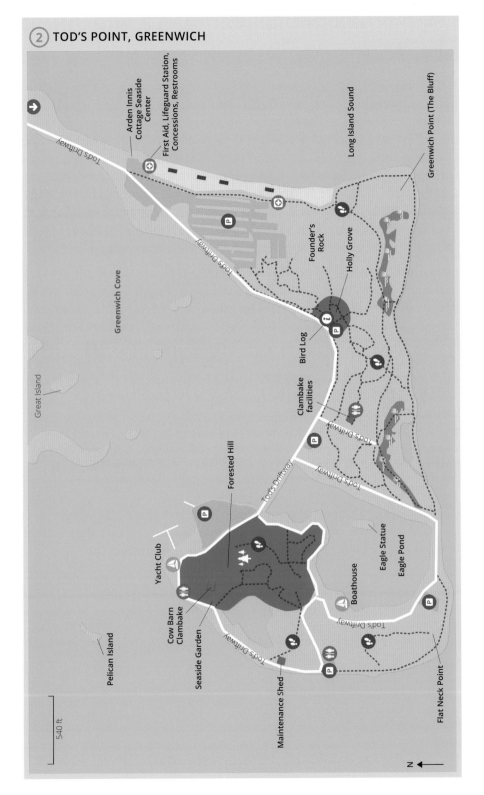

Tod's Driftway

Arden Innis
Cottage Seaside
Center

First Aid, Lifeguard Station,
Concessions, Restrooms

Long Island Sound

Greenwich Point (The Bluff)

Greenwich Cove

Founder's
Rock

Holly Grove

Tod's Driftway

Great Island

Bird Log

Clambake
facilities

Tod's Driftway

Forested Hill

Tod's Driftway

Tod's Driftway

Yacht Club

Boathouse

Eagle Statue

Eagle Pond

Cow Barn
Clambake

Seaside Garden

Tod's Driftway

Tod's Driftway

Pelican Island

Maintenance Shed

Flat Neck Point

540 ft

N

The Birding

Tod's Point, also known as Greenwich Point, is a premier southern Fairfield County birding locale and one of only a few sites statewide with a bird list of more than 300 species. The park rests on a large curved peninsula that forms the eastern and southern borders of Greenwich Cove to the northwest and overlooks Long Island Sound to the south. Greenwich Cove is interspersed with small islands. The park is relatively flat with a few small wooded knolls, a holly grove, and open lawns, along with a small marsh and two ponds. Although nonresidents must pay an exorbitant entry fee from May 1 to December 1, it is worth a visit at any time of year. Fortunately, the birding is still good from late fall through early spring, when access is free.

In summer, breeding songbird numbers are rather lackluster, but Orchard Oriole and Brown Thrasher are found some years. Purple Martin and Northern Rough-winged, Barn, and Tree Swallows all breed locally. Osprey are common and Great and Snowy Egrets visit regularly. Common Terns breed in the area, and they and a few Least Terns can usually be found feeding in the cove or resting on the small islands at low tide. A few American Oystercatchers (may nest), and Spotted Sandpipers (nests) also feed in the area, resting on harbor islands at low tide. Keep an eye out for Black Skimmer, which occurs annually in small numbers. During migration, watch for Piping Plover (uncommon) on the sandy beaches and islands in the bay.

In fall, and especially spring, gulls gather offshore to feed on plankton blooms. Parasitic Jaeger (rare) is possible when these gull congregations occur. Good concentrations of waterfowl, loons, grebes, and gulls can be found from fall through spring, and overwintering fruit- and seed-eaters often linger near the holly grove, the adjacent thickets, and the feeding station. Mega-rarities found in the park have included Gray Kingbird and Burrowing Owl.

From mid to late April, the holly grove and other forested areas also can be good for early spring migrants, such as Yellow-throated Warbler (rare), with other migrant warblers appearing in May. Thirty-four species of warblers have been recorded in the park, so almost anything is possible. Notables include Yellow-breasted Chat, which is seen consistently but in small numbers, usually in September or winter.

The park hosts a decent sparrow migration in spring and, especially, fall. Good numbers of Savannah, Lincoln's, White-crowned, Swamp, and Field Sparrows occur regularly, among which such rarities as Henslow's and, more often, Grasshopper Sparrows have been discovered. Marsh Wren and Brown Thrasher occur during migration, with thrashers nesting in some years.

The ponds, cove, and nearshore waters attract a wide variety of ducks and geese from fall through spring, including Hooded Merganser (common) and Bufflehead. Also look for Long-tailed Duck, White-winged and Surf Scoters, Common Goldeneye, Red-breasted Merganser, particularly on the side nearer Long Island Sound, and both scaup species. Harlequin Duck has been seen on several occasions, usually in rocky areas, such as the point itself. Brant are ubiquitous and may linger well into summer. Both loon species, Great Cormorant, and Horned Grebe are fairly common here in winter; Red-necked Grebe is annual, and Eared Grebe has occurred. Watch for Northern Gannet, especially in April. Check the gull flocks that gather in spring for less common Iceland and Lesser Black-backed Gulls, especially at low tide. Bonaparte's Gulls are seen annually in small numbers, and the rare Little and Black-headed Gulls have occurred, usually in spring. Laughing Gulls are particularly common late summer into November, and a few often linger into winter. It is a good site to find Ruddy Turnstone and the occasional Purple Sandpiper in winter, on the bay edges, islands, and the rocky shores of the sound.

How to Bird This Site

Although the park is fairly large, it is easy to bird, with graded walking paths traversing much of it. The park is visited daily by local birders, and sightings are recorded in a bird log at the kiosk beside the holly grove.

Before entering the park, there is a pull-off just to the left of the entrance booth that gives views of an inlet to the northeast toward Stamford where Horned Grebe, Brant, and a variety of ducks often winter. Eared Grebe has been seen here. Scan from the pull-off or beach.

The park road, Tod's Driftway, goes in a counterclockwise loop from the entrance along the cove shore, past the holly grove, then around the park's western perimeter and pond, before returning through its center to the large main parking lot.

As you enter the park, stop at the first parking lot past the entrance booth on the right. After checking Greenwich Cove to the west, and Long Island Sound (across the street), for waterfowl, shorebirds, and seabirds, drive to the holly grove on the left, just before the stone columns. Peruse the birder's log and map kiosk in the parking lot.

The holly grove is always worth checking for fruit-eaters; in fall and winter, a feeding station for seed-eating species is maintained in a field on the southeast side. In winters when berries are present, the grove holds a few

Hermit Thrushes among the many robins, Cedar Waxwings, and mocking-birds. The thickets have attracted some less common species including Yellow-breasted Chat, Brown Thrasher, and Gray Catbird in winter; oddities also seem to show up, including an Indigo Bunting (very rare in this season), which overwintered here. Behind the holly grove, the open lawns and thicket edges on the hill with the boulder (Founder's Rock) are usually great for sparrows in the fall.

Just past the holly grove, on the left at the one-way road intersection, is the dirt parking lot for the clambake area, which attracts Horned Lark and Savannah Sparrow in winter. Park here and walk south along the maintenance road, blocked by a chain, to the clambake area. There is an active Purple Martin colony here in summer, and this area can be good for sparrows in fall. Henslow's Sparrow was once found on the south side of the field along the edge of the walking path to the marsh. As you continue to drive along Tod's Driftway, stop and scan periodically. There is a parking lot on the right just before the yacht club, and places to pull off (only in winter) near the sailing school building that give good views of the bay and Sand Island. Check the beach and open sandy areas near the boats for wintering Horned Lark, Snow Bunting, or American Pipit. Across the street from the yacht club, there is a driveway that ascends to the Seaside Garden and the lawns near a building known as "the cow barn," overlooking a small pond. At dawn, this area can be good for migrant songbirds in spring and especially in fall.

Farther along the road, the small pond on the left often holds waterfowl all winter, especially Hooded Merganser. The road then makes a loop around the larger Eagle Pond which attracts Bufflehead and other waterfowl. Take advantage of the parking lots and pull-offs all along the road to stop and scan Long Island Sound.

At the southeast end of Eagle Pond, park in the last lot on the right, just before the road turns 90 degrees to the left (and continues around the pond). This is Eagle Pond Lookout. A walking trail parallels the seashore, leading east past a marsh to Greenwich Point, known locally as "the bluff." The bluff gives the best views of Long Island Sound; in winter, watch offshore for Razorbill, and check the lawns for Snow Bunting, which seem to prefer this part of the park. The loop trail that goes around the marsh can be fruitful at any time of year. Clapper Rail occurs most years during migration, and King Rail (rare) also has been found here. In fall, the marsh is a good place to check for migrant Marsh Wren, Saltmarsh Sparrow, and Nelson's Sparrow.

After exploring the marsh and adjacent thickets, continue driving along Tod's Driftway back through the stone pillars, then turn right to return to the main parking lot. During migration, a walk along the entrance road on the lot's east side can be productive for songbirds. Several trails lead from the parking lot to the beach. Another path on the south side of the concession building turns parallel to the beach, leading south to the bluff.

(3) Audubon Center, Greenwich

- Audubon Center
- Fairchild Wildflower Sanctuary

Seasonal rating: Sp *** Su ** F **** W *

Best time to bird: For hawks and landbirds, late August to mid-November, with mid-September to mid-October best; for songbirds, mid-March to early June is good, with late April to May best.

Habitats: Mixed hardwood forest, old fields, apple orchard, a pond, butterfly garden, scrub edge, streams, vernal pools, and a lake.

Bird list for this site:

SPECIALTY BIRDS

Resident – Black Vulture (uncommon), Eastern Screech-Owl, Great Horned and Barred Owls, Pileated Woodpecker, Common Raven (uncommon)

Summer – Wood Duck, American Woodcock, Blue-winged Warbler, Worm-eating Warbler (becoming rare), Louisiana Waterthrush, Orchard Oriole (front fields)

Winter – Red-breasted Nuthatch (numbers fluctuate annually), Yellow-rumped Warbler, Eastern Towhee, Fox Sparrow, Indigo Bunting, Purple Finch (mostly in migration), Pine Siskin (sporadic), Common Redpoll (sporadic), Evening Grosbeak (sporadic)

OTHER KEY BIRDS

Resident – Wild Turkey, Red-bellied Woodpecker, Hairy Woodpecker, Northern Flicker, Eastern Bluebird, Cedar Waxwing

Summer – Ruby-throated Hummingbird, Eastern Wood-Pewee, Great Crested Flycatcher, Yellow-throated Vireo (sporadic at Mead Lake), Tree Swallow, Northern Rough-winged Swallow, Veery, Wood Thrush, Yellow Warbler, Black-and-white Warbler (uncommon), American Redstart, Ovenbird, Common Yellowthroat, Scarlet Tanager, Rose-breasted Grosbeak

Winter – Sharp-shinned Hawk, Cooper's Hawk, Yellow-bellied Sapsucker, Winter Wren, Hermit Thrush, Brown Creeper, American Tree Sparrow

MIGRANTS

Spring and Fall – Common Loon (flybys), Double-crested Cormorant, American Bittern, Green Heron, Solitary Sandpiper, Olive-sided Flycatcher, Willow Flycatcher (has nested), Least Flycatcher, White-eyed Vireo, Blue-headed Vireo, Golden-crowned and Ruby-crowned Kinglets, Blue-gray Gnatcatcher, Brown Thrasher, Northern Parula, Northern Waterthrush; other warblers including Nashville, Mourning (secretive), Palm, Pine, Magnolia, and Canada; Bobolink, Rusty Blackbird

BIRDING IN CONNECTICUT

③ AUDUBON CENTER, GREENWICH

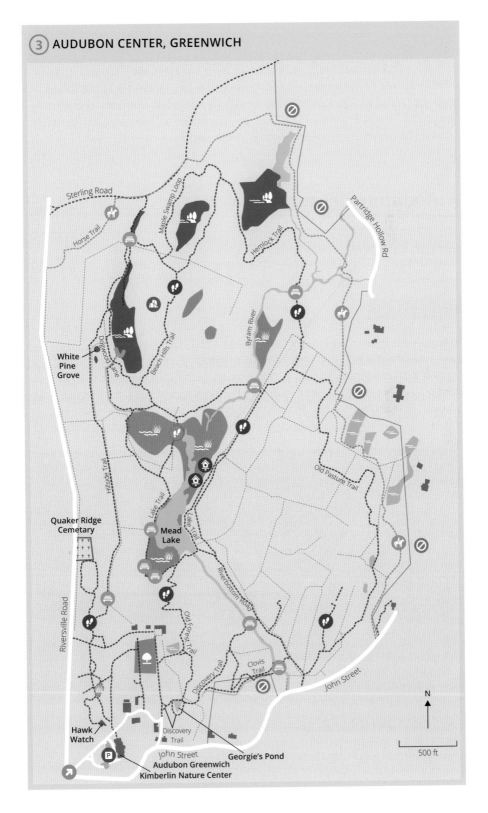

Sterling Road

Horse Trail

Maple Swamp Loop

Hemlock Trail

Partridge Hollow Rd

White Pine Grove

Dogwood Lane

Beach Hills Trail

Byram River

Old Pasture Trail

Hillside Trail

Quaker Ridge Cemetery

Lake Trail

Mead Lake

Lake Trail

Riverbottom Road

Riversville Road

Old Forest Trail

Clovis Trail

John Street

N

500 ft

Hawk Watch

Discovery Trail

P

John Street

Georgie's Pond

Audubon Greenwich Kimberlin Nature Center

3 | Audubon Center, Greenwich

23

Fall – Snow Goose, Black and Turkey Vultures, Osprey, Bald Eagle, Northern Harrier, Sharp-shinned and Cooper's Hawks, Northern Goshawk (uncommon), Red-shouldered and Broad-winged Hawks, American Kestrel, Merlin, Peregrine Falcon, Northern Saw-whet Owl, Common Nighthawk, Red-Breasted Nuthatch (sporadic), Swainson's Thrush, American Pipit; Field, Vesper, Savannah, Lincoln's, and White-Crowned Sparrows; Eastern Meadowlark, winter finches

■ Audubon Center

Location: 613 Riversville Road, Greenwich.
Restrooms: In the nature center building during business hours.

The Birding

Audubon Greenwich opened in 1942 as the National Audubon Society's first environmental education center. Seven miles of trails lead through a wide variety of habitats providing opportunities for birders to see a broad array of species, especially during migration. It is best known as the site of the Quaker Ridge Hawk Watch.

Quaker Ridge Hawk Watch sees mainly buteos, such as Broad-winged Hawk and Red-shouldered Hawk (shown).

Quaker Ridge Hawk Watch

Quaker Ridge is situated along a major migration flyway and has long been recognized as one of the top hawk-watching sites in the Northeast, especially for Broad-winged Hawk and other buteos. It became a full-time fall hawk-watching station in 1985 and boasts an impressive history, averaging more than 19,000 hawks annually since then. From late August to mid-November, a paid hawk-watcher scans the skies, along with volunteers stationed in Adirondack chairs and at picnic tables on the lawn adjacent to the Kimberlin Nature Center parking lot. Broad-winged Hawks are by far the most numerous of the fifteen to seventeen raptor species recorded each year, which include Cooper's and Sharp-shinned Hawks, Bald and Golden Eagles, Osprey, American Kestrel, Merlin, Peregrine Falcon, Northern Harrier, Red-shouldered and Red-tailed Hawks, and, in most years, a few Northern Goshawk. Turkey Vultures move through in good numbers, and Black Vultures are seen throughout the year.

With so many eyes spending long hours staring at the sky each autumn, it's not surprising that a wide variety of species have been recorded at the hawk-watch station, including rarities such as Red-headed Woodpecker (nearly annual), Pomarine Jaeger, Short-eared Owl, Bonaparte's Gull, Sandhill Crane, Anhinga, Swainson's Hawk, Mississippi Kite, and Western Kingbird. Connecticut and Orange-crowned Warblers and even a Boreal Chickadee have been seen at the edge of the meadow and woods bordering the area.

In early fall, Quaker Ridge is a great spot to witness flights of Common Nighthawks passing by at dusk. On some days, Chimney Swifts, Ruby-throated Hummingbirds, and monarch butterflies move through in impressive numbers. Swallows can be abundant, especially in August and September. Tree, Barn, and Rough-winged Swallows are most common, with the occasional Purple Martin, Cliff Swallow, or Bank Swallow mixed in. The "plink" call of the Bobolink is a familiar sound overhead from August into October, and a few stop occasionally in the adjacent meadow. By October, waves of migrating Blue Jays coursing through the treetops are a common sight. In November, thousands of Common Grackles move through as well as skeins of Snow Geese, and sometimes Brant, passing high overhead.

Audubon Center Grounds

Although the Audubon Center in Greenwich is best known for hawk-watching, general birding on the grounds can be quite good, especially in fall and spring. Detailed maps are available inside the center building; it's best to pick one up before setting out on a hike.

If you have less than an hour, concentrate on the meadow, the orchard, and the areas around the Kimberlin Nature Center where, depending on the season, there is generally a good assortment of migrants, nesting, or wintering birds. You can make a loop through the meadow north of the building, connect with the orchard, then check around Georgie's Pond, also known as Indian Spring Pond, before heading back up the hill to the nature center. The small field behind the center is also worth checking. Occasionally, White-crowned, Lincoln's, and Vesper Sparrows can be found at the edges of the fields and lawns in this area. From fall through spring, you can sit inside the building at the observation window to scan the feeders for Black-capped Chickadee, Tufted Titmouse, White-breasted Nuthatch, Downy and Red-bellied Woodpeckers, Blue Jay, Northern Cardinal, Dark-eyed Junco, and Fox, Song, and White-throated Sparrows. Pine Siskin, Purple Finch, and Common Redpoll are seen in some years, while Cooper's and Sharp-Shinned Hawks are often in the vicinity, staking out their next meal. Families of Wild Turkey periodically visit the feeders for seed that has fallen to the ground.

If you have an hour or more, head down the paved driveway from the parking lot and check the thickets on the left for sparrows—including Fox, White-crowned, and Lincoln's—in fall and spring. This is also a good area to find White-eyed Vireo, Brown Thrasher, and Eastern Towhee during migration. Dickcissel has occurred with the House Sparrow flocks. The crabapple trees lining the driveway are attractive to Cedar Waxwing, Purple Finch, and occasionally, Eastern Bluebird or Hermit Thrush, especially fall into early winter. At the bottom of the road, the forest and shrubbery surrounding Georgie's Pond is good for migrants such as Swamp Sparrow, warblers, vireos, grosbeaks, and tanagers. Yellow-throated Warbler (rare) has occurred in spring.

After checking the pond, return to the driveway intersection, then head north down a straight trail to the apple orchard. This is a great spot for migrants, including Yellow-bellied Sapsucker in fall and winter. Breeding species include Eastern Bluebird, House Wren, Eastern Phoebe, Tufted Titmouse, White-breasted Nuthatch, Carolina Wren, American Robin, Song Sparrow, and Indigo Bunting. Pine Warbler has nested in the white pines between the orchard and the Intern House. From the orchard, continue on Lake Trail to Mead Lake, where Belted Kingfisher, Wood Duck, Warbling Vireo, Louisiana Waterthrush, swallows, Eastern Phoebe, and Green Heron can be found from spring through summer. In spring, the forest surrounding the lake is a good site to listen for the drumming of Pileated Woodpeckers.

Follow the trail counterclockwise around the lake, passing through forests where Wood Thrush, Veery, Ovenbird, Great Crested Flycatcher, and Red-eyed Vireo nest, until you come to a boardwalk. Baltimore Orioles commonly nest in trees at the edge of the lake along the way, and Swamp Sparrows breed near the boardwalk. Also keep an eye out for Rusty Blackbirds from fall through spring. The lake usually holds Wood Duck, and occasionally other ducks, including Mallard, American Black Duck, Hooded Merganser, and rarely Green-winged Teal (at the north end). The regularly occurring Green and Great Blue Herons have been joined on rare occasion by American Bittern along the edge of the lake in spring. Red-winged Blackbirds breed in the area and begin singing here in early spring. This is a good spot for migrant warblers, as well as Blue-gray Gnatcatcher, Blue-headed Vireo, and Winter Wren. Rarities spotted near the boardwalk include Virginia Rail and Northern Saw-whet Owl. At quiet times in early morning or late afternoon, the lucky observer may also stumble upon a family of otters.

Continue around the lake to Riverbottom Road. Turn right to head south on the road, then rejoin the Lake Trail. Continue on the trail past the blinds, cross over the dam, then bear left at the intersection to head back up the hill toward the nature center. If time allows, you may wish to leave the Lake Trail and head northwest through the orchard on a path that goes to the meadow. A number of different trails can be taken through or around the meadow, where Eastern Kingbird, Warbling Vireo, Common Yellowthroat, Yellow Warbler, Blue-winged Warbler, Red-winged Blackbird, and Baltimore and Orchard Orioles have been recorded as breeders. Eastern Bluebirds and Tree Swallows use the nest boxes, while American Woodcocks perform their "peent and strut" and aerial displays at dawn and dusk from March to early April. Throughout the meadow, the tops of small saplings and cedar trees are used as singing perches by male Indigo Buntings in spring and summer. Robins, catbirds, mockingbirds, and Song Sparrows nest in the shrubs and thickets. These meadows have attracted a fair selection of rare species, including Sedge Wren, Whip-poor-will, Orange-crowned Warbler, Northern Shrike, and Blue Grosbeak. On several occasions (almost annually), Olive-sided Flycatchers have been discovered perched atop bare snags here in spring and fall, and though secretive, Mourning Warbler occurs with some regularity. Eastern Meadowlarks and Bobolinks pass through during migration and occasionally stop in the meadow.

If you have two or more hours, follow the "hour or more" route described previously to the Lake Trail. At the lake, bear right to continue over the dam and along the east side of the lake, past the bird blinds, then follow Riverbottom Road. This connects with Old Pasture Trail on the right, which heads uphill to the east. The old fields here attract a variety of breeders, including

Eastern Bluebird, Tree Swallow, Indigo Bunting, Blue-winged Warbler, Wild Turkey, Great Crested Flycatcher, Great Horned Owl, and Red-tailed Hawk. The woods come alive in spring and summer with the melodious songs of American Robin, Wood Thrush, and Veery, along with the less musical Red-eyed Vireo, Eastern Wood-Pewee, and Scarlet Tanager. Spring peepers and wood frogs are prevalent in the vernal pools here in early spring.

Other good trails include Hemlock Trail and Maple Swamp Loop, where Barred Owls breed and Winter Wrens can be found during migration and in winter (they sometimes stay to breed as well). Blue Jay, Great Crested Flycatcher, American Redstart, Scarlet Tanager, Pileated Woodpecker, Hairy Woodpecker, and occasionally, Broad-winged Hawk can also be found during the breeding season. Listen for the calls of both cuckoo species in spring and summer. Hillside Trail, which borders the western part of the property, is good for many typical woodland birds. Hooded Warbler has occurred in the spring and has occasionally lingered into early summer.

To return to the nature center, take either Dogwood Lane or Beech Hill Trail, then head south on Lake Trail to the orchard, or take Hillside Trail south through the meadows to the parking lot. (See map for this chapter.)

■ Fairchild Wildflower Sanctuary

Location: A few blocks south of the Audubon Center, 0.5 miles east of Riversville Road on North Porchuck Road, Greenwich.
Restrooms: Portable toilet.
Map: Available at the visitor's center or at http://greenwich.audubon.org/fairchild-wildflower-sanctuary.

The birds here are similar to those found at the Audubon Center, but it is always a good spot to check while in the area, especially around Shadow Pond and the wet meadow. Some of the more colorful or locally less common breeding species here include Great Horned and Eastern Screech-Owls, both cuckoo species (also in migration), Ruby-throated Hummingbird, Blue-winged Warbler, Rose-breasted Grosbeak, Eastern Bluebird, Swamp Sparrow, and Baltimore and Orchard Orioles. During migration, less common species include Solitary Sandpiper and Marsh and Winter Wrens. The variety of thrushes, flycatchers, warblers, and sparrows is like that of the Audubon Center, but at times one location may be more productive than the other. Rarities include American Bittern, Kentucky Warbler (which once bred here), Sedge Wren (recorded in the wet meadow in fall), and Prothonotary Warbler (seen in early spring).

Cove Island Area, Stamford

- Cove Island Park
- Holly Pond
- Shippan Point

Cove Island Park

Seasonal rating: Sp *** Su ** F **** W ***
Best time to bird: September to May.
Habitats: Long Island Sound, tidal pond, estuary, rocky islands, small coastal beach and marsh, open lawns with scattered trees, mixed deciduous forest, old fields, shallow pools, and cedar, holly, and crabapple groves.

Bird list for this site:

SPECIALTY BIRDS
***Resident* –** Wild Turkey, Monk Parakeet, Fish Crow
***Summer* –** Green Heron, Yellow-crowned Night-Heron (uncommon), American Oystercatcher, Least Tern, Willow Flycatcher, Brown Thrasher, Orchard Oriole
***Winter* –** Eurasian Wigeon (uncommon), Brant, Common and Red-throated Loons; Lesser Black-backed Gull, Iceland Gull, Glaucous Gull (some winters)

OTHER KEY BIRDS
***Summer* –** Great and Snowy Egrets, Little Blue Heron (uncommon), Black-crowned Night-Heron, Killdeer, Common Tern, Double-crested Cormorant
***Winter* –** Long-tailed Duck, Common Goldeneye, Bufflehead, White-winged and Surf Scoters, Red-breasted Merganser, Horned Grebe, Red-necked Grebe (occasional)

MIGRANTS
Dabbling and sea ducks, Horned and Red-necked Grebes, Northern Gannet, Bonaparte's Gull, Bald Eagle, hawks and falcons, including Peregrine Falcon (uncommon); Kentucky and Mourning Warblers, Yellow-breasted Chat; Vesper, Grasshopper, Lincoln's, and White-crowned Sparrows; Saltmarsh Sparrow (uncommon), Dickcissel, Rusty Blackbird, and spring and fall rarities

Location: 1281 Cove Island Road, Stamford.
Parking: A Stamford resident's parking permit is required from Memorial Day to Labor Day. Walk-in traffic is allowed, but street-side parking is limited in the summer.
Restrooms: On Cove Island, east of the park entrance, over the footbridge (open year-round); at East Beach Pavilion (summer only).

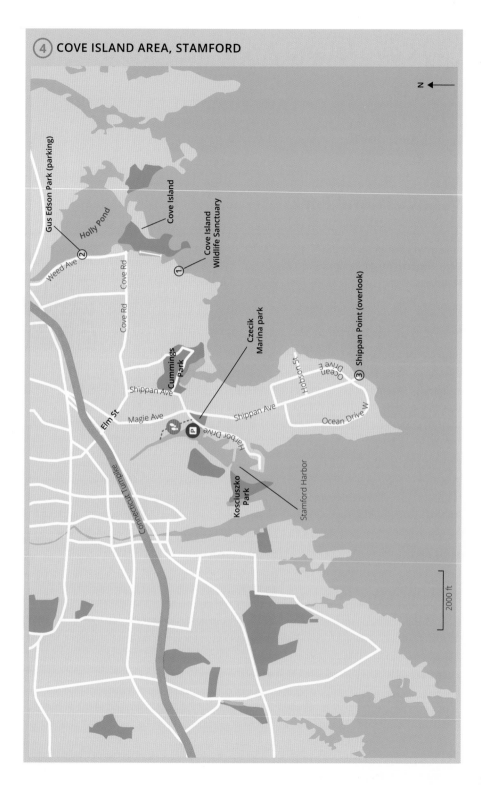

N

Gus Edson Park (parking)

Holly Pond

② Weed Ave

Cove Rd

Cove Rd

Cove Island

① Cove Island Wildlife Sanctuary

Czecik Marina park

Cummings Park

Shippan Ave

Elm St

Magie Ave

Shippan Ave

P

Harbor Drive

Hobson St

Ocean Drive E

Ocean Drive W

③ Shippan Point (overlook)

Connecticut Turnpike

Kosciuszko Park

Stamford Harbor

2000 ft

④ COVE ISLAND WILDLIFE SANCTUARY

Pumping Station

Gate

Holly Grove

Oak Grove

Dogwood Grove

Kiosk

Long Island Sound

Birch Grove

Cedar Grove

Log Pile

Apple Orchard

Swallow Perch

Dune: Protected Habitat – Access Prohibited

SENSITIVE HABITAT

Dogs, bikes, and picnics are not permitted

200 ft

N

The Birding

Stamford's Cove Island Park escaped the notice of most birders until 1995, when Patrick Dugan discovered a wintering Lesser Black-backed Gull here. Since then, Patrick's "patch" has yielded many exciting rarities, from Franklin's Gull and Loggerhead Shrike to Fork-tailed Flycatcher and Painted Bunting.

The park and nearby Holly Pond are classified as an Important Bird Area (IBA) by BirdLife International because of its importance for nesting species and as a stopover for migrating birds. The park's bird list stands at more than 300 species, impressive given the site is only 83 acres. More than 70 butterfly species have been documented here as well.

Cove Island Wildlife Sanctuary

The best birding is generally in the southwest corner of the park, where the city renovated an old brush dump in 2006 to create a 10-acre wildlife sanctuary. Renovations include an information kiosk, perimeter trail, small shallow pools for shorebirds, a butterfly garden, a wire swallow perch, and nesting boxes for Barn Owls, Bluebirds, and Purple Martins. Native grasses and shrubs have been planted, and there are small holly, cedar, and crabapple groves.

This area is rewarding for landbird migrants in spring and particularly fall. In autumn, the edges, brush and stump piles, weedy hummocks, and pools of water provide a haven for seed-loving species. Flocks of Swamp, Song, White-throated, and Savannah Sparrows congregate here to feed, and a few White-crowned, Lincoln's, Fox, and Vesper Sparrows can often be found among them. A couple of Clay-colored Sparrows are found annually after mid-September, and a few Orange-crowned Warblers occur from October to November. Small numbers of Dickcissels and Yellow-breasted Chats are seen from mid-August through November and occasionally later. During migration, Connecticut Warbler occurs rarely, with Mourning Warbler is found more frequently. Blue Grosbeaks are uncommon but regular October migrants, usually in areas with burdock and foxtail grass.

Wild Turkey, Common Yellowthroat, and Orchard and Baltimore Oriole all breed here. Black-crowned Night-Herons and, less commonly, Yellow-crowned Night-Herons roost in the trees adjacent to the harbor. In May and September, look for Spotted and Solitary Sandpipers, Pectoral Sandpiper (rare), Lesser Yellowlegs, and Wilson's Snipe in the rain pools.

Long Island Sound

A walk through the wildlife sanctuary out to the shore can be worthwhile, offering a view of the sound and a small patch of *Spartina* marsh, one of the few left in Stamford. Saltmarsh and Nelson's Sparrows are occasionally found in the marsh during fall migration, usually in October; Seaside Sparrows occur very rarely. Northern Mockingbirds, and occasionally Brown Thrashers, breed in the tangles here. Care should be taken not to trample the delicate *Spartina* and dune grass, or the remaining stands of prickly pear cactus and beach plum. Cove Island harbors some of the area's last remaining populations of these rare plants.

Nesting on the islands offshore are a couple of pairs of American Oyster-catchers, several pairs of Common Terns, and possibly a few Spotted Sand-pipers, along with Double-crested Cormorants, Herring Gulls, and Great Black-backed Gulls. In winter, Brant congregate to feed on eelgrass and sea lettuce and often stay in small numbers into late May. Long-tailed Ducks can be common from November to mid-April. All three scoter species pass by during migration, often in early morning and early evening, although Black Scoter is uncommon. Search among the flocks of wintering Common Gold-eneye, Bufflehead, and Red-breasted Merganser for rarities such as Barrow's Goldeneye, King and Common Eiders, and Harlequin Duck.

Northern Gannets are a regular feature over the sound in spring and fall. A few Red-necked Grebes may mingle among the often abundant Horned Grebes from late fall through early spring, when they are more likely to be seen flying along the horizon early or late in the day. Greater Scaup pass by most mornings and evenings from mid-October through April. Wilson's Storm-Petrels are now rare but expected summer visitors to the sound and seem most abundant in July and August.

Woodlot

The forest to the west of the wildlife sanctuary is an important oasis for woodland migrants, providing shelter and food amid the surrounding urban sprawl. Trails traverse the woods from north to south. At dusk in late April and early May, a few transient Eastern Whip-poor-wills can sometimes be heard from the southeast corner of the woods. Migrating Woodcock display here in mid to late March; listen for their "peent" calls at dusk or dawn. The wetter areas on the west side of the woodlot can attract Gray Catbird, Com-mon Yellowthroat, and Northern Waterthrush during migration. Watch for Ruby-throated Hummingbirds feeding on the jewelweed here in fall. The oaks are especially attractive to migrants; six species of vireos and thirty-six species of warblers have been recorded here. The brushy edges nearest the wildlife sanctuary have attracted such rarities as Connecticut, Prothonotary, and Kentucky Warblers. Both kinglet species are often common during mi-gration, and thrushes can be plentiful in May and October. Fall is generally the best time to see flycatchers, here and elsewhere in the park, including the five *Empidonax* species. Western Kingbird has occurred.

Cove Island

Across a footbridge just to the east of the park entrance is the Holly Pond spillway, the park's eastside beaches, and an expanse of lawns, all of which are worth a visit during fall migration. Although this area of the park is heavily used for recreation, coastal migrants often pass directly overhead. Viewing is best on days with winds from the north, or especially the northwest. Flocks of diurnal migrants such as Red-winged Blackbird, Common Grackle, American Robin, Cedar Waxwing, Blue Jay, Common Nighthawk, Bobolink, and five species of swallows, are seen regularly from late August through mid to late October. American Pipit, Snow Bunting, and Rusty Blackbird occur by mid-October. Lapland Longspur and Horned Lark occasionally stop on the lawns and beach in October and November. Raptors—including Cooper's Hawk, Sharp-shinned Hawk, the increasingly rare American Kestrel, and Merlin—move through in good numbers throughout the period. Osprey can be particularly abundant, and Northern Harriers are common fall migrants. Bald Eagle and Peregrine Falcon pass through in smaller numbers, as do typical ridgeline migrants such as Red-tailed, Red-shouldered, and Broad-winged Hawks. The trees to the west of the shower and concession buildings sometimes hold migrant landbirds, and the dead trees attract woodpeckers.

A small colony of Purple Martins uses the nesting box adjacent to the spillway, and throughout the year, gulls gather on the beach.

■ Holly Pond

Location: Gus Edson Park, Weed Avenue, Stamford.

Holly Pond is a large tidal pond. When the tide ebbs, gulls, shorebirds, and waders gather to rest, feed, and bathe on the exposed mudflats and bars at its north end. Viewing is best two hours before high tide from the small Gus Edson Park pull-off, 0.5 mile north of the Cove Island Park entrance on the right.

Eleven species of gulls have been recorded on the pond. In winter, large numbers of gulls often rest here on the ice. Little and Black-headed Gulls are rare but regular visitors from October through April, but more likely in spring. Little Gulls tend to associate with the many Bonaparte's Gulls that gather here in March, whereas Black-headed Gulls more often congregate with Ring-billed Gulls on the lawns at nearby Cummings Park on Shippan Avenue. Lesser Black-backed Gull and Franklin's Gull (rare) have been observed here.

All thirty-three species of waterfowl that normally occur in Connecticut have been seen either in Holly Pond or on adjacent Long Island Sound. Hooded and Red-breasted Mergansers, Gadwall, American Wigeon, Ring-necked Duck, both scaup species, Green-winged Teal, Common Goldeneye, and Bufflehead are common migrants and winter residents until ice forms on the surface. A few Northern Shoveler, Northern Pintail, Blue-winged Teal, Canvasback, and the occasional Redhead are found each year, usually at the mouth of the inlet, south and east of the pull-off on the opposite shore. Barrow's Goldeneye, Eurasian Wigeon, and Tundra Swan also have occurred.

Shorebirds such as the two yellowlegs species, Killdeer, and Spotted and Least Sandpipers occur with regularity. Scan the trees surrounding the pond for songbirds, and be on the lookout for Cave Swallows in November. Monk Parakeets nest locally; when present, their bulky nests are conspicuous in trees, especially white pines, and on telephone transformers and ball-field light stanchions (Cummings Park).

■ Shippan Point

Location: Adjacent to 2236 Shippan Avenue, Stamford.
Parking: Do not park at the dead end. Use street parking just north of the "no parking" signs (less than a block away).

This is the best place in Stamford from which to view Long Island Sound. All of the sea ducks found in Cove Island Park can also be seen here, with a better chance of finding some less common waterfowl such as Harlequin Duck and Common or King Eider. Horned Grebes and Common and Red-throated Loons are frequent visitors from October through April; these are joined by a few Red-necked Grebes each year. Brant, American Wigeon, and Gadwall winter here with American Black Duck and Mallard; Eurasian Wigeon occurs some winters. Occasionally, a Parasitic Jaeger is seen harassing the gulls that congregate each spring and fall. In summer, the point offers the best local opportunity to view a Wilson's Storm-Petrel from shore; mid-tide seems to be best. Razorbills occur each winter in small numbers. Watch for Northern Gannets, especially from March to April and in November. Rarities discovered here include Manx Shearwater and Black-legged Kittiwake. **Note:** Waterfowl also congregate near the jetty (groin) on Hobson Street, three blocks north. The jetty is straight ahead from where the road turns sharply left. Nearby Stamford Harbor, the Czecik Marina, and Czecik Park, the small park north of the marina on Harbor Drive are all worth checking for waterfowl, gulls, and lingering shorebirds in winter.

(5) Allen's Meadows, Wilton

Seasonal rating: Sp *** Su ** F **** W *
Best time to bird: Late April through May and late August to November with mid-September to early October best for most hawks and landbirds.
Habitats: Small grassland meadow, community garden, brush piles, two small ponds, wooded swamp and scrub edge below forested ridgeline, adjacent to open lawns and athletic fields.

Bird list for this site:

SPECIALTY BIRDS

Resident – Black Vulture, Bald Eagle (sporadic), Red-shouldered Hawk (scarce in winter), Pileated Woodpecker, Common Raven
Summer – Belted Kingfisher (most years), Cliff Swallow (nest at high school), Eastern Bluebird, Brown Thrasher (some years), Field and Savannah Sparrows (small numbers), Indigo Bunting
Winter – Yellow-bellied Sapsucker (sporadic), Winter Wren (uncommon), Hermit Thrush, Fox Sparrow

OTHER KEY BIRDS

Resident – Mallard, Turkey Vulture, Red-tailed Hawk, Mourning Dove, Eastern Screech-Owl, Great Horned Owl, Red-bellied and Hairy Woodpeckers, Northern Flicker, Blue Jay, American Crow, Black-capped Chickadee, Tufted Titmouse, White-breasted Nuthatch, Carolina Wren, American Robin, Northern Mockingbird, Cedar Waxwing, Northern Cardinal, Song Sparrow, Red-winged Blackbird, Common Grackle, Brown-headed Cowbird, American Goldfinch, House Finch, House Sparrow
Summer – Killdeer, Eastern Phoebe, Great Crested Flycatcher, Tree and Barn Swallows, House Wren, Brown Thrasher, Wood Thrush, Warbling and Red-eyed Vireos, Blue-winged Warbler (some years), Yellow Warbler, Black-and-white Warbler, Common Yellowthroat, Chipping and Swamp Sparrows, Rose-breasted Grosbeak, Baltimore Oriole
Winter – Yellow-bellied Sapsucker (sporadic), Northern Flicker, Hermit Thrush, Eastern Bluebird, Gray Catbird, Golden-crowned Kinglet, Cedar Waxwing, American Tree Sparrow, Chipping Sparrow (uncommon), Field Sparrow, Yellow-rumped Warbler, Purple Finch (more common in migration)

MIGRANTS

Spring – Ring-necked and Wood Ducks, Black-crowned Night-Heron, Green Heron, Solitary Sandpiper, Wilson's Snipe, Yellow-billed Cuckoo, Eastern Wood-Pewee, Alder Flycatcher (uncommon), Willow and Least Flycatchers, Yellow-throated Vireo, Northern Rough-winged Swallow, Brown Creeper, Golden-crowned and Ruby-crowned Kinglets, Blue-gray Gnatcatcher; Nashville Warbler, Northern Parula, and Prairie Warbler (fall also); Scarlet Tanager, Rose-breasted Grosbeak, Vesper and Fox Sparrows, Orchard Oriole

⑤ ALLEN'S MEADOWS, WILTON

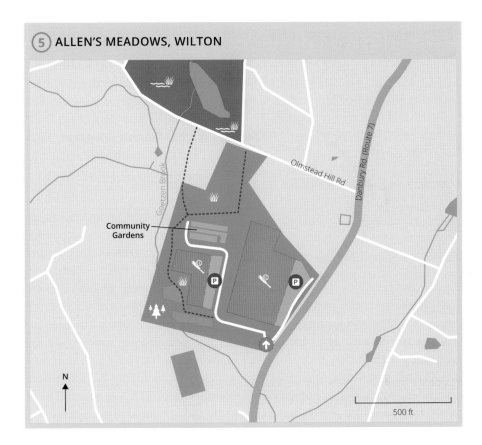

Fall – Red-shouldered Hawk, Cooper's Hawk, Northern Harrier, Merlin, Eastern Phoebe, American Pipit, Horned Lark, Red-breasted Nuthatch (uncommon), Yellow-rumped and Palm Warblers, Indigo Bunting; Field, Savannah, Vesper, Lincoln's, and White-crowned Sparrows; Lapland Longspur, Snow Bunting (uncommon), Eastern Meadowlark, Purple Finch, Pine Siskin (uncommon), Common Redpoll (uncommon)

Location: Allen's Meadows Park, Danbury Road.
Restrooms: Portable toilets spring through fall.

The Birding

Allen's Meadows Park provides grassland habitat in a predominantly urban and forested region of the state. Its small size, diversity of habitats, and level terrain make it easy to explore and an ideal stop when time is limited. The site covers 53 acres, much of which is taken up by athletic fields. The best birding habitat is on the periphery of the fields, especially along the western edge, the community garden, and the small meadow at the end of

5 | Allen's Meadows, Wilton

37

The community gardens at Allen's Meadows attract many sparrow species including Field Sparrow.

the road in the park's northwest section. Such gems as American Bittern, Red-headed Woodpecker, Northern Shrike, Summer Tanager, Clay-colored Sparrow, Blue Grosbeak, Dickcissel, Smith's Longspur, Lark Sparrow, and Harris's Sparrow have been spotted at the site.

The park is nestled between two wooded ridgelines that run north-south and act as migratory corridors for raptors and other birds. Red-tailed Hawks are resident, and Red-shouldered, Broad-winged, Sharp-shinned, and Cooper's Hawks occur during migration. Bald Eagles are uncommon but can be seen at any time of year, especially in winter. Black Vultures are resident in the area and can occasionally be seen soaring above the ridges, usually with Turkey Vultures. Osprey, Northern Harrier, Merlin, American Kestrel, and rarely, Peregrine Falcon also pass by during fall migration. Rough-legged Hawk has occurred (in December). Common Ravens frequent the Wilton landfill a few miles to the north and appear at the meadows on occasion, when they are most often seen flying down the ridge.

The most productive areas are the community gardens and grasslands at the end of the entrance road, at the park's northwest corner. They can be checked in less than an hour, but plan to spend at least an hour or two.

How to Bird This Site

If you have an hour or more, park in the gravel lot across from the second stop sign after entering the park. A short trail leads left (south) to a small pond behind the public works area. Mallards are resident, but occasionally a few Green-winged Teal, Hooded Mergansers, or Wood Ducks occur, usually in March or October. An American Bittern was once found here, but Green, Great Blue, and Black-crowned Night-Herons are more likely, although none are common. In spring, expect a few Solitary Sandpipers to rest and feed along the edge of the pond, especially mid-April to mid-May. The shrubs encircling the pond can harbor decent numbers of migrant songbirds in spring and fall. Eastern Phoebe, Warbling and Red-eyed Vireos, Common Yellowthroat, Common Grackle, Baltimore Oriole, and Yellow, Blue-winged, and Black-and-white Warblers are commonly found during migration and in the breeding season. Dark-eyed Juncos and American Tree Sparrows join the mixed-species flocks here from November through April. Less common birds, such as Hooded Warbler, have been found in this area. Brown Thrashers are fairly regular here in spring and may breed occasionally. In the autumn, fruit-eating birds, such as thrushes and waxwings, target the multiflora rose and wild grape vines.

From the pond, walk northwest across a field toward the ridge (75 yards). A mowed trail along the west side of the field leads north, paralleling a wooded swamp and patches of remnant grassland for less than 200 yards, to the community gardens and meadows. There are several small open wet areas along the way that should be checked for ducks, herons, and shorebirds during migration. Periodically, Wilson's Snipe is found here or in the wetter spots near the community gardens. Red-bellied, Downy, and Hairy Woodpeckers, Pileated Woodpecker (uncommon), and Northern Flicker breed in the area. Yellow-bellied Sapsuckers visit during migration and occasionally linger into winter. Tree Swallows and Red-winged Blackbirds breed throughout the swamp; the swallows breed in tree cavities, while the blackbirds conceal their nests in tussock sedges. Search here for Rusty Blackbirds from late March into April and again in October. Check the larger trees for the hanging nests of Baltimore Orioles. Orchard Orioles are occasionally seen in spring. The Belted Kingfisher's rattling call is heard in the swamp throughout much of the year, but they may be absent in winter. The meadows here also have attracted unusual species such as Northern Shrike (early March and November) and Summer Tanager (May). Continue on to the brush dump and community gardens.

If you have an hour or less, skip the walk and drive straight to the community gardens and small grassland meadow at the end of the road. In the fall, scan the ball fields on the right and the gravel parking lot that parallels the road on the left for American Pipit, Horned Lark, and rarely, Snow Bunting. In spring Vesper Sparrows have been seen feeding among the stubble grass and gravel here.

During migration, especially in fall, American Kestrel, Eastern Meadowlark, and Bobolink use the grasslands. In summer, several uncommon grassland and shrubland species, such as Brown Thrasher, Field Sparrow, and Savannah Sparrow have nested or attempted to nest.

The community garden is incredibly productive in autumn. Early in the season, expect numerous Indigo Buntings; dozens have been seen here in a day. Eastern Bluebirds, which nest in tree cavities in the swamp, can be found in and around the area throughout the year, except perhaps in the dead of winter. They flock to the gardens in the fall, hunting insects and fruit. In late September and early October, the weed and grass seeds in the fallow gardens draw impressive numbers of sparrows. Expect Chipping, Savannah, Song, Swamp, and White-throated Sparrows to be common to abundant. This is one of lower Fairfield County's best sites to see less common sparrows such as Field, Fox, Lincoln's, White-crowned, and especially Vesper Sparrows. American Tree Sparrows are fairly common from November to early April. Be on the lookout for rarities. Blue Grosbeaks have been found here annually since 2006 (expect to see drab brown immature birds). Small numbers of Clay-colored Sparrows occur each fall. Dickcissels have become annual migrants; the few that occur appear in September and October and are most often seen in the shrubs around the community gardens.

In spring and fall, check the hedgerow south of the gardens for migrants. Although the park's warbler diversity is limited, Nashville and Tennessee Warblers are attracted to this area, as are Scarlet Tanagers and, occasionally, Orchard Orioles. Fox Sparrows prefer the hedgerow's west edge closer to the swamp, occurring early October through April, and most commonly in March and November. The park seems especially attractive to Orange-crowned Warblers (rare). Multiple individuals occur most years in fall. Yellow-rumped and Palm Warblers can be common from late September into October.

In winter, the wet sheltered areas throughout the park tend to attract less common wintering species, such as Winter and Carolina Wrens, Hermit Thrush, Gray Catbird, and both Golden-crowned and, occasionally, Ruby-crowned Kinglets.

If time permits, it's worth a quick walk (100 yards) through the small woodlot northwest of the gardens to the wooded swamp and pond on the other side of Olmstead Hill Road. Summer Tanager and Clay-colored Sparrow have been found on the edge of this woodlot. The pond is a good area for ducks, especially Wood Duck, in spring and fall; for Carolina Wren, Swamp Sparrow, and Gray Catbird in winter; and for typical woody swamp-loving species year round.

Fourteen Acre Pond, Norwalk

■ Fourteen Acre Pond
■ Woods Pond

■ Fourteen Acre Pond

Seasonal rating: Sp *** Su ** F *** W ***
Best time to bird: Late summer into early winter for most species, March and April for ducks, and May for songbirds.
Habitats: Lily-covered pond nearly surrounded by riparian woodlands, with adjacent lawns and ball fields within a suburban area.

SPECIALTY BIRDS

Resident – Mute Swan, American Black Duck, Belted Kingfisher
Summer – Wood Duck, Green Heron, Northern Rough-winged Swallow (vicinity), Warbling Vireo, Orchard Oriole
Winter – Northern Pintail, Ring-necked Duck, Northern Shoveler (uncommon), Blue-winged Teal (uncommon)

OTHER KEY BIRDS

Resident – Canada Goose, Mallard, Red-tailed Hawk, Red-shouldered Hawk (vicinity), Mourning Dove, Eastern Screech-Owl, Great Horned Owl (uncommon); Red-bellied, Downy, and Hairy Woodpeckers; Northern Flicker, Blue Jay, American Crow, Black-capped Chickadee, Tufted Titmouse, White-breasted Nuthatch, Carolina Wren, Northern Mockingbird, Song Sparrow, Northern Cardinal, House Finch, American Goldfinch
Summer – Double-crested Cormorant, Chimney Swift, Eastern Wood Peewee, Eastern Phoebe, Great Crested Flycatcher, Eastern Kingbird, Tree and Barn Swallows, House Wren, Wood Thrush, Gray Catbird, Cedar Waxwing, Yellow Warbler, Common Yellowthroat, Chipping and Swamp Sparrows, Rose-breasted Grosbeak, Red-winged Blackbird, Common Grackle, Brown-headed Cowbird, Baltimore Oriole (see also typical riparian woodland species in appendix C)
Winter – Gadwall, American Wigeon, American Black Duck, Green-winged Teal, Bufflehead, Common and Hooded Mergansers, Ruddy Duck (uncommon), White-throated and American Tree Sparrows, Dark-eyed Junco

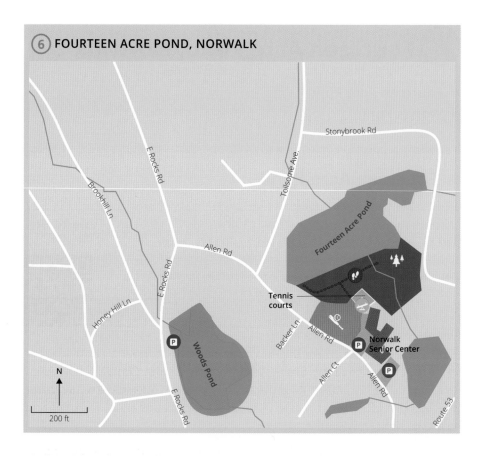

MIGRANTS

Blue-winged Teal (uncommon), Greater Scaup (uncommon), Lesser Scaup (uncommon), Pied-billed Grebe, Bald Eagle (uncommon), Osprey, Cooper's and Sharp-shinned Hawks, Killdeer, Greater and Lesser Yellowlegs; Solitary, Spotted, Semipalmated, and Least Sandpipers; Wilson's Snipe, American Woodcock, Common Nighthawk, Ruby-crowned and Golden-crowned Kinglets, American Redstart; Black-throated Blue, Canada, and Yellow-rumped Warblers; Northern Waterthrush, Scarlet Tanager, Eastern Towhee, Swamp Sparrow, Rusty Blackbird (uncommon)

Location: Norwalk Senior Center, 11 Allen Road, Norwalk.
Restrooms: Fast-food restaurants on U.S. 1 or on Main Avenue in Norwalk.

The Birding

Fourteen Acre Pond is a secluded shallow pond nearly encircled by forest, nestled within a suburban neighborhood. Carpeted with lush aquatic vegetation, it is home to basking painted turtles, cavorting mink, and river otters.

One of the area's best waterfowl havens, its rich plant growth also tempts shorebirds, especially in April and May and from mid-July to mid-September. Herons and egrets are common in late summer.

How to Bird This Site

A spotting scope can come in handy, but binoculars usually suffice. The easiest place from which to view the west end of the pond is the woodlot adjacent to the Norwalk Senior Center. Park at the Senior Center, then walk north across a ball field just to the left of a playground. A trail leads through the woods to the southwest edge of the pond. Another trail goes east, following the south shore. Private houses line the north shore. The densely forested southern shoreline helps conceal your approach, sometimes allowing close views of birds on the pond.

If you are visiting in winter, the east end of the pond may be open even when the rest is frozen, thanks to a stream that crosses beneath Stony Brook Road. Except in the coldest winters, this stream provides enough flowing water to maintain open areas where lingering waterfowl can retreat on both sides of the road. (To get to Stony Brook Road from the Senior Center, follow Allen Road north for 0.1 miles. Take the first right onto Toilsome Avenue. After less than 0.2 miles, take the first right onto Stony Brook Road. The pond will be on the right in 0.3 miles.)

Pied-billed Grebes, at home among the thick emergent vegetation, can be fairly common from March through early May and again in October and November. Resident Belted Kingfishers frequently patrol the shallows in search of fish. Migrating shorebirds include Killdeer (breeds), Greater and Lesser Yellowlegs; Solitary, Least, Semipalmated, and Spotted Sandpipers (may breed); Wilson's Snipe, and occasionally an American Woodcock.

Mute Swan, Mallard, and Canada Geese are resident. Wood Duck is a common breeder; large numbers also gather here late summer and fall, and one or more may linger into winter. Annual and fairly consistent visitors include Gadwall, Ring-necked Duck, Blue-winged and Green-winged Teal, and Northern Pintail, joined occasionally by Ruddy Duck, Lesser Scaup, Bufflehead, Common and Hooded Mergansers, American Wigeon, and rarely, Greater Scaup. Waterfowl numbers peak in March or April and again in October or November. Northern Shoveler is occasionally here in winter.

Spring activity begins in February with the arrival of Red-winged Blackbird and other blackbirds, Tree Swallow, followed by Barn and Northern Rough-winged Swallows, Eastern Phoebe, Northern Waterthrush, and Pine Warbler. Later in April, migrating Bank Swallows (uncommon) and, rarely, Cliff Swallows may be found. During spring and fall migration, the woodlot encircling much of the pond can harbor a nice variety of landbirds, usually a mix of the more common thrushes, vireos, flycatchers, warblers, and sparrows, along with both kinglet species.

In summer, expect the typical riparian species, including Cedar Waxwing, Eastern Kingbird, Eastern Phoebe, Gray Catbird, Warbling Vireo, Yellow Warbler, Common Yellowthroat, and Baltimore Oriole. Other common residents include White-breasted Nuthatch, Carolina and House Wrens; Red-bellied, Downy, and Hairy Woodpeckers; Northern Cardinal, Song Sparrow, House Finch, and American Goldfinch. Orchard Orioles nest along Stony Brook Road.

Fourteen Acre Pond is a reliable inland site to find herons and egrets, especially in August and September. At least one breeding pair of Green Heron is present, augmented by young and migrants in late summer. Great Blue Herons arrive in midsummer, and a few may stay into early winter. Black-crowned Night-Herons are most common in mid to late summer, with sporadic sightings in spring and fall. Little Blue Heron as well as Snowy and Great Egrets are seen occasionally, especially in August, and Glossy Ibis have made rare appearances.

From fall through spring, the area tends to hold flocks of blackbirds. Rusty Blackbirds are seen occasionally, so these flocks are always worth checking.

Reminiscent of rich southern swamps, Fourteen Acre Pond has already enticed one southern wanderer, a White Ibis, and seems likely to attract other vagrants. Whatever the season, this small pond is worthy of a visit.

■ Woods Pond

Seasonal rating: Sp *** Su ** F *** W ***
Location: 98 East Rocks Road, Wilton.
⮕ **Directions:** From the Senior Center, continue north on Allen Road for 0.2 miles. At the second stop sign, turn left onto East Rocks Road. The small signed parking lot for the pond is about 0.1 miles ahead on the left, past Brookhill Lane.

This small pond attracts roughly the same assortment of species as Fourteen Acre Pond and is usually worth a quick peek. The pond is a feeding site for migrating swallows in early spring and occasionally hosts Rusty Blackbirds in spring and fall. It's a good spot for wintering waterfowl, especially Wood Duck (nest locally) and Northern Shoveler.

 Westport Coast

- Sherwood Island State Park
- Nyala Farm
- Burying Hill Beach
- Southport Beach
- H. Smith Richardson Wildlife Preserve and Christmas Tree Farm
- Longshore Golf Club
- Compo Beach
- The Mill Pond
- Grace K. Salmon Park

Sherwood Island State Park

Seasonal rating: Sp *** Su ** F **** W ***
Best time to bird: Year-round—May for landbirds, some hawks, and shorebirds; late August to early November for most hawks and landbirds, with mid-September to mid-October best; early November for vagrants; winter is good after storms.
Habitats: Long Island Sound, estuary, tidal creeks, tidal marshes, large tidal pond, tidal river, sandy and rocky beaches, jetties, mixed deciduous shrubland and woodlots, cedar and pine groves, meadows, open lawns, golf course, brush dump, large gravel and paved parking lots, and a small city park.

Bird list for this site:

SPECIALTY BIRDS

Resident – Mute Swan, American Black Duck, Killdeer, Fish Crow, Monk Parakeet
Summer – Osprey, Clapper Rail, American Oystercatcher, Piping Plover (sporadic), Yellow-crowned Night-Heron, Least Tern, Belted Kingfisher, Willow Flycatcher, Marsh Wren, Brown Thrasher, Warbling Vireo, Saltmarsh Sparrow, Orchard Oriole
Winter – Long-tailed Duck, Northern Gannet, Great Cormorant, Rough-legged Hawk (some years), Iceland Gull (uncommon), Lesser Black-backed Gull, Snowy Owl (some years), Red-breasted Nuthatch (invasion years), "Ipswich" Savannah Sparrow, Lapland Longspur, Snow Bunting, Pine Siskins; winter finches, including Red and White-winged Crossbills (invasion years); Eastern Meadowlark

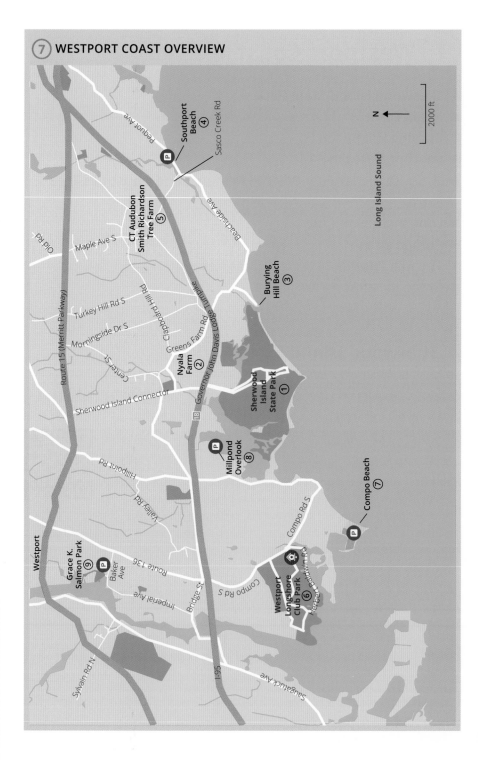

OTHER KEY BIRDS
Resident – Mallard; Great Black-backed, Herring, and Ring-billed Gulls; Great Horned Owl, Mourning Dove; Red-bellied, Downy, and Hairy Woodpeckers; Northern Flicker, Blue Jay, American Crow, Black-capped Chickadee, White-breasted Nuthatch, Carolina Wren, American Robin, Northern Mockingbird, Cedar Waxwing, Song Sparrow, Northern Cardinal, American Goldfinch, House Finch

Summer – Black-crowned Night-Heron, Laughing Gull, Common Tern, Double-crested Cormorant, Eastern Phoebe, Great Crested Flycatcher, Eastern Kingbird, Tree and Barn Swallows, House Wren, Blue-gray Gnatcatcher, Gray Catbird, Yellow Warbler, Common Yellowthroat, Eastern Towhee, Chipping Sparrow, Red-winged Blackbird, Common Grackle, Baltimore Oriole

Winter – Brant, Gadwall, American Wigeon, Greater Scaup, White-winged and Surf Scoters, Common Goldeneye, Bufflehead, Red-breasted Merganser, Common and Red-throated Loons, Horned Grebe, Red-necked Grebe (uncommon), Red-tailed Hawk

MIGRANTS
Spring and Fall – Snow Goose, Northern Shoveler (spring), Northern Pintail, Green-winged Teal (spring), Eurasian Wigeon (uncommon), other dabbling and diving ducks, Red-necked Grebe, Northern Gannet, American Bittern (uncommon), Tricolored Heron (sporadic), Cattle Egret (sporadic), Glossy Ibis, hawks and falcons, Bald Eagle (uncommon), American Coot, Wilson's Snipe, American Woodcock, Bonaparte's Gull, Short-eared Owl (uncommon); *Empidonax* flycatchers including Acadian, Alder, and Yellow-bellied Flycatchers; Brown Creeper, Ruby-crowned and Golden-crowned Kinglets, Eastern Bluebird, Veery, Wood Thrush; Palm Warbler and more than twenty-five other warbler species, including Mourning Warbler (uncommon) and Yellow-breasted Chat (occasional); Eastern Towhee; Fox, Vesper (uncommon), Savannah, Lincoln's, Nelson's, Swamp, White-throated, and White-crowned Sparrows; Dark-eyed Junco, Eastern Meadowlark, Boat-tailed Grackle (spring; occasional)

Location: 420 Sherwood Island Connector, Westport.

Parking: A vehicle entrance fee is charged daily from Memorial Day to Labor Day, and on weekends from late April to Memorial Day and from Labor Day through September. The East and West Beach lots are closed in winter; alternate parking for those sites is at the Central Pavilion lot.

Restrooms: The pavilions have restrooms, but they may be closed in winter.

Hazards: The park is home to a large skunk population that may be active during the day. Healthy skunks are normally timid and, when given a wide berth, tolerant of humans. Keep your distance; if a skunk seems ill or acts strangely, such as showing staggering behavior, alert a park ranger. Keep in mind that skunks can spray accurately to twelve feet.

The Birding

There is little natural coastal habitat remaining in heavily developed south-western Connecticut, and Sherwood Island State Park provides essential resting, feeding, and breeding sites to wildlife. The park consists of 235 acres on a peninsula jutting into Long Island Sound. It encompasses a variety of habitats including a small marsh, a large tidal pond, and rocky and sandy beaches. The park is a wonderful resource for birders and is one of the elite parks to boast a list of 300 or more species.

How to Bird This Site

Much of the park's central section consists of open lawns and gravel parking lots to accommodate the summer beach crowds. Less developed areas lie along the park's periphery. Many of these areas are accessible by car, and most can be checked quickly, but birding the entire park takes several hours. *If your time is limited,* quickly scan the area near the center traffic circle, then proceed to the Main Pavilion parking lot to check Sherwood Point. In spring and fall, the East Beach and its stands of trees, as well as the area near the park entrance, are always worth checking. Check the map for the locations of the following sites within the park.

Spruce and Pine Grove

Park in the West Beach lot, then walk back to the hill west of the entrance booths. The grove is known to local birders as a migrant "fallout" site, especially for thrushes. Veery, along with Swainson's, Hermit, Wood, and a few Gray-cheeked Thrushes, are seen annually. Fox Sparrow (March and November) and other sparrows also congregate here during migration. Small seeps within the grove attract American Woodcock, especially in March and April, and Wilson's Snipe. A pair of Great Horned Owls has nested and roosted here for years.

The cones of spruce and pine attract finches. Migrating Purple Finches often join the resident House Finches and American Goldfinches, and both White-winged and Red Crossbills have been found during "invasion" years. Other winter finches, such as Common Redpolls and Pine Siskins, may drop in anytime from fall through spring. It is also worth checking the bird-feeding station at the east edge of the grove that attracts visiting finches and sparrows along with the local seed-eaters.

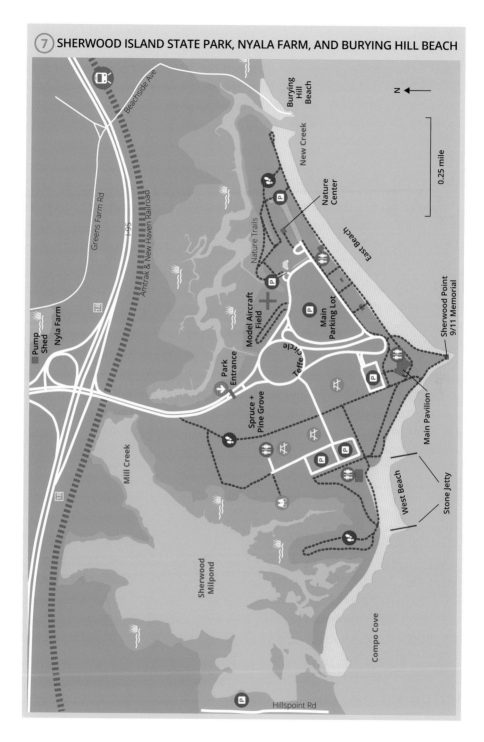

Burying Hill Beach

New Creek

N

0.25 mile

Nature Center

Nature Trails

East Beach

Beachside Ave

Greens Farm Rd

I-95

Amtrak & New Haven Railroad

Pump Shed

Nyala Farm

18

Model Aircraft Field

Main Parking Lot

Sherwood Point 9/11 Memorial

Park Entrance

Teffe Circle

Spruce + Pine Grove

Main Pavilion

Mill Creek

18

West Beach

Stone Jetty

Sherwood Milpond

Compo Cove

Hillspoint Rd

The dead trees to the north of the grove are visited by most of Connecticut's woodpecker species. Red-headed Woodpecker is sighted rarely, usually in fall. Yellow-bellied Sapsucker occurs in the grove during migration. Species typical of this area in summer include White-breasted Nuthatch, Common Grackle, American Robin, Northern Cardinal, Chipping Sparrow, and Baltimore Oriole, all of which nest here. Rarities found in this area include Ash-throated Flycatcher.

The Center Traffic Circle and Rain Pools

It's best to park in the Main parking lot and walk back to scan the lawns in and around the traffic circle. If you pull off to scan the area, be sure not to obstruct traffic. Park police will move you along or may even give you a ticket, especially in summer.

These lawns are home to a few resident Killdeer and Canada Geese and also attract many migrants, especially shorebirds, waders, and grassland species. Check any rain pools that form on the lawns for waders and shorebirds. Glossy Ibis and most of the shorebirds that occur in Connecticut are possible, including American Golden-Plover, Pectoral Sandpiper, and such rare species as Hudsonian Godwit, as well as Baird's and Upland Sandpipers. Red-necked and Wilson's Phalaropes have been found here after severe thunderstorms. Although it has become a rare treat to find a Cattle Egret anywhere in the state, the lawns at Sherwood Island and nearby Nyala Farm provide some of the best chances from April through November. Eastern Meadowlarks, Horned Larks, and Snow Buntings occasionally stop to feed here during migration.

Migrating Canada Geese and occasionally Snow Geese join the park's local goose flocks from fall through spring. Snow Geese are more apt to be encountered flying overhead on crisp fall or early spring days. In recent years, Cackling Geese have appeared with the Canada Geese. Infrequently, Brant also join the flocks on the lawns. Rarely, a Ross's Goose or Greater White-fronted Goose has occurred.

The Main Pavilion Area and Sherwood Point

The trees around the pavilion are home to nesting Fish Crows, whose raucous nasal calls can be heard year-round, and Monk Parakeets. Walk south along the right side of the pavilion to the 9/11 Memorial on Sherwood Point. A spotting scope is very useful here. Scan Long Island Sound for ducks, loons, grebes, and cormorants from fall through spring, and for Northern Gannets, especially in fall or spring. The lengthy list of unusual waterbirds seen from the point includes King and Common Eiders, Barrow's Goldeneye, American White Pelican, and Eared Grebe. Red-necked Grebe is uncommon but regular, fall through spring. The rocky shoreline to the northwest of the point attracts Black-bellied Plover, Ruddy Turnstone, Dunlin, and Sanderling in spring and fall, with a few lingering into December. Purple Sandpipers (rare) can sometimes be found from late fall to early spring, when Brant also congregate in this area. The lawns and beach to the east of the point attract open-field birds, especially Savannah Sparrows, Snow Buntings, Horned Larks, and the occasional Lapland Longspur, autumn through early spring.

The Saltmarsh and Model Aircraft Field

North of the East Beach parking lot, just off the entrance road, there is a smaller gravel lot and a paved runway for radio-controlled planes. Park in this gravel lot, at the north edge near the marsh and away from the runway.

The marsh and nearby grassy fields offer some of the region's best opportunities for finding open-grassland species during migration. Eastern Meadowlarks are seen in March and April, and especially in October or November; at times, a few overwinter. American Pipit, Horned Lark, Snow Bunting, and occasionally Lapland Longspur are also annual visitors. Rarities found among the regulars include Western Meadowlark, Sprague's Pipit, and Smith's Longspur, all seen in the short grass beside the runways. Red-winged Blackbirds are a common presence in the marsh from late February through November. Yellow Warbler and Common Yellowthroat are the common breeding warblers. Look for Baltimore Orioles and sometimes Orchard Orioles to nest in the taller trees overlooking the marsh. Spring sightings of singing male Boat-tailed Grackles have been increasing here and they are a potential nester. Willets return to breed in the marsh around mid-April and linger to at least mid-September. A few Clapper Rails also breed here, and some may stay year-round. Check them carefully; rare King Rails, along with King × Clapper hybrids, have turned up on several occasions. The marsh attracts Black-crowned and a few Yellow-crowned Night-Herons, along with many Snowy and Great Egrets, from spring through fall but especially in late summer, after the breeding season. Although uncommon, Green, Little Blue, and Tricolored Herons are possible, and Glossy Ibis regularly feed on the lawns during migration.

Saltmarsh and Seaside Sparrows arrive in May. The Saltmarsh Sparrows stay to breed in the areas with shorter grasses within the marsh. They are easiest to observe early in the nesting season when males sing conspicuously from perches; they depart by early November. Seaside Sparrows prefer the taller grasses lining the mosquito ditches. They do not breed in the park, so they rarely linger. A few Nelson's Sparrows are found annually from mid-September to mid-November. Look carefully at any of the "marsh" sparrows here, as Le Conte's Sparrow (rare) has occurred.

After checking the marsh and its grassy edges, head south along the tidal creek that runs beside the runway's east edge, from the marsh to the beach. Wilson's Snipe can be common in the channel during migration, and both Clapper and King Rails have been found here. Savannah and other sparrows sometimes congregate to feed along the creek edges, especially in fall and spring. Crossing the small bridge over the creek will take you to the East Beach Nature Trail (see below).

East Beach Nature Trail

Park on the northeast side of the East Beach parking lot adjacent to the road. Across the street at the east edge of the entrance road, you will see a trail crossing a small bridge. On the other side of the bridge, the trail offers three options: one branch heads north (left) along a drainage channel toward the marsh then continues to the east end of the park; another heads south (right) and eventually leads to the beach; the third (straight ahead) takes you east through a grassy field by a bird-feeding station (in winter) and past the nature center on the hill. Purple Martins nest in the gourd trees beside the center. The channel holds Wilson's Snipe during migration. *Allow at least an hour* to check the marsh, wooded copses, and rain pools in this area.

The groves of birches and their catkins attract American Goldfinches year-round, along with Pine Siskins and Common Redpolls (November through mid-April). The birch, basswood, and red maple trees show numerous parallel rows of holes on their trunks from the workings of Yellow-bellied Sapsuckers, which are most often encountered during fall and spring migration. The small groves are favored nesting sites for Baltimore Oriole, the occasional Orchard Oriole, and Brown Thrasher (uncommon). Cedar Waxwings also nest in this area. The groves also serve as resting places for migrant songbirds, especially warblers, vireos, and thrushes. More than thirty species of warblers have been recorded in the park. In fall, look for Yellow-rumped, Palm, Nashville, and occasionally Tennessee Warblers. Less common species to occur include Yellow-breasted Chat and Mourning and Connecticut Warblers (rare). Both Ruby-crowned and Golden-crowned Kinglets can be plentiful in April and October. The rain pools that form in this area have drawn in such rarities as Marbled and Hudsonian Godwits and Cattle Egrets. One autumn, a vagrant Northern Wheatear used a picnic table here as a hunting perch.

The hillside beside the nature center is good for sparrows, especially in autumns when it has not been mowed. Hundreds of birds of several species can be present on good migration days in April or in October and November. Song and Chipping Sparrows are breeders and abundant migrants. They are joined by flocks of Swamp, White-throated, and Savannah Sparrows, and later by American Tree Sparrows (November to March); at least a few of each stay through the winter. A few less common species are often mixed in, such as Lincoln's, White-crowned, Vesper, or Field Sparrows, especially on those days when large numbers of sparrows are present. Rarities found here have included Grasshopper Sparrow (May through October), Clay-colored Sparrow, and Lark Sparrow (fall). This is also a good area in which to look for the scarce Blue Grosbeak or Dickcissel.

The East Beach

A walk from the East Beach parking lot, west along the beach to the Main Pavilion and back, can be productive. *Allow 30 minutes or more.*

The East Beach attracts gulls all year. Resident Ring-billed, Herring, and Great Black-backed Gulls are joined by Laughing Gulls from late summer into fall. In some years, the beach is home to a few wintering Lesser Black-backed Gulls. Bonaparte's Gulls may be seen in small numbers from October to May. During their peak migration in March or April, large flocks gather with other gull species to feed offshore. Iceland and, rarely, Glaucous Gulls, may join the masses in spring and late fall.

Sandy dune-like berms line the walkway that parallels the beach. The seeds of weedy plants growing here are magnets for sparrows, juncos, and finches from fall through spring and especially from late September into October. Both Clay-colored and Vesper Sparrows have been found here. Search for the pale "Ipswich" subspecies of Savannah Sparrow here and along the beach, from mid-October through February.

The gravel parking lots of the East Beach, the lawns, and the beach itself attract Horned Larks, Snow Buntings, and occasionally a Lapland Longspur or two from October to early April. American Pipits also visit the lawns and beaches, especially in April or May, and from mid-September to early November. One or two Red-tailed Hawks have wintered in the park for many years, and at least one pair nests in or close to the park each summer.

The East Beach is also a good site for scanning the ocean. From November through mid-April, flocks of Common Goldeneye gather offshore from adjacent Burying Hill Beach. Search the flocks carefully for Barrow's Goldeneye, known to occur in small numbers annually from mid-November through late April. Long-tailed Ducks, Red-breasted Mergansers, Buffleheads, and all three scoter species may be seen from mid-October through April. Generally, numbers of most of the diving ducks, Common and Red-throated Loons, and Horned and Red-necked Grebes (uncommon) peak from mid-October to November and especially in March or April. The jetties to the east attract roosting gulls and cormorants. In a typical year, Double-crested Cormorants are seen spring through fall then are replaced by Great Cormorants in winter, but a few Double-crested may stay year-round. (Birders may encounter sea mammals as well. In winter, harbor seals are seen with some regularity. Also possible are gray seals, with their large, horsehead-shaped faces, and the more rarely recorded harp seals. **Note:** Seals on the beach should not be approached. They have big teeth, and they know how to use them!)

The fall migration can be remarkable along the East Beach, especially on days with north winds. On good flight days, find a comfortable spot with a clear view for scanning to the east. Diurnal migrants such as robins, Cedar Waxwings, Blue Jays, Purple Martins, swallows, Common Nighthawks, and Bobolinks can pass by in impressive numbers. Common Nighthawks are most active at dawn and dusk, but they may appear at any time. Bobolinks passing over often are heard before they are seen. They utter a "plink" flight call, reminiscent of the sound a tennis ball makes when dropped into a can.

Any of Connecticut's birds of prey are also possible in fall, but falcons and accipiters are especially prevalent. Migrating Northern Harriers are a common sight each spring and fall, coursing down the coast and over the marsh. Migrating Ospreys are common, especially in September and early October. Rough-legged Hawks begin to appear in late October or early November. In some years only a few transients are seen, but in other years one or more take-up winter residence in the park.

From mid-October into November, check the large flocks of migrating Common Grackles and Red-winged Blackbirds for Rusty and Yellow-headed Blackbirds (rare). Late October into November is also the time to look for migrating Cave Swallows.

West Beach and Mill Pond

Follow the indistinct trail from the West Beach parking lot across the grass to an observation deck overlooking the marsh and the south side of the tidal Mill Pond. At high tide, migrant shorebirds and waders roost on the small patches of high ground within the pond. In late summer, there can be large numbers of roosting herons and egrets here. Occasionally a Little Blue Heron is found among the many Black-crowned Night-Herons, Great and Snowy

Egrets, and Great Blue Herons that frequent the area, along with several Yellow-crowned Night-Herons. Most of Connecticut's recorded shorebirds have occurred here at one time or another. A wide variety of dabbling and diving ducks use the pond from fall through spring, including Blue-winged Teal and Canvasback, which are uncommon but regular visitors. Rare Sandhill Crane and American Avocet also have visited the pond. In summer, Brown Thrashers, Eastern Towhees, and Orchard and Baltimore Orioles nest along the pond's wooded edge. This is a good area to search for Marsh Wren, Yellow Warbler, and Common Yellowthroat, spring through fall. Eastern Bluebirds and Tree Swallows occupy the nest boxes here. Ospreys are resident from April into September, and a pair nests on a platform in the pond.

■ The Mill Pond (West Side)

Seasonal rating: Sp *** Su ** F **** W ***
Location: 191 Hillspoint Road, Westport.
Parking: A town parking permit is required during summer months.

The west end of Sherwood Island State Park's Mill Pond can be viewed from this location without entering the park. Look for the same species of dabbling ducks, diving ducks, geese, cormorants, herons, gulls, and shorebirds as mentioned for Sherwood Island.

■ Nyala Farm

Seasonal rating: Sp *** Su ** F *** W *
Location: 196 Greens Farm Road, Westport.

Find a place to pull off the road and scan Nyala Farm's open fields on the right. The farm is a favorite of Cattle Egrets on the rare occasions when they visit the area. A local Red-tailed Hawk favors the roof of the pump shed in the field, and American Kestrels frequent this area during migration. Black Vultures have roosted in the area, and they usually are seen circling overhead. The wetter areas attract migrating Wilson's Snipe and occasionally other shorebird species. A Western Kingbird (rare) spent a period of weeks hunting this field one autumn.

■ Burying Hill Beach

Seasonal rating: Sp *** Su ** F **** W ***
Location: 98 Beachside Common, Westport.
Parking: A town parking permit is required between Memorial Day and Labor Day.

As you enter, check the channel to the right of the entrance road for geese, ducks, waders, shorebirds, and Belted Kingfishers, which perch on the dead snags. American Black Duck, Mallard, both teal species, Bufflehead, and Hooded and Red-breasted Mergansers use the channel from fall through spring, and Ross's Goose (rare) has occurred here.

Offshore, large rafts of diving ducks are present each winter. This is one of the best local sites for finding Barrow's Goldeneye. Lesser Black-backed and Iceland Gulls prefer this beach to East Beach at Sherwood Island State Park and have been reliable from October to April. A prolonged sea-watch may reveal migrating ducks, loons, and grebes, especially in late October or November and March or April. Horned and Red-necked Grebes (occasional) and Common and Red-throated Loons gather here each winter and spring, especially in mid-March.

American Black Ducks winter in the creek at Burying Hill Beach.

■ Southport Beach

Seasonal rating: Sp **** Su ** F *** W ***
Location: 1505 Pequot Avenue, Westport.
Parking: Restricted to Fairfield residents from Memorial Day to Labor Day.

Located at the mouth of Sasco Creek, Southport Beach is a gathering site for waterfowl and gulls, especially in spring, and is the most reliable site in Fairfield County to find Little Gull. As many as five have mixed into the flocks of congregating Bonaparte's Gulls in late March and April. Black-headed, Iceland, Glaucous, Franklin's (rare, in fall), and Mew Gulls (rare) also have been seen. A rising tide is generally best for finding gulls here.

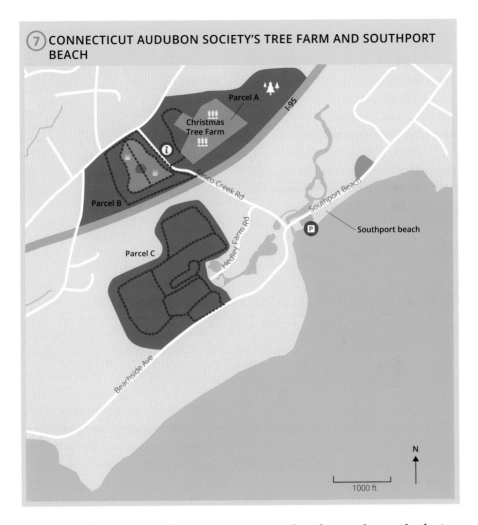

⑦ CONNECTICUT AUDUBON SOCIETY'S TREE FARM AND SOUTHPORT BEACH

The estuary's nutrient-rich waters attract an abundance of waterfowl, similar in scope to that at Burying Hill Beach and Sherwood Island State Park. Brant are particularly common. Eurasian Wigeon is seen most winters among the Gadwall and American Wigeon. Green-winged Teal gather here in spring. Watch for Northern Gannets offshore, especially in spring, and for Great Cormorant in winter. Several of the common shorebirds species typically may be found at low tide during migration. Killdeer and American Oystercatcher breed locally. Any of the swallows are possible in season, and Cave Swallow has passed by in November. In fall, also watch for migrating raptors along the coast.

Across the street, the tidal marshes within Sasco Creek draw ducks, fall through spring, and egrets and ibis in summer. Occasionally, Yellow-crowned

Night-Heron and Green and Little Blue Herons occur. Belted Kingfisher, Osprey, and a few Common Tern hunt the area in summer. In autumn, the marsh sometimes attracts migrant Virginia and Clapper Rails and Saltmarsh Sparrows. Check the Canada Goose flocks that feed on the lawns behind the creek for rarities; Pink-footed Goose has occurred here with them.

In March and April, Bonaparte's Gulls gather at river mouths such as Southport Beach.

■ H. Smith Richardson Wildlife Preserve and Christmas Tree Farm

Seasonal rating: Sp *** Su ** F **** W ***
Location: Sasco Creek Road, Westport.

This wildlife preserve and tree farm, a Connecticut Audubon property, has long been known for attracting landbird migrants, including many less common species, especially in autumn. Boreal Chickadees (rare) once wintered here and could occur again. Western Kingbird has been seen here on several occasions, usually in October or November, and Painted Bunting (rare) has occurred at least once. From late February into April, male American Woodcocks display here at dusk and dawn and often put on quite a show, calling and strutting back and forth across their display mounds. Listen for their characteristic "peent" call and for the distinctive whir of their wings in flight.

■ Longshore Golf Club

Seasonal rating: Sp *** Su ** F **** W ***
Location: 263 Compo Road South, Westport.
Parking: Park beside the pumping station (see map). For access to the Saugatuck River mouth, park in the lot near the clubhouse. Alternatively, drive along the one-way road that makes a loop through the grounds. There are occasional pull-offs along the exit road that will allow you views of Grays Creek.

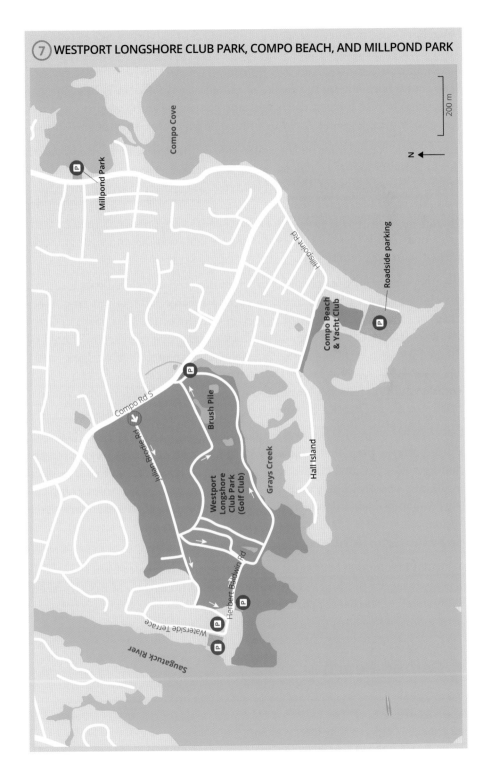

Compo Cove

Millpond Park

200 m

N

Hillspoint Rd

Roadside parking

Compo Beach & Yacht Club

Compo Rd S

Julian Brodie Rd

Brush Pile

Westport Longshore Club Park (Golf Club)

Grays Creek

Hall Island

Herbert Baldwin Rd

Waterside Terrace

Saugatuck River

Longshore's grassy fairways, ponds, and adjacent tidal river are well known for attracting migrating and wintering geese and ducks. Snow, Cackling, Ross's, Barnacle, and Greater White-fronted Geese, as well as Brant, have all been found here among the flocks of Canada Geese. **Note:** Permission has been given to bird the golf club's grounds but can be withdrawn at any time. Please stay off the greens, yield to golfers, and beware of errant golf shots!

Grays Creek, a tidal inlet on the south side of the exit road, is always worth checking for shorebirds, waders, geese, and ducks, even in winter. From fall through spring, Hooded and Red-breasted Mergansers can be fairly common. Often, a few Buffleheads or Common Goldeneyes are mixed among them. Numerous resident American Black Ducks are present, joined by Gadwall, American Wigeon, and Green-winged Teal each fall and spring. Black-necked Stilt has occurred.

The composition of the golf club's brush dump (and occasionally its location) changes from year to year, but it remains a reliable fall migrant trap, especially for sparrows. Bird activity in and around the brush piles peaks in October, when the weedy patches and burdock stands, ripe with seeds, should be checked for such rarities as Blue Grosbeak, Clay-colored, Vesper, Lark (rare), Fox, Lincoln's, and White-crowned Sparrows, and Dickcissel. Eastern Meadowlarks and Bobolink have been found here, and Pine Siskins visit in most years, usually in October or November. From March to May, Fox and White-crowned Sparrows may appear, as well as other less common sparrow species.

Many birds of prey that follow the coast during their fall migration, including the occasional Bald Eagle, pass directly over the golf course. As a result, any of Connecticut's raptor species are possible. The trees lining the driveway and encircling the brush dump attract migrant warblers, vireos, flycatchers, kinglets, and thrushes and are favorite resting sites for Monk Parakeets. Red-headed Woodpecker has visited as well.

A small pond, hidden by a fence, is located across the street from the exit. It is frequented by Black-crowned Night-Herons and egrets. Monk Parakeets have nested in the nearby conifer trees.

■ Compo Beach

Seasonal rating: Sp *** Su ** F *** W ***
Location: 64 Compo Beach Road, Westport.
Parking: Restricted to area residents from May 1 to October 1.

The bird species found here are similar to those seen at Sherwood Island State Park. In winter, the waterbirds include Brant, Long-tailed Duck, and scoters, while Purple Sandpipers can sometimes be found on the jetty. Just offshore, Cockenoe Island (with a long sand spit) and Sprite Island (smaller and to the southwest) attract nesting herons, gulls, and cormorants. Cockenoe Island and Compo Beach often host Snowy Owls during migration, with some individuals remaining through winter. The beach and fields should be checked for open-field birds in fall and spring, including the "Ipswich" subspecies of Savannah Sparrow, Snow Bunting, Horned Lark, American Pipit, and Eastern Meadowlark. Lapland Longspur occurs occasionally.

■ Grace K. Salmon Park

Seasonal rating: Sp *** Su *** F *** W **
Location: Imperial Avenue and Baker Avenue, Westport.

This small park overlooking the Saugatuck River is always worth a quick stop. A wide variety of shorebirds feed here at low tide and roost along the edges at high tide, spring and fall. It is especially productive from roughly three hours before high tide to two hours after. It's possible to find nearly any shorebird feeding on the mudflats, with Baird's Sandpiper and Ruff the most rare species recorded to date. Western Sandpiper are consistently found here, especially in late summer and fall. Pectoral Sandpiper and American Golden-Plover have occurred nearby and are to be expected.

Scan the river for loons and ducks; less common species such as Northern Pintail, both scaup species, and Ring-necked Duck are sometimes among the resident Mallards and American Black Ducks.

The park's ornamental flowers and trees attract a variety of warblers in spring and fall. Baltimore and Orchard Orioles and Cedar Waxwings have all nested here. The shrubs have hosted Yellow-breasted Chat (uncommon) in fall. This small site is surprisingly productive in winter for waterfowl and landbirds. In March, look for Fox Sparrows in the many tangles of multiflora rose. Monk Parakeet can often be found in the area.

⑧ Trout Brook Valley, Weston and Easton

- ▪ Trout Brook Valley Preserve
- ▪ Crow Hill Preserve
- ▪ Jump Hill Preserve
- ▪ Saugatuck Reservoir
- ▪ Aspetuck Reservoir

Note: Detailed maps are available at trailheads.

▪ Trout Brook Valley Preserve

Seasonal rating: Sp *** Su *** F *** W ***
Best time to bird: Late April through November.
Habitats: Large interior deciduous forest tracts, rocky hillsides and forested ridges, hemlock stands, open meadows, regenerating old fields, farm fields, apple and blueberry orchards, freshwater marshes, wood swamps, streams, and vernal pools; adjacent to reservoirs.

Bird list for this site:

SPECIALTY BIRDS
Resident – Bald Eagle, Northern Goshawk (rare), Barred Owl, Pileated Woodpecker, Common Raven, Brown Creeper, Winter Wren
Summer – Green Heron, Black Vulture, Cooper's and Broad-winged Hawks, Yellow-billed and Black-billed Cuckoos, Ruby-throated Hummingbird, American Kestrel (some years), Acadian and Willow Flycatchers, White-eyed Vireo (uncommon), Northern Rough-winged and Cliff Swallows, Eastern Bluebird; Hooded (uncommon), Worm-eating, Blue-winged, and Pine Warblers; Field and Savannah Sparrows, Indigo Bunting, Bobolink, Scarlet Tanager
Winter – Northern Saw-whet Owl, Red Crossbill (sporadic), Common Redpoll (sporadic)

OTHER KEY BIRDS
Resident – Wild Turkey, Turkey Vulture, Red-shouldered and Red-tailed Hawks, Eastern Screech-Owl, Hairy Woodpecker, Northern Flicker, Cedar Waxwing
Summer – Wood Duck, Double-crested Cormorant, Great Blue Heron, Great Egret, Osprey, Chimney Swift, Eastern Wood-Pewee, Least Flycatcher, Eastern Phoebe, Great Crested Flycatcher, Eastern Kingbird; Yellow-throated, Warbling, and Red-eyed Vireos; Blue Jay, Fish Crow, Tree and Barn Swallows, House and Carolina Wrens, Blue-gray Gnatcatcher, White-breasted Nuthatch, Northern Mockingbird, Veery, Wood Thrush,

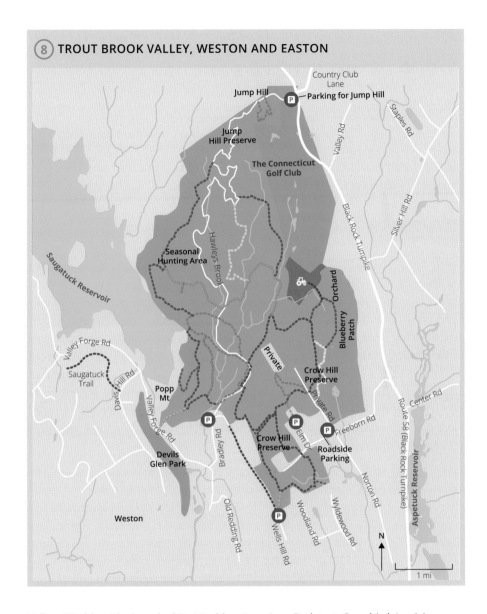

Yellow Warbler, Black-and-white Warbler, American Redstart, Ovenbird, Louisiana Waterthrush, Common Yellowthroat, Chipping and Swamp Sparrows, Eastern Towhee, Rose-breasted Grosbeak, Baltimore Oriole, American Goldfinch
Winter – Woodpeckers, Hermit Thrush, Gray Catbird (uncommon), Golden-crowned Kinglet, winter finches (some years)

MIGRANTS
Common Merganser, scoters, and other ducks (in the reservoirs); hawks and falcons, Common Nighthawk (fall), most flycatchers, all five vireo species, Purple Martin, Bank Swallow, Red-breasted Nuthatch (some years), Ruby-crowned Kinglet; Hermit,

Swainson's, and Gray-cheeked Thrushes; more than 30 species of warblers including Kentucky Warbler (rare), Connecticut Warbler (rare), Mourning Warbler, Northern Waterthrush, and Yellow-breasted Chat (uncommon); Clay-colored (fall), White-crowned, Vesper, and Lincoln's Sparrows; Eastern Meadowlark (fall), Rusty Blackbird, Purple Finch (fall)

Location: 4 Bradley Road, Easton (dirt driveway on the left).

Restrooms: Open seasonally at Aspetuck Park, 369 Black Rock Road (Route 58), Easton.

Hazards: Goshawks nest in remote areas of the preserve. Avoid their active nests, as they are avid defenders of their young.

The Birding

Trout Brook Valley Preserve is a favorite site for birders, hikers, and outdoor enthusiasts. Combined with Crow Hill and Jump Hill Preserves, the total area includes 1,009 acres. The preserve's extensive, well-marked trail systems traverse a diverse array of habitats, providing opportunities for excursions lasting from an hour to a full day. The preserve abuts two other sizable undeveloped areas—Saugatuck Reservoir to the northwest and Aspetuck Reservoir to the southeast—creating a huge expanse of protected habitat. The preserve serves as a nucleus for bird species that require large unbroken tracts of forested land, such as Northern Goshawk and Scarlet Tanager. Saugatuck Reservoir and the Trout Brook Valley watershed also provide a stronghold for Acadian Flycatcher.

From spring to early summer, expect a profusion of birdsong when you arrive in the early morning or at dusk. The preserve hosts an impressive abundance of forest-loving species, and the dawn chorus can almost be felt as well as heard. Common nesting species include Great-crested Flycatcher, Red-eyed Vireo, Wood Thrush, Veery, Ovenbird, Black-and-white Warbler, Scarlet Tanager, and Rose-breasted Grosbeak. Barred Owls are resident and most abundant near the wetter areas. The many dead trees attract all of Connecticut's common woodpeckers.

Northern Goshawks are known to nest in an inaccessible area around Saugatuck Reservoir; they also have been seen off the Popp Mountain (Purple) Trail on rare occasion. During fall migration, the western ridgeline off Bradley Road and the orchard at Crow Hill are good sites to look for raptors, as well as Black and Turkey Vultures. A few Bald Eagles can sometimes be seen soaring over the western ridgeline.

In winter, listen for mixed-species flocks comprised of a few Black-capped Chickadees accompanied by White-breasted Nuthatches and, usually, a

Downy Woodpecker. Other species, including Tufted Titmice and Gold-en-crowned Kinglets, often join them. Watch for flocks of American Robins and Cedar Waxwings, frequently seen in association with one another and occasionally with Eastern Bluebirds.

How to Bird This Site

In order to optimize your visit to this sizable preserve, I have outlined four of my favorite routes. Each encompasses a variety of habitats in a relatively short distance. Depending on your interests, athletic ability, and time sched-ule, however, the preserve can offer countless hours of exploration. The trails vary in difficulty; many of the longer routes pass through unbroken forested areas, and several, including the Red Trail, are quite strenuous. Consult the detailed park map available online or at the park kiosks for route details.

Route 1 (Trout Brook Valley)

Begin at the Bradley Road parking lot. This route offers about a 1-mile round-trip over mostly level terrain, and *can be done in less than an hour*. Fol-low the White Trail from the parking lot, checking the marsh on the left for songbirds and waterbirds. The hillside and hemlock stands, a short distance on the right, are good for thrushes year-round.

In about 0.25 miles, the trail enters an open area cut out of the hillside. This spot is especially productive for migrating sparrows, including Eastern To-whee (breeds), as well as Mourning Warbler (uncommon) in late May and early June. Black-billed and Yellow-billed Cuckoos are found here in most years; they are sedentary, well camouflaged, and best located by sound. Con-tinue on the White Trail to marker 30, at the intersection of the Green/Blue/White Trails, and listen for Acadian Flycatcher, spring through summer.

After another 0.2 miles, the White Trail enters an old field with scattered shrubs. This is one of the best areas in the preserve for spring and fall mi-grants, summering Blue-gray Gnatcatchers, Blue-winged Warblers, Indigo Buntings, and Baltimore Orioles, and a host of other open-field and wood-land-edge species. After searching the fields on both sides of the trail, re-trace your steps to the car.

Route 2 (Trout Brook Valley)

Begin at the Bradley Road parking lot. This 1.5-mile loop passes through a variety of habitats and over generally easy terrain. *It can be done in an hour, but allow at least two.* This is a great loop from which to hear or see Barred

Owls. Their eight-note call, "Who cooks for you, who cooks for you-all," can be heard at dusk or dawn, and even during the day when skies are cloudy.

Follow the White Trail from the parking lot and take the first left onto the Red Trail. The Red Trail crosses an earthen dike that provides great views of the valley's cattail marsh and wooded edges to the north. Cedar Waxwing, Eastern Bluebird, and Song and Swamp Sparrows are resident, although their numbers diminish in winter. The parking-lot edge and the brushy area along the dike are good for migrants, including vireos and a variety of warblers, especially in spring; Mourning Warblers have been found here in late May. Eastern Phoebe, Eastern Kingbird; Warbling, Red-eyed, and Yellow-throated Vireos; Blue-gray Gnatcatcher, Yellow and Blue-winged Warblers, and Baltimore Oriole nest in this area. The marsh holds breeding Wood Duck, at least one pair of Green Heron, Common Yellowthroat, and usually, Tree Swallows. A few Common Ravens frequent the area and are often seen to the west along the ridgeline. The dike is a fine vantage for observing migrating raptors and Common Nighthawks in fall, and migrating swallows in both fall and March or April. Christmas Bird Counts have turned up Common Redpoll and Red Crossbill in this area.

After crossing the dike, bear right onto the Violet Trail, which traverses the base of a hemlock-covered hillside that is home to a small population of resident Winter Wren. Their exuberant chatter emanates from among the many fallen trees scattered along the hillside most years. Louisiana Waterthrushes nest along the stream; they arrive in early April and depart by late August. Most are encountered between the parking lot and marker 15, at the intersection of the Violet and Green Trails. In spring and fall, the hemlocks lining much of the Violet Trail attract migrant warblers, including Black-throated Green, Blackburnian, and Yellow-rumped Warblers. Small numbers of Black-throated Green Warblers may stay to nest. Wood Thrush and Veery commonly nest here, and other thrushes, including Gray-cheeked, are seen during migration.

Acadian Flycatchers can be found about halfway up the Violet Trail. They frequent a semi-open area across the stream to the east, accessible from the Green Trail. Continue north to marker 15 at the intersection of the Violet and Green Trails. In recent years, Hooded Warbler has been heard singing here in spring, and a few may nest. **Note:** If deep-forest species are sought, turn left on the Green Trail, which loops clockwise around to rejoin itself and continues south to the parking lot. This adds an additional 0.8 miles to your route but nearly guarantees Scarlet Tanager, Ovenbird, and Wood Thrush.

To return to the parking lot (0.8 miles) from marker 15, turn right on the Green Trail and follow it south. Acadian Flycatchers can often be found along this sec-

Trout Brook Valley is a great place to find woodland interior nesters, such as Scarlet Tanager.

Photograph courtesy Mark S. Szantyr.

tion of trail. At least three pairs arrive in mid-May to nest, then are gone by the end of August. At marker 3, the trail enters a regenerating old field with scattered shrubs, where the Green and White Trails meet and then run parallel. It can be productive to search the field edges on both sides of the Green Trail at any time of year, but especially during spring and fall songbird migration. Canada and Blackburnian Warblers are fairly regular spring migrants here, and Nashville and Cape May Warblers also have been recorded in spring.

Migrants sometimes concentrate close to the stream at the back of the small field with the granite boulder, west of the trail. Acadian Flycatchers nest in this area as well (this is the same field that lies across the stream from the Violet Trail), and are joined by Least and, occasionally, Yellow-bellied Flycatchers, along with other migrant *Empidonax* flycatchers, in late summer and early fall. In spring and summer, listen for Carolina and House Wrens, and Yellow-billed and Black-billed Cuckoos. The low scattered shrubs provide attractive nesting habitat for Ruby-throated Hummingbirds. The males survey and aggressively defend their territories from favorite exposed perches around the clearings; it usually pays to scan all the bare snags. Blue-gray Gnatcatchers prefer the small copses of oaks within the clearings for feeding and nesting; they can be found spring through fall. Yellow-throated and Warbling Vireos, as well as Blue-winged and Black-and-white Warblers also nest here. This is an excellent place to find breeding Indigo Bunting, Rose-breasted Grosbeak, and Baltimore Oriole; their numbers are augmented by migrants in spring and fall. Scarlet Tanagers and American Redstarts nest in the nearby forest. Sparrows, including the occasional Lincoln's, Vesper, and White-crowned Sparrows, prefer the edges here, especially in autumn.

After leaving the fields, continue south on either the Green or the White Trail, and look for a gravel parking lot carved out of the hillside on the left. The surrounding shrubs attract sparrows during migration. Eastern Towhee nests here and sometimes remains in winter. This is also a good area for both Black-billed and Yellow-billed Cuckoos, and Mourning Warbler has been found here in late May and early June. As you return to the main parking lot (0.25 miles), check the hemlock stands on the left for thrushes year-round. Swainson's, Gray-cheeked, and Hermit Thrushes are seen during migration. A few Hermit Thrushes may remain through the winter. This area looks suitable for finding a (rare) migrant Bicknell's Thrush. Black-throated Blue Warblers may be found in the laurel thickets on the hillside near the entrance during migration.

Route 3 (Elm Drive to Crow Hill)

Begin at the Elm Drive parking lot at the end of a cul-de-sac off Freeborn Road. **Note:** During blueberry season, parking may not be allowed here. There is alternate parking to the east on Freeborn Road (fills quickly); a dirt road east of the pull-off provides access to the Yellow/White and Blue Trails. Another lot on Wells Hill Road adds 30 minutes each way to the walk.

This roughly 2-mile round-trip route to the blueberry and fruit tree orchard at Crow Hill takes *at least an hour*. It is mostly an easy walk, but there are a few hilly areas and a short, fairly steep climb to the orchard. Take the Orange Trail spur to the Blue/Green Trail. Turn right (east) and continue following the Blue Trail when it splits off from the joint Blue/Green Trail. After crossing a dirt road, the trail becomes a boardwalk following the edge of a vernal pool on the left. The dead trees here attract woodpeckers, especially Northern Flicker and Hairy and Red-bellied Woodpeckers. When the Blue Trail meets the Yellow/White, take the Yellow/White toward the Magenta Trail. Turn right on the Magenta Trail and continue uphill until you reach the orchard.

Go through the gate into the orchard and turn right. The small fenced section at the bottom of the hill, planted with blueberry bushes, is part of the preserve and accessible to Aspetuck Valley Land Trust members. The rest of the area to the east, beyond the fence, is a private working farm and closed to the public, but much of the area can be seen through the fence. In summer and fall, when the blueberries ripen and the fields go to seed, the orchard truly comes into its own as a birding site. In August, the blueberry patch and environs attracts scores of fruit-eating birds, including the local woodpeckers, Great-crested Flycatchers, Eastern Bluebirds, Gray Catbirds, Cedar Waxwings, Baltimore Orioles, and even a few Orchard Orioles.

Perched upon a hilltop, the orchard provides sweeping vistas and good hawk-watching opportunities from September through early November. As an inland site, it attracts more buteos than the coastal sites, including many Broad-winged, Red-tailed, and Red-shouldered Hawks. American Kestrels once bred here (and could again); they are still a common migrant. Mississippi Kite (rare) has been seen over the orchard in May.

The fallow fields and farmland adjacent to the orchard provide nesting habitat for a couple pairs of Bobolinks, a few pairs of Savannah Sparrows and Field Sparrows, and a pair or two of Orchard Orioles. The orioles favor the area around the farm buildings to the north, except when the blueberries are in season. The Field Sparrows prefer the south end of the orchard, the Savannah Sparrows the north end.

In autumn, the weedy fields and hedges surrounding the orchard attract many migrant sparrows, warblers, and flycatchers along with a variety of other birds, including some less common species such as Connecticut Warbler and Olive-sided Flycatcher. Just north of the orchard is a farm field accessible to the public. These thickets and farm fields are always worth a visit, especially in fall; Connecticut's third Say's Phoebe was found in this area. To reach the field, continue north on the trail through the orchard. A parallel trail outside the gate runs along the edge of the fence and passes through a second gate into the field. Unfortunately, the orchards and many of the adjacent fields are mowed by mid-October or early November, after which only a few sparrows remain near the farm buildings. Good numbers of American Pipits and a few Horned Larks may visit the plowed fields in autumn, but as often as not, they don't stop and are only heard flying over. Eastern Bluebirds can be found here year-round but are most common in summer and fall. In November, migrating blackbird flocks pass by the hilltop, and Rusty Blackbirds are possible. Finches also pass over in good numbers, especially in flight years. This would be a good site to search for migrating Common Redpoll, Pine Siskin, Purple Finch, or even Evening Grosbeak when those species are being seen in the state.

Winter can provide interesting birding and even a few surprises here. The wetter areas at the bottom of the hill often hold both kinglet species, Hermit Thrush, Gray Catbird, and Eastern Towhee (the latter two also nest in the area). A few Eastern Bluebirds tend to remain throughout the winter, around the orchard, farm buildings, and wetter areas with berries. Common Ravens are heard or seen regularly from the hilltop, and Wild Turkeys visit the mowed and plowed fields. Winter Wren has occasionally been seen in the area, and the dead trees along the orchard edge attract woodpeckers, including Yellow-bellied Sapsucker.

Route 4 (Jump Hill Loop)

Begin at the Jump Hill parking lot (the northeast-most parking lot on the map) opposite Country Club Lane on Route 58. This is a 1.5-mile loop, of medium difficulty, that passes through second-growth forest into deeper woods. From the parking lot, take the White Trail uphill to the first intersection with the Green Trail and turn left onto the combined Green/White Trail, a loop trail of roughly a mile. When it rejoins the White Trail, turn right to return to the car. (Turning left on the White Trail here would lead you south into Trout Brook Valley, with its many trails.) The birds in this area are a mix of second-growth and deep-woods species, including Carolina Wren, Chipping Sparrow, Eastern Towhee, Great-crested Flycatcher, Wood Thrush, Ovenbird, and Scarlet Tanager. Northern Waterthrush has been found in the wetter areas here. Barred Owls frequent this area and can occasionally be heard during the day.

■ Aspetuck Reservoir

Location: Route 58 North, Easton.

The Aspetuck and Hemlock Reservoirs along Connecticut Route 58 (the Black Rock Turnpike) are huge, paralleling the road for over 4 miles, beginning 0.85 miles north of the Merritt Parkway and ending near Freeborn Road, the Crow Hill Orchard entrance to Trout Brook Valley. It is worth checking them for migrant waterfowl and shorebirds in spring and fall, and after severe thunderstorms in late summer. There are a number of pull-offs along the turnpike that provide views of the water; however, do not trespass on water company property.

Center Road, just south of Freeborn Road, crosses the Aspetuck Reservoir's northern end and has ample pull-offs from which to view the water. In fall, Black Scoters and other seaducks make regular, usually brief, stops here, as well as on Hemlock and Saugatuck Reservoirs. Resident Canada Geese are joined annually by migrant flocks, which may contain a few Snow Geese. Goose flocks are worth checking for other less common geese, such as Cackling, Greater White-fronted, and Barnacle. Eurasian Wigeon and Northern Shoveler also have occurred. Center Road is a fine site to check for swallows spring through fall. Several species, including Bank and Cliff Swallows, nest in small numbers in the area. Pine Warblers nest in the pines (appropriately), and Cooper's Hawks have been observed in the area during the breeding season. Both Baltimore and Orchard Orioles are possible in summer.

▪ Saugatuck Reservoir

Location: Valley Forge Road to Route 53, Weston.

Saugatuck Reservoir is the large reservoir situated to the west of Trout Brook Valley Preserve. Like the Aspetuck and Hemlock Reservoirs to the southeast, it attracts migrant waterfowl and wandering eagles. There is a nesting site for Cliff Swallows on one of the structures at the south end near the dam. Northern Goshawks nest on the reservoir property and can sometimes be seen soaring along the ridge between the reservoir and Trout Brook Valley Preserve. Saugatuck Reservoir has few roadside pull-offs but many access points and an elaborate trail system. Maps are available through the Aspetuck Land Trust website. Roadside views are best from the south end on Valley Forge Road near the dam, and at the extreme north end off Route 53 (Newtown Turnpike).

⑨ Bridgeport-Fairfield Coast

- Seaside Park
- Captain's Cove
- Saint Mary's by the Sea Park
- Ash Creek Open Space
- Penfield Reef and Sunken Island

Seaside Park

Seasonal rating: Sp *** Su ** F **** W ***
Best time to bird: October to April.
Habitats: Capped landfill, ball fields, lawns, scattered trees and shrubs, rocky and sandy shore, dirt fields, ponds, wastewater outflow into Cedar Creek Harbor, marina, tidal creek, marsh, estuary, intertidal wetlands, river mouth, coastal scrub, and forest.

Bird list for this site:

SPECIALTY BIRDS

Resident – Mute Swan, Killdeer, Peregrine Falcon, Monk Parakeet, Fish Crow, Common Raven

Summer – Green Heron, Yellow-crowned Night-Heron, Osprey, Clapper Rail, Spotted Sandpiper, Laughing Gull, Common and Least Terns, Forster's Tern (occasional), Caspian Tern (uncommon), Black Skimmer (occasional), Belted Kingfisher, Northern Flicker, Willow Flycatcher, Warbling Vireo, Northern Rough-winged Swallow, Purple Martin (along Fairfield Beach Road), Marsh Wren, Brown Thrasher (some years), Orchard Oriole

Winter – Eurasian Wigeon, American Black Duck, Blue-winged and Green-winged Teal, Northern Shoveler, Northern Pintail, Canvasback, Redhead, Lesser Scaup, Harlequin Duck (rare), Common Eider (uncommon), King Eider (rare), Long-tailed Duck, Northern Gannet, Great Cormorant, Northern Harrier, Rough-legged Hawk (some years), Sanderling; Bonaparte's, Iceland, and Lesser Black-backed Gulls; Snowy Owl (some years), Horned Lark, American Pipit, Lapland Longspur, Snow Bunting; Tree, Field, and Savannah Sparrows

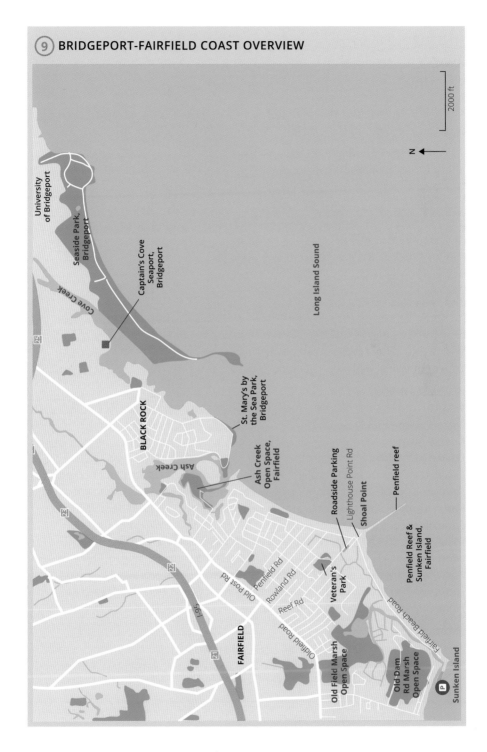

University of Bridgeport

Seaside Park, Bridgeport

Cove Creek

Captain's Cove Seaport, Bridgeport

Long Island Sound

2000 ft

N

BLACK ROCK

Ash Creek

St. Mary's by the Sea Park, Bridgeport

Ash Creek Open Space, Fairfield

Roadside Parking

Lighthouse Point Rd

Shoal Point

Penfield reef

Penfield Rd

Rowland Rd

Old Post Rd

Reef Rd

Veteran's Park

Penfield Reef & Sunken Island, Fairfield

FAIRFIELD

Oldfield Road

Old Field Marsh Open Space

Old Dam Rd Marsh Open Space

Fairfield Beach Road

P Sunken Island

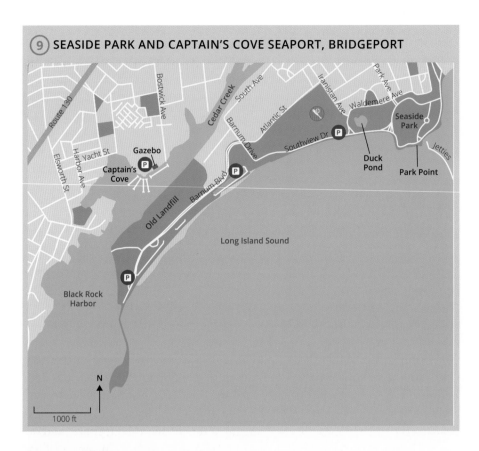

9 SEASIDE PARK AND CAPTAIN'S COVE SEAPORT, BRIDGEPORT

OTHER KEY BIRDS

Resident – Canada Goose, Mallard; Ring-billed, Herring, and Great Black-backed Gulls
Summer – Double-crested Cormorant, Great and Snowy Egrets, Black-crowned Night-Heron, Chimney Swift, Mourning Dove, Eastern Kingbird, Tree and Barn Swallows, Carolina Wren, Northern Mockingbird, Gray Catbird, Cedar Waxwing, Common Yellowthroat, Yellow Warbler, Red-winged Blackbird, Baltimore Oriole
Winter – Brant, Gadwall, American Wigeon, Greater Scaup, Bufflehead, Common Goldeneye, Hooded and Red-breasted Mergansers, Red-throated and Common Loons, Horned Grebe, Great Blue Heron, American Coot, Dunlin, Dark-eyed Junco, White-throated and Savannah Sparrows

MIGRANTS

Pied-billed Grebe, raptors (fall), Bald Eagle, American Oystercatcher, Merlin, vireos, Cave Swallow (almost annual), thrushes; Palm Warbler, Yellow-rumped Warbler, and other warblers; Swamp Sparrow and other sparrows

Location: 6 Park Avenue, Bridgeport.
Parking: Parking lots and roadside parking throughout the park. Entrance fee in summer.
Restrooms: On site (may be closed in winter).

The Birding

Seaside Park is a large and very popular coastal park in urban Bridgeport. Its 300 acres encompass the old city landfill, beaches, playgrounds, and the historic Fayerweather Island Lighthouse at its west end. On the east side, there are ball fields, open lawns, and a duck pond. The entire south edge of the park overlooks Long Island Sound. The park offers good birding year-round but can be quite crowded in summer.

Gulls tend to gather here, fall through spring, on the lawns by the duck pond, on the west-end beaches, and particularly on or near the rock jetty, sandbars, and breakwater at the east end, off Park Point. Laughing Gull is a regular summer visitor, and Iceland and Lesser Black-backed Gulls occur in small numbers most winters, usually around the duck pond or off Park Point, and occasionally remain into summer. Black-headed Gull has occurred in spring, and Franklin's Gulls (rare) put on quite a show here in 2015 when more than fifteen were seen in a single day. The lawns attract Canada Geese and the occasional Cackling or Snow Goose most winters. Rarely, a Ross's Goose has turned up here. Brant can sometimes be found on the lawns and are common along the shore, fall through late spring. In winter, Horned Grebe and both loon species are common here. Look for the occasional Red-necked Grebe, especially in early spring. Northern Gannets pass by, fall through spring, especially in October and March. The lawns and parking lots also attract Horned Lark, Snow Bunting, a few Lapland Longspurs, and occasionally an American Pipit. Migrant Western Kingbird (uncommon) has been seen in the park in fall.

In summer and early fall, Common and Least Terns gather on the west-end beaches. A few Forster's Terns may occur with them and could linger into late fall. The park's coastal location also makes it ideal for viewing migrant raptors in fall, especially Osprey, accipiters, falcons, and harriers; a Northern Harrier and a Cooper's Hawk often hang around all winter. In spring, there is usually a decent landbird migration, including a broad selection of wood warblers; in autumn, the park attracts sparrows, including American Tree, Field, and Savannah Sparrows.

A boat ramp off the northwest parking lot overlooks the mouth of Cedar Creek and Black Rock Harbor, which is great for scaup, Ring-necked Duck, and other *Aythya* ducks.

It is easiest to start at the east end and drive to the west, stopping periodically to scan or to walk the fields and beaches. There are plenty of places to park along the route. Remember to check the Park Point area for gulls, shorebirds, and waterfowl, especially in winter. The gulls often roost on Pleasure Beach and Long Beach, across the channel in Stratford. Also scan the power plant outside the park's northeast perimeter. Both Common Raven and Peregrine Falcon have nested on it.

▪ Captain's Cove

Seasonal rating: Sp *** Su * F *** W ****
Location: 1 Botswick Avenue, Bridgeport.
Parking: Park in the southeast corner of the parking lot near the gazebo, if possible.
Restrooms: In the restaurant from Mother's Day to September 1 (a purchase is encouraged).

The Birding

Captain's Cove is a privately owned restaurant and marina complex adjacent to the water treatment plant at the head of Cedar Creek Harbor, opposite Seaside Park in Bridgeport. Warm outflow from the treatment plant keeps the harbor from freezing completely, allowing diving ducks and other waterfowl to congregate here fall through spring. It is a great place to study scaup and their close relatives in the genus *Aythya*: six species of *Aythya* have been found together here in winter, and large groups of Lesser and Greater Scaup are joined by a few Canvasbacks, Redheads, and good numbers of Ring-necked Ducks most winters. Tufted Duck (rare) has occurred here occasionally. Gadwall, American Black Duck, and American Wigeon are among the many dabbling ducks that also frequent the area. Eurasian Wigeon occurs most winters and remains into early spring, and a few Northern Shoveler and Northern Pintail usually visit during migration. All three mergansers are expected in winter.

As winter progresses and inland waters freeze, the harbor and outflow area attract American Coot, both cormorant species, and the occasional loon. Horned Grebes are often common in the area, and Pied-billed and Red-necked Grebes are possible. Great Blue Heron, late shorebirds, and other

Greater and Lesser Scaup gather at Captain's Cove along with other *Aythya* ducks in winter.

waders should be searched for along the shoreline at least into January. Belted Kingfishers may be present year-round. Northern Harrier, Red-tailed Hawk (resident), Cooper's Hawk, and occasionally Bald Eagle and other raptors hunt the area from fall through spring, especially the capped landfill at Seaside Park across the channel. Wild Turkeys feed and roost at the landfill as well. Both American and Fish Crows are resident. Scan any gull flocks; occasionally an Iceland or Bonaparte's Gull is found, and Franklin's Gulls (rare) were once found in the harbor mouth.

In summer, the area is crowded with boaters and restaurant-goers. Parking is at a premium, and birds are generally few. Great and Snowy Egrets do hunt the channel edges; Monk Parakeet, Common Tern, and Osprey visit and nest nearby.

How to Bird This Site

A scope is recommended here. There is easy viewing from a gazebo overlooking the marina, the upper harbor channel, and the north side of Seaside Park. The gazebo has its own small parking lot, east of the main parking lot and restaurant buildings. Other views of the main harbor and adjacent Burr Creek can be had from the south and west sides of the main parking lot beside the small cottages. The Captain's Cove restaurant serves good seafood, and its owner has been amenable to visiting birders; let's keep it that way. Avoid blocking access to the boat slips or any business activities, and remember that the docks are off limits in summer. In winter, please do not venture onto the docks without permission.

◼ Saint Mary's by the Sea Park

Seasonal rating: Sp *** Su * F *** W ****
Location: 11–37 Eames Boulevard, Bridgeport.
Parking: Along the roadside.
Hazards: Because this is an urban park, commonsense safety precautions should be taken; birding with friends is recommended.

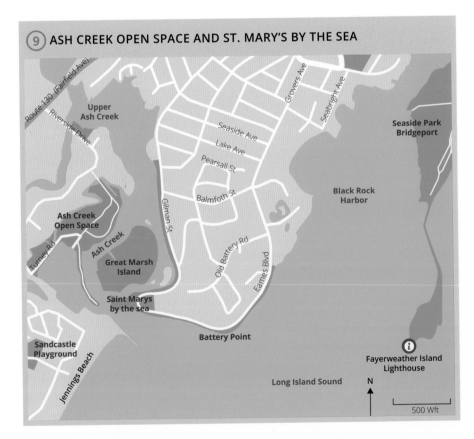

9 ASH CREEK OPEN SPACE AND ST. MARY'S BY THE SEA

Route 130 (Fairfield Ave)
Riverside Drive
Upper Ash Creek
Seaside Ave
Lake Ave
Pearsall St
Grovers Ave
Seabright Ave
Seaside Park Bridgeport
Balmfoth St
Gilman St
Black Rock Harbor
Ash Creek Open Space
Ash Creek
Turney Rd
Great Marsh Island
Old Battery Rd
Eames Blvd
Saint Marys by the sea
Sandcastle Playground
Jennings Beach
Battery Point
Fayerweather Island Lighthouse
Long Island Sound
N
500 Wft

The Birding

Saint Mary's by the Sea is a linear park that parallels Eames Boulevard and Gilman Street, just a couple miles to the south of Captain's Cove, where Cedar Creek drains into Black Rock Harbor. Part of the park perches on a bluff that rims the outer edge of Battery Point, overlooking Long Island Sound, with the mouth of Black Rock Harbor to the east and Ash Creek to the west.

The birdlife found here is nearly identical to that at Captain's Cove. As the birds move in and out of Cedar Creek with the changing tides, Saint Mary's provides an alternate location from which to search for them. Common Goldeneye seem to prefer this more open area to the shallower waters within Cedar Creek Harbor, and large rafts of them often congregate here. Barrow's Goldeneye and Barrow's × Common hybrids have been spotted here. Long-tailed Ducks are usually conspicuous here as well. Clear views into Long Island Sound provide opportunities for finding Northern Gannet and other open-water species. Within the park proper, something like a Snowy Owl or Lapland Longspur may show up, though the sightings have been rare.

How to Bird This Site

The park is very busy throughout the year, especially on weekends and on nice weekdays after about three o'clock, even in winter. On the west side, a grassy area with parking overlooks Ash Creek. It can be worth a visit for landbirds and a quick scan of the creek.

■ Ash Creek Open Space

Seasonal rating: Sp *** Su ** F *** W ****
Location: near South Benson Marina, 555 Turney Road, Fairfield.
Parking: The main entrance and parking lot is off Turney Road.

The Birding

The scenic 40-acre Ash Creek Open Space is a tree-lined meadow surrounded by saltmarsh. This town-owned preserve sits at the mouth of Ash Creek Harbor, overlooking an intertidal estuary almost in downtown Fairfield. A wide variety of waterfowl and waterbirds gather here in winter, very similar to those at Captain's Cove. Fall through spring, this is arguably the best place in Fairfield to find the less common ducks, such as wintering Eurasian Wigeon, Canvasback, and occasionally Redhead, Northern Pintail, or Blue-winged Teal. Tufted Duck (rare) has occurred. Ash Creek attracts more shorebirds and waders than Captain's Cove, including both Yellow- and Black-crowned Night-Herons, Green Heron (may breed), Little Blue Herons (uncommon), and Snowy and Great Egrets. Least Bittern (rare) has been seen in spring. Clapper Rails breed in good numbers in the marsh. Most of Connecticut's commonly occurring shorebirds are seen annually, with Red Knot and Whimbrel the rarest seen so far. In late March, watch for Osprey to arrive on their Great Marsh Island nesting platform within the river mouth. They generally remain until at least September.

How to Bird This Site

The park rests within a tidal estuary, so bird abundance changes with the tide. Ducks prefer mid-tide, while mid-tide or lower is best for shorebirds and waders. The park's main trail leads east from the lot through an open shrubby meadow edged with trees. At meadow's end, two trails loop back through the trees in either direction to the lot, while the main trail continues northwest across a dike that overlooks marsh on the left and creek and mudflats on the right, ending at Riverside Drive. This patch of marsh is consistently the best place in the park to find dabbling ducks, including Eurasian Wigeon (annual) in winter, and feeding herons and egrets in summer. The ring of trees and brush around the meadow can be a great trap for migrant warblers, thrushes, and vireos in the spring, and the meadow itself is excellent for fall sparrows, especially in October. Field and Savannah Sparrows often winter in the meadow. Orchard Orioles breed here. Check the pines ringing the meadow for wintering owls; although infrequent, visits from Great Horned, Barred, and Long-eared Owls have occurred.

Another path, the Point Trail, starts at the southeast corner of the parking lot and goes straight along a wooded dike to a point overlooking the mouth of Ash Creek, across from Saint Mary's by the Sea. This path is worth checking for songbird migrants, especially in fall. Brown Thrasher has nested along the dike.

While you are in the area, it is also worthwhile to check out Upper Ash Creek, which is great for ducks. It is viewable from the parking lot of the Jewish Home for Elderly, 1 Post Road, Fairfield, by the bridge.

Penfield Reef and Sunken Island

Seasonal rating: Sp *** Su * F *** W ****
Location: Lighthouse Point, off Fairfield Beach Road, Fairfield.
Parking: There is roadside parking by the Seagrape Café at 1144 Reef Road, about a 2-minute walk away. Alternate parking is available back at Veteran's Park on Edward Street, a five minute walk north on Reef Rd.

Penfield Reef, which can be viewed from the end of Lighthouse Point, is known for attracting waterfowl, including all three scoter species, Common and Barrow's Goldeneye, and Harlequin Duck. Terns mass here in summer, and gulls in winter and early spring. Black, Roseate, and Caspian Terns (uncommon), and Black Skimmer are found occasionally among the many Common Terns. A scope is essential here.

Sunken Island is a group of submerged rocks visible at low tide from the end of Fairfield Beach Road. Ducks tend to congregate here, and it is especially good for Harlequin Duck (uncommon) in winter. Park in the turnaround at the end of the road and look south.

⑩ Lordship Tour, Stratford

- ▣ Railroad Trail and Warehouse Fields
- ▣ Warehouse Pond
- ▣ Sikorsky Airport
- ▣ Long Beach
- ▣ Stratford Seawall
- ▣ Stratford Point
- ▣ Short Beach
- ▣ Frash Pond
- ▣ Access Road Ponds
- ▣ Birdseye Street Boat Ramp
- ▣ Shelby Pond, Shakespeare Theatre
- ▣ Broad Street Pilings

Seasonal rating: Sp *** Su *** F **** W ***
Best time to bird: Year-round.
Habitats: Long Island Sound, Housatonic River, estuary, tidal creeks, large saltmarsh, tidal and freshwater ponds, sandy and rocky beaches, breakwaters, barrier dunes, mixed woodlands, open lawns, municipal airport grasslands surrounded by industry and residences.

Bird list for this site:

SPECIALTY BIRDS

Resident – Mute Swan, Gadwall, American Black Duck, Bald Eagle (uncommon), Northern Harrier (uncommon), Fish Crow, Peregrine Falcon, Monk Parakeet, Common Raven (uncommon), Boat-tailed Grackle

Summer – Osprey, Little Blue Heron (uncommon), Green Heron, Yellow-crowned Night-Heron (fairly common), Glossy Ibis (uncommon), Clapper and Virginia Rails, Piping Plover, American Oystercatcher, Willet, Common and Least Terns, Belted Kingfisher, Willow Flycatcher, Purple Martin, Bank Swallow, Marsh Wren, Brown Thrasher (sporadic), Eastern Towhee (uncommon), Saltmarsh and Seaside Sparrows, Orchard Oriole

Winter – Eurasian Wigeon, Canvasback, Long-tailed and Ruddy Ducks, Northern Gannet, Great Cormorant, American Bittern (rare), Rough-legged Hawk (invasion years), Purple Sandpiper (jetties), Razorbill; Iceland, Lesser Black-backed, and Glaucous Gulls (uncommon); American Coot, Snowy Owl (invasion years), Horned Lark, "Ipswich" Savannah Sparrow, Snow Bunting, Lapland Longspur

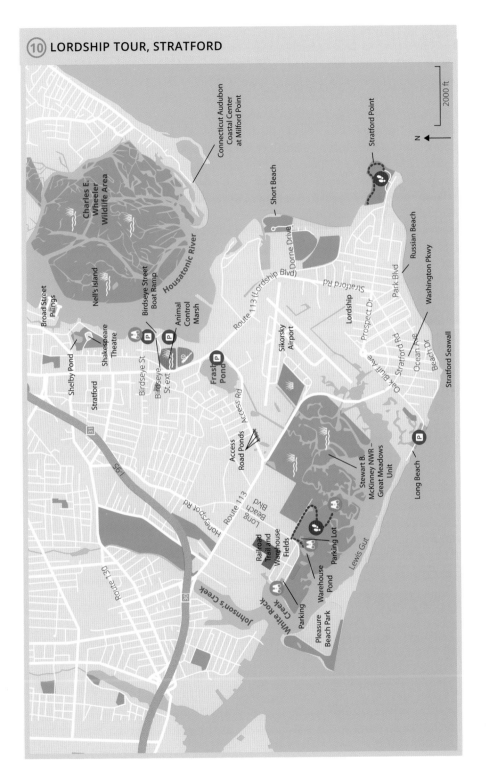

OTHER KEY BIRDS

Resident – Mallard, Wild Turkey, Double-crested Cormorant, Great Blue Heron, gulls, Mourning Dove; Red-bellied, Downy, and Hairy Woodpeckers; Northern Flicker, Blue Jay, American Crow, Black-capped Chickadee, White-breasted Nuthatch, Carolina Wren, American Robin, Northern Mockingbird, Cedar Waxwing, Northern Cardinal, Song Sparrow, American Goldfinch, House Finch

Summer – Great and Snowy Egrets, Black-crowned Night-Heron, Double-crested Cormorant, Killdeer, Spotted Sandpiper, Laughing Gull, Yellow-billed and Black-billed Cuckoos (uncommon), Chimney Swift, Eastern Phoebe, Eastern Kingbird; Northern Rough-winged, Tree, and Barn Swallows; House Wren, Gray Catbird, Common Yellowthroat, Yellow Warbler, Chipping Sparrow, Baltimore Oriole, Red-winged Blackbird, Common Grackle

Winter – Brant, American Wigeon, Ring-necked Duck, Greater and Lesser Scaup, Long-tailed Duck; White-winged, Surf, and Black Scoters (uncommon); Common Goldeneye, Bufflehead; Hooded, Common, and Red-breasted Mergansers; Common and Red-throated Loons, Horned Grebe, Black-crowned Night-Heron (a few), American Tree Sparrow, Dark-eyed Junco

MIGRANTS

Dabbling and sea ducks, Red-necked Grebe (uncommon), Northern Gannet, American Bittern, hawks and falcons, Common Gallinule (rare); shorebirds, including Long-billed Dowitcher and rarities; Bonaparte's Gull; Roseate, Black, and Forster's Terns; Black Skimmer, Short-eared Owl; *Empidonax* flycatchers (August and September), including Acadian, Alder, and Yellow-bellied Flycatchers; swallows, Brown Creeper, kinglets, Veery, Wood Thrush; thirty warbler species, especially Yellow-rumped, Pine and Palm Warblers; Clay-colored Sparrow (occasional), Swamp and White-throated Sparrows (common); White-crowned, Lincoln's, Nelson's and Vesper Sparrows (uncommon); Dickcissel (fall), Bobolink, Eastern Meadowlark (uncommon), Rusty Blackbird (uncommon)

Restrooms: Short Beach; Dunkin' Donuts on Lordship Boulevard and at the corner of Main Street and Access Road; in summer at Birdseye Street Boat launch.
Hazards: Some sites in Lordship are remote; birding with friends is recommended. Ticks can be plentiful.

The Birding

Lordship is situated upon a wide peninsula (once an island) jutting into Long Island Sound. It forms the western shore of the mouth of the Housatonic River, one of Connecticut's larger waterways, with its origin in northern Massachusetts. The area's closely spaced and varied habitats, and strategic location at the confluence of two migration corridors within the Atlantic Flyway, contribute to its status as one of the state's premier birding areas. Lordship is not the most picturesque site, however. While partly residential, especially along the shore, the area is predominantly industrial and includes a municipal airport and a capped landfill (now a park).

Lordship also encompasses one of the state's largest un-ditched saltmarshes, an extensive coastal dune/beach/mudflat complex, and fairly extensive areas of town, state, and federal open space. It boasts a cumulative bird species list of more than 300, and Great Meadow Marsh, Long Beach, and Frash Pond together have been nominated as an Audubon Important Bird Area (IBA), constituting some 700 acres of protected upland and marsh.

Great Meadow Marsh is a great draw for birds and birders. Although years of uncontrolled development have reduced it to a small remnant of its former size, it remains a critical resource to many species. The area's extensive marsh complex contains one of the few remaining nesting sites in Connecticut for Northern Harriers, while the refuge protects critical dune habitat for several endangered or threatened species, including nesting Piping Plovers, Least Terns, and Barn Owls, and is used extensively by Snowy and Great Egrets, Black-crowned and Yellow-crowned Night-Herons, and a host of other uncommon species. The refuge and adjacent preserves also protect rare coastal plants and insects.

How to Bird These Sites

This chapter is arranged as a tour of twelve sites in Lordship. Although the tour *can be done in less than two hours*, it could easily warrant half a day or more. A spotting scope is recommended at all of the sites. Check the tides before arriving; low tide is better for shorebirds, ducks, and gulls at Short Beach and the Access Road tidal pools. Mid- to high tide is good for shorebirds at Stratford Point, the Sikorsky Airport, the Broad Street Pilings, and the warehouse fields near the Railroad Trail, where birds get pushed into upland areas.

Note: Do not enter posted U.S. Fish and Wildlife restricted areas (unless being prosecuted for trespassing is in your plans).

■ Railroad Trail

Location: Opposite 500 Long Beach Boulevard, Stratford.
⊃ **Directions:** If coming from the southwest, take I-95 to Exit 30, Lordship Boulevard. At the end of the ramp, turn right onto Lordship Boulevard and head east. After 0.5 miles, turn right onto Long Beach Boulevard. Continue just over 0.3 miles, cross the

railroad tracks, and park on the left in the U.S. Fish and Wildlife Service's small public gravel lot beside the warehouse pond (see description below). The trailhead is back across the railroad tracks, on the right. If arriving from the northeast, turn left off the exit onto Surf Avenue. Continue 0.2 miles and turn left onto Lordship Boulevard. Long Beach Boulevard is 0.4 miles on the right. Proceed as above. **Note:** Do not park in the warehouse parking lots or trespass on their property. Although the road itself is private, there is a public right of way to Fish and Wildlife Service property.

Hazards: From late spring through the summer, be prepared for mosquitoes the size of small birds; long sleeves and repellent are essential. On calm days, gird your loins; it is impossible to bird without bathing in DEET!

The entrance to the Railroad Trail is on the north side of the railroad tracks. This level, gravel trail runs southeast into a marsh, paralleling the tracks. Remain on the trail and out of the posted areas.

This area is best known for its small population of resident Boat-tailed Grackles, which established Connecticut's first breeding colony, two males and three females, after Hurricane Gloria in 1985. More than thirty birds now frequent the Lordship area year-round, although they often disappear for a while in midwinter. They feed in the marsh, nest in the trees rimming the warehouse pond, and often roost by the Sikorsky Airport entrance at night. Listen for their bizarre videogame-like squawks and squeals, especially in spring.

In spring and fall, search for migrants in the hedgerows lining the path. Hermit Thrush, sparrows, and a wide variety of warblers, including Palm and Wilson's Warblers, seem especially attracted to this area. Willow Flycatcher and Eastern Kingbird breed locally, and other flycatchers pass through during migration. Eastern Towhee, Gray Catbird, Northern Mockingbird, and Brown Thrasher (some years) breed in the thickets here. Other breeders include Gadwall (uncommon), Belted Kingfisher, Marsh Wren, Warbling Vireo, Yellow Warbler, and Common Yellowthroat. Resident Cedar Waxwings are often conspicuous; in winter they concentrate in areas with berries. In some years, Yellow-billed Cuckoo breed here, and Black-billed Cuckoo is possible.

The trail leads to a marsh restoration area on the left that can be scanned both from the trail and from an observation platform farther down. It is home to breeding Willet and Killdeer, which often nest quite close to the tracks and feign injury as a distraction if nest or young are approached too closely. Pools within the marsh draw a nice variety of waders and shorebirds from mid-March into November, and are most productive from mid-tide rising and back to mid-low, especially in May and from mid-July to mid-September. Less common species recorded here include Pectoral, White-rumped, and Baird's Sandpipers, "Western" Willet, American Golden-Plover, and Whimbrel. Glossy Ibis and Yellow-crowned Night-Herons nest locally, and

Little Blue and Tricolored Herons visit irregularly, spring through fall. Clapper Rails can be conspicuous.

From the platform, look northeast across the marsh to the long tree-covered dike, a favorite resting area for raptors, woodpeckers, and other birds, year-round. Late fall through spring, Rough-legged Hawks are possible. From mid-July to mid-September, all five of Connecticut's nesting swallow species often roost here or feed over the marsh, with Cliff Swallow being the least common. Purple Martins occur in small numbers from spring into fall, and Cave Swallows (rare) are possible, late October through November. Tree Swallows breed in nest boxes within the marsh, and Northern Rough-winged Swallows nest locally.

The trail takes a 90-degree turn after the platform and heads southwest, eventually turning back east to another observation platform that provides stunning views of Great Meadow Marsh and Long Beach. Migrating sparrows, kinglets, vireos, warblers, and thrushes frequent the weedy areas adjacent to the trail, especially in late summer and fall. Swamp, Song, White-throated, Chipping, and Savannah Sparrows can be plentiful, and White-crowned, Lincoln's, Field, and other less common sparrows may occur. Saltmarsh and Seaside Sparrows nest in the marshes, and it is a good area to search for Nelson's Sparrows in fall.

Twenty yards down the trail is an observation blind overlooking a hidden pond on the right. *Walk quietly here.* The far shore is a favorite roosting site for egrets and night-herons. Blue and Green-winged Teal, Gadwall, American Black Duck, Hooded Mergansers, Wood Duck, and other dabbling ducks also seek this secluded refuge, especially in spring and fall.

The channel on the left, just before a gate, attracts diamond-backed terrapins, Connecticut's only brackish water turtles, which nest along the path.

If the gate is open, continue on to the outer observation platform. A pair of Willets displays and roosts on the platform, and Marsh Wrens nest near it. Waders and shorebirds sometimes feed in the channels visible from the platform. In winter, scan the duck blinds, posts, and any high ground for Snowy Owls, which are often difficult to spot amidst the frozen landscape. A few Short-eared Owls are seen fall through spring, usually at dawn or dusk. Northern Harrier has nested in this area.

This is also an excellent site for butterflies and dragonflies, including seaside dragonlet.

■ Warehouse Pond and Fields

Location: Opposite 500 Long Beach Boulevard, Stratford.
➲ **Directions:** From the trailhead for the Railroad Trail, walk back to the parking lot. The small pond is visible from the road edge, 30 yards past the parking lot, but can best be viewed from a short, gated spur trail off the parking lot. **Note:** At this time, it is permissible to access the pond's observation blind on the north end beyond the gate, but do not pass the wooden barrier in the main trail.

In spring, the area around the parking lot and spur trail can be inundated with migrants, particularly warblers, vireos, and flycatchers. The section of wooded edge along the road, from the railroad trail to the parking lot and past the pond, can be particularly birdy. Migrants often feed in the many blooming crabapple and other fruit trees that line both sides of the road. On a good day, twenty or more species can be seen in a morning. Unlike many other locations, here the birds are often at or below eye level!

In summer, Boat-tailed Grackles nest in the trees and in the reeds on the pond's small islands. Pied-billed Grebe and Least Bittern are seen infrequently but have nested. Green Heron, Mute Swan, Gadwall (uncommon), American Black Duck, and Mallard breed here as well, and June visitors may be treated to the sight of the females trailing their downy young. During migration, a wide variety of ducks are possible; regulars include small numbers of Blue and Green-winged Teal, American Wigeon, Ring-necked Duck, and Hooded Merganser. A few American Coots are seen and Common Gallinule occurs irregularly.

Connecticut's first established Boat-tailed Grackle colony nests around the pond at the end of Long Beach Boulevard, Stratford.

In late summer and early fall, herons, egrets, and a few Glossy Ibis congregate in and around the pond; White Ibis (rare) has occurred. Tricolored and Little Blue Herons are found occasionally. Regular migrants include Spotted Sandpiper (may nest), Solitary Sandpiper, both yellowlegs species, Killdeer (nest in the gravel areas along the entrance road), and Least and Semipalmated Sandpipers. Northern Waterthrush visit the pond margins in early spring and in July and August. Search the trees and shrubs adjacent to the pond for songbird migrants. Wild Turkeys frequent the entire area.

A short walk north along the road past the pond and beside the warehouses leads to an open grassy area on the left that may attract Eastern Meadowlark, Horned Lark, American Pipit, and other grassland species. Pleasure Beach in Bridgeport can be seen across the marsh. There are active Osprey nests visible; in winter, raptors tend to perch in the trees there. Willets nest in the marsh, which is a good place to find Whimbrel and Pectoral Sandpiper during migration. At high tide, shorebirds sometime gather on the lawns or on similar fields on the opposite side of the warehouses. Raptors—including Merlin, Kestrel, and Peregrine Falcon—hunt this area, especially in fall. Red-tailed Hawk breeds locally, and Rough-legged Hawk sometimes overwinters. At the end of the road, there are a couple of parking spots for the Fish and Wildlife Service's observation area overlooking White Rock and Johnson's Creeks. An obscure path leads down across the lawn to the creek edge. The creeks attract a variety of waterfowl year-round. Spring through fall, watch for Great and Snowy Egrets and migrating shorebirds at low tide. Resident Gadwall and American Black Duck frequent the area, especially fall through early summer, and Eurasian Wigeon has wintered here on more than one occasion.

■ Igor I. Sikorsky Memorial Airport

Location: 1000 Great Meadow Road, Stratford.
⊃ **Directions:** From Long Beach Boulevard, turn right onto Lordship Boulevard, continue 0.3 miles to the light, then turn right to stay on Lordship Boulevard. The road crosses the marsh. (Watch for Yellow-crowned Night-Herons.) About halfway across (0.4 miles), there is a pull-off on the left next to the airport fence. Although this spot is posted, birders use it to scan the marsh and fields adjacent to the runways. A designated free parking area inside the airport, halfway around the airport entrance road, can be used to scan other parts of the runways.

During migration, especially from mid to late July into September, the airport fields are used as resting and feeding sites by shorebirds at high tide. Most species are possible, but American Golden-Plover, along with Buff-breasted, Upland, and Baird's Sandpipers, occur almost annually. Whimbrel is a regular migrant in small numbers, and both Marbled and Hudsonian Godwits are found occasionally. Migration also brings Eastern Meadowlark, Horned Lark, Snow Bunting, American Pipit, and the occasional Lapland Longspur to the fields; a variety of sparrows, especially Savannah Sparrow, gather on the edges and along the fences. Clapper Rail and Saltmarsh and Seaside Sparrows breed in the marsh, while Yellow-crowned Night-Herons feed here spring through fall. Snowy and occasionally Short-eared Owls, Rough-legged Hawks, and other raptors use the marsh in many winters. Northern Harriers hunt here year-round.

Thirty yards southwest of the airport entrance, along Lordship Boulevard, are pools that attract Sora and Virginia Rail. Boat-tailed Grackles gather year-round in the trees to the left of the airport most evenings.

■ Long Beach

Location: Long Beach Park.
➲ **Directions:** Leave the airport and continue south across the marsh on Lordship Boulevard, 0.7 miles to a stop sign. Turn right onto Oak Bluff Avenue, and go 0.3 miles to the entrance to Long Beach Park. (Scan the marsh along this stretch of Oak Bluff Avenue for Yellow-crowned Night-Heron. It's a favored feeding area for this uncommon Connecticut breeding bird.) The park is open dawn until dusk; an entrance fee is charged in summer.

Stop near the beginning of the parking lot to scan the ocean and beaches to the east before continuing to the end of the lot. From fall through spring, this area provides a fine vantage point from which to search for water-birds, including Northern Gannet, Long-tailed Duck, Common Goldeneye, Red-breasted Merganser, King Eider (rare), and all three scoter species. A good variety of ducks, gulls, loons, and grebes are usually present in winter, and it's a great site for finding lingering sea ducks in summer.

The numbers of gulls and sea ducks often build offshore in November and in March and April, with the occasional rarity found among them. This is a particularly good site to find wintering Iceland, Glaucous (uncommon), and Lesser Black-backed Gulls, all of which have at times lingered well into spring. Black-headed and Little Gulls sometimes occur, especially in spring when Bonaparte's Gulls become more plentiful.

Check the beaches for Dunlin and especially Sanderling, and the jetties for Purple Sandpiper and Ruddy Turnstone, in season. On crisp fall days, mi-grating swallows stream down the beach, heading south. Cave Swallow is possible from late October through November. Belted Kingfishers are fre-quently sighted over the marsh, while ducks, shorebirds, and waders gather to feed in the channels during much of the year. As previously mentioned, Yellow-crowned Night-Herons often feed near the park entrance on the marsh side.

At the far end of the parking lot is a row of boulders, beyond which are the dunes of Long Beach. From here you can walk on a path through the dunes to Pleasure Beach, a 2-mile roundtrip that requires *at least an hour*. However, many of the area specialties can be found within the first 50 to 100 yards of dunes. Please remain on the path or beach to avoid trampling the fragile dune grass or disturbing nesting birds.

From March through September, Long Beach hosts several breeding pairs of Piping Plover, a threatened species. Least Terns are sporadic nesters, but the colony here can hold sixty or more pairs. Common Terns feed locally, and Roseate Tern can make a rare appearance in spring or fall. The dunes here and at Milford Point are the area's best sites for finding the "Ipswich" sub-species of Savannah Sparrow, November through March. Roosting Short-eared Owls may be found mid-October through April. Horned Larks are reliable visitors from fall through spring, and are joined by Snow Buntings in most winters. Orange-crowned Warbler has been found in the dunes in fall and winter. Raptors and diurnal landbird migrants pass through in good numbers, especially in fall.

State-threatened Least Terns nest at Long Beach in Stratford; their numbers fluctuate, often dramatically, from year to year.

Stratford Seawall

Location: 53 Beach Drive, Stratford.
➲ **Directions:** Leave Long Beach, go 0.2 miles, and take the second right onto Ocean Avenue. Continue 0.2 miles, then turn right onto Washington Parkway. In 0.1 miles, the parkway becomes Beach Drive and bends left to follow the water. Just after the curve, there is a parking lot on the right overlooking Long Island Sound.

The same variety of waterbird species that can be seen off Long Beach occurs here. Lesser Black-backed and Iceland Gulls seem to prefer this stretch of beach to those nearby.

Stratford Point

Location: Opposite 1098 Prospect Drive, Stratford.
➲ **Directions:** From the Stratford Seawall, continue northeast on Beach Drive 0.1 miles onto Jefferson Street. Go 0.2 miles, then turn right onto Stratford Road and continue 0.4 miles to a three-way intersection. Turn right onto Prospect Avenue and continue 0.7 miles to the entrance to a fenced-in area on the left. This area of short-grass fields and buildings is Stratford Point. If the gate is open, enter and park by the last building to the east. If the gate is closed, no access is possible.

Once the site of the historic Lordship Gun Club, Stratford Point includes 28 acres of open coastal meadows overlooking the mouth of the Housatonic River and Milford Point to the east. To remove lead shot from the area, the DuPont Corporation is performing extensive environmental remediation activities. The National Audubon Society conducts conservation work, scientific studies, and some public programs here and allows public access when their staff is onsite, generally on weekdays from 9:00 to 5:00, and on some weekends. They make a special effort to remain open when rarities are present.

Given the site's location, an increase in public access, and the extensive habitat restoration underway, birders can expect good things to come. Thus far, the species list here is similar to those of Short and Long Beaches, and to Milford Point (Chapter 18). Rarities recorded include both American White and Brown Pelicans, Swainson's Hawk, Gull-billed and Sandwich Terns, Chuck-wills-widow, Western Kingbird, Yellow-headed Blackbird, and Grasshopper and Clay-colored Sparrows. Connecticut's only recorded White-tailed Kite spent months here.

Stratford Point affords wonderful views of the estuary mouth, jetties, and sandbars across the river at Milford Point from mowed trails that run along the periphery. It is a stellar site for viewing wintering sea ducks, storm-driven pelagics, summering and migrating terns, and feeding flocks of gulls (fall and spring). Large rafts of scaup (mostly Greater Scaup) and White-winged and Surf Scoters (in the thousands) build here from November to March, usually moving between nearby Russian Beach (off Park Boulevard) to the west and the mouth of the Housatonic River to the east, where Brant and other waterfowl also congregate. A sighting or two of Common Eider or Harlequin Duck are expected most winters. King Eider has occurred. Eurasian Wigeon is nearly annual among the many Gadwall, American Wigeon, American Black Duck, and other waterfowl in the river mouth, fall through spring. In winter, look for Great Cormorant on and near the jetty in the river mouth, and expect Northern Gannet to pass by in fall and spring. Migrating raptors move through in good numbers, especially in fall. Snowy Owls seem to favor the rocks and bluffs here in most years, and occasionally a Short-eared Owl or Rough-legged Hawk will overwinter.

During migration, decent numbers of shorebirds gather on the rising tide along the Stratford Point shore of the river's mouth and roost on the concrete reef balls in the cove toward Short Beach (north). These usually include many Semipalmated Plovers and Least and Semipalmated Sandpipers, along with a few White-rumped Sandpipers, Ruddy Turnstones, and Short-billed Dowitchers.

The point is also a migrant trap for landbirds. A butterfly garden and water feature near the main building are always worth checking for them. Fall through spring, the fields and gravel parking lots are reliable for Savannah Sparrow (including the "Ipswich" subspecies), Snow Bunting, Horned Lark, and American Pipit (fall), with occasional visits from Eastern Meadowlark and Lapland Longspur. Field and American Tree Sparrows overwinter in the fields and along the hedges that line the fence on the park's west side. Sedge Wren (rare) has been found in the fields in October, and Grasshopper Sparrows have been teased out from the brush along the fence during migration. The thickets here also have drawn a variety of other less common landbirds, including Gray-cheeked Thrush, and various warblers, such as Yellow-breasted Chat and Connecticut, Mourning, Kentucky, and Orange-crowned Warblers. The fields hold great potential for attracting migrant grassland-loving shorebirds such as American Golden-Plover or Buff-breasted Sandpiper.

■ Short Beach

Location: Dorne Drive, Stratford.

➲ **Directions:** Leave Stratford Point on Prospect Avenue. After 0.1 miles, turn right onto Riverdale Dive, go 0.4 miles, and turn right onto Lighthouse Avenue. In less than 0.1 miles, turn left onto Short Beach Road, continue 0.3 miles and turn right onto Dorn Drive, the entrance to Short Beach. Proceed 0.2 miles, straight through the intersection, and either park directly ahead (left of the walkway and pavilion) or turn left and continue another 0.2 miles, then park at the curb in the rotary. An entrance fee is charged in summer.

This town park provides access to the sandy beaches of the inner Housatonic River mouth. There are several trails to the beaches, including a path across from the entrance road and another near the rotary at the park's north end. The brushy areas lining the beach and the perimeter fence of the old land-fill should be checked for migrant songbirds. Sparrows frequent the area in winter, including American Tree Sparrow and, occasionally, Field and White-crowned Sparrows. The planted pines sometime attract winter finches, in-cluding crossbills, during invasion years.

A walk along the beach, fall through spring, may produce Horned Lark, Snow Bunting, and "Ipswich" Savannah Sparrow. The park's observation platforms provide excellent views of the estuary mouth and Milford Point's outer sand-bars and rock jetties. This area is a mecca for shorebirds, terns, gulls, ducks, loons, and grebes. (See the lists given for Milford Point and Stratford Point.)

At low tide, up to twenty species of migrating shorebirds may be seen feed-ing on the mudflats, rebuilding fat reserves for their arduous journeys. High tide finds them resting on the sandbars and jetties. Killdeer, Black-bellied and Semipalmated Plovers, both yellowlegs species, Short-billed Dowitcher, and Semipalmated and Least Sandpipers are the most likely. White-rumped Sand-piper, Stilt, Red Knot, and many other less common sandpipers also occur.

Up to eight species of gulls visit annually, and winter brings concentrations that can build into the thousands by April. Check for a few Iceland, Lesser Black-backed, and Glaucous Gulls (least common) among the masses. Bona-parte's Gulls visit in March and April, and Laughing Gulls occur in summer. Franklin's Gull (rare) has been found here.

Waterfowl also use the small pond by the rotary year-round. Gadwall, American Black Duck, and Mallard are common and breed locally. Hooded Merganser, Bufflehead, teal, especially Green-winged, American Coot, and Pied-billed Grebe are regular visitors. Egrets, Glossy Ibis, herons, including Green (may nest), and Black- and Yellow-crowned Night-Herons visit spring through fall. Brown Thrasher and Wild Turkey scrape out a living on the old landfill adjacent to the inlet, and the turkeys roost nightly in huge trees on the beach. Monk Parakeet and Fish Crow patronize the golf course at the entrance. In fall, Savannah Sparrow and Palm and Yellow-rumped Warblers feed among the dune plants. Many landbirds pass through during migration.

Mute Swans are a permanent fixture here, and Brant are common, fall through spring. Flocks of hundreds build into March or April with a few lingering into summer. In winter, search the jetties for Purple Sandpiper and Great Cormorant (by mid-October). American Oystercatchers (four to five pairs) nest at Milford Point; they are vocal and conspicuous on the jetties and sandbars all summer. Common wintering ducks include Gadwall, American Wigeon, American Black Duck, Bufflehead, and Red-breasted Merganser. Eurasian Wigeon is found annually.

In addition to the commonly occurring species, the area vaunts an impressive list of rarities, including White Ibis, both pelican species, White-faced Storm Petrel (only continental U.S. record), Thick-billed Murre, King Eider, and Gyrfalcon, along with rare shorebirds, grebes, and ducks.

◼ Frash Pond

Location: 48 Access Road, Stratford.
➲ **Directions:** Leave Short Beach and head west 0.1 miles, then turn right onto Stratford Road (Connecticut 113). Continue 0.8 miles, then turn left onto Access Road; Frash Pond is immediately on the right, behind the shopping center. Park in the shopping center lot.

This small trash-lined pond may not be picturesque, but it is a magnet for migrating waterfowl and often holds wintering waders, waterbirds, and gulls. It's the local hotspot for Canvasback, late October through April, whenever the pond has open water, and is reliable for Common and Hooded Mergansers, Bufflehead, both scaup species, Ring-necked and Ruddy Ducks, and an occasional Redhead. Gulls and cormorants roost on the ice in winter. The pond has held wintering Great Egret, Black-crowned Night-Heron, and Great Blue Heron. Rarely, an American Bittern shelters in the reeds lining the shore. American Coot is expected annually, and Pied-billed Grebe and Belted Kingfisher are frequent visitors.

Access Road Ponds

Location: Opposite 840 Access Road, Stratford.
➲ **Directions:** Leave Frash Pond and turn right, continuing southwest on Access Road for 0.8 miles. Most birders park in the lot of the R.E. Michel Company, the small brick building just past Sunset Avenue, before the light at Lordship Boulevard. **Note:** This is private property; please do not disrupt business traffic.

The small tidal ponds just across the street are best at low tide, when shorebirds, waders, rails, and ducks use the exposed mudflats. These ponds are always worth a stop, having attracted more than their share of rare shorebirds, especially from late July to mid-September. Wilson's Phalarope, Ruff, and Baird's Sandpiper have all been seen here. This is a regular feeding site for Glossy Ibis (check for White-faced Ibis as well), and for Belted Kingfisher, which breed in the area. Clapper, King (rare), and Virginia Rails have bred here. The list of nesting and migrating landbirds is similar to that at the Railroad Trail, including Marsh Wren, Cedar Waxwing, Eastern Kingbird, and Willow Flycatcher. In winter, the brushy area west of the brick building has held Fox Sparrow, and the local flock of Boat-tailed Grackle has roosted in the trees here.

It is a short walk to a large tidal saltpan on the south side of Lordship Boulevard, near the intersection, that often holds shorebirds, including White-rumped Sandpiper. **Note:** Traffic is heavy here.

Birdseye Street Boat Ramp

Location: 180 Beacon Point Road, Stratford.
➲ **Directions:** Leaving the Access Road Ponds, proceed east on Access Road back toward Frash Pond, 0.9 miles to the light at Main Street. Turn left onto Main Street, go 0.3 miles, then bear right onto Elm Street. Continue 0.2 miles and turn right onto Birdseye Street. The boat ramp is at the end of the street. **Note:** The Birdseye Street Extension (the last right before the boat ramp) offers more views of the river and its mudflats. At the end of that road, there is parking in the Animal Control lot; the marsh by the ball fields across from the lot attracts shorebirds and waders, and is especially good for Lesser Yellowlegs and Stilt Sandpiper. Ruff (rare), American Bittern, and Glossy Ibis have been seen in that marsh, and Bobolink has been found in the fields adjacent to the building. Orchard Orioles breed locally.

The area near the boat ramp is best on a falling tide. To the left of the ramp, an observation platform provides a clear view of the Housatonic River and the west side of Nell's Island in Milford's Wheeler Saltmarsh. (See Milford

Point for species list). This area can be quickly checked, and a wide variety of water, marsh, and beach-loving species is possible.

Mute Swans (often fifty or more), Canada Geese, ducks, and gulls are fed here. In winter, American Coots join the masses and can be fairly common, especially in the channel on the south side of the parking lot, where Gadwall (common), Northern Shoveler, and Green-winged and Blue-winged Teal also have been found. Rare Tundra and Trumpeter Swans have occurred with the Mute Swans. Check the river for Brant,

Mute Swans often gather at the boat ramp in winter.

loons, and grebes from fall through spring, and look in the drainage ditch that parallels the north side of the entrance road for shorebirds; Wilson's Snipe are regular in March or April and again in September and October. American Bittern also has occurred in the drainage channel, as well as the small patches of marsh at either end of the parking lot. In summer, egrets, both night-herons, and Glossy Ibis can be conspicuous in these small marshes and in the Wheeler Saltmarsh. Terns and gulls feed over the river and the Wheeler Marsh, and Black Skimmers are sometimes seen, usually on the sandbars across the river. Less common species, such as Forster's and Black Terns, occur during migration. It's worth scanning the Wheeler Marsh for raptors year-round, especially for Bald Eagle and Peregrine, which nest locally, and Northern Harrier (rare nester).

■ Shelby Pond and Shakespeare Theatre

Location: 1850 Elm Street, Stratford.
➲ **Directions:** Leaving Birdseye Street Boat Ramp, take the first right onto Elm Street. Continue less than 0.4 miles and turn right into the entrance to Stratford's Shakespeare Theatre. Shelby Pond is on the left.

This small pond attracts ducks, especially Gadwall, American Black Duck, and Blue-winged and Green-winged Teal, along with Hooded Merganser and an occasional Pied-billed Grebe or American Coot during migration. Scan the trees that surround the pond for migrating songbirds. Orchard Oriole has nested here, and Monk Parakeet nests in the pines beside the theatre and in nearby residential areas. A small colony of Yellow-crowned Night-herons often nests in the sycamores across the road from the theatre entrance; they feed in the marsh on the property's south side.

■ Broad Street Pilings (Shorebird Roost)

Location: 649 Broad Street, Stratford.
➲ **Directions:** Leaving the Shakespeare Theatre, continue north on Elm Street for less than 0.1 miles and turn right at the light onto Ferry Boulevard. Go 0.2 miles, then turn right at the light onto Broad Street. Stop almost immediately on the right, where a small stream channel crosses under the road.

This is a well-known roosting site for shorebirds, especially Greater and Lesser Yellowlegs, along with Short-billed Dowitcher during fall migration. It is also one of the most reliable sites in Connecticut to find Long-billed Dowitcher in fall. Hudsonian Godwit has occurred. At high tide or at dusk (when the birds come to roost), hundreds of birds can sometimes be seen standing on the pilings in the channel.

Wimisink Preserve, Sherman

Seasonal rating: Sp *** Su **** F *** W *
Best time to bird: Mid-April to October, especially May through August.
Habitats: Wooded swamp, marsh, open water, shrubby edge, beaver pond, adjacent to forested ridgelines.

Bird list for this site:

SPECIALTY BIRDS
Resident – Belted Kingfisher, Common Raven
Summer – Wood Duck, Hooded Merganser, American Bittern (some years), Great Blue and Green Herons, Virginia Rail, Broad-winged Hawk, Yellow-billed Cuckoo, Pileated and Hairy Woodpeckers, Ruby-throated Hummingbird, Willow and Least Flycatchers, Warbling Vireo, Bank and Cliff Swallows (uncommon), Marsh Wren, Eastern Bluebird, Cedar Waxwing, Swamp Sparrow, Scarlet Tanager

OTHER KEY BIRDS
Turkey Vulture, Cooper's and Red-shouldered Hawks, Chimney Swift, Eastern Phoebe, Eastern Kingbird; Northern Rough-winged, Tree, and Barn Swallows; Veery, Wood Thrush, Common Yellowthroat, Rose-breasted Grosbeak, Indigo Bunting

MIGRANTS
Great Egret (uncommon), Little Blue Heron (uncommon), Common Gallinule (rare; potential nester)

Location: 167 Gaylordsville Road, Sherman.
Restrooms: Public restrooms in Kent, 6.6 miles north. The diner and restaurants on Route 7 in Gaylordsville town center, 0.5 miles south of Route 55, have restrooms but may require a purchase.

The Birding

This lovely 55-acre inland wetland, with its shrubby border and scattered dead trees, is managed by the Naromi Land Trust. The preserve rests in a valley encircled by forested ridges a mile from the New York line. It came to the birding community's attention in 2014 when a pair of American Bitterns, a rare local breeder, raised three young here. The family was often visible from the 100-yard boardwalk that leads from the parking area into the edge of the marsh. The presence of so many visiting birders revealed this to be a vibrant birding site, with a diversity of the typically more northern-nesting Connecticut species. This wetland is representative of the many small swamps and marshes in the area, and its easy accessibility makes it worth visiting.

How to Bird This Site

A scope is recommended here. Follow the short boardwalk to the end, where there is a viewing platform. Search among the reeds for breeding waterfowl which include Wood and American Black Ducks along with Hooded Merganser (most years), a quite localized breeder, restricted in range statewide. Virginia Rail, Red-winged Blackbird, Marsh Wren (most years), Common Yellowthroat, and Swamp Sparrow nest in tussocks and reeds within the marsh and are generally quite vocal in summer. The shrubby edges support breeding Green Heron, Willow and possibly Least Flycatchers, Eastern Kingbird, the secretive Yel-

The small marsh at Wimisink is home to nesting American Bitterns.

Photograph courtesy Mark S. Szantyr

low-billed Cuckoo, Cedar Waxwing, Gray Catbird, and Ruby-throated Hummingbird. Male Ruby-throats are most conspicuous, as they tend to perch at the tips of dead snags within their territories. Nesting Eastern Bluebird, Tree Swallow, Black-capped Chickadee, and other species take advantage of the holes in dead trees created by local woodpeckers, including Hairy and Pileated Woodpeckers. Bank Swallow, another less common and localized breeder, is reliably found here. Along with Chimney Swifts and Barn, Northern Rough-winged, Tree, and (rarely) Cliff Swallows, they feed on insects over the marsh. Broad-winged, Cooper's, and Red-shouldered Hawks all breed locally and can be consistently seen circling over the ridges, along with Common Raven, Turkey Vulture, and sometimes Black Vulture.

The marsh edge can attract shorebirds, herons, and egrets in summer. Least, Solitary, and Spotted Sandpipers are the likeliest of their family. Great Blue

Heron breeds locally, and look for Great Egret and even Little Blue Heron in late July or August during their post-breeding dispersal. A wide variety of songbirds frequents the trees surrounding the marsh, including American Goldfinch, House Finch, Common Grackle, and the occasional Rose-breasted Grosbeak or Indigo Bunting. The forests adjacent to the marsh host Scarlet Tanager, Veery, Wood Thrush, Red-eyed Vireo and other forest-nesting species.

Note: There is another trailhead, with sign and kiosk, about 0.1 miles south of the parking lot, on the same side of the road. This trail, which can be muddy at times, leads west through meadow and forest, across a bridge, and ultimately to a platform overlooking open water and marsh. Across the street and a short walk farther south is the trailhead to the Giddings Preserve. That trail ascends steadily for 300 feet (and continues for at least a mile) through a forest that is home to typical upland deciduous and mixed woods species.

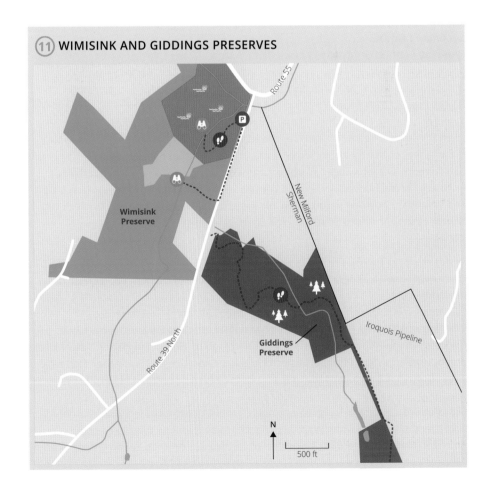

11 WIMISINK AND GIDDINGS PRESERVES

Route 55

Wimisink Preserve

New Milford Sherman

Iroquois Pipeline

Giddings Preserve

Route 39 North

N

500 ft

(12) Kent

- Kent School Bridge
- Skiff Mountain Road
- River Road
- Schaghticoke Road

Seasonal rating: Sp **** Su *** F ** W *
Best time to bird: Late April to early August, but especially May and early June.
Habitats: River, streams, forested ridgelines, lowland riparian woodlands, small hemlock ravines, farm fields, open lawns and athletic fields, regenerating old fields, open meadows, scrub edge, power-line cuts, small ponds, wooded swamps, sewage ponds, wet areas with thick understory.

Bird list for this site:

SPECIALTY BIRDS

Resident – Ruffed Grouse (declining), Black Vulture, Sharp-shinned Hawk (uncommon), Cooper's Hawk, Northern Goshawk (rare), Bald Eagle (uncommon), Broad-winged Hawk, Yellow-bellied Sapsucker, Pileated Woodpecker, Common Raven, Purple Finch (local)
Summer – Common Merganser, American Kestrel (decreasing); Acadian, Willow, and Least Flycatchers; Yellow-throated and Warbling Vireos, Purple Martin, Cliff Swallow, Brown Creeper, Winter Wren (some years), Brown Thrasher (local), Hermit Thrush (uncommon), Golden-winged Warbler (rare), Cerulean and Worm-eating Warblers, Northern Parula, Hooded and Prairie Warblers (local), Canada Warbler (sporadic), Field and Savannah Sparrows (local), Bobolink, Eastern Meadowlark, Orchard Oriole (local)
Winter – White-throated Sparrow, Pine Siskin (sporadic)

OTHER KEY BIRDS

Resident – Wild Turkey, Double-crested Cormorant, Turkey Vulture, Eastern Screech-Owl, Great Horned and Barred Owls, Hairy Woodpecker, Northern Flicker, Fish Crow (uncommon)
Summer – Wood Duck, Hooded Merganser, Great Blue and Green Herons (uncommon), Osprey, Killdeer, Spotted Sandpiper, Black-billed and Yellow-billed Cuckoos, Chimney Swift, Ruby-throated Hummingbird, Belted Kingfisher, Eastern Wood-Pewee, Eastern Phoebe, Eastern Kingbird, Great Crested Flycatcher, Red-eyed Vireo; Northern Rough-winged, Tree, and Barn Swallows; House and Carolina Wrens, Blue-gray Gnatcatcher, Eastern Bluebird, Veery, Wood Thrush, Northern Mockingbird, Gray Catbird, Cedar Waxwing; Blue-winged, Yellow, Chestnut-sided, Black-throated Green, and Black-and-white Warblers; Blackburnian and Pine Warblers (local), American Redstart, Ovenbird, Louisiana Waterthrush, Common Yellow-throat, Scarlet Tanager, Eastern Towhee, Swamp Sparrow, Rose-breasted Grosbeak, Indigo Bunting

(local), Red-winged Blackbird, Common Grackle, Baltimore Oriole
Winter – Northern Shrike (occasional), winter finches

MIGRANTS
Spring – Solitary Sandpiper, Common Nighthawk, Olive-sided Flycatcher (uncommon), Alder Flycatcher (uncommon), Blue-headed Vireo, Bank Swallow, Red-breasted Nuthatch (spring and fall), Ruby-crowned Kinglet, Golden-crowned Kinglet (local; nearby nester), Gray-cheeked and Swainson's Thrushes, any of Connecticut's warbler species, White-crowned and White-throated Sparrows (spring and fall), Dark-eyed Junco (spring and fall)
Fall – Warblers

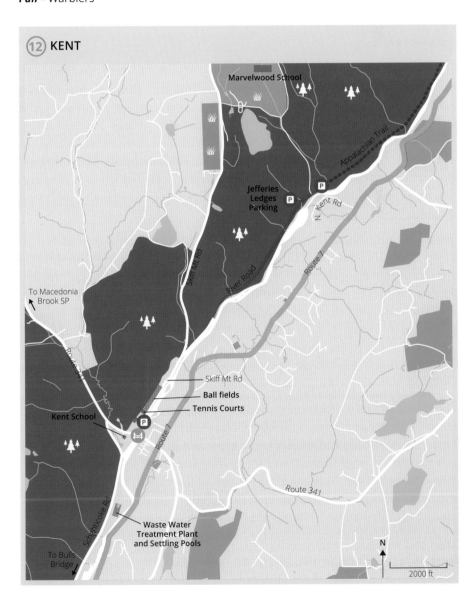

Location: Intersection of Connecticut Routes 7 and 341, Kent.

Restrooms: There are public restrooms in Kent; the bookstore in Kent also allows use of their facilities.

Hazards: The meadows and old fields at the end of River Road have *abundant* deer ticks, which may carry Lyme disease. Wear light-colored clothing, tuck pants into socks, and check for ticks regularly while in this area and upon returning home. Black flies and mosquitoes can be bad from early spring into mid-summer. The road is not maintained and can have large potholes. Carry a map, water, and food if you venture past the trailhead.

The Birding

The sites in this chapter are nestled in the Housatonic Valley in Connecticut's heavily forested northwest highlands. This area alongside the Housatonic River is uniquely situated between moist riparian woodlands and steep-sloped forested ridgelines. The river and ridgelines create a major north-south migration corridor for birds. Within this vast and largely undeveloped region are a mosaic of numerous microhabitats, including regenerating old fields, live and dead pine stands, hemlock ravines, wet and dry meadows, plowed farm fields, wooded swamps, and small ponds and streams.

The area's location, topography, size, and habitats make it attractive to an extensive assortment of bird species. It is the ideal location for finding spring migrant songbirds and several of Connecticut's more unusual nesting species, including those like Cerulean Warbler that require large tracts of undisturbed forest near water. Also to be found are species with restricted ranges in the state, such as Golden-winged Warbler (rare). Occasionally, species at the extreme edge of their range, such as Yellow-throated Warbler (rare), are lured here to very specific habitats—in this case large sycamores and cottonwoods growing along streams.

The area is situated within an ecotone, a transition zone where the flora and fauna of both north and south blend. Northern plant species such as white birch, hobble bush, and bunch berry grow alongside southern species like cardinal flower and columbine. Bird species from the north, such as Common Raven, Winter Wren, and Yellow-bellied Sapsucker, rub shoulders with their southern cousins such as Fish Crow (rare), Black Vulture, Tufted Titmouse, and Red-bellied Woodpecker. It is the only area in Connecticut at which I've recorded more than ninety species in a morning!

Note: Acadian Flycatcher regularly breeds along the entrance road at nearby Macedonia Brook State Park, off Connecticut 341.

This chapter outlines a 15-mile roundtrip route to four main areas; it usually takes *at least four hours to do this circuit*. Be sure to **set your odometer to zero** where indicated, as subsequent directions are given in tenths of a mile.

Much of this route travels along River Road, which is paved for the first 20 yards then turns to dirt. The road is not maintained and there are some potholes, but it is usually passable without four-wheel drive. Even in summer, the valley doesn't really awaken until about 7:00 a.m., when the sun finally clears the eastern ridges. If you arrive at dawn, I recommend checking the meadows at the top of Skiff Mountain Road for grassland species such as Bobolink, Eastern Meadowlark, Savannah Sparrow, and American Kestrel before venturing down River Road. Because grassland species are often active throughout the day, a post–River Road visit also can be productive. Note that sunset arrives early in the valley.

■ Kent School Bridge

○ **Directions:** From the intersection of Connecticut Routes 7 and 341 in Kent, go west 0.3 miles on Route 341, over a bridge across the Housatonic River, then take your first right onto Skiff Mountain Road. Most birders pull into the parking lot immediately on the left, park to the side, then walk across the street and down the driveway to the river. **Note:** This is private property; proceed at your own risk. There also is a pull-off on the right, less than 0.1 miles farther along Skiff Mountain Road.

Most years, a few pairs of Cliff Swallows, very local breeders in Connecticut, nest under the bridge, while Rough-winged Swallows nest in the embankments. It may be necessary to walk under the bridge to view the nests of either of these swallows, but as often as not the birds can be seen feeding over the river, resting on the wires, or soaring around the athletic fields. All of Connecticut's resident swallows, including Purple Martin, occur here in spring migration, sometimes in good numbers. Although Tree and Barn Swallows arrive in March and the other swallows by mid-April, the martins don't arrive until very late April or early May. Chimney Swifts nest in the chimneys of the Kent School, across Connecticut Route 341 to the south; their distinctive silhouette—cigar-shaped body with sickle-shaped wings—is a common sight over the playing fields.

This is a great spot from which to scan the ridgelines to the west for raptors, Black and Turkey Vultures, and Common Raven, especially later in the

12 | Kent

morning when they tend to soar above the ridge. Red-tailed Hawks are common residents, and occasionally Red-shouldered and Broad-winged Hawks, or even a Bald Eagle, are seen. Cooper's and Sharp-shinned Hawks hunt the area, and Northern Goshawk (rare) is possible. Ospreys are fairly common spring through fall. Pileated Woodpeckers are frequently heard and occasionally seen flying along the ridge. Eastern Kingbird, Yellow-throated and Warbling Vireos, American Redstart, Yellow Warbler, Baltimore Oriole, and Chipping Sparrow are a few of the typical nesting songbird species to be found here and along the route.

■ Lower Skiff Mountain Road

⮑ **Directions: Set your odometer to zero** and continue north on Skiff Mountain Road. After 0.2 miles, stop at the tennis courts. **Note:** Do not reset your odometer at the tennis courts, as additional directions appear below.

The Housatonic River Valley is the center of Black Vulture abundance in Connecticut. The dead trees on the east bank, across the river, are a favored and well-known roost site. Small numbers of Eastern Bluebirds frequent the playing fields all along Skiff Mountain Road and can sometimes be found sitting on the fences by the tennis courts. Occasionally, Orchard Orioles are found along this stretch of the river in spring and summer.

Continuing along the road, stop at the pull-off when your odometer *reads 0.8 miles*. This pull-off affords great views up and down the river. Scan the river, sandbars, and boulders for Wood Duck, the occasional Hooded Merganser, and Common Merganser, a very local breeding species in Connecticut that nests along the river in holes in large trees, often sycamores. In summer, female Common Mergansers can be seen trailing lines of babies through the river's currents and eddies. The river's many sandbars also attract Spotted Sandpiper (nests) and, in spring, migrant Solitary Sandpiper.

Continue to another pull-off *at 0.9 miles* on your odometer. Park here and walk back to view the pastures across the street to the west. Scores of species visit this idyllic little glade during migration; many stay to breed, including Great Crested Flycatcher, Eastern Kingbird, Indigo Bunting, Chipping Sparrow, and Yellow-throated and Warbling Vireos. During the breeding season, the many birdhouses here are occupied by Black-capped Chickadees, Tufted Titmice, Tree Swallows, Eastern Bluebirds, and House Wrens. This is also another good spot from which to watch the ridgeline for raptors, vultures, and ravens.

Upper Skiff Mountain Road

➲ **Directions:** Continue to 1.1 miles on your odometer from Lower Skiff Mountain Road. Here the road forks, with Skiff Mountain Road continuing to the left and River Road on the right. **Note: Reset your odometer to zero** here, then continue up the hill on Skiff Mountain Road. (Or see River Road below, if you wish to start there.)

At *1.5 miles* on your odometer, stop at the pull-off on the right. The nearby wetland across the street sometimes holds Wood Duck and Solitary Sandpiper during migration.

Continue on Skiff Mountain Road, passing Fuller Mountain Road on the left. At the top of the hill, *at 1.8 miles* on your odometer, a house on the right has both Purple Martin and Eastern Bluebird boxes in the yard. Park in the small pull-off just past the property, on the right, taking care not to block the road. In most years, martins nest here in small numbers, while bluebirds are usually plentiful. Pine Warblers breed in the evergreens across the street.

Continue along Skiff Mountain Road. When the odometer *reads 2.7 miles*, begin checking the farm fields on the road's west side. These fields are home to Eastern Meadowlark, Bobolink, Savannah Sparrow, and in most years, a pair of Kestrels. Wild Turkeys frequent the area as well. Warbling Vireo and Eastern Bluebird nest in the residential neighborhood.

At *3.1 miles* on your odometer, turn around in the entrance road for the Marvelwood School, then stop and look east. There is a small pond behind the residential neighborhood that can be scanned from the entrance road. Ringnecked and Wood Ducks, and occasionally scaup or other species, may be found here during migration.

River Road

Retrace the 3.1 miles to River Road, then turn left at the base of the hill. Look for a sign for the Appalachian Trail on the left. **Note: Reset your odometer to zero** here.

If you have yet to see Common Merganser on this trip, park on the left, just after the road turns to dirt, and look upstream. You'll see a group of boulders on which Common Mergansers often rest. Search carefully, as sleeping female mergansers are especially difficult to see.

One effective way to find birds on River Road is to drive slowly with the windows open, looking and listening. *If time is short*, the best birding is usually from Saint John's Ledges (1.7 miles on your odometer) to the road's end (2.8 miles), especially around the parking area there. **Note:** On weekends from July 1 to Labor Day, the last mile of road is closed to vehicles but remains accessible by foot or bicycle.

At 0.2 miles on your odometer, there is a bridge over a stream and a beautiful hemlock ravine on the left. Louisiana Waterthrush nests along this stream (and along most of the other streams that cross River Road). Small side ravines like this one are good places to find Black-throated Green Warbler and Winter Wren during migration; the warblers prefer the hemlocks, while the wrens frequent areas with deadfalls. Occasionally both species stay to nest. Any of the hemlock stands along the road may attract migrating Black-throated Green, Blackburnian, Yellow-rumped, and Blackpoll Warblers, and occasionally Tennessee, Nashville, Pine, and other warblers. After mid-May, these streams should be checked for Acadian Flycatcher, an uncommon/sporadic nester here. Blue-headed Vireos also prefer areas with conifers, especially hemlocks; these birds usually arrive in mid-April, and are seen through May.

From 0.3 to 0.5 miles, the moist lowlands and drier hillsides hold typical woodland breeding species, including Eastern Wood-Pewee, Hairy Woodpecker, Scarlet Tanager, and other common species of mixed-deciduous and riparian woods. This is usually the first area in which Yellow-bellied Sapsucker appears along the road.

From 0.5 to 0.8 miles, there is a flat wet area good for nesting Louisiana Waterthrush, which frequents both sides of the road.

Just past 0.8 miles on your odometer, a pull-off on the right overlooks a sandbar that sometimes holds shorebirds, ducks, and geese. Cedar Waxwings seem to prefer this section of the river edge. These wetter areas along the road harbor lowland deciduous and riparian forest-loving species such as Eastern Kingbird, American Redstart, and Warbling Vireo.

At 0.9 miles, a stream comes in from the left. On the right, you can walk down a dirt road to the river's edge for a view of the other side of the sandbar. This is one of the better sites to try for Acadian Flycatcher in late spring. It's also the beginning of a stretch of road where Worm-eating Warbler normally occurs; typically, you can hear breeding birds sing from the steep hillsides between 0.9 and 1.9 miles on your odometer.

At 1.4 miles, the low shrubby areas support a rich diversity of species, including Yellow-bellied Sapsucker, Veery, Wood Thrush, Scarlet Tanager, Red-eyed Vireo, American Redstart, and Black-and-white Warbler. Rose-breasted Grosbeaks are usually fairly conspicuous as well. This is a good location to look for

Canada Warbler, which can occur during migration in any of the wetter, over-grown areas along the river; it's possible that some even stay to nest.

At 1.7 miles, the parking lot at Saint John's Ledges marks the typical start of breeding territories for Cerulean Warbler; these continue intermittently to the end of the road (2.8 miles). The easiest place to see Cerulean Warbler is often in the last 0.1 miles of the road, especially around the parking area at the end. Golden-winged Warbler once nested in very small numbers along River Road, mainly in old fields at the end, although one with an odd song held a territory just north of the Saint John's Ledges parking lot, in an old tree-fall area. Tree-falls occur periodically along the road, and any forest opening or clearing could still attract this species. Because Blue-winged and Golden-winged Warblers can mimic each other, it's worth paying attention to any bird singing either one's song. Belted Kingfishers also may nest near the Saint John's Ledges parking area, possibly in the embankment a little farther north on the left.

At 2.0 miles, there is a particularly good site for woodpeckers, where all six of Connecticut's typical breeding species occur. Cerulean Warbler and Eastern Phoebe are often on territory here as well. The next half-mile (from 2.0 to 2.5 miles on the odometer) is generally good for woodpeckers, vireos, warblers, and Rose-breasted Grosbeak.

Worm-eating Warblers are found on rocky forested hillsides.
Photograph courtesy Mark S. Szantyr

At 2.8 miles, the road dead-ends at a metal gate, behind which the Appalachian Trail continues north. Parking is permitted along the road edge and in an upper parking lot to the left. It is worth spending some time around the upper lot, and on the trail at its northwest corner that follows the telephone right-of-way uphill to a power-line cut. The right-of-way is steep, rocky, and sometimes slippery, but it offers a fine view of the surrounding area. It is an excellent site from which to see migrant thrushes, vireos, orioles, tanagers, and warblers. Indigo Bunting and Ruby-throated Hummingbird typically sit on or near the phone wires, or on exposed branches along the forest edges, along with the occasional Eastern Bluebird. Black-and-white, Yellow, and Chestnut-sided Warblers, along with American Redstart, Eastern Towhee, Gray Catbird, and sometimes Brown Thrasher, breed along the right-of-way. On several occasions, Common Nighthawks have been found roosting in the trees edging the trail, or circling over the clearing during migration. A pair of Blue-winged Warblers usually has a territory at the edge of the clearing, and Golden-winged Warbler is occasionally seen here.

As previously noted, the parking area has been a good place to see Cerulean Warbler. A territorial male often sings from atop the lot's tallest trees, remaining conspicuous until the trees leaf out and his thin song becomes difficult to pinpoint among the dense foliage. Fortunately, the pair's nest is often fairly obvious—sometimes directly over the road—and the female easily seen.

The River Road, Kent, is home to Cerulean Warblers which nest in large forested tracts of land.

Photograph courtesy Mark S. Szantyr

Below the parking lot, where the road ends, a towering sycamore overhangs the river and attracts a host of birds. All spring and summer, pairs of Cedar Waxwings sally forth from its crown, hawking insects, while nesting Baltimore Orioles, Eastern Kingbirds, Least Flycatchers, and Yellow-throated and Warbling Vireos sing from within its sprawling canopy. Locally uncommon species, such as Purple Finch and Orchard Oriole, are attracted to this tree as well. Common Yellowthroat, Louisiana Waterthrush, and during migration, Canada Warbler patrol the thickets along the river's edge. Spotted Sandpipers nest and feed on the riverbanks and sandbars, joined periodically by Killdeer and migrant Solitary Sandpipers. Swallows and swifts can be abundant here in spring, especially in the morning, when they feed over the river or swirl above the clearing. Scan the flocks carefully; there are often a few Purple Martins and Bank Swallows mixed in.

After checking the right-of-way and parking areas, walk north past the gate on the Appalachian Trail for about 50 yards, to a clearing on the left. This stretch of trail is often alive with bird activity and is typically within the territory of a pair of Least Flycatchers. If it's been maintained, take the small spur trail into the clearing, once an old housing site. The clearing is bordered to the north by a stream lined with large sycamores and cottonwoods, with an old stand of red pines situated across the stream. Louisiana Waterthrush breeds along this stream from April to early August. A pair of Yellow-throated Warblers, rarely found in Connecticut, once attempted to nest within the clearing for several years in a row. **Note:** This area is especially bad for deer ticks!

All of the small fields in the immediate area have long been left to revert to forest. As expected, the numbers of early succession–dependent species, such as Blue-winged and Golden-winged Warblers, have declined. Unless the area is actively managed for them or a storm creates new clearings, this location will soon be unsuitable for these species.

After returning to the Appalachian Trail, continue north across the stream to an area on the left with mostly dead and dying red pines. Brown Creepers often breed here, building their nests under the loose bark of dead trees. It's always a treat to hear their exuberant song each spring, such a contrast to their thin, weak "zzzzz" heard in the remainder of year. The pines and nearby hillside also attract thrushes; it is an especially productive site in May, when Swainson's, Gray-cheeked (uncommon), and Bicknell's (rare) move through the area. Blackburnian and (usually) Black-throated Green Warblers nest here as well. Also look for Red-breasted Nuthatch, Golden-crowned Kinglet, and Winter Wren, all of which may breed in some years. Black-and-white Warbler and Ovenbird are common here.

The Appalachian Trail continues along the river for another 6 miles or so, before reaching Connecticut Route 4. The terrain is mostly level and easy to walk, meandering through a variety of habitats similar to those along River Road. Within the first 2 miles, the trail passes another stand of pines, now mostly fallen or cut down, some young regenerating forest areas, and a power-line cut that may hold Blue-winged Warbler and Indigo Bunting. It's usually not worth going beyond the power-line cut unless a longer walk is desired.

Retrace your steps to the parking lot. Looking across the river, you can see the fields on North Kent Road, off Route 7, that hold nesting Prairie Warbler, Eastern Towhee, Field Sparrow, Indigo Bunting, and Orchard Oriole. The wet areas along the dirt road past the parking lot attract Wood Duck, Hooded Merganser, and other waterfowl, and Cerulean Warbler has nested in the forest here. **Note:** On weekends from July 1 to Labor Day, North Kent Road is gated and closed.

■ Schaghticoke Road

⊃ **Directions:** Drive back along River Road until it reunites with Skiff Mountain Road. Continue on Skiff Mountain Road until you reach the Kent School Bridge, at the intersection with Route 341. Turn right onto Route 341, continue 0.4 miles, and take the first left onto Schaghticoke Road. **Note: Reset your odometer to zero** here. Continue 1.0 mile to the Kent School's wastewater facility on the left. If the gate is open, pull in the driveway and park to the right, out of the way of traffic. If the gate is closed, park at the nearest roadside pull-off.

The trees and hedgerow to the left of the entrance are furnished with bird-houses. Many pairs of Tree Swallows, along with a few Eastern Bluebirds, nest in these boxes. An Eastern Phoebe is often seen in the area, perched on the fences or buildings. Scan the plowed farm fields and sewage impoundments for Barn and Rough-winged Swallows and for Killdeer, which nest near the sewage ponds. These ponds also occasionally attract Spotted and Solitary Sandpipers as well as swallows, during migration. Indigo Buntings breed along the field edge, and Scarlet Tanagers and Rose-breasted Grosbeaks nest on the hillside across the street from the entrance. This is private property so behave accordingly. If in doubt, ask at the office for permission to bird the area, or bird from the road.

Continue along Schaghticoke Road *to 1.4 miles* on your odometer, then park before a small bridge with a concrete abutment. The 50 yards between the bridge and the spot where the road starts up a hill is often the territory of at least two pairs of Hooded Warblers (there are just a few pairs in this area). The warblers can be found on either side of the road, in the areas with a dense understory of barberry shrubs. Males sing all day, but are most active in the morning and late afternoons. Patience is often required to see them, so leave ample time for your visit. **Note:** Please do not play recorded songs! This is a highly birded area, and studies have shown that repeated exposure to recordings can cause birds to abandon their territories. Along the road, midway up the hill, listen for Northern Parula (a rare breeder), which sometimes nest here.

Although the fastest way to Connecticut Route 7 is to return to the monument in Kent town center, Schaghticoke Road continues south through the Schaghticoke Indian Reservation (public road access only), passing steep hillsides that sometimes hold Winter Wren. The road eventually turns to dirt, skirts some open wet areas, and passes by a few pine stands that host nesting Pine Warblers. Most species found along River Road also occur on Schaghticoke Road. At the end of the road, turn left. You'll pass through the covered Bull's Bridge and end up back at Connecticut Route 7, south of Kent.

(13) Mohawk Mountain Area, Cornwall

- Mohawk Mountain State Park
- Route 4 Swamp
- Route 43 Swamp
- Coltsfoot Valley and Great Hollow Road
- Housatonic Meadows State Park
- Rattlesnake Road Swamp

Seasonal rating: Sp *** Su **** F **/*** W *
Best time to bird: May through September.
Habitats: Mohawk Mountain, open farmland, old fields in early succession, grasslands, second-growth deciduous forests, old-growth (and planted) pine stands, hemlock ravines, black spruce "bog" (fen), streams, small ponds, wooded swamps, wet meadows, and cattail marshes.

Bird list for this site:

SPECIALTY BIRDS

Resident – Ruffed Grouse (declining), Black Vulture, Northern Goshawk (rare), Long-eared and Northern Saw-whet Owls (very local), Yellow-bellied Sapsucker, Pileated Woodpecker, Common Raven, Purple Finch

Summer – Hooded and Common Mergansers, Pied-billed Grebe (rare), American and Least Bitterns (very local), Broad-winged Hawk, American Kestrel, King Rail (very local), Virginia Rail, Sora, Eastern Whip-poor-will (declining), Ruby-throated Hummingbird, Least and Alder Flycatchers, Acadian Flycatcher (occasional), Blue-headed and Yellow-throated Vireos, Bank Swallow, Red-breasted Nuthatch (red pines), Brown Creeper, Winter and Marsh Wrens, Golden-crowned Kinglet, Hermit Thrush, Brown Thrasher; Blue-winged, Magnolia, Black-throated Blue, Yellow-rumped, Prairie, Cerulean (uncommon), Worm-eating, and Canada Warblers; Nashville Warbler (rare breeder), Northern Waterthrush, Dark-eyed Junco, White-throated Sparrow (very local), Indigo Bunting, Bobolink, Eastern Meadowlark (very local), Orchard Oriole

Winter – Rough-legged Hawk, Northern Shrike, winter finches including both crossbill species, Common Redpoll, Pine Siskin, and Evening Grosbeak (sporadic)

OTHER KEY BIRDS

Resident – Wild Turkey, Cooper's and Red-shouldered Hawks, Eastern Screech-Owl, Great Horned and Barred Owls, Carolina Wren, Eastern Bluebird, Cedar Waxwing
Summer – Wood Duck, Great Blue and Green Herons, Killdeer, Spotted Sandpiper, American Woodcock, Belted Kingfisher, Black-billed and Yellow-billed Cuckoos; Red-bellied, Downy, and Hairy Woodpeckers; Northern Flicker, Eastern Wood-Pewee, Eastern Phoebe, Willow and Great Crested Flycatchers, Eastern Kingbird, Warbling

⑬ MOHAWK MOUNTAIN AREA, CORNWALL

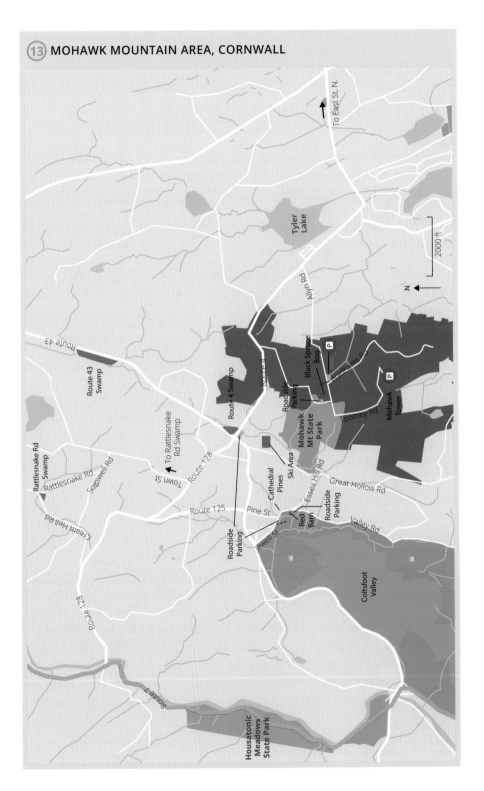

To East St. N.

Tyler Lake

2000 ft

N

Route 43

Route 43 Swamp

Black Spruce Bog

P

Wadhams Rd

P

Route 4 Swamp

Route 4

Roadside Parking

Mohawk Tower

Toomey Rd

Mohawk Mt State Park

Allyn Rd

To Rattlesnake Rd Swamp

Rattlesnake Rd Swamp

Rattlesnake Rd

Sogswell Rd

Town St

Route 128

Route 125

Ski Area

Cathedral Pines

Essex Hill Rd

Great Hollow Rd

Pine St

Red Barn

Roadside Parking

Valley Rd

Cream Hell Rd

Roadside Parking

Jewell St

Route 128

Coltsfoot Valley

Route 7

Housatonic Meadows State Park

13 | Mohawk Mountain Area, Cornwall

115

Vireo, Northern Rough-winged Swallow, House Wren, Blue-gray Gnatcatcher, Veery, Wood Thrush; Black-throated Green, Chestnut-sided, Blackburnian, Pine, and Black-and-white Warblers; American Redstart, Ovenbird, Louisiana Waterthrush, Scarlet Tanager, Eastern Towhee; Chipping, Savannah, and Swamp Sparrows; Rose-breasted Grosbeak, Baltimore Oriole

Winter – White-throated and Fox Sparrows, Dark-eyed Junco

MIGRANTS

Spring – Both teal species, Common and Hooded Mergansers, Solitary Sandpiper, Wilson's Snipe, Cliff Swallow (Housatonic River); other possibilities include all the thrushes, warblers, vireos, and flycatchers, along with most other landbirds that normally occur in the state

Fall – Rough-legged Hawk, American Pipit, Dark-eyed Junco; White-throated, American Tree, and Fox Sparrows

---

Restrooms: Outhouses are available at several locations within Mohawk Mountain State Forest and Housatonic Meadows.
Hazards: Venomous snakes.

■ Mohawk Mountain State Park

Location: Intersection of Connecticut Route 4 and Toomey Road, West Cornwall.

The Birding

Mohawk Mountain is a 1,683-foot peak located in Connecticut's northwest highlands. Because every thousand-foot rise in elevation is the climatic equivalent of driving 200 miles north, the birding in the park's higher elevations is similar to that experienced 300 miles to the north, in Canada. In effect, the top of Mohawk Mountain is a northern island set within a sea of farm fields and forest. Its altitude, combined with diverse habitats such as black spruce bogs and mixed coniferous and deciduous forest, create a bastion for species that either do not breed or are much less common at lower elevations in the state, including Hermit Thrush, Blue-headed Vireo, Golden-crowned Kinglet, and Magnolia and Yellow-rumped Warblers. The park's size—more than 2,900 acres—also makes it ideal for species dependent on large tracts of land, such as Northern Goshawk and Scarlet Tanager.

During peak migration in May, more than twenty-five species of warblers are possible along the 3-mile road to the summit; finding at least fifteen species is usually fairly easy. Migrating birds can be encountered in almost any habitat in the park; during the breeding season, however, some species are restricted to very specific habitats and may only be encountered at certain sites along the road. For instance, specialists such as Worm-eating Warbler are only found on hillsides and talus slopes, while Northern Waterthrush breeds only in boggy areas.

How to Bird This Site

An extensive system of paved roads allows easy access by car, and most species can be seen from the roadside. To take full advantage of this wonderful site, it is best to drive slowly, stopping frequently to get out and listen in a variety of habitats. Walking is necessary only at the black spruce bog. For those less ambulatory, most of the specialty species that breed in the bog may be seen from the roadside rest area adjacent to it, although the birds may be more difficult to find. The park also features an extensive trail system, including a section of the Appalachian Trail. The terrain is very steep in some sections.

Be sure to set your odometer to zero where indicated, as subsequent directions are given in tenths of a mile.

Lower Toomey Road Section

The park entrance is at the intersection of Toomey Road and Connecticut Route 4. Turn onto Toomey Road and **set your odometer to zero**. Fifty yards in from the entrance, there is a stand of pines and hemlocks on the left, opposite a wet area. These evergreens are good for migrants such as Black-throated Blue and Black-throated Green Warblers, and Northern Parula. Blackburnian Warblers have bred in or around the hemlocks, and Yellow-throated and Red-eyed Vireos, Common Yellowthroat, and Eastern Towhee all nest in the area.

At 0.2 miles, the first territorial Black-throated Blue Warblers are usually encountered. Listen for their songs beginning in late April; most are gone by early October. The dead trees in this area also make it attractive to woodpeckers, including Yellow-bellied Sapsucker and Hairy Woodpecker. American Redstart, Veery, Eastern Towhee (in open drier areas), and Red-eyed Vireo are common nesters along this stretch of road.

From 0.2 to 0.4 miles, pay particular attention to the right-hand side for breeding Chestnut-sided Warblers. These may also be found in any of the scrubby clearings that are regenerating to forest, or in more open forest with understory shrubs. On either side of the road, listen for the sweet song of Blue-headed Vireos, which breed in this area, along with Yellow-throated Vireo, Scarlet Tanager, and Ovenbird. Steep hillsides, especially rocky ones, are preferred sites throughout the park for Worm-eating Warbler, and one is occasionally found in this stretch.

Between 0.4 and 0.5 miles on your odometer, there are typically Least Fly-catchers.

At 0.7 miles, there is a pull-off on the right next to a small stand of white pines that occasionally attracts Bay-breasted Warblers during migration. Black-and-white Warbler is common here; listen for a squeaky-wheel-like song: "teesee, teesee, teeesee." This is a good area to find the cavity-nesting Great Crested Flycatcher and to listen for the plaintive "pee-o-wee" of the Eastern Wood-Pewee, which usually arrives in mid-May to breed. Ovenbird and Blackburnian Warbler are also sometimes found here.

At 0.9 miles, there are picnic tables and pit toilets. This is one of the better areas in the park for Blue-headed Vireo.

From 0.9 miles to 1.1 miles, where there is a scenic overlook, Chestnut-sided Warblers are generally common. This stretch of road is another good spot for Blue-headed Vireo as well. Indigo Buntings frequent the open area around the overlook and other open scrubby areas throughout the park.

Blue-headed Vireo on nest.

Roadside Rest Area

At 1.2 miles, stop at a pull-off on the left. This pull-off is situated at the northern edge of a black spruce bog. While there is no access to the bog itself here, you can walk to its edge. Most species that breed within the bog visit this edge at least occasionally. One of the more consistent "northern" breeding species to be found here is Yellow-rumped Warbler, which frequents the tamarisks at the bog edge and the oaks by the parking area. Yellow-bellied Sapsucker, Blue-headed Vireo, and Black-throated Green Warbler also breed here. Canada Warbler and Northern Waterthrush are often heard singing within the bog, but only occasionally make an appearance near the road. The oaks and tamarisks seem to attract migrants as well, so this area is worth a stop from spring through summer. Occasionally, Winter Wren is found near the bog edge, visible from the roadside. Cerulean Warbler (uncommon) has reportedly been heard here in spring; however, be careful of Black-throated Blue Warblers singing their alternate Cerulean-like song, which is commonly heard throughout the upper reaches of the park in spring and summer.

The Black Spruce Bog is home to Canada Warbler and other highland breeding warblers.
Photograph courtesy Mark S. Szantyr

Black Spruce Bog

Continue to the stop sign *at 1.4 miles* on your odometer, then turn left, onto Wadhams Road (may be unmarked). Continue *just under 0.2 miles*, where you will see storage buildings on the right. Pull into the entrance road; there is a parking area on the left.

Check around the storage buildings for migrating sparrows and Dark-eyed Juncos. Chipping Sparrows breed in the area, as do American Goldfinches, House Finches, and a few Purple Finches. The road edge opposite the parking area is often good for migrants, including Tennessee Warbler, and Nashville Warbler, which may breed in very small numbers. Breeding Yellow-rumped and (sometimes) Blackburnian Warblers, along with Blue-gray Gnatcatchers (in oaks), can be found as well.

Walk north across the road to the trailhead for the bog. The trail climbs over a small hill, passes through a power-line cut, then descends through mountain laurel thickets onto a short, level boardwalk that traverses part of the bog.

The power-line cut is often good for Indigo Bunting, cuckoos, and Eastern Towhee. As you enter the laurel thickets, be on the lookout for Black-throated Blue, Magnolia, and Canada Warblers. Black-throated Green Warblers can be found in the evergreens. Yellow-rumped Warblers also seem to prefer the spruce and tamarisks but feed throughout the bog. A couple of pairs of Northern Waterthrush breed here and generally frequent the wetter areas farther into the bog; their ringing songs and loud chip notes can be heard throughout the day. Winter Wrens are a sporadic breeder; they prefer areas with blown-down trees. Barred Owls also have bred here.

Clear-cut

Leaving the storage buildings' parking lot across from the bog, *return 0.2 miles* to the stop sign. **Reset your odometer to zero** here, then continue through the intersection, *0.1 miles uphill* on Toomey Road to a pull-off on the right; park near the outhouse.

The regenerating clear-cut uphill (to the left) of the pull-off has attracted Mourning Warblers in June; they could conceivably nest here on rare occasions. In summer, this area and its forested edge is home to Gray Catbird, Eastern Towhee, Chestnut-sided Warbler, Indigo Bunting, and Rose-breasted Grosbeak. Scarlet Tanagers breed within the forest nearby. This site is good for finding Cedar Waxwing and Purple Finch year-round. During migration, hordes of White-throated Sparrows visit the brushy areas and roadsides.

Upper Toomey Road

Continue uphill until your odometer reaches *0.3 miles*. Park on the left in the pine grove picnic area. Any pine stand along the upper road is worth checking for less common breeding species such as Red-breasted Nuthatch, Golden-crowned Kinglet, and Brown Creeper. This particular pine stand attracts an array of the northern specialties. In most years, this grove and the surrounding forest holds breeding Yellow-bellied Sapsucker, Red-breasted and White-breasted Nuthatches, Blue-headed Vireo, Brown Creeper, and

Black-throated Green, Black-and-white, Blackburnian, and occasionally Pine Warblers. Rose-breasted Grosbeak nest nearby, and this is a very reliable area to find breeding Purple Finch. Pileated Woodpecker, Hermit Thrush, Winter Wren, and Northern Waterthrush have bred on the back side of this grove, downhill from the picnic area, and can often be heard from here. If Yellow-rumped Warblers aren't nesting here, then try along the next 0.1 miles of road.

At 0.4 miles, check the pine stand on the left for Yellow-bellied Sapsucker and especially Red-breasted Nuthatch. Golden-crowned Kinglets have nested here. In the past, White-throated Sparrow (very rare breeder) has been heard singing here during breeding season.

From 0.4 to 0.7 miles, search for all the thrushes during migration, along with Wood Thrush, Veery, and Hermit Thrush during the breeding season. In summer, listen for Great Crested Flycatcher, woodpeckers, Ovenbird, Black-throated Blue Warbler, Scarlet Tanager, and Purple Finch.

At 0.8 miles, the mountain laurel is prime habitat for breeding Black-throated Blue Warblers. Eastern Wood-Pewee, Great Crested Flycatcher, Northern Goshawk (rare breeder), and Broad-winged Hawk are sighted in this area spring through fall.

At 1.3 miles, the summit offers spectacular vistas of the northwest highlands of Connecticut. To the northwest is an unobstructed view of the Housatonic River Valley and the Berkshire Mountains. The view to the south is just as lovely, overlooking a beaver swamp at the base of the mountain. Great Blue Herons and occasionally Green Herons frequent this swamp spring through fall. These views alone make the peak worth a visit at any time of year. In October, at the height of fall colors, one is inspired to paint.

Indigo Bunting, Chestnut-sided Warbler, Chipping Sparrow, and Wood Thrush are usually conspicuous on and around the summit. Dark-eyed Juncos have bred here in the past and can be fairly conspicuous during migration, when they mix with the flocks of White-throated Sparrows and other sparrows. The summit is great for viewing raptors at any time of year, but especially during autumn migration. In summer, Broad-winged, Red-shouldered, Red-tailed, Sharp-shinned (rare), and Cooper's Hawks, as well as Goshawks (rare), are all possible. Turkey and Black Vultures are seen year-round. Listen for the croaking calls of Common Ravens, which nest locally and can sometimes be seen soaring above the treetops. Pine, Black-and-White, Prairie (uncommon), and Chestnut-sided Warblers, along with Yellow-bellied Sapsuckers, may also be found. If birds are not readily visible from the overlook, search the trails and fire access road.

During summer, especially on weekends, the summit can get crowded with people. At other times, it can be quite peaceful; little noise, other than wind and birdsong, typically reaches this area.

To return to the park entrance, drive back down Toomey Road.

■ Route 4 Swamp

Location: Connecticut Route 4, near the intersection of Routes 4, 128, and 43, Cornwall.
⭢ **Directions:** From the Toomey Road entrance of Mohawk Mountain State Park, head west on Route 4 for 1.1 miles, then stop at a pull-off on the left, opposite a marsh and wooded swamp. (The marsh is at the bottom of the hill, 0.1 miles from the intersection of Routes 4, 128, and 43.)

This swamp is always worth a check! It appears small but connects to an extensive marsh system extending north along nearby Route 43. It attracts a wide variety of interesting species that breed or feed here, including Belted Kingfisher, Green Heron, Warbling Vireo, and Swamp Sparrow. Great Blue Herons visit spring through fall, and the site is favored by feeding swallows, especially in July. Barn and Tree Swallows are common, and Bank and Rough-winged Swallows also occur here. Spring through fall, Common Yellowthroats, Yellow Warblers, and Red-winged Blackbirds sing from the shrubs and reeds. Scan the trees and bushes for Eastern Bluebird, Eastern Kingbird, and Cedar Waxwing in summer, and check the water's edge and any muddy areas for Solitary Sandpiper, Wilson's Snipe, and other shorebirds during migration. Veery sing from the wooded hillsides, which are also home to Northern Flicker, Pileated Woodpecker, and other woodpeckers. American Bittern has bred here, and this is the kind of place one might find Common Gallinule, Sora, Virginia Rail, Wood Duck, or possibly Marsh Wren.

■ Route 43 Swamp

Location: Route 43, Cornwall.
⭢ **Directions:** From the intersection of Routes 4, 128, and 43 in Cornwall, turn right (north) onto Route 43. Continue for 1.7 miles, just past a yellow sign on the right, and stop at an obscure pull-off on the right, next to a pine stand that is on a slight rise. There is faint evidence of an old dirt road angling off to the right. Go slowly, as this pull-off is easy to miss.

Yellow-bellied Sapsucker, Red-eyed and Blue-headed Vireos, Black-capped Chickadee, Hairy Woodpecker, and American Redstart nest in or around the pines. Cedar Waxwings hunt over the swamp across the street. Swamp Sparrows breed in this swamp and can be heard singing spring and summer. Least Bitterns also have been heard here. Winter Wrens nest behind the swamp, but their exuberant song carries to the road. Just south of the pines, on the same side of the road, is a wet expanse; this is one of the better sites in the area to find Canada Warbler and Northern Waterthrush. Both are skulkers, but can usually be enticed to appear with the aid of some judicious "pishing." For the Canada Warblers, check the mountain laurels and rhododendrons.

■ Coltsfoot Valley and Great Hollow Road Tour

Location: Intersection of Valley Road and Essex Hill Road, Cornwall.
➲ **Directions:** This tour stops at sites in the Coltsfoot Valley and along Great Hollow Road, Cornwall. Be sure to set your odometer to zero where indicated, because subsequent directions are given in tenths of a mile. Beginning from the intersection of Routes 43, 4, and 128 in Cornwall, drive west on Route 4 for 1.0 miles, passing the Cornwall Cemetery on the right, then turn left onto Pine Street. **Note: Reset your odometer to zero** here. Pass through Cornwall town center and, after 0.3 miles, turn left onto Valley Road. Park at the roadside and scan the valley for American Kestrel. Then continue on Valley Road until 0.5 miles on your odometer and park on the right at the red barn, opposite Essex Hill Road. This area is known as the "Corner of the Pines."

This tranquil valley, named for the yellow coltsfoot flowers that bloom here in early spring, hosts a healthy population of Bobolinks. Their incessant videogame-like chatter can be heard from spring through early summer. The former dairy farm is now under state stewardship and is mowed annually to preserve the meadow. A pair or two of Eastern Meadowlarks also nest here some years. Eastern Bluebird and Barn Swallow are common summer residents. The swallows can usually be seen gracefully traversing the fields, catching insects, while the bluebirds breed in the nest boxes. In July and August, during migration, swallow numbers build until they create an aerial ballet. At dawn, the song of Carolina Wrens often rings loudly through the valley, accompanied by Veery and Wood Thrush from the hillside.

The dead trees across the road are the remnants of a majestic old-growth white pine stand owned by the Nature Conservancy. Known as the Cathedral Pines, the stand was destroyed by a tornado in the late 1980s. Pileated Woodpecker holes riddle the skeletal pine trunks, and the birds themselves can be conspicuous in spring, especially during courtship and while feeding their young. Look for active nest cavities high on the dead trunks. Their old cavities have been used as homes by a nesting pair of American Kestrels, which are often seen hunting the meadows. In some years, the kestrels occupy the nesting box on a tree in the meadow.

Continue on Valley Road. *Between 0.6 and 0.8 miles*, stop to look and listen for Willow Flycatcher ("fitz-bew") and Alder Flycatcher ("fee-be-o"). Both are possible throughout the valley, especially in the wetter areas where there are alder thickets. Eastern Towhees, along with cavity-nesting Tree Swallows and Eastern Bluebirds, are common in the valley, especially near 0.8 miles on your odometer, where there are several nest boxes for the use of the latter two species.

At 0.8 miles, turn around and return to the red barn. Just past the barn, turn right onto Essex Hill Road and go uphill.

You will pass through a hemlock ravine that hosts Pine Warbler, Hairy Woodpecker, Red-eyed Vireo, Wood Thrush, Veery, and Scarlet Tanager.

A half-mile after the barn, you will reach the intersection of Essex Hill Road and Great Hollow Road, facing Mohawk Mountain. **Note: Reset your odometer to zero** here. Turn right onto Great Hollow Road and *proceed 0.4 miles* looking carefully for a metal gate on the left. Pull off the road near the gate, but don't obstruct it. Beyond the gate, there is a dirt track that leads down into a wet area. (This is private property, so proceed accordingly.)

A pair of White-throated Sparrows has bred here sporadically over the years, the only confirmed nesting pair in the area. Willow and Alder Flycatchers and Cooper's Hawks nest locally, with the hawks often seen hunting along the ridge. Wood Duck and possibly Hooded Merganser and Belted Kingfisher breed in this valley, while Green Heron is sometimes seen here. Migrating Nashville and Wilson's Warblers have been found in the understory.

Continue south on Great Hollow Road, bearing left *at 0.7 miles* on your odometer onto Great Hill Road, where Great Hollow Road splits off to the right. *At about 0.8 miles*, pull off and park on the right at the bottom of the hill. A swamp is on the left.

The hill behind the house on the right sporadically hosts Eastern Whip-poor-will, now a very local and rare breeding species in the state; these birds usually begin singing around dusk, from late April into July. (Other traditional areas to try for this species include the hills opposite this site and the area behind the Mohawk Mountain ski area, back toward Route 4 on Great Hollow Road. If these spots are unrewarding, check other hillsides in the area at dusk, keeping in mind that Eastern Whip-poor-wills have become fairly scarce.) Ruby-throated Hummingbirds nest in this valley and are occasionally spotted on exposed perches along the roadside. The swamp across the road is home to Cedar Waxwing, Willow and sometimes Alder Flycatchers, Eastern Kingbird, Yellow Warbler, Common Yellowthroat, Swamp Sparrow, Baltimore Oriole, and Red-winged Blackbird. Red-tailed Hawks breed in the area, and Red-eyed Vireo, Veery, and Wood Thrush sing from the hillsides.

The Great Hollow Road tour ends here. To return to Route 4, retrace your route toward Essex Hill Road, then continue on Great Hollow Road, passing the entrance to Mohawk Mountain ski area on the right. Turning right on Route 4 will bring you to the intersection of Routes 4, 128, and 43 near Rattlesnake Road Swamp (page 126). Turning left takes you to the intersection of Routes 4 and 7 in Cornwall Bridge. From there, continuing north on Route 7 brings you first to Housatonic Meadows State Park, then to Kent Falls State Park.

■ Housatonic Meadows State Park

Location: Route 7, Sharon.
⊃ **Directions:** From the junction of Routes 4 and 7 in Cornwall Bridge, head west (Route 7 north) over the bridge 0.2 miles and turn right, staying on Route 7. Travel 1.4 miles and turn right into the main entrance of Housatonic Meadows State Park and Campground. **Note:** It might be prudent to ask at the office for permission to drive around the camp loop to the right of the entrance.

The park is adjacent to the Housatonic River and is home to species typical of riparian habitats. The pine groves within the campground support a substantial population of breeding Pine and Blackburnian Warblers, and this may be one of the easier places to see both in the entire area. Chipping Sparrow, White-breasted Nuthatch, several species of woodpecker, Brown Creeper, Baltimore Oriole, Great Crested Flycatcher, Eastern Wood-Pewee, Eastern Phoebe (may nest under eaves of some buildings), Cedar Waxwing, Eastern Bluebird, Barn and Tree Swallows, and American Goldfinch are all commonly seen here. Osprey can be found along the river, especially in migration, but a few pairs nest in the area. Check the river for Common Merganser, spring through fall; holes in the sycamores and other large trees lining the bank provide nesting sites. Spotted Sandpiper sometimes feeds along the river during migration. All five of our nesting swallow species are seen over the river during migration. Watch the ridgelines for raptors and both Black and Turkey Vultures. Bald Eagles are seen on rare occasion.

▪ Rattlesnake Road Swamp

Location: Intersection of Rattlesnake Road and Cream Hill Road, Cornwall.
➲ **Directions:** From the intersection of Routes 4, 43, and 128, take Route 128 west toward Cornwall. After 0.8 miles, turn right on Town Street to North Cornwall. Continue 1.1 miles, then take a left onto Cogswell Road. (The swamp on Cogswell Road has had American Bittern and Virginia Rail.) Take the first right onto Rattlesnake Road and continue 0.8 miles, to just before the road meets Cream Hill Road. The swamp spans both sides of Rattlesnake Road.

The beaver pond and wet meadow has the site's best birding. There are breeding Hooded Merganser, Wood Duck, Mallard, Great Blue Heron, and Belted Kingfisher, and Sora has been recorded in summer in the wet meadow. Sharp-shinned and Cooper's Hawks, as well as Black Vulture, are regularly seen, and the two hawks likely nest in the area. Ruby-throated Hummingbirds perch on the dead snags on the creek side. Both Willow and Alder Flycatchers nest here. Blue-headed Vireo, and Yellow-rumped, Blackburnian, and Black-throated Green Warblers occur in the bordering white pines. Tree Swallow and Eastern Bluebird breed in the nest boxes in the meadow. When water levels are down, this can be a great inland spot for shorebirds. Greater Yellowlegs and Spotted, Solitary, and Least Sandpipers are the most common during migration. Bank Swallows are regularly seen over the pond and field, especially during migration.

(14) Winter Birding Trail: Goshen to Norfolk

- ◼ Goshen
- ◼ Canaan Mountain
- ◼ Norfolk

Seasonal rating: Sp *** Su *** F *** W ****
Best time to bird: November to March.
Habitats: Open farmlands, shrubby meadows, riparian woodlands, streams, and lakes, but mostly steep forested hillsides with evergreen and mixed evergreen-hardwoods; ornamental plantings in small towns.

Bird list for this site:

SPECIALTY BIRDS
Resident – Common Raven, Red-breasted Nuthatch, Purple Finch
Summer – Golden-crowned Kinglet (uncommon); Magnolia, Yellow-rumped, Black-throated Green, Blackburnian, and Pine Warblers; Northern Waterthrush
Winter – Rough-legged Hawk, Northern Shrike, Fox Sparrow, Pine Grosbeak, Red and White-winged Crossbills, Common Redpoll, Pine Siskin, Evening Grosbeak

OTHER KEY BIRDS
Resident – Wild Turkey, Eastern Screech-Owl, Great Horned and Barred Owls, Cedar Waxwing
Summer – See list in chapter 13
Winter – Raptors, including Rough-legged Hawk (invasion years), Tree and Fox Sparrows

MIGRANTS
Cape May, Black-throated Blue, Bay-breasted, and Blackpoll Warblers, as well as other warblers

Restrooms: In Goshen on Routes 4 and 63, in Canaan on Routes 63 and 7, and in Norfolk on Routes 44 and 272.
Hazards: This is a rural area with unimproved roads, so take caution in winter. In summer, beware of bears and venomous snakes.

The Birding

Connecticut's northwestern highlands has habitat similar to boreal forests farther north, including large tracts of cone-bearing evergreen woodlands. In addition, many of the small towns in this region are planted with

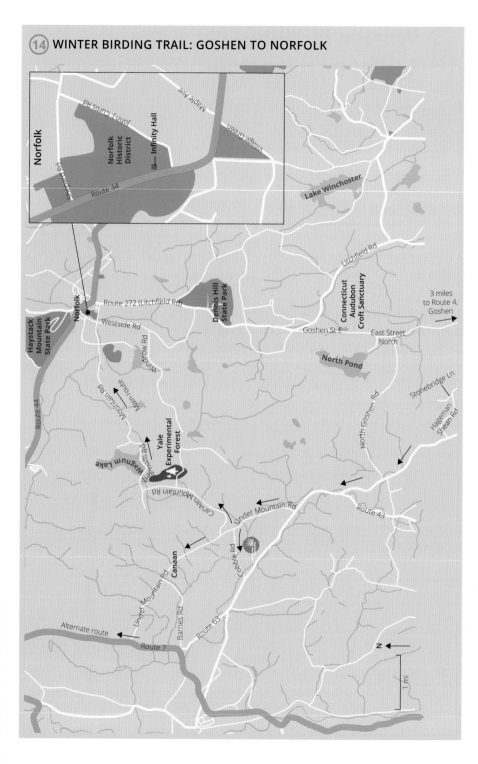

ornamental crabapple, viburnum, mountain ash, spruce, and rose, providing readily available food sources for birds in winter. These two factors have combined to attract winter finches, waxwings, and other fruit- and seed-eating species to the area in some years. Connecticut birders now make annual winter pilgrimages here, in search of these ever-elusive irruptive species. As the term "irruptive" suggests, numbers of each species vary dramatically from year to year, sometimes with several years between sightings of the least common species, such as Bohemian Waxwing, Hoary Redpoll, and Pine Grosbeak. Common Redpoll, Pine Siskin, Purple Finch, and both crossbills are more consistent winter visitors, although they too can be scarce in some years, especially the crossbills. Evening Grosbeaks are also unpredictable winter visitors to the area.

How to Bird These Sites

Many birders simply drive the roads looking for cone- and fruit-bearing trees and houses with bird feeders. (Please be respectful of homeowners.) This chapter includes one such route that has proven productive over the years. **Note:** Be sure to set your odometer to zero where indicated, because the subsequent directions are given in tenths of a mile.

When they occur, rare Bohemian Waxwings typically join Cedar Waxwings to feed on berries.
Photograph courtesy Mark S. Szantyr

Checking trees and bushes with berries can be a rewarding way to find Bohemian Waxwing and Pine Grosbeak. Pine or spruce stands with abundant cones may harbor Red-winged and White-winged Crossbills, Pine Grosbeak, Red-breasted Nuthatch, and Pine Siskin. Alder and birch stands with catkins are visited by Common and Hoary Redpolls (very rare) and Pine Siskin. Bird feeders in the area are always worth a look; Evening Grosbeaks tend to be attracted to them. In addition, hilltops and ridgetops are worth checking for raptors and Common Raven, while open areas may harbor Northern Shrike.

■ Goshen

Location: Intersection of Route 4 and East Street North, Goshen.
⮑ **Directions:** Turn onto East Street North heading north. After you turn, pull off the road.

Scan the first two fields on the left for Northern Shrike. Rough-legged Hawk has also been found here.

Set your odometer to zero and continue north along East Street North. Check any spruce and pine stands with cones, as well as houses with feeders, for winter finches and Red-breasted Nuthatch. Scan open fields and farms for raptors and shrikes. There are apple and crabapple trees and berry bushes all along the road, especially on the right (east) side; these may attract waxwings, robins, and grosbeaks.

Between 2.5 and 3.0 miles on your odometer is an area with apple trees where Bohemian Waxwings and Pine Grosbeaks have congregated in the past.

At 3.0 miles, turn left onto Hageman Shean Road (dirt for first 1.3 miles). Continue *to 4.5 miles* on the odometer, then turn right on Stonebridge Lane.

The apple, crabapple, and other fruit-bearing trees and shrubs along this road also can attract waxwings, robins, and grosbeaks. The fields opposite the entrance to Stonebridge Lane, and the feeders at the house there, have attracted large flocks of Common Redpoll, numbering over a hundred at times. Although very rare, Hoary Redpoll is always a possibility. Common Ravens are resident along the route and often fairly conspicuous; if not seen flying around, they sometimes frequent a white pine grove farther along Stonebridge Lane on the left, *at 4.7 miles* on your odometer. The marshy swamp, encircled in pines, at the end of Stonebridge Lane can be worth a check, especially earlier in the fall when there is open water.

At this point in the tour, you can continue to Canaan (see below) or, if you prefer, go to the nearby Richard G. Croft Memorial Preserve in Goshen (see chapter 15), an 8- to 10-minute drive. To visit Croft, return to the intersection of East Street North and Hageman Shean Road. Continue north on East Street North for 2 miles, then start looking carefully for a small dirt parking area on the right. A little sign identifies Croft Preserve as a Connecticut Audubon Society property. Follow the dirt road uphill into the preserve. **Note:** The trails are not maintained and, without snowshoes, may be impassable in winter.

■ Canaan

⤺ **Directions:** From Stonebridge Lane, return to Hageman Shean Road, turn right, and drive west for 1.1 miles until you reach Route 63. Turn right onto Route 63 and go north for 3.8 miles (passing Route 43 at 2.7 miles), then turn right onto Under Mountain Road. **Note: Set your odometer to zero** here.

The mixed-conifer forest along the beginning of Under Mountain Road may support resident Brown Creeper (uncommon in winter), Red-breasted and White-breasted Nuthatches, Downy Woodpecker, and, occasionally, other species, including Pileated Woodpecker, American Goldfinch, and winter finches, especially Pine Siskin.

At 0.4 miles on the odometer, after passing through the forest, the road enters an open farm area on the right, at the base of the steep wooded slopes and stark cliffs of Canaan Mountain. Stop where there is a good view of the rugged cliff face, then scan the ridgeline. Pileated Woodpeckers are sometimes seen darting along the treetops. Especially on sunny days, Common Ravens, which nest locally and are fairly common in the area, often soar about the cliff face, usually in the company of raptors, which they tend to harass. Their aerial maneuvers can be quite entertaining, especially in early spring when they are also actively courting.

Raptors are a common sight above the cliffs. Red-tailed Hawk, Northern Goshawk (rare), Cooper's Hawk, and (probably) Sharp-shinned Hawk are resident nesting species. Broad-winged Hawk also breeds in the area. There is a possibility of finding a Golden Eagle from late fall through early spring, when Rough-legged Hawk and Northern Harrier are also occasionally seen hunting over the farm fields.

At *1.4 miles* on the odometer, Cobble Road appears on the left (Chubby Bunny Farm). This mile-long dirt road connects to Route 63. **Note:** The road may be closed to vehicle traffic in winter or flooded in spring, but is usually passable on foot. Please respect private property and remain on the road.

In winter, especially late December through February, look for Northern Shrike in the open farm areas along both Cobble Road and Barnes Road, 1.8 miles farther along Under Mountain Road, and along the Wangum River, at the west end of both roads. Resident species along the Wangum River include Eastern Bluebird, Cedar Waxwing, White-breasted Nuthatch, Hairy Woodpecker, and Northern Flicker. In winter, American Tree Sparrow can usually be found, and sometimes Fox Sparrow. Areas with alder and birch catkins may attract American Goldfinch, redpolls, and Pine Siskin. Scan the yards with bird feeders for Red-breasted Nuthatch, Evening Grosbeak, Common Redpoll, and other winter finches. Pine Grosbeaks occasionally turn up along Under Mountain Road to feed on cones and berries, or to pick gravel off the freshly sanded roads. The area also supports a healthy Wild Turkey population, and it's not unusual to spy them feeding in the fields along Under Mountain, Cobble, and Barnes Roads. Belted Kingfisher occasionally overwinters. In spring, this is a good area for Solitary Sandpiper, American Bittern, and swallows. Please do not play recordings for bitterns; they may nest here.

From the intersection with Cobble Road, you have two options. You can continue north on Under Mountain Road for 1.8 miles to Barnes Road, or turn right after 0.2 miles onto Canaan Mountain Road and head north to Norfolk (see below).

If you choose Barnes Road, it appears on the left *at 3.3 miles* on your odometer. Barnes Road is about 2 miles long. It parallels Cobble Road and connects with Route 63 near its intersection with Route 7, in South Canaan. The possible bird species are essentially the same as for Cobble Road. Check the fields along its length and the edge of the Wangum River near the road's western end. This road has minimal maintenance in winter and can be slippery or impassable.

■ Norfolk

⮑ **Directions:** From Cobble Road, return to Under Mountain Road. Turn left and drive north 0.2 miles, then turn right onto Canaan Mountain Road. Canaan Mountain Road goes steeply uphill, heading northeast for 2.4 miles until it meets Wangum Road. **Note:** Canaan Mountain and Wangum Roads are unimproved in areas and can be slippery or impassable in winter. A four-wheel drive vehicle is recommended when the roads are snowy. (If conditions are bad, an alternate route to Norfolk follows Route 63 north to Route 7. Continue north on Route 7 to Route 44 in Canaan. Turn right on Route 44 and go east to Norfolk.)

Canaan Mountain Road traverses miles of mixed evergreen and hardwood forests. There are numerous stands of pines and spruce that can be scanned from the road for winter finches. The Yale Experimental Forest, near the intersection with Wangum Road, has many cone-bearing trees, and Pine Grosbeaks have been found here. In winter, the open fields are worth a check for Northern Shrike and for raptors. Areas with fruiting bushes may harbor Cedar Waxwing, possibly Bohemian Waxwing (rare), and Eastern Bluebird. **Note:** Please respect private property; some homeowners have been suspicious of strangers.

At the intersection with Wangum Road, turn right. Wangum Lake soon appears on the left; it warrants a quick scan from spring through fall for waterfowl.

Continue east on Wangum Road for 3.8 miles (its name becomes Mountain Road after 2.1 miles) until you reach Route 272 (Litchfield Road). Turn left onto Route 272, bear right at the fork, then continue to the intersection with Route 44.

The crabapple trees in Norfolk attract Pine Grosbeaks some winters.

Across the street (east of this intersection), there are some crabapple trees worth checking. In fact, the village of Norfolk is interspersed with crabapple trees; these have consistently attracted Pine Grosbeak in most of the winters when they have occurred in the state.

Turn left on Route 44 and head west into Norfolk. Within a block or so, a line of crabapple trees will be on your left, across from John J. Curtis Road (Speckled Hen Pub).

After scanning these trees, continue north 0.2 miles on Routes 44/272, then turn right onto Shepard Road. At the bottom of the hill (less than 0.1 miles), pull off on the right, opposite the entrance to the Meadowbrook Senior Living complex.

Crabapple trees line the long driveway into Meadowbrook as well as the front of the Lion's Club building, thirty yards farther along Shepard Road. Walking this area may be the easiest way to find grosbeaks. They are often vocal in flight and, when perched, generally tolerant of humans.

After checking this area, continue east on Shepard Road for 0.1 miles, then turn right onto John J. Curtis Road and follow it through the village back to Routes 44/272 near the pub.

Bohemian Waxwing and Pine Grosbeak also have been found well north of here, near the Massachusetts border. To scout this area, turn right on Routes 44/272, bearing right at the fork to stay on Route 272 north, then check any fruit trees along the roadside.

To reach Connecticut Audubon's Croft Preserve, turn left on Routes 44/272 and then right onto Route 272 south. After 4.4 miles, following a left-hand bend, bear right onto Goshen Street East. Continue 1.5 miles (the road becomes East Street North); the sanctuary is on the left.

(15) Connecticut Audubon Society's Richard G. Croft Memorial Preserve, Goshen

Seasonal rating: Sp *** Su *** F *** W *
Best time to bird: May through mid-November; winters with finch invasions.
Habitats: Forested hillsides, some steep, with mixed hardwoods, northern hardwoods, and mixed evergreens, ranging in age from early successional to mature forest; hemlock ravines, isolated white and red pine stands, open scrub, a small pond, wooded swamps, boggy areas, streams, and vernal pools.

SPECIALTY BIRDS
Resident – Ruffed Grouse, Northern Goshawk, Yellow-bellied Sapsucker, Pileated Woodpecker, Common Raven, Red-breasted Nuthatch, Purple Finch (unconfirmed)
Summer – Wood Duck, Hooded Merganser, Broad-winged and Red-shouldered Hawks, American Woodcock, Ruby-throated Hummingbird, Least Flycatcher, Yellow-throated and Blue-headed Vireos, Brown Creeper, Winter Wren, Golden-crowned Kinglet (unconfirmed), Hermit Thrush; Blue-winged, Magnolia (unconfirmed), Chestnut-sided, Black-throated Blue, Yellow-rumped (unconfirmed), Black-throated Green, Blackburnian, and Cerulean Warblers; Northern Waterthrush, White-throated Sparrow (unconfirmed), Dark-eyed Junco
Winter – Hermit Thrush (uncommon), Pine Siskin, Common Redpoll (some years)

OTHER KEY BIRDS
Resident – Wild Turkey, Turkey Vulture, Cooper's and Red-tailed Hawks, Mourning Dove, Great Horned and Barred Owls; Red-bellied, Downy, and Hairy Woodpeckers; Northern Flicker, Blue Jay, American Crow, Black-capped Chickadee, Tufted Titmouse, White-breasted Nuthatch, Carolina Wren, American Robin, Cedar Waxwing, Song Sparrow, Northern Cardinal, House Finch, American Goldfinch
Summer – Wood Duck, Great Blue Heron, Eastern Wood-Pewee, Eastern Phoebe, Great Crested Flycatcher, Eastern Kingbird, Red-eyed Vireo, Tree and Barn Swallows, Blue-gray Gnatcatcher, Veery, Wood Thrush, Gray Catbird, Black-and-White and Yellow Warblers, American Redstart, Ovenbird, Louisiana Waterthrush, Common Yellowthroat, Song and Swamp Sparrows, Rose-breasted Grosbeak, Scarlet Tanager, Red-winged Blackbird, Common Grackle, Brown-headed Cowbird, Baltimore Oriole
Winter – American Tree and White-throated Sparrows, as well as other sparrows; winter finches

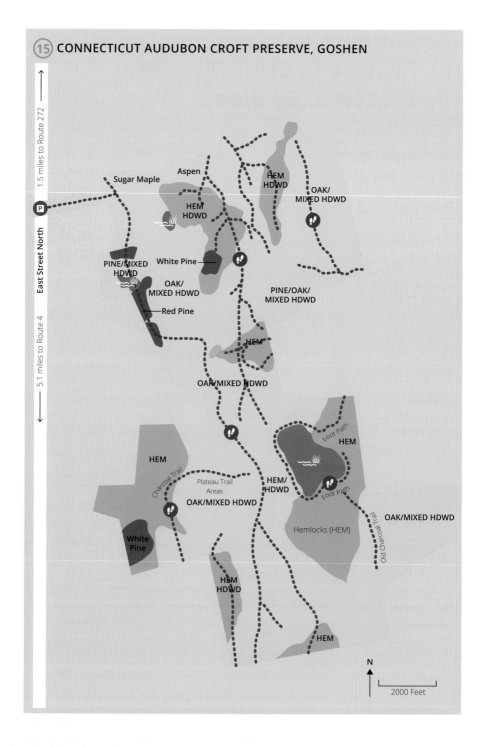

1.5 miles to Route 272 →

P

East Street North

← 5.1 miles to Route 4

Sugar Maple

Aspen

HEM HDWD

OAK/ MIXED HDWD

HEM HDWD

PINE/MIXED HDWD

White Pine

OAK/ MIXED HDWD

Red Pine

PINE/OAK/ MIXED HDWD

HEM

OAK/MIXED HDWD

Foot Path

HEM

HEM

Charcoal Trail

Plateau Trail Areas

HEM/ HDWD

OAK/MIXED HDWD

Foot Path

Old Charcoal Trail

OAK/MIXED HDWD

White Pine

Hemlocks (HEM)

HEM HDWD

HEM

N

2000 Feet

MIGRANTS

Canada Goose, *Empidonax* flycatchers, Golden-crowned and Ruby-crowned Kinglets; all of Connecticut's thrushes, including Bicknell's Thrush (theoretical); most of Connecticut's warbler species; sparrows including American Tree, Swamp, and White-throated Sparrows; Dark-eyed Junco

---

Location: East Street North, Goshen.
⮑ **Directions:** From the north, take Route 8 south to Exit 44. Turn right onto Route 4 and follow the directions below. From the south, take Route 8 north to Exit 44, Route 202 toward Route 4 (Downtown Torrington). At the end of the ramp, go straight for one block, then turn left at the light onto Route 4. Follow Route 4 west for 5.0 miles, then turn right onto East Street North and proceed north for nearly 5.2 miles. The sanctuary is on the right.
Parking: Go slowly, looking for a small dirt parking area on the right, with a little sign identifying it as Connecticut Audubon Society property. Walk the dirt road uphill into the preserve.
Restrooms: In Litchfield.
Hazards: Moose and black bear roam the property; give them a wide berth.

The Birding

The Connecticut Audubon Society acquired the 694-acre Richard G. Croft Memorial Preserve from Jean B. Croft in 1986. The park opened to the public in the fall of 2008, after controlled logging to enhance habitat diversity also provided road access to much of the property. Although Croft Preserve may seem like a sea of forested hills and valleys, it contains a multitude of habitats, from shrubby meadows and early successional woodland to mature forest tracts, hemlock ravines, and pure stands of pine. There are streams, swamps, and countless vernal pools. The preserve is seldom visited and has yet to be fully explored.

The Croft Preserve is within the enormous northwest highlands forest block. It abuts other large protected tracts owned by Goshen Land Trust and Torrington Water Company, which together create a huge expanse of undeveloped land.

How to Bird This Site

The preserve is roughly a mile in length and is situated on hilly but generally accessible terrain. The areas of roughest topography are along the eastern border. The entrance road is fairly steep for the first 0.5 miles and can be muddy, especially in spring and fall; most other sections of road are more level and provide relatively easy walking. Access in winter requires snow-shoes or cross-country skis, as there is no trail maintenance in winter.

The total distance from the north entrance to the southern border is about 3 miles roundtrip; there are some steep sections, so *give yourself at least 4 or 5 hours*. If time is short, work the first 0.75 to 1.0 miles of the entrance road, perhaps venturing as far as the pond and stream crossing. This covers a majority of the available habitats.

The first 0.5 miles of the entrance road traverses a wooded hillside of mixed hardwoods and conifers before descending to the right into an open shrubby area interspersed with stands of hemlock and white and red pines. This section of road has yielded Ruffed Grouse, Barred Owl, all six of Connecticut's commonly breeding woodpeckers, both nuthatch species, Brown Creeper, Blue-headed Vireo, and a collection of migrant warblers, including Pine, Magnolia, Black-throated Blue, Black-throated Green, Black-and-White, Blackburnian, and Blackpoll Warblers. Black-throated Blue, Black-throated Green, and Black-and-White Warblers nest in the preserve; all of the others, except Blackpoll Warbler, probably breed on the site as well. The road edge is good for sparrows, thrushes, and Dark-eyed Juncos, especially in spring and fall; the juncos breed here in small numbers. Listen for mixed-species flocks of Black-capped Chickadees, Tufted Titmice, both nuthatch species, and perhaps a kinglet or Downy Woodpecker, late fall through spring. Wild Turkeys are common throughout the preserve, and Common Ravens nest nearby. The evergreen stands provide nesting sites for accipiters, Great Horned Owl, Black-throated Green Warbler, and Brown Creeper (especially where there are hickories available). Cedar Waxwings are resident and also seem to prefer small evergreens in which to nest. Northern Goshawk, a rare and local breeder in Connecticut, nests in the preserve, as might Sharp-shinned Hawk. Broad-winged Hawks breed on the property as well and are known to nest along trails.

In summer, shrubby areas are ideal for Blue-winged and Chestnut-sided Warblers, American Redstart, Common Yellowthroat, Rose-breasted Grosbeak, Eastern Towhee, American Goldfinch, both cuckoos, Ruffed Grouse, Ruby-throated Hummingbird, and potentially Brown Thrasher or Indigo Bunting. A rare Connecticut Warbler was found in the roadside shrubs shortly after the park opened, in fall 2008. Habitat attractive to a migrant Connecticut Warbler may well entice a Mourning Warbler, Yellow-breasted Chat, or Lincoln's Sparrow in spring or fall. American Woodcock prefers the wetter edges of early successional areas and likely breeds on the preserve. Listen for them in early morning and evening.

After leaving the shrubby area, the road takes a sharp left within 0.25 miles and descends to a stream crossing beside a pond. In spring and summer, listen for Cerulean Warbler along this quarter-mile stretch. Louisiana Waterthrush may be heard along the stream in summer. Be on the lookout for Eastern Kingbird, Yellow-throated and Red-eyed Vireos, Least Flycatcher, Eastern Wood-Pewee, and Great Crested Flycatcher. The pond should be checked for marsh and waterbirds in season. Spotted Sandpiper has been seen around the pond. In summer, the dead snags provide nesting sites for Eastern Bluebird and Tree Swallow; during migration, they offer perches for flycatchers. Rusty Blackbirds are found here on occasion in fall and spring. In late 2008, an 18-acre area of early successional habitat was created just south of the pond, and Connecticut Audubon continues to maintain substantial areas of scrub and young forest within this large forest block. Perhaps 0.5 miles farther along is a large swamp on the left, concealed behind a stand of hemlocks and mixed hardwoods. Marsh and waterbirds visit here, and it's worth checking for Wood Duck, Hooded Merganser, Sora, Virginia Rail, and possibly bitterns. Spring through fall, look for Eastern Phoebe and perhaps Willow and Alder Flycatchers, which may be found regionally in wet areas, especially where alder thickets thrive.

The road continues south to a fork; both roads lead another 0.5 miles farther to the property line. The left skirts more hemlock forest; the right traverses a variety of mixed forest types, mostly hardwoods with some evergreens. Scarlet Tanager is found throughout the area.

The property has potential to support rare and local Connecticut highland breeders, such as Golden-crowned Kinglet, and Nashville, Magnolia, or even Mourning Warblers. Worm-eating and Canada Warblers and Purple Finch are also potential breeders, as is White-throated Sparrow.

Nearly the entire eastern edge of the property is composed of steep hills and ravines with limited access, and it has been little explored. Other hemlock ravines in the region hold Red-shouldered Hawk, Barred Owl, Winter Wren, Black-throated Green Warbler and Hermit Thrush, and all breed elsewhere on the property.

White Memorial Foundation and Conservation Center, Litchfield

Seasonal rating: Sp **** Su *** F *** W **
Best time to bird: May and June.
Habitats: Large tracts of hemlock, white pine, spruce, mixed coniferous, mixed coniferous/deciduous, and mixed deciduous forests; Bantam Lake (large), forested beaver swamps and ponds, cattail marshes, streams, bogs and fens, wet and dry meadows, and open lawns.

Bird list for this site:

SPECIALTY BIRDS

Resident – Mute Swan, American Black Duck, Hooded Merganser, Sharp-shinned Hawk, Northern Goshawk (rare), Bald Eagle, Ruffed Grouse (uncommon), Yellow-bellied Sapsucker, Pileated Woodpecker, Common Raven, Red-breasted Nuthatch, Brown Creeper, Golden-crowned Kinglet (local), Winter Wren, Dark-eyed Junco (rare breeder), Purple Finch

Summer – American and Least Bitterns (rare breeders), Great Blue Heron, Broad-winged Hawk, Virginia Rail, Sora (rare breeder); Acadian (uncommon), Alder, Willow, and Least Flycatchers; Purple Martin (some years), Bank Swallow, Marsh Wren, Brown Thrasher (rare breeder), Hermit Thrush, White-eyed Vireo (rare breeder), Blue-headed and Yellow-throated Vireos; Blue-winged, Magnolia, Black-throated Blue, Yellow-rumped, Blackburnian, Worm-eating, Prairie, and Canada Warblers; Northern Waterthrush, Eastern Towhee, Field Sparrow (rare breeder), Savannah Sparrow (uncommon), Bobolink, Eastern Meadowlark (rare breeder), Orchard Oriole (uncommon)

Winter – Pine Siskin and other winter finches (some years)

OTHER KEY BIRDS

Resident – Wild Turkey; Cooper's, Red-shouldered, and Red-tailed Hawks; Belted Kingfisher, Downy and Hairy Woodpeckers, Northern Flicker, Blue Jay, American and Fish Crows, Black-capped Chickadee, Tufted Titmouse, White-breasted Nuthatch, Eastern Bluebird, American Robin, Cedar Waxwing, Song Sparrow, Red-winged Blackbird, Common Grackle, Brown-headed Cowbird, American Goldfinch, House Finch

Summer – Double-crested Cormorant, Turkey and Black Vultures, Killdeer, Spotted Sandpiper, American Woodcock, Black-billed Cuckoo, Yellow-billed Cuckoo (uncommon), Eastern Screech-Owl, Great Horned and Barred Owls, Chimney Swift, Ruby-throated Hummingbird, Eastern Wood-Pewee, Eastern Phoebe, Great-crested Flycatcher, Eastern Kingbird; Northern Rough-winged, Tree, and Barn Swallows; Carolina Wren (uncommon), House Wren, Blue-gray Gnatcatcher, Northern Mockingbird, Gray Catbird, Veery, Wood Thrush, Warbling and Red-eyed Vireos; Yellow, Chestnut-sided, Black-throated Green, Pine, and Black-and-white Warblers; American Redstart, Ovenbird, Louisiana Waterthrush, Common Yellowthroat, Northern Cardinal, Chipping and Swamp Sparrows, Rose-breasted Grosbeak, Indigo Bunting, Scarlet Tanager, Baltimore Oriole

Winter – American Coot; American Tree, White-throated, and Fox Sparrows; Dark-eyed Junco

MIGRANTS

Waterfowl, Common and Red-throated Loons, Pied-billed Grebe (has bred), Horned and Red-necked Grebes, Common Gallinule (rare breeder), American Kestrel (rare breeder), gulls and terns, Common Nighthawk, Philadelphia Vireo (fall); flycatchers, including Olive-sided and Yellow-bellied Flycatchers; swallows, kinglets, thrushes, more than twenty species of warblers, White-crowned and Lincoln's Sparrows, Rusty Blackbird

Location: 80 Whitehall Road, Litchfield.
Restrooms: White Memorial Conservation Center building; pit and portable toilets available on site.

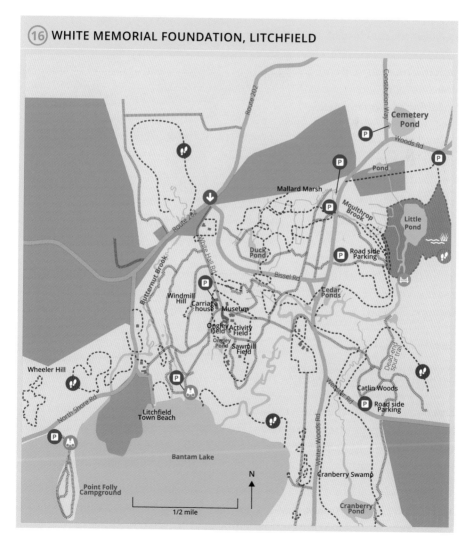

16 WHITE MEMORIAL FOUNDATION, LITCHFIELD

The Birding

The picturesque White Memorial Foundation encompasses 4,000 acres of diverse habitats in the northwest highlands of Litchfield and Morris. This private reserve is open to the public, providing one of the finest inland birding sites in Connecticut. Over a third is forested, much of it in evergreens; the rest is marsh and beaver ponds, streams and lakes, and shrubby and open meadows. Its forests have a boreal feel, shaded and cool in summer, quiet in winter. White Memorial is so vast it feels like wilderness and, in some ways, it is—yet with amenities nearby.

Barred Owls hunt the deep forests of White Memorial.

More than 275 species of birds have been recorded here, more than at many coastal sites. Of these, 116 are known to have bred, including 8 species of raptors, 7 flycatchers, 6 woodpeckers, 5 vireos, and an impressive 18 species of warblers.

How to Bird This Site

Upon arrival, visit the museum building to obtain a detailed map, bird lists, and trail and program information. There are some 35 miles of well-marked trails and carriage roads on the property. The majority of trailheads are marked with map kiosks, and many of the trails are fairly easy loops.

There are several areas along the Bantam River and Bantam Lake where canoes can be launched (ask at the museum). Birding by canoe allows you into areas where some less common breeding species, such as bitterns and rails, are more likely to be encountered, such as the north end of Little Pond. A canoe trip from the Whites Woods Road boat launch to Bantam Lake is very scenic and can be a relaxing and rewarding experience. **Note:** Beavers are active in the area and their dams may impede access to some sites.

Museum Grounds

The museum grounds are an excellent area for birds, year-round, with many feeders and plantings to attract them. The deck feeders behind the building are best viewed from within the exhibit hall (there is an entrance fee), but also can be seen from outside. The raptor cages on the building's east side have housed hawks and owls over the years. A long wooden observation blind known as the Holebrook Bird Observatory overlooks an additional battery of feeders. Fall through spring, a wide assortment of sparrows and finches, including Dark-eyed Junco and American Tree, White-throated, White-crowned (uncommon), and Fox Sparrows, visit these feeders. The feeders often attract winter finches as well, especially Pine Siskins, resident Purple Finches, and Common Redpolls (during invasion years). These two feeding stations have attracted Evening Grosbeaks from September through April, although even here they are few and far between. In summer, Rose-breasted Grosbeaks sometimes utilize the feeders, and, if oranges or fruit are supplied, Baltimore Orioles have been known to pay a visit. Both species nest in the vicinity.

Throughout the year, American Robins, Cedar Waxwings, and occasionally Eastern Bluebirds take full advantage of the bounty from the berry bushes on the museum grounds. These bushes sometimes draw in other thrushes, including Hermit Thrush, and on rare occasions Pine Grosbeaks visit, attracted by crabapples and berries. Watch for accipiters around the building; Cooper's and Sharp-shinned Hawks may patrol the feeders, especially in winter.

Lake Trail

The Lake Trail is about a mile-long loop beginning just west of the museum parking-lot entrance. It passes a number of outbuildings where Chipping Sparrow, Barn Swallow, Northern Mockingbird, and the occasional House or Carolina Wren are conspicuous in summer.

Continue on the trail as it descends through the rolling lawns of Ongley Meadow, watching for resident Northern Flickers.

The trail then skirts Ongley Pond, which attracts a few dabbling ducks during migration; a spur loop trail goes around the pond. American Kestrels can be seen in the field above the pond, most often during fall migration in September and October.

Once past the pond, the trail enters low wet forest then passes through an area of cattails and shrubby or wooded swamp. The marshy areas and brushy edges support Marsh Wren, Common Yellowthroat, and Swamp Sparrow, spring through fall. Breeding species common in the woodland include Great-crested Flycatcher, Eastern Wood-Pewee, Red-eyed Vireo, White-breasted Nuthatch, House Wren, Veery, Wood Thrush, Gray Catbird (wetter areas), Black-and-white Warbler, Ovenbird, and American Redstart. In summer, look for both Black-billed and Yellow-billed Cuckoos, especially in years with gypsy-moth caterpillar outbreaks. The area along the Bantam River to the east supports Willow Flycatcher, Eastern Kingbird, Warbling and Yellow-throated Vireos, Cedar Waxwing, Yellow Warbler, and Baltimore Oriole. In spring and fall, this is a good trail for migrants, especially flycatchers, vireos, warblers, and sparrows.

The trail leads to an observation platform that provides a fine view of Bantam Lake, Connecticut's largest natural lake. Large inland lakes are worth checking year-round, but especially after storms from early spring through fall, when rarities such as scoters, phalaropes, rare terns, and even jaegers may be forced down. The lake freezes in most winters, but many birds use the lake fall through spring, including numerous species of ducks, both diving and dabbling: American Coot (common), the occasional Common Loon or Red-throated Loon (rare), Pied-billed and Horned Grebes, Red-necked Grebe (uncommon), and both cormorant species. Several species of gulls are seen annually, with Ring-billed, Herring, and the occasional Great Black-backed Gull the most often encountered. Rarely, Bonaparte's Gull or Black Tern occurs. **Note:** Point Folly, on North Shore Road, a short drive to the west, offers an even better view of the lake than this trail.

Driving Route: Museum to "Chickadee Bridge" to Little Pond

From the museum parking lot, turn right and follow Whitehall Road (the dirt entrance road) past the museum to a T-intersection. Directly across the intersection, behind some boulders, is a footpath to "Chickadee Bridge," which spans the Bantam River. Park in the pull-off. **Note:** This area may be closed in winter or impassable after heavy rains.

The footpath winds through a shrubby marsh to a boat launch on Whites Woods Road. Staff or volunteers often leave seed along this trail in winter, attracting sparrows and finches. Red-breasted Nuthatches sometimes visit the area, and this is a good spot to look for Rusty Blackbirds from fall through spring.

Return to your vehicle and continue driving north from the intersection. Scan the dead snags in the marsh on the left for Olive-sided Flycatchers (rare) during migration. The hemlock woods beyond the marsh host a wide variety of landbirds, including nesting Brown Creepers and Yellow-rumped, Pine, Black-throated Green, and occasionally, Blackburnian Warblers. The river edge is home to Eastern Bluebirds and Cedar Waxwings year-round and Eastern Kingbirds and Baltimore Orioles in summer. Belted Kingfishers can usually be found along the river as well.

Continue driving through the hemlock woods until the next T-intersection, at Bissell Road. The trail across from the intersection attracts thrushes in migration.

Turn right onto Bissell Road, then bear left at the fork; Bissell Road soon meets Whites Woods Road. Turn left, continue less than 100 yards, and park on the right near a kiosk and gate; this is the trailhead to Little Pond.

Little Pond

The entrance trail to Little Pond passes through second-growth forest, with hemlock and pine woods on the left. Brown Creepers breed here, and their delightful song often reverberates through the forest in spring. Check the hemlock and pine stands for breeding Blackburnian, Pine, Black-throated Green, and Yellow-rumped Warblers. During migration, this is a good area for thrushes, especially Hermit and Swainson's Thrush. Other species typical in the area include Yellow-bellied Sapsucker, Great-crested Flycatcher, Red-breasted and White-breasted Nuthatches, Brown Creeper, Veery, Wood Thrush, Scarlet Tanager, Black-and-white Warbler, and Ovenbird. There have been a few surprises here over the years, including a singing Yellow-throated Warbler.

Within 200 yards, an old field with scattered white pines and shrubby second-growth opens on the right, behind which is an open (often plowed) field obscured from view, but accessible by side trails. The open shrubby areas sometimes attract less common breeding species, including Brown Thrasher, Field Sparrow, and Eastern Towhee, but they are more frequently encountered here as migrants. Eastern Bluebirds, Tree Swallows, and occasionally, Black-capped Chickadees or House Wrens take advantage of the bird boxes erected here. Song and Chipping Sparrows are resident in summer. Besides these common breeding sparrows, this area also attracts migrating sparrows in fall and spring, including Swamp, White-throated, American Tree, Fox, and the occasional White-crowned and Lincoln's Sparrows. Migrating Palm Warblers seem to favor this site from April to May and again in October.

Just past this semi-open area, the entrance trail intersects the loop trail for Little Pond. Turn right on the loop trail, and you will soon reach the start of a 1-mile raised boardwalk that encircles Little Pond. After passing through tall reed grass (*Phragmites*), the trail continues over a metal bridge that spans the Bantam River just south of Little Pond. A broad cattail marsh and shrubby swamp line the shores of the river and pond.

The bridge is a great place from which to view the marsh and pond. Mute Swans, Canada Geese, Mallards, American Black Ducks, and Wood Ducks typically breed here and can be seen north of the bridge, while Belted King-fishers often patrol the river to the south. Beaver and river otter are seen here occasionally as well. If you stand on the bridge in early spring, you will be met with waves of sound emanating from the vibrating vocal sacs of spring peepers and wood frogs. These two diminutive denizens of the muck produce a deafening array of trills and quacks to rival any bird. To this din are added the "conkarees" of Male Red-winged Blackbirds, which arrive here in late February to stake out territories. These are joined by noisy flocks of migrating Common Grackles, many of which nest in the nearby pines. This is also one of the better areas on the property to find Rusty Blackbirds, especially in late March or early April, then again in October.

In spring and fall, scores of migrating swallows invade the area, searching the pond and river for flying insects. Purple Martin and Tree, Barn, Rough-winged, Bank, and Cliff Swallows are seen annually, though Cliff Swallow is the least common and the only one that does not nest nearby. Migrating ducks gather on Little Pond and in the surrounding marsh, especially in April. Wood Ducks and Ring-necked Ducks can be plentiful, while Hooded Merganser and Green-winged and Blue-winged Teal (former breeder) visit in good numbers. Common Merganser, Lesser Scaup, American Wigeon, Gad-wall, and other species are possible.

This is an excellent area to find migrating shorebirds as well, from April to May and from August to September. The usual species include Killdeer (breeds), Spotted Sandpiper (breeds), Solitary and Least Sandpipers, Great-er Yellowlegs, and the secretive Wilson's Snipe. Lesser Yellowlegs, Pectoral Sandpiper, and a few other species are possible. American Woodcock (breeds) are often heard and seen here at dawn and dusk, especially in spring.

Some inhabitants of cattail marshes rarely encountered in Connecticut—such as Pied-billed Grebe, American and Least Bitterns, and Common Gal-linule—may sometimes be found here. All are suspected of nesting on occasion, with Least Bittern and gallinule known to do so, at least sporadically; bitterns utilize cattails, while gallinules seem to prefer the thick emergent vegetation at the pond's north end. Green Heron and Virginia Rail are fairly common breeding species. Soras occur as migrants and may nest here in small numbers. Great Blue Herons are common visitors, spring through fall.

If time is short, it is faster to return to the parking area by retracing your steps to the entrance trail. Otherwise, continue east from the bridge along the boardwalk. At first, it meanders through the marsh and shrubby swamp at the forest edge; it then traverses a small woodlot before again crossing the Bantam River, this time at the inflow to Little Pond. The trail eventually loops around the pond's north edge and returns through cattail marsh and alder thickets to the entrance trail. In spring, the blooming wildflowers can be spectacular along the way.

While traveling the boardwalk in spring and summer, the slow reedy trill of the Swamp Sparrow, the rattle of the Marsh Wren, and the "witchity, witchity" of the Common Yellowthroat are frequent accompaniments. Riparian species inhabit the trees at the periphery of the marsh, including Warbling and Yellow-throated Vireos, Eastern Phoebe, Eastern Kingbird, Cedar Waxwing, Rose-breasted Grosbeak, Baltimore Oriole, and Blue-winged and Yellow Warblers. Chestnut-sided Warbler, Eastern Bluebird, and Tree Swallow are also fairly common sights around the pond in summer. The latter two nest in tree cavities and boxes set out in the area.

Scan the bushes and dead snags throughout the marsh for flycatchers from spring through fall. Both the "fitz-bew" of the Willow Flycatcher and the "fee-be-o" of the Alder Flycatcher can be heard here in summer. Both species arrive in mid-May to breed and depart by mid-September. Alder Flycatcher is the less common of the two and more likely to be encountered toward the north end of the pond. Least Flycatcher breeds in the nearby wooded areas, and Yellow-bellied Flycatcher is sometimes seen during migration mid-May to June and mid-August to September.

Little Pond is also known as a good area to find rare northern butterflies, such as Arctic skippers.

Mallard Marsh and Northern Pike Impoundment

Location: Whites Woods Road, Litchfield. From the Little Pond lot, the trailhead is 0.4 miles north on the left. There is overflow parking at 0.3 miles on the left.

When you park at the pull-off for these sites (see map), you will see a paved path on both sides of the road. A brief walk to the west along this old railroad bed offers a fine view of the large Mallard Marsh. Many of the species found at Little Pond and Cemetery Pond can also be found here. Virginia Rail—fairly common, yet difficult to see—inhabits the area spring through fall. Common Gallinule and American and Least Bittern have been seen here in spring and early summer; they may breed, but the dense marsh grasses make it difficult to see them. (Their vocalizations are often the only indication of their presence.) Swamp Sparrow, Red-winged Blackbird, and Yellow Warbler are common here in summer, and Marsh Wren may sometimes be found. Blue-winged Teal occur in the wetter areas on both sides of the road during migration in September and October. This marsh also supports a population of state-endangered northern leopard frogs, which can sometimes be seen along the grassy edges. Fully protected by law, these spotted, bright green frogs should not be disturbed.

Across the street, to the east, the trail heads through shrubby wetland toward Northern Pike Impoundment, situated along the feeder stream connecting Cemetery and Little Ponds. As the name implies, this is a breeding site for pike (they spawn in April). The impoundment also provides habitat for marsh- and swamp-loving birds, including Blue-winged Teal and Pied-billed Grebe. Willow and Alder Flycatcher breed here in summer.

Just to the south, Pine Island (including Duck Pond) is a known breeding site for Common Ravens, which nest in the tall pines of the cool, shady forest. (Ravens also nest on the far east side of White Memorial Foundation property, near Plunge Pool.)

Cemetery Pond

Location: 17-21 Constitution Way, Litchfield. From Little Pond, drive 0.7 miles north on Whites Woods Road; from Mallard Marsh, drive 0.3 miles north. Turn left onto Constitution Way and look for a pull-off on the right.

This small beaver pond—lined with shrubs, cattails, and reeds—may be one of the area's more easily accessible and reliable sites to find the rare Common Gallinule, which occasionally nests here. Gallinules are adept at concealment and often missed among the reeds. Other rare Connecticut breeding species also have been found here, including Pied-billed Grebe, Blue-winged Teal, and Least Bittern.

The shrubby border and marsh grasses hold small breeding populations of Marsh Wren; Willow, Alder, and Least Flycatchers (wooded edges); Eastern Kingbird, Gray Catbird, Yellow Warbler, Common Yellowthroat, and Swamp Sparrow. Tree Swallows, Eastern Bluebirds, and Eastern Phoebes are regular sights around the pond, spring through fall. In summer, look for the hanging nests of Baltimore Orioles in the trees in the cemetery across the street. Rose-breasted Grosbeak, Chipping Sparrow, American Goldfinch, House Finch, and Purple Finch (uncommon) all breed in the area as well.

The cemetery is worth checking in spring and fall for migrant vireos, warblers, and sparrows. In winter, American Tree Sparrow and Dark-eyed Junco feed here.

During migration, a variety of shorebirds frequents the muddy shores and bars within the pond, including Killdeer (breeds), Spotted Sandpiper (breeds), both yellowlegs species, Least Sandpiper, and occasionally Pectoral Sandpiper. Solitary Sandpiper can be common in late April or early May and late July or early August. Wilson's Snipe should be looked for in March and April and in September and October. During the breeding season, American Woodcock can usually be heard here. The pond is also attractive to waders, especially during post-breeding dispersal: in July and August, inland rarities such as Great Egret and Little Blue Heron have occurred. Green Heron nests in the area, while Great Blue Heron is a regular visitor.

Watch for raptors here as well. Turkey Vulture and Red-tailed, Cooper's, and Sharp-shinned Hawks are often seen circling on thermals or patrolling the pond and cemetery. Northern Goshawk (rare), Red-shouldered Hawk (uncommon), and Broad-winged Hawk (fairly common) all nest in the area. Black Vulture and Common Raven (nests) are increasingly common sights over the preserve.

Catlin Woods

Location: Webster Road. From Little Pond, drive 0.5 miles south on Whites Woods Road, then turn left onto Webster Road; the trailhead is about 0.2 miles ahead, on the left.

Several trails of differing lengths traverse these woods. Two roughly half-mile loops can be done fairly quickly, but are worth *at least an hour*.

The more productive of these loops takes the main trail north, ignoring the trail that soon forks to the left. When you reach a T-intersection, turn left (west); at the next intersection, turn right onto a scenic—and often birdy—dead-end spur. This leads north into a marsh and brushy swamp, good for Rusty Blackbird, Swamp Sparrow, and other marsh birds. (This area floods in spring.) Retrace your steps to the trail, then turn right. Bear left at the fork to loop back through forest to Webster Road. **Note:** For details on other trails, consult the White Memorial Foundation maps and proceed carefully; it is easy to get lost in some areas.

Catlin Woods is an old hemlock forest: cool, moist, dark, and reminiscent of northern woodlands. Entering its mature groves gives an inkling of what forests were like in colonial times. The forest interior is a world of shadows and shifting light, where verdant lichens coat the trees and the moist, rich odors of decomposition mix with the scent of pine. Many species typical of more northern climes are resident. These woods are the haunt of Purple Finch, Pine Siskin (rare breeder), and Great Horned Owl.

Prehistoric-looking Pileated Woodpeckers wander here, leaving huge rectangular holes in decaying trees and littering the forest floor with massive chip piles. It is a place to find breeding Blue-headed Vireo, Red-breasted Nuthatch, Winter Wren, and Yellow-rumped, Black-throated Green, and Blackburnian Warblers. In spring and summer, the ethereal sounds of Wood Thrush and Veery greet each dawn and dusk. During migration, insects on the soft forest floor entice Swainson's, Gray-cheeked, and Hermit Thrushes. Each spring, these woods resound with the thumping of Ruffed Grouse, the explosive expletives of the Brown Creeper, and the "teacher, teacher" of the Ovenbird. Yellow-bellied Sapsuckers add their staccato tapping to the dawn chorus and leave rows of weeping holes on trees—telltale signs of their presence. Northern Waterthrush, another dweller of boggy northern haunts, nests in the wetter forest periphery along the east path. Canada Warblers occur during migration and are possible nesters. Throughout the summer, listen for the "chick-bur" call of the Scarlet Tanager, which is a common migrant as well.

More typically northern breeding species of flycatchers and warblers stop here during migration, including Yellow-bellied Flycatcher and Olive-sided Flycatcher (occasional), Northern Parula, and Nashville, Magnolia, and Bay-breasted Warblers. Tennessee, Cape May, and Mourning Warblers also are observed annually in small numbers.

In winter, check for Pine Siskin, Purple Finch (resident), and other winter finches. During invasion years, Pine Grosbeak and both Red-winged and White-winged Crossbills have been found, but there are sometimes years between visits.

Infrequently, a pair of Northern Goshawks (rare) has nested at Cranberry Pond, on the opposite side of Webster Road. The pond can be reached by walking 0.5 miles along the trail that runs south from the parking area. These large predators hunt for small mammals and birds within dense forest and, like other accipiters, have broad wings and long tails to allow them to maneuver through dense cover. If present, avoid disturbing the pair in spring and summer, when they can be both vocal and physical defenders of their nest; listen for repeated "keks" to warn that you are approaching their nesting territory.

Bantam Lake (Point Folly)

Location: 92-98 North Shore Road, Bantam.

Bantam Lake—especially Keeler Cove, directly opposite the Point Folly parking lot—is known for some of the state's largest concentrations of American Coot and Ruddy Duck, from October through December. Mute Swan, Canada Goose, Mallard, and American Black Duck are common residents, while Wood Duck, Green-winged Teal, Ring-necked Duck, and Hooded and Common Mergansers are plentiful migrants. Many other species of waterfowl occur annually, at least in small numbers, including Northern Pintail (fall), American Wigeon, Blue-winged Teal, Canvasback, Lesser Scaup, Common Goldeneye, Bufflehead, all three scoter species, and Long-tailed Duck. Common Loon, Pied-billed and Horned Grebes, and Double-crested Cormorant are also annual visitors, and, on rare occasion, a Red-throated Loon, Red-necked Grebe, or Great Cormorant are seen. Other rare species have included Tundra Swan, Snow Goose, Redhead, Barrow's Goldeneye, Iceland Gull, and Eared Grebe. Bonaparte's Gull, Forster's and Black Terns, and other gulls and terns should be looked for in migration.

Migrating landbirds often congregate in the trees lining the lake, preferring areas with oaks, especially on peninsulas jutting into the water, such as Folly Point. From the parking lot, a 0.85-mile loop road traverses Folly Point, with a spur trail that cuts through the forested center of the peninsula. This loop and spur are worth walking in fall and spring for migrant warblers, vireos, thrushes, and a host of other landbirds; in winter, the same route is good for viewing waterfowl. The lively public campground on the point makes birding difficult in summer.

The first part of the road provides a view of the back of a marsh to the north, where Rusty Blackbirds frequently congregate. There is an observation platform 400 yards down the road, on the left, that gives a raised view of the marsh, the mouth of the Bantam River, and the east end of the lake (known as North Cove).

Bantam Lake is a high-use recreation area in summer, crowded with boaters, anglers, and families out to enjoy the beaches. Waterbirds do stop by in summer, but rarely remain much past sunrise—when human activity increases. The lake can be worth checking after thunderstorms, however, when migrants are sometimes forced to take shelter on the lake and human disturbance is at a minimum. Exciting rarities, such as phalaropes or rare gulls and terns, are sometimes sighted after such storms.

Apple and Laurel Hills, on the southern portion of the lake, near Morris, are good from spring through fall for old field, northern forest, and swamp species. The trailhead is on East Shore Road, opposite Marsh Point Road. White-eyed Vireo might be found here.

Southbury Area

- Mitchell Farm and Housatonic River
- Old Southbury Training School Farm
- Bent of the River Audubon Sanctuary

▪ Mitchell Farm and Housatonic River

Seasonal rating: Sp ** Su ** F *** W ***
Habitat: River, riparian forest, forested ridges, fallow and active farm fields, wet and dry meadows, lawns.

Bird list for this site:

SPECIALTY BIRDS
Resident – Cooper's Hawk, Bald Eagle, Red-shouldered Hawk, Black Vulture, Common Raven, Fish Crow, Belted Kingfisher, Pileated Woodpecker, Eastern Bluebird
Summer – Black-crowned Night-Heron, Least Flycatcher, Cliff Swallow, Brown Thrasher, Prairie Warbler
Winter – White-fronted Goose (uncommon); Iceland, Lesser Black-backed, and Glaucous Gulls (uncommon); Mew Gull (rare), Rough-legged Hawk (invasion years); American Tree, Field, Fox, White-crowned, and Savannah Sparrows; Vesper Sparrow (uncommon)
Migrants – Least Flycatcher, Lincoln's Sparrow, Rusty Blackbird (uncommon)

OTHER KEY BIRDS
Resident – Wild Turkey, Great Horned Owl, Northern Flicker, Carolina Wren, Cedar Waxwing, Swamp Sparrow
Summer – Common woodland and shrubland birds, Osprey, Killdeer, Great Crested Flycatcher, Eastern Kingbird, swallows, Carolina Wren, Blue-gray Gnatcatcher; White-eyed, Warbling, Yellow-throated, and Red-eyed Vireos; Yellow and Black-and-White Warblers, American Redstart, Common Yellowthroat, Scarlet Tanager, Rose-breasted Grosbeak, Eastern Towhee, Red-winged Blackbird
Winter – Bald Eagle, Northern Harrier, sparrows

MIGRANTS
American Woodcock (spring), *Empidonax* flycatchers, both kinglet species

Location: 51 Purchase Brook Road at junction with River Road, Southbury.
Parking: It is best to park along the side of River Road. Take care to avoid soft shoulders and lawns. Please do not park or trespass on farm property nor impede farm access.

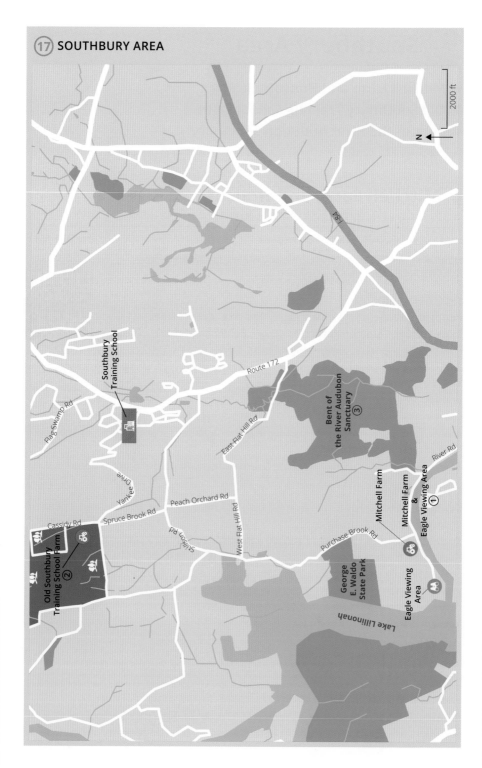

2000 ft

N

Southbury Training School

I-84

Flag Swamp Rd

Route 172

Bent of the River Audubon Sanctuary ③

East Flat Hill Rd

Yankee Drive

Cassidy Rd

Peach Orchard Rd

Spruce Brook Rd

Old Southbury Training School Farm ②

Sullison Rd

West Flat Hill Rd

Purchase Brook Rd

Mitchell Farm

Mitchell Farm & Eagle Viewing Area ①

River Rd

George E. Waldo State Park

Eagle Viewing Area

Lake Lillinonah

Restrooms: Dunkin' Donuts at Exit 14 off I-84; Bent of the River Audubon Sanctuary.
Additional information: Shepaug Dam is accessible by reservation only. To make a reservation, go to http://www.shepaugeagles.info/

The Birding

Mitchell Farm is now Connecticut's best inland site for rare gulls. Ring-billed Gulls gather by the hundreds, sometimes thousands, along with Herring Gulls, to feed on silage and spoiled farm produce deposited in the fields surrounding the barns. The gulls bathe en masse in the adjacent Housatonic River, just below Lake Zoar. A few Iceland and Lesser Black-backed Gulls, along with the odd Glaucous Gull, can usually be found among them. Mew Gull (rare) has occurred repeatedly.

The brushy hillside beside the barns attracts a variety of sparrows, including Fox, American Tree, and White-crowned Sparrows, fall through spring. This hillside and other brushy areas along the roads can also harbor overwintering fruit- and seed-eaters such as Gray Catbird, Brown Thrasher, and Eastern Towhee. Eastern Bluebirds are resident throughout the area, and this is one of the better local sites to find Fish Crow. Common Ravens (resident) and Black and Turkey Vultures often soar over the ridges, while Bald Eagles winter along the river in good numbers, and at least one pair nests locally. Check fields and wet areas for wintering blackbirds; Rusty Blackbird (uncommon) is possible. The riverside trees attract a variety of landbirds.

Mitchell's Farm is a premier location for finding less common gulls, such as Iceland Gull, and Lesser Black-backed Gull (shown in foreground).

In winter, the Housatonic River draws waterfowl; a few American Coot, Hooded Mergansers, and Ring-necked Ducks are usually among the many Common Mergansers. In addition to resident Canada Geese, migrant flocks visit fall through spring, at times accompanied by less common species, such as Greater White-fronted and Snow Geese.

Shepaug Dam is just past the farm on River Road. In winter, the public eagle-viewing platform is worth a visit. In summer, there is a sizable colony of Cliff Swallows in residence. Below the dam, there is usually a nesting pair of Black-crowned Night-Herons (uncommon inland). Watch for Brown Thrasher (uncommon) in the hedgerows and nesting Prairie Warbler and Least Flycatcher along the road to the dam.

■ Old Southbury Training School Farm

Seasonal rating: Sp *** Su **** F *** W***
Best time to bird: May to December.
Habitat: Fallow and active farm fields, farm pond, hedgerow thickets, wet and dry meadows, lawns, upland forest, orchards.

SPECIALTY BIRDS
Resident – Black Vulture, American Kestrel, Fish Crow, Common Raven, Eastern Bluebird
Summer – Yellow-billed and Black-Billed Cuckoos, White-eyed Vireo (some years), Willow and Alder Flycatchers, Cliff Swallow, Brown Thrasher, Blue-winged and Chestnut-sided Warblers, Field and Savannah Sparrows, Indigo Bunting, Bobolink, Eastern Meadowlark (some years), Orchard Oriole
Winter – Northern Harrier, Rough-legged Hawk (some years), other raptors, Short-eared Owl (some years); American Tree, Field, Fox, and White-crowned Sparrows

OTHER KEY BIRDS
Resident – Wild Turkey, Turkey Vulture, Red-tailed Hawk, Northern Flicker, Carolina Wren, Cedar Waxwing
Summer – Killdeer, Chimney Swift, Ruby-throated Hummingbird, Eastern Phoebe, Eastern Kingbird; Yellow-throated, Warbling, and Red-eyed Vireos; Tree and Barn Swallows, House Wren, Northern Mockingbird, Gray Catbird, Yellow Warbler, Common Yellowthroat, Chipping Sparrow, Eastern Towhee
Winter – Merlin

MIGRANTS
Wilson's Snipe, American Woodcock, Least Flycatcher, Horned Lark (uncommon), American Pipit, Yellow-breasted Chat (uncommon), Lincoln's Sparrow

Location: Intersection of Purchase Brook, Spruce Brook, and Cassidy Roads and Yankee Drive, Southbury.

Parking: Along the roadside. Take care to avoid soft shoulders and lawns. Please do not park or trespass on farm property nor impede farm access (unless you long to meet an irate farmer).

Restrooms: Dunkin' Donuts at Exit 14 off I-84; Bent of the River Audubon Sanctuary.

The Birding

The old Southbury Training School farm is a patchwork of fallow and active farmland lined with extensive hedgerow. The area is wonderful year-round for a mix of shrub- and grassland species. Breeders include Bobolink (common), Field Sparrow (fairly common), and a few pairs of Savannah Sparrow. There are healthy populations of American Kestrel and Brown Thrasher; in some years, Eastern Meadowlark, a rather rare and local nester in Connecticut, takes up residence. All but the Bobolink may linger into winter. Watch for American Kestrels around nesting boxes located throughout the area. Yellow-billed and Black-billed Cuckoos, House Wren, Willow Flycatcher, Alder Flycatcher (uncommon); Blue-winged, Yellow, and Chestnut-sided Warblers; Indigo Bunting, Eastern Towhee, and Chipping Sparrow nest along the field edges.

White-crowned Sparrows are often found in *Multiflora* rose thickets, such as those along Cassidy Road.

Chimney Swifts and swallows, mainly Barn and Tree Swallows, are common over the farmland in summer. Cliff Swallow (uncommon) has nested on the barn. Watch for Wild Turkeys in the fields year-round. Killdeer and Eastern Bluebirds are resident. White-eyed Vireos pass through, have nested in thickets nearby, and could easily nest here. **Note:** White-eyed Vireos nest in hedgerow thickets along the south side of East Flat Hill Road near its intersection with Peach Orchard Road. This is state and town land.

Check any wet areas for shorebirds and ducks during migration, especially in spring. American Woodcock breeds in early successional forest near the wetter areas. Killdeer nest in the dryer gravelly areas, while Spotted and Solitary Sandpipers and Wilson's Snipe (March or April) pass through. The wet areas along Cassidy Road occasionally attract migrating Sora and Virginia Rail.

Fall through spring, the hedges attract numerous migrant sparrows, including Lincoln's (rare, winter), White-throated, and American Tree Sparrows. The multiflora rose thickets are particularly good for White-crowned Sparrows, even in winter. In fall and winter, the plowed fields here are the most likely in the area to attract American Pipits and the occasional Horned Lark.

The resident Red-tailed, Red-shouldered, and Cooper's Hawks are joined by migrant and wintering Northern Harrier, Merlin, and other raptors; in some winters, Rough-legged Hawk, Short-eared Owl, and Northern Shrike are found. Resident Black Vulture and Common Raven are fairly common.

How to Bird This Area

It can be productive to drive slowly along the roads, listening for birdsong. When you hear something interesting, find a safe place to pull over, then walk along the road. Birding is typically best within a half-mile or so of the intersection, especially on Cassidy Road.

Territorial Yellow-breasted Chat (rare breeder) has been found along Spruce Brook Road, just south of Cassidy Road, but with extensive suitable habitat, one could occur anywhere in this area. The orchard and vicinity on Spruce Brook can be quite birdy and are worth a visit. Yankee Drive is excellent for landbird migrants in May. From the intersection, Yankee Drive passes through farmland into forest before descending to Route 172 in Southford, by the Southbury Training School.

Audubon Center Bent of the River

Seasonal rating: Sp **** Su **** F *** W ***
Habitat: River, riparian forest, hilly upland forest, hemlock ravines, wet and dry meadows, lawns, vernal ponds.

SPECIALTY BIRDS
Resident – Cooper's Hawk, Bald Eagle, Eastern Screech-Owl, Great Horned and Barred Owls, Belted Kingfisher, Yellow-bellied Sapsucker, Pileated Woodpecker, Fish Crow, Common Raven, Eastern Bluebird
Summer – Common Merganser, Broad-winged Hawk, American Woodcock, both cuckoo species, Acadian Flycatcher, White-eyed Vireo (some years), Winter Wren, Brown Thrasher (some years), Louisiana Waterthrush, Northern Parula (some years); Worm-eating, Blue-winged, Hooded, Magnolia, and Prairie Warblers; Field Sparrow, Indigo Bunting, Orchard Oriole
Winter – Rough-legged Hawk (invasion years); Field, Fox, and White-crowned Sparrows; Purple Finch, Pine Siskin (invasion years)

OTHER KEY BIRDS
Resident – Wild Turkey, Hairy Woodpecker, Northern Flicker, Carolina Wren, Cedar Waxwing, Swamp Sparrow
Summer – Common deciduous forest and shrubland birds, Cooper's Hawk, Eastern Wood-Pewee, Eastern Phoebe, Great Crested Flycatcher, Eastern Kingbird; Warbling, Yellow-throated, and Red-eyed Vireos; Northern Rough-winged Swallow, Carolina Wren, Blue-gray Gnatcatcher, Veery, Wood Thrush; Yellow, Black-and-White, and Pine Warblers; American Redstart, Ovenbird, Common Yellowthroat, Scarlet Tanager, Rose-breasted Grosbeak, Eastern Towhee, Red-winged Blackbird, Baltimore Oriole
Winter – Common Merganser, American Black Duck, accipiters, Golden-crowned Kinglet

MIGRANTS
American Woodcock (spring), Northern Saw-whet Owl, American Kestrel, Least Flycatcher and other *Empidonax* flycatchers, both kinglet species, Hermit Thrush; most warblers, including Yellow-throated Warbler (rare), Cape May, Bay-breasted, Blackburnian, and Canada Warblers; Lincoln's, Fox, and Savannah Sparrows

Location: 185 East Flat Hill Road, Southbury.
Parking: The main parking area is near the entrance; another with handicapped access is 0.3 miles farther along, near the nature center buildings.
Restrooms: Inside the nature center during business hours.

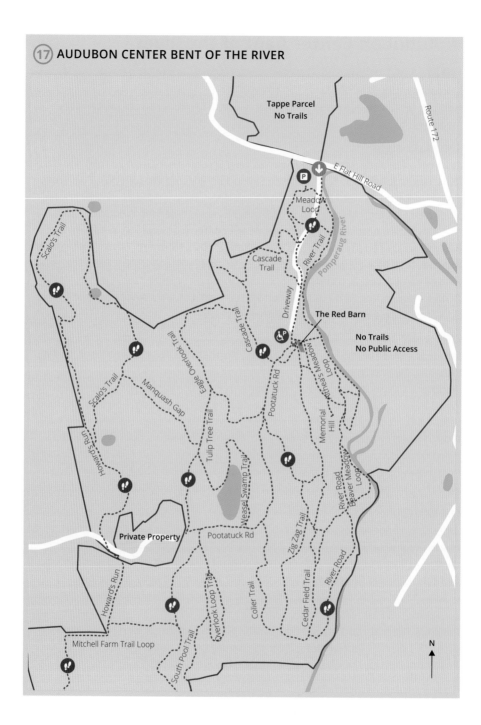

Tappe Parcel
No Trails

Route 172

E Flat Hill Road

Meadow Loop

River Trail

Cascade Trail

Pomperaug River

Scalo's Trail

Driveway

The Red Barn

No Trails
No Public Access

Cascade Trail

Poorutuck Rd

Althea's Meadow Loop

Scalo's Trail

Manquash Gap

Eagle Overlook Trail

Tulip Tree Trail

Memorial Hill

Howard's Run

Weasel Swamp Trail

Beaver Meadow Loop

River Road

Private Property

Pootatuck Rd

Zig Zag Trail

Howard's Run

Overlook Loop Trail

Coller Trail

Cedar Field Trail

River Road

Mitchell Farm Trail Loop

South Pool Trail

N

The Birding

Audubon Center Bent of the River is a 700-acre wildlife sanctuary that encompasses a broad array of habitats. It is the area's best site for finding migrant and nesting landbirds.

Breeding species along the Pomperaug River include Common Merganser, Belted Kingfisher, Louisiana Waterthrush, Baltimore and Orchard Orioles, Eastern Phoebe, Great Crested Flycatcher, Cedar Waxwing, and Rose-breasted Grosbeak. During migration, the river edge is good for viewing an array of migrants, including Black-throated Green, Pine, Palm, and Black-and-white Warblers, and even the occasional Yellow-throated Warbler (rare). The river also attracts swallows, especially during spring migration. All but Cave Swallow are possible. Olive-sided Flycatcher (uncommon) has been seen perching on snags over the river.

The riverside meadows, especially Cedar Fields and Althea's Meadow (behind the barn), are good for nesting Blue-winged and Prairie Warblers, Indigo Bunting, Eastern Towhee, and Field Sparrow, and attract a diverse group of migrant sparrows and shrub-loving species, including White-eyed Vireo and Brown Thrasher, both potential nesters. Medici Meadow hosts nesting Indigo Bunting, Orchard Oriole, and Black-and-white Warbler. Both cuckoo species breed in edge habitat in the area; Black-billed Cuckoos are usually seen near the barn, while Yellow-billed Cuckoos often appear along the Cedar Fields Trail.

The best migrant birding areas are generally the large oaks along the driveway near the barn and—when they're in bloom—the apple trees beside the barn. These trees have held ten species of warblers at once and twenty species over the course of a day. The list includes Canada, Bay-breasted, Tennessee, and Nashville Warblers. Yellow-bellied Flycatcher and Mourning Warbler are among the noteworthy species to also have occurred. The nature center's feeders and gardens are always worth checking, as they attract birds year-round. During fall migration, viewing from the barn's birding balcony can be quite productive, particularly in the afternoon or early morning. In winter, the feeders here consistently attract less common sparrows, including White-crowned, Fox, and Lincoln's. Fall through spring, resident House Finch and American Goldfinch are joined occasionally by Purple Finch, Common Redpoll, and Pine Siskin. All the resident woodpeckers can be expected at the feeders, except Pileated, which is regular in the deeper forest.

Note: Please do not bird near the staff housing across from the barn.

Very close to the staff parking area, beyond the red barn, Hooded and Worm-eating Warblers have nested on the first hill along Pootatuck Road Trail. Most of the Hooded Warblers are found just past the barn as you enter the forest; some are encountered farther into the forest, and just a few near the River Trail. In the forest interior, Acadian Flycatcher and Black-throated Green Warbler breed in the hemlock ravines, most often near the Cascades, the wet area along Pootatuck Road (easiest to access), and along Zig Zag Trail; Barred Owl is a resident breeder in the same habitat and can sometimes be heard during the day. In some years, Blackburnian and Magnolia Warblers, along with Blue-headed Vireo, have nested in the higher mixed-forest terrain; these are found most reliably at the top of Cascades Trail, along Tulip Tree Trail, and at Eagle Overlook. Winter Wren nests only on the steeper terrain of the Tulip Tree and Cascades Trails, usually in areas with downed trees. Yellow-bellied Sapsucker nests near Weasel Swamp. Scarlet Tanager, Wood Thrush, Veery, Eastern Wood-Pewee, and Red-eyed Vireo are ubiquitous breeders. During migration, Swainson's, Gray-cheeked, and other thrushes are found foraging on the ground of the wooded trails.

How to Bird This Site

A trail map is essential here, especially when visiting the interior forest. Maps are available at the red barn, and there are information kiosks at each parking lot. Walking through the meadows, along the river edge, or on the entry road is fairly easy. Beyond the second parking area, however, the terrain is mostly steep forested hillsides and ravines. The River Trail and Althea's Meadow Trail are the least strenuous trails and also quite birdy.

The most accessible and productive areas to bird are along the driveway, the river and its adjacent meadows, the old orchard, and the nature center buildings and gardens, especially during migration. Most visiting birders concentrate their efforts within the first half-mile of the entrance and on the meadows just beyond the red barn, which are excellent for riparian, edge-loving, and field-loving species, and for migrants from spring through fall.

If your interest is deep-forest species, you can explore the center's 15 miles of forest trails. Because Bent of the River is so large and its bird populations ever-changing, it is advisable to visit the center during business hours to obtain current information before venturing out. The Audubon Society has birders on staff to answer your questions.

The Grand Loop

This roughly 1.5-mile loop is designed to maximize the possible number of species. It *can be walked in 35 minutes*, but on a good day in May typically takes 2 hours. The best overall birding on this route is usually along the Cedar Fields Trail, with almost all of the local specialties nesting in this area, including White-eyed Vireo and Northern Parula in some years.

From the first parking lot, walk east along the River Trail, a relatively flat trail through riparian habitat adjacent to fields, with one short steep spot.

When you arrive at the red barn, continue southwest and uphill, following Pootatuck Road through mixed forest. Stop and listen for birdcalls at the intersections with Cascades and Tulip Tree Trails. (Depending on what you hear, you may wish to make a short detour.)

Turn left on Zig Zag Trail, which proceeds mostly downhill through wet hemlock forest, then merges with the Cedar Fields Trail, which passes through rolling terrain with shrubland habitat.

Continue downhill to the forested Beaver Meadow Loop, then proceed north along the River Road, through mixed riparian forest, into Althea's Meadow, mostly flat terrain and shrubland habitat. Continue back to the barn.

(18) Milford Tour

- Milford Point
- Jonathan Law High School Pond (Beaver Brook Ponds)
- Mondo Ponds Park
- Silver Sands State Park and Charles Island
- Wilcox Park

■ Milford Point

Seasonal rating: Sp **** Su **** F **** W ***
Best time to bird: Year-round; shorebird migration is best from May to mid-June and from mid-July through mid-September.
Habitats: Tidal estuary, saltmarsh, sandbars, breakwater, small barrier dunes, open lawns with scattered trees, mixed deciduous forest, old-field habitat, cedar groves, and a butterfly garden.

Bird list for this site:

SPECIALTY BIRDS

Resident – Mute Swan, American Black Duck, Gadwall, Bald Eagle, Northern Harrier (rare local nester), Great Blue Heron, Clapper Rail, Peregrine Falcon, Monk Parakeet, Fish Crow, Common Raven (occasional)

Summer – American Oystercatcher, Piping Plover, Willet, Least and Common Terns, Black Skimmer (nonbreeder), Yellow-crowned Night-Heron, Little Blue Heron (most years), Glossy Ibis, Willow Flycatcher, Purple Martin, Marsh Wren, Brown Thrasher (some years), Saltmarsh Sparrow, Seaside Sparrow, Boat-tailed Grackle (occasional), Orchard Oriole

Winter – Eurasian Wigeon (most winters), Canvasback, Red-necked Grebe (occasional); Iceland, Lesser Black-backed, and Glaucous Gulls (all uncommon); Short-eared Owl (uncommon), Snowy Owl (invasion years), Rough-legged Hawk (invasion years), American Tree Sparrow, "Ipswich" Savannah Sparrow, Fox Sparrow

OTHER KEY BIRDS

Resident – Common Loon (nonbreeder), Red-tailed Hawk, Ring-billed Gull (nonbreeder), Herring and Great Black-backed Gulls, Belted Kingfisher, Northern Flicker

Summer – Double-crested Cormorant, Great and Snowy Egrets, Green Heron

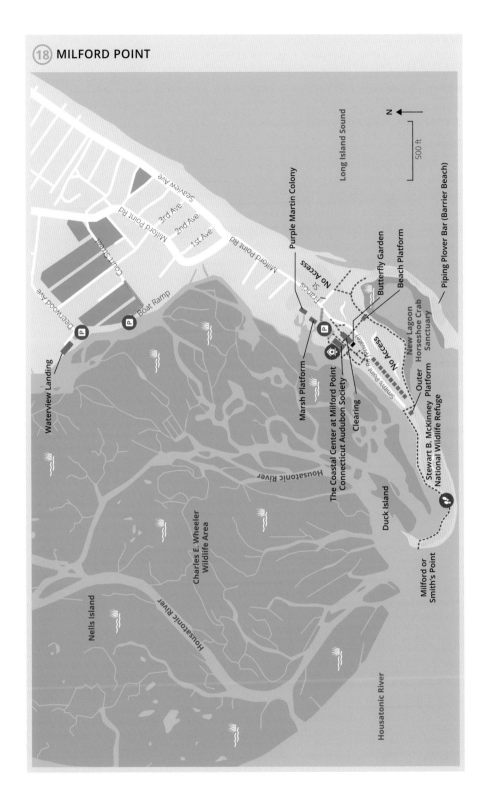

N

500 ft

Long Island Sound

Seaview Ave

3rd Ave

2nd Ave

1st Ave

Milford Point Rd

Milford Point Rd

Court Street

Deerwood Ave

Boat Ramp

Waterview Landing

Francis St

NO ACCESS

Purple Martin Colony

Butterfly Garden

Beach Platform

Piping Plover Bar (Barrier Beach)

Marsh Platform

The Coastal Center at Milford Point
Connecticut Audubon Society

Clearing

Smith's Point Rd (private)

NO ACCESS

New Lagoon

Outer
Horseshoe Crab
Sanctuary

Stewart B. McKinney
National Wildlife Refuge

Housatonic River

Housatonic River

Duck Island

Charles E. Wheeler
Wildlife Area

Nells Island

Housatonic River

Milford or
Smith's Point

(uncommon), Black-crowned Night-Heron, Osprey, Killdeer, Spotted Sandpiper, Laughing Gull, Eastern Kingbird, Common Yellowthroat, Yellow Warbler, Eastern Towhee (some years), Baltimore Oriole

Winter – Brant, American Wigeon, Greater Scaup, Long-tailed Duck, Common Goldeneye, Bufflehead, Red-breasted Merganser, Common and Red-throated Loons, Horned Grebe, White-throated Sparrow, Dark-eyed Junco

MIGRANTS

Blue-winged and Green-winged Teal, "Eurasian" Green-winged Teal (most years), Northern Shoveler, Northern Pintail, all three scoter species, and most other waterfowl; American Bittern, Sora, Virginia Rail, raptors, Caspian and Royal Terns (uncommon); Forster's, Roseate, and Black Terns; rare terns, American Coot, Northern Gannet, American Avocet (nearly annual), American Golden-Plover (fall); Whimbrel, Hudsonian and Marbled Godwits (fall), Red Knot, and most other shorebirds; Bonaparte's Gull, Alder and Yellow-bellied Flycatchers, Brown Creeper, both kinglet species, Mourning Warbler and Yellow-breasted Chat (uncommon); Palm, Yellow-rumped, and most other warblers; most sparrows, including White-crowned, Vesper, Lincoln's, Seaside, and Nelson's Sparrows; Lapland Longspur, Snow Bunting, Bobolink, Dickcissel (uncommon), Rusty Blackbird

---

Location: Connecticut Audubon Society Coastal Center, 1 Milford Point Road, Milford
Parking: The parking lot is locked from dusk to dawn, and is closed on July 4. A permit and key may be obtained (for a small fee) to enter after dark. Inquire at the center.
Restrooms: Inside the Coastal Center.
Hazards: Hunting is permitted fall through spring, except on Sundays, in the Wheeler Marsh. A breach in the barrier beach is impassable at high tide. No-see-ums can be extremely bothersome here in spring and summer.
Additional information: Enquire about summer and fall canoe tours of the Wheeler Marsh led by Connecticut Audubon Society staff; these provide an excellent opportunity to view marsh birds. Navigating the marsh without a guide requires careful timing with the tides. There is no public boat ramp at the Coastal Center. The ramp is on Court Street.

The Birding

Milford Point is a premier Connecticut coastal birding site, one of two with a bird list of more than 325 species. Most of the state's endangered or threatened bird species, as well as species of special concern, nest, feed, or rest during migration at Milford Point each year. The site consists of three sections. Connecticut Audubon Society operates its Coastal Center on an 8.4-acre area of upland, dunes, and barrier beach known as the Smith-Hubbell Wildlife Refuge. The 840-acre, state-owned Wheeler Wildlife Management

Area (Wheeler Marsh) is situated to the north of the Coastal Center. To the center's southwest, beyond a private residential area, is the 9-acre Smiths Point, a federally owned piece of the Stewart B. McKinney National Wildlife Refuge. **Note:** The upland area of Smiths Point is closed year-round. On the marsh (north) side, limited access to the point is permitted below the high-tide line.

Milford Point is located at the confluence of two major migration routes: the Connecticut coastline and the Housatonic River. The river mouth and its protected areas provide a large expanse of diverse habitats essential for both breeding species and migrants. It's not surprising, then, that many of Connecticut's rare shorebirds were first observed here, including Black-tailed Godwit and all three records for Red-necked Stint. Ruff and Curlew Sandpiper have been found in spring and Black-necked Stilt and American Avocet in summer. A staggering array of rare landbirds, waterfowl, gulls, terns, and waders have occurred here. Knowing that nearly anything is possible is one of the joys of birding Milford Point!

How to Bird This Site

The area surrounding the Coastal Center features scattered fruit and hardwood trees, cedar groves, old-field habitat, thickets, and a butterfly garden. In July and early August, the ripened fruit of the mulberry trees near the building attracts many birds, including Rose-breasted Grosbeak, Baltimore and Orchard Orioles, Common Grackle, Red-winged Blackbird, and a host of other species. Even the Boat-tailed Grackle flock from nearby Stratford has been known to appear when the mulberries are ripe.

The red cedars scattered throughout the property attract Purple Finches from late August through mid-April in most years. Monk Parakeets visit the cedar and mulberry trees in season and the Coastal Center feeders throughout the year. Cedar Waxwings, American Robins, and Hermit and other thrushes eat the berries of the red cedar in fall.

It is permitted to walk along the private road within the refuge; this area can be very birdy, but beware of traffic and avoid trespassing onto posted land. The vine tangles alongside the road and paths, along with the tall trees surrounding the building, are attractive to migrants; on "fall-out" days, the area can be dripping with birds. Ruby-crowned and Golden-crowned Kinglets, Brown Creeper, and a wide variety of flycatchers, vireos, thrushes, sparrows, and warblers—including some less common species such as Mourning Warbler—visit in spring and especially in fall.

Several pairs of Baltimore Orioles, along with a pair or two of Orchard Orioles, nest at the clearing edge. In some years, Brown Thrasher and Eastern Towhee breed in the roadside thickets or dunes; their numbers are augmented by migrants in spring and fall. A pair or two of Northern Flickers, as well as Hairy, Downy, and Red-bellied Woodpeckers, are generally present year-round.

The covered multilevel **observation tower** attached to the Coastal Center is roughly 40 feet high. It provides spectacular views of Wheeler Marsh and the many waterbirds that use it, along with distant views of the sandbars on Long Island Sound. The tower is also an excellent spot from which to observe migrating diurnal landbirds and raptors, especially in fall.

The **marsh platform** at the corner of the parking lot provides a clear view of the southeast section of the marsh. Shorebirds, waders, and ducks are generally most visible around mid-tide. The gourd trees next to the platform house a vibrant colony of Purple Martins, typically from mid-April through early August. The martins are best seen early or late in the day; at midday they may be absent or off feeding. Tree Swallows also nest in boxes near the platform.

The **beach platform**, at the end of a path leading from the Coastal Center through the dunes, overlooks Long Island Sound, the outer barrier beach, and the inner tidal lagoon with its mudflats and adjacent sandbars. It is a good place from which to observe terns and shorebirds at high tide.

To the west, at the base of Smiths Point, the **outer platform** overlooks the river mouth and outer sandbars, as well as a few channels in the marsh that are hidden from the observation tower and marsh platform. A path cuts across the dunes from the lagoon-edge beach to the raised observation deck. **Note:** Please do not use the private road. A walk from the platform to the point on the marsh (north) side, below the high-tide line, can be productive, especially in winter. (The point's south shore is closed to foot traffic.) In fall and winter, look for Snowy and Short-eared Owls, Horned Lark, Snow Bunting, and "Ipswich" Savannah Sparrow. Swamp, Savannah, Saltmarsh, Seaside, and Nelson's Sparrows, and occasionally Lapland Longspur and Eastern Meadowlark, are seen in fall. Northern Wheatear, Sedge Wren, and Dickcissel are a few of rarities that have been found in this area.

The Coastal Center's **exhibit hall** has huge picture windows offering stunning views of Wheeler Marsh. Ospreys nest on a platform in the marsh 50 yards from the window. The pair arrives in late March and departs by September, with young-of-the-year sometimes lingering later. Three spotting scopes mounted by the windows allow close scrutiny of the nest and marsh. A video camera mounted on the nest platform is linked to a viewing monitor in the exhibit hall, treating visitors to intimate views of nesting activity. (The video feed is also available online at www.ctaudubon.org.) In winter, watch for Northern Harrier, Rough-legged Hawk, Snowy Owl, and Bald Eagle (sometimes more than a dozen). Bird feeders below the windows are stocked from fall through spring and attract a wide variety of migrants. Monk Parakeets visit regularly, and Fox and White-crowned Sparrows stop by during migration. American Tree Sparrows visit in winter, when Pine Siskins and Common Redpolls can also occur.

Mid-tide is usually the best time to observe **Wheeler Marsh**. At high tide, when the marsh is flooded, birds either concentrate on the periphery or roost on the higher sandbars in Long Island Sound. At low tide, when extensive mudflats are exposed, the birds are often distant and difficult to observe from this vantage point. (The exposed mudflats can be better viewed from Court Street or Waterview Landing.)

Small groups of Canvasbacks arrive at Wheeler Marsh in February (most years). Along with the returning Red-winged Blackbirds, these migrants foretell the coming of spring. Duck numbers and diversity build through early spring, with large numbers of Gadwall, American Wigeon, and Green-winged Teal joining the resident American Black Ducks, Mallards, and abundant Mute Swans in the marsh. Blue-winged Teal, Northern Shoveler, Northern Pintail, Eurasian Wigeon, and "Eurasian" Green-winged Teal (the Eurasian form of Green-winged Teal) are annual in small numbers.

From spring through fall, Tree and Barn Swallows are often abundant over the marsh. Diligent searching usually reveals a few Bank, Rough-winged, and Cliff Swallows as well. By mid-April, Clapper Rails begin to call, especially at dawn and dusk. They are occasionally seen feeding on the mudflats and along the periphery at high tide or wading the channels as the tide changes. Clapper Rails stay well into fall and can overwinter.

During peak shorebird migration, from May to early June, then from mid-July through September, thousands of shorebirds are seen feeding here, splitting their time between the marsh and the sandbars. Typical species include Sanderling, Semipalmated and Least Sandpipers, Dunlin, Ruddy Turnstone, Greater and Lesser Yellowlegs, and Short-billed Dowitcher. Red Knot and White-rumped Sandpiper are less common but regular visitors, in May and June, then again from August into October. A few Western Sandpipers intermingle with the flocks, especially in fall.

In summer, Wheeler Marsh hosts one of the state's highest concentrations of Yellow-crowned Night-Herons. It also is one of west-central Connecticut's few reliable sites for Glossy Ibis. Both Black-crowned and Yellow-crowned Night-Herons frequently roost in the trees around the Coastal Center building or by the entrance, and on the roofs of houses along Milford Point Road. In summer, a couple of Little Blue Herons usually feed in the marsh (take care: Yellow-crowned Night-Herons look similar in flight), while both Snowy and Great Egrets are common and the occasional Tricolored Heron turns up. Great Blue Herons are ubiquitous in season.

Small numbers of Seaside Sparrows breed in the tall *Spartina alterniflora* grasses throughout the marsh. The more numerous Saltmarsh Sparrows breed in the shorter *Spartina patens*, better viewed from Court Street and Fair View Landing. In summer, males of both species are sometimes seen from the marsh observation towers, singing from atop the grasses, but a canoe trip offers the best chance to encounter these elusive marsh dwellers. In fall, they are easiest to observe at high tide along the marsh edge near Smiths Point and in the small marsh at the base of the barrier beach east of the beach platform; at this time, they are joined by migrating Nelson's Sparrows.

While there are only a few September records for King Rail, both Sora and Virginia Rail are fairly numerous (though inconspicuous) migrants. They are generally found deep in the marsh and only occasionally heard from shore. Rare Black and Yellow Rails also have been heard. Least Bitterns are known to nest occasionally in pools hidden within the marsh but are rarely encountered. American Bitterns arrive in autumn; a few overwinter, but most are seen in flight.

At least one pair each of Northern Harrier, Bald Eagle, and Peregrine Falcon hunts Wheeler Marsh year-round. The eagles are seen infrequently in summer but are often conspicuous fall through spring, especially when the upper Housatonic River freezes. Their nest is on the west edge of the marsh in a residential neighborhood. The site is closed during nesting season to minimize disturbance, but an adult roosts regularly by the Court Street boat ramp. During autumn migration, there are good flights of hawks over the marsh and the distant tree line along I-95. Cooper's and Sharp-shinned Hawks, Merlin, Kestrel, Northern Harrier, and Osprey are the most abundant species, but anything is possible—even Gyrfalcon and Swainson's Hawk have occurred.

In fall, migrating waterfowl begin appearing in late August or early September with the arrival of Blue and Green-winged Teal. Numbers of most species build after mid-October through mid-November, with many species remaining through the winter. Numbers peak again from mid-March to mid-April, with all three scoter species lingering well into May on Long Island Sound. Most loons and grebes move at these times as well. Any duck that occurs in Connecticut may appear at Milford Point. Long-tailed Duck numbers peak from mid-March to early April. Flocks of scoters (mostly Surf and White-winged) and Greater Scaup build into the thousands as they prepare to migrate north in spring. A few Lesser Scaup, and occasionally Redheads, are typically mixed in. Check for Barrow's Goldeneye bobbing among the flocks of Common Goldeneye in winter. Although rare, Common and King Eider are possible in winter as well. If inland lakes and reservoirs freeze, expect to see freshwater-loving species such as Common and Hooded Mergansers along the coast.

At high tide, shorebirds, terns, gulls, and cormorants congregate on the barrier beach and **exposed sandbars** in Long Island Sound. These are best viewed from the beach platform or from "the hot corner," a section of high ground along the lagoon shore, 50 yards to the west of the platform and close to the inner barrier beach and bars. At low tide, the birds are dispersed across the extensive mudflats. **Note:** A spotting scope is essential to take full advantage of these birding opportunities.

The **dunes** along the way to the beach platform are home to nesting Willow Flycatcher, Tree Swallow, Northern Mockingbird (resident), Gray Catbird, Common Yellowthroat, and Song Sparrow (resident). During migration, these dunes can be inundated with landbirds, especially in fall. Spring through fall, watch for Eastern Towhee and Brown Thrasher; both are potential breeders here. Palm Warbler and Savannah Sparrow are often conspicuous in spring and fall. **Note:** Please bird from the path; the dunes are fragile and closed to foot traffic year-round.

As many as nine pairs of federally threatened Piping Plovers nest at Milford Point.

In most years, from mid-March to mid-April, thousands of gulls—primarily Ring-billed and Herring Gulls, with lesser numbers of Great Black-backed Gulls—gather offshore and in the river mouth to feed on barnacle larvae. Close scrutiny usually reveals a few Iceland and Lesser Black-backed Gulls, and rarely a Glaucous Gull. Bonaparte's Gulls often join the feeding frenzy, and it can pay to search among them for Black-headed and Little Gulls, especially in March. Laughing Gulls are an area staple in late summer and early fall.

Tern numbers peak in August, with hundreds to thousands of Common and Least Terns gathering on the outer bars, frequently with a few Roseate, Black, and Forster's Terns intermixed. The Forster's Terns will often linger into November. Small numbers of Royal and Caspian Terns occur annually spring into fall, and Black Skimmers are regular spring and summer visitors. Milford Point is arguably the best site in Connecticut to find rare terns: Sooty (after hurricanes), Arctic, Sandwich, and Gull-billed Terns have all made the list.

Fall through spring, the beaches also attract American Pipit, Horned Lark, Snow Bunting, and a few Lapland Longspur. **Note:** In summer, the high barrier beach opposite the beach platform is cordoned off by the Connecticut Department of Energy and Environmental Protection (DEEP) to protect nesting Piping Plovers (a threatened species), Least and Common Terns, and several pairs of American Oystercatchers. To minimize disturbance to the breeding birds, please refrain from walking on the barrier beach at or near high tide, or near the string fencing at any time. These birds are best viewed from the beach platform, the outer platform, "the hot corner," or the base of the barrier beach, accessed by walking from the beach platform along the lagoon edge or from the public right-of-way off Francis Street, east of the refuge entrance.

▪ Jonathan Law High School Pond (Beaver Brook Ponds)

Seasonal rating: Sp *** Su * F *** W ***
Best time to bird: Late fall through spring.
Habitats: Pond, stream, second-growth forest, and schoolyard.

SPECIALTY BIRDS
Resident – Fish Crow, Carolina Wren
Summer – Osprey, Belted Kingfisher
Winter – Puddle ducks, including Wood Duck, Gadwall, American Wigeon, Eurasian Wigeon (uncommon), American Black Duck, Green-winged Teal (uncommon), Hooded Merganser

MIGRANTS
Wood warblers (fall)

Location: 20 Lansdale Avenue, Milford.
Parking: Drive along the north side of the building toward the back of the school. Park on the right overlooking the pond. Avoid restricted parking areas and do not block driveways or entrances. Parking may not be possible during school hours. Alternate parking is available near the ball fields on Lawman Road.
Restrooms: At fast-food restaurants on U.S. 1 (Bridgeport Avenue).

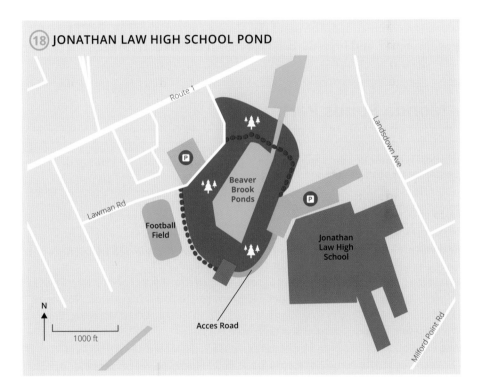

The Birding

This small pond down the hill from the northwest side of the high school's parking lot may be Connecticut's best place to find Eurasian Wigeon from fall through spring, while the water remains open. Four at once have been seen among the many visiting American Wigeon and Gadwall. Any of the pond-loving waterfowl are possible.

Belted Kingfisher hunt the area and nest nearby. On good migration days, especially in fall, the trees along the brook can hold a nice assortment of landbirds, especially warblers, kinglets, vireos, and woodpeckers, while assorted thrushes and Carolina Wrens feed in the understory. When viewed from the parking area, the birds are often close to eye level. Common riparian forest species breed here.

How to Bird This Area

A paved trail leads down from the parking lot along the east side of the pond to a flat area near the brook that provides a fairly unobstructed view. **Note:** A scope is recommended. The pond can also be viewed from the parking area, at least in winter, and from the ball fields down the hill at the pond's south end.

■ Mondo Ponds Park

Seasonal rating: Sp **** Su *** F *** W ***
Best time to bird: Year-round.
Habitats: Small lake, secluded vegetated pond, wet and dry woodlands, pine/spruce forest, swamp, rocky outcrops, and brushy thickets.

SPECIALTY BIRDS
Resident – Wood Duck, Fish Crow, Common Raven (uncommon), Cooper's Hawk, Belted Kingfisher, Hairy Woodpecker, Northern Flicker
Summer – Spotted Sandpiper, Great Egret, Green Heron, Black-crowned Night-Heron, Osprey, Chimney Swift, Eastern Phoebe, Eastern Kingbird, Warbling Vireo, Northern Rough-winged Swallow, Purple Martin (a few), Wood Thrush, Cedar Waxwing, Pine Warbler (some years), Orchard and Baltimore Orioles
Winter – Puddle ducks, including Wood Duck, Gadwall, American Wigeon, and Eurasian Wigeon (uncommon); Canvasback, Redhead (some years), Lesser and Greater Scaup (both uncommon), Ring-necked Duck, Ruddy Duck (uncommon), Hooded and Common Mergansers, American Coot, Pied-billed Grebe, Bald Eagle, Red-breasted Nuthatch, Brown Creeper, Winter Wren, both kinglet species

MIGRANTS
Solitary Sandpiper, Greater Yellowlegs (large numbers some years), Short-billed and Long-billed Dowitchers (rare), vireos, Bank Swallow, thrushes, wood warblers, Fox Sparrow, Eastern Towhee, Rose-breasted Grosbeak, Rusty Blackbird (uncommon)

Location: 1352 Naugatuck Avenue, Milford.
Parking: Dirt parking lot (can be closed in winter). Alternate parking is available at the John F. Kennedy School, 404 West Avenue, Milford; park in the back lot nearest the pond.
Restrooms: At U.S. 1 fast-food restaurants.

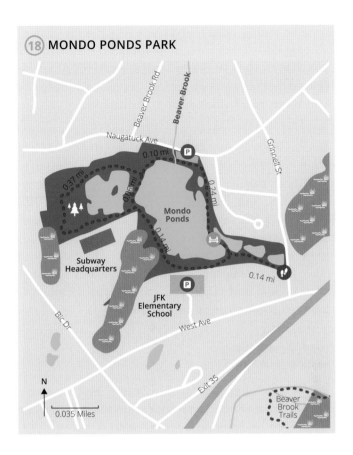

18 MONDO PONDS PARK

The Birding

Mondo Ponds Park is a lovely place, especially in autumn, when the leaves reflect off the water. The park's 36.7 acres include five ponds. The two largest—the spring-fed main lake and the secluded west pond—are covered here. This scenic park, with its nice diversity of habitats, is among my favorite sites to visit in Milford. The generally flat terrain, with the exception of a small hill at the west end, makes for easy walking, although the trails can get icy in winter, then muddy and wet in spring. The 0.65-mile loop trail around the main lake can be walked in 15 minutes, and the 0.25-mile west pond loop in 10 minutes, but to cover the park well, *1 to 3 hours are recommended.*

Mondo Ponds is known for attracting waterfowl from late August through April, including such less common species as Eurasian Wigeon, Northern Shoveler, Canvasback and Redhead. Because the main lake is spring-fed, it remains open along its north shore most winters, often allowing Ring-necked

Duck and Common and Hooded Mergansers to gather in sizable flocks. Any of the pond-loving duck species might be found in the main lake (or in the west pond, for that matter), and it is a reliable site for American Coot and Pied-billed Grebe from fall through spring. Occasionally both scaup species, Common Golden-eye, and Bufflehead join the masses.

A few less common nesting species include Wood Duck (west pond), American Black Duck, Green Heron (west pond), Spotted Sandpiper (islands), Belted Kingfisher, Northern Rough-winged Swallow, Warbling Vireo, and Orchard Oriole (both ponds). There are four species of resident woodpeckers: Northern Flicker and Downy, Hairy, and Red-bellied Woodpeckers. Yellow-bellied Sapsucker is seen in migration, and Pileated Woodpecker has occurred. Black-crowned Night-Heron, Great Egret, and Osprey frequently visit in summer. Bald Eagles hunt here most winters. Check the islands in the main lake for roosting shorebirds—Spotted and Solitary Sandpipers (spring), the occasional dowitcher, and especially in October, Greater Yellowlegs (as many as 105 have been seen at once).

How to Bird This Area

The best birding is generally on the peninsula adjacent to the parking lot and west along the north side of the main lake, from the parking lot to the start of the west pond loop, and around the west pond.

Check the peninsula directly south of the parking lot. A trail leads to it through the spruce grove. Migrants, especially warblers and kinglets, tend to congregate here. Orchard and Baltimore Orioles nest here and at the west pond, as do Cedar Waxwings and many Warbling Vireos. The low wet area on the peninsula's east side is hunted by Green Herons spring through fall; during migration, it attracts Northern Waterthrush and an occasional Solitary Sandpiper. Resident Belted Kingfisher and nesting Eastern Kingbird often hunt from bare perches overlooking the lake or on islands.

After checking the peninsula, head west (away from the condos) along the north edge of the lake, checking the trailside thickets for migrants and scanning the lake through openings in the vegetation. In spring, Yellow-throated Warbler (rare) and White-eyed Vireo (uncommon) have occurred in these thickets, while Pine Warbler (nests) is usually found in the evergreens by the parking lot. Just after the trail bends to the left (south), there are fruit trees and grapevines on both sides of the trail; these are especially attractive to migrants. Brown Thrasher, Gray-cheeked Thrush, Philadelphia Vireo, and Fox Sparrow are just a few of the goodies found in this area. One large opening in the vegetation here gives great views of the lake, especially in the afternoon when the light is behind you. This also is a good spot to scan for swallows. On some mornings during migration, the skies above the lake are filled with hunting Chimney Swifts and Northern Rough-winged, Tree, and Barn Swallows, joined occasionally by a few Purple Martins or Bank and Cliff Swallows. Double-crested Cormorants (spring through fall) and Herring and Ring-billed Gulls often rest on or bathe by the islands.

A little farther on, the loop trail that encircles the west pond veers off to the right. At this juncture, be sure to check the rocky outcrops and vernal pools directly ahead for Swainson's Thrush, Veery, and other thrushes; warblers and other migrants also seem to prefer this area. Scan for migrant Northern Waterthrush and Solitary Sandpiper along the pool edge. The next 50 yards or so along the main lake trail can be very birdy, especially in the morning or late afternoon, when the sun hits the trees. Along the way, short side trails to the right give views of the west pond. Continue past the junction with the south side of the west pond loop trail and check the wet areas along the main trail adjacent to Subway's brick office building; look for Winter Wren, fall through spring, and the occasional Rusty Blackbird (spring). Then retrace your steps to the initial fork in the trail and go left to check the north side of the west pond.

The birches along this trail attract finches, including Purple Finch, Pine Siskin, and Common Redpoll some winters. Thickets on the right, especially toward the west end of the pond, have held Mourning Warbler, Indigo Bunting, and a variety of sparrows, including Fox Sparrow (in March) and Swamp Sparrow. House and Carolina Wrens breed here, along with both oriole species, Eastern Kingbird, Cedar Waxwing, and Warbling Vireo.

The beech and oak hillside on the west end of the pond overlooks skunk-cabbage-filled vernal pools and is probably the best spring birding site in the park. Hooded, Blackburnian, and Worm-eating Warblers have been found here. Green Heron, Wood Duck, Wood Thrush, Rose-breasted Grosbeak, American Goldfinch, and all four of the common woodpeckers nest in this area. Scarlet Tanagers are seen in migration, and Common Ravens prefer this area in spring. As you first enter the woods from the north side, a set of stairs leads to the hilltop. At the top of the stairs, an obscure side trail to the right leads northwest to a wet area that, during migration, can be great for Canada and Magnolia Warblers, as well as Black-and-white Warbler and Common Yellowthroat. **Note:** Beware of deer ticks here.

Complete the loop around the west pond by scanning the treetops for migrants, especially along the south shore. The south shore birches may hold Rose-breasted Grosbeak and Purple Finch in spring, and a slew of warbler species has been found in this area. Check the pond for Gadwall, American Wigeon, Hooded Merganser, and other ducks. In summer, Green Herons nest here. Great Egret and Black-crowned Night-Heron visit regularly, and Great Blue Heron is possible late summer through spring.

The loop around the main lake is lovely but often not very birdy, except near the southeast corner, where a side trail leads past a third small pond to a house with bird feeders. The best views of the main lake, however, are from its east side in the morning light.

■ Silver Sands State Park and Charles Island

Seasonal rating: Sp *** Su *** F **** W ***
Best time to bird: Year-round.
Habitats: Long Island Sound, tidal saltmarsh, Charles Island, rocky tombolo, sandbars, beach, mudflats, a jetty, small barrier dunes, open lawns with scattered trees, mixed deciduous forest, old-field habitat, and capped landfill.

SPECIALTY BIRDS
Resident – Mute Swan, American Black Duck, Gadwall, Ring-necked Pheasant, (declining), Wild Turkey, Fish Crow
Summer – Clapper Rail, Piping Plover (some years), Killdeer, American Oystercatcher, Willet, Common and Least Terns, Great and Snowy Egrets, Yellow-crowned Night-Heron, Little Blue Heron (some years), Glossy Ibis, Osprey, Willow Flycatcher, Eastern Kingbird, Warbling Vireo, Northern Rough-winged Swallow, Purple Martin, Marsh Wren, Brown Thrasher (some years), Yellow-breasted Chat (sporadic), Saltmarsh Sparrow, Orchard Oriole
Winter – Brant, Horned Grebe, loons, Northern Harrier, Red-shouldered Hawk, Rough-legged Hawk (invasion years), Iceland and Lesser Black-backed Gulls (uncommon), Short-eared and Long-eared Owls, Snowy Owl (invasion years), Horned Lark, Snow Bunting; American Tree, Field, and Fox Sparrows; "Ipswich" Savannah Sparrow

MIGRANTS
Wilson's Snipe, American Woodcock and other shorebirds, raptors, Eastern Phoebe and other flycatchers, Bank Swallow and other swallows, kinglets, American Pipit; Palm, Yellow-rumped, and other warblers; Nelson's, Saltmarsh, and other sparrows; Indigo Bunting, Dickcissel (uncommon); Bobolink, Eastern Meadowlark, and other blackbirds; Purple Finch

Location: Silver Sands State Park Way, Milford.
Restrooms: Portable toilets available spring through fall.

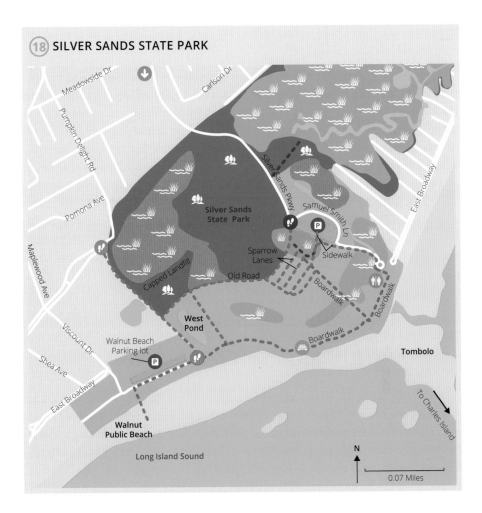

18 SILVER SANDS STATE PARK

(Map labels:)
Meadowside Dr
Carlson Dr
Pumpkin Delight Rd
Pomona Ave
Maplewood Ave
Viscount Dr
Shea Ave
East Broadway
Silver Sands Pkwy
Samuel Smith Ln
East Broadway
Silver Sands State Park
Sparrow Lanes
Sidewalk
Old Road
Boardwalk
Boardwalk
Boardwalk
Capped Landfill
West Pond
Walnut Beach Parking lot
Tombolo
To Charles Island
Walnut Public Beach
Long Island Sound
N
0.07 Miles

The Birding

Silver Sands State Park is a reclaimed landfill site tucked along the coast just 2 miles east of Milford Point. The park is open from 8:00 a.m. to sunset. It has a 1.5-mile boardwalk, restored coastal dunes and saltmarshes, woodlots, brushy thickets, lawns, open meadows, and marshy seeps. A tidal creek runs through a saltmarsh on the east side, and there is a tidal pond on the west end. The park also includes the Charles Island Natural Area, home to one of the largest heronries in the state.

The park's coastal location and varied habitats make it an ideal location for finding birds, especially during migration. In summer, when the park is often quite crowded with beachgoers, birding is best early or late in the day.

Entrance is currently free, but plans for new bathhouses and concession stands include admission fees.

The park attracts a broad array of landbird migrants and is best known as a prime autumn location for finding sparrows, especially such less common species as Lincoln's, Clay-colored, and Vesper Sparrows. Savannah Sparrows are a particularly abundant migrant and may breed here in small numbers; the "Ipswich" subspecies can sometimes be found in the beach dunes. The tall weedy areas on both sides of the entrance road, the grasses lining the landfill perimeter fence, and the park's meadows and lawns are all frequented by migrating sparrows. The site's premier location for sparrows and other seed-eaters, however, is the grassy overflow parking area—known locally as the "sparrow lanes"—just west of the paved parking lot. Fourteen sparrow species have occurred here. Indigo Bunting and Bobolink also can be fairly common in the lanes during migration, and small numbers of Blue Grosbeak and Dickcissel occur with regularity.

The weedy areas adjacent to the creek on the park's northeast side have drawn their share of sparrows and warblers as well, including, the "Audubon's" race of Yellow-rumped Warbler (rare). Wilson's Snipe feed in the wet channels and pools paralleling the fence. Wild Turkeys are often seen beside the entrance road, especially at dusk, and typically roost in the trees on the east side near the marsh.

The autumn raptor migration is noteworthy, especially for the coastal migrants, falcons, accipiters, Northern Harrier, Osprey, and Bald Eagle. Swallows are conspicuous from late summer into fall, and Cave Swallow (rare) has occurred in November. Rarities such as Brown Pelican and Sandhill Crane have been seen.

In winter and early spring, this is Connecticut's best site for viewing Long-eared and Short-eared Owls without disturbing them. Viewers wait quietly along the old road at dusk, when the owls usually appear (the Short-eared less consistently) along the landfill perimeter fence or over the marsh. Occasionally a Snowy Owl or Rough-legged Hawk also visits in winter. **Note:** The Silver Sands parking lot typically closes at sunset, though the gate sometimes remains open in winter; owl-seekers may need to park at adjacent Walnut Beach.

The 0.2-mile section of boardwalk that leads from the parking lot to the beach traverses a small restored marsh used by herons, egrets, Clapper Rail, Glossy Ibis, and, rarely, American Bittern (fall and spring). It provides a superb vantage point to see Clapper Rail, especially in midsummer, when chicks are often visible.

In some years, a pair of Piping Plovers nests on the sandy sections of beach adjacent to the boardwalk. Killdeer breed in the gravelly areas along the boardwalk and on parking lot edges.

Wilson's Snipe, Greater and Lesser Yellowlegs, Black-bellied and Semipalmated Plovers, and Least and Semipalmated Sandpipers visit the marsh and rain pools on the mowed lawns during migration, sometimes in good numbers. Over the years, rarities such as Buff-breasted Sandpiper, Cattle Egret, and White-faced Ibis have been seen on the lawn near the main parking lot. American Wood-

Long-eared (shown) and Short-eared Owls often winter at Silver Sands State Park, appearing at dusk to hunt over the marsh.

cock breed in the old landfill area and display conspicuously at dusk, especially in March and April. American Oystercatchers are often seen on the rocky jetties, bars, and Charles Island, while Least and Common Terns feed in the area in summer.

There is a small river and marsh along the park's eastern edge that can be viewed from a pull-off just northeast of a parking circle at the south end of the entrance road. Look north along what appears to be a canal. Glossy Ibis, Yellow-crowned and Black-crowned Night-Herons, and egrets can usually be seen from April through September. A White Ibis was found here one fall.

Charles Island is closed to public access during the heron breeding season, from mid-April to Labor Day; during the rest of the year, access is possible via a 0.7-mile tombolo that is exposed at extremely low tides. (Connecticut Audubon provides guided tours in season.) **Note:** Extreme care should be taken when visiting the island, as the part of the bar nearest the island submerges much earlier than the section near the mainland. Many have been stranded after the tide rises, and some have drowned attempting to return. The island's interior is inaccessible—and festooned with poison ivy.

As many as 300 pairs of herons and egrets nest on Charles Island, mostly Black-crowned Night-Heron and Great and Snowy Egrets, with several pairs of Glossy Ibis, a few Yellow-crowned Night-Herons, and periodically, a pair of Little Blue Herons. Many of the nesting trees, already weakened by fungal blight, were destroyed by recent hurricanes, but Connecticut DEEP is working to restore the habitat. The island remains a productive heronry, although heron and egret numbers are depressed locally and will likely remain so until the habitat improves. In summer, the birds fly to and from the island and mainland marshes, including Wheeler Marsh to the west, especially at dusk and dawn. Gulls, along with American Oystercatchers and other shorebirds, feed on the island's shores and on the tombolo. Lesser Black-backed and Iceland Gulls have been found with them.

How to Bird This Area

An often productive 1.3-mile loop begins at the northwest side of the parking lot on the old road adjacent to the landfill. **Note:** This route is ideal if you are visiting the park in the morning. In the afternoon, reverse the described course so the sun stays at your back while on the road.

From the parking lot, walk west along the old road (beside the chain-link fence) searching the thickets on both sides. In autumn, these thickets have attracted several species famous for skulking in the underbrush: MacGillivray's Warbler (very rare), Connecticut Warbler (rare), Mourning and Orange-crowned Warblers, and Yellow-breasted Chat. A male chat has sung for several springs along this road and may breed in some years.

During migration (especially in fall), a detour into the grassy "sparrow lanes" on the left often yields a wide assortment of sparrows, including less common species such as Lincoln's and Clay-colored Sparrows. Orchard and Baltimore Orioles, along with grassland species such as Bobolink, Dickcissel, and Eastern Meadowlark, also are attracted to this area, especially in spring. Any of the grassland species, particularly Bobolink, could potentially breed in the old landfill area behind the fence.

Baltimore and Orchard Orioles, Cedar Waxwing, Willow Flycatcher, Eastern Kingbird, Warbling Vireo, Yellow Warbler, Common Yellow-throat, and occasionally a pair of Brown Thrasher breed along the old road. Near the end of the road is a gate on the left. Go through the gate and onto a gravel path, then take the side trail on the right. This trail passes through birches to an area with a good view of a pond where you may find waterfowl and shorebirds, including egrets, herons, Glossy Ibis, Wilson's Snipe, both yellowlegs species, and all the common plovers and sandpipers, as well as the less common White-rumped or Baird's Sandpipers (occasional). Belted Kingfisher is resident. Green Heron nests locally. A pair of Red-shouldered Hawks winter in the park and are often seen in this area from fall through spring. Ring-necked Pheasant prefer this area, and this is one of the few coastal sites where they may still breed.

To complete the loop, return to the gravel path and continue south toward the boardwalk that follows the shore; turn left toward Charles Island and return to the parking lot along the boardwalk, watching for Piping Plover, Killdeer, and other shorebirds, waders, and waterfowl from spring through fall. **Note:** A right turn leads to a bridge overlooking the pond, an area especially good for Wilson's Snipe in spring, then continues to Walnut Beach and the shops (including Walnut Beach Creamery) beyond.

In winter, a nice variety of ducks—along with Common and Red-Throated Loons, Horned Grebe, and an occasional Red-necked Grebe—tuck in behind Charles Island. Harbor seals also visit occasionally. Large rafts of Greater Scaup, with smaller numbers of Common Goldeneye, Bufflehead, Long-tailed Duck, and Red-breasted Merganser, feed in the water between Charles Island and Stratford Point to the west. Search for less common species such as Barrow's Goldeneye, Lesser Scaup, and Redhead among the flocks. All three scoter species are possible here but uncommon. Rarities seen from shore have included Brown Pelican, American White Pelican, and Harlequin Duck. In March or April and sometimes October, large gatherings of gulls, mainly Ring-billed, Herring, and Laughing Gulls, congregate offshore to eat fish fry and barnacle larvae. Less common species have been found with them, including Lesser Black-backed, Iceland, Glaucous, and Mew Gulls (rare). Keep an eye out for Parasitic Jaegers (rare), which sometimes appear to harass the gulls. When Bonaparte's Gulls are present, search for Little and Black-headed Gulls. Scan for Northern Gannets, especially in October or November, and again in March. During fall migration, landbirds and raptors often pass by along the shore.

■ Wilcox Park

Seasonal rating: Sp *** Su ** F *** W *
Best time to bird: Mid-April to May and all fall.
Habitats: Coastal forest, harbor, mudflats, lawns, residential neighborhood, and ball field.

SPECIALTY BIRDS
Resident – Mute Swan, American Black Duck, Great Horned Owl, Belted Kingfisher, Monk Parakeet, Fish Crow, Carolina Wren
Summer – Black-crowned and Yellow-crowned Night-Herons (nest), Great Egret, Osprey, Least Tern (uncommon), Chimney Swift, Northern Flicker, Hairy Woodpecker,

Northern Rough-winged Swallow, House Wren, Cedar Waxwing
Winter – Bufflehead, Hooded and Red-breasted Mergansers, other ducks, Red-throated and Common Loons, American Coot (most years), Pied-billed Grebe (some years), Ring-billed Gull, and other gulls

MIGRANTS
Landbirds, especially kinglets, thrushes, and warblers

Location: Shipyard Lane, Milford.
Parking: There is public parking beside the ball field, but it's often easiest to park along Harborside Drive near Elton Street, opposite Shipyard Lane.
Restrooms: Portable toilets available seasonally; otherwise at the Milford Public Library.

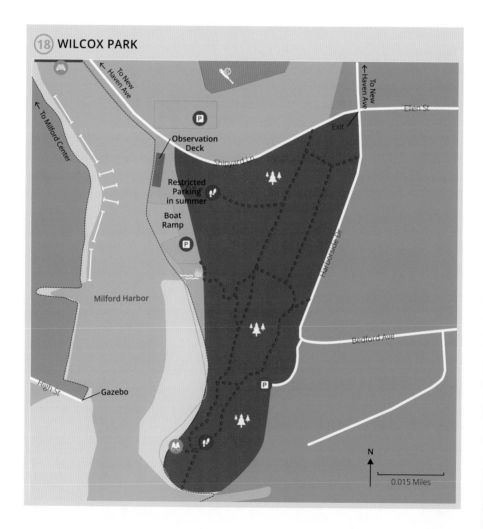

The Birding

This 20-acre oak-covered coastal upland provides a wooded oasis in an urban center. The park hugs the east side of Milford Harbor and *can be birded in an hour*, but you'll probably want more time. The wooded southern section is 0.25 miles long, but only 0.1 miles wide; it creates an ideal migrant trap in spring and especially in fall. The park's bird list includes nearly 170 species.

Songbird activity tends to be focused early in the day at the southern end and among the trees that border Harborside Drive. The birds arrive from the east and south at dawn then work northward as the day progresses. By 9:00 a.m. the oaks near the Shipyard Lane exit, along with the trees on Harborside Drive, can be very active. Late afternoon by the Shipyard Lane exit can also be rewarding; just stand on the lawns and watch the birds crossing the road. Spring mornings have produced more than ten species of warblers, including Magnolia, Blackburnian, Black-throated Green, Bay-breasted, and Cape May Warblers; the park is especially good for Black-throated Blue Warbler and Northern Parula. Other migrants include Veery, Wood Thrush, Blue-headed and Red-eyed Vireos, Scarlet Tanager, and Rose-breasted Grosbeak.

Cedar Waxwing, White-breasted Nuthatch, Baltimore Oriole, and all four of the common woodpecker species—along with, possibly, Wood Thrush and Cooper's and Red-tailed Hawks—breed in the uplands, while Belted Kingfisher and Barn, Tree, and Rough-winged Swallows nest along the harbor. In some years, Yellow-crowned Night-Herons nest along Harborside Drive or at the south end of the park. They often gather at dusk in summer and roost together with Great Egrets and Black-crowned Night-Herons in the trees edging the harbor. During migration, the harbor can hold a few shorebirds, mainly Greater and Lesser Yellowlegs and Least and Spotted Sandpipers (may nest), along with waders and ducks. Common and Red-throated Loons, American Coot, Bufflehead, and Hooded Merganser are present most winters and Pied-billed Grebe some winters. Red-necked Grebe (uncommon) also has occurred in winter.

How to Bird This Area

In spring and fall, park along Harborside Drive or in the small parking area at the south end of the park and work north to Shipyard Lane. To reach the south end, proceed south on Harborside Drive to a stop sign, then continue straight into what looks like a driveway to a dirt parking lot. A trail leads to the south observation platform, which overlooks the lower and central harbor and a nearby inlet (to the left) where ducks and geese hang out year-round. Other trails loop through the park, and all are worth walking.

In fall and winter, parking is usually available off Shipyard Lane, beside the ball fields, or by the north observation platform. It can be very rewarding to scan the fall skies for raptors and other diurnal migrants from the platform. Bald Eagles, Peregrine Falcons, and most of the state's other raptors have been seen from here. This platform also affords the best views of the harbor. Barn Swallows nest under it in summer.

Coastal West Haven Tour

- Sandy Point
- West Haven Boat Ramp
- Bradley Point Park
- South Street Beach
- Oyster River
- Merwin Point

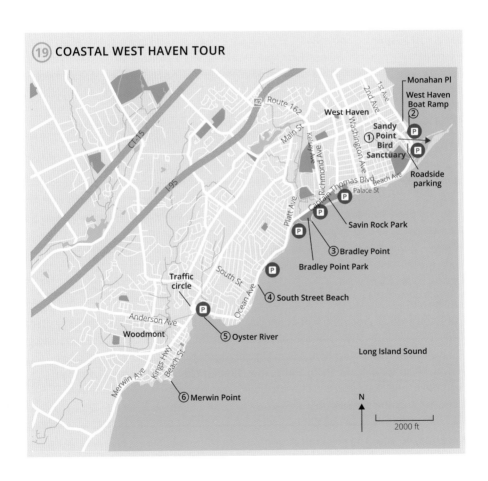

19 COASTAL WEST HAVEN TOUR

■ Sandy Point

Seasonal rating: Sp **** Su **** F **** W ***
Best time to bird: Year-round.
Habitats: Harbor, tidal river and lagoon, extensive sandy beaches, *Spartina* marsh, rock jetties, adjacent residential area, and wastewater treatment plant.

Bird list for this site:

SPECIALTY BIRDS

Resident – Mute Swan, American Black Duck, Peregrine Falcon (uncommon), Monk Parakeet, Fish Crow

Summer – Little Blue Heron (uncommon), Yellow-crowned Night-Heron, Glossy Ibis (uncommon), Piping Plover, Killdeer, American Oystercatcher, Willet, Spotted Sandpiper, Osprey, Clapper Rail, Laughing Gull, Common and Least Terns, Black Skimmer (most years), Willow Flycatcher, Warbling Vireo, Northern Rough-winged Swallow, Marsh Wren, Saltmarsh Sparrow, Seaside Sparrow (some years), Baltimore Oriole, Orchard Oriole (uncommon)

Winter – Lesser Scaup and Redhead (uncommon), Purple Sandpiper, Horned Lark, Snow Bunting, Lapland Longspur (uncommon), "Ipswich" Savannah Sparrow

OTHER KEY BIRDS

Resident – Herring, Great Black-backed, and Ring-billed Gulls (nonbreeders)

Summer – Great and Snowy Egrets, Black-crowned Night-Heron, Double-crested Cormorant, Mourning Dove, Northern Flicker, Downy Woodpecker, Eastern Kingbird, Tree and Barn Swallows, Yellow Warbler, Common Yellowthroat, Baltimore Oriole, Red-winged Blackbird, Common Grackle, Brown-headed Cowbird

Winter – Brant, Common and Red-throated Loons, Horned Grebe, Greater Scaup, Long-tailed Duck, Common Goldeneye, Bufflehead, White-winged and Surf Scoters, Red-breasted Merganser

MIGRANTS

Waterfowl, loons, grebes, any of Connecticut's shorebirds; Bonaparte's, Black-headed, Little, Lesser Black-backed, and Iceland Gulls (uncommon); Mew Gull (rare); Roseate, Forster's, Black, and other terns; Bald Eagle, Osprey, Northern Harrier and other hawks, falcons, swallows, Palm and Yellow-rumped Warblers; Swamp, Savannah, Saltmarsh, and Nelson's Sparrows (October); Seaside Sparrow (fairly common), Bobolink and other blackbirds

Location: 46 Beach Street, West Haven.

➲ **Directions:** Coming from I-95, take First Avenue south. At a stop sign near the bird sanctuary, First Avenue turns into Beach Street. In 0.3 miles, Second Avenue is on the Right (a good place to park in summer to avoid the parking fee at the lot). To reach the main Sandy Point parking lot, continue another 0.1 miles. The lot is on the left.

Parking: Nonresidents must pay a parking fee year-round at the main parking lot. Street parking is often limited along Second Avenue and Beach Road in the summer.

Free walk-in traffic is allowed.

Restrooms: Portable toilets in the parking lot.

Hazards: The inner bar floods near high tide—keep careful watch to avoid getting stranded. Because this is a city park, commonsense safety precautions should be taken: hide valuables and bird with friends.

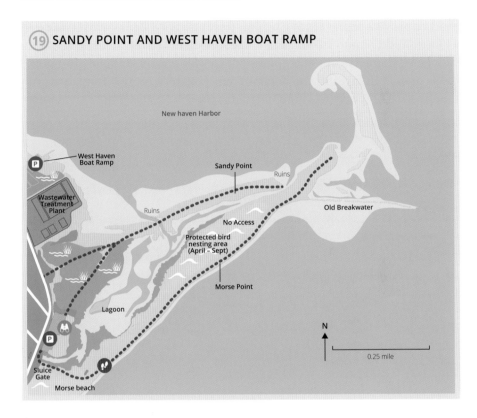

19 SANDY POINT AND WEST HAVEN BOAT RAMP

New haven Harbor

West Haven Boat Ramp

Sandy Point

Ruins

Ruins

Old Breakwater

Wastewater Treatment Plant

No Access

Protected bird nesting area (April – Sept)

Morse Point

Lagoon

N

0.25 mile

Sluice Gate

Morse beach

The Birding

Sandy Point is one of Connecticut's most popular and productive coastal birding sites. The bird sanctuary is actually comprised of two sand spits—a shorter inner bar (Sandy Point) and a longer outer one (Morse Point)—that enclose a tidal lagoon, known collectively as Sandy Point. The park offers a variety of habitats in close proximity, providing the chance to view a wide range of species in a small area—one-stop shorebirding, so to speak. It is ideally situated to attract migrants: the point sticks nearly a half-mile into New Haven Harbor and is located across the water from Lighthouse Point Park, the state's premier coastal hawk and landbird migration site. Equally important, there are few broad stretches of water or marsh to isolate the birds from observers; if care is taken, many species will tolerate fairly close approaches. **Note:** Several of the nesting species are threatened or endangered and protected by law.

Shorebirds, terns, and waders are the main attractions, but a wide variety of landbirds and raptors also can be seen. Sandy Point's extensive sandy beaches provide prime nesting habitat for threatened Piping Plovers, as well as Least and Common Terns and a few American Oystercatchers, and once supported Connecticut's only colony of Black Skimmers. Because storms can cause drastic changes in the habitat from year to-year, the annual nesting numbers of these species often fluctuates widely.

American Oystercatchers often nest in the same areas as Least Terns and Piping Plovers.

Sandy Point's list of rare terns and shorebirds is impressive, including Arctic and Sandwich Terns, Wilson's Plover, and Connecticut's first Snowy Plover and Little Stint. It is one of the better places in the state to find the rare but nearly annual American Avocet; most have occurred at the height of shorebird migration in August or September.

All three jaeger species (rare) have been recorded; the best chance to see one is when tern numbers peak in late summer. Tricolored Heron and, more commonly, Little Blue Heron occur here with consistency from spring into early autumn. The Osprey that nest locally often fish in the harbor in summer, and impressive numbers of migrant Osprey can be seen here, especially in autumn. During fall migration, most if not all of Connecticut's raptor species pass over Sandy Point. Gyrfalcon has occurred more than once, while

Peregrine Falcons often nest on the I-95 Quinnipiac River Bridge visible to the north; that pair typically hunts the harbor and Sandy Point.

If you're visiting from mid-October through May, expect to see Brant. Hundreds often congregate in the shallows around the point to feed on eelgrass and sea lettuce. New Haven Harbor attracts thousands of Greater Scaup in winter; Lesser Scaup and the occasional Redhead or Canvasback may join them. In season, Red-throated and Common Loons and Horned and Red-necked Grebes (uncommon) can be found in the harbor or in the deeper waters off the outer bar. Be on the lookout for lingering loons, grebes, and waterfowl in summer; Sandy Point seems to attract them.

Landbird rarities have included Northern Wheatear and a few migrant Cave Swallows (November). Purple Martins, as well as Barn, Tree, Rough-winged, Bank, and Cliff Swallows, are regular migrants. Tree Swallows sometimes stop here to feed on poison ivy and bayberry fruit in fall. It's always a treat to see dozens of them carpeting the bushes. It never hurts to check the thickets here for migrants, especially in autumn. Look for kinglets and a variety of sparrows and warblers, including both races of Palm Warblers. Yellow-rumped and Yellow Warblers, along with Common Yellowthroat, are fairly regular visitors. Song, Swamp, and Savannah Sparrows can be abundant. Impressive flights of Common Nighthawks may occasionally be seen here from late May to early June but more often from late August to mid-September.

Sandy Point is a picturesque site at any time of the year—a mild surprise given its proximity to a wastewater treatment plant. In September, the petite purple blossoms of sea lavender carpet the area with delicate beauty. As this plant's range is fairly restricted in Connecticut, please leave it for others to enjoy. Sea pickle or *Salicornia* covers the ground in scarlet in autumn, when migrant butterflies and dragonflies are moving through. Strikingly patterned monarch butterflies and both black saddlebag and green darner dragonflies can be abundant here. In winter, Sandy Point has a desolate, windswept beauty. Because there is little cover, it can get quite blustery and cold.

How to Bird This Site

Late afternoon on Sandy Point's inner bar provides the best light for birding. In autumn, the *Spartina* grasses glow with a rich golden hue.

It is still worth checking Sandy Point in the morning, but any birds on the east shore of the inlet or on Morse Point's outer bar, where the terns and Piping Plovers nest, will be backlit. For this reason, morning birders may find it more rewarding to work Morse Point first. This will keep the sun at your back. It is best to avoid birding Morse Point at high tide during the breeding season (from May through mid to late July) to minimize disturbance to nesting birds.

A spotting scope is highly recommended! The trailhead for the inner bar is located at the northeast corner of the main parking lot, beyond the guard-rail. It is about a 1-mile roundtrip from the parking lot to the end of the inner bar, though you generally need not walk more than half that far. If you use a scope, most of the birds can be seen from the mouth of the inlet at the base of the bar.

As you proceed on the path, stop periodically to scan the marsh edges. At low tide, extensive mudflats are exposed in the tidal lagoon between the two bars. These areas attract feeding waders and shorebirds. In summer, a little patience may be rewarded with a view of a Clapper Rail darting across the mudflats or feeding among the muddy mounds of *Spartina* grass. Salt-marsh Sparrow and Marsh Wren are also possible. To the north, Baltimore Orioles, Eastern Kingbirds, and Yellow Warblers nest in the trees and shrubs adjoining the wastewater treatment plant. Monk Parakeets nest on the pow-er poles and in trees in the local neighborhoods and sometimes along Beach Street; they regularly visit the trees near the treatment plant, year-round.

A few Piping Plovers—and sometimes impressive numbers of Snowy and Great Egrets—can be found feeding along the edges of the bars or on the mud-flats or resting on the sandbar near the mouth of the lagoon, from mid-March through at least October. Beginning in late April, they are typically joined by Least and Common Terns and a variety of other terns, shorebirds, and waders.

Stop where the bar narrows at the mouth of the lagoon and look across to Morse Point. In summer, the fenced-in area is where Least and Common Terns nest; the wire cages are "exclosures" that protect Piping Plover nests from predators. Black Skimmers (uncommon) visit occasionally, from May through September, and are most often seen feeding in the channel or at the harbor edge in mid to late summer.

If you continue out along the bar, stop to check the rocky north shore and the jetties to the east for shorebirds, waders, terns, and gulls. In summer, Dou-ble-crested Cormorants are commonly seen on the jetties. Great Cormorants replace them in winter, but a few Double-crested often remain, at least through early winter. This is a good place to find Belted Kingfisher at any season, but they can be scarce in winter; scan the jetties, buoys, and pilings. Laughing Gulls begin frequenting the area in July and can be quite common into October.

From late March through mid-June, then again from July through October, the mudflats can be covered with migrating shorebirds at low tide. Most of these birds will roost on the sandbars or shoreline when the tide becomes too high for them to feed. This is one of the better coastal sites to find Red Knot, Whimbrel, and Buff-breasted Sandpiper (uncommon) from July to September. A very few Upland Sandpipers are expected each year. Several American Golden-Plovers are found annually among the many Black-bellied Plovers from mid-July through mid-October. Semipalmated Plovers and Semipalmated Sandpipers can be very common on the mudflats, joined by Least Sandpipers and the chance Western Sandpiper. Ruddy Turnstones and Short-billed Dowitchers are fairly common migrants; the former prefer the rocky areas, the latter the mudflats. Expect to see good numbers of Sanderling in season; along with Dunlin, these often overwinter.

Migrant Pectoral Sandpipers begin to arrive at about the same time as the yellowlegs species, in late March or early April. A few may be seen from July through October, with a second peak in September. When Baird's Sandpipers put in a rare appearance, they generally frequent the grassy edges. Look for them from late July through September. Solitary Sandpiper is encountered infrequently here.

A few Hudsonian Godwits occur from late July through mid-November, but their stays are often brief. Marbled Godwits may occur as well, but only a few are reported each year statewide. Stilt Sandpipers are most likely from July through September.

Common and Least Terns, along with other terns, congregate at Sandy Point in late summer before they depart for the winter.

Farther along Sandy Point, just north of the jetty, is a low area where thousands of terns congregate in August and September. Search among the many Common Terns for the less abundant Roseate, Forster's, and Black Terns. Roseate Terns can be hard to pick out among the throngs of Commons: search for brighter orange-red legs, a paler, almost white plumage, and listen for their grating calls. Although Forster's Terns are a nonbreeding species in Connecticut, their numbers may exceed a hundred in a day in September and especially October; this is currently the most reliable site to see them in the state. The larger Royal and Caspian Terns make occasional appearances.

To reach **Morse Point**, head southwest from the parking lot entrance, around the head of the inlet before turning back north along the beach. Scan the inlet for night-herons and Clapper Rail. Access is restricted to certain areas during the breeding season.

Anglers congregate along the beach here, especially in summer and fall. The best birding is usually toward the end of the point away from the crowds. Walking the outer bar requires more time than checking the inner bar, but it remains accessible regardless of the tide. *Allow an hour or more to complete the loop.*

Stop along the way to scan the distant jetties and open water to the east. A variety of sea ducks, loons, and grebes can usually be found here, especially from October through May. The terns and Piping Plovers nest in a level area with short grass near the point. In spring and summer, avoid approaching the nesting area too closely. Common Terns aggressively defend their nests and may strike the unwary. Check any gull flocks for less common species such as Iceland or Glaucous Gull. There is at least one record of Black-legged Kittiwake resting on the sandbar here.

From late October through March, the outer bar is a good place to search for flocks of Snow Bunting and Horned Lark. Scrutinize these flocks for Lapland Longspur, which usually occur in small numbers. The dunes attract Savannah Sparrows, mainly from September through early May; this is a good place to find the pale "Ipswich" subspecies from November through February.

When you reach the end of Morse Point, scan the jetties and north shore. The same species mentioned in the description of Sandy Point can be seen from here as well. You can return the way you came or continue around the tip and then return along the edge of the lagoon. Stay below the high-tide line and avoid walking on the *Spartina* and dune grasses, whose fragile roots die when trampled.

The grasses along the edge of the lagoon are a good place to find Saltmarsh and, occasionally, Seaside Sparrows. A few Saltmarsh Sparrows may nest, but they are most abundant during migration from August through November. Nelson's Sparrows are possible in May and early June, then again in late September and especially October. Swamp, Song, and Savannah Sparrows can also be abundant here during migration. Clapper Rails can sometimes be found feeding along the edge, while Northern Harriers and Short-eared Owls occasionally roost in the grass during migration. In the years when Snowy Owls occur, they seem to prefer the dunes.

◾ West Haven Boat Ramp

Seasonal rating: Sp *** Su *** F **** W ****
Location: 1 Monahan Place, West Haven.
⮕ **Directions:** From Sandy Point, turn right out of the parking lot and drive 0.4 miles to a stop sign. Turn right into the parking lot for the boat ramp. Park on either side of the ramp but do not obstruct access to it.

The areas adjacent to the boat ramp provide fine views of the harbor as well as the sandbars at Sandy Point, to the south. In winter, this is a great place to look for loons, grebes, and waterfowl, and to study the scaup flocks; hundreds of Greater Scaup tend to concentrate here. Lesser Scaup, the occasional Redhead, and (rarely) a few Canvasbacks can be found among them. American Black and Mallard Ducks are common year-round, while Brant are often plentiful from fall through spring. Bufflehead, Common Goldeneye, and Red-breasted Mergansers are common sights from fall through spring. A few Gadwall and American Wigeon can usually be found in winter, and it's always worth looking for Eurasian Wigeon (rare); the West Haven coast has a fair number of records for this striking species. The power poles and trees throughout this area support nests of Monk Parakeets. If you didn't see any on your drive in, then canvass the local neighborhoods, either by car or foot, and you're almost sure to find some; look for large stick nests.

The ducks, geese, swans, and gulls are used to being fed here. They may approach quite closely if it appears that a potential meal is at hand. Iceland, Black-headed, "Thayer's", and Franklin's Gulls (rare), as well as Connecticut's first California Gull, have been found among the more common Herring, Ring-billed, and Great Black-backed Gulls. Sometimes, hundreds of Mute Swans congregate here in winter; scan them closely for Tundra or even Trumpeter Swans (rare), which have both occurred here.

Osprey, as well as Common and Least Terns, can be common in summer. During migration, scan the shoreline for shorebirds. Nearly any of the species listed for Sandy Point may occur here. Rough-winged and Barn Swallows nest locally.

Bradley Point Park

Seasonal rating: Sp *** Su ** F *** W **
Location: 482 Captain Thomas Boulevard, West Haven.
⮑ **Directions:** Turn left out of the Sandy Point parking lot and travel 0.7 miles, parallel to the beach. Beach Street then takes a sharp bend to the right and becomes Washington Avenue. Continue 0.1 miles, then turn left at the stop sign, onto Captain Thomas Boulevard. Travel 0.4 miles, then turn left into the parking lot adjacent to expansive lawns overlooking the beach. (Look for Jimmies of Savin Rock Restaurant on the left. The lot is just past the restaurant.)

The lawns of Bradley Point Park attract a variety of gulls at high tide. Occasionally a Lesser Black-backed or Iceland Gull turns up. Laughing Gulls are regular visitors in summer and join the many Herring, Ring-billed, and Great Black-backed Gulls patrolling the lawns and beaches for food. (I saw my first Connecticut Lesser Black-backed Gull here in the pouring rain.) Monk Parakeets nest in the neighborhoods nearby, and Fish Crows are usually in the area.

During migration, shorebirds stop to rest and feed when rain pools form. Least and Semipalmated Sandpipers, both yellowlegs species, and the occasional Pectoral or White-rumped Sandpiper may be found. It's always worth a quick check and seems a likely spot for Whimbrel, a godwit, or even Buff-breasted Sandpiper to pause during migration. Don't leave without scanning Bradley Point, the rocky islands to the south, and their adjacent mudflats, especially at low tide: Connecticut's first documented Mew Gull was found here in early spring 2009. Least and Common Terns, shorebirds, and waterfowl often roost on the rocky islands in summer.

South Street Beach

Seasonal rating: Sp ** Su ** F *** W ***
Location: 523 Ocean Avenue, West Haven.
⮑ **Directions:** From Bradley Point Park, continue south on Captain Thomas Boulevard, which quickly becomes Ocean Avenue, for about 0.5 miles. Look on your left for the parking area across from Mevlana Camii Mosque.

The parking lot at South Street Beach is a convenient place from which to view Long Island Sound. Large flocks of Greater Scaup sometimes gather here in winter, and a variety of sea ducks, loons, and grebes can be seen in season. Pacific Loon (rare) has been found here. It is best known as a consistent place to find Eurasian Wigeon. Most years, one or two males are found wintering with the American Wigeon, Gadwall, and American Black Ducks that congregate here from mid-October to mid-April. If you don't find one here, check the next stop on the West Haven tour: Oyster River.

■ Oyster River

Seasonal rating: Sp **** Su ** F *** W **
Location: Beside 63 Ocean Avenue, West Haven.
⮑ **Directions:** Continue west from South Street Beach on Ocean Avenue. The small parking lot for Oyster River is off the traffic circle, opposite Route 162 and a row of stores. To reach it, drive two-thirds of the way around the circle; the parking lot will be on your right. (If there are no spaces there, park in the store lot across the street.)

The sandbars and flats at the mouth of the Oyster River are known for attracting Bonaparte's Gull (decreasing in numbers) and other gulls. When gull numbers build in March and April, watch for Iceland, Glaucous, and Lesser Black-backed Gulls among the fray. Multiple Mew Gulls (rare) also have been found here. Local birders search the flocks of Bonaparte's Gulls for the rare but regularly occurring Little and Black-headed Gulls. This site is renowned for the 1984 appearance of a Ross's Gull (very rare), which attracted hundreds of people from all over the United States. The sheltered inlet also provides a haven for ducks, geese, and swans. Eurasian Wigeon occurs here with some consistency from mid-October to mid-April. In winter, a few Red-throated and Common Loons and Horned and Red-necked Grebes (occasional) can usually be found.

■ Merwin Point

Seasonal rating: Sp *** Su * F *** W ****
Location: Opposite 108 Beach Avenue, Milford.
Parking: Merwin Point is in a residential neighborhood, and parking is always a challenge (most birders briefly scan from their cars). Parking is not allowed on Beach Avenue but is sometimes available on side streets.

In winter, Merwin Point's rocky shoreline attracts rarities, such as Harlequin Duck and King and Common Eiders, more frequently than any other site in the area. It is also reliable for Purple Sandpipers from late fall well into May.

(20) Western New Haven Parks

- Edgewood Park
- West Rock Playground
- West River Memorial Park

Seasonal rating: Sp **** Su ** F *** W **
Best time to bird: Fall and spring, though winter can bring surprises.
Habitats: River, floodplain forest, wooded hillsides, freshwater cattail marshes, tidal marshes, several small ponds, meadows, open lawns, and athletic fields.

Bird list for this site:

SPECIALTY BIRDS

Resident – Mute Swan, Wood Duck (may be absent in winter), American Black Duck, Peregrine Falcon (West Rock), Black Vulture, Monk Parakeet, Belted Kingfisher, Fish Crow, Common Raven (West Rock)
Summer – Green Heron, Black-crowned Night-Heron, Osprey, Killdeer, Spotted Sandpiper, Northern Rough-winged Swallow, Willow Flycatcher, Yellow-throated Vireo, Warbling Vireo, Brown Thrasher, Worm-eating Warbler (West Rock)
Winter – Yellow-bellied Sapsucker (most years), Winter Wren, Field Sparrow (uncommon), Rusty Blackbird (most years)

OTHER KEY BIRDS

Resident – Canada Goose, Mallard, Double-crested Cormorant, Turkey Vulture, Red-tailed Hawk, Mourning Dove, Eastern Screech-Owl; Red-bellied, Downy, and Hairy Woodpeckers; Northern Flicker, American Redstart, Song Sparrow, Northern Cardinal, House Finch, American Goldfinch
Summer – Great Egret (late summer), Chimney Swift, Eastern Wood-Pewee, Eastern Phoebe, Great Crested Flycatcher, Eastern Kingbird, Red-eyed Vireo, Tree and Barn Swallows, House Wren, Blue-gray Gnatcatcher, Wood Thrush, Gray Catbird, Cedar Waxwing, Yellow Warbler, Common Yellowthroat, Chipping and Swamp Sparrows, Rose-breasted Grosbeak, Red-winged Blackbird, Common Grackle, Brown-headed Cowbird, Baltimore Oriole
Winter – Great Blue Heron, Hermit Thrush (most years), Gray Catbird (some years), American Tree and White-throated Sparrows, Dark-eyed Junco

MIGRANTS

Spring – Common Loon (flyover), American Woodcock (uncommon), Greater and Lesser Yellowlegs, Solitary Sandpiper, Least Sandpiper (uncommon), Wilson's Snipe (uncommon), Ruby-throated Hummingbird
Fall – Osprey, Bald Eagle (uncommon); Cooper's, Sharp-shinned, Red-shouldered, Broad-winged, and Red-tailed Hawks; American Kestrel, Merlin, Common Nighthawk, Eastern Bluebird (uncommon)

Both Spring and Fall – Gadwall, Green-winged Teal, Northern Pintail (uncommon), Ring-necked Duck, Greater Scaup, Lesser Scaup (uncommon), Bufflehead, Hooded Merganser, Ruddy Duck, Pied-billed Grebe, both kinglet species, Veery, Swainson's and Gray-cheeked Thrushes (uncommon), Scarlet Tanager, Eastern Towhee, Swamp Sparrow, Indigo Bunting, Rusty Blackbird (uncommon)

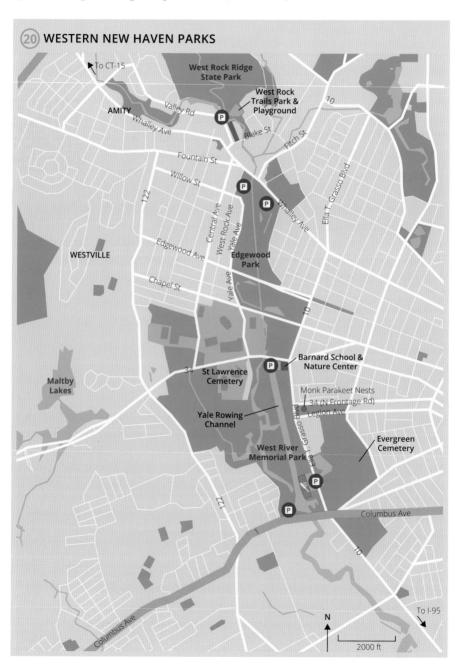

Edgewood Park

Location: 357 West Rock Avenue, New Haven.
Parking: Enter the driveway heading toward the tennis courts; take the first right and park in the small lot west of the courts. **Note:** The main entrance to Coogan Pavilion, on Whalley Avenue opposite Fitch Street, is not always open.
Hazards: Because this is a city park, commonsense safety precautions should be taken; birding with friends is recommended.
Restrooms: Available seasonally at the ranger station on Edgewood Avenue, at Barnard Nature Center, and at Coogan Pavilion.

The Birding

Edgewood is a linear 121-acre park, nearly a mile in length. Once the farm of landscape architect Donald G Mitchell, the park was designed in 1910 by Frederick Law Olmsted, Jr. The grounds straddle the West River in the Westville neighborhood of New Haven. Though surrounded by steep wooded hillsides, much of the park rests in the West River floodplain, where river soils support shallow-rooted trees such as box elder, silver and red maples, elm, ash, and willow.

Although smaller and less well known to birders than East Rock Park across town, Edgewood is a fine birding site, rivaling East Rock in the diversity of bird species to be found in spring and fall. Both Edgewood Park and West River Memorial Park (to the south) were designated as Important Bird Areas in 2016.

Edgewood provides food, water, and cover to birds throughout the winter. Wetter areas—especially along the white trail on the park's west side, the Lily Pond area, and behind the Parks Department—generally hold Carolina Wren, a good mix of sparrows, and often a few less common species such as Yellow-bellied Sapsucker, Winter Wren, Gray Catbird, Hermit Thrush, or Fox Sparrow, along with the occasional Brown Thrasher, Brown Creeper, or kinglets. The park also is one of the most reliable places along the coast to find wintering Rusty Blackbirds.

At Edgewood's southern end, the *Phragmites* (reed grass) stands at the corner of Connecticut Route 10 (Ella T. Grasso Boulevard) and Route 34 (Derby Avenue) are an autumn roosting site for 3,000 to 5,000 blackbirds in most years; in some years the flock remains from November through the winter. Rusty and Yellow-headed Blackbirds are always possibilities as well.

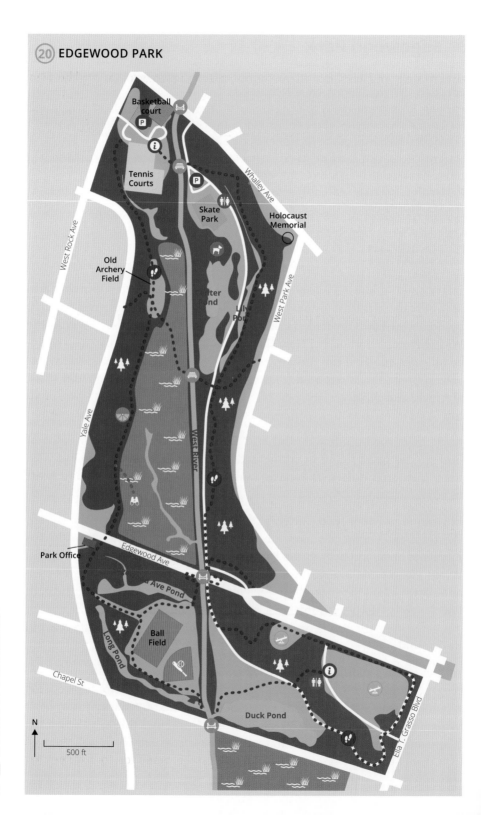

The gravel roofs of downtown New Haven were once the summer homes of nesting Common Nighthawks, but now they nest only sporadically. In late summer and early fall, flights of migrating nighthawks can still be seen passing over the city and through Edgewood and West River Memorial Park. On peak nights from late August into early September, dozens may be seen hawking insects above the trees, or winging south high overhead.

How to Bird This Site

The park's most productive sections can be covered in a morning, with several variations possible to shorten or lengthen your walk.

West Rock Avenue Walking Loop

This easy 2-mile loop begins at the north end of the park. The walk *usually takes 2 to 3 hours, but it can be done in 1.5 hours*. The trailhead is just inside the West Rock Avenue entrance, west of the tennis courts.

The trail (marked by white rectangles) runs south along the base of the forested hillside. After less than 10 yards, it begins to follow Iris Pond—more of a long vernal pool—just behind the tennis courts. Spring through fall, this little pool attracts Green Herons and dabbling ducks, including Wood Ducks. Also look for Northern Waterthrush here; in spring and fall they may be found throughout the wetter areas of the park.

You will pass a concrete catch basin on the left and then come to a small clearing lined with shrubs on its eastern edge; this was once an archery field. During migration and in winter, check the edges for White-throated, Song, Swamp, and American Tree Sparrows as well as Dark-eyed Junco. Less common species to have occurred here include White-eyed Vireo, Winter Wren, and a male Summer Tanager (rare), discovered in early May behind the catch basin.

The forest along the riverbank is home to breeding Warbling and Yellow-throated Vireos, Eastern Kingbird, Cedar Waxwing, and American Redstart. The wetter areas also support a few Willow Flycatcher. Rough-winged Swallows nest in the riverbanks themselves, while Wood Ducks make their homes in natural or man-made cavities. Although uncommon and elusive, both Yellow-billed and Black-billed Cuckoos pass through the park in spring and fall and may nest in some years.

Two trails leave the clearing at the south end of the field. **Note:** To shorten your walk to less than 1 mile, take the trail to the left. It passes through sandy floodplain forest where American Redstarts breed to a footbridge over the West River, then meets the central paved park road. Bear left and follow the road back to the tennis courts, checking Center Pond, the dog run, and Lily Pond on the way.

To continue the 2-mile loop, take the right-hand fork. The initial 150 yards of trail offer some of the best birding in the park. The trail passes the amphitheater and marsh observation boardwalk (on the left) before rising through upland forest toward the Parks Department building. During migration, more than twenty-five species of warblers can occur here. Rarities seen in the area include Alder and Olive-sided Flycatchers, White-eyed and Philadelphia Vireos, Pileated Woodpecker, Prothonotary Warbler (spring), and Evening Grosbeak (fall and winter).

The boardwalk and marsh observation deck provide access to the park's largest remaining cattail marsh. Sora and Virginia Rail (both uncommon), as well as Wilson's Snipe, American Woodcock, and Marsh Wren have been heard and seen here in spring. The adjacent river edge attracts waterthrushes and twice enticed a Prothonotary Warbler in early May. Woodland raptors such as Sharp-shinned and Cooper's Hawks seem to prefer this area when wintering in the park.

Continue south across Edgewood Avenue, then enter the Parks Department driveway. Follow the dirt road at the southeast corner of the parking lot, which leads to Edgewood Avenue Pond (on the left), Long Pond (on the right), and the ball fields adjoining the West River. Edgewood Avenue Pond is best viewed from either end, but in winter, after the leaves fall, it can also be seen by walking along Edgewood Avenue. A similar rule applies to Long Pond, which can be scoped from Yale Avenue in winter.

The ponds and nearby fields are the best spots in the park for finding Solitary Sandpiper, Wilson's Snipe (uncommon), and other shorebirds in spring and fall. Occasionally, American Woodcock, Greater and Lesser Yellowlegs, Least Sandpiper, and Pectoral Sandpiper (rare) are found. In summer, look for Green Heron, Black-crowned Night-Heron, and occasional Great or Snowy Egrets.

After checking the two ponds, make a counterclockwise circuit of the fields and river edge. In summer, look for a rich variety of riparian songbird species here. Field, Lincoln's, White-crowned, and Vesper Sparrows visit infrequently, usually in October. Watch for Fox Sparrow as well, especially in November and March. Grasshopper Sparrows are a rare visitor.

The weedy edges attract Indigo Bunting and Bobolink, especially in fall. In late summer and early autumn, check for migrating flycatchers: Willow,

Least, and Yellow-bellied Flycatchers have been seen here (Willow Flycatcher breeds). Rarely, an Eastern Meadowlark, Horned Lark, or American Pipit alights during migration, but most are heard passing overhead.

Once you've finished your circuit, go up the stone stairway on the southwest side of the Edgewood Avenue Bridge. (Be aware that the homeless sometimes shelter under the bridge, especially in winter.) Continue across Edgewood Avenue to the north side of the street, walk east over the bridge, then take a left down another set of stairs. You should find yourself on the paved park road, heading north.

To make a side-trip to Duck Pond, turn left after descending the stairs and pass underneath the bridge. The pond is a short walk to the south. Eastern Phoebe sometimes nests beneath the bridge or near Duck Pond. Gadwall, American Wigeon, Wood Duck and teal are possible on the pond, while Hooded and Common Mergansers, along with the occasional Bufflehead, use the river fall through spring. One November, a rare Cackling Goose spent a few weeks feeding on the lawns here. The weeping willows lining the pond provide cover and food to migrants, especially in spring. Monk Parakeets have a small colony near the pond, at the corner of Chapel Street and Route 10. Shorebirds frequent the rain pools that form on the lawns: Killdeer (nests), both yellowlegs species, and Least and Solitary Sandpiper have been seen here. On rare occasion, other shorebirds have been found, including White-rumped Sandpiper, Wilson's Snipe, and Black-bellied Plover.

To continue the 2-mile loop, walk north on the paved park road, which leads from the Edgewood Avenue Bridge, past Coogan Pavilion and back to the tennis courts. The oaks and other trees that line the road are often productive for migrants.

About 0.25 mile north of Edgewood Avenue, look for a footbridge across the river on your left, at the edge of the field. The footbridge allows unobstructed views of the West River. Look for Hooded Merganser in winter and Hairy Woodpecker year-round. The many dead trees in the valley attract Great Crested Flycatchers—these take advantage of the many woodpecker cavities for nesting. Warbling Vireo and Baltimore Oriole nest in the elms by the footbridge, while Eastern Phoebes usually nest under it. Watch for shad and herring in spring when they swim upstream to spawn. **Note:** The path over the bridge leads back to the archery field and can be used to return to your car.

After surveying the river from the footbridge, return to the paved road and continue north past the Coogan Pavilion to the tennis courts, checking Center Pond and the dog run area (on the left) and Lily Pond (on the right) along the way. Tree, Barn, and Rough-winged Swallows forage the area in early spring then again in fall, infrequently accompanied by a few Bank and Cliff Swallows. Rough-wing Swallows have nested in the riverbanks, Barn Swallows on the Coogan Pavilion, and Tree Swallows in the birdhouses by the pond. (Another trail goes behind Center Pond to the Pavilion.)

From spring through fall, check Center Pond for Green Heron and Wood Duck and other dabbling ducks. Baltimore Oriole, Cedar Waxwing, Eastern Kingbird, and Warbling Vireo have nested in the trees around the pond. Concentrate on the brushy edge behind the pond and the fenced dog run to the north; both attract sparrows and thrushes during migration and are good areas to search for Fox Sparrow and Eastern Towhee. Brown Thrasher (uncommon) may nest in this area.

The standing dead trees in the dog run attract woodpeckers. In the past, this woodlot has hosted two wintering Red-headed Woodpeckers (rare). Yellow-bellied Sapsuckers are regular visitors, fall and spring, and sometimes take up winter residence. During migration and in winter, Rusty Blackbirds prefer this general area, especially the shores of Lily Pond, across the park road. Lily Pond also is one of the more reliable spots in the park for Solitary Sandpiper in spring.

The face of West Rock Ridge, visible to the north above Westville Center, is home to several species of nesting raptors, including Red-tailed Hawk and Peregrine Falcon, while Turkey and Black Vultures breed along the ridgeline (see Chapter 21: Konold's Pond). In autumn, large numbers of migrating hawks funnel down the ridgeline on their journey south, using warm updrafts to aid their progress; many of these birds pass over Edgewood. In mid-September, kettles of 500 or more Broad-winged Hawks may form over the ridgetop and the Southern Connecticut State University parking lots near its base. The lawns north of Coogan Pavilion offer a good vantage point from which to watch the ridge. All of Connecticut's raptors are possible.

In the fall, a large crow roost forms on the West Haven–Orange town line. From fall through spring, American and Fish Crows on their way to roost often stream over Edgewood Park late each afternoon. It is an amazing spectacle to see and hear as hundreds—even thousands—of corvids pass overhead. The best vantage places are the Coogan Pavilion area, the fields behind and across from the Park Department, and the fields in West River Memorial Park. Arrive at least an hour before sunset.

For a shorter visit to Edgewood, find a place to park near the New Haven Department of Parks and Recreation, at 720 Edgewood Avenue. A walk behind the office building, around the brushy wet edges of the ball fields adjoining Long Pond, the West River, and Edgewood Avenue Pond can be rewarding at any time of year and *requires less than an hour*. In summer, Green Heron, Black-crowned Night-Heron, the occasional Great Egret or Great Blue Heron, Belted Kingfisher, Wood Duck, and other dabbling ducks use the ponds. In spring and fall, the pond edges are visited by migrating shorebirds. These are also good times to look for flycatchers and migrant songbirds. From fall through spring, the fields and road edges attract sparrows while the ponds continue to hold waterfowl. Long Pond is spring-fed and usually remains at least partially open all winter. It is especially good for Gadwall, Green-winged Teal, Wood Duck, and the occasional Nortern Pintail or American Wigeon, in addition to resident Mallard and American Black Duck. Both Long and Edgewood Avenue Ponds can be scoped from the roadside in winter.

West Rock Playground

Location: 1 Valley Street, New Haven.
⮂ **Directions:** Leaving Edgewood Park, turn right on West Rock Avenue. At the intersection of West Rock and Whalley Avenues, turn left and head north on Whalley 0.1 miles, then turn right onto Blake Street. Take the first left onto Valley Street. After passing the long brick Blake Street Center Building (on your right), turn right into the parking lot. Park on the left, near the footbridge. The face of West Rock Ridge (State Park) will be directly in front of you.
Hazards: Because this is a city park, commonsense safety precautions should be taken; birding with friends is recommended.
Restrooms: At fast-food restaurants on Whalley Avenue.

Worm-eating Warblers breed along the talus slopes at the base of West Rock. To reach them, walk across the West River footbridge into Amhryn Field. Turn left and follow the field edge to a trail behind the backstop that angles left and leads northwest up West Rock Ridge. It is unnecessary to climb to the ridgetop to see or hear the warblers. Prairie Warbler and Indigo Bunting breed farther up the hill but can sometimes be heard or seen from the base. Watch for raptors, vultures, and ravens, especially in autumn.

■ West River Memorial Park

Location: 200 Derby Avenue, New Haven.

Parking: At the park's north end, use the Barnard Nature Center parking lot at 200 Derby Avenue. At the south end, parking is available at the canoe launch, opposite 40 Boston Post Road, West Haven.

Hazards: Because this is a city park, commonsense safety precautions should be taken; birding with friends is recommended.

Restrooms: At fast-food restaurants on Whalley Avenue (north) and along Route 10 and U.S. Route 1 (south).

The Birding

The 200-acre West River Memorial Park lies just south of Edgewood Park. Like Edgewood, it includes both banks of the West River. Although the two parks have nearly identical lists of nesting landbirds—including the less common local breeders, Brown Thrasher and Willow Flycatcher—West River Park offers a somewhat different migrant and winter bird diversity. Because it's closer to the coast and includes more open water, it hosts more species of ducks and gulls than its smaller northern neighbor. Least Terns hunt the river and Yale's Rowing Channel in summer. Ospreys nest on platforms along the river's edge from April to September, and resident Bald Eagles can be seen at any time. The park's broad thickets attract a variety of sparrows and other shrub-loving species, fall through spring, in good numbers.

Much of the property along the park's east side is developed, while the southern section abuts an industrial and economically depressed area. Barnard Nature Center is located in the park's northeast corner, while public playing fields occupy much of its eastern edge.

How to Bird This Area

The marsh and northern section of the river and rowing channel can be scanned from the Barnard Nature Center parking lot or from the bridge on Derby Avenue. Much of the park's east side, including the rowing channel, can be seen from the soccer fields across from Evergreen Cemetery.

Monk Parakeets nest in the trees of the otherwise grassy median at the junction of North Frontage Road and Ella T. Grasso Boulevard (Route 10). Park at Barnard Nature Center and walk south 150 yards to scope them from Ella T. Grasso Boulevard. The nearby playing fields, along with the Evergreen

Cemetery Pond across the street, are congregating sites for gulls, mostly Ring-billed, Herring, and a few Great Black-backed Gulls. In late summer, Laughing Gulls join the flocks, and on rare occasions Lesser Black-backed, Black-headed, Glaucous, or Iceland Gulls are seen, usually in winter or spring. Canada Geese graze the fields in winter, sometimes attracting other, less common geese. Wild Turkeys display on the playing fields in spring. After rain, the fields are worth checking for shorebirds, especially in late summer and early autumn.

Birds of prey take advantage of the undisturbed west side of the river to hunt and rest during migration. In addition to the common species, Rough-legged Hawk (rare), and Great Horned, Snowy, and Short-eared Owls have occurred. In fall, Northern Harriers are a fairly common sight above the marsh. On rare occasions, Red-shouldered Hawk has wintered in the park.

To check the southern section of the West River, park at the canoe launch off Boston Post Road. A dead-end path leads northeast from the parking lot to the canoe ramp and offers a good vantage upriver. Wild Turkey and, occasionally, Red-shouldered Hawk (fall and winter) can be seen here. Brushy areas attract sparrows, including Eastern Towhee and American Tree and Field Sparrows, in winter. Other trails lead north into the forest, paralleling the river; however, these and other areas along the west side of the river have been used as homeless camps and should probably be avoided.

21 Konold's Pond and the Chain Lakes, Woodbridge

- Konold's Pond
- Lakes Dawson and Watrous (The Chain Lakes)

Konold's Pond

Seasonal rating: Sp *** Su ** F **** W **
Best time to bird: Fall and spring; winter can be good for ducks and gulls when the water remains open.
Habitats: Broad shallow pond, West Rock Ridge, West River, early second-growth forest, wooded hillsides, freshwater cattail marshes, red maple–tussock sedge swamp, residential and industrial neighborhoods.

Bird list for this site:

SPECIALTY BIRDS
Resident – Mute Swan, Wood Duck (can be absent in winter), American Black Duck, Peregrine Falcon, Black Vulture, Belted Kingfisher, Fish Crow, Common Raven
Summer – Green Heron, Killdeer, Spotted Sandpiper, Northern Rough-winged Swallow, Willow Flycatcher (possible), Yellow-throated Vireo (possible), Warbling Vireo
Winter – Trumpeter Swan (rare), waterfowl and gulls (when water remains open), Winter Wren (some years), Rusty Blackbird (some years)

OTHER KEY BIRDS
Resident – Canada Goose, Mallard, Double-crested Cormorant, Turkey Vulture, Red-tailed Hawk, Mourning Dove, Eastern Screech-Owl; Red-bellied, Downy, and Hairy Woodpeckers; Northern Flicker, Blue Jay, American Crow, Black-capped Chickadee, Tufted Titmouse, White-breasted Nuthatch, Carolina Wren, American Robin, Northern Mockingbird, European Starling, Song Sparrow, Northern Cardinal, House Finch, American Goldfinch
Summer – Great Egret, Chimney Swift, Eastern Wood-Pewee, Eastern Phoebe, Great Crested Flycatcher, Eastern Kingbird, Red-eyed Vireo, Tree Swallow, Barn Swallow, House Wren, Blue-gray Gnatcatcher, Wood Thrush, Gray Catbird, Cedar Waxwing, Yellow Warbler, Common Yellowthroat, Chipping and Swamp Sparrows, Rose-breasted Grosbeak, Red-winged Blackbird, Common Grackle, Brown-headed Cowbird, Baltimore Oriole
Winter – Great Blue Heron, Hermit Thrush (most years), Gray Catbird (some years), American Tree and Fox Sparrows (uncommon), White-throated Sparrow, Dark-eyed Junco

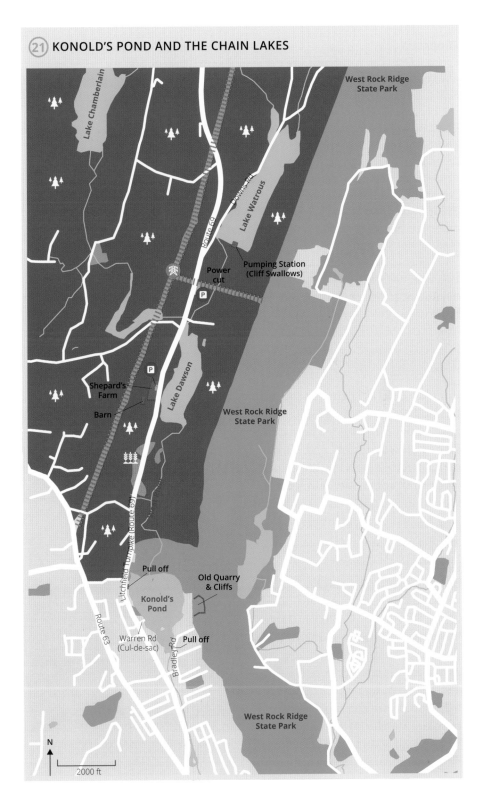

Spring – American Woodcock, Greater and Lesser Yellowlegs; Solitary, Semipalmated, and Least Sandpipers; Pectoral Sandpiper (uncommon), Ruby-throated Hummingbird

Fall – Bald Eagle (uncommon but increasing); Broad-winged, Cooper's, and Sharp-shinned Hawks; Rough-legged Hawk (uncommon), American Kestrel (declining), Common Nighthawk, Eastern Bluebird (uncommon)

Both Spring and Fall – Trumpeter Swan (rare), Snow Goose (uncommon), Gadwall, American Wigeon, Northern Shoveler (uncommon), Green-winged Teal, Northern Pintail (uncommon), Ring-necked Duck (abundant), Greater Scaup (uncommon), Lesser Scaup, Bufflehead, Hooded and Common Mergansers, Ruddy Duck, Pied-billed Grebe, Wilson's Snipe, most *Empidonax* flycatchers, both kinglet species, thrushes, more than twenty species of warblers, Scarlet Tanager, Eastern Towhee, Indigo Bunting, Rusty Blackbird

---

Location: Warren Road and Bradley Road, Woodbridge.

Restroom: At fast-food restaurants along Connecticut Route 69 (Whalley Avenue) south toward New Haven.

The Birding

Konold's Pond is a dammed section of the West River. Broad and shallow, the pond is bordered by marsh, second-growth forest, and shrubs on its north side, and by West Rock Ridge to the east. The south edge is mostly industrial, while the west edge is partially residential.

The pond's north end is choked with pickerelweed, tussock sedge, and water lilies, providing ideal cover for reclusive species such as Pied-billed Grebe, Common Gallinule (rare), Wood Duck, Wilson's Snipe, and Rusty Blackbird. As spring advances, the entire pond develops floating and emergent aquatic plants. Pied-billed Grebe are common migrants from late March into April and again in September and October. Common Gallinule is seen irregularly,

Common Ravens nest on West Rock Ridge behind Konold's Pond.

usually in April and May or August and September. American Coot is annual, but not abundant. The north end is very reliable for Wilson's Snipe in March and early April. The shoreline and mud bars there also attract Greater and Lesser Yellowlegs, Least and Solitary Sandpipers, and less frequently, Pectoral and Semipalmated Sandpipers and Semipalmated Plover. American Woodcock has been heard displaying in spring, but their preferred early successional habitat is slowly becoming forest. Rusty Blackbird (uncommon) may appear anywhere around the pond in spring or fall and occurs sporadically into early winter.

Konold's Pond has long been recognized as a gathering site for waterfowl, especially from March to April and from October to November. Almost any of the diving and dabbling ducks may occur, including Bufflehead, Ring-necked Duck (in large numbers), Greater and Lesser Scaup, and Ruddy Duck. It's one of a few remaining local sites where Canvasback still occurs in some years, and Redhead is possible.

Blue-winged Teal (uncommon) and Green-winged Teal begin arriving in August. Hooded and Common Mergansers arrive in early October; some may stay into early winter, then return again in late February to early March. In fall and spring, large numbers of Mute Swans gather on the pond, but by the breading season, only two or three nesting pairs remain. Large concentrations of Wood Ducks, at times numbering over a hundred, gather here each March and again from late July through at least mid-October; if the water stays open, some remain into December. Less common annual visitors include Northern Pintail, Common Goldeneye, and Red-breasted Merganser. Irregular visitors include Tundra Swan (rare), Snow Goose, and Northern Shoveler. Canada Geese, Mallard, and American Black Duck are resident. Connecticut's first accepted sighting of Trumpeter Swan was made here.

Connecticut's first accepted Trumpeter Swan record was from Konold's Pond.
Photograph courtesy Mark S. Szantyr

In winter, the pond becomes a gathering site for gulls. Herring and Ring-billed Gulls make up the majority, with a few Great Black-backed Gulls and an occasional Glaucous or Iceland Gull. Lesser Black-backed Gull should be anticipated as its numbers are increasing in the northeast. A few Black Terns are seen in spring as they migrate to inland breeding sites far to the north.

Tree Swallows arrive beginning in early or mid-March; they are soon followed by Barn, then Northern Rough-winged Swallows, which gather to feed on insects hatching from the pond. In late April, Bank and Cliff Swallows (nest nearby) join the feeding swarms over the water; watch carefully for Purple Martins (uncommon).

In addition to Tree and Barn Swallows, the usual breeding landbirds include Hairy, Downy, and Red-bellied Woodpeckers; Northern Flicker, Fish and American Crows, Mourning Dove, White-breasted Nuthatch, Black-capped Chickadee, Tufted Titmouse, Eastern Kingbird, Cedar Waxwing, Yellow Warbler, Common Yellowthroat, Song Sparrow, American Goldfinch, Red-winged Blackbird, Common Grackle, and Baltimore Oriole.

The less common breeding species consist of Wild Turkey, Pileated Woodpecker (ridgeline), Belted Kingfisher, Spotted Sandpiper, Green Heron (on the north side), Rough-winged Swallow, and Orchard Oriole (fields along Bradley Road). Willow Flycatchers can be found during migration and may breed as well. Warbling Vireo (and possibly Yellow-throated Vireo) breed along the edge, while Swamp Sparrow nests in the marsh at the north end.

Common Raven, Peregrine Falcon, Turkey Vulture (and probably Black Vulture) nest on West Rock Ridge, often on or near the cliff face of the abandoned quarry above the pond. **Note:** A good view of this cliff can be had from Warren Road in early spring and from Bradley Road later on. The pair of Peregrines is one of the very few that nest on cliffs in Connecticut; most others choose man-made structures. Courtship flights are worth watching in mid to late winter, when each species vigorously defends its territory from all comers. The birds can put on quite an air show: cavorting over the cliff face and diving and chasing one another.

The ridgeline serves as a natural migration corridor, connecting with Edgewood Park and West River Memorial Park to the south via the West River to create a greenway that birds follow to and from the coast. Raptors utilize the ridgeline thermals during spring and especially in fall. Any of Connecticut's birds of prey are possible, with mid-September to mid-October the peak for most species and late October into November for larger buteos and Goshawk. Red-tailed, Red-shouldered, and Cooper's Hawks, and possibly Broad-winged Hawk, all nest locally. During flight years, winter finches have been seen moving along the ridgeline as well, occasionally stopping to feed in the trees around the pond. In autumn, migrating landbirds typically pause at Konold's Pond while following the river south. They usually congregate first along the north shore (difficult to access), then move downstream around either side of the pond.

How to Bird This Site

Because both access and parking are limited, most birders scan from the roadsides. A spotting scope is recommended. Please do not obstruct driveways or trespass on private lawns.

The best place from which to view the lake and the West Rock ridgeline, until the vegetation grows up in late spring, is from the end of **Warren Road**, where you can park in the cul-de-sac. Some of the pond's north end can be scoped from here; there is otherwise no good access to it.

Bradley Road provides the best vantage for viewing the pond's south end and east side and gives closer, but more restricted views of the cliff face. From Connecticut Route 69, turn east onto Bradley Road, proceed to a stop sign, then turn left. After 0.1 miles, pull off opposite the spillway.

Lake Dawson and Lake Watrous (the Chain Lakes)

Location: Alongside Connecticut Route 69, Woodbridge.

The Birding

These two reservoirs on the West River are much deeper than Konold's Pond. Although they do not attract as many waterfowl as that body of water, much the same species mix is possible. They are especially worth checking after thunderstorms, spring through fall.

How to Bird This Site

The following instructions describe a 3.5-mile driving tour, beginning at the intersection of Connecticut Route 69 (Litchfield Turnpike) and Warren Road in Woodbridge. **Note: Set your odometer to zero**, then proceed north on Connecticut Route 69.

At 0.9 miles on your odometer, there is a farm field on the left. If you can find a safe place to pull over, check here for Horned Larks in winter.

At 1.4 miles, you begin to pass Lake Dawson on the right, but there is not much access for viewing the lake here.

At 1.6 miles on your odometer, look on the left for Shepard's Farm (closed indefinitely). Pull into the parking lot. From mid-April through summer, scan the barn for Cliff and Barn Swallows. Blue-winged Warbler nests in the fields left of the barn.

At 2.3 miles, pull off on the right at a power-line cut near a pine stand. In summer, check for nesting Pine Warbler in the pines and listen for Eastern Towhee, Prairie and Blue-winged Warblers, and Indigo Bunting along the power-line cut and in the fields across the street. Yellow-billed Cuckoo and occasionally Black-billed Cuckoo can sometimes be heard here as well.

At 2.5 miles, turn right onto Downs Road and **reset your odometer to zero**. Stop at the first pull-off on the left (1,000 feet) and scan the Lake Watrous dam area. Cliff Swallows nest on the pump house and feed near the dam.

At 0.6 miles on the odometer, stop at the pull-off on the left to scan the lake. Watch for Eastern Bluebirds, which nest near the grassy knolls at this stop. This is also a good site for watching raptors migrate along the ridge in spring and fall. Look for swallows over the lake in early spring. Other migrant songbirds move along the road edge, especially in spring.

At 0.8 miles, at the north end of Lake Watrous, there is a small impoundment on the left. Continue 0.1 miles to the intersection of Brooks Road, park on the right, then walk back on Downs Road. Green Heron and dabbling ducks are sometimes seen here, and you may be rewarded with a glimpse of a river otter. This also is a good area for finding both migrant and breeding songbirds.

Before getting back into your car, scan the north end of Lake Watrous from Brooks Road. There are often swallows hunting over the water, including Northern Rough-winged and Cliff Swallows. The pines at the intersection can be good for both nuthatch species in season, breeding Pine Warbler, and wintering Brown Creeper. Cooper's Hawk nests locally and can be quite vocal here some years. In spring and fall, this is another good place to watch for migrating raptors along the ridgeline. Common Raven and Black and Turkey Vultures are seen regularly above the ridge.

22 East Rock Park Area, New Haven

- East Rock Park
- Regional Water Authority (RWA) Recreational Space
- Edgerton Park
- Lake Whitney

East Rock Park

Seasonal rating: Sp **** Su ** F *** W *
Best time to bird: Mid-April to early June.
Habitats: Traprock ridge, steep wooded hillsides with dense understory, hemlock forest, dry upland forest, Mill River, floodplain forest, freshwater cattail and tidal marshes, Lake Whitney, meadows, open lawns and athletic fields.

Bird list for this site:

SPECIALTY BIRDS
Resident – Mute Swan, American Black Duck, Wood Duck, Black Vulture (occasional), Peregrine Falcon, Monk Parakeet, Belted Kingfisher, Fish Crow, Common Raven
Summer – Green Heron, Black-crowned Night-Heron, Killdeer, Northern Rough-winged Swallow, Warbling Vireo, Blue-gray Gnatcatcher, Veery, Wood Thrush; Blue-winged, Prairie, and Worm-eating Warblers; Scarlet Tanager, Indigo Bunting, Orchard Oriole
Winter – Common and Hooded Mergansers, Yellow-bellied Sapsucker (most years), Red-breasted Nuthatch (some years), Winter Wren (uncommon), Golden-crowned Kinglet (uncommon), Ruby-crowned Kinglet (occasional), Hermit Thrush

OTHER KEY BIRDS
Resident – Canada Goose, Mallard, Wild Turkey, Red-tailed Hawk; Ring-billed, Herring, and Great Black-backed Gulls; Rock Pigeon, Mourning Dove, Eastern Screech-Owl, Great Horned Owl; Red-bellied, Downy, and Hairy Woodpeckers; Northern Flicker, Red-eyed Vireo, Blue Jay, American Crow, Black-capped Chickadee, Tufted Titmouse, White-breasted Nuthatch, Carolina Wren, American Robin, Northern Mockingbird, European Starling, Cedar Waxwing, Song Sparrow, Northern Cardinal, House Finch, American Goldfinch
Summer – Double-crested Cormorant, Osprey, Great and Snowy Egrets (both uncommon), Chimney Swift, Eastern Wood-Pewee, Eastern Phoebe, Great Crested Flycatcher, Eastern Kingbird, Red-eyed Vireo, Tree and Barn Swallows, House Wren, Wood Thrush, Gray Catbird, Yellow and Black-and-white Warblers, American Redstart,

Davis St

Lake
Whitney

North
Meadow

Armory St

Dam

RWA

Covered
Bridge

Ridge Rd

Eli Whitney
Museum

Archery
Field

Edge Hill Rd

Whitney
Peak

Pardee Rose
Garden
& Greenhouse

Edgerton Park

Cliff St

Park
Maintenance
Dept

Mill River

Park Dr

East Rock Rd

Whitney Ave

Everit St

Farnham Dr

English Drive

State St

Ranger
Station

Livingston St

College
Woods

Giant Steps

Indian
Head

Cold Spring St

Giant Steps
Trailhead

Cold
Spring

Roadside
Parking

Wilbur Cross
High School

Rice
Field

Snake
Rock

Mill River

East
Gate

Rock St

Michell Dr

N

1000 ft

Willow St

Common Yellowthroat, Chipping Sparrow, Eastern Towhee, Rose-breasted Grosbeak, Red-winged Blackbird, Common Grackle, Brown-headed Cowbird, Baltimore Oriole
Winter – Great Blue Heron, White-throated Sparrow, Dark-eyed Junco

MIGRANTS
Spring and Fall – Common Merganser, Common Loon (flyovers), Spotted Sandpiper, Solitary Sandpiper (spring), Greater Yellowlegs (uncommon), both cuckoo species, Ruby-throated Hummingbird, Willow and Least Flycatchers, vireos, both kinglet species, thrushes, more than thirty warbler species, Eastern Towhee, Swamp Sparrow and other sparrows
Fall – Osprey, Bald Eagle (uncommon); Cooper's, Sharp-shinned, Red-shouldered, Broad-winged, and Red-tailed Hawks; Common Nighthawk, Merlin, Peregrine Falcon

---

Location: Hamden and New Haven.
Parking: At the Eli Whitney Museum, 915 Whitney Avenue, Hamden. Additional parking at North Meadow, the summit, and along English Drive beside Rice Field.
Restrooms: Ranger station at College Woods, corner of Cold Spring and Orange Streets. Seasonally, portable toilets are located at the summit and at Rice Field.
Hazards: Because this is a city park, commonsense safety precautions should be taken; birding with friends is recommended.

The Birding

The 435-acre East Rock Park includes a 350-foot basalt outcrop with a towering war memorial at its summit. Much like Central Park in New York, the park is a forested island within a city and an oasis for migrating birds, providing them with food, water, and shelter.

East Rock is an Audubon-sanctioned Important Bird Area, with a bird list of more than 220 species. It is known regionally as *the place* to find warblers in spring: 36 warbler species have been identified in the park, nearly as many as in the entire state. Spring migration begins in early April with the arrival of Louisiana Waterthrush (rare here), then Northern Waterthrush and Pine, Palm, and Black-and-white Warblers. Activity peaks in mid-May, then tails off in late May and early June with the passage of most Mourning and Blackpoll Warblers. Fall migration begins in early to mid-July with the departure of Louisiana Waterthrush and Cerulean (rare) and Yellow Warblers—an event that often goes unnoticed by birders more attuned to watching shorebirds at this time of year.

A fall visit to the park can be just as rewarding as one in spring. Besides the abundance of warblers (now in less colorful garb), sparrows, thrushes, and other songbirds also pass through the park, while hawks glide by the summit, sometimes in impressive numbers (during northwest winds). Common Nighthawks push south as well, often hawking insects over the ball fields as they go.

In winter, the lingering birds include Hermit Thrush, Swamp Sparrow, Eastern Towhee, and both kinglet species. If you don't mind snow-covered trails, you can find American Tree Sparrow, Dark-eyed Junco, and the occasional Field Sparrow or Winter Wren.

Except in severe winters, Carolina Wrens are fairly common; in some years, Yellow-bellied Sapsuckers also overwinter. Hooded and Common Mergansers, Great Blue Heron, and Belted Kingfisher can usually be found along the Mill River, while at least one Cooper's Hawk or Sharp-shinned Hawk joins the resident Red-tailed Hawks each winter. All four of Connecticut's breeding corvids are resident. Fish Crows are often seen near the ranger station and ball fields, while the ravens prefer the summit.

In summer, the wooded hillsides and forested edges support not only the ubiquitous species but also breeding Great Horned Owl, a variety of woodpeckers (including Hairy), Wood Thrush, Veery, Eastern Wood-Pewee, Great Crested Flycatcher, Blue-gray Gnatcatcher, Red-eyed Vireo, Black-and-white Warbler, Rose-breasted Grosbeak, and Chipping Sparrow. The conifers hold nesting Fish and American Crows and numerous Common Grackles.

The riverbank forests hold breeding Eastern Screech-Owl, Warbling and Yellow-throated Vireos (some years), Eastern Kingbird, Cedar Waxwing, American Redstart, Yellow Warbler, Baltimore Oriole, and House Finch. The cattail marshes support thriving populations of Red-winged Blackbirds. Eastern Phoebes build their mossy nests under the bridges, Barn Swallows nest on the pavilions and buildings, and Tree Swallows breed both in tree cavities and birdhouses.

Specialized habitats, such as old-field areas and the park's summit face and rocky talus slopes, have their own assortments of species, including Worm-eating Warbler (talus slopes), Prairie Warbler, Indigo Bunting, and Eastern Towhee. Blue-winged Warbler can usually be found in these more open habitats as well. Peregrine Falcon and Common Raven nest along the west summit face.

How to Bird This Site

Mill River Loop Trail

The birding along the Mill River is some of the best and most beautiful in the park. *Allow 2 to 3 hours* to enjoy this 1.5-mile route.

From the northeast side of the Eli Whitney Museum's parking lot, walk through the covered bridge below the Lake Whitney spillway to the east side of the river. In summer, Eastern Phoebes commonly nest on or near the bridge and are usually conspicuous around it. The spillway area attracts Double-crested Cormorants, while Black-crowned Night-Herons hunt all along the river, especially at dawn and dusk. Chimney Swifts and Rough-winged, Tree, and Barn Swallows usually breed in the area; they feed over the river and the reservoir.

Just after the covered bridge, take the right fork of the trail, paralleling the river. This stretch is the haunt of Green Heron, Great Egret, Belted Kingfisher, and Wood Duck. It also may be Connecticut's most reliable place to find Prothonotary Warbler (rare) in late April or the first week in May. Kentucky and Mourning Warblers also have been found here, as have most of Connecticut's other migrant warblers, including Northern Parula and Magnolia, Black-and-white, Blackburnian, and Black-throated Green Warblers. The maple, willow, elm, and ash trees of the floodplain forest and the shrubby rose thickets harbor a wide variety of landbirds during migration.

Watch for Canada Warblers skulking in the thick streamside vegetation and hillside laurel thickets, for Wilson's, Chestnut-sided, and Yellow Warblers in the willows, and for Northern Waterthrush on the riverbanks. House and Carolina Wrens are vocal members of the old-field and riverside communities. Check the many dead snags for Eastern Kingbird (nests) and migrating Least Flycatcher, along with other *Empidonax* flycatchers.

The trail bends 90 degrees to the left, then eventually comes to a footbridge over the river. Along the way, the wetter flooded areas on the left often shelter Wood Ducks. The shrubs and willows in this stretch attract Cedar Waxwing, Baltimore Oriole, Eastern Kingbird, and migrant warblers; this area is particularly good for finding Prairie, Black-throated Blue, Blue-winged, and Magnolia Warblers, Northern Parula, and Northern Waterthrush. At the footbridge, stop to scan the river in both directions. Check for Solitary and Spotted Sandpipers, herons, and egrets on the riverbanks and cormorants in the river itself. Common and Hooded Mergansers are common on the river from fall through early spring. Although rare, both bittern species have been seen in the marshes near the bridge. Tree, Barn, and Rough-winged

Swallows often hunt over the river, joined by Bank Swallow in spring and fall and Common Nighthawk in late summer. Visitors also occasionally see river otter and beaver (rare).

After crossing the bridge, turn left at the T-intersection. The trail climbs slightly and eventually passes through dense rhododendron thickets—quite beautiful when blooming in late May or early June—then meets East Rock Road.

Turn left and walk along the sidewalk over the East Rock Road Bridge. Common Raven and Peregrine Falcon nest on the ridge directly opposite the bridge. The ravens are usually noisy and obvious, but finding the Peregrines may require a fair bit of searching; look to the south high on the cliff face. Just past the bridge, turn left onto a path that leads back toward the footbridge. Swamp Sparrow breeds in the cattail marshes here. Watch the thickets for Carolina and House Wrens, Common Yellowthroat, Gray Catbird, Northern Cardinal, Eastern Towhee, and the occasional Brown Thrasher.

After passing the footbridge, bear slightly right at the fork onto the white trail (the left-hand fork leads back to the covered bridge on the path along the river). This trail eventually heads up a slight incline into the forest. American Robin and Wood Thrush and other spotted thrushes, along with the occasional Eastern Bluebird, work the vine tangles for fruit here, especially in autumn. At the next fork, stay left; the trail goes slightly north, then arcs west, back to the covered bridge, passing through an upland forest of beech, oak, maple, and hickory. This area is good for thrushes, sparrows, warblers, and other migrants; the warblers often feed in the treetops here.

For a potentially rewarding detour, take the first trail on the right that angles uphill to an overlook. This area provides treetop views of migrating birds and can be good for warblers, including Blackburnian, Cape May, Nashville, Tennessee, and Black-throated Blue Warblers. Look for Bay-breasted Warbler in the evergreens along the slope.

Otherwise, continue on the white trail through regenerating old field and back to the covered bridge. (This last stretch can be very birdy.) Cross the covered bridge to return to the museum parking lot. **Note:** Before leaving the parking lot, see the RWA Recreation Space and Edgerton Park site descriptions in this chapter, as these sites are quite close.

The Archery Field

Because the archery field greets the sun before the valley below, it is a good place to start the day. *Allow 30 to 45 minutes* to bird this 150-yard trail.

To drive there from the Eli Whitney Museum parking lot, head south on Whitney Avenue for 0.4 miles, then turn left at the light onto East Rock Road. Continue 0.2 miles to the T-intersection with Farnam Drive. Turn left and follow winding Farnam Drive for 0.7 miles, then turn right onto the road to the summit. The narrow North Meadow parking lot is on the left; park at the far end.

The trailhead is difficult to see, concealed at the back edge of the grassy hillside across the street from the parking lot, adjacent to a large tree and bench. The unmarked trail leads from the lawn edge up a slight grade to a weedy field carved out of a rocky hilltop. The shrubs and trees lining the field are home to Northern Mockingbird, Gray Catbird, Blue-winged and Yellow Warblers, American Redstart, Common Yellowthroat, Eastern Towhee, Song and Chipping Sparrows, Indigo Bunting, Northern Cardinal, and American Goldfinch in summer. Worm-eating Warbler and Wood Thrush both breed on the rocky forested hillsides. Cuckoos visit in migration and may nest in years with caterpillar outbreaks. Watch for migrating raptors in fall and Common Raven year-round. During migration, the field edge attracts Scarlet Tanager and Rose-breasted Grosbeak, along with warblers, vireos, thrushes, and sparrows. The thrushes prefer to feed along the roadside, while sparrows frequent the shrubs encircling the field and flycatchers perch on the dead snags at the forest edge. Connecticut's first Hermit Warbler was discovered here on May 1, 1977.

Trowbridge Drive

Trowbridge Drive is an old fire-access road that connects Farnam Drive with State Street along the park's east slope. Now closed to vehicle traffic, it is open to use by mountain bikers, joggers, and hikers. *Allow 1 to 2 hours* for the 1-mile roundtrip.

To reach Trowbridge Drive from the North Meadow parking lot on the summit road, walk up the road for 0.3 miles. The entrance is on the left behind a barricade of stones. **Note:** Do not park at this entrance: you will be ticketed and towed.

The paved road provides a pleasant walk, with stone footbridges, laurel thickets, and shady mixed forest. Trowbridge Drive has the added benefit of providing eye-level views of birds feeding in the treetops, a welcome relief from springtime "warbler neck." Most birders concentrate their efforts in the first 0.4 miles of road—and particularly around the first bridge, which overlooks a seep that attracts birds year-round. Both waterthrush species visit the seep during migration. All six of the spotted thrushes are possible along the road; Veery and Wood Thrush breed in the area and are the most common, while Gray-cheeked and Bicknell's Thrush are the least. The laurels and rhododendrons lining the road attract Black-throated Blue, Magnolia, and occasionally Canada Warblers; although uncommon, Mourning, Kentucky (rare), and Hooded Warblers also slink through these thickets from time to time. American Redstart can be abundant here.

Lush groves of hemlocks once lined the roadway beyond the first footbridge; sadly, most were destroyed in the 1980s by woolly adelgids. Now only tree skeletons remain, but the many dead trees attract nearly the full complement of Connecticut's woodpeckers year-round, along with flycatchers, especially during migration. Black-throated Green Warblers have bred in this section of the park, and the remaining evergreens also attract some less common migrants, including Blackburnian, Pine, Bay-breasted, and Cape May Warblers (spruce).

The wooded hillsides host all the typical migrants mentioned earlier and can be especially good for Blue-headed, Yellow-throated, and Red-eyed Vireos; both kinglet species, Brown Creeper, most of the eastern *Empidonax* and other flycatchers, cuckoos (uncommon), Hermit Thrush, and Scarlet Tanager. Olive-sided Flycatchers are seen occasionally, usually hunting from a dead snag. Great Crested Flycatcher breeds in the area, nesting in old woodpecker holes. This area attracts more than twenty-five species of warblers each spring.

The New Haven Bird Club, the East Rock Rangers, and Sunrise Birding (a private company) lead guided walks along Trowbridge Drive in spring. Few birders come here in autumn, but the area is worth checking from late August into November for its abundance of migrants. Check starting in mid-July for early migrants.

The Summit

To reach the summit, drive from North Meadow past Trowbridge Drive then up and along the western edge of the park. There are several parking and picnic areas near the monument. The summit gets crowded with people in summer. **Note:** The summit road may be closed in winter.

Aside from the exciting raptor-watching in fall, the birding can be sparse at the summit itself. The soils are relatively poor and thin, and the trees and plants that survive here are all adapted to living on the arid cliffs. These include pitch pine, red cedar, native yucca, and scrub, chestnut, and other oaks. In summer, the bird species mix can be similar to that of the archery field. Indigo Bunting and Prairie and Blue-winged Warblers all have nested below the summit, while Peregrine Falcon nests along the ridge. Turkey and Black Vultures and Red-tailed Hawks are often in view. Common Raven, a relatively new arrival in coastal Connecticut, has nested on or near the cliff face since 2004 and is generally conspicuous. Even when the birding is slow, however, the views of New Haven are worth the visit.

English Drive and The Giant Steps

This paved, 1.4-mile section of English Drive is closed to vehicles. From the trailhead at the English Drive gate, on the north side of Rice Field, it gradually wends its way up through forest, past talus slopes, then around Indian Head. It then leads literally to giant steps below the East Rock summit and on to the park entrance road. For the more adventurous, a 285-foot climb to the summit can be made from the Giant Steps Trail, marked with red triangles. The best birding is usually within the first 0.25 miles of road. Most of Connecticut's warblers, vireos, and thrushes, along with a wide variety of other species, can be found along English Drive during migration, making this a favored site for local birders; spring is typically very birdy. Expect to find Veery, Wood Thrush, Indigo Bunting, Eastern Towhee, Rose-breasted Grosbeak, Scarlet Tanager, and Blue-winged, Prairie, and Worm-eating Warblers spring through fall. Aside from migrating raptors overhead, the birding is often slow here in autumn.

■ RWA Recreational Space

Location: Opposite 915 Whitney Avenue, Hamden.
Parking: Pull in the driveway, then take the first right. There is a small parking area on the left at the trailhead.

Across the street from the entrance to the Eli Whitney Museum, the Regional Water Authority has created a lovely little park with small ponds and easy-to-navigate walking trails. This park hosts breeding Baltimore and Orchard Orioles and can be quite good for passerine migrants in spring and fall. The other possible birds are similar to those of the adjacent Edgerton Park and lower East Rock Park. See map page 226.

Edgerton Park

Location: 75 Cliff Street, New Haven.

Parking: There is no vehicle access. Park on the street, then enter on foot at 75 Cliff Street or from Edgehill Road.

Restrooms: In the greenhouse on Saturdays or at the East Rock Ranger Station at the corner of Cold Spring and Orange Streets.

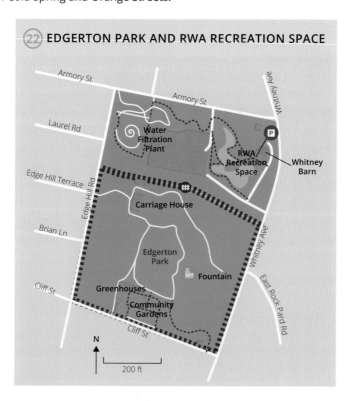

The Birding

This 27-acre park was once a richly landscaped private estate, with flower gardens, arboretum plantings, a fountain, and a greenhouse, surrounded by a high sandstone wall. Although the estate's mansion has been torn down, the gardens and greenhouse are still standing.

The park's southeastern portion is mostly lawn with scattered trees, but there are stands of cedars and ornamental evergreens throughout and quite a number of ornamental berry bushes around the buildings. The laurel-covered hillside at the northeast corner of the park is good for thrushes and sparrows in spring and fall. Look for Dark-eyed Junco and White-throated, Song, and occasional American Tree Sparrows in winter. Fox Sparrows can be found under the pines at the north edge of the big lawn and in the brushy areas at the edge of the road in March. The berry bushes attract Cedar Waxwings during migration, along with American Robins and other thrushes. The many cedars and exotic evergreens are attractive to Golden-crowned Kinglet, the occasional Ruby-crowned Kinglet, and Carolina Wren in winter. White-breasted Nuthatches are resident, while Red-breasted Nuthatches and Brown Creepers occur during migration and sometimes overwinter. Pine Siskins and redpolls occur some winters, usually in the birches. Baltimore and Orchard Orioles nest in the park, as do Cedar Waxwings and Tree and Barn Swallows.

Evening Grosbeaks have been recorded as flyovers, and hawks often travel over the park, especially during fall migration. Both Northern Goshawk and Rough-legged Hawk have occurred.

How to Bird This Site

Starting at the Cliff Street entrance, follow the park road to the north. This road makes a loop around the center of the park. Depending on the time of day, you can follow the loop in a clockwise or a counterclockwise direction, keeping the sun mostly at your back. Other trails connect to the road, including one that traverses the northeast corner of the park; these can be worth checking as well.

Lake Whitney

Location: Davis Street, Hamden.
Parking: In a pull-off on Davis Street, just to the east of the causeway.
Restrooms: At the Eli Whitney Museum, 915 Whitney Avenue.

Lake Whitney is a Regional Water Authority property, and its shores are strictly off-limits to foot traffic. Even so, the good views from Davis Street make it worth a stop. Swallows congregate over the lake in April and May to feed on hatching insects, while diving and dabbling ducks appear in small numbers in both fall and spring. Common Nighthawks are fairly common in late summer, especially at dusk. Great Blue Heron, Black-crowned Night-Heron, the occasional Green Heron, and Snowy and Great Egrets visit in season, and Double-crested Cormorants are common spring through fall. A rare Summer Tanager was once found in the small park east of the spillway in spring. Other views of Lake Whitney can be had by driving north on Whitney Avenue then turning left on Waite Street. An Anhinga (rare) was once found in the northernmost impoundment.

(23) Lighthouse Point Park and East Shore Park, New Haven

- Lighthouse Point Park
- East Shore Park

Lighthouse Point Park

Seasonal rating: Sp *** Su ** F **** W **

Best time to bird: Mid-September to mid-October for most hawks and landbirds; late April through May can also be good.

Habitats: Long Island Sound, New Haven Harbor, sandy and rocky beaches, breakwaters, jetties, small marsh and tidal creek, open lawns with scattered trees, mixed oak-hickory-sassafras woodlots, scattered conifers, and butterfly garden.

Bird list for this site:

SPECIALTY BIRDS

Resident – Mute Swan, American Black Duck, Peregrine Falcon (uncommon), Fish Crow

Summer – Killdeer, American Oystercatcher, Willet, Laughing Gull, Common and Least Terns, Belted Kingfisher (most years), Brown Thrasher (sporadic), Willow Flycatcher, White-eyed Vireo (some years), Purple Martin

Winter – Brant and other waterfowl, Common and Red-throated Loons, Horned Grebe, Great Cormorant, Iceland Gull (uncommon) and other gulls, Snowy Owl (invasion years), Purple Sandpiper, Horned Lark, "Ipswich" Savannah Sparrow (beaches), Lapland Longspur, Snow Bunting

OTHER KEY BIRDS

Resident – Typical urban, suburban, and ubiquitous species

Summer – Double-crested Cormorant, Great and Snowy Egrets, Black-crowned Night-Heron, Osprey, Chimney Swift, Eastern Phoebe, Great Crested Flycatcher, Eastern Kingbird; Tree, Rough-winged, and Barn Swallows; House Wren, Wood Thrush, Gray Catbird, Warbling and Red-eyed Vireos, Cedar Waxwing, Yellow Warbler, Common Yellowthroat, Rose-breasted Grosbeak, Eastern Towhee, Chipping Sparrow, Baltimore Oriole

MIGRANTS

Fall – Anything is possible here, especially known for hawks and diurnal landbirds.

Location: 2 Lighthouse Point Road and Park Avenue, New Haven.

Parking: An entry fee is charged daily from April 1 to Labor Day and on weekends from Labor Day to November 1. The park is open from 7:00 a.m. to sunset, year-

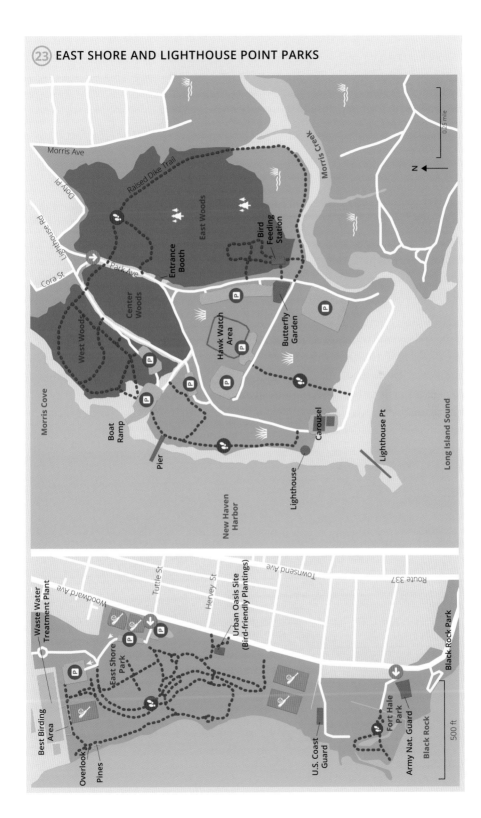

round, but the gate may remain closed as late as 9:00 a.m., especially in winter. There is limited legal parking on side streets off Lighthouse Point Road, a 5- to 10-minute walk from the park.

Restrooms: In the bathhouse in season; there are portable toilets in the park from spring through fall.

The Birding

The 82-acre Lighthouse Point Park is situated on a peninsula that juts into Long Island Sound at the entry to New Haven Harbor. It rests along the Atlantic Flyway, nestled between Saltonstall Ridge to the east and the Quinnipiac River, which empties into the harbor. During the right wind conditions, southbound birds following the ridgeline, coast, or river are all funneled into the park.

Lighthouse Point is one of New England's premier autumn hawk-watching sites and second only to Cape May, New Jersey, among Northeast coastal sites. An average of 15,000 hawks are seen annually from late August through November, with numbers peaking from mid-September to mid-October. Migrating hawks also can be seen here in spring, especially in mid-April when winds are from the south. However, fewer are seen in spring, as the migration is spread over a broader front.

Lighthouse Point Park is known for its fall hawk migration, especially for accipiters such as this young Cooper's Hawk.

The park is less well known for its even more extensive diurnal songbird migration, reflected in the park's impressive bird list: more than 290 species, recorded mainly in autumn. Most of the fall migrant species mentioned in this chapter may also be found in spring, though usually in smaller numbers.

The park *can be covered in a few hours*, but many birders stay from early morning into early afternoon to enjoy the show. To fully appreciate the scope of the migration spectacle, plan to visit over several days when conditions are favorable.

If songbirds are of particular interest, it's best to arrive early and walk the trails near Morris Creek and in the woodlots, especially the eastern woodlot. Much of the best songbird activity is missed by the masses who arrive later to view hawks.

In autumn, southbound nocturnal migrants that find themselves over Long Island Sound at dawn often reverse course and head for the nearest available land. The first rays of the sun cresting the trees above Morris Creek may reveal owls coming to roost, rails dropping into the marsh, and thrushes descending from their nocturnal sojourns, still uttering their flight calls. As the sun clears the horizon, jays, robins, bluebirds, swallows, waxwings, hawks, and many other diurnal migrants begin passing over the point.

Summer is generally slow, but birders willing to brave the beach crowds in July and August can be rewarded with interesting discoveries when winds are from the northwest. This is the time to find *Empidonax* flycatchers and early departing warblers in the woods or, following thunderstorms, vagrant shorebirds resting in rain pools on the lawns near the hawk-watching station. *Ichneumon* wasps periodically swarm over the park in late summer and fall, when swirling clouds of gulls can be seen hawking them out of the sky. In summer, also check for nesting Killdeer on the gravelly areas adjacent to the parking lots; during migration, they are seen regularly on the lawns as well.

How to Bird This Site

The official hawk-watching station on the park's central lawns is staffed daily by volunteers from late August through November. There's almost always a crowd of birders on weekends at this time; during the peak season, weekdays can be busy as well. At inland sites such as Quaker Ridge in Greenwich, the majority of raptors are Broad-winged Hawks and other buteos. At Lighthouse Point, the bread-and-butter birds of prey are the accipiters, especially Sharp-shinned Hawks, along with falcons, harriers, and Osprey.

Hawk watchers at the hawk-watch station at Lighthouse Point Park.

The highest hawk counts occur on mornings with clear blue skies and northwest winds, when the hawks fly high and sunglasses come in handy. By mid-afternoon, when thermals reach their peak, the hawks often rise too high to be seen with the naked eye; beginning birders may find it frustrating trying to identify the tiny specks high overhead. While there may be fewer hawks on overcast days, they are easier to see—this can provide a more enjoyable situation for the novice hawk-watcher. Hawks also tend to fly lower on windy days; sometimes they traverse the lawns at eye level, banking, swerving, and putting on quite a show. Watch for Merlins and American Kestrels, which snack on the go, catching and eating migrating dragonflies and butterflies. Autumn days with north or northeast winds also can bring good numbers of hawks, but southerly winds tend to slow down the action.

Although the thermals diminish later in the day, late afternoon can remain productive. Harriers, osprey, and falcons are often still moving after 3:00 p.m. Close to sunset, it's not unusual to see a few Merlins and American Kestrels perched on snags overlooking Morris Creek. Because falcons rely less on thermals than do other raptors and fly in any weather, even rainy days can produce a decent falcon count.

An annual hawk-watch festival is held at Lighthouse Park in September, typically on the third Saturday of the month. There are live birds of prey on display, along with bird-banding demonstrations and guided bird walks. Check local newspapers or the New Haven Bird Club webpage: www.newhavenbird-club.org.

While the hawk migration can be spectacular, the songbird migration is even more impressive. From mid-September through mid-November, the same lawns that host the hawk-watching station provide a good site for viewing passing diurnal migrants such as swallows, robins, and blackbirds, including Rusty Blackbird (uncommon). Other migrating species include Common Nighthawk, Blue Jay, Cedar Waxwing, Eastern Bluebird, and Eastern Meadowlark. Eastern Kingbirds can stage impressive flights from mid-August through early September. Scan the wires, telephone poles, and dead snags for vagrant Western Kingbirds; a few are recorded each fall. It's common to hear the "plink" flight calls of Bobolinks passing high overhead from mid-August to mid-September and the "pip, pipit" call of the American Pipit later in the fall; occasionally, one even hears the distinct "raspberry-like" call of the Dickcissel.

In November, when the winds turn to the north or northwest after several consecutive days of southwest winds, watch for Cave Swallows and other southwestern vagrants. November rarities have included Connecticut's only Tropical Kingbird, White-winged Dove, American White Pelican, and Ash-throated Flycatcher. Huge numbers of blackbirds can pass through in early November: 10,000 Red-winged Blackbirds and 110,000 Common Grackles have been recorded in a single day.

Large flocks of Snow Geese banking high overhead provide one of the great thrills of the fall migration here. They are joined by flocks of Canada Geese from October through December, usually on the same days that bring abundant hawks.

The irruptive "winter finches" vary dramatically in abundance year to year, from zero to hundreds to sometimes thousands in a single day. Purple Finches arrive first, in July and August. They are followed by Pine Siskin and crossbills in early October (Red Crossbills outnumber White-winged), with Common Redpolls arriving by early November. A few Evening Grosbeaks occur most years, seen or heard in flight; their call is a House Sparrow–like "chup, chup."

The masses of jewelweed growing in the park's wetter areas attract migrant Ruby-throated Hummingbirds, especially in late August and September, when they often streak past the hawk-watching station like little darts. Scrutinize any hummingbird after mid-October, when Rufous Hummingbird or other western species are more likely.

The **butterfly garden** near the hawk-watching station (nearly fifty butterfly species have been recorded here) is stocked with several hummingbird feeders. The garden plantings and feeders have attracted some uncommon species, including Calliope Hummingbird and Orange-crowned Warbler. This garden and the woodland borders and weedy edges throughout the park should be checked for migrating sparrows in the fall, especially in October. Among the numerous Song, Swamp, Savannah, and White-throated Sparrows, you might find some less common Lincoln's, White-crowned, or Vesper Sparrows, which skulk in brushy areas like the trails near Morris Creek. Field Sparrows can be fairly common in spring, often associating with large flocks of migrant Dark-eyed Juncos, Chipping Sparrows, and American Tree Sparrows. Both Song and Chipping Sparrows nest in the park.

On days with good sparrow flights, look for Blue Grosbeaks (uncommon) in brushy areas, especially where there is abundant burdock, a favorite food. Indigo Buntings are fairly common in May and again from July through mid-October, but expect to see brown-plumaged birds in fall.

During migration, landbirds can be plentiful in the east, center, and west **woodlots**. Each attracts a slightly different mix of species, with some overlap, and all are worth checking. The east and west woods have extensive trail systems and can be productive throughout; typically, only the periphery of the center woods is productive. All are hunted by Cooper's and Sharp-shinned Hawks and occasionally by Northern Goshawks during fall migration.

In the morning, the oaks along the sunny south and east edges of the center woodlot are especially active, often attracting warblers, vireos, and kinglets. Most of Connecticut's warbler species have been seen here at one time or another. Fall numbers for most warblers peak in September, with Palm and Yellow-rumped Warblers peaking in October. Check the Virginia creeper and Asiatic bittersweet vine tangles for feeding American Robins and other thrushes. Veery, along with Wood, Swainson's, and Hermit Thrushes, are expected, but Gray-cheeked or Bicknell's (rare) Thrush also are possible, especially in September. Wood Thrush has bred here.

From July through mid-September (with a peak in August), the woods can harbor any of the five species of migrant *Empidonax* flycatchers—Least, Willow, Alder, and the less common Yellow-bellied and Acadian.

Spring or fall, the woodlots' many rocky knolls and moss-covered hillsides attract thrushes, Eastern Towhee, and sparrows, including Fox Sparrow. Brown Creepers favor the hickory trees from late March to mid-April, then again from mid-October to mid-November. During cold weather, they roost together under upturned bark. Migrant Blue-gray Gnatcatchers can be found in the oaks; a few stay to nest.

In late fall and winter, mixed feeding flocks of Black-capped Chickadees and Tufted Titmice—often with a few White-breasted Nuthatches, a Downy Woodpecker, or some kinglets—traverse the woodlots. Both kinglet species are especially prevalent as migrants in mid-October. Occasionally, Pine, Palm, Yellow-rumped, and other warblers join the flocks, especially later in the fall. White-breasted Nuthatches breed here, while migrant Red-breasted Nuthatches are seen most years. Eastern Wood-Pewee and Great Crested Flycatchers can be conspicuous from July into September. Eastern Phoebes are common migrants as well; a few stay to breed.

The east woodlot is a particularly good place for woodpeckers, thrushes, warblers, and vireos. Downy Woodpeckers are common year-round, while Hairy Woodpeckers occur in small numbers. In fall, numbers of migrant Northern Flickers, Yellow-bellied Sapsuckers, and Red-headed Woodpeckers (rare) peak from mid-September through mid-October. Look for both cuckoo species in May and September or October. About halfway round the east woodlot's loop trail, a side trail runs east into the marsh along a raised dike (often overgrown and impassable in fall). The dike backs up against residential homes with feeders and offers limited views of the marsh and Morris Creek. With luck, Belted Kingfisher and a few night-herons and egrets will be seen in the marsh, and a rail might be heard. In summer, the brushy areas along the marsh edge are good for Eastern Towhee, Carolina and House Wrens, Gray Catbird, and the occasional Brown Thrasher, which breeds most years here or in the northwest corner of the park. Unusual for lower New Haven County, a pair or two of White-eyed Vireos nest here on occasion.

Banding data shows that species such as Yellow-breasted Chat, Connecticut and Mourning Warblers, and Lincoln's Sparrow occur in the thickets along **Morris Creek** and on the dike edge, on a rare but regular basis during fall migration. Quiet patience and luck are required to find these secretive species.

Migrant songbirds are attracted to the willows and locust trees overlooking the creek. Watch also for the Cooper's and Sharp-shinned Hawks that pursue them. These willows also have attracted Long-eared, Great Horned, Barred, and Barn Owls (rare), as well as Eastern Screech-Owls. Baltimore Orioles commonly nest in the creek-edge trees, as do Warbling Vireos and Eastern Kingbirds. Belted Kingfishers are found from April into December, sometimes later. Both crow species breed locally, and Connecticut's first Boat-tailed Grackles (rare) were found here.

Black-crowned Night-Herons roost in trees on the far side of Morris Creek; these can be seen leaving the roost at dusk or returning at dawn. Occasionally, a Yellow-crowned Night-Heron is among them. Rarely, American Bittern or Cattle Egret are seen in the marsh. Sora and Clapper and Virginia Rails occur during migration.

A walk to the **western shore**, near the old park entrance, can provide spectacularly close views of some raptor species as they turn north to avoid crossing the harbor. Red-headed Woodpeckers (rare) favor the trees in this corner of the park, with most records coming from mid-September to mid-October. Brown Thrasher has nested in this area.

The boat ramp and fishing pier here provide clear views of New Haven Harbor. In winter, Brant are ubiquitous and the harbor holds large flocks of Greater Scaup, often just around the bend in Morris Cove. Careful scrutiny of the flocks usually produces a few Lesser Scaup and occasionally a Redhead or the increasingly uncommon Canvasback. Search the small groups of Long-tailed Ducks, Common Goldeneye, and Red-breasted Mergansers for less common species such as Barrow's Goldeneye. All three scoter species occur here, generally in small numbers. Horned Grebes, along with Common and Red-throated Loons, are fairly common and sometimes overwinter. Red-necked Grebe occurs occasionally, and Eared Grebe has been seen in Morris Cove. A few Bonaparte's Gulls sometimes overwinter, and the gull flocks that may occur from mid-March to mid-April are always worth checking for rare Little and Black-headed Gulls. Iceland and Lesser Black-backed Gulls also are seen among the larger gulls from time to time.

The **beach and jetties** east of the point can be productive for shorebirds and others. In the morning, it is best to walk along the beach toward the lighthouse, keeping the sun at your back (reverse course in the afternoon). Purple Sandpipers can be fairly common in winter on the rock jetties to the east, but a spotting scope is needed to see them; occasionally, they rest on the rocky shore near the lighthouse. Ruddy Turnstone, Sanderling, Dunlin, and less frequently, American Oystercatcher also use the breakwaters offshore, especially during migration. Great Cormorants roost on the breakwaters in winter, while Double-crested Cormorants can be found year-round, though only a few overwinter. In April, then again from September through mid-October, large lines of migrating Double-crested Cormorants often are seen on the horizon. They circle regularly in the thermals, almost like hawks.

The beach attracts gulls year-round, including Laughing Gull in summer. It also may harbor Snow Bunting, Horned Lark, and Lapland Longspur from late October to early April; usually only a few of these overwinter, along with small numbers of the "Ipswich" subspecies of Savannah Sparrow.

■ East Shore Park

Seasonal rating: Sp *** Su * F **** W ***
Best time to bird: September to May.
Habitats: Open lawns, ball fields, hedgerows, small woodlots, pine stands, and New Haven Harbor.
Location: At the intersection of Woodward Avenue and Tuttle Street, New Haven.

Parking: Once inside the park, turn right and follow the road northwest to the parking lot.
Restrooms: There are portable toilets in the park from spring through fall.

East Shore Park hugs the edge of New Haven Harbor, between a wastewater treatment facility to the north and Nathan Hale Park to the south. The raptor, waterbird, and songbird species found here are similar to those at Lighthouse Point Park, and the site offers great potential for the discovery of rarities.

The best birding is at the northwest edge of the park, along the fence adjacent to the wastewater treatment plant. The plant's settling pools support significant insect swarms in winter, attracting lingering insectivores. The hedges and trees along the fence have held an impressive array of species into early winter, including Blue-headed Vireo, American Redstart; Black-and-white, Palm, Pine, and Nashville Warblers; Ovenbird, Common Yellowthroat, and Yellow-breasted Chat, as well as Eastern Phoebe and Baltimore Oriole.

Other noteworthy species—including Red Crossbill, Red-breasted Nuthatch, Yellow-bellied Sapsucker, and Brown Creeper—also have been found in the pines that line the fence and shore. The settling pools also regularly attract late-staying Tree, Northern Rough-winged, and rare Cave Swallows in November and early December. To get another view of the pools, walk west to the beach, then north along the shore and up to the chainlink fence. Check any of the wetter areas and willows for migrants.

In November, rare Cave Swallows and other migrants are attracted to insects at the wastewater treatment plant adjacent to East Shore Park.

The trails along the western edge of the park provide fine views of the harbor. Gulls found on the beach or just offshore have included Iceland Gull and Black-headed Gull. Flocks of Brant and Greater Scaup tend to linger in the area from fall through spring.

Ecology Park and Shoreline Greenway Trail, Branford

Seasonal rating: Sp *** Su * F **** W **
Best time to bird: Mid-October to April.
Habitats: Grass-covered hilltop (capped landfill), mixed deciduous forest, small pond, shrubby borders; overlooks marsh, river, Long Island Sound, and urban areas.

Bird list for this site:

SPECIALTY BIRDS
As Ecology Park was new at the time of this writing, little data was available to compile a species list.
Resident – Common Raven (uncommon)
Summer – Osprey, Red-tailed Hawk, Orchard Oriole

OTHER KEY BIRDS
Resident and Summer – Typical urban, suburban, and ubiquitous species

MIGRANTS
Fall – Anything is possible here: hawks, blackbirds, swallows—including Cave Swallow (November)—sparrows, warblers, and other landbirds

Location: 100 Tabor Drive, Branford. The park is also accessible on foot via the Shoreline Greenway Trail and Branford Walking Trail.
Parking: There is a small parking area just inside the entrance and handicapped parking at the summit.
Restrooms: At Branford town center.

The Birding

Ecology Park was opened in 2014, the splendid result of the reclamation of Branford's capped landfill. A gazebo at the park's summit provides spectacular views of Long Island Sound, Stony Creek, and the Thimble Islands to the south, and the Branford River, church steeples, and shops of Branford center to the north. This park has incredible potential as a hawk-watching site and migrant trap, especially in fall. It could easily come to rival Lighthouse Point Park in nearby New Haven for species diversity.

An array of migrants passes through from late August to November, similar in scope and variety to Lighthouse Point Park. Any of Connecticut's hawks are possible. As with other coastal sites, watch for Cave Swallows on days with north winds from late October into November, when you also can expect large mixed flocks of Common Grackles and other blackbirds. On one November day here, observers recorded 11 Cave Swallows, 1 Sandhill Crane, 300 Cedar Waxwings, 130 Purple Finches, 18 American Pipits, 22 Eastern Bluebirds, and 6 Horned Larks—along with nine species of raptors. There have been days in mid-November with 5,000 Red-winged Blackbirds and 10,000 grackles.

24 ECOLOGY PARK AND SHORELINE GREENWAY TRAIL, BRANFORD

In summer, Ospreys nest on the cell tower just to the northeast of the park. Great views of the nest can be had with a spotting scope from the summit. Expect typical resident woodland species in the forested areas year-round; during migration anything is possible, especially in fall.

How to Bird This Site

The most productive approach during migration is to scan the skies from the summit, with occasional forays along the walking trail that encircles the hilltop to search for songbirds. A comfortable chair, along with sunscreen, hat, and a spotting scope, are recommended; views of passing raptors and other migrants can be quite distant.

The walking trail and weedy edges should be checked for Savannah, American Tree, and other sparrows in fall and spring, while the grassy hilltop itself is likely to attract migrant Horned Lark, American Pipit, Snow Bunting, the occasional Eastern Meadowlark, and American Golden-Plover or other shorebirds. Eastern Bluebirds prefer the forested edges.

At the bottom of the hill opposite the parking lot is an old brush dump surrounded by thickets and forest—good for landbirds. A nearby pond is accessible from the Shoreline Greenway Trail or a small spur trail across from the parking lot. This area is worth checking at any season, but especially in fall and winter. Thicket-loving species such as Gray Catbird and Eastern Towhee, along with American Tree Sparrow and other sparrows, have overwintered here, and the pond has held Black-crowned Night-Heron as well as other waders and waterfowl.

Shell Beach, Guilford

Seasonal rating: Sp **** Su *** F **** W **
Best time to bird: March through November.
Habitats: Tidal saltmarsh impoundments, sheltered bay, roadside thickets, coastal forest, and suburban neighborhood.

Bird list for this site:

SPECIALTY BIRDS

Resident – Mute Swan, American Black Duck; Cooper's, Red-shouldered, and Red-tailed Hawks; Belted Kingfisher (some years), Fish Crow

Summer – Great and Snowy Egrets; Green, Little Blue, and Tricolored Herons; Glossy Ibis, Osprey, Killdeer, Spotted Sandpiper, Willet, Least Tern, Yellow-billed Cuckoo, Purple Martin, Brown Thrasher (some years), Eastern Bluebird, Orchard Oriole (some years)

Winter – Sea ducks, loons, grebes (bay only), Great Blue Heron, raptors

OTHER KEY BIRDS

Summer – Double-crested Cormorant, Black-crowned Night-Heron, Common Tern, Chimney Swift, Eastern Phoebe, Eastern Kingbird; Northern Rough-winged, Tree, and Barn Swallows; Cedar Waxwings, Yellow Warbler, Common Yellowthroat, Baltimore Oriole

MIGRANTS

Spring – Puddle ducks, shorebirds, waders (herons and egrets), Clapper and Virginia Rails (uncommon)
Summer – Shorebirds, waders
Fall – Waders, some puddle ducks, shorebirds, raptors

Location: 2 Shell Beach Road off Connecticut Route 146, Guilford.
Restrooms: At Guilford town center.

The Birding

Shell Beach is a series of flooded marsh impoundments used for grazing cattle, opposite Island Bay. A causeway (Shell Beach Road) divides the marsh from the bay. There is an active Osprey nest at the western edge of the marsh, right beside the causeway.

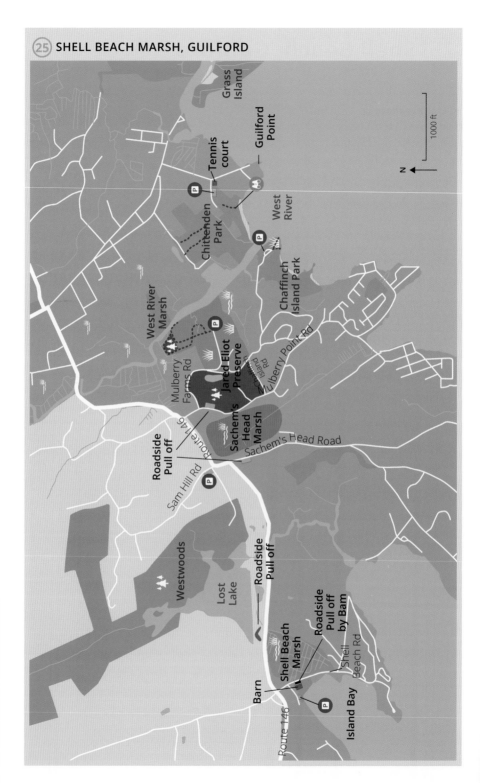

25 SHELL BEACH MARSH, GUILFORD

Grass Island

Tennis court

Guilford Point

1000 ft

N

West River

Chittenden Park

Chaffinch Island Park

West River Marsh

Mulberry Point Rd

Mulberry Farms Rd

Jared Eliot Preserve

Oyster Island Rd

Route 146

Sachem's Head Marsh

Roadside Pull off

Sachem's Head Road

Sam Hill Rd

Westwoods

Lost Lake

Roadside Pull off

Roadside Pull off by Barn

Shell Beach Marsh

Shell Beach Rd

Barn

Route 146

Island Bay

Nearly two hundred species of birds have been found in and around this small marsh, and it is one of the most productive and popular wader and shorebird sites in the state, especially for several less common species. Little Blue Heron, for example, visits regularly in small numbers; in late summer, their presence is augmented by the influx of white first-year birds. Their favored roost trees are on a small island on the northeast side of the marsh, near the road. Tricolored Heron (rare) has occurred consistently and should be looked for in June and July. Glossy Ibis are often observed among the many Snowy and Great Egrets.

Uncommon shorebirds drawn consistently to these impoundments include Stilt Sandpiper, Baird's Sandpiper (September), and Western and White-rumped Sandpipers, while Pectoral Sandpipers are found annually in small numbers. Look for early arriving shorebirds in March and lingering ones in late May. Lesser Yellowlegs is reliable here. Mid-May is best for northbound migrants and mid-July through September for southbound birds. Killdeer are common breeders, along with a few pair of Willet and Spotted Sandpiper.

Shell Beach also serves as a stopover point for several of the less common dabbling ducks. It is a great place to find Gadwall, Blue-winged and Green-winged Teal, Northern Shoveler, and Northern Pintail from late March into April. American Black Duck and Mallard breed here, while Gadwall is a potential nester. Migrant dabbling ducks tend to linger here into late May.

Rarities discovered here include White-faced Ibis, Cattle Egret, Sandhill Crane, Wilson's and Red-necked Phalarope, Upland and Buff-breasted Sandpipers, Ruff, and American Avocet.

Shell Beach attracts a wide variety of shorebirds, waterfowl, and waders, including Lesser Yellowlegs (shown).

How to Bird This Area

Turn south onto Shell Beach Road from its intersection with Connecticut 146. Park at the pull-off beside the red barn, 100 yards farther on the right. From here, you can scope the west side of the marsh impoundments across the street.

An access road near the barn leads to a parking lot at the beach that overlooks sheltered Island Bay. The bay attracts sea ducks, including Long-tailed Duck, as well as loons and grebes from fall through spring, with some lingering here well into May. Terns, mostly Common and Least Terns, hunt here in summer. Black-headed Gull (rare) and Red-necked Grebe (uncommon) have occurred here in spring.

To view the east end of the marsh, return to Connecticut Route 146, then turn right and drive east for 0.3 miles. Park in the pull-off on the north side of the road, just before the trees end and before the road continues across a causeway. **Note:** Please do not block the access to the railroad tracks. There is space to scope the marsh behind the guardrail across the street. Shorebird diversity decreases dramatically when the empoundments are flooded.

(26) West River Marsh Complex, Guilford

- Jared Eliot Preserve
- Chaffinch Island
- Chittenden Park
- Sachem's Head Marsh
- Westwoods

SPECIALTY BIRDS
Resident – American Black Duck, Belted Kingfisher (some years), Fish Crow
Summer – Great and Snowy Egrets, Green Heron (uncommon), Osprey, Willet, Common Tern, Yellow-billed Cuckoo, Purple Martin, Marsh Wren, Warbling Vireo, Brown Thrasher (some years), Eastern Bluebird, Orchard Oriole (some years)
Winter – Sea ducks, loons and grebes (Chaffinch Island area), Great Blue Heron, raptors

Bird list for this site:

OTHER KEY BIRDS
Summer – Double-crested Cormorant, Black-crowned Night-Heron, Chimney Swift, Eastern Phoebe, Eastern Kingbird; Northern Rough-winged, Tree, and Barn Swallows; House and Carolina Wrens, Northern Mockingbird, Cedar Waxwing, Yellow Warbler, Common Yellowthroat, House Finch, Baltimore Oriole

MIGRANTS
Spring – American Woodcock (display), Great Horned Owl, warblers
Fall – Diurnal migrants, Ruby-throated Hummingbird, swallows, Philadelphia Vireo, sparrows, blackbirds, Bobolink

Jared Eliot Preserve

Seasonal rating: Sp *** Su ** F **** W *
Best time to bird: May through November.
Habitats: Open meadows, thickets, coastal forest, ponds, saltmarsh, tidal river, and suburban neighborhood.
Location: 199 Mulberry Farms Road, Guilford.
⮕ **Directions:** From Connecticut Route 146, take Mulberry Point Road south, then take the first left onto Mulberry Farms Road. **Note:** The road may be unmarked.

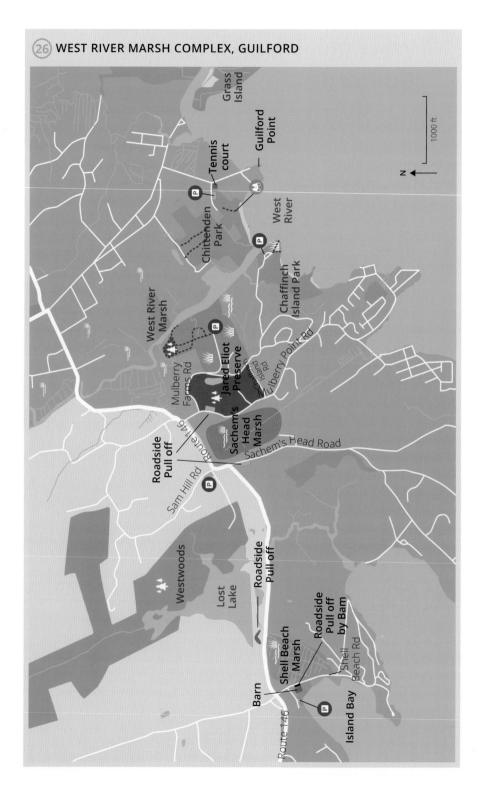

Restrooms: At Guilford town center.

Additional information: The park protects rare plants, especially grasses, and historic plantings that attract birds and butterflies. The Connecticut Butterfly Association visits annually; see www.ctbutterfly.org for a schedule.

The Birding

The 36-acre Jared Eliot Preserve, once known as Mulberry Farm, is nestled in a coastal valley south of the Amtrak rail line. The wooded western section of the park, adjacent to Mulberry Point Road, is made up of regenerating coastal forest within a suburban neighborhood. The eastern section of the preserve has open meadows, thickets, a remnant arboretum, and abuts the extensive saltmarsh of the tidal West River. This secluded coastal site, with its varied habitats, is ideally situated as a migrant trap.

How to Bird This Site

There is parking for the western side of the preserve on Mulberry Point Road, on the left, just south of the intersection with Mulberry Farms Road. During migration, it can be very rewarding to park at this pull-off and walk at least the first 75 yards of Mulberry Farms Road, especially early in the morning. This forested area is a fantastic migrant trap and often holds warblers, vireos and other landbirds. Pay particular attention to the power-line cut to the south, where fifteen species of warblers and Philadelphia Vireo (uncommon) have been recorded in fall.

After birding this area, return to your car, then drive east down Mulberry Farms Road 0.2 miles to the fork at Pinewood Road; park off the roadside. The first 50 yards of Pinewood Road feature a secluded pond on the right and a swamp on the left. Green Heron and Mallard nest by the pond, and an assortment of ducks, including Wood Duck (may nest), visit during migration. The trees lining the road edge are often good for migrant landbirds, including Philadelphia Vireo, especially in fall.

Return to Mulberry Farms Road and continue to the east for 0.1 miles (you can walk or drive), passing through open meadow until you reach the parking area on the left. Watch the wires and road edges for migrants on your way. Western Kingbird (rare), assorted raptors, Eastern Bluebird, and most of Connecticut's swallows have been seen on these wires. Dead trees along the marsh edge on the road's south side provide convenient hunting perches for resident and migrating raptors, especially Osprey (nests) and Red-tailed Hawk. Peregrine Falcon, Merlin, and Bald Eagle also have been recorded.

In autumn, this meadow section of Mulberry Farms Road offers unobstructed views of passing diurnal migrants; the birding can be quite exciting on days with north or northwest winds. On good flight days, expect a steady stream of raptors, swallows, Bobolinks, waxwings, robins, Blue Jays, and other migrants, passing from east to west. Ruby-throated Hummingbirds are often seen streaking by from late August into September. Large mixed flocks of blackbirds also move through, particularly in October and November, and one should watch for Rusty Blackbird and Yellow-headed Blackbird (rare). In mid-March, American Woodcock display here, and by late April, Purple Martins occupy a box across the meadows near the railroad tracks.

Moving on from the parking area, you can walk along a mowed path that winds its way through thickets then ends at the river edge, overlooking an extensive marsh. The meadows and thickets provide ample habitat for a nice assortment of sparrows—including Clay-colored Sparrow (uncommon)—and other seed-eaters during migration; Brown Thrasher, Eastern Bluebird, and both Baltimore and Orchard Orioles nest here in summer.

The main path has two spur trails that split off shortly after leaving the parking lot. The side trail on the right leads east toward the caretaker's home into an old arboretum with magnolia and black walnut trees; this can be particularly good for Brown Thrasher and other thicket-loving species. Farther along the main trail, another trail leads to the left; it passes along forest edge and a cedar-covered knoll before looping back to the main trail. This loop trail is often good for warblers, thrushes, woodpeckers, and sparrows, especially during fall migration.

When you reach the river edge and saltmarsh at the end of the main trail, watch for resident Belted Kingfisher, Double-crested Cormorant, and a variety of migrant waterfowl. Listen for migrant Clapper Rail, Marsh Wren, and Saltmarsh Sparrow, all of which are potential nesters. Check the marsh and channel edges for shorebirds, including nesting Willet (common), Marbled Godwit (rare), yellowlegs, and others. Snowy and Great Egrets feed in the saltmarsh from spring through fall; they are joined later in the season by Great Blue Heron, a few of which overwinter.

▪ Chaffinch Island Park

Seasonal rating: Sp *** Su ** F *** W **
Location: 348 Chaffinch Island Road, Guilford.
Restrooms: Portable toilets on site.

Chaffinch Island Park is a small, rocky peninsula overlooking the mouth of the West River and Guilford Harbor, just south of the Jared Eliot Preserve. The park is mostly lawn with scattered trees, many of them hackberry, which are attractive to a variety of rare butterflies. The park's western section includes a marsh and a sandy beach.

Expect the same bird species here as at Jared Eliot Preserve, with the addition of a greater number and variety of shorebirds and waterbirds. The peninsula offers a good vantage point to scan for sea ducks, loons, grebes, and gulls during migration and in winter. Carefully check the water's edge and any partially submerged rocks for shorebirds. In summer, Common and Least Terns are often found resting on rocks just off the peninsula, while Great Horned Owls nest and roost in the area most years. Within the marsh, there are nesting Osprey (on a platform) and Clapper Rail. The park has attracted rarities including Marbled Godwit and American White Pelican.

■ Chittenden Park

Seasonal rating: Sp *** Su ** F *** W **
Location: 2-40 Field Road, Guilford.
Parking: On Field Road, off Seaside Avenue.
Restrooms: At Guilford town center. Seasonal portable toilets on site.

Chittenden Park is located on the east side of the West River, opposite Chaffinch Island Park. Walk southwest across the ball field to reach the beach and river mouth. The beach and its nearby marshy pools provide attractive habitat for a variety of shorebirds and waders. Rarities such as Marbled Godwit, Ruff, and Cattle Egret have been found here.

■ Sachem's Head Marsh

Seasonal rating: Sp *** Su *** F *** W *
Location: Sachem Head Road, Guilford.
⊃ **Directions:** From the intersection of Connecticut Route 146 and Sachem Head Road, turn south on Sachem Head Road and look for a pull-off immediately on the right.
Restrooms: At Guilford town center.

Scope the marshy inlet here. Puddle ducks, especially Green-winged Teal, shorebirds, and waders visit these pools during migration, especially when water levels are low. This is a favored site for Lesser Yellowlegs, Least and Semipalmated Sandpipers, and Semipalmated Plovers. Egrets tend to gather here in summer. The marsh also supports an active Purple Martin box.

■ Westwoods

Seasonal rating: Sp *** Su *** F *** W *
Location: 1 Sam Hill Road, Guilford.

Westwoods is a 1,200-acre forested site that includes Lost Lake. The site has 20 miles of trails and a large diversity of habitats. In addition to the standard deep-forest species, Prothonotary Warbler (rare) has been found along the small seep to the left of the entrance in spring. The edges can sometimes be good for migrants. Lost Lake attracts an assortment of waterfowl and waders from spring through early winter. **Note:** A detailed map is available at https://guilfordlandtrust.org/wordpress/properties/westwoods.

Madison Shoreline

■ East Wharf Beach to West Wharf Beach
■ Circle Beach
■ East River State Boat Launch

■ East Wharf Beach to West Wharf Beach Tour

Bird list for this site:

Seasonal rating: Sp *** Su *** F *** W ***
Best time to bird: Year-round.
Habitats: Long Island Sound, sandy beaches, rocky outcrops, near and offshore islands, and residential neighborhoods.

SPECIALTY BIRDS
Resident – Monk Parakeet, Fish Crow
Summer – Herons and egrets, including Yellow-Crowned Night-Heron, Little Blue Heron, and Glossy Ibis; American Oystercatcher, Spotted Sandpiper, Roseate Tern (uncommon), Common and Least Terns, Purple Martin, Orchard Oriole
Winter – Common Eider, all three scoter species, sea ducks, loons, grebes, Ruddy Turnstone, Purple Sandpiper

MIGRANTS
Waterfowl, especially scoters and eiders, loons, grebes, Northern Gannet, gulls, Royal and Caspian Terns (both uncommon), Purple Sandpiper

Locations: East Wharf Beach, 122 East Wharf Road, Madison; West Wharf Beach, adjacent to 94 West Wharf Road, Madison.
Restrooms: East Wharf has a portable toilet; Dunkin' Donuts in Madison.

The Birding

The 1-mile stretch of rocky coastline along Middle Beach Road, between East Wharf Beach and West Wharf Beach, is one of the better sites in the area to find sea ducks, grebes, and loons from fall through spring. All three scoter species, Common Eider, Long-tailed Duck, Common Goldeneye, Bufflehead, scaup, and other ducks frequent the area. Less common species also occur, including Barrow's Goldeneye and Harlequin Duck. Both loon species and Horned Grebe are usually plentiful, while Red-necked Grebe is seen occa-

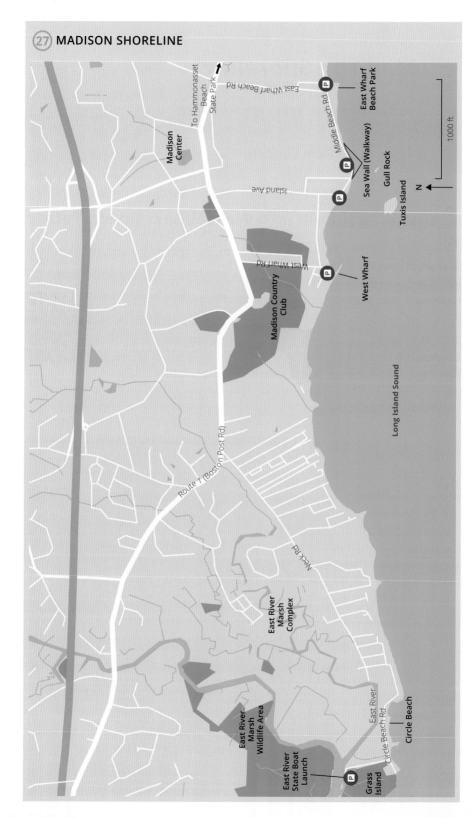

To Hammonasset Beach State Park

East Wharf Beach Rd

Middle Beach Rd

East Wharf Beach Park

Madison Center

Island Ave

Sea Wall (Walkway)

Gull Rock

Tuxis Island

N

1000 ft

West Wharf Rd

West Wharf

Madison Country Club

Long Island Sound

Route 1 (Boston Post Rd)

Neck Rd

East River Marsh Complex

East River Marsh Wildlife Area

East River State Boat Launch

Grass Island

East River

Circle Beach Rd

Circle Beach

sionally. The many small, rocky islands frequently hold Purple Sandpiper well into May.

In summer, Tuxis Island, the large near-shore island off Middle Beach, supports one of Connecticut's largest heronries, with many pairs of Great and Snowy Egrets, Black-crowned Night-Heron, and Glossy Ibis, and a few pairs of Little Blue Heron and Yellow-Crowned Night-Heron. Keep an eye out for Tricolored Heron and White-faced Ibis; both are seen in local heron colonies in summer and could occur here. The island also supports a thriving Double-crested Cormorant colony. Osprey, Green Heron, American Oystercatcher, Spotted Sandpiper, and Common Tern also breed on the island.

Roseate Terns visit occasionally in summer (they breed on Falkner Island, the island with the lighthouse). Both Caspian and Royal Terns also have been seen, usually in late summer and fall. Snowy Owl has been found in winter. East Wharf Park has breeding Orchard Oriole, and Monk Parakeets nest in the parking lot pines and the nearby neighborhood. Purple Martins have a nest box between the two wharfs, beside the second Middle Beach parking lot. Fish Crow is common in this area. At low tide, the shoreline and sandbars provide roosting and feeding sites for gulls and shorebirds.

How to Bird This Site

If birding in the morning, begin your tour at East Wharf Beach and work west along Middle Beach Road to West Wharf Beach, as described below. If arriving in the afternoon, reverse the directions to keep the sun at your back. **Note:** A scope is needed for this tour.

East Wharf Beach Park is located at the intersection of East Wharf Road and Middle Beach Road in Madison. The parking lot is open only to residents in summer but can usually be accessed early or late in the day, when no attendant is present; at other times of the year, the lot is accessible to all.

After checking the coastline here, turn left out of the parking lot and proceed west on Middle Beach Road for 0.5 miles to a small parking area on the left. If this lot is full, there is another 0.1 miles farther on, just before the road makes a 90-degree turn to the right and becomes Island Avenue.

Stop here and check the coast again. A Barrow's Goldeneye has wintered near the seawall on multiple occasions. Gull Rock is the smaller and closer of the two islands; the larger one is Tuxis Island.

Continue north on Island Avenue, then take the first left onto Middle Beach Road West. At the stop sign, turn left onto West Wharf Road. The parking lot is at the end of the road, past the Madison Beach Hotel. Although the lot can be crowded in summer, there is usually ample parking fall through spring.

This wharf gives unobstructed views of the west side of Tuxis Island.

■ Circle Beach

Seasonal rating: Sp *** Su * F *** W ***
Location: 67 Circle Beach Road, Madison.
⊃ **Directions:** From U.S. 1 in Madison, drive southwest on Neck Road for 1.3 miles, then turn left onto Ridgewood Avenue. Ridgewood Avenue makes two 90-degree turns then becomes Circle Beach Road.
Restrooms: Portable toilet at East River State Boat Launch (see next site description).

Circle Beach is a private beach. Roadside parking is generally tolerated in winter, but avoid parking here in summer. The beach is known as a reliable wintering site for Iceland Gull. The waters and rocky offshore islands attract sea ducks, including all three scoter species. Ruddy Turnstone, Dunlin, and Sanderling visit frequently, and Purple Sandpiper occurs late fall through spring. American Oystercatcher nests nearby.

Circle Beach is a reliable place to find Iceland Gull in winter.

■ East River State Boat Launch

Seasonal rating: Sp *** Su **** F *** W **
Location: Entrance road opposite 169 Circle Beach Road, Madison.
Restrooms: Portable toilet on site.
Hazards: Hunting is allowed in season.

The Birding

The East River State Boat Launch is located across the river from the East River Marsh Wildlife Area and adjacent to Grass Island. The access road passes through a high marsh comprised of *Spartina patens* (saltmarsh hay). This is the easiest place in the state to view high-marsh nesting species such as Willet, Clapper Rail, and Saltmarsh Sparrow, all of which are common to abundant breeders here. There are also healthy populations of Marsh Wren and Seaside Sparrow, which nest along the mosquito ditches in the marsh.

Herons, egrets, and ibis from nearby Tuxis Island feed in the East River marsh complex from spring through fall, with a few egrets and herons often lingering into winter. A diverse array of migrant shorebirds frequents the marsh and river edges. Scope the tip of the peninsula on Grass Island to the west, where Least and Semipalmated Sandpipers, Sanderling, Dunlin, and Black-bellied and Semipalmated Plovers often congregate. Recently, Boat-tailed Grackles have set up a small colony there. Bald Eagles are resident in the area, while Osprey nest and congregate here in amazing numbers—up to twenty in summer and thirty-eight during migration. In winter, look for Northern Harrier, Rough-legged Hawk, and the occasional Snowy Owl.

Eastern Willet is an abundant breeder in the marsh.

How to Bird This Site

A scope is highly recommended. Park only in the designated spots for non-boaters, and be sure to avoid blocking access to the ramp itself. No parking is allowed along the access road, but there are pull-offs where you may stop to scan the marsh as long as you remain in your car. Be certain to pull completely off the road so as not to obstruct vehicles towing boats with trailers. **Note:** Those disobeying posted signage have been ticketed.

Hammonasset Beach State Park, Madison

Seasonal rating: Sp *** Su *** F **** W ***
Best time to bird: Year-round.
Habitats: Long Island Sound, nearby islands, estuary, tidal creeks, large tidal marshes, small pond, sandy and rocky beaches, rocky headlands, breakwaters, jetties, open lawns, large gravel and asphalt parking lots, scattered rain pools, mixed deciduous and coniferous woodlots, coastal forest, cedar and pine groves, campgrounds, and butterfly garden.

Bird list for this site:

SPECIALTY BIRDS

Resident – Mute Swan, American Black Duck
Summer – Osprey, Clapper Rail, Piping Plover, Killdeer, American Oystercatcher, Least Tern (east beaches), Roseate Tern (nests on Falkner Island), Great and Snowy Egrets, Little Blue Heron, Tricolored Heron (most years), Little Blue × Tricolored Heron, Glossy Ibis, Willow Flycatcher, Purple Martin, Marsh Wren, Brown Thrasher, Eastern Towhee, Saltmarsh and Seaside Sparrows, Boat-tailed Grackle, Orchard Oriole
Winter – Northern Gannet, Great Cormorant, American Bittern, Bald Eagle (most years), Northern Goshawk (some years), Rough-legged Hawk (invasion years), Purple Sandpiper, Razorbill and other alcids; Iceland, Lesser Black-backed, and Glaucous Gulls (all uncommon); Snowy Owl (invasion years), Red-breasted Nuthatch (invasion years), "Ipswich" Savannah Sparrow (beaches), Snow Bunting, Lapland Longspur, Red and White-winged Crossbills (invasion years), Common Redpoll (invasion years)

OTHER KEY BIRDS

Resident – Herring, Great Black-backed, and Ring-billed Gulls (nonbreeder); Red-bellied, Downy, and Hairy Woodpeckers; Northern Flicker, Blue Jay, American and Fish Crows, White-breasted Nuthatch, Carolina Wren, Eastern Bluebird, Northern Mockingbird, Cedar Waxwing, Red-winged Blackbird, Common Grackle, American Goldfinch, House Finch
Summer – Black-crowned Night-Heron, Belted Kingfisher (most years), Laughing Gull, Common Tern, Double-crested Cormorant, Eastern Phoebe, Eastern Kingbird, Tree and Barn Swallows, House Wren, Gray Catbird, Red-eyed Vireo, Yellow Warbler, Common Yellowthroat, Chipping Sparrow, Baltimore Oriole
Winter – Greater and Lesser Scaup, Long-tailed Duck; White-winged, Surf, and Black Scoters (uncommon); Common Goldeneye, Bufflehead, Hooded and Red-breasted Mergansers, Common and Red-throated Loons, Horned and Pied-billed Grebes, Great Blue Heron, Northern Harrier, Black-bellied Plover, Ruddy Turnstone, Sanderling, Dunlin, Hermit Thrush, Yellow-rumped and Pine Warblers (uncommon); American Tree, White-throated, and Fox Sparrows; Dark-eyed Junco

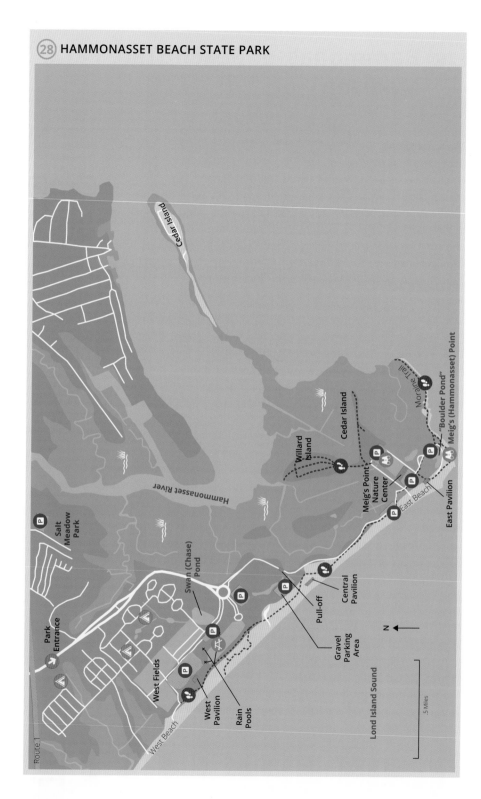

(28) HAMMONASSET BEACH STATE PARK

Route 1

Park Entrance

Salt Meadow Park

West Fields

West Beach

West Pavilion

Rain Pools

Swan (Chase) Pond

Gravel Parking Area

Central Pavilion

Pull-off

Hammonasset River

Willard Island

Cedar Island

Cedar Island

Meig's Point Nature Center

East Beach

East Pavilion

Moraine Trail

"Boulder Pond"

Meig's (Hammonasset) Point

Lond Island Sound

N

.5 Miles

MIGRANTS

Spring and Fall – Dabbling and diving ducks, Red-necked Grebe, hawks and falcons, Golden Eagle (rare), American Coot, Bonaparte's Gull, Short-eared Owl; *Empidonax* flycatchers (August or September), including Acadian, Alder, and Yellow-bellied Flycatchers; Brown Creeper, both kinglet species, Veery, Wood Thrush, thirty-one warbler species; many sparrow species, including Grasshopper (uncommon), Field, White-crowned, White-throated, Vesper, Savannah, Swamp, and Clay-colored Sparrows; Rusty Blackbird

Fall – American Golden-Plover, Buff-breasted Sandpiper, Upland Sandpiper (uncommon)

Location: 1288 Boston Post Road, Madison.

Parking: An entrance fee is charged from Memorial Day to Labor Day and on weekends from late April to Memorial Day and from Labor Day through September. Season passes are available at the entrance booths.

Restrooms: At bathhouses from Memorial Day through Labor Day; portable or pit toilets are available year-round by the bathhouses, Willard Island, and in the West Beach parking lot.

The Birding

If I could visit just one site in Connecticut, it would be Hammonasset Beach State Park. The incredible array of habitats included in the park's 919 acres has attracted at least 325 species of birds; not surprisingly, it is designated an Important Bird Area.

Most of Connecticut's songbird migrants—including more than thirty warbler species—occur annually, at least in small numbers. Songbird migration peaks in May, then again from mid-August to mid-October. On fall days with north winds, hordes of diurnal landbird migrants—including waxwings, robins, jays, swallows, and blackbirds—stream through the park. Rarities can be expected: Western Kingbird, Northern Wheatear, and Cave Swallow have all occurred on more than one occasion.

Nearly all Connecticut's waders and migrant shorebird species also have been sighted at Hammonasset. A few species, such as Willet, are active and vocal nesters in the park's marshes. In summer, they commandeer posts and signs as display perches and embark on vocal flying sorties. Migrating Whimbrel seem partial to the entrance-road borders and the field edges between the traffic circle and the West Beach parking lot, from mid-April into May, then again from July through September. Hudsonian Godwits have turned up along the road edge or near the picnic pavilions in autumn as well.

Hammonasset Beach State Park is known for attracting rarities, including Hudsonian Godwit.

Great and Snowy Egrets and Little Blue Herons frequent the park's marshes from mid-March through October. They are joined spring through fall by Great Blue Herons, a few of which overwinter. Green Herons are encountered from late April through September and may breed in small numbers. Tricolored Herons are rare but annual, and the state's only recorded Tricolored × Little Blue hybrids can be found here.

During the height of sparrow migration—in March and April then again in October—the park is a reliable place to find most of the sparrows that occur in the state, including Clay-colored Sparrow (uncommon) and Fox Sparrow, which winters in small numbers. White-throated, Song, and Chipping Sparrows are abundant, while Savannah and Swamp Sparrows are common, especially along the marsh and road edges. The abundance of cedars and bayberry allow Yellow-rumped Warblers to winter in the park; these are sometimes joined by Pine, Palm, or rarely, Orange-crowned Warblers.

Hammonasset also is one of the better places in Connecticut to find migrating or wintering raptors and owls. Northern Harriers patrol the marshes throughout the park from fall through spring, although few remain in midwinter. A Short-eared Owl is occasionally seen perched on a post or hunting the marsh between the traffic circle and Meigs Point, generally at dusk or dawn, from mid-October through early April. The beach and marshes at the park's east end are dependable sites for wintering Snowy Owls and Rough-legged Hawks whenever these species occur in the state.

Tree Swallows use nest boxes placed in the marshes, while Barn Swallows nest in many of the bathhouses and buildings. Tree Swallow numbers build in fall; hundreds or even thousands can be seen gathering to roost here. Cave Swallows (rare) are observed in late fall nearly every year.

How to Bird This Site

Hammonasset's sandy beaches attract hordes of beachgoers in summer, but the park's size means that birders can find relatively secluded corners even in the busiest season. (Parking, on the other hand, can be a problem.) At the height of the summer shorebird migration, it is best to come early and leave before the multitudes arrive. Late afternoon, after the crowds have dissipated, can also be productive. A scope is recommended.

Stopping along the roadside is allowed only in some parts of the park. **Note:** These places are not always clearly marked. If you do stop, obey all traffic signs and pull completely off the road. The park is open to vehicle traffic from 8:00 a.m. to sunset, daily, but is often closed following snowstorms.

A birder's logbook, maintained by Menunkatuck Audubon Society, is currently attached to the east wall of the nature center. The logbook can be a valuable resource: please leave details of your sightings for other birders.

Swan (Chase) Pond

This pond on the park's west side can be reached by taking the first right off the entrance-road traffic circle. From September through May, for as long as the water remains open, it may host Bufflehead, Hooded and Red-breasted Mergansers, Green-winged and Blue-winged Teal (uncommon), Gadwall, American Wigeon, as well as Greater and, occasionally, Lesser Scaup. American Black Duck, Mallard, and Belted Kingfisher are resident, while Pied-billed Grebe and American Coot are expected visitors from October through April. Rarely, the resident Mute Swans are joined by a migrant Tundra Swan. Double-crested Cormorants are nearly permanent fixtures from March through November.

The pond also attracts as many as seven swallow species annually. In summer, a colony of Purple Martins uses the nearby nest boxes. Tree Swallows breed in the birdhouses here. Herons and egrets feed along the edge, spring through fall.

As you walk back toward the traffic circle, scan the marshy edge of the pond for Wilson's Snipe and Pectoral and Least Sandpipers. Check the reeds lining the pond carefully for American Bitterns, which are regularly encountered here from October through April. Glossy Ibis, herons, and egrets feed along the edge or in the pools across the street, spring through fall.

The berry-like cones of the area's cedars draw Cedar Waxwing, American Robin, Eastern Bluebird, and other thrushes, year-round. They are also attractive to kinglets, the occasional Brown Creeper, and during migration, a wide variety of vireos and warblers.

There are several Osprey platforms in the marsh to the east of the traffic circle. Most platforms host nesting pairs from April through early September. In the off-season, other raptors use them as hunting perches, so they are always worth a check—everything from Bald Eagle to Goshawk is possible.

West Fields and Rain Pools

These fields have consistently lured Buff-breasted Sandpipers from late July through early October. One or two individuals are typical, but six or more have occurred together. Killdeer nest here and can be plentiful during migration, both spring and fall. A variety of other migrating shorebirds visit the many rain pools that form in these fields, including American Golden-Plover and Pectoral Sandpiper (July through October). Upland Sandpiper can occur in April and at any time from July through September. Least Sandpipers are found with regularity, while Stilt and White-rumped Sandpipers appear occasionally, and Baird's Sandpiper (rare) has been observed along the grassy edges. One rain pool near the southeast edge of the West Beach parking lot has attracted Ruff (very rare) in April and September; the same pool often holds common species such as Greater and Lesser Yellowlegs, Semipalmated Sandpiper, and Semipalmated Plover.

West Beach Parking Lot

Gulls and shorebirds roost on this parking lot, especially at high tide. From fall through spring, they are often joined by flocks of Horned Lark and Snow Bunting. Caspian, Royal, and Forster's Terns, Black Skimmers, and Iceland and Lesser Black-backed Gulls have appeared among the usual contingent of Ring-billed, Great Black-backed, and Herring Gulls. Laughing Gulls can be numerous from July through September. Look carefully, as rarities can be easily missed among the many gulls; one of the state's few records of Mew Gull was found here in the 1980s, and a California Gull was seen on the nearby beach. Black-bellied Plover, Killdeer, and the occasional American Golden-Plover sometimes mingle among the masses. Any rain pools, particularly at the southeast end of the parking lot, should be checked for shorebirds.

West Beach Pines and West Beach

The scattered black pines throughout the park are known for attracting Red Crossbills and, occasionally, White-winged Crossbills during irruption years. The pines along the south side of the West Beach parking lot were especially productive until most were storm-damaged and then removed in 2016. Young trees were planted, but it may be a few years before crossbills again frequent this area. Crossbills do not appear annually but can be fairly common when they do occur. Check for them from October through April, with Red Crossbills occasionally appearing into May. Other irruptive species such as Common Redpoll and Pine Siskin are also drawn to the park's pines from October through April. Red-breasted Nuthatches favor pines as well and may be present from mid-August through April; their numbers vary widely from year to year.

It is often worth a quick walk to the beach here to scan Long Island Sound. Good numbers of Horned Grebes, Common and Red-throated Loons, and some sea ducks can gather off this beach from fall through spring. Long-tailed Duck, Red-breasted Merganser, and flocks of Common Goldeneye frequent this area. Watch for Northern Gannets and flocks of Double-crested Cormorants, and Greater Scaup flying along the horizon. These are sometimes joined by scoters, especially from mid-October to mid-November, then again from mid-March to mid-May. Harbor seals and, less frequently, gray seals winter on Falkner Island (the island with the lighthouse) and are occasionally observed here. Rarely, small young harp seals are seen as well.

Both Red Crossbill (shown here) and White-winged Crossbill invade our area some winters to feed on conifer seeds.

A walk east on the path behind the dunes can be rewarding for migrating and wintering sparrows, and for Yellow-rumped and Palm Warblers in autumn. Mixed flocks of Dark-eyed Juncos and American Tree Sparrows frequent the area fall through spring.

Center Pavilion Gravel Parking Area

The gravel lot due west of the pavilion's main lot, 0.3 miles east of the traffic circle, floods when it rains, attracting shorebirds. Wilson's Snipe seem to prefer these rain pools to many of the others that form in the park. When the park's maintenance crew piles brush in this lot, migrating sparrows also may appear. Connecticut's first Lazuli Bunting was unexpectedly found here.

Meigs (Hammonasset) Point

Many exciting seabird sightings have been made at the point over the years, often after storms. Rarities include Harlequin Duck, Eared Grebe, Manx Shearwater, Wilson's Storm-Petrel, American White Pelican, Brown Pelican, Black-legged Kittiwake, Common and Thick-billed Murres, Dovekie, and Black Guillemot. This is also one of the more consistent locations for finding King Eider in Connecticut. All three scoter species may be seen from fall through spring, although Black Scoter is uncommon. Northern Gannets are seen almost daily in fall and spring, with sporadic winter and early summer reports. Common and Red-throated Loons, along with Horned Grebes, are generally plentiful, fall through spring. A few migrant Red-necked Grebes can usually be found from mid-October into early November, and again from mid-February to mid-May.

The jetties (groins) to the southwest and northeast attract Great Cormorant, Purple Sandpiper, Ruddy Turnstone, Sanderling, Black-bellied Plover, and Dunlin, fall through spring. The Purple Sandpipers usually appear in November and stay, at least in small numbers, through May. Anglers who use the west jetty may scare birds to the rocks off the jetty's tip. Be patient: sometimes the birds roost on the south side, out of sight.

East Beach (Moraine Trail)

The East Beach, at the end of the Moraine Trail, hosts nesting pairs of several rare or uncommon species, including Piping Plover, American Oystercatcher, and Least and Common Terns. These species are joined by roosting shorebirds during migration, and by the occasional Roseate Tern spring through fall. (Roseate Terns nest on Falkner Island.) In summer, Double-crested Cormorants roost on the rocks just off the beach. In winter, these are largely replaced by Great Cormorants, although a few Double-crested may remain. The rocks also have attracted King and Common Eiders, all three scoter species, and seals. Spring through fall check the saltpans and pools in the marsh along the way for shorebirds and waders. Migrating White-rumped Sandpipers, Lesser Yellowlegs, and a few Stilt Sandpipers and Whimbrels consistently utilize this area of marsh. **Note:** The beach is closed to public access during the breeding season. Foot traffic is allowed on the beach at other times, but parts of the trail flood around high tide. The platform at the end of the Cedar Island trail (see below) also provides good views of this area. A scope is recommended.

A few Lapland Longspurs occur annually in the fields near the Meigs Point Nature Center.

Meigs Point Nature Center

From October to April, the grassy fields adjacent to the Meigs Point Nature Center consistently attract flocks of Horned Larks and Snow Buntings, along with a few Lapland Longspurs. During high tides, migrating shorebirds roost in these fields. Killdeer, Semipalmated and Black-bellied Plovers, Dunlin, and Least Sandpiper are commonly seen. It is a reliable site for American Golden-Plover from August through at least mid-October, and for Pectoral Sandpiper in April and September. The field edges are worth checking for sparrows. Chipping Sparrows can be common spring through fall, and Savannah Sparrows from October through April. Check any flock carefully for Clay-colored Sparrow, now an annual occurrence. A few White-crowned Sparrows join the flocks of White-throated Sparrows that gather each fall, especially in October and November. Buffy-striped young birds are most likely, but black-and-white-striped adults are seen as well. Extreme rarities such as Le Conte's and Henslow's Sparrows, and Lark Buntings have all been recorded.

Brown Thrashers nest throughout the park in small numbers and frequent the shrubs and lawns around the nature center building and along the marsh edge. In spring, watch for males to sing from exposed perches. Also near the building are a butterfly garden, a birdbath, and Purple Martin boxes. The martin boxes are active from mid-April through August, although the martins themselves are often out of sight during the heat of midday, carried high into the sky by thermals. In the fall, check the garden carefully: migrating landbirds are attracted to the plantings that have gone to seed.

The hillside fields adjacent to the nature center provide an excellent vantage point for observing hawks and other diurnal migrants, such as swallows, Common Nighthawk, Blue Jay, American Robin, Cedar Waxwing, and Northern Flicker. Fall hawk flights can be good here, especially when there are northwest winds.

The marsh and pools to the east are consistently good for shorebirds and waders, from spring through fall. Both Glossy Ibis and Little Blue Heron nest nearby. (If you don't find a Little Blue Heron in these pools, check the "boulder pond" by Meigs Point.) White-faced Ibis is now an annual visitor, typically in spring. (If the ibis flock is not in this section of marsh, check the marsh between Willard and Cedar Islands, which can be viewed from the road at the base of Willard Island or from several points on the trail through Cedar Island.) Wilson's Phalarope (rare) is recorded almost annually, usually from May into early June or in August and September.

The pools and marsh are also the easiest locations in the park to see Saltmarsh and Seaside Sparrows. Saltmarsh Sparrows breed from late May to August; their quiet song is reminiscent of the sizzle of hot metal quenched in water and can be difficult to hear unless you are close. The less numerous Seaside Sparrows nest from early June to late July and sound like tiny, distant Red-winged Blackbirds. Both species will sit up when they sing, so scan the grasstops (a scope is useful for this). Most Seaside Sparrows depart by the end of August, but Saltmarsh Sparrows may stay, at least in small numbers, until November. Migrating Nelson's Sparrows appear from May to early June and then again in October.

An observation blind is hidden in the brush at the northeast edge of the nature center fields. The blind overlooks a small tidal marsh created as part of a habitat restoration project. American Bittern is seen here regularly from fall through spring, and this also can be a good spot for rails and roosting shorebirds.

Willard Island and Picnic Grove

The picnic grove beside the parking lot for Willard and Cedar Islands holds a small population of breeding Boat-tailed Grackles, rare and local nesters in Connecticut. The nearby cedar groves on Willard Island attract a variety of migrant landbirds; when food is plentiful, they can hold numerous species through the winter. Black-throated Gray Warbler (rare) has occurred here more than once. In late fall or winter, check the feeding flocks of Black-capped Chickadees for Boreal Chickadee—although very rare, they do occur.

Willard Island was once a farm orchard; its central section is now maintained in early successional habitat, predominantly cedars and fruit-bearing shrubs, interspersed with open areas. The dense vegetation provides food and cover for birds throughout the year.

Along the southern half of Willard's Island, the marsh approaches closely on each side. The northern end is close to the mouth of the Hammonasset River. Paved paths encircle and divide the area. At the southern end, there is a good spot to scan the marsh for ibis and other waders. The small tidepools that form near the road attract American Bitterns and rails, with Clapper and Virginia Rails most likely, although Yellow Rail (very rare) also has been seen feeding here.

The north end is dominated by a sassafras, oak, and hickory woodlot (habitat unique to coastal Connecticut) that provides a magnet for migrant songbirds. Songbirds seem to work their way north as the morning progresses, often appearing in the woodlot or the shrubs along the trail to the marsh and Hammonasset River overlook by late morning. A wide variety of thrushes, warblers, and vireos can occur. Baltimore Oriole, Rose-breasted Grosbeak, and Scarlet Tanager are fairly common migrants. During migration, the vine tangles at the north end attract Great Horned and Barred Owls. Saw-whet Owls often show up in the cedars and may overwinter (care should be taken not to disturb them). One of Connecticut's only recent records of Great Gray Owl occurred here in January 1996. Yellow-breasted Chat is a regular, yet elusive visitor to vine tangles along the east path. Brown Thrasher nests here most years. House Finch and American Goldfinch are resident, while Purple Finch can be found at almost any time of year but especially in spring and fall (annual numbers vary widely).

The area overlooking the marsh and Hammonasset River can be reached by continuing north via an extension of the center trail through scattered trees and shrubs. The marsh here supports all the species common to the park's other marshes, including breeding Willets and feeding Glossy Ibis. Both dabbling and diving ducks frequent the river, fall through spring. American Black Duck and Mallard breed here, while Gadwall is a possible breeder. During migration, Bufflehead and Common Goldeneye appear, and all three merganser species are possible. Forster's Tern and other terns are sometimes seen along the river in fall. Check the shoreline for herons and other waders: American Avocet has been seen here.

The island's sandy soil supports many other interesting plants and animals. The rare New England Cottontail Rabbit has been seen here, but is difficult to distinguish from the more numerous Eastern Cottontails.

Cedar Island

Cedar Island is a small woodlot located across the picnic grove lawns to the south and east of Willard Island. A trail leads northeast through stands of oak, hickory, sassafras and maple onto a boardwalk that ends at an observation deck overlooking marshes and East Beach. This is a great area to hear and see Clapper Rail, feeding Glossy Ibis, egrets, and Little Blue Heron. Both cuckoo species have been found along the trail, usually in May or in August and September. The landbird species found on Willard Island occur here as well.

Clapper Rails are seen and heard from mid-April through August, with a few remaining into the fall. Breeding Seaside and Saltmarsh Sparrows are common in season. Flocks of Glossy Ibis feed here from late March through early October, with occasional stragglers remaining into November. The large boulders that can be seen due east along the shore are always worth scanning for terns, gulls, and shorebirds. Occasionally, a wayward Royal or Caspian Tern is found here.

Raptors hunt these woods during migration, with Sharp-shinned and Cooper's Hawks, Merlin, and American Kestrel the most frequently encountered. Northern Goshawk and Rough-legged Hawk have wintered here occasionally; these can turn up anywhere in the park from mid-October through mid-March. Sometimes a Bald Eagle or two will set up winter residence, but most are seen during fall migration. Rarely, a Golden Eagle is sighted in autumn, usually after mid-October.

THE CENTRAL INTERIOR

(29) Winter Geese and Duck Tour, Enfield and Somers

- Donald W. Barnes Boat Launch
- King's Island Boat Launch
- Somersville Pond

▦ Donald W. Barnes Boat Launch

Seasonal rating: Sp *** Su * F *** W ****
Best time to bird: Late December through March.
Habitats: A tree-lined section of the Connecticut River adjacent to an urban center, with farmland nearby.

Bird list for this site:

SPECIALTY BIRDS
Resident – Bald Eagle, Red-tailed Hawk
Summer – Common riparian species, Chimney Swift
Winter – Barrow's Goldeneye, rare geese and ducks, Red-necked Grebe, Iceland Gull, Fish Crow, Common Raven

MIGRANTS
Ducks and geese

Location: 14 South River Street, Enfield (opposite Asnuntuck Street).
Restrooms: Dunkin' Donuts on Route 140W near I-91, exit 45.

The Birding

The Enfield Rapids area of the Connecticut River has long been a reliable inland site to find wintering Barrow's Goldeneye (January to February) among the many Common Goldeneye, along with Common Merganser, Bufflehead, and rare geese (late December to April). Pink-footed, Barnacle, Greater White-fronted, Snow, and Cackling Geese have been found among the wintering hordes of Canada Geese. In February and March, as migration inten-

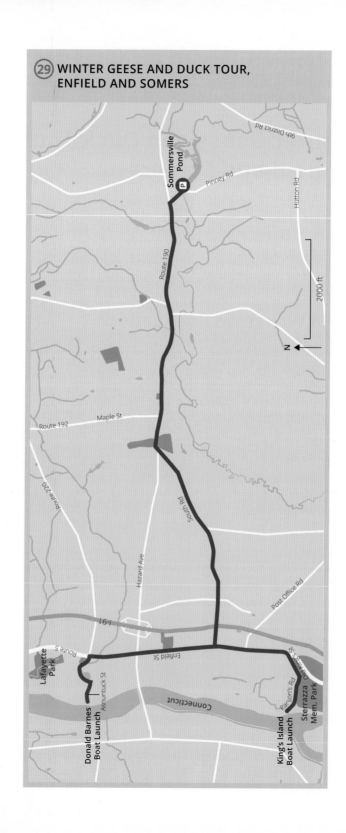

29 WINTER GEESE AND DUCK TOUR,
ENFIELD AND SOMERS

Sommersville
Pond

P

Pinney Rd

9th District Rd

Hutton Rd

2000 ft

N

Route 190

Route 192

Maple St

Route 220

South Rd

Hazard Ave

Post Office Rd

I-91

Route 5

Enfield St

Parson's Rd

Old King's St

Lafayette
Park

Asnuntuck St

Donald Barnes
Boat Launch

Connecticut

King's Island
Boat Launch

Sterrazza
Mem. Park

Most winters, the Enfield Rapids attract Barrow's Goldeneyes.
Photograph courtesy Mark S. Szantyr

sifies, expect fluctuating numbers of American Black Duck, Canvasback, Greater Scaup, Ring-necked Duck, Northern Pintail, and Wood Duck, with occasional visits from less common species including Redhead and Lesser Scaup.

Pay close attention to the gulls and waterbirds. Iceland Gull (January to February) and Red-necked Grebe (February to March) visit with some regularity; Glaucous Gull is possible. It's also worth scanning the skies for raptors. Bald Eagles are common in winter and seen in small numbers year-round; Red-tailed Hawks are resident; and Peregrine Falcon, Cooper's Hawk, and other raptors occur periodically. Common Raven and Fish Crow are seen occasionally, especially in winter and spring. Riparian woodland species—especially woodpeckers, White-breasted Nuthatch, and Eastern Kingbird (summer)—frequent the trees along the river.

How to Bird This Site

A scope is needed here. The goldeneyes and other ducks move up and down the river constantly, while the geese move to and from the nearby farm fields all day. Patience and repeated scanning (and visits) may be necessary to find any given species. If the sought-after birds are absent from the Donald W. Barnes Boat Launch, try the other sites described in this chapter.

King's Island Boat Launch

Seasonal rating: Sp ** Su * F ** W ****
Location: 49 Parson's Road, Enfield.
Restrooms: Portable toilet in season.

Farther downriver from Enfield Rapids, the King's Island Boat Launch is an alternate site to check for Barrow's Goldeneye and geese. It is adjacent to Angelo Joseph Sferranza Memorial Park, a wooded linear park with trails along the river, which holds typical riparian species.

Somersville Pond

Seasonal rating: Sp ** Su * F *** W ****
Location: Viewing from behind the Village Players theater, 55 School Street, Somers.
Restrooms: None.

Somersville Pond and the surrounding farmland off Connecticut Route 190E are likely spots for wintering geese. Most of Connecticut's rare geese have been seen in the area. The pond is best viewed from the parking lot behind the Village Players theater, by the boat launch at the far end of the lot.

Flocks of geese also visit the extensive farm fields to the south along Pinney Road, Maple Street, Billings Road, Hutton Road, and 9th District Road. Use the triangle formed by Route 190, Pinney Road, and 9th District Road to outline your search.

# (30) Broad Brook Millpond, East Windsor

---

Seasonal rating: Sp *** Su * F **** W ****
Best time to bird: Mid-October to April.
Habitats: Small pond surrounded by trees near open farmland and adjacent to an urban center.

Bird list for this site:

SPECIALTY BIRDS

Resident – Belted Kingfisher
Summer – Killdeer, Spotted Sandpiper, Green Heron, Great Egret
Winter – Rare geese, including Pink-footed, Barnacle, Greater White-fronted, Ross's, and Cackling Geese; American Coot, ducks

MIGRANTS

Bald Eagle, Lesser Yellowlegs (uncommon); Solitary, Least, and Semipalmated Sandpipers; Common Raven (mainly fall)

Location: Opposite 20 Depot Street, Broad Brook.
Parking: There is a small parking lot on the pond, off Depot Street.
Restrooms: Dunkin' Donuts on Route 140W near I-91, exit 45.

Fall through spring, as many as eight species of geese gather to rest and bathe on Broad Brook Millpond, leaving each evening to feed in nearby cornfields.

The Birding

This small pond is arguably the best place to find rare geese in New England from mid-October through March. Eight of the nine species to occur in Connecticut have been seen here. Pink-footed, Barnacle, Greater White-fronted, Brant (rare inland), Snow, and Cackling Geese, along with the very rare Ross's Goose, have all been found—sometimes in a single day or week—among the thousands of Canada Geese that congregate here. Hooded and Common Merganser are regular winter visitors. Unusual duck species to occur include Black Scoter and Canvasback.

Scan the skies for raptors as well. Bald Eagles are uncommon winter visitors, while Red-tailed Hawks are resident and Peregrine Falcons and other raptors visit periodically. Resident Belted Kingfishers breed nearby. Scan the ever-present gull flocks for Iceland Gull and other less common species. The pond edge can attract shorebirds, herons, and egrets in summer. Resident landbirds frequent the trees that surround the pond. Common Ravens are seen occasionally, especially in fall.

How to Bird This Site

A scope is needed here. The geese move back and forth between the pond and nearby farm fields all day, often returning in mid or late afternoon to bathe and drink. Patience, along with repeated scanning of the pond and adjacent lawns, may be necessary to find a given species among the tightly packed throngs of birds. At dusk, the geese leave the pond, often en masse—an awesome spectacle to witness.

If you are looking for a particular bird that has been reported at the pond but find it absent when you visit, drive 1.1 miles east to East Road. The fields along East Road, both to the north and the south, are favored feeding areas and worth checking. Frog Hollow Road in Ellington also should be checked. To get there, head south on East Road to Chamberlain Road, then turn left and drive east; Chamberlain Road soon becomes Frog Hollow Road.

(31) Station 43, South Windsor

Seasonal rating: Sp **** Su *** F **** W **
Best time to bird: Spring and fall.
Habitats: Open agricultural fields, Connecticut River floodplain, riparian woodlands, farm pools, densely vegetated marsh, small ponds, and old residential neighborhoods.

Bird list for this site:

SPECIALTY BIRDS

Resident – Mute Swan, American Black Duck, Bald Eagle
Summer – Least Bittern, American Kestrel, King Rail (some years), Sora, Bank Swallow, Bobolink
Winter – Rough-legged Hawk (invasion years), Northern Shrike (some years), Horned Lark, Snow Bunting

OTHER KEY BIRDS

Resident – Wood Duck, Ring-necked Pheasant, Virginia Rail, Cooper's Hawk, Eastern Screech-Owl, Great Horned Owl, Belted Kingfisher, Cedar Waxwing
Summer – Green Heron, Chimney Swift, Willow Flycatcher, Eastern Kingbird, Northern Rough-winged Swallow, Marsh Wren, Warbling Vireo, Swamp Sparrow, Rose-breasted Grosbeak, Orchard Oriole
Winter – Northern Harrier, other raptors

MIGRANTS

Snow Goose, Gadwall, Northern Shoveler, Blue-winged Teal, Great Egret, Merlin, Peregrine Falcon, American Coot, Pectoral Sandpiper, Wilson's Snipe, Common Nighthawk, Ruby-throated Hummingbird, Cliff Swallow, American Pipit, Wilson's Warbler, Northern Waterthrush; Vesper, Lincoln's, White-crowned, and other sparrows; Indigo Bunting, Rusty Blackbird

Location: Intersection of Main Street and Vibert Road, South Windsor.
Restrooms: Dunkin' Donuts on the corner of Route 5 and Pleasant Valley Road.
Hazards: Deer and pheasant are hunted here. During hunting season, heed "no trespassing" signs, wear blaze orange, and take extreme care when on foot. Check with the Department of Energy and Environmental Protection (DEEP) for official hunting dates.

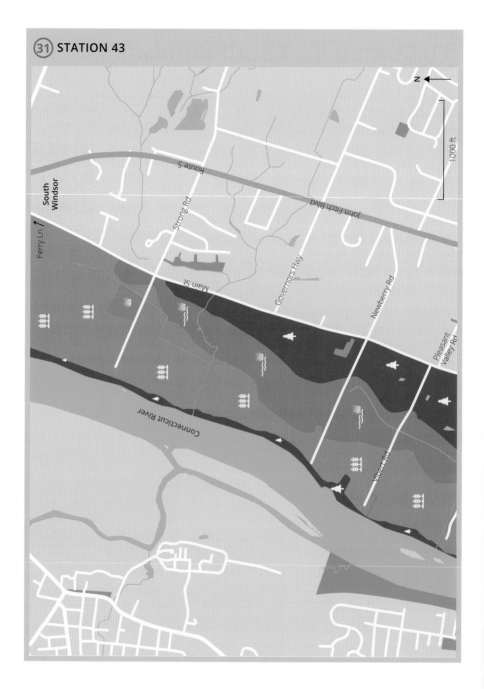

The Birding

Station 43, also known as South Windsor Meadows, is a large wetland, now an Important Bird Area, nestled within fertile agricultural lands in the Connecticut River floodplain, once part of a glacial lake. It is a premier inland birding location, offering an impressive variety of habitats.

This wetland is a verdant place of rich mud and lily pads, of painted turtles, pickerelweed, and muskrats. The haunt of waterbirds, it's where one goes to glimpse a fleeing rail or to stalk a bittern. In summer, the air is filled with the sounds of croaking frogs, buzzing insects, quacking ducks, and the paddling of webbed feet across water. (It also is a good place to feed the mosquitoes.)

Station 43 is reliable for Least Bittern, Virginia Rail, Sora (in wet years), Wood Duck, Marsh Wren, and Swamp Sparrow. King Rail is found in some years. It is also the place I saw my first Sandhill Crane.

In late fall and winter, large flocks of Common Grackle, Red-winged Blackbird, and Brown-headed Cowbird stage here in late afternoon before flying to roost in Manchester. Rusty Blackbird appears in small numbers (October to early May), and Yellow-headed Blackbird (rare) also has occurred. In December and January, an impressive flock of crows (5,000 or more) often gathers here at dusk before heading off to roost in West Hartford. The entire area is great for raptors in winter and can attract Northern Shrike as well. Bald Eagles nest locally and are a common wintering species along the Connecticut River south to Essex.

How to Bird This Site

Station 43 gets its name from the bus stop designation at the corner of Newberry Road and Main Street. Each of its different access roads offers a different mix of species, with habitats ranging from farm fields to wetlands to riparian forest. This chapter describes a route from south to north that covers several of the most productive and easily accessed areas. **Note:** Make sure to reset your odometer to zero where indicated, as subsequent directions are given in tenths of a mile.

Access can be impeded after heavy rain, and flooding is common. In winter, some roads are not plowed and may require four-wheel drive. In spring, expect mud up to your eyes. Always bring boots! **Note:** Much of the area is private property. To assure continued access, please heed "no trespassing" signs and always stay on roads and paths.

Vibert Road

The marshy areas alongside Vibert Road (just south of Newberry Road) attract typical wetland and wetland-edge species including Willow Flycatcher, Eastern Kingbird, Eastern Phoebe, Warbling Vireo, Common Yellowthroat, Yellow Warbler, Swamp Sparrow, and Baltimore Oriole. **Note: Set your odometer to zero** at the intersection of Main Street and Vibert Road, then drive west along Vibert Road.

At 0.1 miles, stop and scan the area around the sewage plant on the left for Eastern Bluebird. The fields on the right sometimes attract Ring-necked Pheasant.

At 0.2 miles, the road surface turns to dirt. In the scrubland on the right, look for Indigo Bunting, Brown Thrasher, and other shrub-loving species. Indigo Buntings can be plentiful, especially from late August to mid-September. Yellow Warbler is common in spring and summer. Cooper's Hawks have nested in the distant woodlot to the south. In fall, this is a great place to find sparrows. Song, Swamp, White-throated, and Chipping Sparrows are most common, but look for Savannah, White-crowned, and later in the fall, American Tree Sparrows as well. Vesper, Lincoln's, and even Grasshopper Sparrows (rare) are possible.

At 0.4 miles on your odometer, pull off on the right, just after crossing Newberry Brook. (Although small, the brook can flood in spring, leaving the road impassable.) Check the moist fields on both sides of the road for Killdeer and other shorebirds, spring through fall. The marshy areas near the bridge hold breeding Swamp Sparrow, Common Yellowthroat, and Yellow Warbler. Both Baltimore and Orchard Oriole nest locally. The Orchard Orioles seem to prefer the woodlot north of the road. Red-tailed Hawks also nest in this north woodlot; in winter, their nest may be used by Great Horned Owls. The owls are sometimes visible from the road (February to April). Please do not trespass to get closer nor use recorded calls. In winter, check any geese feeding in the farm fields. Pink-footed Goose and other rare species have occurred here.

The dirt farm road along the edge of the cornfields leads to fields where bobolinks breed; these are accessible on foot.

To check the wet meadows south of the road, walk back over the brook. You may find shorebirds as well as dabbling ducks here, including Wood Duck, Green-winged Teal, and occasional Blue-winged Teal. In March and April, then again in September and October, Wilson's Snipe are usually plentiful, while Solitary Sandpiper is reliable in April and May. Less common but still regular visitors include Greater and Lesser Yellowlegs and Least Sandpiper. A few Great Egrets stalk the wetter areas occasionally, spring through summer, while Cattle Egret (rare) has occurred. Look for Northern Harriers fall through spring.

The hedgerows lining the road for the next 0.4 miles are worth walking, spring and fall. Those closest to the public boat launch, *at 0.8 miles* on your odometer, are especially good for White-crowned Sparrows, which may remain into winter. At the boat launch, a public trail runs south through the huge sycamores that line the river. These trees are home to many typical riparian species, including Eastern Screech-Owl, Black-capped Chickadee, Eastern Kingbird, Warbling Vireo, and Baltimore Oriole. In late fall and early winter, check for Brown Creeper and American Tree Sparrow. This also is a good area for woodpeckers; all but Pileated Woodpecker occur regularly.

Because the Connecticut River acts as a corridor for migrant land- and waterbirds, seventy-five species or more may be found in a single spring day along Vibert Road. Check the river itself from fall through spring for cormorants and a variety of ducks, including Bufflehead and Common and Hooded Mergansers. Both Great and Double-crested Cormorants use the river, with Great Cormorants (rare) found only in winter. A colony of Bank Swallows nests in the riverbank a quarter-mile north of the boat ramp. In spring, all five of Connecticut's breeding swallows—Bank, Rough-winged, Tree, Barn, and Cliff—can be seen feeding along the road. Raptors frequent the area year-round, including resident Bald Eagles.

When the river is low, especially in summer and fall, the banks may attract migrating shorebirds, including Spotted, Solitary, and Least Sandpipers.

Newberry Road

Return along Vibert Road to Main Street, then turn left and drive 0.4 miles north to Newberry Road. Park along Main Street before the intersection, making sure not to obstruct driveways, bus stops, or mailboxes. The trail into the marsh is opposite Newberry Road, on the west side of Main Street, and looks like an old dirt road to the right of a house. (Look for small Hartford Audubon Nature Reserve signs on the trees.) This trail is often very wet; boots are necessary.

As you enter the rutted dirt trail, check the first line of trees, at the northwest edge of the yard, for migrants; this area can be especially good for warblers in spring and fall.

The first 50 yards of trail traverses shrubby wet areas that also attract migrants in spring, as well as Rusty Blackbirds from fall through spring.

The shrubs then give way to a marsh on the left, home to resident Swamp Sparrows; tread carefully to avoid flushing birds—you are approaching open water on the right. In spring and fall, the lily-covered beaver ponds can harbor large numbers of dabbling ducks. Wood Duck and Ring-necked Duck are often plentiful, joined by varying numbers of Northern Pintail, Green-winged Teal, Gadwall, American Wigeon, American Black Duck, Mallard, Hooded Merganser, the occasional Common Merganser, and often a pair of Mute Swans. This is a reliable place to find Blue-winged Teal and Northern Shoveler, both uncommon.

The marshes of Station 43 attract rare waterbirds, including migrants such as Common Gallinule (shown).

These pools are well known for their breeding Least Bittern, especially in the reeds southwest of the trail, along with Green Heron, Virginia Rail, Belted Kingfisher, Marsh Wren, and the occasional Sora. King Rail and American Bittern are found during migration and may infrequently stay to breed. American Coot and Common Gallinule occur as migrants, although gallinule is rare. Migrant Pied-billed Grebe patrol the quiet lily-shrouded backwaters, while Sandhill Crane (very rare) has visited.

Wild Turkeys are common and may be seen on the trail or roosting in the trees by the marsh. Great Blue Herons visit year-round, and Great Egrets occasionally in summer. During spring and fall, a variety of sandpipers—including Spotted, Solitary, and Least Sandpipers—as well as Wilson's Snipe and Greater and Lesser Yellowlegs, capitalize on the abundant food and shelter here. American Woodcock breed in the area; their nasal "peents" and chirping wing-whir may be heard from dusk to dawn. The landbirds here are those typical of wet marsh-edge habitat (see Vibert Road section).

The trail is usually flooded and impassable beyond these pools. If not flooded, you can continue through shrubby forest to the edge of farm fields where Bobolink has nested and a variety of sparrows visit, especially in fall.

Newberry Road to Strong Road

Reset your odometer to zero at the intersection of Newberry Road and Main Street, then continue north on Main Street. The old chimneys of this historic neighborhood attract nesting Chimney Swifts from mid-April to mid-October. Common Nighthawks also frequent this area, from mid-May to mid-June, then again from mid-August to mid-September.

At 0.9 miles on your odometer, pull off by the small bridge, overlooking a farm on the right. Northern Rough-winged Swallows nest in the embankment here.

Continue to 1.2 miles on your odometer and turn left onto Strong Road.

Strong Road

Strong Road is usually bumpy but passable, except after rains or winter storms when four-wheel drive may be necessary. **Note: Reset your odometer to zero here**.

The trees near the intersection attract woodpeckers, including Hairy Woodpecker. The road descends gradually into a fertile floodplain. At the bottom of the hill, a shallow pool on the right, near the field's edge, attracts many Wilson's Snipe in March and April.

At 0.2 miles on your odometer, the small pools on both sides of the road are reliable breeding sites for Sora in most (wet) years and may harbor Great Blue Heron year-round. The plowed fields are magnets for flocks of American Pipit, fall through spring, but especially in April and October. **Note:** This is private land; please do not trespass into these fields. Farmers have been tolerant of birders; we wish to keep it that way. Stay on the road!

At 0.3 miles, the weedy fields north of the road have attracted Sedge Wren (rare breeder) in late spring and early summer.

At 0.5 miles, look near the barns for Horned Lark and Snow Bunting in winter. In fall, the vegetable fields attract flocks of sparrows, including Grasshopper Sparrow (rare). This valley also is a magnet for migrating and wintering raptors.

Return to Main Street and turn left. Drive north for 1 mile, then turn left onto Ferry Lane.

Ferry Lane

Reset your odometer to zero here, then continue west on Ferry Lane.

At 0.4 miles on your odometer, the hedgerows are great for sparrows during migration, including the occasional Vesper or Savannah Sparrow. Eastern Bluebirds breed in nest boxes here.

At 0.5 miles, stop near the gates and scan the trees to the north across the field. A Bald Eagle nest is often visible from the road (it's a good distance north and may appear below the treetops). Watch for American Kestrels on the wires; a box on one of the telephone poles near the barns is usually active.

Both vegetables and sod are farmed here; in summer and fall, the sod fields (usually on the right) attract many shorebirds. This is a good place to find Buff-breasted and Pectoral Sandpipers, with a few American Golden-Plover appearing annually. These are mixed in with the many Killdeer, along with Black-bellied and Semipalmated Plovers, Least Sandpiper, and the occasional yellowlegs.

The road ends at 1 mile on your odometer, near a house and the historic site of the Bissell Ferry. There are often American Kestrels along this stretch of road. Bird only from the roadside, and turn around before reaching the end. There is no parking in the private lot at the end, and I recommend avoiding this area.

(32) The Hoppers—Birge Pond Nature Preserve, Bristol

Seasonal rating: Sp *** Su **** F *** W *
Best time to bird: May through October.
Habitats: Grassland, scrubland, forest, pond, stream, and glacial features (kettle holes and eskers).

Bird list for this site:

SPECIALTY BIRDS
Summer – Eastern Bluebird, Brown Thrasher (some years), Prairie Warbler, Grasshopper, Field and Savannah Sparrows, Eastern Towhee, Indigo Bunting, Bobolink
Winter – Typical woodland species

OTHER KEY BIRDS
Resident – Red-tailed Hawk
Summer – Great Crested Flycatcher, Eastern Kingbird, House Wren, Wood Thrush, Warbling Vireo, Yellow Warbler, Common Yellowthroat, Chipping Sparrow

MIGRANTS
Eastern Meadowlark

Location: 400 Perkins Street, Bristol.
Restrooms: Dunkin' Donuts, Bristol.

The Birding

This park rests within a recessional moraine created during the melting of the Laurentide Ice Sheet more than 12,000 years ago. Although a majority of the preserve is forested, most birders visit solely for the chance to see nesting grassland specialists in Robert's Field, the roughly 40-acre grassland at the park's north end. Robert's Field is nestled in a glacial formation called a kettle hole, known locally as a "hopper." This relatively small grassland is perhaps Connecticut's most accessible site for viewing breeding Grasshopper Sparrows, which usually arrive in early May and are relatively conspicuous through July, often singing throughout the day and night. Other breeding species include Field and Savannah Sparrows, Bobolink, Prairie Warbler, and Indigo Bunting. **Note:** Breeding Grasshopper Sparrows are endangered in Connecticut; playback is not allowed.

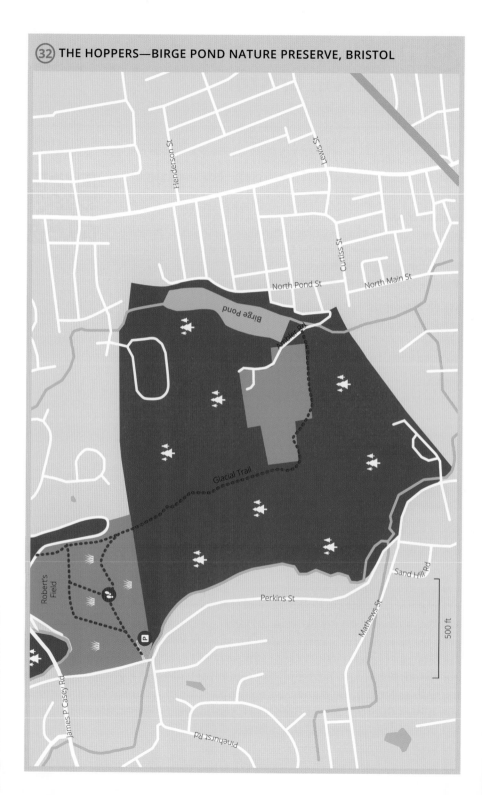

Henderson St

Lewis St

Curtiss St

North Pond St

North Main St

Birge Pond

Amblene

Glacial Trail

Robert's Field

Perkins St

Mathews St

Sand Hill Rd

James P Casey Rd

Pinehurst Rd

P

500 ft

As the season progresses, Grasshopper Sparrows sing consistently only in the early morning. Along with Field, Savannah, Song, and Chipping Sparrows, they may linger into October, when migrating White-throated, Swamp, and other sparrows frequent this site. Barn Swallows hunt the grassland spring through fall, joined occasionally by other swallows. Eastern Meadowlark has occurred during fall migration.

The forest to the south (along the Glacial Trail) is home to typical edge and forest nesters, including Baltimore Oriole, Great Crested Flycatcher, Warbling and Red-eyed Vireos, Tufted Titmouse, Wood Thrush, and Veery. Watch the thickets for Brown Thrasher and Eastern Towhee, which nest most years. During spring and fall, expect migrant warblers such as Ovenbird and Black-and-White Warbler, along with thrushes, kinglets, flycatchers, and vireos.

This is one of the best sites to see Grasshopper Sparrows in Connecticut.
Photograph courtesy Mark S. Szantyr

How to Bird This Site

The main path from the parking lot traverses the open swale where the grassland species nest. Two side trails angle to the left, joining a trail that parallels the main one. Both the main trail and its parallel cousin end in T-intersections. Turn right to head south on the Glacial Trail, which leads 1.2 miles along a glacial ridge or esker to Lookout Point, Ambler Road, and Birge Pond. A *minimum of 1 hour* is recommended to explore the grassland, but allow at least 2 hours if you wish to hike into the forest.

There is a paved handicapped-accessible trail near Birge Pond, off Beech Street. A yellow-blazed trail encircles the pond and includes a boardwalk through a marsh. The red-blazed Indian Trail is across the bridge spanning the spillway; it leads to the blue-blazed Old Colonial Road that connects to the Glacial Trail.

(33) Rocky Hill

- Rocky Hill–Glastonbury Ferry Parking Lot
- Rocky Hill Meadows

■ Rocky Hill–Glastonbury Ferry Parking Lot

Seasonal rating: Sp *** Su *** F *** W **
Best time to bird: The peak times for most shorebirds are mid-March to June, and August to mid-September. Mid-September to mid-October is best for most hawks and landbirds. Winter can be hit-or-miss.
Habitats: Vegetable and sod-farm fields (both fallow and active) within the Connecticut River floodplain, mature riparian forest, early successional forest, wet and dry meadows, small freshwater marshes, and Connecticut River.

Bird list for this site:

SPECIALTY BIRDS
Resident – Bald Eagle, Belted Kingfisher
Summer – Wood Duck, Green Heron, Killdeer, American Woodcock, American Kestrel (sporadic nester), Willow Flycatcher, Bank Swallow, Brown Thrasher, Warbling Vireo, Eastern Towhee, Savannah Sparrow, Orchard Oriole
Winter – Common Merganser, Rough-legged Hawk (invasion years), Horned Lark, Snow Bunting (uncommon), Lapland Longspur (uncommon)

OTHER KEY BIRDS
Resident – Red-shouldered and Red-tailed Hawks, Eastern Screech-Owl, Great Horned and Barred Owls, Black Vulture (uncommon), Turkey Vulture, Ring-billed Gull (nonbreeder), Mourning Dove; Pileated, Red-bellied, Downy, and Hairy Woodpeckers; Northern Flicker, Fish Crow, Tufted Titmouse, Carolina Wren, American Robin, Northern Mockingbird, Cedar Waxwing, Northern Cardinal, Song and Swamp Sparrows, Red-winged Blackbird, Common Grackle, American Goldfinch, House Finch
Summer – Double-crested Cormorant, Osprey, Eastern Phoebe, Great Crested Flycatcher, Eastern Kingbird; Tree, Northern Rough-winged, and Barn Swallows; House Wren, Gray Catbird, Veery, Wood Thrush, Yellow-throated Vireo, American Redstart, Blue-winged Warbler, Rose-breasted Grosbeak, Chipping Sparrow, Baltimore Oriole
Winter – Northern Harrier, Cooper's Hawk, Merlin, Peregrine Falcon (occasional); sparrows, especially Song, White-throated, American Tree, and Savannah Sparrows; Dark-eyed Junco

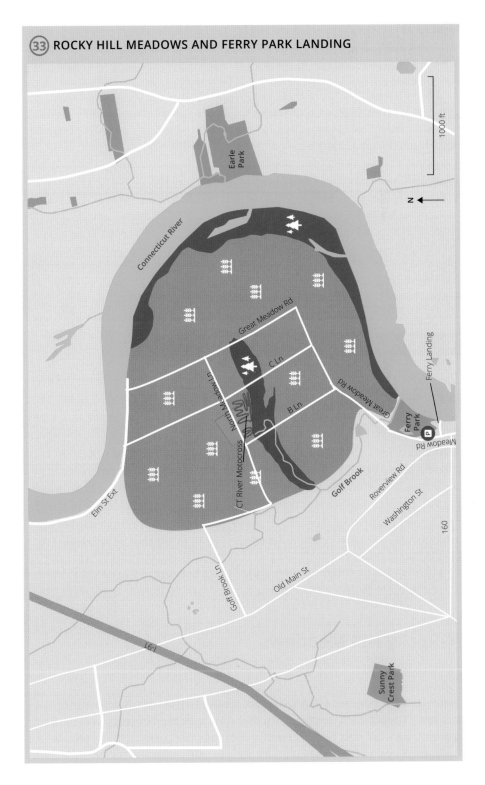

MIGRANTS

Shorebirds, including Upland, Buff-breasted, and Baird's Sandpipers and American Golden-Plover; Short-eared Owl (some years), dabbling and diving ducks, Great and Snowy Egrets (both uncommon), hawks and falcons, American Coot; *Empidonax* flycatchers (August and September), including Acadian, Alder, and Yellow-bellied Flycatchers; Brown Creeper, both kinglet species, all the thrushes; warblers, including Yellow-breasted Chat; Swamp, Song, White-throated, American Tree, White-crowned, Vesper, and Lincoln's Sparrows; winter finches, Rusty Blackbird

Location: Connecticut Route 160 (Meadow Road), Rocky Hill.

➲ **Directions:** Take Exit 24 from I-91 to Connecticut Route 99S (Rocky Hill). At the end of the ramp, turn left (south) onto Route 99 and proceed 1.3 miles. Turn left onto Elm Street (Connecticut Route 160E), then bear right at the fork, following the signs for the Rocky Hill–Glastonbury Ferry. Continue 0.4 miles, then turn left at the stop sign onto Meadow Rd. In 0.2 miles, you will come to another stop sign; the ferry terminal is on the right.

Restrooms: In season, there are public restrooms at the ferry terminal.

The Birding

The Rocky Hill–Glastonbury Ferry is the oldest continually operated ferry in the country; for birders, the terminal's parking lot offers a convenient vantage point for viewing the Connecticut River, both upstream and downstream. This section of river is used extensively by a variety of dabbling and diving ducks fall through spring. In winter, large numbers of Common Mergansers move up and down the river each day, especially at dawn and dusk. Bufflehead and Common Goldeneye are fairly common, while a little searching will usually turn up Hooded Merganser, Ring-necked Duck, and Greater and Lesser Scaup. Occasionally a Wood Duck will remain into winter. Both loon species also are possible in winter, though neither is common. As a general rule, Great Cormorants are seen in winter and Double-crested Cormorants in summer, but a few Double-crested may stay year-round.

■ Rocky Hill Meadows

➲ **Directions:** From the Rocky Hill–Glastonbury Ferry parking lot, turn right and continue north on Meadow Road. The road surface turns to dirt as you enter the meadows. **Note:** Due to vandalism, the meadows have been closed to vehicles from spring through fall, until further notice, and perhaps permanently. Foot and bike traffic are allowed. Park at the Ferry Landing. Currently, vehicles may still enter from

Goff Brook Lane and go partway to the motocross track on North Meadow Lane. This provides the closest access to some of the fields where Buff-breasted Sandpiper occurs. All the roads may open to traffic after the first frost each year.

Restroom: Seasonal portable toilets are available in the ferry landing parking lot.

Hazards: The area is used by hunters in season.

The Birding

The Rocky Hill Meadows are located in a broad fertile floodplain tucked within a bend of the Connecticut River. The rich alluvial soils have been put to the plow since the mid-seventeenth century. Riparian forest lines the river, with patches of trees filling the spaces between numerous agricultural fields. The town of Rocky Hill owns the meadows, but much of the land is leased to private farming interests that grow sod and vegetables.

The sod fields attract migrating shorebirds, including hundreds of Killdeer annually.

To many Connecticut birders, the Rocky Hill Meadows are known for resident Bald Eagles and migrant shorebirds, especially Upland and Buff-breasted Sandpipers in late summer. Aside from a handful of locals, few birders are aware of the variety of species that visit this area. It is a superb site for migrating sparrows spring and fall, and for wintering Horned Lark, Snow Bunting, and Lapland Longspur. It also attracts fair numbers of migrating hawks, especially in fall, and is a fairly reliable wintering site for Rough-legged Hawk. In summer, the area supports some uncommon nesting species, including Bobolink, Savannah Sparrow, and Bank Swallow.

Each year, the farm fields and rain pools host a few migrating Buff-breasted and Baird's Sandpipers along with American Golden-Plover; numbers generally peak from the last week in August into the third week of September. The first week of September can be very good for Buff-breasted Sandpiper, with the possibility of seeing several in a day. Even on the best days, however, expect numbers of each species to remain in the single digits. Only a very few Upland Sandpipers are found most years, but the last week in July through the second week of August is optimal; this is also the time to find hundreds of Least Sandpipers. Killdeer, which may number in the hundreds, peak from the last week in August to the third week of September. Individual White-rumped Sandpipers have occurred on several occasions in mid-August. Small numbers of other shorebirds occur annually, including Lesser and Greater Yellowlegs, Short-billed Dowitcher, Spotted Sandpiper, and Semipalmated Plover, with an occasional Black-bellied Plover or Semipalmated Sandpiper. Other possibilities include Wilson's Snipe, American Woodcock, and Solitary Sandpiper.

Eastern Bluebirds breed in tree cavities throughout the meadows and are noticeably common during fall migration, from late October to mid-November. Migrating Eastern Meadowlarks also visit the weedy fields at this time. Young Eastern Meadowlarks have been seen in summer, suggesting that at least some nesting occurs. October and April are good months to look for American Pipit in the open fields; in fall, daily pipit totals may exceed a hundred.

Barn, Tree, and Bank Swallows are a common sight over the farm fields in summer; these are joined occasionally by Northern Rough-winged and Cliff Swallows during migration. Bank Swallows, very local breeders in Connecticut, excavate nest holes in the riverbanks here, as do Belted Kingfishers.

During migration, especially in autumn, check the fallow fields, hedgerows, and road edges for sparrows and other migrants. Song, White-throated, Swamp, Savannah, and Chipping Sparrows lead the parade, with Dark-eyed Junco and American Tree Sparrow arriving in late fall. Be on the lookout for less common species such as White-crowned, Lincoln's, and Vesper Sparrows, especially in April or May and October or November. Weedy edges have repeatedly attracted rarities such as Dickcissel and Blue Grosbeak.

The rich moist woodlots are home to typical riparian breeding species, including Eastern Kingbird, Great Crested Flycatcher, Wood Thrush, Veery, Warbling and Red-eyed Vireos, Yellow Warbler, American Redstart, and Baltimore Oriole.

Wood Duck, Green Heron, Common Yellowthroat, and Red-winged Blackbird nest in the wetter areas. The location of these wet areas—some of which are concealed within woodlots—varies with the amount of rainfall and flooding. There are a few in the woods between C-Lane and Great Meadows Road; you could also try the far north end of the property on the east side of 2nd Lane.

How to Bird This Site

Crop plantings in the meadows change every year, making it difficult to predict the precise locations of particular species. The most efficient way to find shorebird flocks in summer, as well as Horned Lark and Snow Bunting in winter, is to bike, walk, or drive (when possible) the several miles of roads that skirt the fields, making periodic stops to scan. Look for rain pools and examine areas where sod is being harvested in late August or early September; these can attract shorebirds at any time of day. Scan hedgerows and fallow fields for sparrows, bobolinks, and meadowlarks, and check wooded edges for landbirds. **Note:** Although the roads are public, the fields should be treated as private property. Avoid blocking access, and yield to farmers and their machinery. The following instructions describe one possible route.

Continue north on Meadow Road from the Rocky Hill–Glastonbury Ferry parking lot until you reach the gate for Rocky Hill Meadows. **Note: Set your odometer to zero here**. Subsequent directions are given in tenths of a mile. Although road names appear on the map in this chapter, there are no road signs at the site.

Meadow Road becomes Great Meadow Road. The forested first 0.2 miles can be good for migrant songbirds in spring and fall and riparian breeding species in summer.

At 0.3 miles on your odometer, you will pass B Lane on your left. (B Lane is closed.) After entering the fields, the road bends 90 degrees to the left, then quickly intersects with C Lane (*0.6 miles* on your odometer). Turn right to remain on Great Meadow Road, and pull off near the corner.

In summer, the unplowed fields support nesting Bobolink and Savannah Sparrow. As with the shorebirds, their numbers and locations will depend on field usage, but the 0.2-mile stretch of C Lane that heads north from the intersection with Great Meadow Road to a line of trees is often a good place to check for them.

Continue east on Great Meadow Road to a T-intersection *at 0.9 miles* on your odometer. Turn left and drive north, passing small woodlots on the left and a radio-controlled plane site on the right. The forest tracts can be checked for landbirds; when flooded, these may harbor Wood Duck, Green Heron, and other water-loving birds.

At 1.5 miles on your odometer, Great Meadow Road intersects with North Meadow Lane on the left. From here, you have two options. You can either continue north to the Connecticut River or turn left and follow North Meadow Lane west for about 2 miles, eventually exiting from Goff Brook Lane onto Old Main Street. The last 0.8 miles of this route passes through wooded areas that can be good for landbirds.

If you continue north, you will reach the river in 0.2 miles. A pair of Bald Eagles nests along this stretch, and it's possible to see eagles here year-round. Many Bald Eagles concentrate along the lower Connecticut River in winter. Occasionally, a Golden Eagle or two overwinters, so scrutinize all dark-headed eagles carefully. The area also supports a variety of other raptors. It's not unusual to find a Merlin or Cooper's Hawk hunting the area, and occasionally a Peregrine Falcon will put in an appearance. American Kestrels stage here during fall migration. Red-tailed and Red-shouldered Hawks are resident, and one or both can usually be found during a visit (Red-shouldered Hawks tend to perch low and can be inconspicuous). Turkey Vultures are frequent visitors year-round but especially in summer, while Black Vultures are becoming more common each year. Short-eared Owls, although uncommon, occur during migration and may stay into the winter on rare occasion.

After scanning the river, you can return to the ferry the way you came, or turn left and explore more of the area. The road (labeled Elm Street Extension and 2nd Lane on the map in this chapter) follows the river for about 1.7 miles and then comes to a T. To the right, a spur of Great Meadow Road enters an extensive forest that extends east for 0.5 miles. The woods hold typical riparian species, including Veery, Warbling Vireo, and American Redstart. The road to the left takes you through field and forest, leaving the meadows in about 0.4 miles.

③④ Wallingford-Meriden Area

- North Farms Reservoir
- Bishop's Pond

■ North Farms Reservoir

Seasonal rating: Sp *** Su ** F *** W ***
Best time to bird: Mid-October to April.
Habitats: Shallow lily-covered reservoir, riparian woodland, thickets, lawns, adjacent farmland; near an urban center.

Bird list for this site:

SPECIALTY BIRDS
Resident – Mute Swan, Bald Eagle
Summer – Double-crested Cormorant, Green and Great Blue Herons, American Coot (some years), Killdeer, Spotted Sandpiper, Belted Kingfisher, Orchard Oriole (most years)
Winter – Geese and ducks, American Coot

OTHER KEY BIRDS
Canada Goose, Mallard, Chimney Swift, Eastern Kingbird, swallows, Warbling Vireo, Cedar Waxwing, blackbirds, Baltimore Oriole

MIGRANTS
Swans, geese, ducks, Osprey, Pied-billed Grebe, Common Nighthawk, Fish Crow

Location: Leigus Road, Wallingford.
Restrooms: Gas stations and fast-food restaurants on Connecticut Route 5.

The Birding

This shallow, lily-cloaked 60-acre reservoir just off I-91 sits between farm fields to the east and an urban center to the west. It is known for hosting American Coot nearly year-round, and it is one of the only sites statewide where they may sometimes be found in summer, though breeding has not been confirmed. The dense plant cover also attracts Pied-billed Grebe in spring and fall. A small colony of Great Blue Herons nests on the larger of two islands at the reservoir's north end; a few often remain into winter. Resident Bald Eagles nest on this island as well. Ospreys are regular visitors, spring

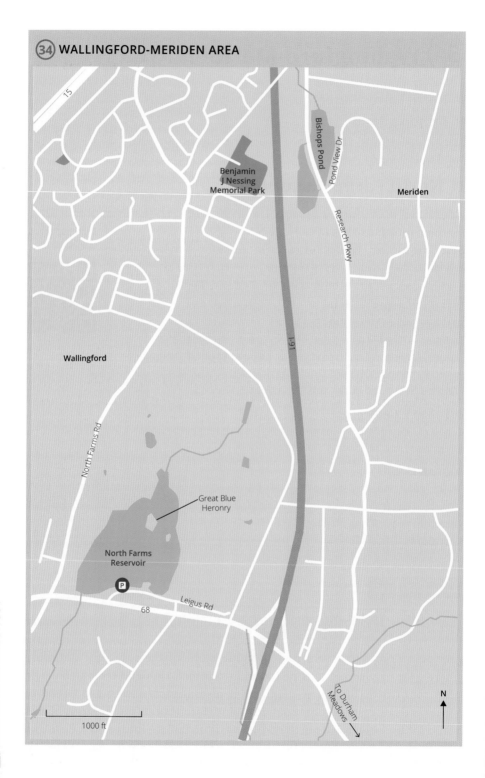

through fall, while Belted Kingfisher is seen often and may breed nearby. Scan the edges of the reservoir for Spotted Sandpiper spring through fall, and check the parking lot for Killdeer.

The numbers of resident Mute Swans and Canada Geese swell with the arrival of fall migrants; by winter, these birds nearly carpet the pond. On rare occasions, Greater White-fronted and Snow Geese, along with Brant (rare inland) and Tundra Swan, have been found among them. (There is also a flock of domestic geese here.) Until the pond freezes, wintering ducks regularly include American Black, Ring-necked, and Ruddy Ducks, especially in January, and Hooded and Common Mergansers, with the occasional visit from Northern Pintail and Northern Shoveler. Wood Duck, Green-winged and Blue-winged Teal (uncommon), and Bufflehead collect here in small numbers in March and April. Rarities have included Redhead and Canvasback in winter, and Black Scoter in fall. Ring-billed, Herring, and Great Black-backed Gulls congregate here fall through spring; these have been joined by Iceland, Black-headed, and Laughing Gulls (rare inland).

Breeding songbirds include the common riparian and edge species, such as Eastern Kingbird, Warbling Vireo, Cedar Waxwing, Northern Mockingbird, Yellow Warbler, American Goldfinch, and Orchard Oriole (most years). Connecticut's four common woodpecker species frequent the pond-side trees. Rusty Blackbirds have occurred with the flocks of other blackbirds in fall.

How to Bird This Site

A scope is recommended here. There is easy viewing from the parking lot and picnic grove on the south shore. A short trail runs along this shore west of the boat ramp; its weedy edges can provide some cover when you are approaching birds and may also harbor songbirds during migration.

■ Bishops Pond

Seasonal rating: Sp *** Su ** F *** W ***
Location: Near 996 Research Parkway, Meriden.
Restrooms: Gas stations and fast-food restaurants on Connecticut Route 5.

Bishops Pond is nestled within an office complex in Meriden. Research Parkway bisects the pond, and either side can be productive for waterfowl. Unfortunately, there is no designated parking area. Birders generally park on the grassy roadside to the west, but great care should be taken as traffic moves quickly here. The nearby office lots are private property; please do not trespass.

All of the species mentioned for North Farms Reservoir may be found here as well; until the pond freezes, this can be a particularly good site for finding less common dabbling ducks. Blue-winged Teal have occurred here in September and October, while Eurasian Wigeon, Ruddy Duck, Northern Shoveler, and Northern Pintail are seen from October into December.

Other fall visitors regularly include Pied-billed Grebe and American Coot, while Common Gallinule (rare) is possible. Raptors pass along the I-91 corridor during migration, particularly in fall. Both Black and Turkey Vultures are seen regularly, while Rough-legged Hawk has been found in winter.

Killdeer breed, and Solitary and Spotted Sandpipers, as well as other shorebirds, visit during migration. This also is a good summer site for Black-crowned Night-Heron, Great Blue Heron, Great Egret, and Belted Kingfisher. The grassy margins have attracted migrant Eastern Meadowlarks, while the thickets surrounding the ponds have yielded Indigo Bunting and White-crowned, Savannah, and American Tree Sparrows among a variety of others. Scan the area for American Pipit in fall.

Nesting species are similar to those at North Farms Reservoir; these include Baltimore Oriole and, in some years, Orchard Oriole.

(35) Durham Meadows, Durham and Middlefield

- Greenbacker Farm Pond
- Skating Pond
- Durham Fair Grounds
- Durham Meadows Wildlife Management Area
- Lyman Orchards Pond and Cornfields

Seasonal rating: Sp *** Su *** F *** W ***
Best time to bird: Year-round.
Habitats: Wetlands, farm ponds, brooks, rivers, riparian forest, upland forest, agricultural fields, and hedgerows.

Bird list for this site:

SPECIALTY BIRDS

Resident – Cooper's and Red-shouldered Hawks, Black Vulture, Eastern Screech-Owl, Great Horned and Barred Owls, Belted Kingfisher, American Kestrel, Common Raven, Eastern Bluebird

Summer – Green and Great Blue Herons, Killdeer, American Woodcock (spring), Virginia Rail, Yellow-billed Cuckoo, Willow Flycatcher, Marsh Wren, Swamp Sparrow, Indigo Bunting, Bobolink, Eastern Meadowlark (some years), Orchard Oriole (uncommon)

Winter – Geese and ducks, Northern Harrier and other raptors, Winter Wren; Field, Fox, and other sparrows; Rusty Blackbird, large blackbird flocks (Lyman Orchards)

OTHER KEY BIRDS

Resident – Red-tailed Hawk, Northern Flicker

Summer – Chimney Swift, Eastern Phoebe, Great Crested Flycatcher, Eastern Kingbird, Warbling Vireo; Northern Rough-winged, Tree, and Barn Swallows; Blue-gray Gnatcatcher, Northern Mockingbird, Gray Catbird, Cedar Waxwing, Common Yellowthroat, Yellow Warbler, Baltimore Oriole

MIGRANTS

Pied-billed Grebe, bitterns (occasional), Sora (uncommon), King Rail (rare), Solitary and Pectoral Sandpipers, Wilson's Snipe, Osprey, Common Nighthawk, Peregrine Falcon, Horned Lark, American Pipit, Palm Warbler and other warblers; sparrows, including American Tree and Savannah Sparrows; Rusty Blackbird (spring and fall)

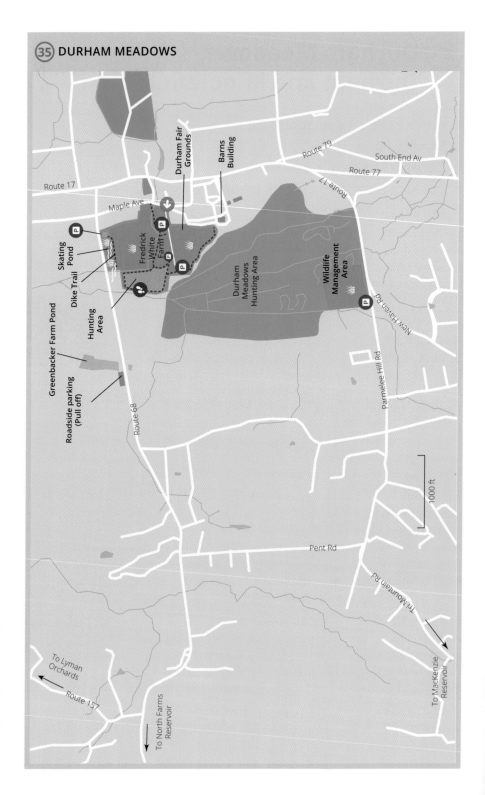

Route 79
South End Av
Route 77
Route 17
Route 17

Durham Fair Grounds

Barns Building

Maple Ave

Fredrick White Farm

Skating Pond

Dike Trail

Hunting Area

Durham Meadows Hunting Area

Wildlife Management Area

New Haven Rd

Greenbacker Farm Pond

Roadside parking (Pull off)

Route 68

Parmelee Hill Rd

Pent Rd

Trl Mountain Rd

1000 ft

To Lyman Orchards

Route 157

To North Farms Reservoir

To MacKenzie Reservoir

Durham Meadows encompasses myriad habitats in a picturesque valley, including vast and varied wetlands, farmland, forests, fields, thickets, and streams. The most accessible sites are in the southern portion of the preserve.

■ Greenbacker Farm Pond

Location: 153-465 Wallingford Road (Connecticut Route 68), Durham.
Parking: There is a pull-off next to the pond, on the north side of Route 68, 0.3 miles east of Clearidge Road. **Note:** Please do not block the gate to the field or trespass beyond the fence.
Restrooms: Fast-food restaurants in Durham.

The pond at Greenbacker Farm attracts geese fall through spring as long as there is open water. Pink-footed, Greater White-fronted, Snow, Barnacle, and Cackling Geese have all been seen here or nearby. A nice selection of ducks also occurs fall through spring, including Ring-necked Duck, both scaup species, Green-winged Teal, Northern Pintail, Northern Shoveler, Ruddy Duck, and Hooded and Common Mergansers. Both Green and Great Blue Herons nest and feed locally, while Great Egret visits the area in summer.

During migration, check the pond edges for shorebirds; the site reliably attracts Killdeer (may nest), Lesser Yellowlegs, Pectoral Sandpiper, Solitary Sandpiper, and Spotted Sandpiper (has nested), with fewer numbers of Wilson's Snipe, Least Sandpiper, and others. The hedgerow thickets are good for sparrows and the occasional Indigo Bunting. Scan the cornfields for Horned Lark, American Pipit, and perhaps a Lapland Longspur or Snow Bunting (rare), fall through spring. The field edges are home to resident Eastern Bluebird. Belted Kingfisher nests locally and hunts here on occasion, as do Eastern Kingbird, Willow Flycatcher, and Northern Rough-winged, Tree, and Barn Swallows.

■ Skating Pond

Address: 36-146 Wallingford Road (Connecticut Route 68), Durham.
Parking: There is ample parking on the pond's east side.
Restrooms: Fast-food restaurants in Durham.

A scope is recommended here. From mid-March to mid-April, this area often teems with migrating Wilson's Snipe; double-digit counts are common. Scan the pond edges next to the parking lot, then walk to the end of the dike along the pond's south side to check the floodplain on both sides of the brook. Snipe are masters of concealment; watch for their movements in the grass as they feed. American Woodcock are occasionally seen here as well; they may be heard displaying at dusk from March to June, but are more common in the nearby Wildlife Management Area. Virginia Rail, Swamp and Song Sparrows, Marsh Wren, and Common Yellowthroat breed in the adjacent wetlands. In years with higher water levels, Sora (uncommon) may stop during migration. From late spring into summer, a pair or two of Yellow-billed Cuckoos usually haunt the swamp edges. Wood Duck and Green Heron breed locally and feed in the area. Sparrows frequent the site from fall though spring. White-crowned (uncommon), Lincoln's (uncommon), and LeConte's Sparrow (rare) have been seen along the dike in October. During migration, rarities such as King Rail, American Bittern, and Common Gallinule have been found in the wetlands across the road (access via trails near the brook).

The many dead trees lining the brook southwest of the dike are used as hunting perches year-round by raptors. Resident Red-tailed and Red-shouldered Hawks, along with American Kestrel, are the most likely species.

In summer, Eastern Bluebird (resident), Tree Swallow, Great Crested Flycatcher, and other cavity nesters capitalize on the abundant holes created by Northern Flicker and Hairy, Downy, and Red-bellied Woodpeckers.

■ Durham Fair Grounds

Location: 73 Maple Avenue, Durham.

The diverse habitats of the Durham Fair Grounds, also known as White's Farm, can be productive at any time of year. With close proximity to open water, plentiful shelter, and an ample food supply, this is an ideal wintering site for sparrows, blackbirds, and other seed- and fruit-eaters, especially in years with an abundant berry crop. It also seems well-suited for attracting scrub-loving rarities such as Yellow-breasted Chat and Connecticut or Orange-crowned Warblers.

This section of the valley holds raptors year-round; scan the sky and any dead snags, especially for resident American Kestrel. Peregrine Falcon,

Merlin, and Northern Harrier frequently overwinter here. Black and Turkey Vultures and Common Raven regularly circle overhead as well; the vultures come to roost in the area before dusk. Great Horned Owl, Eastern Screech-Owl, and Barred Owl breed in the valley and may be heard calling in the evening, especially while courting (from late November to January for Great Horned Owl, and from March to May for Barred Owl and Screech-Owl). Common Nighthawks frequent the valley during migration (mid-May into June and late August into September); they are most often seen at dusk.

A few grassland specialists breed here in summer, including Bobolink, Savannah Sparrow, and sometimes a pair or two of Eastern Meadowlarks. Eastern Meadowlarks also visit during migration, and a few may linger into winter. Ring-necked Pheasant (released for hunting) can sometimes be found as well. Common riparian species, including Willow Flycatcher, Eastern Kingbird, Warbling Vireo, Gray Catbird, Cedar Waxwing, Northern Cardinal, and Baltimore Oriole, are seen here in summer. During years with winter incursions, the valley can be a good place to find Rough-legged Hawk and Northern Shrike.

There are three small parking areas at the foot of the entrance road. On the north side of the first two parking areas, to the right of the entrance road, a trail follows Allyn Brook north toward the Skating Pond on Route 68. The brook typically remains open well into winter, and the shrubs that line the banks provide food for a variety of sparrows. The area is particularly good for Fox, Field, American Tree, and Savannah Sparrows, fall through spring. Swamp and Song Sparrows are resident nesters, and Chipping Sparrow breeds here in summer. The dead trees attract woodpeckers. Look for Yellow-bellied Sapsucker to occur fall through spring.

Another trail leads west from the third parking area to the trees along the Coginchaug River and the Durham Meadows Hunting Area beyond, before turning north along the river. Two other parallel trails head north, on either side of a line of trees, to join the trail along Allyn Brook. The alder and multiflora rose thickets here hold the same array of birds mentioned in the previous paragraph.

Note: The Durham Fair Grounds are very popular with dog owners, and dogs are often allowed to roam free. The Durham Meadows Hunting Area, which extends to the west and south, should be avoided during hunting season; blaze-orange clothing is recommended when birding nearby.

■ Durham Meadows Wildlife Management Area

Location: 77 Parmelee Hill Road, Durham.
Restrooms: Fast-food restaurants in Durham.

This wildlife management area, just off Connecticut Route 17S, includes open-field habitat managed for deer and game birds by the Connecticut Department of Energy and Environmental Protection. American Woodcock display here at dusk and dawn from late February into June, but especially in March. Wilson's Snipe frequently visit during migration, and both species may be seen together. The birdlife here is similar to that of the valley's other sites. In spring and summer, Virginia Rail can be heard calling from the east or northeast. Migrating Common Nighthawks are seen hunting over the area in spring and late summer through early autumn, and Bobolinks and Eastern Meadowlarks feed here in fall. Northern Shrike (rare) has been found in winter. Check the forest edges for landbird migrants. Black and Turkey Vultures roost nearby and pass through at dusk.

■ Lyman Orchards Pond and Cornfields

Location: S Street Extension, near the junction of Connecticut Routes 147 and 157, Middlefield.
Restrooms: Lyman Orchards' farm market, and fast-food restaurants in Durham.

The pond beside the Lyman Orchards' farm market attracts waterfowl, including some unusual geese, from fall through spring. **Note:** Lyman's cider and doughnuts are delicious. Also, try the local macoun apples.

The corn-maze fields at the intersection of Routes 147 and 157 often hold large mixed flocks of migrating or wintering Common Grackles and Red-winged Blackbirds, as do other cornfields in the area. Yellow-headed Blackbird (rare) and Rusty Blackbird (uncommon) can be found with them, but careful scrutiny is required. Other field-loving species, including American Pipit, Horned Lark, and Eastern Bluebird, are also possible. In winter, scan the hedgerows for sparrows and watch for Rough-legged Hawk and other raptors, as well as Northern Shrike (rare). The abundance of both natural and cultivated fruit in the surrounding orchards often results in good numbers of wintering frugivores such as robins and waxwings, with good potential for rarer species to occur.

(36) MacKenzie Reservoir Area, Wallingford

- MacKenzie Reservoir
- Whirlwind Hill Road
- Pistapaug Pond
- Vietnam Veterans Memorial Park

■ MacKenzie Reservoir, Whirlwind Hill Road, and Pistapaug Pond

Seasonal rating: Sp *** Su *** F **** W ****
Best time to bird: October to April.
Habitats: Open country, farmland, farm ponds, wet meadows, large reservoirs, riparian and upland forest, hedgerows, and rural residential neighborhoods.

Bird list for this site:

SPECIALTY BIRDS
Resident – Red-shouldered Hawk, Black Vulture, Belted Kingfisher, American Kestrel, Common Raven, Eastern Bluebird
Summer – Osprey, Killdeer, American Woodcock (spring), Northern Rough-winged Swallow, Savannah Sparrow, Indigo Bunting, Bobolink
Winter – Rare geese, ducks, Bald Eagle, American Pipit, Horned Lark, Rusty Blackbird (uncommon)

OTHER KEY BIRDS
Summer – Eastern Wood-Pewee, Eastern Phoebe, Eastern Kingbird, Warbling Vireo, Blue-gray Gnatcatcher, Veery, Wood Thrush, Cedar Waxwing, Rose-breasted Grosbeak, Baltimore Oriole
Winter – Waterfowl and raptors

MIGRANTS
Wilson's Snipe, Solitary and Spotted Sandpipers, Eastern Meadowlark (uncommon), Rusty Blackbird (uncommon)

Locations: MacKenzie Reservoir, 2013 East Center Street, Wallingford; Pistapaug Pond, 1678 Whirlwind Hill Road, Wallingford.
Restrooms: Seasonal portable toilets at Vietnam Veterans Memorial Park near the ball fields.

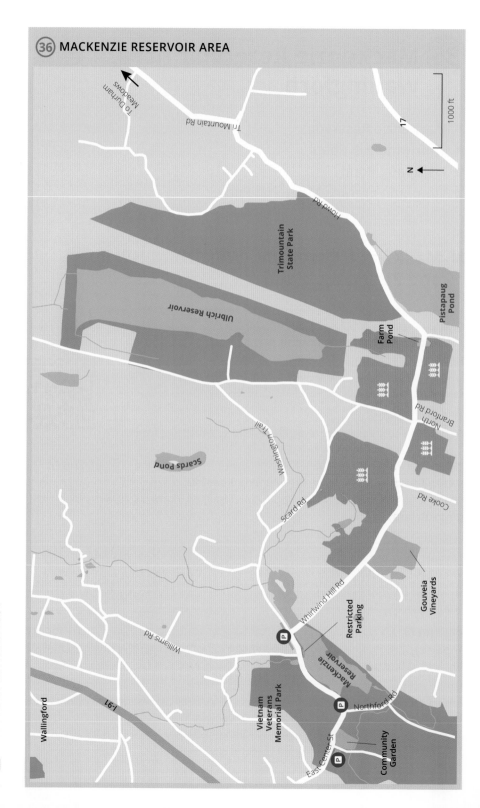

To Durham Meadows

Tri Mountain Rd

17

1000 ft

N

Howd Rd

Trimountain State Park

Ulbrich Reservoir

Pistapaug Pond

Farm Pond

North Branford Rd

Washington Trail

Scards Pond

Scard Rd

Cooke Rd

Whirlwind Hill Rd

Restricted Parking

Gouveia Vineyards

Williams Rd

Wallingford

I-91

Mackenzie Reservoir

Vietnam Veterans Memorial Park

Northford Rd

East Center St

Community Garden

The Birding

Whirlwind Hill Road stretches for 2 miles from Pistapaug Pond (south section) northwest and over a hill to MacKenzie Reservoir. The many farm fields along the road—especially those nearest the reservoir and pond—draw geese from fall through spring. Small numbers of Cackling and Greater White-fronted Geese are seen annually. Barnacle and Snow Geese occur occasionally, and the extremely rare Greylag Goose has occurred. The geese generally rest and bathe in MacKenzie Reservoir. A nice variety of ducks also visits MacKenzie and, to a lesser extent, Pistapaug; regulars include Wood and American Black Ducks, Hooded and Common Mergansers, Green-winged Teal, the occasional Lesser or Greater Scaup, and Ring-necked and Ruddy Ducks. Bald Eagles are often in the area, especially in winter and spring. Osprey fish the reservoirs in summer. Geese also regularly visit the pond and fields at Gouveia Vineyards, on the hill. The hilltop itself provides a good vantage for spying out soaring raptors. Any of the state's familiar raptors are possible, including Northern Harrier and Rough-legged Hawk (uncommon), late fall into winter. American Kestrel is a consistent feature in the area and nests locally in some years.

Fall through spring, check plowed fields for American Pipit, Horned Lark, and Lapland Longspur (rare). Eastern Meadowlark and other open-country birds are possible, especially in grassy fields. Eastern Bluebird is resident. In summer, look for Indigo Bunting, Bobolink (uncommon), and resident Savannah Sparrow, which usually breeds in small numbers at the vineyard. Both cuckoo species have been heard along the field edges. Swallows and swifts course over the fields and reservoirs spring through fall. The hillsides opposite MacKenzie and Pistapaug host the standard array of woodland and edge species, including Eastern Wood-Pewee, Blue-gray Gnatcatcher, Veery, and Wood Thrush. Eastern Phoebe, Cedar Waxwing, Warbling Vireo, House Finch, and Baltimore Oriole nest around the reservoirs.

At the eastern end of Whirlwind Hill Road, near Pistapaug Pond, the farm ponds and wet areas on both sides of the road are attractive to ducks, Killdeer (breed), Wilson's Snipe, and American Woodcock, which display locally in spring. Pectoral Sandpiper has been found in autumn. The roadside hedgerows are always worth checking for sparrows. Most of the common migrants can be found, including American Tree Sparrow, along with a few of the less common White-crowned and Fox Sparrows (fall and winter); goodies like Vesper Sparrow (uncommon) also have occurred.

How to Bird This Site

Pistapaug Pond can be viewed from pull-offs on Whirlwind Hill Road. To view MacKenzie Reservoir, there are pull-offs on East Center Street, opposite Whirlwind Hill Road, at the midway point of the reservoir (handicapped access), and at the west end. A scope is recommended.

Because traffic can be heavy, set up your scope well off the road. Be especially careful while birding from the roadside along Whirlwind Hill Road. Care should be taken to avoid soft shoulders and lawns. **Note:** Please respect private property and avoid impeding farm access.

Gouveia Vineyards is open to the public from 11:00 a.m. to 8:00 p.m. most days, with more restricted hours in winter. It is a nice place to bring lunch and take a wine tour. However, remember to bird only from the roadside and parking area and not to stray into the vineyards themselves. The pond here usually freezes by January.

Rare geese, such as this Greylag Goose—a first in the Lower 48—have been found here in winter.

Photograph courtesy Mark S. Szantyr

Vietnam Veterans Memorial Park

Seasonal rating: Sp *** Su ** F **** W **
Location: 1058 East Center Street, Wallingford.
Restrooms: Seasonal portable toilets near the ball fields.

The park is just west of MacKenzie Reservoir on East Center Street. In fall, the community gardens and adjacent brushy areas east of the first parking lot attract sparrows and other fruit- and seed-eaters, including less common species such as Blue Grosbeak, Clay-colored Sparrow, and Orange-crowned Warbler. Because access to the gardens themselves is restricted to plot-holders, please bird from the perimeter. The park is large with lots of habitat worth checking. Eastern Bluebird is resident, and a variety of raptors is often seen. **Note:** The park is not plowed and may be closed after snowstorms.

(37) Winter Eagle and Raptor Tour, Lower Connecticut River

- Eagle Landing State Park
- Parkers Point Boat Launch
- Chester Ferry Dock
- Deep River Depot
- Riverview Cemetery
- Essex Town Dock

Seasonal rating: Sp **/*** Su * F ** W ****
Best time to bird: Mid-January to mid-March
Habitats: Forested ridgelines, riparian woodlands, wet and dry meadows, islands, bays, inlets, and marshes, interspersed with urban areas.

Bird list for this site:

SPECIALTY BIRDS

Resident – Mute Swan, American Black Duck, Black Vulture (uncommon), Bald Eagle (numbers increase dramatically in winter), Sharp-shinned and Cooper's Hawks, Northern Goshawk (rare), Red-shouldered Hawk, Peregrine Falcon, Belted Kingfisher, Pileated Woodpecker, Common Raven (uncommon), Fish Crow
Summer – Green Heron, Osprey, Broad-winged Hawk, Bank Swallow
Winter – Canvasback (uncommon), Ring-necked Duck, Lesser Scaup, Common Merganser, Great Cormorant, Northern Harrier, Rough-legged Hawk (most years), Merlin, American Coot, Yellow-bellied Sapsucker, Red-breasted Nuthatch (some years), American Tree and Fox Sparrows, Purple Finch, winter finches

OTHER KEY BIRDS

Resident – Canada Goose, Wood Duck (few in winter), Mallard, Wild Turkey, Turkey Vulture, Red-tailed Hawk; Ring-billed, Herring, and Great Black-backed Gulls; Red-bellied, Downy, and Hairy Woodpeckers; Northern Flicker
Summer – Double-crested Cormorant
Winter – Greater Scaup, Bufflehead, Common Goldeneye, Hooded Merganser, Red-breasted Merganser (uncommon), Pied-billed Grebe, Great Blue Heron, Golden-crowned Kinglet, Eastern Bluebird, Hermit Thrush (uncommon), Northern Mockingbird, Gray Catbird (uncommon)

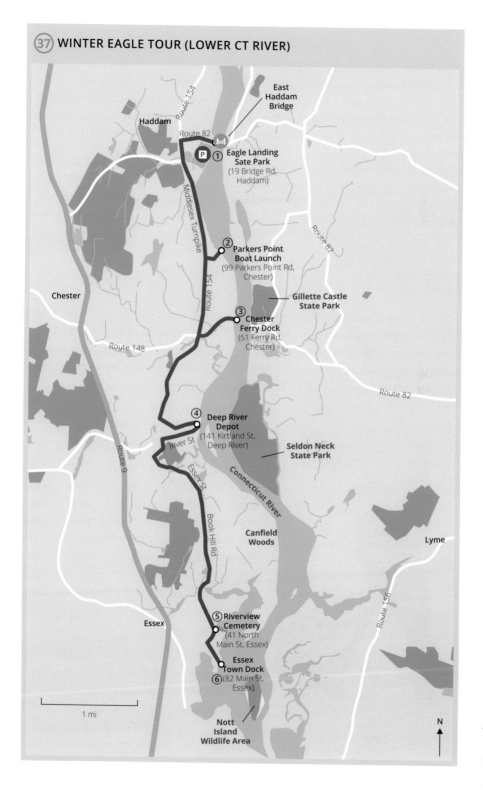

37 WINTER EAGLE TOUR (LOWER CT RIVER)

East Haddam Bridge

Haddam

Route 154

Route 82

P ① Eagle Landing Sate Park
(19 Bridge Rd, Haddam)

Middlesex Turnpike

Route 154

② Parkers Point Boat Launch
(99 Parkers Point Rd, Chester)

Chester

Gillette Castle State Park

③ Chester Ferry Dock
(51 Ferry Rd, Chester)

Route 148

Route 82

④ Deep River Depot
(141 Kirtland St, Deep River)

River St

Route 9

Seldon Neck State Park

Connecticut River

Essex St

Book Hill Rd

Canfield Woods

Lyme

Essex

Route 156

⑤ Riverview Cemetery
(41 North Main St, Essex)

Essex Town Dock
⑥ (82 Main St, Essex)

Nott Island Wildlife Area

1 mi

N

MIGRANTS

Gadwall, American Wigeon, Northern Pintail (uncommon), Green-winged Teal, Ruddy Duck, Wilson's Snipe, American Kestrel, Bonaparte's Gull

Restrooms: In Haddam, Citgo and Haddam Pizza, near the corner of Routes 82 and 154, allow use of their restrooms, although a purchase is expected. There are public restrooms in Essex, as well as restrooms at the gas stations on Route 154 and Dunkin' Donuts near Eagle Landing.

Additional information: Eagle cruises on the *RiverQuest* are offered from mid-January through mid-March. Contact them at 860-662-0577. The Connecticut Audubon Society's EcoTravel Department also offers cruises; to make reservations, call 860-767-0660. The Audubon Shop in Madison, Connecticut, offers guided land-based tours; visit www.theaudubonshop.com.

The Birding

Several pairs of resident Bald Eagles nest along the lower Connecticut River. Migrant eagles begin arriving in fall, but concentrations of eagles aren't seen here until winter. Numbers rise through mid-January and typically peak in mid-February, when upper stretches of the river freeze. At these times, fifty or more eagles can be seen along the lower river in a single day.

More than seventy Bald Eagles have been recorded wintering on the lower Connecticut River.

How to Bird These Sites

The route described in this chapter covers the lower Connecticut River from Eagle Landing State Park, at the East Haddam Bridge, south to Essex. In winter, it is prime territory for viewing Bald Eagle and, occasionally, Golden Eagle. The eagles tend to sit on exposed snags along the river, but are also seen soaring overhead or floating downriver on the ice floes.

This section of river is excellent for other raptors, including Rough-legged and Red-shouldered Hawks, as well as waterbirds such as Great Cormorant and Common Merganser and other ducks. Because the choice viewing areas can often get crowded, the route is designed in the reverse order from standard eagle tours; this should minimize your overlap with other groups touring the river. The route can be easily completed in half a day, but a relaxed pace, with longer stops, could fill an entire day.

■ Eagle Landing State Park

Location: 19 Bridge Road, Haddam.

Eagle Landing State Park in Haddam provides easy access to prime Bald Eagle viewing. (The historic Goodspeed Opera House is visible across the river.) Roosting eagles often sit in the trees just north of the East Haddam Bridge, and on Lord Island, south of the bridge. When there is ice on the river, eagles can be seen riding the floes downriver. This also is a good area to look for Red-shouldered Hawk and Pileated Woodpecker. In winter, Common Merganser, Ring-necked Duck, Common Goldeneye, Bufflehead, and the occasional Hooded Merganser are the regular fare along the river; these mix with the resident American Black Ducks, Mallards, and Canada Geese. Occasionally, Lesser and Greater Scaup, Wood Duck, Green-winged Teal, Northern Pintail, Gadwall, or American Wigeon join the flocks. Black and Turkey Vultures often roost near the landing.

■ Parkers Point Boat Launch

Location: 99 Parkers Point Road, Chester.
➲ **Directions:** Turn left out of Eagle Landing onto Route 82, then drive 0.5 miles to the traffic light. Turn left onto Routes 82/154 (also 9A) and continue on Route 154 south for 1.9 miles, then turn left on Parkers Point Road. Bear left at the fork and proceed to the end of the road, overlooking the river.

The Parkers Point Boat Launch, known locally as the Chester Town Dock, offers views of the south side of Lord Island, an area where eagles often congregate, along with good views of the river. There are often rafts of Common Mergansers, Black Ducks, and Canada Geese upriver (toward the East Haddam Bridge). Check these flocks for Common Goldeneye, Bufflehead, and Ring-necked Duck, along with an occasional Hooded Merganser or two. The marsh edges along the far shore are a favored area for wintering Great Blue Heron. Belted Kingfisher occur sporadically, and there is often a large contingent of Great Cormorants nearby. The trees that line the river and entrance road are worth checking for landbirds, including Golden-crowned Kinglet; American Tree, White-throated, and Song Sparrows; and other songbirds.

■ Chester Ferry Dock

Location: 51 Ferry Road, Chester.
◗ **Directions:** Return to the intersection of Parkers Point Road and Route 154, then turn left. Continue south on Route 154 for 1.2 miles, then turn left onto Route 148 (Ferry Road). Drive to the ferry dock at road's end.

The Chester Ferry, our country's second-oldest ferry, operates from April 1 through November 30. The ferry dock provides excellent views of the river in both directions. On the hill across the river is the historic Gillette Castle, brought from England by William Gillette and reassembled on site. It is now a state park, open from Memorial Day to Labor Day. This is one of the best sections of the river for observing the few Golden Eagles that occur most winters. Both adults and young birds are typically seen, usually as they soar above the far ridgeline. Bald Eagles can be common and frequent both sides of the river. The ridge also is a good place to scan for other raptors, including Red-tailed and Red-shouldered Hawks, Northern Harrier, Cooper's Hawk, Sharp-shinned Hawk, and the occasional American Kestrel. Turkey Vulture is fairly common in winter, while Black Vultures are becoming increasingly evident each year. The river hosts the normal array of ducks, Great Cormorants, the occasional Double-crested Cormorant, a few American Coot, and rarely, a loon.

The alder-lined wetland on Ferry Road's south side, about 50 yards from the dock, usually offers excellent birding. Eastern Bluebird, Northern Flicker, White-breasted Nuthatch, Northern Cardinal, and a variety of sparrows are staple winter visitors. In some years, a few Swamp Sparrows linger in the marsh, joining the more common American Tree, White-crowned, and Song Sparrows; and Dark-eyed Juncos. It also is a good site for woodpeckers (any of the common species are possible) and Carolina Wren. The alder catkins draw in American Goldfinch, House Finch, and sometimes Purple Finch. Check for a lingering Gray Catbird, Common Yellowthroat, or Winter Wren, and watch for the accipiters that hunt the area. It's also a place that turns up rarities such as Northern Shrike or Yellow-breasted Chat. **Note:** During late spring and summer, a visit to Hartman Park, 57 Gungy Road, across the river in Lyme, is often productive and should produce Cerulean Warbler and Acadian Flycatcher.

Deep River Landing (Depot)

Location: 141 Kirtland Street, Deep River.
⮑ **Directions:** From Ferry Road, return to the intersection with Route 154 and turn left. Drive about 1.5 miles south on Route 154, then turn left onto Kirtland Street. Follow Kirtland Street to the parking lot at the end.

In addition to eagles and other raptors, this is a good area for finding ducks, especially Ring-necked Duck, Common and Hooded Mergansers, Common Goldeneye, and an occasional Canvasback or scaup. The flocks of Common Merganser along the river can be quite impressive, sometimes numbering in the dozens.

Riverview Cemetery

Location: Entrance adjacent to 41 North Main Street, Essex.
⮑ **Directions:** Bear left out of the parking lot at Deep River Landing onto River Street. Turn left at the second stop sign onto High Street, then continue to a T-intersection. Turn left onto Essex Street. Follow Essex Street to a four-way stop, then bear left onto River Road toward Essex. Continue 4.8 miles on River Road, which becomes North Main Street. After passing New City Street on the left, you will see two stone pillars that mark the entrance to the cemetery. Go slowly, as the pillars are easy to miss. Turn left into the cemetery, drive to the end, and park near the water. **Note:** This is a private cemetery. Please respect the rules and avoid interfering with funerals or other activities.

This is often the most productive stop on the tour, with eagles of all ages visible along this stretch of the river. For years, a pair of Bald Eagles has nested on Nott Island, to the southeast. The nest may be visible from the knoll to the right of the parking circle. Scan southeast over the treeline and across the river for a large stick nest in a tree. The eagles often reuse the same nest from year to year, but may sometimes build a new one. You may see eagles in the nest in January or especially February, when they are tending eggs. (This is one of the earliest nesting pairs in New England.) The young hatch in April. Closer views of the nest can be had from the Essex Town Dock, but parking at the dock can be difficult after mid-January, when eagle boat tours are running. **Note:** The eagle's nest may also be on the hillside behind the island.

The cove adjacent to the cemetery has repeatedly harbored rare wintering waterfowl, such as Tundra Swan and Barrow's Goldeneye, and often holds an array of other ducks. In addition to the standard species, look for lingering Green-winged Teal, Ruddy Duck, American Wigeon, and Gadwall. Raptors are often conspicuous; this is one of the better areas along the river to see Rough-legged Hawk, Red-shouldered Hawk, and Northern Harrier. The Rough-legged Hawks seem to prefer the marsh north of the cemetery, Nott Island, and the large marshy areas to the south. Peregrine Falcons nest on the I-95 bridge downriver.

Eastern Bluebirds can usually be found in the cemetery, which also supports a variety of landbirds, especially sparrows.

■ Essex Town Dock

Location: 82 Main Street, Essex.
◔ **Directions:** Turn left onto North Main Street from Riverview Cemetery and continue south through Essex Center. At the rotary, head east on Main Street. The dock is at the end of the street.
Parking: There is limited parking at the Connecticut River Museum and along Main Street.

The Bald Eagle nest on Nott Island is often more easily seen from here than from Riverview Cemetery; it's generally on the back left side of the island. Flocks of ducks tend to congregate around the boat docks and often contain something interesting, such as a Wood Duck or Green-winged Teal. American Coot can usually be found here in winter.

(38) Cornfield Point Scenic Viewing Area, Old Saybrook

Seasonal rating: Sp *** Su ** F *** W ****
Best time to bird: October to March, and before and after storms, from late summer through spring.
Habitats: Residential neighborhood, Willard Bay, and Long Island Sound.

SPECIALTY BIRDS
Resident – Double-crested Cormorant (few in winter)
Summer – Wilson's Storm-Petrels (July), American Oystercatcher, Osprey
Winter – Common Eider, Black Scoter, Red-necked Grebe (December–January), alcids, Northern Gannet, Great Cormorant, Black-legged Kittiwake (rare)

OTHER KEY BIRDS
Summer – Great and Snowy Egrets, Osprey

MIGRANTS
Waterbirds, including Surf and White-winged Scoters, Horned Grebe, and loons

Location: 98 Hartlands Drive, Old Saybrook.
Parking: There are only three spaces here, one of which requires a handicapped permit. No street parking is available. Carpooling is recommended.
Restrooms: Downtown Old Saybrook.

The Birding

Cornfield Point juts south into Long Island Sound. The scenic viewing site is on the point's east side, perched at the edge of a residential neighborhood overlooking Willard Bay. It offers unobstructed views to the south toward Plum Island and Orient Point, New York, and to the east toward the mouth of the Connecticut River and distant Fishers Island, New York.

During winter storms, be on the lookout for rare alcids, such as Dovekie.

Most birders visit from late summer through spring, after hurricanes and winter nor'easters, when high winds can drive rare pelagic species close to shore. Hurricanes have produced such rarities as Great, Cory's, and Manx Shearwaters; Leach's and Wilson's Storm-Petrels, Red Phalarope, Dovekie, Black-legged Kittiwake, Royal Tern, and Parasitic Jaeger. Winter rarities have included Common Murre. During storms, almost anything is possible.

Aside from storm-driven birds and the occasional Wilson's Storm-Petrel, summer here is slow. The residents include Osprey, Double-crested Cormorant, and the common gulls, joined later in the season by Laughing Gull. Spring through fall, any of the tern species may occur, with Common and Least Tern most likely, and Forster's Tern generally seen later into fall than the others.

Fall through spring, this is a good site to look for sea ducks, including Common Eider, along with Long-tailed Duck, all three scoter species, both cormorant species, Common and Red-throated Loons, Horned and Red-necked Grebes (uncommon), Northern Gannet, as well as Razorbill (uncommon) and other alcids (rare). If there are gull flocks in the area after a storm, watch for Parasitic Jaegers (which may harass them) and the occasional Bonaparte's Gull. Bald eagles winter in the area, as do small numbers of Purple Sandpiper, Dunlin, Sanderling, and Ruddy Turnstone. Gray and harbor seals also are seen here, especially in winter.

How to Bird This Site

A spotting scope is essential here as the birds can be quite distant. On calm days, the birding can be very pleasant, but there is little protection during storms, especially if winds are from the east. Under some conditions, it may be necessary to bird from your vehicle or to use it as a windbreak. Storm-driven birds may pass close by, providing good (though often brief) views; vigilance is necessary in order not to miss them. Continuous scanning and patience is needed to find birds on the water, especially when they are diving or in heavy surf.

Note: Although the list of storm-driven birds here is impressive, any coastal site offering clear views can be productive following severe weather, and success at any given site varies from storm to storm. For safety's sake, it is better to bird before or after a storm, not during it. Sites that offer shelter from wind and rain are generally preferable, but open shelters should be avoided during lightning storms.

(39) Old Lyme Area

- Ferry Landing State Park
- Great Island Boat Launch

Ferry Landing State Park

Seasonal rating: Sp *** Su *** F **** W ***
Best time to bird: Year-round.
Habitat: freshwater marsh, tidal wetlands, tidal rivers, intertidal mudflats, thickets, coastal forest, boardwalk, lawns, picnic area.

Bird list for this site:

SPECIALTY BIRDS

Resident – Mute Swan, Bald Eagle, Belted Kingfisher, Fish Crow
Summer – Green Heron (uncommon), Snowy and Great Egrets, Black Vulture, Osprey, Willow Flycatcher, Marsh Wren, Warbling Vireo
Winter – American Black Duck, Gadwall, Green-winged Teal, Great Cormorant (uncommon), Rough-legged Hawk (invasion years), Winter Wren, kinglets (some winters), Hermit Thrush, Brown Thrasher (uncommon); American Tree, Field, Fox, White-crowned, and Swamp Sparrows

OTHER KEY BIRDS

Summer – Black-Crowned Night-Heron, Double-crested Cormorant; Rough-winged, Tree, and Barn Swallows; House Wren, Cedar Waxwing, Common Yellowthroat, Yellow Warbler, Chipping Sparrow
Winter – Loons, grebes, Yellow-rumped Warbler, Pine Siskin (invasion years), Purple Finch (some years)

MIGRANTS

Scaup (spring), Bufflehead, Common Goldeneye (spring), mergansers (spring), American Bittern (late fall), Eastern Towhee, Savannah Sparrow and other sparrows, thicket-loving species, Rusty Blackbird (fall; uncommon)

Location: 398 Ferry Road, Old Lyme.
Restrooms: On site (closed in winter).
Additional information: The park is open from sunrise to sunset. The Connecticut DEEP Marine Fisheries office at 333 Ferry Road is open weekdays from 8:30 a.m. to 4:00 p.m. Some areas are wheelchair accessible.

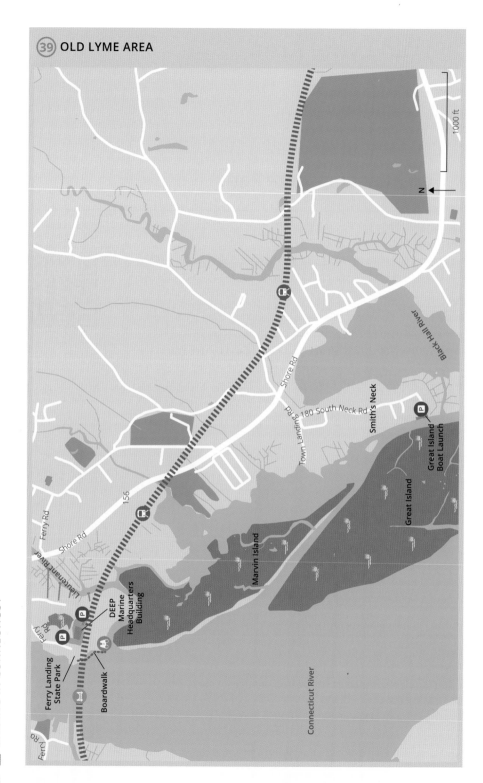

The Birding

Ferry Landing Park is a small coastal preserve only a few minutes from I-95 that allows wonderful views of the lower Connecticut and Lieutenant Rivers and their wildlife-rich marsh complex. It is known locally as a place to find waders in summer and landbird migrants, especially in fall; it often holds thicket-loving species fall through spring.

How to Bird This Site

A 300-yard boardwalk on the park's southwest side leads south along the Connecticut River, passes under a railroad trestle, and ends at a raised platform overlooking the extensive tidal marshes and mudflats at the mouth of the Lieutenant River. Great Island, Saybrook Point, and the two Saybrook lighthouses can be seen to the south. This lovely boardwalk provides opportunities to view a wide variety of marsh- and waterbirds throughout the year. In summer, watch for Clapper Rail, egrets, Green Heron and other herons, Glossy Ibis (uncommon), and shorebirds. American Bittern has been found in fall. Ospreys are abundant in summer, Rough-legged Hawks visit in some winters, and resident Bald Eagles frequent the area year-round. Loons, grebes—including the occasional Red-necked Grebe—and a wide variety of ducks can be seen fall through spring. Great Cormorant occur in winter, and Double-crested Cormorant in summer. Northern Rough-winged, Tree, and Barn Swallows are common spring through fall.

To the east, behind the DEEP building, is a small pond edged by marsh that attracts waders and migrant waterfowl, including Gadwall, American Wigeon, and Green-winged Teal in fall, and Blue-winged Teal in April. The pond is surrounded by forest and thickets that often hold migrant sparrows and thicket-loving species such as Brown Thrasher and Eastern Towhee, especially in autumn. It is also a reliable site to find lingering Common Yellowthroat, Gray Catbird, and Hermit Thrush, and it's the type of place one might find a wintering Yellow-breasted Chat. American Tree, Song, and White-throated Sparrows are common in winter, and Fox Sparrows are regular in small numbers. By wandering the pond and thicket edges, it's usually possible to find a Field or White-crowned Sparrow as well. Swamp Sparrow, Winter Wren, and Yellow-rumped Warblers often overwinter near the pond. In summer, Willow Flycatcher, House Wren, and Carolina Wren may nest in the uplands, while Marsh Wren is fairly common in the saltmarshes (off the boardwalk). Watch for Rusty Blackbirds (uncommon) near the pond in fall. Noteworthy visitors have included the very rare Fork-tailed Flycatcher.

■ Great Island Boat Launch

Seasonal rating: Sp ** Su *** F *** W ***
Location: 98 Town Landing Road, Old Lyme.
Restrooms: Portable toilet on site.

The Birding

The observation platform at the Great Island boat launch looks across to the Great Island marsh. The Great Island area, near the confluence of the Connecticut and Black Hall Rivers, is especially good for finding Osprey, Clapper Rail, waders, shorebirds—including nesting Willet and the occasional Whimbrel (uncommon)—Common and Least Terns, and Saltmarsh and Seaside Sparrows in summer. Spotted Sandpipers are fairly common nesters, while American Oystercatchers and Piping Plovers breed locally. American Bittern (uncommon) occurs in fall. It is also quite reliable for raptors in winter, especially Northern Harrier, Bald Eagle, and Rough-legged Hawk (in invasion years). Search for Short-eared Owl (uncommon) at dusk, especially in fall, and for Snowy Owl in winter. A variety of ducks frequent the area late fall into spring. Migrant landbirds drop into the trees along Town Landing Road, especially in fall, and the adjacent fields are worth checking for Eastern Meadowlark, American Pipit, and possibly Lapland Longspur or Snow Bunting, especially in winter.

How to Bird This Area

A scope is needed here, as Great Island is fairly distant. To check the fields, park by the platform, then walk back up the road.

ⓘ Waterford and New London Area

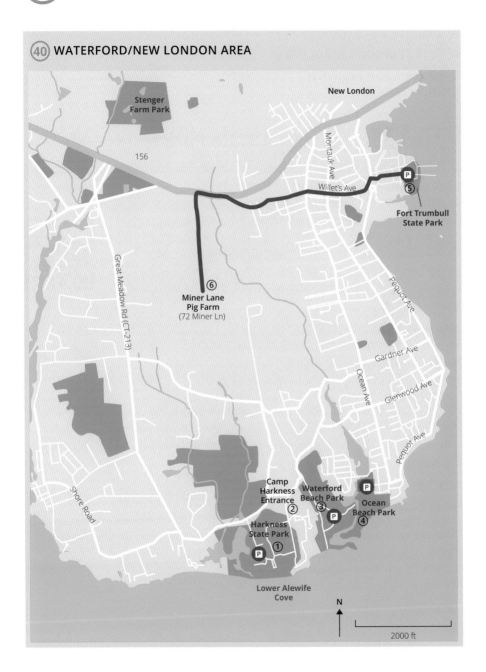

ⓘ WATERFORD/NEW LONDON AREA

New London

Stenger Farm Park

156

Montauk Ave
Willet's Ave

P
⑤
Fort Trumbull
State Park

Great Meadow Rd (CT-213)

Pequot Ave

⑥
Miner Lane
Pig Farm
(72 Miner Ln)

Gardner Ave

Ocean Ave
Glenwood Ave

Pequot Ave

Shore Road

P
Camp
Harkness   Waterford
Entrance   Beach Park
②   ③
P   Ocean
     Beach Park
     ④
Harkness
State Park
P ①

Lower Alewife
Cove

N

2000 ft

40 | Waterford and New London Area

321

- Harkness Memorial State Park
- Camp Harkness
- Waterford Beach Park and Town Beach
- Ocean Beach Park
- Fort Trumbull State Park
- Miner Lane Pig Farm

■ Harkness Memorial State Park

Seasonal rating: Sp ** Su **/*** F *** W ****
Best time to bird: Summer for Roseate Tern and Wilson's Storm-Petrel; winter for seabirds, waterfowl, and Purple Sandpiper; fall for sparrows.
Habitats: Expansive manicured lawns, ornamental trees, formal gardens, tidal inlets, small tidal marsh, rocky and sandy beaches, Long Island Sound, shrubby meadows, small copses of trees, and brush dump.

Bird list for this site:

SPECIALTY BIRDS
Resident – Mute Swan, American Black Duck, Fish Crow
Spring – Black-headed Gull (occasional)
Summer – Wilson's Storm-Petrel (most years), Least Tern (nests), Roseate Tern, Orchard Oriole
Winter – "Black" Brant, King Eider (rare), Common Eider (fairly common), Black Scoter (uncommon), Red-necked Grebe (most years), Great Cormorant, Purple Sandpiper, Little Gull (rare), Razorbill (most years), Snow Buntings (occasional), Lapland Longspur (uncommon)

OTHER KEY BIRDS
Resident – Canada Goose, Belted Kingfisher, Eastern Bluebird (scarce in winter, common migrant)
Summer – Herons and egrets, Osprey, Common Tern, European Starling (flocks)
Winter – Brant, sea ducks, White-winged and Surf Scoters, Long-tailed Duck, Bufflehead, Common Goldeneye, Hooded Merganser, Red-breasted Merganser, Red-throated and Common Loons, Horned Grebe, Horned Lark

MIGRANTS
Spring and Fall – Northern Gannet, Wilson's Snipe, American Pipit
Fall – Raptors, especially Osprey, Northern Harrier, accipiters, and falcons, including Peregrine Falcon (uncommon); flycatchers, Palm Warbler and other warblers, sparrows, diurnal landbirds

40 HARKNESS STATE PARK & CAMP HARKNESS

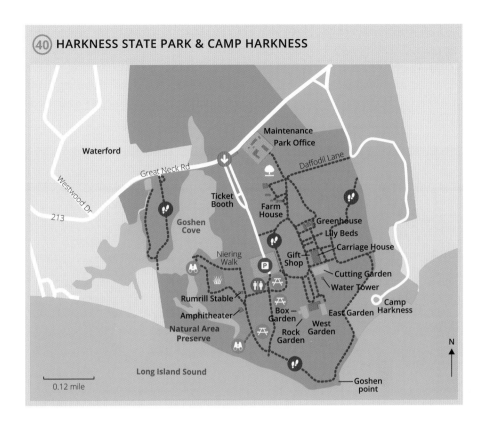

Location: 275 Great Neck Road (Connecticut Route 213), Waterford.

Parking: Entry fee from Memorial Day through Labor Day, plus weekends from late April to Memorial Day and Labor Day into mid-September.

Restrooms: On site; may be closed in winter.

Additional information: Rocky Neck State Park, about a 30-minute drive to the west, is also an excellent birding site, with similar seabirds but more marshland.

The Birding

Harkness Memorial State Park was once a grand coastal estate. Its forty-two-room mansion is perched on a peninsula overlooking Long Island Sound, with sweeping lawns, ornamental shade trees, and lavish formal gardens. Although much of the park's 230 acres remain heavily manicured, the gardens, meadows, and shoreline—along with a tidal inlet and marsh—attract a wide variety of birds. The park is well worth a visit at any time of year.

During migration, any birds following the Thames River or Connecticut coastline, especially on their southbound journeys, pass directly over the park. Accipiters, falcons, Northern Harrier, and Osprey stream by each autumn in the company of migrating Eastern Kingbird, Bobolink, swallows, Cedar Waxwing, Blue Jay, and American Robin. In autumn, the lawns, thickets, weedy fields, hedges, and gardens are rich with ripening fruit and seed, attracting thrushes, sparrows, finches, and other fruit and seed-eaters.

Watch for King Eider among the many Common Eider that frequent Harkness Memorial State Park. Female and young male King Eiders are seen most often.

Photograph courtesy Mark S. Szantyr

In winter, Harkness's rocky shoreline is known as a place to find Purple Sandpiper and to search Long Island Sound for rare waterfowl and seabirds, including Razorbill, Red-necked Grebe, and Northern Gannet. It is a very reliable site for Common Eider and, less frequently, King Eider, with occasional occurrences of Harlequin Duck, late fall through spring. Northern Gannets, sometimes in the hundreds, appear during the same period.

Local birders also watch for storm-driven birds at Harkness. Hurricanes can blow in rare terns and other seabirds, including shearwaters, pelicans, and jaegers. Parasitic Jaeger has been seen as late as October. Even a summer thunderstorm can drop shorebirds such as phalaropes into the rain pools. Winter nor'easters are best for stray ducks, Black-legged Kittiwake (rare), and gulls. Other than Razorbill, alcids are very rare in Long Island Sound; stiff east winds offer the best chance of seeing one here or elsewhere in Connecticut.

In summer, those willing to contend with beach crowds and entrance fees may be rewarded with views of Roseate, Least, and Common Terns. More than a dozen Wilson's Storm-Petrels (rare) have been seen from shore in a single day, usually in July and August.

In the tidal area, birds ebb and flow with the fluctuating food supply. It can pay to visit at different tides, as well as at different times of day. Not only will the numbers of a given species vary, but also the mix of species. While few birds may be present at high tide, there might be hundreds at low water. Dawn and dusk may reveal flights of waterfowl, herons, gulls, and other species, whereas dead noon may often be just that: dead.

How to Bird This Site

On the tree-lined entrance road, scan the fields to the west and the wet grassy meadows to the east. In winter, the fields attract Horned Lark, occasional Snow Bunting, and rarely Lapland Longspur, all of which may turn up anywhere on the lawns throughout the park. American Pipit also visit occasionally, fall through spring (rare in winter). The wet meadows, especially the one hidden beyond the wall east of the entrance, are favored sites for Wilson's Snipe and Eastern Meadowlark (uncommon) in fall and spring. Forty snipe have been found concealed in the grass in a single day, but careful scrutiny is required. Killdeer and other shorebirds frequent the wet areas and rain pools in migration. Baltimore Oriole and occasionally Orchard Oriole nest in the ornamental trees surrounding the many buildings. Eastern Bluebirds breed in the nest boxes.

In autumn, the brush piles and weed-covered dirt mounds near the dilapidated greenhouse, along with the large grassy meadow behind it, host sparrows, Indigo Bunting, and American Goldfinch, which feast on the bountiful weed seeds. Savannah, Song, Swamp, White-throated, and later, American Tree Sparrows, are joined by less common diners such as Field, White-crowned, and the skulking Lincoln's Sparrows. Rarities such as Blue Grosbeak and Clay-colored and Lark Sparrows have been found by a fortunate few. In the gardens, passing flocks of Eastern Bluebird mix with Eastern Phoebe and tail-wagging Palm Warbler, snapping up any remaining insects or gorging on available berries. In late summer, large groups of European Starling form to take advantage of plentiful food.

After perusing the fields and gardens near the entrance, park in the northwest corner of the main parking lot. A 0.4-mile loop trail leads west toward **Goshen Cove** through tall grass and scrubby meadows; these are good for sparrows, fall through spring, and shrub-loving species such as Eastern Towhee and Common Yellowthroat in summer. *Allow 45 minutes to 1 hour for this trail.* The inner cove can be viewed from a small peninsula 0.1 miles from the trailhead. This area is popular with feeding and roosting Least Tern (which nest here), Common Tern, and endangered Roseate Tern (uncommon) spring through fall. Migrating shorebirds arrive from spring through fall, while gull and waterfowl concentrations occur fall through spring.

The trail then turns south, passing through tall grasses and shrub edge good for migrating sparrows—such as White-throated, Song, Swamp, and Savannah Sparrows—to a blind overlooking the cove mouth.

From the blind, check the flats for shorebirds during migration, including both yellowlegs species, Least and Semipalmated Sandpipers, and Semipalmated and Black-bellied Plovers. The park gained statewide notoriety when Connecticut's first Black-tailed Godwit was relocated here in April 2001. Belted Kingfisher is common in the cove, and Ospreys nest on the platforms. Watch for American Black Duck, Green-winged Teal, American Wigeon, Bufflehead, Hooded Merganser, and the occasional Northern Pintail or Gadwall, fall through spring.

In winter, there is a roost of gulls in the cove, mostly Herring, Ring-billed, and Great Black-backed Gulls, but Iceland (occasional), Glaucous (rare), and Lesser Black-backed (rare) do occur. Bonaparte's Gulls congregate here in late fall, then again in March and April; when they gather, be alert for Black-headed Gull (rare), now annual in small numbers, and Little Gull (very rare). Double-crested Cormorants are conspicuous, but are generally replaced by Great Cormorants through the colder months.

After checking the blind, continue on the loop south, then east to a break in the hedge at the next bend. Behind the hedge, you will see lawns and a building. The trees beyond the building are good for landbird migrants in fall. The hedge by the building is great for White-crowned Sparrow in fall.

Go through the hedges, then head south across the lawn, past the building on the left, to a dirt road. Follow the road south through a picnic grove toward Goshen Point. **Note:** A paved road by the building leads east past the restrooms, then hooks back to the parking lot.

The trail to **Goshen Point** provides views of the shoreline and Long Island Sound. A boardwalk side trail leads to a viewing platform overlooking the breachway and dunes; Least Terns breed on the beach in summer, and shorebirds and ducks gather in the channel during migration. The main trail continues southeast along the shore to the point. In winter, check the lawns for geese, including Canada Goose, Brant, and Snow Goose (uncommon), as well as Snow Bunting and the other grassland birds. Rare "Black" Brant, a subspecies from the High Arctic of western North America, has been found here and at Waterford Beach Park. In summer and fall, Laughing Gulls gather, sometimes in flocks of more than a hundred, joining the larger gulls resting on the lawns. Watch for Sanderling and Dunlin along the sandy stretches of beach, and Ruddy Turnstone and Purple Sandpiper (winter) in the rocky areas.

Common and Red-throated Loons, Horned Grebe, and a variety of sea ducks visit the waters offshore from fall through spring, including Black Scoter (uncommon), White-winged and Surf Scoters, Long-tailed Duck (uncommon), Red-breasted Merganser, Bufflehead, and Common Goldeneye. Red-necked Grebe (occasional) and Eared Grebe (rare) have occurred. Roseate Tern and other terns feed offshore in summer. In autumn, watch for Forster's Tern, especially in September or October. Be alert in fall and winter for raptors; Rough-legged Hawks are possible.

■ Camp Harkness

Seasonal rating: Sp ** Su ** F *** W ***
Location: Near 295 Great Neck Road, Waterford.
➲ **Directions:** From Harkness Memorial State Park, turn right on Great Neck Road. Proceed east 0.2 miles, then turn right, staying on Great Neck Road. Continue 0.3 miles to the entrance, turn around by the guardhouse, and pull off the road.

Camp Harkness is private property. The fields by the entrance are worth scanning for geese, gulls, and shorebirds, fall through spring.

■ Waterford Beach Park and Town Beach

Seasonal rating: Sp *** Su ** F *** W ***
Location: 305 Great Neck Road, Waterford.
➲ **Directions:** From Camp Harkness, turn right and continue east on Great Neck Road. Turn right after 0.2 miles, following the sign for the Eugene O'Neill Theater. Continue 0.1 miles, then turn right into Waterford Beach Park and proceed 0.4 miles to the parking lot.
Parking: There is an entrance fee in summer unless you purchase a town beach sticker.

Scope the lawns for gulls and geese year-round; less common birds such as Snow Geese or white-winged gulls may occur in winter. The marsh to the south (lower Alewife Cove) can be reached by a short walk through the trees. Northern Harrier and Rough-legged Hawk have wintered here, and a variety of ducks visit in spring and fall. Osprey and Willet nest here, while herons, egrets, and terns visit in summer.

To reach Town Beach, continue south through the marsh over a footbridge. The waterbirds possible here are the same as those listed for Harkness Memorial State Park.

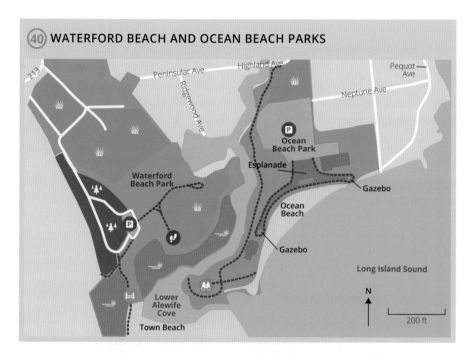

■ Ocean Beach Park

Seasonal rating: Sp ** Su *** F *** W ***
Location: 76 Neptune Avenue, New London.
⊃ **Directions:** Leaving Waterford Beach Park, turn right on Great Neck Road and continue northeast for 0.4 miles. Turn right onto Ridgewood Avenue, drive south 0.4 miles, then turn left onto Peninsular Avenue. Go 0.2 miles, continuing onto Highland Avenue, then turn right onto Stuart Avenue. Proceed one block to Neptune Avenue and turn right into the park.

Ocean Beach is a good seabird-watching spot, year-round. It is a reliable site for Fish Crow, and Osprey nest in the parking lot. The boardwalk provides good views of Long Island Sound. Look for Horned Grebe, Common and Red-throated Loons, sea ducks, and Northern Gannet, fall through spring. The small islands off the point to the west consistently attract all three scoter species, Common Goldeneye, and Red-breasted Merganser, along with Common Eider; in winter, search the rocks for Purple Sandpiper and harbor seals. Great Cormorant (winter) and Double-crested Cormorant (summer) frequent the rocks and buoys to the east. Brant and Mute Swan are often numerous. Razorbill and other alcids are possible, especially after a nor'easter.

In July and August, Wilson's Storm-Petrels have been seen here. To avoid the summer beach crowds, arrive early or late in the day. Common, Least, and Roseate Terns roost on the rocks, spring through fall; these are joined occasionally by other terns. Roseate Terns are most common in late summer, when they wander here from the colony at Great Gull Island, New York. American Oystercatchers occur.

The channel and marsh to the west are part of Alewife Cove. To view these areas, walk west along the boardwalk toward the point. Behind the last pavilion is a trail that leads to an observation platform. Watch for Rough-legged Hawk (some years) and Great Blue Heron in winter. The marsh offers shelter to Mute Swan and a variety of ducks, including American Black Duck, Hooded Merganser, and others. Belted Kingfisher is possible.

■ Fort Trumbull State Park

Seasonal rating: Sp ** Su ** F *** W ***
Location: Off Pequot Avenue, New London.
➲ **Directions:** Leaving Ocean Beach Park, head east on Neptune Avenue until you reach Pequot Avenue, then turn left. Continue north along the shore on Pequot Avenue. (The birding can be productive here; stop wherever vantage points are available.) At the rotary, take the second right onto Goshen Street, then the first right onto Trumbull Street.
Parking: Free parking for the fort is on East Street.
Restrooms: On site (in season).

The boardwalk at Fort Trumbull State Park provides clear views of the mouth of the Thames River. Fall through spring, this site almost always harbors Brant, Common and Red-breasted Mergansers, and a variety of other waterfowl, including loons, Horned Grebe, and the occasional Red-necked Grebe.

Pacific Loon (rare) has been seen in the area in winter. Occasionally, a Razorbill or other alcid has been found. It is reliable for wintering Double-crested Cormorant and American Coot; both often congregate around the many pilings and docks. Black-legged Kittiwake (rare) has been seen in this area, off Ocean Beach, and from Avery Point in Groton.

Note: You may wish to continue the coastal tour one more stop to the east, over the river to Avery Point, in Groton. In winter, that area also is productive for seabirds, including Razorbill, as well as waterfowl; in summer, Wilson's Storm-Petrels are possible.

■ Miner Lane Pig Farm

Seasonal rating: Sp *** Su ** F *** W ***
Location: 72 Miner Lane, Waterford.
⟳ **Directions:** From the parking lot at Fort Trumbull State Park, turn right on East Street, then left onto Walbach Street. Drive 0.4 miles, then turn left onto Harris Street. Enter the traffic circle and take the second exit onto Willets Avenue. Continue 1.1 miles, then turn left onto U.S. 1. After 0.2 miles, turn left onto Miner Lane. Continue 0.6 miles and look for the farm on the left. Pull safely off the road and view from the roadside.

This unique farm can be excellent for gulls, sparrows, and raptors, fall through early spring. Although this is a hit-or-miss sort of place, it is a local favorite for Glaucous, Iceland, and Lesser Black-backed Gulls, which scavenge along with the Ring-billed, Herring, and Great Black-backed Gulls. Raptors, including Cooper's and Red-shouldered Hawks, patrol the area. Sparrows frequent the many thickets in season. In spring, scan the wet seep across the street for American Woodcock and Wilson's Snipe. Shrub-nesting species are here in summer.

Note: Rocky Neck State Park, to the west on Route 156 in Niantic, is worth a visit. It has similar species to Harkness State Park but more shorebirds, waterfowl, and waders.

New London–Orient Point Ferry

Seasonal rating: Sp *** Su **/*** F *** W ****
Best time to bird: October through March.
Habitats: Mouth of the Connecticut River, river edge, open bay, Long Island Sound, islands, jetties, rocky outcrops, sheltered coves, marinas, and urban neighborhoods.

Bird list for this site:

SPECIALTY BIRDS
Resident – Mute Swan, American Black Duck, Double-crested Cormorant, Peregrine Falcon
Summer – Shearwaters (rare), Wilson's Storm-Petrel (July and August), American Oystercatcher, Roseate Tern, Osprey, Parasitic Jaeger (rare)
Winter – Brant, Common Eider, scoters, Long-tailed Duck, Red-necked Grebe (December and January), American Coot, Purple Sandpiper, Razorbill, Common and Thick-billed Murres (both uncommon), Northern Gannet, Great Cormorant, Black-legged Kittiwake (rare); Iceland, Glaucous, and Lesser Black-backed Gulls (all uncommon)

OTHER KEY BIRDS
Summer – Great and Snowy Egrets
Winter – Common Goldeneye, Bufflehead

MIGRANTS
Brant, sea ducks, Horned Grebe, loons

Location: 2 Ferry Street, New London.
Parking: At the terminal (come early), or in a garage across the street. There is a fee.
Restrooms: At the ferry terminals and onboard.
Hazards: Slippery or icy decks in winter; on rough days, seasickness for those who are susceptible.
Additional information: It is permissible to disembark in New York, but your ticket is required to reboard. The boat leaves for the return trip 30 minutes after docking. Even if you stay on the boat, a roundtrip ticket is required.

The Birding

A roundtrip voyage on the New London to Orient Point Ferry offers the chance to see pelagic species such as Wilson's Storm-Petrel (summer), Parasitic Jaeger, alcids (winter), Cory's Shearwater (late summer and fall), and some uncommon-to-rare ducks, gulls, loons, and grebes. Winter trips have produced such rarities as Pacific Loon (in New London Harbor), Common and Thick-billed Murres, and Black-legged Kittiwake. Razorbills are expected in winter, as are good numbers (sometimes hundreds) of Common Eider, with the chance to see all three scoter species, Long-tailed Duck and other sea ducks, Horned and Red-necked Grebes, Purple Sandpiper, and Iceland, Glaucous (uncommon), and Lesser Black-backed Gulls, as well as a slew of other species. Northern Gannets occur regularly, especially in November and December, then again in March and April.

Red-breasted Mergansers are a common sight during crossings from fall through spring.

How to Bird from the Ferry

Pick one of the two ferries with good upper-deck access to the bow: the *John H.* or the *Mary Ellen*. Avoid the *Cape Henlopen* and *Susan Anne*, which have limited bow access. The roundtrip *takes approximately 3 hours*.

Before departure, be sure to scan the area for loons and grebes; they often feed under the docks across from the ferry. Pacific Loon was recorded here one winter among the many Common and Red-throated Loons. American Coots tend to winter with dabbling ducks around the ferry slip itself. A few Purple Sandpiper, along with Ruddy Turnstone, Dunlin, and Sanderling, are often seen on the docks themselves or on the rocks and jetties lining the harbor, along with Double-crested Cormorant (year-round) and Great Cormorant (winter). Common Goldeneye, Bufflehead, and Red-breasted and Common Mergansers move up and down the river daily. Common Mergansers prefer the area upriver near the bridge, while Red-breasted Mergansers tend toward the river mouth. Peregrine Falcons nest on the I-95 bridge to the north, so scan the bridge and rooftops while you wait to leave. Turkey and Black Vultures roost in the area and sometimes soar over the river.

Watch for Glaucous and Iceland Gulls (both have spent entire winters here) among the many Herring, Ring-billed, and Great Black-backed Gulls that loiter near the terminal.

During the crossing, scan all islands, marker buoys, jetties, and rock outcroppings for Great Blue Herons, cormorants, shorebirds (including Purple Sandpiper and Ruddy Turnstone), and eiders, scoters, and other ducks. While en route, watch for loons, grebes, and alcids on the water or in flight. Razorbill is the most commonly encountered alcid, but both murres (rare) have been seen in winter, and Dovekie (very rare) is possible. Northern Gannets are sighted on many of the crossings, fall through spring, and Black-legged Kittiwake, though rare, is seen regularly, especially in January.

In winter, dress in layers. Warm boots, gloves, hat, and a windproof outer layer are essential. The wind can be quite harsh, and the metal deck sucks heat through poorly insulated footwear. Wear sunscreen even in winter: the glare off the water can cause quite a burn.

Birding from a moving platform takes practice and certainly isn't for everyone. Constant scanning is necessary just to find birds, while identifying birds on the water or in flight, often at a distance, is an acquired skill. No two trips are alike, and the return trip can be vastly different from the outbound one. One never knows: though many are lackluster, some are fantastic.

Note: If you're working on a state list, use your phone's GPS capabilities to monitor your location, and record the time and coordinates for any rarities.

(42) Bluff Point Coastal Reserve and Haley Farm, Groton

- ◼ Bluff Point State Park and Coastal Reserve
- ◼ Haley Farm State Park

◼ Bluff Point Coastal Reserve

Seasonal rating: Sp *** Su ** F **** W **
Best time to bird: Fall.
Habitats: Forested peninsula, bluffs, open and shrubby meadows, thickets, marshes, small wetlands, small pond, inlets, bays, river estuary, dunes, and barrier beach.

Bird list for this site:

SPECIALTY BIRDS
Resident – Belted Kingfisher
Summer – Wilson's Storm-Petrel (some years), Osprey, Piping Plover (some years), American Woodcock (Haley Farm), Least Tern (some years), Willow Flycatcher, White-eyed Vireo (declining), Brown Thrasher (declining)
Winter – Great Cormorant, Virginia Rail (Haley Farm), Horned Lark, Snow Bunting

OTHER KEY BIRDS
Resident – Carolina Wren, Cedar Waxwing, Eastern Towhee
Summer – Great and Snowy Egrets, Black-crowned Night-Heron, Double-crested Cormorant, Common Tern, Eastern Wood-Pewee, Eastern Kingbird, Blue Jay, Tree and Barn Swallows, House Wren, Wood Thrush, Gray Catbird, Red-eyed Vireo, Scarlet Tanager; Blue-winged (declining), Chestnut-sided (declining), and Black-and-white Warblers; Ovenbird, Common Yellowthroat, Rose-breasted Grosbeak
Winter – Sea ducks, including Surf, White-winged, and Black Scoters (uncommon) and Long-tailed Duck; Red-throated and Common Loons, Horned Grebe, Red-necked Grebe (uncommon)

MIGRANTS
Northern Gannet, Bonaparte's Gull, Forster's Tern, most raptors, Clapper Rail; nearly all of Connecticut's landbird migrants are possible here during late summer and fall cold fronts, including Philadelphia Vireo, Dickcissel, Yellow-breasted Chat, and Cape May, Bay-breasted, Connecticut, and Mourning Warblers

Location: Depot Road, Groton.
Restrooms: There are composting toilets at the entrance and near the point.

BIRDING IN CONNECTICUT

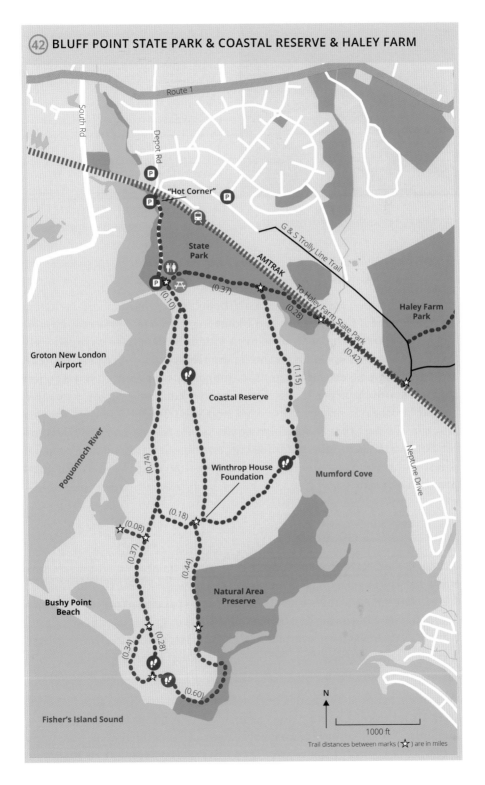

42 BLUFF POINT STATE PARK & COASTAL RESERVE & HALEY FARM

Route 1

South Rd

Depot Rd

P

P "Hot Corner" P

State Park

G & S Trolly Line Trail

AMTRAK

To Haley Farm State Park

(0.37)

(0.28)

(0.42)

Haley Farm Park

Groton New London Airport

Coastal Reserve

(1.15)

(0.10)

Poquonnoch River

(0.74)

Winthrop House Foundation

Mumford Cove

(0.18)

(0.08)

(0.37)

(0.44)

Natural Area Preserve

Bushy Point Beach

(0.34)

(0.28)

(0.60)

Neptune Drive

Fisher's Island Sound

N

1000 ft

Trail distances between marks (★) are in miles

The Birding

Bluff Point is known for its fall songbird migration, especially flights of warblers.

Bluff Point State Park and Coastal Reserve is a forested peninsula that juts into Long Island Sound on the eastern end of Connecticut. Considered to be Connecticut's (and perhaps New England's) best passerine migrant trap, it is similar to Higby Beach, the famous landbird migrant trap in Cape May, New Jersey, though smaller in scope. Given the sheer numbers of birds seen each autumn, Bluff Point may be the most likely place in the state to stumble upon a great songbird rarity in the fall.

Many less common species are annual (though sparse in number), including Orange-crowned, Connecticut, and Mourning Warblers. Some real rarities, such as Northern Wheatear, have been found. Birders have recorded sixty to seventy species—including eighteen warbler species—on a peak September day. Hundreds, even thousands, of individuals can be seen in just a few hours. It's awe-inspiring to watch the myriad kingbirds, vireos, sparrows, finches, grosbeaks, orioles, Blue Jays, and even Scarlet Tanagers moving through. The best time for warbler variety is late August and early September. For maximum numbers of birds but fewer species, the end of September is best. For western rarities, try October into November; Western Kingbird is seen most years.

How to Bird This Site

Although Bluff Point covers 800 acres of varied habitat, most birders visit only what is known as "the hot corner" near the park's north end. They go there in late summer and early fall, following the passage of a cold front, for a chance to view the impressive flights of landbird migrants passing overhead. Wind direction plays a major role in their success: north-northwest is best. There can be many slow days between spectacular ones, so repeated visits are recommended. It's a hit-or-miss sort of place, but anything is possible.

The hot corner is at the park's northwest edge, next to the railroad tracks. After a cold front, birders gather at first light, awaiting the dawn push of landbirds. (Birds that have traveled overnight and find themselves over water at dawn will return to the nearest land.) Before continuing their migration south, birds rest and feed at Bluff Point while working north through the park. A bottleneck forms where the peninsula meets the mainland. Birds amass in the trees south of the tracks, then launch themselves skyward. To observe these migrants, station yourself between the trees and the mainland, with the railway fence behind you. **Note:** Keep your distance from the fence. Visitors who get too close are sometimes forced to leave by railway police.

The hot corner is perhaps the most reliable site in Connecticut for finding Philadelphia Vireo and Mourning Warbler (late August and early September). It is dependable for several other less common, but annual migrants, including Red-headed Woodpecker, Dickcissel, and Clay-colored Sparrow (all in September and October), Yellow-breasted Chat, Connecticut Warbler (late August into October), Bay-breasted Warbler, Cape May Warbler, and Orange-crowned Warbler (October and November). It also is one of the few places locally where migrating Golden-winged Warblers are encountered (August and September). Rare fall sightings of Prothonotary Warblers have occurred as well.

Finding any of these species takes work and a little luck. Identifying warblers in low light while they flit high overhead takes practice, and many individuals pass unidentified even by experienced birders.

After the morning madness dies down, take a quick walk around the semi-open trails adjacent to the hot corner. Earlier in the season, adult warblers tend to linger in the park instead of zipping out. Latecomers are often still feeding in the bushes, including thrushes, sparrows, vireos, flycatchers, and even cuckoos. Connecticut Warbler and Blue Grosbeak are possible here in season. White-eyed Vireo, Eastern Towhee, and Brown Thrasher breed in the area.

■ Haley Farm State Park

Seasonal rating: Sp *** Su *** F **** W **
Location: Haley Farm Lane, Groton.
Restrooms: Pit toilets on site.

This is a good general birding site close to Bluff Point. The trails through the park traverse a number of habitats—including meadows, marsh, thicket, forest, and ponds—and offer a wide variety of species, especially in fall. Many of the trails can be done as loops. Together, Bluff Point and Haley Farm State Parks protect more than 1,000 acres. Haley Farm is open from 8:00 a.m. to sunset.

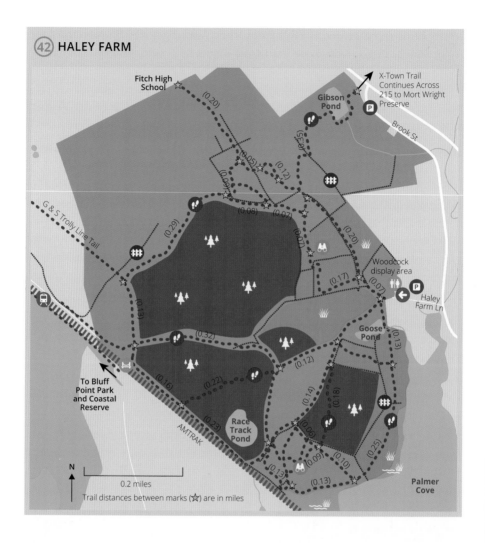

42 HALEY FARM

This is one of the best places to observe American Woodcock in the area. During peak migration, as many as twenty have been seen in the fields close to the entrance parking lot at dusk. Yellow-breasted Chat occurs most winters in the marsh and upper thickets near Fitch High School. The marsh is also dependable in winter for Virginia Rail. In summer, less common breeders include Brown Thrasher. **Note:** The park's meadows also attract a nice variety of butterflies.

(43) Stonington Point

Seasonal rating: Sp *** Su ** F *** W ****
Best time to bird: October to April.
Habitats: Harbor, rock jetties, breakwaters, near and offshore islands, and Long Island Sound.

Bird list for this site:

SPECIALTY BIRDS
Resident – Mute Swan, Common Eider, American Black Duck, Double-crested Cormorant
Summer – Wilson's Storm-Petrel (July), American Oystercatcher, Least and Roseate Terns, Fish Crow
Winter – Common Eider, King Eider (rare), Black Scoter, Red-necked Grebe (December to January), Northern Gannet, Great Cormorant, Purple Sandpiper, Razorbill and other alcids, Black-legged Kittiwake (rare), Black-headed Gull (rare)

OTHER KEY BIRDS
Summer – Great and Snowy Egrets, Black-crowned Night-Heron, Osprey, Spotted Sandpiper, Willet, Common Tern, Northern Rough-winged Swallow
Winter – Brant, Long-tailed Duck, Surf and White-winged Scoters, Horned Grebe, loons, Bonaparte's Gull

Location: End of Water Street, Stonington.
Restrooms: Downtown Stonington.

The Birding

Stonington Point overlooks Rhode Island's Napatree Point, New York's Fishers Island, and the entrance to Long Island Sound. Because of its proximity to the open waters of the Atlantic Ocean, it offers the possibility of seeing pelagic species that are less common in Long Island Sound proper. It is also the most reliable site in Connecticut to see Common Eider, while Razorbill occurs regularly from fall through spring.

Common Eiders can be seen in the area year-round.

All three scoter species also are seen regularly, with Surf Scoter the most common and Black Scoter the least. There are good numbers of Long-tailed Duck, Bufflehead, Common Goldeneye, Red-breasted Merganser, Common and Red-throated Loons, and Horned Grebe, fall through spring, along with a few Red-necked Grebe. Pacific Loon has been recorded here in late October. When conditions are right, the point gives birders a fighting chance to find rarities such as Dovekie and Black-headed Gull, rare pelagic species such as Black-legged Kittiwake, or the extremely rare Northern Fulmar.

Scan the rocks and breakwaters for Common Eider and Purple Sandpiper, fall through spring; a few Common Eider, perhaps nonbreeders, often summer in this general area as well. American Oystercatcher occurs spring through fall, Double-crested Cormorant is resident, and Great Cormorant appears in winter. Roseate, Common, and Least Terns nest on offshore islands in nearby Rhode Island waters. During fall migration, they are usually joined by at least a few Black and Forster's Terns before the tern flocks leave the area. Resident Herring and Great Black-backed Gulls nest locally, while Ring-billed Gulls, although resident, breed inland. Laughing Gulls can be common from July through fall.

How to Bird This Site

Birding can be done right from the parking lot. A spotting scope is recommended.

Barn Island Wildlife Management Area, Stonington

Seasonal rating: Sp **** Su *** F *** W **
Best time to bird: Spring and fall.
Habitats: Expansive tidal marshes and impoundments, open salt water, sheltered inlets, coastal woodlands, shrubland, and thickets.

Bird list for this site:

SPECIALTY BIRDS

Resident – Mute Swan, American Black Duck, Great Blue Heron, Fish Crow

Summer – Great and Snowy Egrets, Little Blue and Green Herons, Glossy Ibis, Virginia Rail, Willet, American Oystercatcher, Least Tern, Black-billed Cuckoo, Whip-poor-will, Willow Flycatcher, Marsh Wren, White-eyed and Yellow-throated Vireos, Bank Swallow, Brown Thrasher (declining), Blue-winged and Prairie Warblers, Yellow-breasted Chat (some years); Field, Saltmarsh and Seaside Sparrows; Orchard Oriole, Purple Finch

Winter – Great Cormorant, Snowy and Short-eared Owls (invasion years), Rough-legged Hawk (invasion years)

OTHER KEY BIRDS

Resident – Wild Turkey, Northern Flicker, Carolina Wren, Cedar Waxwing, Swamp Sparrow

Summer – Common woodland, shrubland, and marshland birds, along with Black-crowned Night-Heron, Osprey, Clapper Rail, Killdeer, Spotted Sandpiper, Laughing Gull, Common Tern, Ruby-throated Hummingbird, Belted Kingfisher, Eastern Wood-Pewee, Eastern Phoebe, Great Crested Flycatcher, Eastern Kingbird, swallows, Blue-gray Gnatcatcher, Veery, Wood Thrush, Warbling Vireo, Black-and-White and Pine Warblers, American Redstart, Ovenbird, Scarlet Tanager, Rose-breasted Grosbeak, Indigo Bunting, Eastern Towhee

Winter – Brant, Common Goldeneye, Bufflehead, Hooded and Red-breasted Mergansers, Great Egret (some years), Hermit Thrush

MIGRANTS

Blue-winged and Green-winged Teal (spring), Greater Scaup and other diving ducks, American Bittern (uncommon), Tricolored Heron (spring), White-faced Ibis (rare; spring), Horned Grebe, coastal migrating hawks and falcons, Northern Harrier, Bald Eagle, Virginia Rail, Sora (fall); most shorebirds, including Whimbrel, White-rumped and Pectoral Sandpipers; American Woodcock (spring), Forster's Tern, kinglets, Eastern Bluebird; most warblers, including Palm Warbler and Yellow-breasted Chat; Nelson's Sparrow as well as some less common sparrows, including White-crowned and Vesper Sparrows; Purple Finch

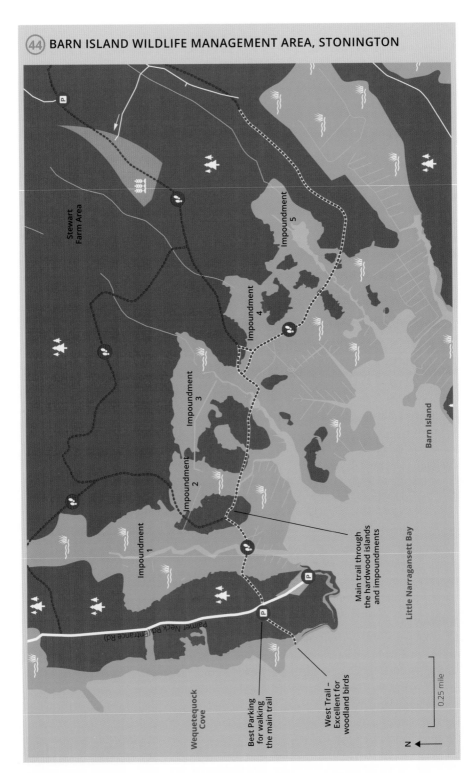

Location: 279 Palmer Neck Road, Stonington.

Restrooms: Along U.S. 1.

Hazards: This is a heavily hunted area from mid-September to mid-February, even on weekdays; blaze orange clothing is a must. There is no hunting on Sunday. Ticks, biting flies, and mosquitoes can be plentiful in season.

The Birding

Barn Island is actually a peninsula. A series of dikes traverses its marshy impoundments and connects a chain of wooded copses. If you are looking for a site in southeastern Connecticut to find waders and shorebirds, along with a few of the less common shrub-nesting species, with the added potential for turning up rarities, this is the place! The list of regularly occurring species includes at least 250, and the list of rare species is impressive. Most shorebirds that occur in Connecticut appear at Barn Island over the course of the season, and a number of rarities have been found with some regularity, including Black-necked Stilt and American Avocet. The area's 800 total acres include 350 acres of saltmarsh and may receive recognition as a globally important site for Saltmarsh Sparrows.

Barn Island is wonderful for warblers and other songbird migrants in late May, as its forests are generally late to leaf out; spring is also best for shorebirds. Although declining, shrubland breeders such as White-eyed Vireo and Brown Thrasher are still present in small numbers. During fall migration, nearly every species of warbler, along with many other migrant passerines, come through; the parade begins in mid-summer for many species, including Golden-winged Warbler (rare), which occurs most years. In autumn, watch for migrating raptors, including American Kestrel, Merlin, Cooper's and Sharp-shinned Hawks, Osprey, and Northern Harrier. Peregrine falcons and eagles are possible and becoming more common. Most sparrow species that occur in Connecticut have been recorded at Barn Island; fall is generally best for finding them.

How to Bird This Site

Because shorebirds and waders can be quite distant, a scope is recommended. The following tour of the site *can take from 3 to 6 hours*, with generally easy walking. **Note:** The Main Trail impoundments can be done in *1 or 2 hours*.

Palmer Neck Road Fields

From the intersection of Greenhaven Road and Palmer Neck Road, drive 0.5 miles south on Palmer Neck Road, then pull off to the side when you reach two fields on the right.

Bobolinks are regular visitors in spring and fall and may breed here. Any flooded areas may attract Glossy Ibis in May or June, and White-faced Ibis (rare) has visited. Cattle Egrets have occurred here occasionally in spring. Check any rain pools for Wilson's Snipe, Pectoral Sandpiper, and dabbling ducks during migration. A very rare Fork-tailed Flycatcher was once discovered in this area, and Greater White-fronted Goose has occurred in winter.

Barn Island Boat Ramp

Continue south to the boat ramp at the end of Palmer Neck Road, where you can scan Little Narragansett Bay for seabirds. If you're visiting in summer, arrive early in the day, as heavy boat traffic can disperse the birds. The boat-ramp area and adjacent Wequetequock Cove are good sites for finding waterfowl in winter and tend to hold lingering Brant, Red-breasted Merganser, Bufflehead, and Long-tailed Duck into at least May or even June. Horned Grebe and both loon species can usually be found in winter. Least and Common Terns feed here in summer, when they are joined occasionally by Black Skimmers. Look for shorebirds as well, including American Oystercatcher, which may also appear in Wequetequock Cove.

Wequetequock Cove Spur Trail

The trailhead for this short trail is about 0.1 miles north of the boat ramp, on the road's west side. Parking is available in the small pull-off adjacent to the barricade. *Allow 30 to 40 minutes* for the 0.2-mile roundtrip.

The trail leads west along a dirt track. Shrubland species nest along the trail, including Brown Thrasher and Prairie and Chestnut-sided Warblers. Yellow-breasted Chat (may nest) has been heard singing here in spring. Saltmarsh Sparrows breed in the marsh to the north (and in saltmarshes throughout the reserve); walk along the marsh edge for closer looks. Terns hunt the bay from spring through fall; look for Forster's Tern in late summer or early fall, when Laughing Gulls are also fairly common. Egrets and herons hunt this marsh, including Little Blue Heron and rarely Tricolored Heron, while shorebirds visit the small beach during migration. Purple Martins (nest locally) and other swallows can often be seen here as well.

Main Trail

The dirt road across Palmer Neck Road from the Wequetequock Cove Spur Trail is the beginning of the wildlife management area's main walking trail. *Allow at least 1.5 hours* for the 3-mile roundtrip, although a productive walk might occupy 3 hours or more. The main trail traverses scrub and forested habitat interspersed between four old waterfowl impoundments, now reverting into saltmarsh. Spur trails branch off to the north, usually into forested uplands. Keep right at all intersections to visit the four impoundments. In the shrubby woodlands between the trailhead and the first impoundment, be alert for Black-billed Cuckoo, Gray Catbird, Brown Thrasher, White-eyed Vireo, Blue-winged Warbler, American Redstart, and Common Yellowthroat, all of which nest. At dusk or dawn, listen for Whip-poor-wills, especially in spring. Ruby-throated Hummingbird (nests) may be seen throughout the area, especially during August and September migration.

The first impoundment is a large marsh, cut by a wide channel; there are extensive mudflats on the north side, exposed at low tide. Glossy Ibis, egrets, and herons frequent this area; in spring and summer, look out for Little Blue and Tricolored Herons. White Ibis has occurred here and elsewhere in the preserve. A wide variety of shorebirds visits the mudflats during migration, and terns cruise the main channel in summer. Watch for Saltmarsh and Seaside Sparrows, which breed in the area. Belted Kingfisher can usually be found somewhere along the trail. This is a good section for American Kestrel during migration, and for Rough-legged Hawk and Short-eared Owl in winter.

After the first impoundment, the trail enters a wooded area that is good for landbirds, including Carolina Wren, Black-capped Chickadee, White-breasted Nuthatch, Great Crested Flycatcher, the occasional Black-and-white Warbler, and Eastern Towhee. In winter, Northern Saw-whet Owl, Great Horned Owl, and other owls sometimes use the scattered evergreens for roosting. Special care should be taken not to disturb them. Hermit and other thrushes move through in fall.

When the trail forks, stay to the right to reach the second impoundment. This small strip of marsh is typically not very productive, but egrets or herons—including Green Heron—are occasionally seen in the channel here.

The next woodland hosts breeding Veery and Wood Thrush, and is often good for migrants.

The third impoundment is probably the best spot on the trail for shorebirds and waders. Tricolored Heron has been found here, and Little Blue Heron seems to favor this marsh in spring. At low tide, the exposed mudflats can attract some less common migrants, including Western and White-rumped Sandpipers (late May), and occasionally Baird's (late summer or early fall) or Stilt Sandpipers. Shorebird rarities discovered here include American Avocet, Curlew Sandpiper, Wilson's Phalarope, and Hudsonian Godwit. Check the area near the active Osprey platform for roosting shorebirds at high tide. Scissor-tailed Flycatcher has occurred once here.

Barn Island is a reliable place to find Little Blue Herons, especially mottled young birds.

The mosquito ditches here and elsewhere on Barn. Island are popular feeding sites for Swamp Sparrow and other marsh sparrows, Clapper Rail, herons, and egrets. Least Terns also patrol the ditches in summer, hunting small fish, while swallows quarter the marsh, spring through fall. During migration, all of the state's six species of breeding swallows, including Purple Martin, are possible.

The trail continues across the marsh and into the forest. At the junction, turn right to proceed to the fourth impoundment, roughly 100 yards ahead. Check any patches of cattail for Swamp Sparrow and Marsh Wren; during fall migration, look here for Sora and Virginia Rail. The extensive saltmarsh on the right should be checked for waders, shorebirds, and other marshland species. This is a good area for Yellow Warbler, and Willow Flycatcher nests in the shrubby areas farther along the impoundment, on the left. Nesting Orchard Oriole and Purple Finch also have been found in this area.

The last area of open water on the left attracts dabbling ducks such as Gadwall, American Wigeon, and teal during migration. At low tide, the exposed mudflats here are very good for migrating shorebirds, including Short-billed Dowitcher and Solitary Sandpiper. This also is a consistently good area to find Glossy Ibis and other waders. Rarities discovered in this general area have included Black-necked Stilt, White Ibis, and Yellow Rail. Fish Crows nest nearby and frequent the area in summer, while Eastern Meadowlarks are seen in migration. The brushy areas harbor typical scrub-nesting species.

From the fourth impoundment, you can either return to the trailhead the way you came, or walk an additional 1.5-mile loop through Stewart Farm by continuing southeast past the fifth impoundment. The trail enters forest and turns north.

Stewart Farm Loop

This trail enters the woods just past a small patch of saltmarsh on the right with an active Osprey platform. *Allow 50 to 90 minutes or more* to complete the 1.5-mile loop. The trail continues north through scrubby woods for roughly a quarter-mile then meets a paved road, Brucker Pentway. Walk north on the road another quarter-mile. At the fork where the pentway meets Stewart Road, bear left and continue northwest a short way to a Cul-de-sac. On the southwest (left) side of the cul-de-sac, take a short trail through the trees into a field. Continue southwest through the field on the trail, which cuts through the regenerating fields, forested swamp, and upland forest of Stewart Farm, passes behind the fourth impoundment, and leads back to a junction on the main trail between the third and fourth impoundments. In summer, this loop can yield Ring-necked Pheasant, Wild Turkey, Whip-poor-will (dusk), Black-billed Cuckoo, Red-eyed Vireo; Blue-winged, Yellow, Chestnut-sided (declining), and Hooded Warblers (rare); Ovenbird, Scarlet Tanager, Rose-breasted Grosbeak, and a host of other forest and scrubland species.

THE NORTHEAST HIGHLANDS

㊺ University of Connecticut Storrs Campus Area

- Lot W
- Mirror Lake
- Horsebarn Hill Loop
- Pumping Station Road

Seasonal rating: Sp *** Su *** F *** W ***
Best time to bird: May through August for grassland breeders, spring or fall for migrating landbirds, and October through April for geese, winter finches, and Horned Lark.
Habitats: Agricultural fields, old fields, wet and dry meadows, thickets, second-growth forest, pine woods, hemlock ravines, riparian forest, cattail marsh, reservoirs, and ponds.

Bird list for this site:

SPECIALTY BIRDS
Resident – Black Vulture, Ruffed Grouse (uncommon), Common Raven, Pileated Woodpecker
Summer – American Woodcock, American Kestrel, Least and Willow Flycatchers, Brown Thrasher (rare breeder), White-eyed Vireo (uncommon); Blue-winged, Prairie, Canada (most years), and Worm-eating Warblers; Eastern Towhee, Field and Savannah Sparrows, Bobolink, Eastern Meadowlark
Winter – Greater White-fronted, Snow, and Cackling Geese (all uncommon); Rough-legged Hawk (some years), Northern Shrike (invasion years), Bohemian Waxwing (rare; invasion years), Horned Lark, Lapland Longspur, Snow Bunting, Pine Grosbeak (invasion years), crossbills (invasion years), Common Redpoll (invasion years), Pine Siskin

OTHER KEY BIRDS
Resident – Cooper's and Red-shouldered Hawks, Eastern Screech-Owl, Great Horned and Barred Owls, Belted Kingfisher (uncommon in winter); Red-bellied, Downy, and Hairy Woodpeckers; Northern Flicker, White-breasted Nuthatch, Carolina Wren, Northern Mockingbird, Eastern Bluebird
Summer – Wood Duck, Great Blue and Green Herons, Killdeer, Spotted Sandpiper, Wild Turkey, Broad-winged Hawk, Ruby-throated Hummingbird, Black-billed and Yellow-billed Cuckoos, Warbling and Yellow-throated Vireos; Tree, Bank, Northern Rough-winged, and Barn Swallows; Brown Creeper, House Wren, Blue-gray

THE NORTHEAST HIGHLANDS

348

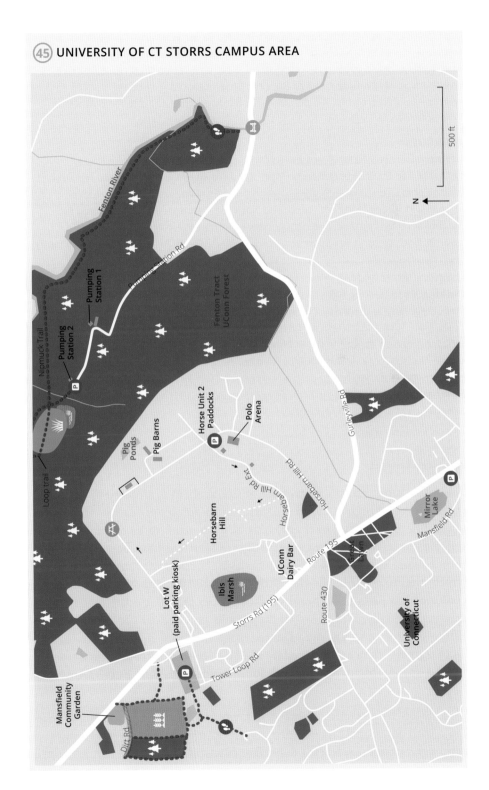

500 ft

N

Fenton River

Pumping Station 1

Pumping Station 2

Nipmuck Trail

Depot Station Rd

Fenton Tract UConn Forest

Gurleyville Rd

Loop trail

Horse Unit 2 Paddocks

Polo Arena

Pig Barns

Pig Ponds

Horsebarn Hill Rd Ext

Horsebarn Hill Rd

Horsebarn Hill

Mirror Lake

Mansfield Rd

Lot W (paid parking kiosk)

Ibis Marsh

UConn Dairy Bar

Route 195

Route 430

Storrs Rd (195)

University of Connecticut

Mansfield Community Garden

Tower Loop Rd

Dirt Rd

Gnatcatcher, Gray Catbird, Veery, Wood Thrush, Cedar Waxwing; Blue-winged, Black-throated Green, Yellow, Chestnut-sided, Pine, Prairie, and Black-and-white Warblers; American Redstart, Louisiana Waterthrush, Northern Waterthrush (uncommon), Ovenbird, Scarlet Tanager, Indigo Bunting, Rose-breasted Grosbeak

Winter – Golden-crowned Kinglet, Dark-eyed Junco, White-throated and American Tree Sparrows

MIGRANTS

Northern Harrier, Merlin, Peregrine Falcon, Solitary Sandpiper, Wilson's Snipe, Yellow-bellied Sapsucker, American Pipit, Ruby-crowned Kinglet, Blue-headed Vireo, Philadelphia Vireo (uncommon), Swainson's and Gray-cheeked Thrushes (uncommon); warblers, including Northern Parula and Nashville, Tennessee, Black-throated Blue, Magnolia, Yellow-rumped, and occasionally Mourning Warblers; White-crowned, Swamp, Lincoln's, and Fox Sparrows (some winters); Rusty Blackbird (may overwinter)

Location: Storrs and Mansfield.

Parking: Read parking signs and follow regulations carefully, as the campus police patrol regularly and are quick to give tickets. Visitor parking is available at university parking garages and in designated PayByPhone spaces in Lot W and other commuter lots. Information about the PayByPhone service (along with an app) are available online at http://park.uconn.edu/guest-visitor-parking/. No university parking permits or payments are required to park after 5:00 p.m. weekdays or on weekends.

Restrooms: In restaurants in Storrs Center on Route 195, opposite E.O. Smith High School.

The Birding

The main campus of the University of Connecticut is situated in the state's rural northeast highlands, where farms are a dominant feature of the landscape. The university's own agricultural fields used to be among the more reliable places to find rare geese in Connecticut but have become less so in recent years. This is due to the university's efforts to prevent Canada Geese, which used to occur in the thousands, from roosting on Mirror Lake in the center of campus. A few hundred Canada Geese still use the fields around campus annually, and these flocks should be checked for Snow, Greater White-fronted, and Cackling Geese, especially from mid-October through Thanksgiving, then again from late March to early April. Barnacle Geese and Brant also have occurred, and both Pink-footed Geese and Ross's Geese have been seen not far away.

In addition to attracting geese, the farm fields harbor wintering Horned Lark, with occasional Snow Bunting, American Pipit, and Lapland Longspur. Although not annual, Northern Shrikes frequently spend the winter. Winter finches such as Common Redpoll and Pine Siskin can be common in some years.

During the breeding season, many of these same fields support some of the state's less common grassland species, including Bobolink, Savannah Sparrow, American Kestrel, and Eastern Meadowlark. Shrub-nesting species such as Eastern Towhee breed here, and Brown Thrasher and Field Sparrow also are present in some years.

The fields in the Storrs area attract rare geese in winter, including Pink-footed Goose.

Note: For information on other campus-area birding sites, see http://birds. uconn.edu/birding-on-campus/. Try the nearby Moss tract in the UConn Forest for nesting Winter Wren, Hermit Thrush, Blue-headed Vireo, and Northern Waterthrush.

How to Bird This Area

The following descriptions include a selection of the most productive birding spots in the Storrs area. As a general note, many of the university's extensive ornamental plantings produce berries that are attractive to birds. In winter, large flocks of Cedar Waxwings and American Robins often can be found on campus, along with smaller groups of Eastern Bluebirds. In invasion years, these plantings are well worth checking for irruptive species such as Bohemian Waxwing, Pine Grosbeak, Pine Siskin, Common Redpoll, and Red and White-winged Crossbills.

If time permits, the farm fields along Stearns Road, midway between Storrs and Willimantic, are also worth checking for geese, raptors, and open-field passerines, such as Horned Lark and Snow Bunting, in winter.

◼ Lot W

Location: Opposite the intersection of Connecticut Route 195 (Storrs Road) and Horsebarn Hill Road, Storrs.
➲ **Directions:** The entrance for Lot W is on the west side of Route 195, across from

a big barn at the north end of Horsebarn Hill Road. Park in designated PayByPhone spots; see details above, under Parking.

Start by a small, tree-lined pond near the northwest corner of the parking lot. Check the thickets along the pond's eastern edge first. Song Sparrows nest here, Dark-eyed Juncos are regular during migration and winter, and American Tree Sparrows are common from late fall through winter. The thickets and particularly the grassy edges between the pond and the cornfield are good areas to look for White-crowned, Field, Vesper, and Fox Sparrows, especially in April or May then again in October. Lark and Grasshopper Sparrows have occurred.

Walk the dirt road west along the pond's north edge, with a cornfield on your right. Check the pond edge for shorebirds, especially in fall. Solitary and Spotted Sandpipers are annual visitors, while Pectoral Sandpiper and Greater Yellowlegs are occasional. Killdeer nest in the area. A small shallow seep paralleling the track on the right is frequented by Wilson's Snipe in March and April then again in fall.

Just past the pond on the left, a path leads south. From here, you have several choices.

If you have less than an hour, take the path south and circle the pond. The vine tangles and dense cover in this area regularly attract Lincoln's Sparrows, especially in May and October, and have harbored Yellow-breasted Chat, Dickcissel, and Orange-crowned Warbler in fall. Hedgerow species are common, with Northern Flicker, American Robin, and Cedar Waxwing found year-round. Both Common Redpoll and Pine Siskin have occurred here.

If you have more than an hour, walk north and follow the perimeter of the cornfield. When you reach the field's north end, turn right and follow the dirt track toward Route 195 to visit the Mansfield Community Garden (on the left), before looping back to the parking lot along the field's east side.

The forest and hedgerows along the cornfield's edges attract uncommon migrants such as Swainson's Thrush and Wilson's Warbler. This is also a good area to find Eastern Bluebird and large numbers of migratory sparrows (especially Song and Savannah Sparrows) and warblers (especially Palm Warbler).

The cornfield itself draws raptors year-round. Northern Harriers are regularly seen, except during the breeding season, while Peregrine Falcon and Merlin are occasional during migration. American Kestrel and Red-tailed and Red-shouldered Hawks nest and hunt in the area, and Rough-legged Hawks have been observed, usually in late fall or winter. Look for a large flock of Horned Lark during winter, sometimes with Snow Bunting or Lapland Longspur mixed in. Migrating Savannah Sparrow and American Pipit use these fields in spring and fall, while dozens of Bobolink may congregate in the corn in autumn. Fall through spring, the local goose flock regularly feeds here. Exceptional sightings in the cornfield include Northern Lapwing, Gyrfalcon, Snowy Owl, and Northern Wheatear.

The Mansfield Community Garden is a good place to find sparrows, among many other species, especially in fall. A *Selasphorus* hummingbird was once found here. As you return to Lot W along the east edge of the cornfield, you will pass behind Mansfield Supply, a hardware store. The bushes and trees behind the store have attracted several unusual species over the years, including Lark Sparrow, Dickcissel, and Northern Shrike. Eastern Towhee and Fox Sparrow can be found during migration.

◼ Mirror Lake

Location: Mansfield Road, Storrs.
➲ **Directions:** From Lot W, turn right onto Route 195 and proceed 0.8 miles, watching for the pond on your right. Just past the pond's south end, turn right onto Mansfield Road. **Note:** There is no road sign for Mansfield Road.
Parking: A few metered parking spaces are available at the pond's south end.

This small pond is worth a quick look at any time of year. A spotting scope is helpful but not essential.

Mirror Lake attracts a variety of waterfowl and gulls year-round—more than might be expected given its size. It has hosted five species of geese as well as other regional rarities, including Great Egret, Common Tern, Iceland Gull, and Tundra Swan. A Yellow-throated Warbler was once found in the small woodlot nearby.

In winter, the warm-water discharge from campus buildings keeps Mirror Lake open later than other bodies of water in the area. Mallards and a few American Black Ducks are the standard fare, with some hybrids in the mix, but the pond also receives regular though infrequent visits from other species, including Common and Hooded Mergansers, Ring-necked Duck, Gadwall, and Blue-winged Teal. Both Green-winged Teal and American Wigeon have overwintered in recent years.

Migrant Canada Geese used to roost here in the thousands, but the university has taken steps to reduce their presence in recent years, making the site far less suited to the discovery of rare geese than in the past.

Throughout the year, the lake hosts a few Ring-billed and Herring Gulls, along with the occasional Great Black-backed Gull. Lesser Black-backed and Iceland Gulls are very rare, but have been seen here and elsewhere in the vicinity. Other species to look for on or around the lake include Double-crested Cormorant, Great Blue Heron, Belted Kingfisher, Cooper's Hawk, Northern Flicker, and Eastern Bluebird; during migration, Osprey stop to snack on the resident carp.

◼ Horsebarn Hill Loop

Location: Horse Unit 2, Horsebarn Hill Road, Storrs.
⊃ **Directions:** Leaving Mirror Lake, drive north on Route 195 for 0.3 miles, then turn right onto Gurleyville Road. The road forks almost immediately: bear left onto Horsebarn Hill Road. Continue 0.5 miles, scanning the fields to the right for geese and shorebirds, then park at the polo arena on the left, opposite the buildings for Horse Unit 2.
Additional information: The UConn Dairy Bar, 3636 Horsebarn Hill Road Extension, is in one of the buildings on the hill's southwest side. It serves soft drinks and wonderful homemade ice cream!

Horsebarn Hill Road forms a 1.2-mile, U-shaped loop off Route 195. The road is lined with farm fields, agricultural buildings, and small woodlots and wet areas. You can walk around the hill *in about an hour*, or drive and scan the fields from the road.

The paddocks at Horse Unit 2 support large mixed flocks of blackbirds in March and April, then again in October and November. Barn Swallows often appear around the animal buildings (they nest in many of them). Common woodland and hedgerow species can be found behind these buildings, while White-crowned Sparrow, American Pipit, and Dickcissel also have occurred here.

Check the wet areas in the fields opposite the polo arena, known as Valentine's Meadows, which draw Wilson's Snipe and other shorebirds during migration. Greater and Lesser Yellowlegs (uncommon), Solitary and Spotted Sandpipers, and other shorebirds have occurred. Geese and ducks regularly use the area, as do migrant Eastern Meadowlark and American Pipit.

After visiting the paddocks and checking Valentine's Meadow, return to the northwest corner of the polo arena parking lot, then walk west on Horse Barn Hill Extension. Going uphill along the tree-lined road, you will pass a few houses, then meet a trail on the right. Take this trail, which leads over the hilltop. Turn right when the trail intersects a road, then right again onto the northern part of Horsebarn Hill Road, which will return you to the polo arena.

Eastern Bluebirds are a common sight on the telephone wires and fences in this area. Killdeer nest in the paddocks; in early spring and fall, the local breeders are joined by numerous migrating Killdeer. Red-tailed and Cooper's Hawks are commonly seen year-round, while Sharp-shinned Hawk and Merlin are fairly regular occurrences.

In spring and summer, grassland species such as Savannah Sparrow, Bobolink, Eastern Meadowlark, and American Kestrel can be found in the open fields anywhere along this loop, but especially around the hilltop. Nest boxes have been erected for Eastern Bluebird, Tree Swallow, and American Kestrel, and all three species breed here. Kestrels may overwinter when conditions are mild. Upland Sandpiper and Grasshopper Sparrow have been seen in summer but are not known to nest.

During migration, the thickets and woodland edges on Horsebarn Hill can be quite good for landbirds. Walking the hedgerows in summer usually produces the common edge species along with the occasional Cedar Waxwing or Baltimore Oriole. Chimney Swifts are usually around from late April into mid-September. Fall through spring, a variety of songbirds frequent the hedges and field edges, including Song, Savannah, White-throated, Swamp, and American Tree Sparrows, Dark-eyed Junco, Northern Cardinal, Indigo Bunting, and American Goldfinch. Less common sparrows, such as Lincoln's, Vesper, and White-crowned Sparrows, occur periodically. Small numbers of Purple Finches may occur at any time of the year.

The hilltop provides a splendid and rather scenic vantage point from which to view migrating hawks. Northern Harrier, Osprey, Merlin, American Kestrel, and Sharp-shinned, Cooper's, Red-tailed, and Red-shouldered Hawks are regular migrants, though none in significant numbers. Most species are seen hunting the fields and woodlot edges rather than as passage-migrants, high overhead. Annually, the occasional Peregrine Falcon or Bald Eagle is sighted, but Golden Eagle is very rare. Turkey Vultures are common year-round, while Black Vultures are becoming more frequent in the area. The hilltop is also a good site to scan for diurnal landbird migrants. Common Nighthawks pass by on evenings in May and early June, then again from late August into September.

From October through April, a flock of up to 150 Horned Larks—sometimes with American Pipits, Snow Buntings, and a few Lapland Longspurs mixed in—can usually be found on the grassy hilltop. These birds also may visit the manure piles behind the barns to the southeast.

The cattail marsh to the west of the hilltop once hosted a flock of Glossy Ibis (very rare inland), and is always worth a look; ibis also have been seen in the wet seeps at the bottom of the east slope. There are often Red-tailed Hawks perched in the taller trees or on the roofs of nearby buildings. Swamp Sparrow can sometimes be found in the marsh as well.

As you walk back along Horsebarn Hill Road toward the polo arena, you will pass a small picnic area at the northeast corner of the loop. Northern Saw-whet, Great Horned, and Barred Owls have been heard in the nearby woods in winter and spring. In summer, these woods host Veery, Wood Thrush, Red-eyed Vireo, Scarlet Tanager, Rose-breasted Grosbeak, and other species typical of second-growth forest. The fenced paddocks, just south of the picnic area on the east side of the road, and the polo arena itself are both good spots to look for nesting Killdeer; search any wet areas along the road for shorebirds and waterfowl.

◼ Pumping Station Road

Location: Off Gurleyville Road, Storrs.
⮑ **Directions:** Drive east on Gurleyville Road from its intersection with Horsebarn Hill Road for 1.1 miles. At the bottom of a long hill, where the road bears sharply to the right, take a sharp left turn onto a poorly maintained dirt road. Although it may appear as if you're turning into a driveway, this is Pumping Station Road. (The university allows public access.) Continue on Pumping Station Road for about 0.6 miles, passing a power-line cut, after which the road takes a sharp right turn then comes to the first pumping station. Park on the right, where the road turns sharply left. **Note:** Pumping Station Road also can be reached on foot from the Nipmuck Trail. The trailhead is another 0.1 miles east on Gurleyville Road, by a bridge over the Fenton River.

Pumping Station Road parallels the Nipmuck Trail along the west side of the Fenton River and ends at the second of two pumping stations. The road traverses a nice cross-section of habitats, including second-growth hardwoods, pine and hemlock stands, wet and dry meadows, a beaver pond, and riparian forest.

Fifteen or more species of warblers are possible in May, then again in August and September. Breeders include Ovenbird, American Redstart, and Black-and-white and Worm-eating Warblers in the hardwood forests, Pine and Black-throated Green Warblers in the conifers, Yellow and Blue-winged Warblers in the shrubby fields, and Common Yellowthroat and Louisiana Waterthrush along the Fenton River. During migration, these are joined by Nashville, Chestnut-sided, and Yellow-rumped Warblers; Northern Parula, and Northern Waterthrush, along with such less common species as Tennessee, Black-throated Blue, Blackburnian, and Wilson's Warblers. Search for Canada Warbler in the dense laurel thickets near the Fenton River, especially in May; a few may occasionally breed here.

Dawn birders may catch the thumping serenade of Ruffed Grouse in spring, although there have been few reports in recent years. Males display by drumming from atop fallen logs, especially in the early mornings from April through June. It is a display seldom witnessed, and a sound that's felt more than heard. Listen for the songs of Wood Thrush and Veery in spring and summer. Thickets along the road provide cover for breeding Eastern Towhee, Chipping Sparrow, Northern Cardinal, and Song Sparrow; the same thickets can be full of sparrows in winter as well. Scan the power lines and any exposed perches along the power-line cut for Ruby-throated Hummingbirds spring through fall.

The typical residents of second-growth forest include Black-capped Chickadee, Tufted Titmouse, White-breasted Nuthatch, Blue Jay, and various woodpeckers. Although the Brown Creeper's thin call can easily go unnoticed, their explosive song is hard to miss in spring. These fascinating little birds feed by starting at the base of a tree, toggling up the trunk to the top, then flying to the base of the next tree to repeat the process. They seem to prefer areas with at least some evergreens, but conceal their nests under the loose bark of shagbark hickory or of dead trees. They often roost communally in winter, sheltering together under bark.

Summer migrants include the diminutive Blue-gray Gnatcatcher, which seems to prefer oaks for its nests. Although tiny, these birds are active and vocal, constantly flitting through the trees and uttering their "mew" call. Great-crested Flycatchers can be conspicuous along this stretch of road, where they use tree cavities as nest sites. In spring and summer, listen for the "chick-bur" call of the Scarlet Tanager, the warbling, robin-like song of the Rose-breasted Grosbeak, and the slow monotonous musings of the Red-eyed Vireo. Eastern Wood-Pewee is also heard here, especially in early morning and late afternoon.

From the first pumping station, you can walk south on a trail that runs alongside the river, continue north along the road to an open meadow, or backtrack west along the road to check out the power-line cut.

Eastern Phoebe, one of the earliest migrants to our area, usually arrives in March and often uses the eaves of the pumping station for nesting. They generally stay through October (rarely into December). The trail along the river passes through the breeding territories of Black-throated Green Warbler, Louisiana Waterthrush, and Warbling and Yellow-throated Vireos. The Warbling Vireo has a lively song, but the Yellow-throated's tune is raspy and slow, similar to a Red-eyed Vireo trying to sing like a Scarlet Tanager. Blue-headed Vireo can be found during migration.

The dead pines to the north of the pumping station attract Northern Flicker and Red-bellied, Downy, Hairy, and Pileated Woodpeckers, all of which breed in the surrounding area. Occasionally, Yellow-bellied Sapsuckers visit during migration, preferring live maple, basswood, apple, and aspen on which to leave their signature rows of shallow holes. Any of the live pine stands may contain breeding Pine Warblers, which sing a soft liquid trill.

It is usually worthwhile to walk back along Pumping Station Road toward Gurleyville Road, at least to the power-line cut. This area can produce breeding Worm-eating Warblers, allowing you to compare their buzzy trill with that of the more numerous Chipping Sparrows and Pine Warblers. This is also a good place to look for migrant landbirds.

If you continue on from the first pumping station (either by car or on foot), you will come to the second pumping station and a small parking area at road's end, with a sign for the Nipmuck Trail. The trail goes north, crosses a small stream, then continues into a shrubby field and the woods beyond.

Just after the small stream is a marshy area with a beaver pond on the left. Common Yellowthroat breeds in the marsh, and possibly Swamp Sparrow. Solitary and Spotted Sandpipers are sometimes seen during migration. Common Grackle and Red-winged Blackbird frequent the pond edge; the dead snags around the pond house nesting Eastern Bluebird and Tree Swallow.

A pleasant loop trail passes through the shrubby field then returns along the river. It's an easy 15-minute walk, but *allow at least 45 minutes* for birding. Yellow and Blue-winged Warblers, Northern Cardinal, Song Sparrow, House Wren, Baltimore Oriole, and Ruby-throated Hummingbird all breed in the area. Field Sparrow, Indigo Bunting, and Prairie Warbler are sometimes seen during migration; these may occasionally nest here as well. Both cuckoo species occur in the area in some years.

In March, male American Woodcock perform their comical mating displays in the meadow, complete with strutting, "peenting," and energetic flights into the ether. To witness the festivities, it is best to arrive a half-hour before sunset, then wait quietly for the show to commence. Avoid using flashlights once activities start as the light may disturb them. This meadow also attracts Wild Turkey from time to time.

The evergreens along the river draw in migrating Blackburnian Warbler in spring and fall, and are home to nesting Black-throated Green Warbler from late April onward. Eastern Screech-Owl and Great Horned and Barred Owls all occur in the area. Ospreys hunt the Fenton River during migration, especially in September and October, joining resident Belted Kingfishers. The kingfishers nest in holes in the banks. If the river ices over, the kingfishers may depart in winter.

Fall through spring, the many shrubs and weedy plants in the meadow attract a variety of seed- and fruit-eating species, including sparrows, Cedar Waxwing, American Robin, and Eastern Bluebird. This is a good site for wintering American Tree Sparrow, as well as a lingering Hermit Thrush or Gray Catbird. A few White-crowned Sparrows usually turn up in late September or early October, then again in May, often in association with White-throated Sparrows and multiflora roses.

Boston Hollow Tour, Ashford

Seasonal rating: Sp *** Su *** F ** W *
Best time to bird: Mid-May to mid-June
Habitats: Hemlock ravine with white pine and spruce stands, forested ridgeline, early successional forest, bare cliff faces, beaver ponds, tussock and cattail marshes, open meadows, farmland, and small streams.

Bird list for this site:

SPECIALTY BIRDS
Resident – Ruffed Grouse, Northern Goshawk (rare), Yellow-bellied Sapsucker, Pileated Woodpecker, Common Raven, Red-breasted Nuthatch, Brown Creeper (uncommon in winter), Golden-crowned Kinglet, Purple Finch, White-winged Crossbill (sporadic)
Summer – Broad-winged Hawk, Yellow-billed and Black-billed Cuckoos, Ruby-throated Hummingbird; Acadian (most years), Alder (uncommon), and Least Flycatchers; Yellow-throated and Blue-headed Vireos, Winter Wren, Hermit Thrush; Magnolia, Yellow-rumped, Black-throated Blue, Blackburnian, Canada, and Worm-eating Warblers (possible); Northern Waterthrush, Field Sparrow (uncommon)
Winter – Crossbills (sporadic), Common Redpoll (sporadic), Pine Siskin (sporadic)

OTHER KEY BIRDS
Resident – Wild Turkey, Great Blue Heron; Cooper's, Red-shouldered, and Red-tailed Hawks; Great Horned and Barred Owls, Belted Kingfisher; Red-bellied, Downy, and Hairy Woodpeckers; Northern Flicker, Eastern Bluebird
Summer – American Woodcock, Eastern Wood-Pewee, Eastern Phoebe, Willow and Great Crested Flycatchers, Eastern Kingbird, Warbling and Red-eyed Vireos; Tree, Northern Rough-winged, and Barn Swallows; White-breasted Nuthatch, Carolina and House Wrens, Blue-gray Gnatcatcher, Veery, Wood Thrush, Cedar Waxwing; Yellow, Chestnut-sided, Black-throated Green, Pine, Prairie (some years), and Black-and-White Warblers; American Redstart, Ovenbird, Louisiana Waterthrush, Common Yellowthroat, Scarlet Tanager, Eastern Towhee, Chipping Sparrow, Rose-breasted Grosbeak, Indigo Bunting, Baltimore Oriole
Winter – American Tree, Fox, and White-throated Sparrows; Dark-eyed Junco

MIGRANTS
Gray-cheeked (uncommon) and Swainson's Thrushes, Nashville Warbler (may breed), Northern Parula; Cape May, Bay-breasted, Blackpoll, and Palm Warblers; Cerulean and Hooded Warblers (uncommon), Rusty Blackbird (uncommon)

Location: Intersection of Connecticut Route 89 and Boston Hollow Road, Ashford.
Restrooms: At Cumberland Farms, 33 Pompey Hollow Road (U.S. Route 44), Ashford; also at Travel Centers of America (TA), just off I-84 at exit 71.

Boston Hollow is a 2-mile-long ravine through Yale Forest lands. A small stream runs its length, shaded by hemlocks, with steep forested hills and scattered cliffs on either side. It is home to porcupines, fishers, and bobcats, with a nice variety of breeding amphibians in its swamps and vernal pools. Winter Wrens nest among the many deadfalls, while pink lady's slippers and maple-leafed viburnum bloom on its hillsides.

Many of the breeding birds are representative of more northern climes, and the area offers a sizable collection of species in a relatively small area. Hermit Thrush—a very uncommon or local breeder in the state—can be heard singing from the hillsides. Louisiana Waterthrush and Belted Kingfisher patrol the stream and pond edges, and the wetter swampy areas are home to breeding Northern Waterthrush and Canada Warbler. Areas with a shrub understory (especially laurel) support Black-throated Blue Warbler. Spruce stands may hold nesting Golden-crowned Kinglet or Magnolia Warbler. Evidence of Pileated Woodpeckers can be found throughout the hollow, and Least Flycatcher, Blue-headed Vireo, and Brown Creeper are heard along much of its length. Although seen infrequently, Northern Goshawk, the quintessential raptor of northern woodlands, hunts these forests.

How to Bird This Area

The following paragraphs describe a 6-mile tour through Boston Hollow that *requires at least 2 hours*. **Note:** Be sure to set your odometer to zero where indicated, as subsequent directions are given in tenths of a mile.

The roads on this route are unpaved. The west end is plowed in winter, but the east end, along Axe Factory Road, is not maintained in winter and may be closed. Although in a relatively remote area, the roads are well-traveled, so take care when stopping along the roadside. Because the ravine is shaded in early morning, it can be well past first light before bird activity picks up.

At the intersection of Route 89 and Boston Hollow Road, turn east onto Boston Hollow Road. After 0.3 miles, the road surface turns to dirt where Eastford Road bears to the right. **Note: Set your odometer to zero here**, then continue on Boston Hollow Road.

In the first 0.3 miles of unpaved road, the typical breeding species include all of Connecticut's woodpeckers (except Red-headed Woodpecker), along with Great Crested Flycatcher, Eastern Wood-Pewee, Scarlet Tanager;

Yellow-throated, Blue-headed, and Red-eyed Vireos; Blue-gray Gnatcatcher, Veery, Wood Thrush, and Rose-breasted Grosbeak.

At 0.6 miles on your odometer, look for a very large boulder on the left. Just after the boulder is a hemlock stand with nesting Blackburnian and Black-throated Green Warblers. This is also a good area for Pileated Woodpecker and Rose-breasted Grosbeak.

Between 0.7 and 0.9 miles, listen for Black-throated Blue Warbler on the hill to the right, and Canada Warbler and Northern Waterthrush in the flooded swamp on the left.

At 1.0 miles, there is a slope on the left with scattered dead trees that can be good for Winter Wren.

At 1.1 miles on your odometer, look for some cliffs up the hill on the left (it can be difficult to see through the trees). These cliffs are one of several traditional nesting sites for Common Raven in the hollow. There is a pull-off on the left *at 1.2 miles* which offers a convenient place to stop and check the area. A trail leads uphill toward the cliffs. Ravens are often vocal around the nest and may be heard or seen anywhere along the road.

Between 1.1 and 1.5 miles, the low areas are generally good for breeding Acadian Flycatcher from mid-May through August. *At 1.4 miles* on your odometer, there is another pull-off on the left. The trail here leads to the cliffs where the area's first Common Raven nest was located.

At 1.5 miles, just after passing a house, look for a white pine grove on the left. This grove can be birdy at any time of year. Pine and Blackburnian Warblers nest here and in most of the pine stands along the road. In winter, this is a good place to look for Golden-crowned Kinglet as well as mixed-species feeding flocks.

At 1.7 miles, turn left onto an unmarked road. Known as Axe Factory Road or Barlow Mill Road, this road may be closed in winter or in mud season. **Note: Reset your odometer to zero here**.

Soon after the intersection, Axe Factory Road traverses an open wet area that is home to breeding Purple Finch. Willow Flycatcher nests at the fringes of the marsh, while Magnolia Warbler may breed in the small conifers to the right of the road. Northern Goshawks are sometimes seen in this area, and Common Ravens frequent the ridge to the left. In early spring, the "peent" of the American Woodcock can be heard here at dusk and dawn, as well as in another open area 0.3 miles farther on.

At about 0.2 miles on your odometer, stop just after a small pond on the left. Ruffed Grouse are sometimes heard on the hillside behind the pond, and a rare Brewster's Warbler (Golden-winged × Blue-winged hybrid) was once found here.

At 0.4 miles, Black-throated Green Warblers are fairly common in the stretch of hemlocks that begins here.

When the road takes a sharp turn to the left and comes to a bridge overlooking two small ponds, check exposed perches for resident Belted Kingfisher. American Black Duck (a fairly uncommon inland breeder) has bred in these small wetlands, as has Wood Duck and possibly Hooded Merganser.

At 1.1 miles on your odometer, bear right where the unmarked Hillside Road goes to the left. At this point, Axe Factory Road becomes Kinney Hollow Road. The road now passes through some areas of dense hemlock and a swamp.

At 1.8 miles, Bigelow Brook will appear on the right. This is a worthwhile place to get out of the car and walk a bit. In summer, it is a good site for Least Flycatcher and sometimes Willow Flycatcher or Swamp Sparrow.

From 1.9 to 2.0 miles, an area of recently harvested white pines is great for Pine Warbler. It's also a good spot to look for Nashville Warbler during migration (though not a confirmed breeder, any area with conifers less than 15 feet tall should be checked for this species).

At 2.5 miles on your odometer, the spruce stand on the right is one of the best areas to find breeding Golden-crowned Kinglet and Blackburnian and Black-throated Green Warblers. Red-breasted Nuthatches are sometimes found during migration and may breed here as well. White-throated Sparrow and Yellow-rumped Warbler breed along the road and frequent this area during migration.

At 2.6 miles, Kinney Hollow Road makes a sharp left, then heads uphill. Kinney Pond appears shortly on the left, with parking available on the pond's west side. The pond's walking trails can be productive during migration.

At 2.8 miles, there is another spruce stand worth checking for Golden-crowned Kinglet; this stand also has attracted Pine Grosbeak (uncommon) in winter. The wet area near it is a gathering site for migrating Tree, Barn, and Northern Rough-winged Swallows, especially March through May, then again in August and September. Belted Kingfishers hunt the open water on both sides of the road.

At 2.9 miles, the open area is a good site for Chestnut-sided Warbler, spring through summer.

At 4.1 miles, there is an apple orchard on the right. This area—along with the crabapples 0.1 miles farther on, at the intersection with Town Hall Road—should be checked in winter for Pine Grosbeak, Cedar Waxwing, and Bohemian Waxwing (rare). Eastern Bluebird and American Robin are also possible.

To return to I-84, continue on Kinney Hollow Road to its intersection with Connecticut Route 190, then turn left. *If you have more time*, it's a short drive to Bigelow Hollow State Park, which hosts a similar mix of species. To get there, turn right on Town Hall Road, then turn right onto Route 190. Continue 0.2 miles, then turn right onto Connecticut Route 171, toward North Ashford. Proceed 1.2 miles to Bigelow Hollow State Park on the left.

(47) Pomfret Loop

- Connecticut Audubon Society's Bafflin Sanctuary
- Wyndham Land Trust Preserve
- Duck Marsh
- Natchaug State Forest
- Cul-de-sac
- Lyon Preserve
- Meadow Ledge
- Mashamoquet Meadow
- Needles Eye Road
- Air Line Trail

Seasonal rating: Sp *** Su **** F *** W *
Best time to bird: mid-April through October
Habitats: Open farmland, old fields, grasslands, second-growth deciduous forest, pine stands, hemlock ravines, streams, small ponds, wooded swamps, wet meadows, cattail marshes, and shallow ponds.

Bird list for this site:

SPECIALTY BIRDS

Resident – Ruffed Grouse, Ring-necked Pheasant, Common Raven, Purple Finch
Summer – Blue-winged Teal (very local), Green-winged Teal (sporadic; very local), Pied-billed Grebe, American Bittern (sporadic), American Woodcock, Black-billed and Yellow-billed Cuckoos, American Kestrel, Least and Willow Flycatchers, Purple Martin (sporadic), Red-breasted Nuthatch (red pines), Brown Thrasher, White-eyed Vireo; Blue-winged, Prairie, Canada, and Worm-eating Warblers; Field and Savannah Sparrows, Bobolink, Orchard Oriole
Winter – Northern Harrier, Rough-legged Hawk (some years), Long-eared Owl, Northern Saw-whet Owl (common migrant), American Tree Sparrow

OTHER KEY BIRDS

Resident – Wild Turkey, Cooper's and Red-shouldered Hawks, Eastern Screech-Owl, Great Horned and Barred Owls
Summer – Wood Duck, Hooded Merganser, Great Blue and Green Herons, Turkey Vulture, Virginia Rail, Sora, Killdeer, Spotted Sandpiper, Broad-winged Hawk, Ruby-throated Hummingbird, Belted Kingfisher, six nesting woodpecker species, Warbling and Yellow-throated Vireos, Bank and Northern Rough-winged Swallows, Brown Creeper, Blue-gray Gnatcatcher, Eastern Bluebird, Veery, Wood Thrush, Cedar Waxwing; Black-throated Green, Chestnut-sided, Blackburnian, Pine, and Black-

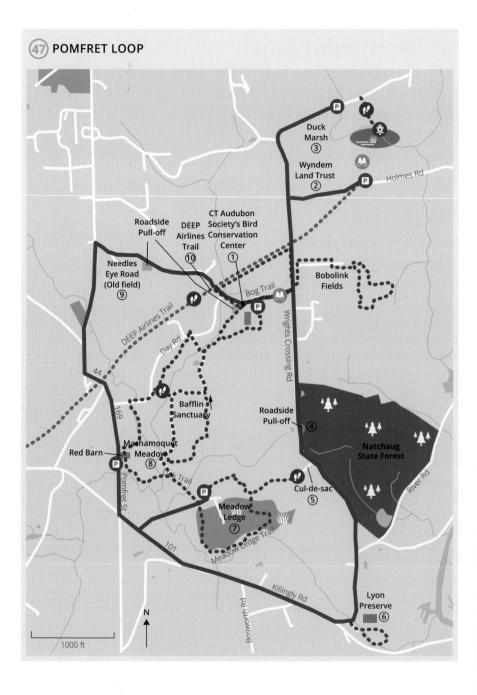

Duck
Marsh
③

Wyndem
Land Trust
②

Holmes Rd

Roadside
Pull-off

DEEP
Airlines
Trail
⑩

CT Audubon
Society's Bird
Conservation
Center
①

Needles
Eye Road
(Old field)
⑨

Bobolink
Fields

Bog Trail

DEEP Airlines Trail

Day Rd

44

Wrights Crossing Rd

Bafflin
Sanctuary

169

Roadside
Pull-off
④

Natchaug
State Forest

River Rd

Mashamoquet
Meadow
⑧

Red Barn

Trail

Cul-de-sac
⑤

Pomfret St

Meadow
Ledge
⑦

Meadow Ledge Trail

101

Killingly Rd

Bosworth Rd

Lyon
Preserve
⑥

N

1000 ft

and-white Warblers; American Redstart, Louisiana and Northern Waterthrushes, Ovenbird, Scarlet Tanager, Indigo Bunting, Rose-breasted Grosbeak, Eastern Towhee, Swamp Sparrow

Winter – Common Merganser, Bald Eagle, Horned Lark, Fox Sparrow

MIGRANTS
Spring – Blue-headed Vireo; thrushes, including Swainson's and Gray-cheeked Thrushes; warblers, including Northern Parula and Nashville, Tennessee, Black-throated Blue, Magnolia, Yellow-rumped, and Mourning

Fall – American Pipit, Ruby-crowned and Golden-crowned Kinglets, Blue-headed and Philadelphia Vireos, Yellow-rumped Warbler, Dark-eyed Junco; White-throated, White-crowned, Swamp, Lincoln's, American Tree, and Fox Sparrows

---

Restrooms: At the Connecticut Audubon Society's Bafflin Sanctuary, 218 Day Road.

Wild Turkeys are a common sight in the Pomfret area.

The Birding

Enter Pomfret and you enter a town with a longstanding tradition of agriculture. One with barnyards and cornfields, rock walls and hedgerows, where grain silos and corncribs still stand, and Holsteins walk to the barn to be milked. It is a place to buy milk from the maker. With one look at the surroundings in summer, a birder's thoughts turn to American Kestrel,

Bobolink, Savannah Sparrow, and Eastern Meadowlark. In winter, you find your eyes scanning the hawthorn bushes and barbed wire for signs of Northern Shrike. Full crabapple trees elicit visions of Bohemian Waxwing or Pine Grosbeak among the many flocks of Cedar Waxwing. Open expanses draw your eye to exposed perches in hopes of a Rough-legged Hawk. Plowed fields conjure thoughts of Horned Lark and maybe a Snow Bunting or Lapland Longspur. It's a place to glimpse a Northern Harrier cruising over the cornfields and to wonder if Northern Bobwhite are around.

During harvest season, the old barnyards and hedgerow thickets are ripe for views of migrating sparrows. Hidden in the seemingly uniform agricultural landscape are also some surprises: hemlock ravines with nesting Black-throated Green Warbler and Winter Wren, talus slopes where Worm-eating Warbler sings and searches dead leaves for food, and dense laurel thickets where Canada Warbler breeds. There are moist bogs harboring Northern Waterthrush; kettle-hole ponds with nesting teal, rails, and bitterns; and wet meadows with dancing woodcock.

How to Bird These Sites

The 700-acre Bafflin Sanctuary, owned by the Connecticut Audubon Society (CAS), is the largest piece in a mosaic of protected properties; the others are owned by Wyndham Land Trust and the state. Combined, they create over 1,300 acres of protected habitat. This chapter describes a 9.6-mile loop through these properties, visiting a variety of productive habitats while highlighting sites for shrubland and grassland species. The loop *can be done in a few hours by car*, but it can easily take a full day, especially if you hike on some of the trails.

■ Connecticut Audubon Society Center at Pomfret

Location: 218 Day Road, Pomfret.

The Pomfret center serves as the gateway to the Bafflin Sanctuary's forests, streams, and rolling meadows. The sanctuary's bird list includes more than 200 species and is still growing. Numerous tracts of land, each more than 200 acres, are managed specifically for shrub- and grassland-dependent species. While such species are disappearing due to development and forest regeneration elsewhere in the state, they are doing relatively well here. Several sites are managed as food plots—planted with grains attractive to a variety of seed-eating species. Bobolinks, large flocks of Indigo Buntings, and mixed groups of sparrows gather at these sites in late summer and early fall. In late October or early November, hordes of sparrows visit these sites. Eastern Meadowlarks occur regularly as migrants. Sadly, Northern Bobwhite is gone.

The small grove of mature trees on the hill adjacent to the parking lot seems an unlikely migrant trap, but it attracts Yellow-throated Vireo, Yellow and Pine Warblers, and Baltimore Oriole, along with the occasional Orchard Oriole. Indigo Bunting and both cuckoo species also have been found here. A Golden Eagle has even spent time resting in these trees. Bobolinks nest in the nearby meadows; from August to October, large post-breeding flocks gather in the wet areas here to eat smartweed and other seeds. A pair of American Kestrels (increasingly rare) nest in a box just northeast of the Nature Center.

Look in the parking area for a sign marking the trailhead for the Ravine Trail. Take this short loop in summer to find nesting Black-throated Green Warbler in the hemlocks and Louisiana Waterthrush in the wet areas. The ravine also attracts migrants, especially thrushes, in spring and fall.

■ Observation Platform (Bog Trail)

⊃ **Directions:** From the parking lot, turn right (east) on Day Road. After 0.1 miles, stop at an observation platform on the left, overlooking a marsh.

Though sometimes obscure, the Bog Trail begins just to the right of the platform; it leads down to the left through a field, bends east, then traverses the southeast edge of the marsh (there is a boardwalk at the eastern end). The trail then circles behind the marsh and returns to the parking lot. The loop is about 1 mile and usually worth the walk, especially spring through fall. Prepare for mud in the spring.

Virginia Rail nests in the cattails, and some may linger into winter. Blackpoll, Wilson's, and Canada Warblers seem especially attracted to this area during migration. American Woodcock can sometimes be found along the wet edges of the marsh, and a rare Sedge Wren was once seen here. Willow Flycatcher breeds along the perimeter and Least Flycatcher in the woods behind the marsh. The many nest boxes you see here (and elsewhere throughout the preserve) are for Eastern Bluebird and Tree Swallow but may also attract Black-capped Chickadee, House Wren, and other cavity-nesting species. Bluebirds and Tree Swallows are conspicuous here spring through fall. The American Kestrels that nest nearby are frequently seen in the fields across the road from the observation platform. In autumn, the platform also is a good place to watch for migrating hawks, although numbers and diversity are generally low compared to the coast or the western end of the state.

◼ Wyndham Land Trust Preserve

⊃ **Directions:** From the observation platform, continue east on Day Road to the T-intersection with Wrights Crossing Road. (Directly across the intersection is the most densely populated Bobolink nesting area in the sanctuary; in spring, these fields resonate with the complex song of the males.) Turn left onto Wrights Crossing Road and proceed 0.5 miles, then turn right onto Holmes Road (a dirt road). Continue 0.4 miles on Holmes Road to a pull-off on the left.

This site is a 146-acre preserve owned by the Wyndham Land Trust. It is a short walk (north) over the hilltop to an observation platform overlooking a wetlands complex. A spotting scope can be useful here. The marsh and beaver ponds attract waterfowl spring through fall. Numbers and species composition are dependent on the season and water levels, but there is usually something of interest to see here year-round. Blue-winged and Green-winged Teal, Wood Duck, and Hooded Merganser, as well as American Bittern, have nested in the marsh. The hilltop and platform are good vantage points from which to watch for migrating raptors in fall; Bald and Golden Eagles (rare) have been seen, and Rough-legged Hawks can occur here in late fall and winter. In late summer and fall, the fields are carpeted in goldenrod, a favorite food plant of many butterfly species, including migrating monarchs. Keep an eye out for bobcats, which are sometimes seen around the beaver ponds or resting at the tops of dead snags during mating season.

◼ Duck Marsh

⊃ **Directions:** Return to Wrights Crossing Road and turn right. Continue on Wrights Crossing Road (it takes a sharp bend to the right) for 0.7 miles to a small parking area on the right, marked with a Land Trust sign.

The Duck Marsh is part of the same preserve you viewed from the hilltop on Holmes Road. To reach the trail for the observation blinds, walk east on the road until you cross a small brook. The trailhead is on the right. Follow the trail south along the field and through the trees to the blinds.

This is one of the best birding sites in the region. The area *can be checked in less than an hour but allow at least twice that,* with some time spent in each blind and wandering the trails. Which species one encounters depends in part on the activities of the resident beavers. When the area is flooded, the conditions favor waterfowl, while low water levels benefit migrating shore-birds. Regionally uncommon species recorded here include Northern Pintail, Gadwall, American Wigeon, and Ruddy Duck; Northrn Shoveler has been found in spring twice. This also may be the best site in northeast Connecti-cut to find migrating Glossy Ibis, in either spring or summer.

In spring or fall, when water levels are low, check the pond edges and open muddy areas for Killdeer, both yellowlegs species, and Soltary, Spotted, Pec-toral, Least, and less frequently, Semipalmated Sandpipers; Dunlin occur very rarely. American Woodcock display at the edge of the wetter areas from March through May and are quite common in the region. Listen for males at dawn and especially at dusk. Males "peent" and strut across display mounds at wet meadow edges, launch themselves skyward, then descend with their wings creating an unearthly syncopated whir.

A number of Connecticut's rare breeding birds have nested here, including American Bittern, Blue-winged Teal, and possibly Green-winged Teal. (Both teal species have been seen in the beaver ponds in summer, but only Blue-winged has been observed with young.) Hooded Merganser, Sora, Virginia Rail, Willow Flycatcher, Brown Thrasher, White-eyed Vireo, and Orchard Oriole also breed here. The more typical nesting birds include Tree and Barn Swallows, both cuckoo species, Gray Catbird, Eastern Bluebird, Warbling Vireo, Yellow and Blue-winged Warblers, Common Yellow-throat, and Eastern Towhee.

The fields across Wrights Crossing Road are home to Bobolinks and a few Savannah Sparrows, spring through fall. Migrant Canada Geese use these and other fields nearby fall through spring. They are occasionally joined by a few Snow Geese, and Greater White-fronted Geese (rare) have occurred. American Kestrels nest in the box in front of the parking area, and Merlins have been seen during migration. Red-shouldered Hawk and Great Horned Owl nest locally.

Natchaug State Forest

● **Directions:** From the Duck Marsh parking area, turn left onto Wrights Crossing Road and return the way you came (passing Holmes Road). Continue past Day Road as well. About 1.9 miles from Duck Marsh, look for a pull-off on the left at a pine stand.

This is a trailhead for Natchaug State Forest land. The trail is worth a walk from May through September and *can be accomplished in 30 to 45 minutes* if you limit your stops. Follow the trail east (it eventually connects to River Road), taking care not to divert onto spur trails or logging roads. The pines near Wrights Crossing Road support nesting Pine Warbler, and Canada Warbler may breed in small numbers farther in, preferring wet areas with rhododendron. Louisiana Waterthrush is also present.

Cul-de-sac

● **Directions:** From the Natchaug State Forest trailhead, continue south on Wrights Crossing Road about 0.1 miles, looking for a metal gate between two stone walls on the right. Park at the entrance to this abandoned road.

This property, saved by the Wyndham Land Trust from becoming a housing development, is a local favorite for viewing migrants in spring and fall. The old road provides easy access through the forest, ending at a cul-de-sac that gives a panoramic view of the wooded edge. Mixed flocks of vireos, warblers, thrushes, and tanagers pass through during migration, including some of the more unusual species, such as Cape May Warbler. Just about anything is possible; on good days, birding groups can spend entire mornings here. The area has a rich diversity of breeding species including plentiful Wood Thrush and Veery, with the occasional Hermit and Swainson's Thrushes visiting during migration. Barred Owl, Pileated Woodpecker, Eastern Wood-Pewee, Blue-gray Gnatcatcher, Yellow-throated Vireo, Chestnut-sided and Worm-eating Warblers, and Scarlet Tanager all breed at this site. Another trail, less than a mile long, leads from the end of the cul-de-sac through the forest to Meadow Ledge Trail in the Bafflin Sanctuary.

Lyon Preserve

➲ Directions: From the cul-de-sac, continue 0.9 miles south on Wrights Crossing Road. Look for a gate and dirt track entering an old field on the left, just before a bridge. This is Lyon Preserve, another Wyndham Land Trust parcel. Turn left and drive 0.1 miles, past a barn, then stop.

You have a few choices here. One is a continuation of the entrance road that returns to the barn and can be driven, but is easy to walk. The first left on this loop is a short dead-end trail that can be worth a walk during migration. The second left is a walking trail that descends to the river, then loops back to the barn.

This is a wonderful site for finding shrubland- and grassland-loving species, year-round. Most of the habitat here is maintained in a state of early succession to keep it suitable for shrub-nesting species such as American Woodcock, Brown Thrasher, White-eyed Vireo; Prairie, Blue-winged, and Yellow Warblers; Indigo Bunting, Eastern Towhee, Orchard Oriole, and Field Sparrow (abundant in spring and summer). Fox Sparrows are usually present in winter.

Purple Finches nest in the spruce grove on the hilltop, and a few remain through winter. Pine Warblers nest in the hilltop pines. In fall, a variety of seed-eaters are attracted to the area, including Northern Cardinal (resident), Dark-eyed Junco, and Fox, Field, White-throated, and Song Sparrows; all usually overwinter. Savannah Sparrows may occur during migration. Occasionally, Sharp-shinned Hawks are seen here in summer, and it is possible that a pair breeds in the area; one patrols the area most winters. American Woodcock display at dusk in the low wet areas here from March through May. Four species of vireos nest in the area: White-eyed Vireo prefers the shrubs; Red-eyed, the forest; and Yellow-throated and Warbling, the wetter areas near the river on the walking trail. A loop down to the river will add species more typical of riparian forest, such as woodpeckers, Black-and-white Warbler, and American Redstart.

Meadow Ledge

➲ Directions: From Lyon Preserve, continue south on Wrights Crossing Road, across the bridge to a stop sign. Turn right and proceed to the next stop sign at Connecticut Route 101. Turn right on Route 101, continue for approximately 1 mile, then take a right onto Bosworth Road. Proceed to the roadside parking area at the end.

This section of Bafflin Sanctuary is just west of the cul-de-sac on Wrights Crossing Road. Walk 100 yards back down the road to the trailheads.

The cornfield to the north attracts American Pipit during fall migration. The Link Trail heads northwest to the Old Barn, and the trail to the cul-de-sac heads northeast. To the south, the Meadow Ledge Trail passes through old fields before reaching a wet area along a stream. If time is short, walk to the stream and back; otherwise, the full loop *can be walked in under 45 minutes*. Be prepared for mud, especially in spring. Brown Thrasher, White-eyed Vireo, Prairie Warbler, Field Sparrow, and other typical old-field species are found here. Closer to the stream, species such as Willow Flycatcher, American Redstart, and Scarlet Tanager may be encountered. Indigo Bunting and Eastern Towhee are common during nesting season.

◼ Mashamoquet Meadow

➲ **Directions:** From Bosworth Road, return to Route 101 and turn right. Continue north for 0.3 miles, to the intersection with Connecticut Route 169. Turn right on Route 169 and continue about 0.7 miles to a parking area on the right, next to a large red barn (just after the Bafflin Sanctuary sign).

Across the road from the parking area is a small Wyndham Land Trust property. It has a short loop trail traversing a field used by Bobolink and Indigo Bunting spring through fall, and a woodlot used by Hairy Woodpecker and other woodpeckers. Barn Swallows nest in the red barn, and rarely, Purple Martins breed in a nearby nest box. Tree Swallows are common. American Kestrels often breed in the nest box just beyond the barn. The grassy areas and edges attract sparrows in fall. The trail enters areas where Willow Flycatchers breed. Black-billed Cuckoos, along with meadow and meadow-edge species, can usually be found here as well.

◼ Needles Eye Road

➲ **Directions:** From Mashamoquet Meadow, continue north on Route 169 for 1.1 miles, then take a right onto Needles Eye Road. Continue 0.4 miles and pull off at the second gate on the right.

The hillside across the road (north) hosts breeding Worm-eating Warbler. To the south is a small regenerating old field with cedars that is home to breeding Blue-winged Warbler and Indigo Bunting. Occasionally, Prairie Warblers breed here, too. Although it's hard to tell, you're on a hilltop. The area is used by spring migrants, especially warblers, vireos, and Scarlet Tanagers. This is often a birdy spot even when other sites are quiet. Walking along the road is the simplest way to check this area.

■ Air Line Trail

⊃ **Directions:** Continue east along Needles Eye Road for another 0.3 miles, then pull off on the right just past an old granite bridge abutment near the junction with Day Road. Walk back to the Air Line Trail, which crosses the road and follows a former railway bed.

The Air Line is so named because the railroad was once the fastest route from New York to Boston. The trail to the southwest, over the hill, enters a hemlock ravine where Wood Thrush, Scarlet Tanager, and Rose-breasted Grosbeak can be plentiful spring through fall. A variety of warblers are attracted to this area during spring migration; a few, including Pine and Worm-eating Warblers, stay to breed. Migrant Mourning Warblers have been found here in late May and early June. In spring, migrants seem to funnel across the road right above the parking area; on some days, this can be a productive place to stand.

Walking southeast along Day Road also can be rewarding. There are food plots a short distance down the road on the left, where the woods open up to fields in a state of early succession. Heading northeast from the roadside near the food plots, along the Bog Trail mentioned earlier in this chapter, you'll meet the Air Line Trail behind the marsh. Large flocks of tanagers, orioles, and grosbeaks move through the thickets here during spring and fall, and it's an excellent place to look for breeding White-eyed Vireo and Blue-winged Warbler in summer. In autumn, the food plots fill with a variety of sparrows and finches. Hordes of Indigo Buntings can often be found with Bobolinks feeding in these cultivated patches of sunflower, sorghum, and millet from August to early October.

To return to the Connecticut Audubon Society's Center at Pomfret, continue on Day Road for another 0.2 miles.

Quinebaug Valley Fish Hatchery, Plainfield

Bird list for this site:

Seasonal rating: Sp *** Su ** F *** W ****
Best time to bird: October through March.
Habitats: Ponds, fields, deciduous and pine forests, and rivers.

SPECIALTY BIRDS
***Resident* –** Great Blue Heron, Bald Eagle, Belted Kingfisher, Pileated Woodpecker
***Summer* –** Wood Duck, Green Heron, Osprey, Spotted Sandpiper, American Kestrel, White-eyed Vireo, Purple Martin, Bank Swallow, Indigo Bunting, Orchard Oriole
***Winter* –** Common Merganser, Ring-necked Duck, Northern Pintail, Wilson's Snipe, Eastern Phoebe, Winter Wren, Ruby-crowned Kinglet, Hermit Thrush, American Pipit, Gray Catbird; Field, Fox, White-crowned, and Swamp Sparrows; Rusty Blackbird, Purple Finch

OTHER KEY BIRDS
***Resident* –** Wild Turkey, Red-tailed Hawk, Red-shouldered Hawk, Eastern Bluebird
***Summer* –** Wood Duck, Killdeer, Broad-winged Hawk, Ruby-throated Hummingbird, Eastern Wood-Pewee, Black-billed and Yellow-billed Cuckoos, Warbling and Yellow-throated Vireos, Northern Rough-winged Swallow, Blue-gray Gnatcatcher, Veery, Wood Thrush, Cedar Waxwing; Black-throated Green, Pine, and Black-and-white Warblers; American Redstart, Yellow Warbler, Common Yellowthroat, Louisiana Waterthrush, Ovenbird, Scarlet Tanager, Rose-breasted Grosbeak, Eastern Towhee
***Winter* –** Brown Creeper, Golden-crowned Kinglet

MIGRANTS
***Spring* –** Green-winged Teal, Blue-headed Vireo, Yellow-rumped and Palm Warblers
***Fall* –** Common Nighthawk, Yellow-bellied Sapsucker, American Pipit, Ruby-crowned and Golden-crowned Kinglets, Blue-headed Vireo, Yellow-rumped Warbler, Dark-eyed Junco; White-throated, White-crowned, Swamp, Lincoln's, American Tree, and Fox Sparrows

Location: 141 Trout Hatchery Road, Plainfield.
Restrooms: In main headquarters building, open daily 8:00 a.m. to 3:00 p.m.

The Birding

Connecticut's largest fish hatchery is situated on approximately 2,000 acres of state-owned land. Bordered by the Quinebaug and Moosup Rivers, its ponds, fields, and deciduous and pine forests provide diverse habitats for birds and wildlife. Migrants following the Quinebaug River are funneled into the site.

48 QUINEBAUG VALLEY FISH HATCHERY, PLAINFIELD

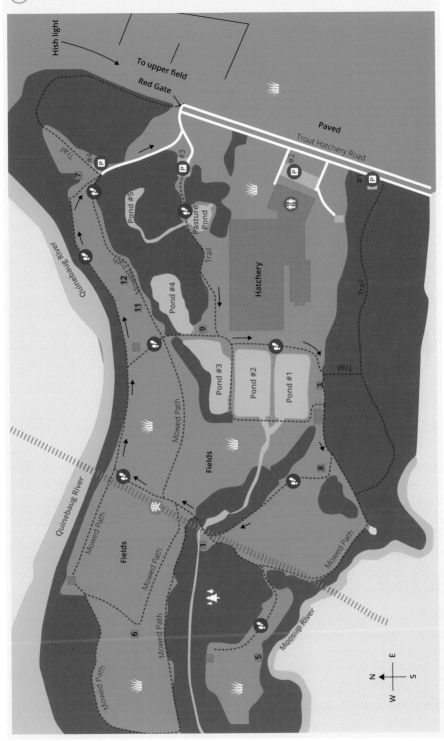

The most interesting time to bird the hatchery is in winter. Because the water flowing from the fish-growing tanks into the ponds is temperature-controlled, the ponds provide some of the only open water in Windham County, attracting both waterfowl and some species otherwise difficult to find inland in winter, such as Wilson's Snipe and Eastern Phoebe. The area holds a few less common breeders, such as White-eyed Vireo and American Kestrel, and also is worth visiting during spring and fall migration. Gravel roads and well-maintained paths provide easy access to nearly all of the property.

How to Bird This Site

For an easy 2-mile walk that's often *worthy of 2 to 3 hours* of birding, start at the Pasture Pond parking area (Lot 3) at the end of Trout Hatchery Road. Scan the feeders here for Fox, White-crowned, and other sparrows before heading to Pasture Pond itself. Peruse the vegetation along the stream entering the pond for Hermit Thrush, Ruby-crowned Kinglet, and Winter Wren. Continue on the path to the main ponds, where a variety of ducks, along with Bald Eagle, Great Blue Heron, Belted Kingfisher, Wilson's Snipe, Eastern Phoebe, and Swamp Sparrow, can often be found. Go either way around Ponds 1 and 2, then take the gravel road on the south side toward Well House 8 and head northwest toward Well House 1. The woodland stream to the right of the road can be good for Wilson's Snipe and Rusty Blackbird. Watch for Purple Finches foraging in the sycamores. Beyond Well House 1, near the meadow, the stream flows under the road. Look there for Wilson's Snipe, Rusty Blackbird, Winter Wren, and sparrows.

Here, you can either take a mowed path east past Ponds 3, 4, and 5 to Parking Lot 4, or take one of two loops through the meadow, which is good for finding sparrows and raptors. The longer loop begins on the first grassy road to the left and follows the forest edge; the shorter loop begins at the second left, toward Well House 6. The two trails meet at the meadow's north side near the river, then continue east along the river and field edge. Continuing east eventually leads you to Parking Lot 4. Either way, it's a short walk along the road from Lot 4 to Lot 3.

This same walk can be productive in spring and summer for nesting American Kestrel and Orchard Oriole around the ponds, Willow Flycatcher and Indigo Bunting in the shrubby borders, and Green Heron and Spotted Sandpiper along the pond edges. Wood Thrush, Veery, Rose-breasted Grosbeak, and Scarlet Tanager are common in the mature woods at the end of the loop. **Note:** The upper fields (beyond the red gate on the map) host nesting White-eyed Vireo, Indigo Bunting, and Willow Flycatcher.

APPENDIX A

Species Status Bar Graphs

■ How to Use Bar Graphs

These bar graphs show the relative abundance of bird species in Connecticut throughout the year, making them valuable tools for helping you find birds. Please note that the bar graphs represent occurrence in a general sense; individual occurrence will vary from region to region according to species distribution, habitat preferences, and other factors (see QR codes for specific sites, Appendix B: Annotated Species List, and Appendix C: Species by Habitat).

KEY

····························	Rare
———————	Uncommon
▬▬▬▬▬▬▬	Fairly common
▬▬▬▬▬▬▬	Common
▬▬▬▬▬▬▬	Abundant
◀——————▶	Breeding season
▪	Very rare (block = 1 record)
▪	Historic very rare record
– – –	Irruptive or irregular
●	Unseasonable record
N	Isolated nesting records
Xr	Extirpated as a Breeding Sp.
(c)	Primarily coastal
(C)	Almost exclusively coastal
(r)	Extensively released
(p)	Pelagic
(f)	Favors freshwater
?	Status obscured by identification problems
Ø	No recent records

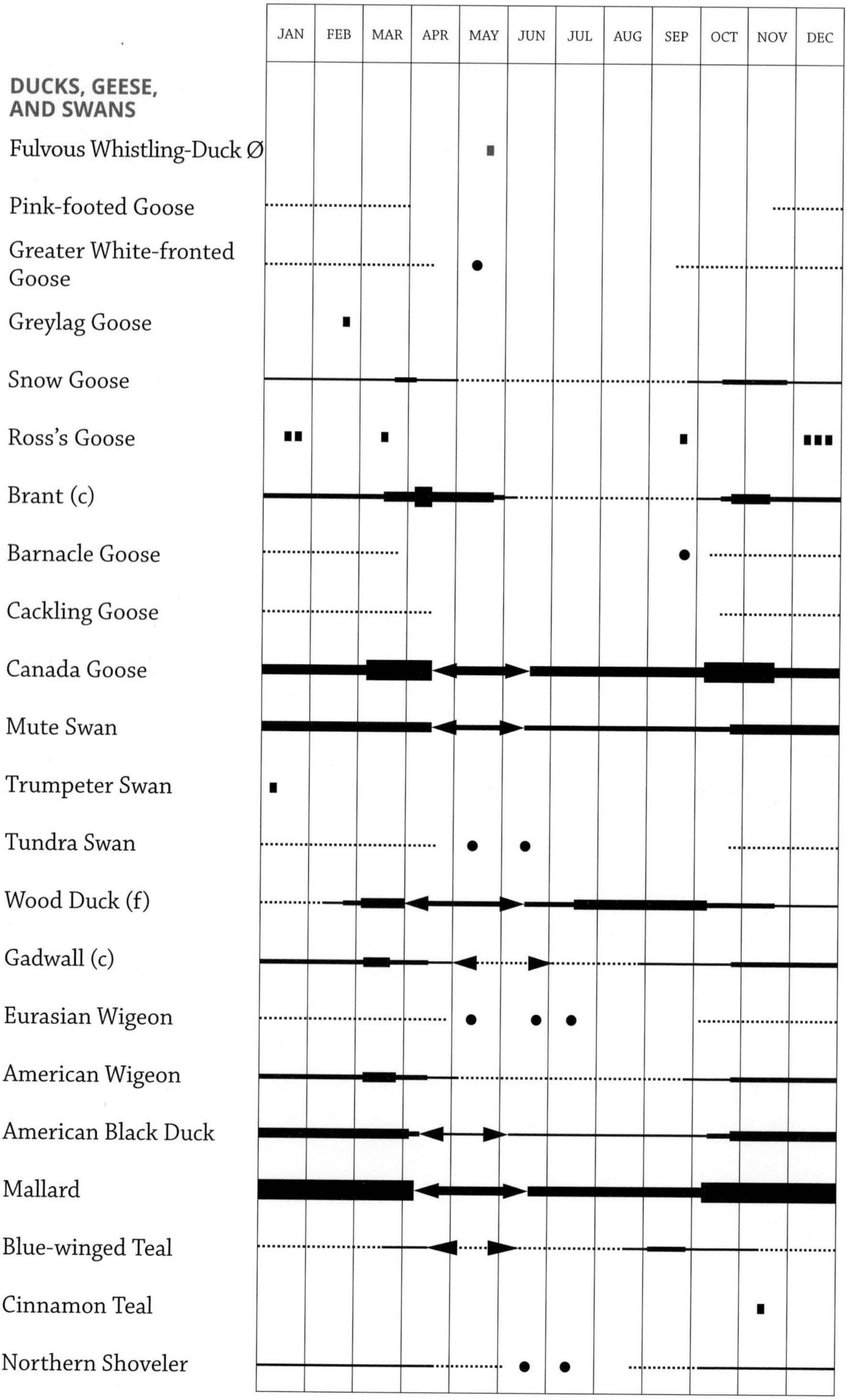
JAN
FEB
MAR
APR
MAY
JUN
JUL
AUG
SEP
OCT
NOV
DEC
DUCKS, GEESE, AND SWANS
Fulvous Whistling-Duck Ø
Pink-footed Goose
Greater White-fronted Goose
Greylag Goose
Snow Goose
Ross's Goose
Brant (c)
Barnacle Goose
Cackling Goose
Canada Goose
Mute Swan
Trumpeter Swan
Tundra Swan
Wood Duck (f)
Gadwall (c)
Eurasian Wigeon
American Wigeon
American Black Duck
Mallard
Blue-winged Teal
Cinnamon Teal
Northern Shoveler

	JAN	FEB	MAR	APR	MAY	JUN	JUL	AUG	SEP	OCT	NOV	DEC

Northern Pintail

Green-winged Teal

Canvasback (c)

Redhead (c)

Ring-necked Duck (f)

Tufted Duck (c)

Greater Scaup (c)

Lesser Scaup

King Eider (C)

Common Eider (C)

Harlequin Duck (C)

Surf Scoter (c)

White-winged Scoter (c)

Black Scoter (c)

Long-tailed Duck (c)

Bufflehead

Common Goldeneye

Barrow's Goldeneye

Hooded Merganser

Common Merganser (f)

Red-breasted
Merganser (c)

Ruddy Duck

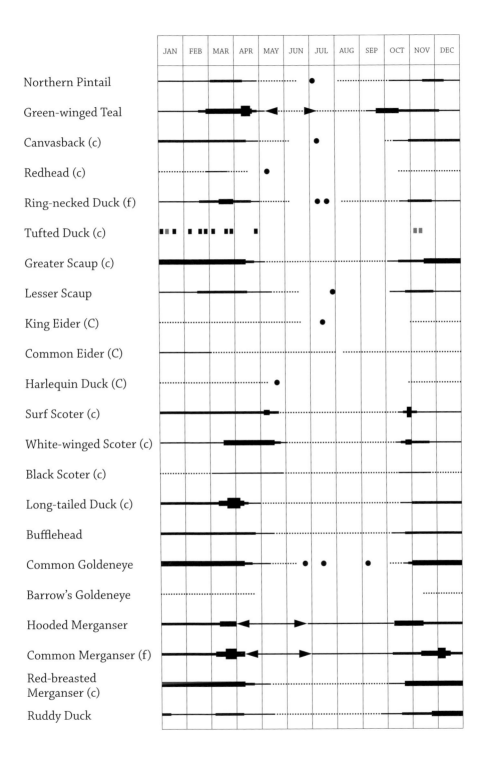

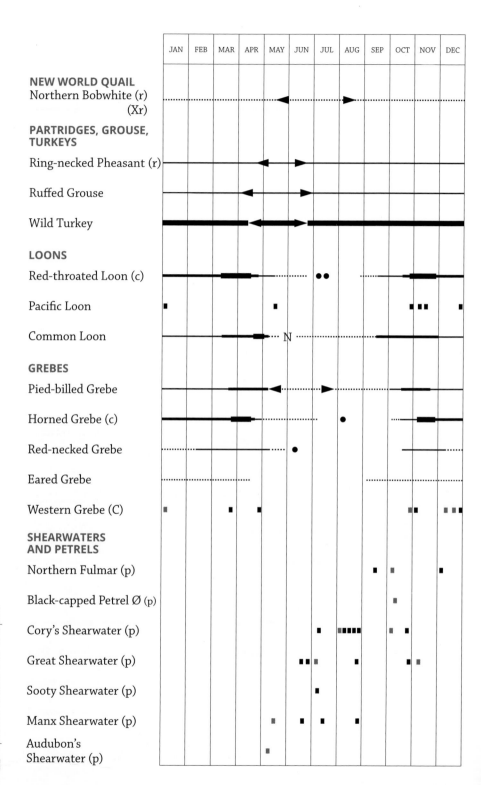

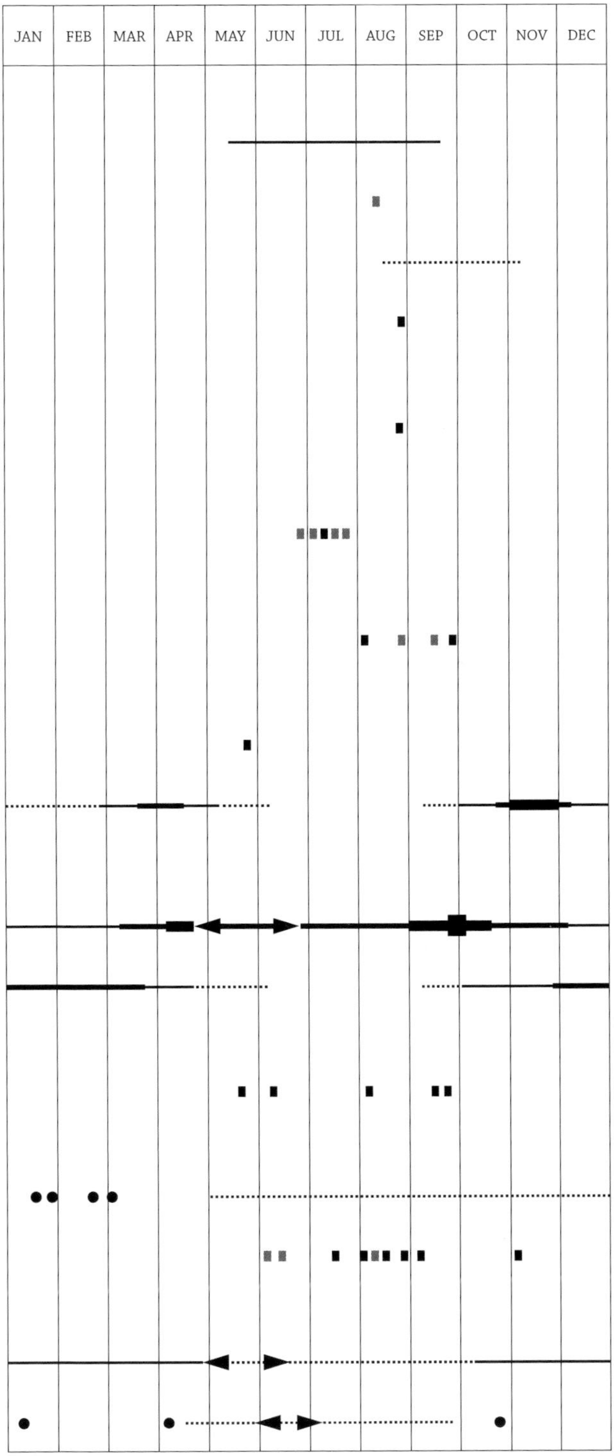

	JAN	FEB	MAR	APR	MAY	JUN	JUL	AUG	SEP	OCT	NOV	DEC

STORM-PETRELS

Wilson's Storm-Petrel (p)

White-faced Storm-Petrel (p) Ø

Leach's Storm-Petrel (p)

Band-rumped Storm-Petrel

TROPICBIRDS

White-tailed Tropicbird

STORKS

Wood Stork

FRIGATEBIRDS

Magnificent Frigatebird

GANNETS

Brown Booby

Northern Gannet (C)

CORMORANTS

Double-crested Cormorant

Great Cormorant (c)

DARTERS

Anhinga

PELICANS

American White Pelican (c)

Brown Pelican (C)

BITTERNS AND HERONS

American Bittern

Least Bittern

	JAN	FEB	MAR	APR	MAY	JUN	JUL	AUG	SEP	OCT	NOV	DEC
Great Blue Heron												
Great Egret (c)												
Snowy Egret (c)												
Little Blue Heron (c)												
Tricolored Heron (C)												
Cattle Egret												
Green Heron												
Black-crowned Night-Heron (c)												
Yellow-crowned Night-Heron (C)												

IBISES

	JAN	FEB	MAR	APR	MAY	JUN	JUL	AUG	SEP	OCT	NOV	DEC
White Ibis (C)												
Glossy Ibis (c)												
White-faced Ibis (C)												

NEW WORLD VULTURES

	JAN	FEB	MAR	APR	MAY	JUN	JUL	AUG	SEP	OCT	NOV	DEC
Black Vulture												
Turkey Vulture												

OSPREYS

	JAN	FEB	MAR	APR	MAY	JUN	JUL	AUG	SEP	OCT	NOV	DEC
Osprey												

HAWKS, KITES, AND EAGLES

	JAN	FEB	MAR	APR	MAY	JUN	JUL	AUG	SEP	OCT	NOV	DEC
White-tailed Kite												
Swallow-tailed Kite												
Mississippi Kite												
Golden Eagle												
Northern Harrier												

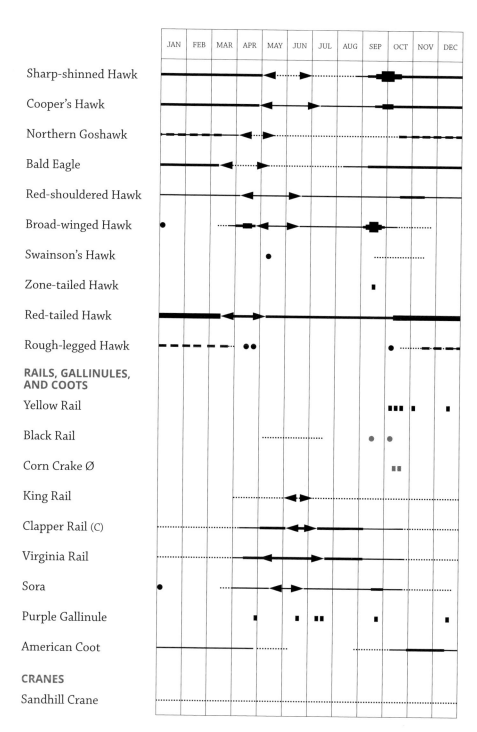

	JAN	FEB	MAR	APR	MAY	JUN	JUL	AUG	SEP	OCT	NOV	DEC
Sharp-shinned Hawk												
Cooper's Hawk												
Northern Goshawk												
Bald Eagle												
Red-shouldered Hawk												
Broad-winged Hawk												
Swainson's Hawk												
Zone-tailed Hawk												
Red-tailed Hawk												
Rough-legged Hawk												

RAILS, GALLINULES, AND COOTS

Yellow Rail

Black Rail

Corn Crake Ø

King Rail

Clapper Rail (C)

Virginia Rail

Sora

Purple Gallinule

American Coot

CRANES

Sandhill Crane

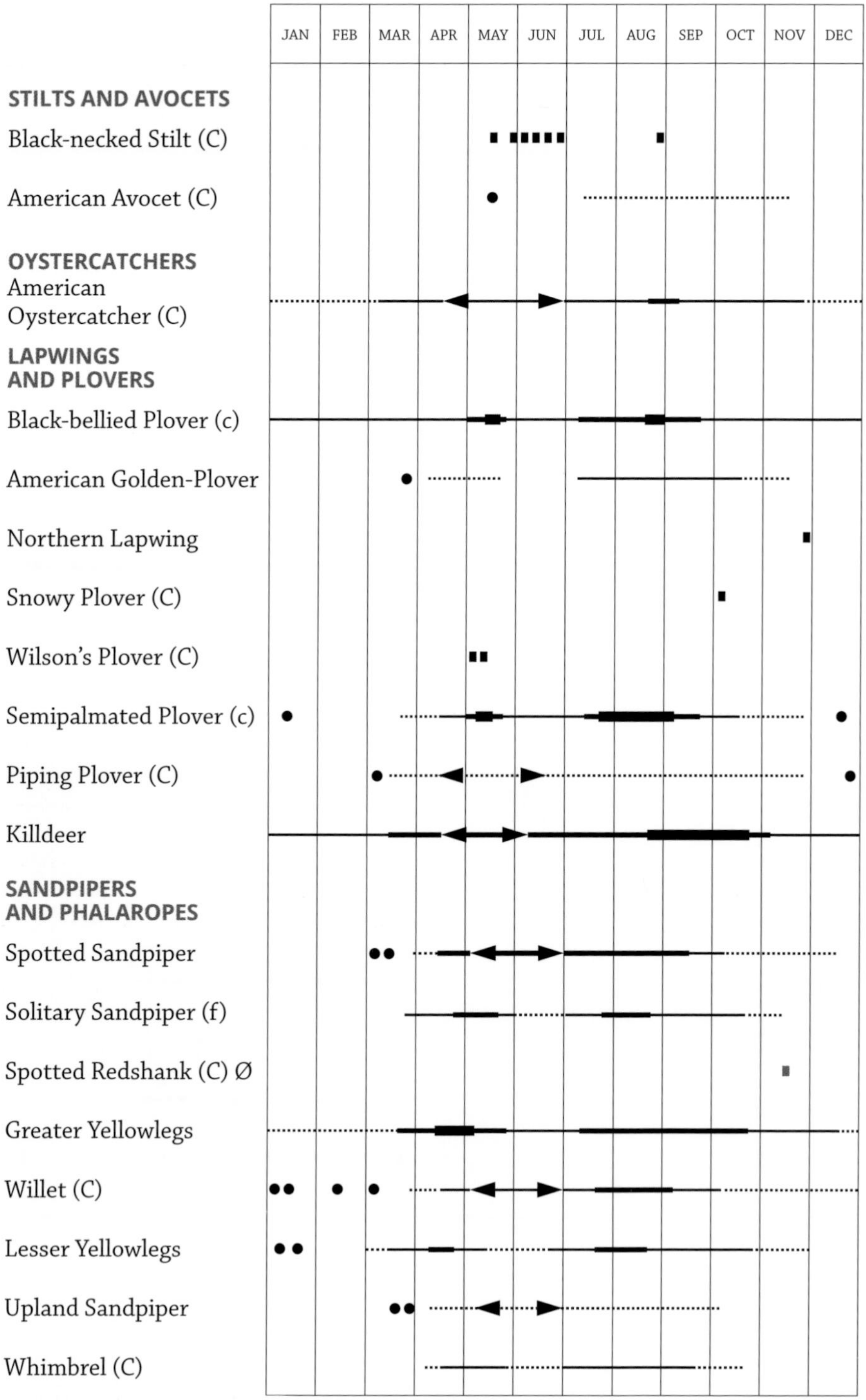

	JAN	FEB	MAR	APR	MAY	JUN	JUL	AUG	SEP	OCT	NOV	DEC

STILTS AND AVOCETS

Black-necked Stilt (C)

American Avocet (C)

OYSTERCATCHERS

American
Oystercatcher (C)

**LAPWINGS
AND PLOVERS**

Black-bellied Plover (c)

American Golden-Plover

Northern Lapwing

Snowy Plover (C)

Wilson's Plover (C)

Semipalmated Plover (c)

Piping Plover (C)

Killdeer

**SANDPIPERS
AND PHALAROPES**

Spotted Sandpiper

Solitary Sandpiper (f)

Spotted Redshank (C) Ø

Greater Yellowlegs

Willet (C)

Lesser Yellowlegs

Upland Sandpiper

Whimbrel (C)

Species Status Bar Graphs

	JAN	FEB	MAR	APR	MAY	JUN	JUL	AUG	SEP	OCT	NOV	DEC
Long-billed Curlew												
Black-tailed Godwit (C)												
Hudsonian Godwit (c)												
Bar-tailed Godwit (C)												
Marbled Godwit (C)												
Ruddy Turnstone (c)												
Red Knot (C)												
Ruff (C)												
Sharp-tailed Sandpiper												
Stilt Sandpiper (c)												
Curlew Sandpiper (C)												
Red-necked Stint (C)												
Sanderling (C)												
Dunlin (C)												
Purple Sandpiper (C)												
Baird's Sandpiper												
Little Stint												
Least Sandpiper												
White-rumped Sandpiper (c)												
Buff-breasted Sandpiper												
Pectoral Sandpiper												
Semipalmated Sandpiper (c)											?	
Western Sandpiper (c)												

Species Status Bar Graphs

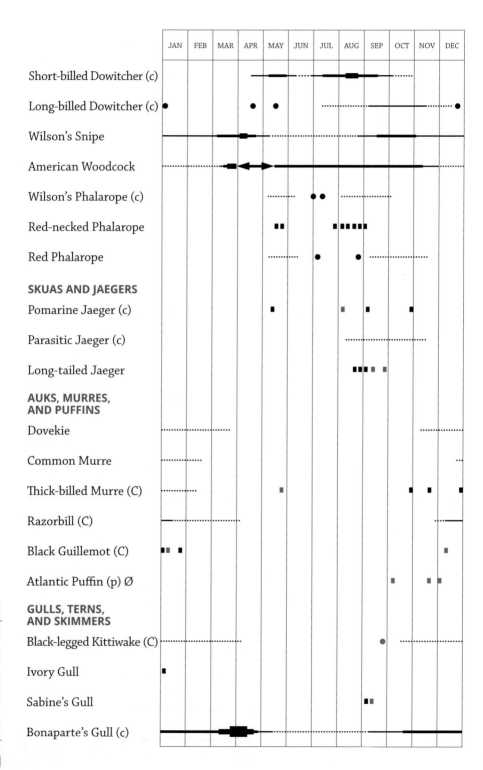

	JAN	FEB	MAR	APR	MAY	JUN	JUL	AUG	SEP	OCT	NOV	DEC

Short-billed Dowitcher (c)

Long-billed Dowitcher (c)

Wilson's Snipe

American Woodcock

Wilson's Phalarope (c)

Red-necked Phalarope

Red Phalarope

SKUAS AND JAEGERS

Pomarine Jaeger (c)

Parasitic Jaeger (c)

Long-tailed Jaeger

**AUKS, MURRES,
AND PUFFINS**

Dovekie

Common Murre

Thick-billed Murre (C)

Razorbill (C)

Black Guillemot (C)

Atlantic Puffin (p) Ø

**GULLS, TERNS,
AND SKIMMERS**

Black-legged Kittiwake (C)

Ivory Gull

Sabine's Gull

Bonaparte's Gull (c)

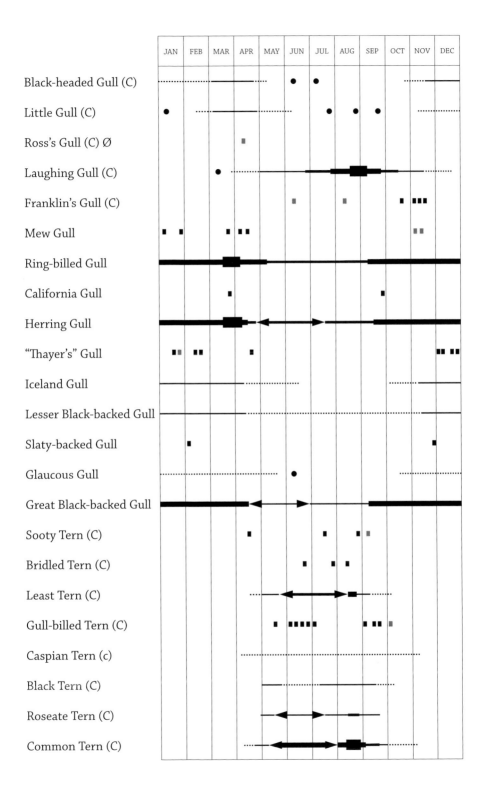

	JAN	FEB	MAR	APR	MAY	JUN	JUL	AUG	SEP	OCT	NOV	DEC
Black-headed Gull (C)												
Little Gull (C)												
Ross's Gull (C) Ø												
Laughing Gull (C)												
Franklin's Gull (C)												
Mew Gull												
Ring-billed Gull												
California Gull												
Herring Gull												
"Thayer's" Gull												
Iceland Gull												
Lesser Black-backed Gull												
Slaty-backed Gull												
Glaucous Gull												
Great Black-backed Gull												
Sooty Tern (C)												
Bridled Tern (C)												
Least Tern (C)												
Gull-billed Tern (C)												
Caspian Tern (c)												
Black Tern (C)												
Roseate Tern (C)												
Common Tern (C)												

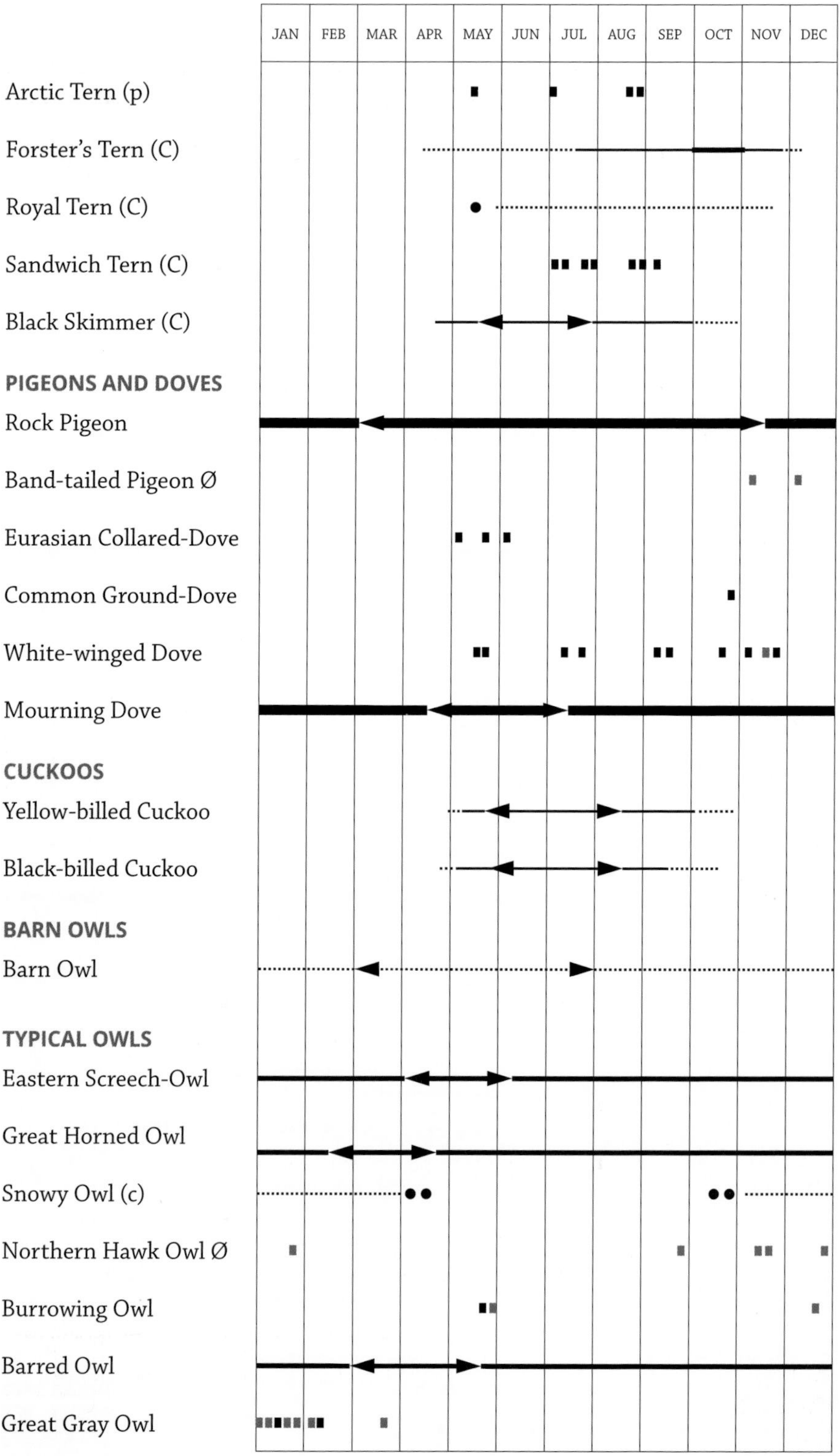

	JAN	FEB	MAR	APR	MAY	JUN	JUL	AUG	SEP	OCT	NOV	DEC

Arctic Tern (p)

Forster's Tern (C)

Royal Tern (C)

Sandwich Tern (C)

Black Skimmer (C)

PIGEONS AND DOVES
Rock Pigeon

Band-tailed Pigeon Ø

Eurasian Collared-Dove

Common Ground-Dove

White-winged Dove

Mourning Dove

CUCKOOS
Yellow-billed Cuckoo

Black-billed Cuckoo

BARN OWLS
Barn Owl

TYPICAL OWLS
Eastern Screech-Owl

Great Horned Owl

Snowy Owl (c)

Northern Hawk Owl Ø

Burrowing Owl

Barred Owl

Great Gray Owl

Species Status Bar Graphs

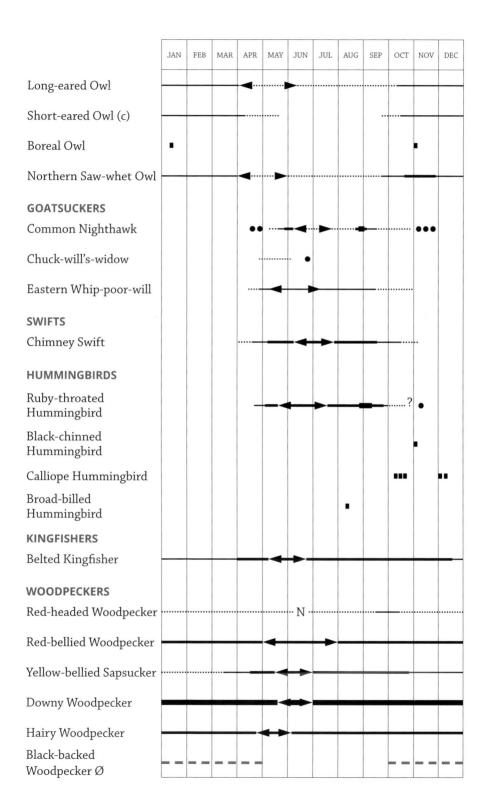

	JAN	FEB	MAR	APR	MAY	JUN	JUL	AUG	SEP	OCT	NOV	DEC

Long-eared Owl

Short-eared Owl (c)

Boreal Owl

Northern Saw-whet Owl

GOATSUCKERS
Common Nighthawk

Chuck-will's-widow

Eastern Whip-poor-will

SWIFTS
Chimney Swift

HUMMINGBIRDS
Ruby-throated
Hummingbird

Black-chinned
Hummingbird

Calliope Hummingbird

Broad-billed
Hummingbird

KINGFISHERS
Belted Kingfisher

WOODPECKERS
Red-headed Woodpecker

Red-bellied Woodpecker

Yellow-bellied Sapsucker

Downy Woodpecker

Hairy Woodpecker

Black-backed
Woodpecker Ø

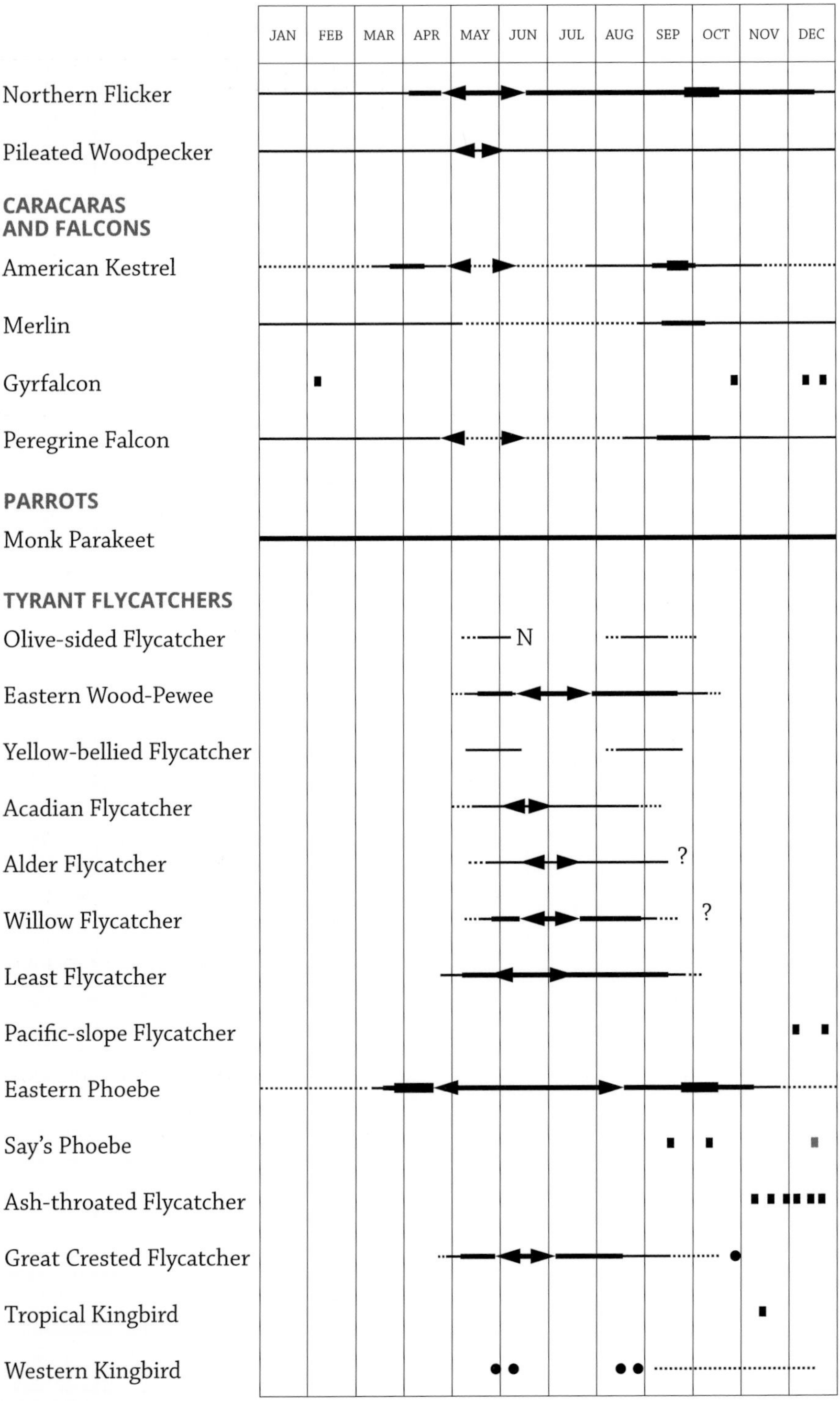

	JAN	FEB	MAR	APR	MAY	JUN	JUL	AUG	SEP	OCT	NOV	DEC

Northern Flicker

Pileated Woodpecker

CARACARAS AND FALCONS

American Kestrel

Merlin

Gyrfalcon

Peregrine Falcon

PARROTS

Monk Parakeet

TYRANT FLYCATCHERS

Olive-sided Flycatcher N

Eastern Wood-Pewee

Yellow-bellied Flycatcher

Acadian Flycatcher

Alder Flycatcher ?

Willow Flycatcher ?

Least Flycatcher

Pacific-slope Flycatcher

Eastern Phoebe

Say's Phoebe

Ash-throated Flycatcher

Great Crested Flycatcher

Tropical Kingbird

Western Kingbird

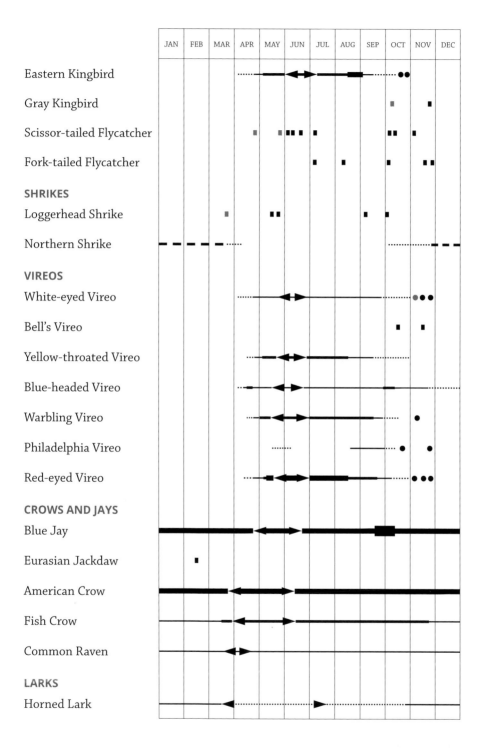

	JAN	FEB	MAR	APR	MAY	JUN	JUL	AUG	SEP	OCT	NOV	DEC

Eastern Kingbird

Gray Kingbird

Scissor-tailed Flycatcher

Fork-tailed Flycatcher

SHRIKES
Loggerhead Shrike

Northern Shrike

VIREOS
White-eyed Vireo

Bell's Vireo

Yellow-throated Vireo

Blue-headed Vireo

Warbling Vireo

Philadelphia Vireo

Red-eyed Vireo

CROWS AND JAYS
Blue Jay

Eurasian Jackdaw

American Crow

Fish Crow

Common Raven

LARKS
Horned Lark

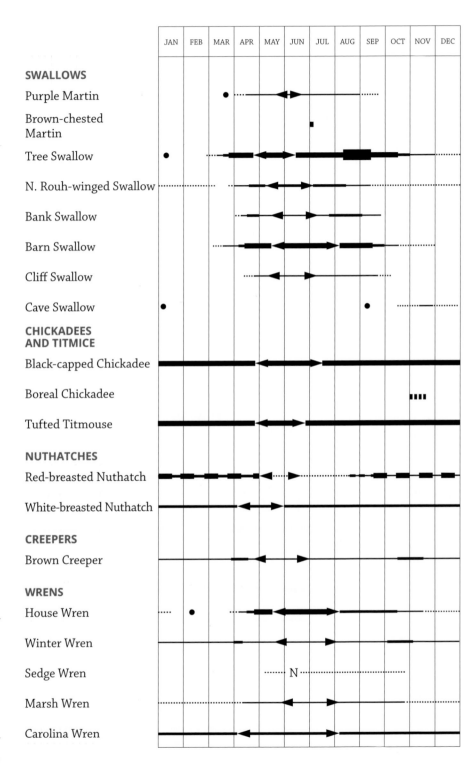

	JAN	FEB	MAR	APR	MAY	JUN	JUL	AUG	SEP	OCT	NOV	DEC

SWALLOWS

Purple Martin

Brown-chested Martin

Tree Swallow

N. Rouh-winged Swallow

Bank Swallow

Barn Swallow

Cliff Swallow

Cave Swallow

CHICKADEES AND TITMICE

Black-capped Chickadee

Boreal Chickadee

Tufted Titmouse

NUTHATCHES

Red-breasted Nuthatch

White-breasted Nuthatch

CREEPERS

Brown Creeper

WRENS

House Wren

Winter Wren

Sedge Wren

Marsh Wren

Carolina Wren

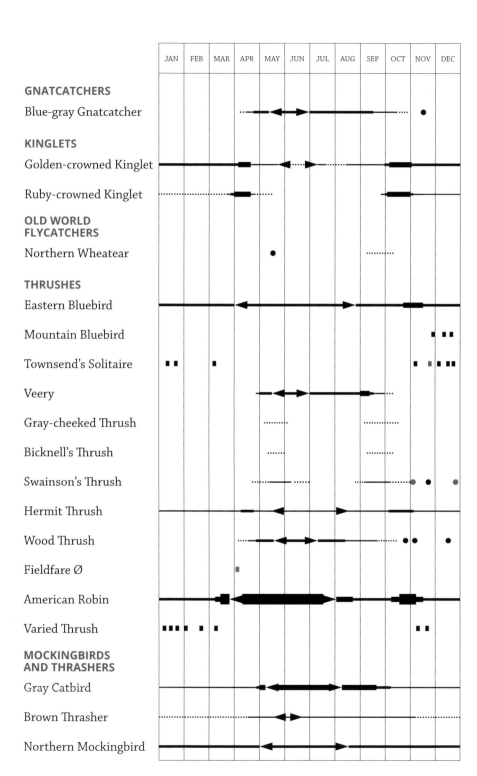

	JAN	FEB	MAR	APR	MAY	JUN	JUL	AUG	SEP	OCT	NOV	DEC

GNATCATCHERS

Blue-gray Gnatcatcher

KINGLETS

Golden-crowned Kinglet

Ruby-crowned Kinglet

OLD WORLD FLYCATCHERS

Northern Wheatear

THRUSHES

Eastern Bluebird

Mountain Bluebird

Townsend's Solitaire

Veery

Gray-cheeked Thrush

Bicknell's Thrush

Swainson's Thrush

Hermit Thrush

Wood Thrush

Fieldfare Ø

American Robin

Varied Thrush

MOCKINGBIRDS AND THRASHERS

Gray Catbird

Brown Thrasher

Northern Mockingbird

Species Status Bar Graphs

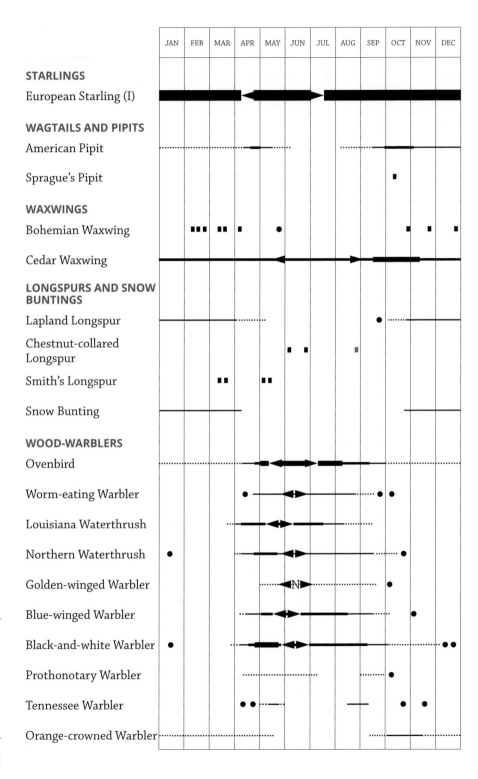

	JAN	FEB	MAR	APR	MAY	JUN	JUL	AUG	SEP	OCT	NOV	DEC

STARLINGS
European Starling (I)

WAGTAILS AND PIPITS
American Pipit

Sprague's Pipit

WAXWINGS
Bohemian Waxwing

Cedar Waxwing

LONGSPURS AND SNOW BUNTINGS
Lapland Longspur

Chestnut-collared Longspur

Smith's Longspur

Snow Bunting

WOOD-WARBLERS
Ovenbird

Worm-eating Warbler

Louisiana Waterthrush

Northern Waterthrush

Golden-winged Warbler

Blue-winged Warbler

Black-and-white Warbler

Prothonotary Warbler

Tennessee Warbler

Orange-crowned Warbler

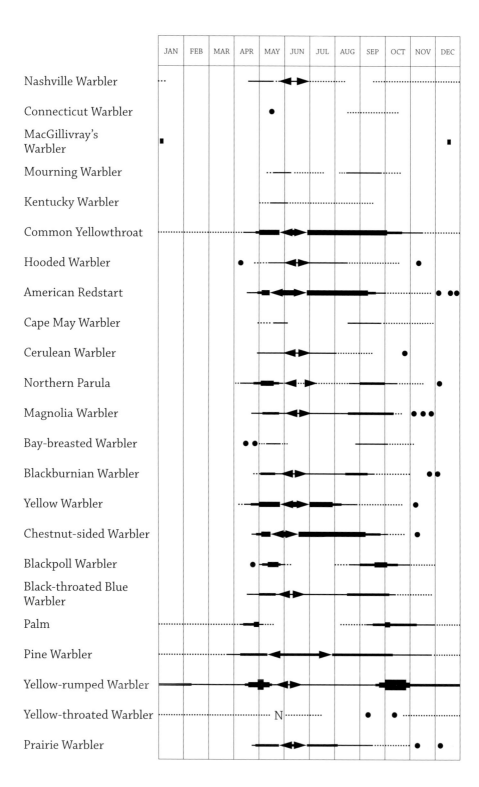

	JAN	FEB	MAR	APR	MAY	JUN	JUL	AUG	SEP	OCT	NOV	DEC

Nashville Warbler

Connecticut Warbler

MacGillivray's Warbler

Mourning Warbler

Kentucky Warbler

Common Yellowthroat

Hooded Warbler

American Redstart

Cape May Warbler

Cerulean Warbler

Northern Parula

Magnolia Warbler

Bay-breasted Warbler

Blackburnian Warbler

Yellow Warbler

Chestnut-sided Warbler

Blackpoll Warbler

Black-throated Blue Warbler

Palm

Pine Warbler

Yellow-rumped Warbler

Yellow-throated Warbler

Prairie Warbler

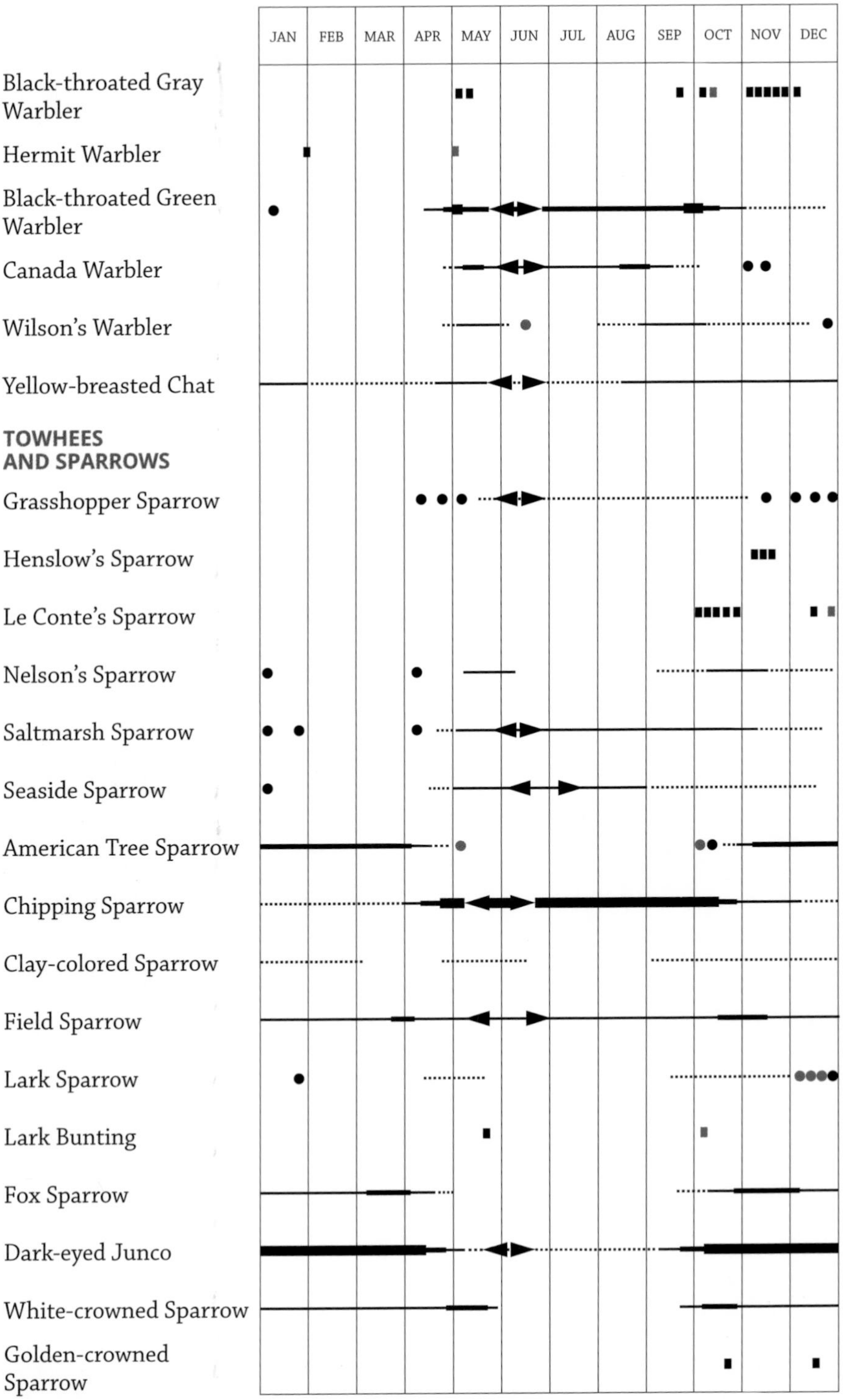

	JAN	FEB	MAR	APR	MAY	JUN	JUL	AUG	SEP	OCT	NOV	DEC

Black-throated Gray Warbler

Hermit Warbler

Black-throated Green Warbler

Canada Warbler

Wilson's Warbler

Yellow-breasted Chat

TOWHEES AND SPARROWS

Grasshopper Sparrow

Henslow's Sparrow

Le Conte's Sparrow

Nelson's Sparrow

Saltmarsh Sparrow

Seaside Sparrow

American Tree Sparrow

Chipping Sparrow

Clay-colored Sparrow

Field Sparrow

Lark Sparrow

Lark Bunting

Fox Sparrow

Dark-eyed Junco

White-crowned Sparrow

Golden-crowned Sparrow

	JAN	FEB	MAR	APR	MAY	JUN	JUL	AUG	SEP	OCT	NOV	DEC

Harris's Sparrow

White-throated Sparrow

Vesper Sparrow

Savannah Sparrow

Song Sparrow

Lincoln's Sparrow

Swamp Sparrow

Green-tailed Towhee

Spotted Towhee

Eastern Towhee

**CARDINALS
AND TANAGERS**

Summer Tanager

Scarlet Tanager

Western Tanager

Northern Cardinal

Rose-breasted Grosbeak

Black-headed Grosbeak

Blue Grosbeak

Lazuli Bunting

Indigo Bunting

Painted Bunting

Dickcissel

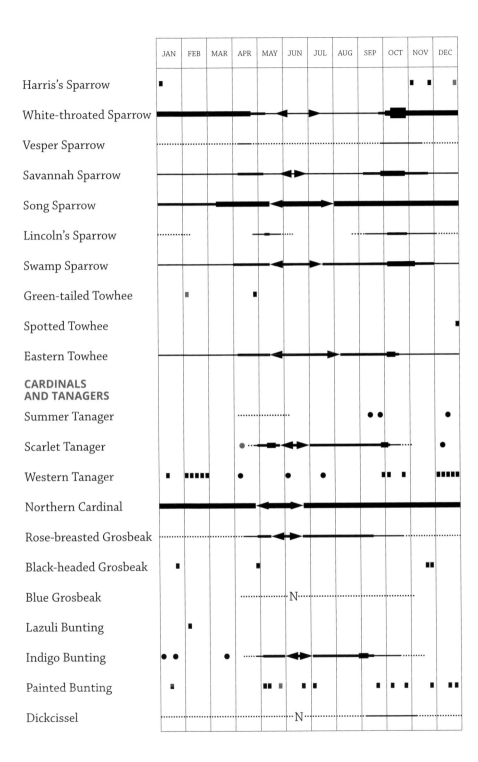

Species Status Bar Graphs

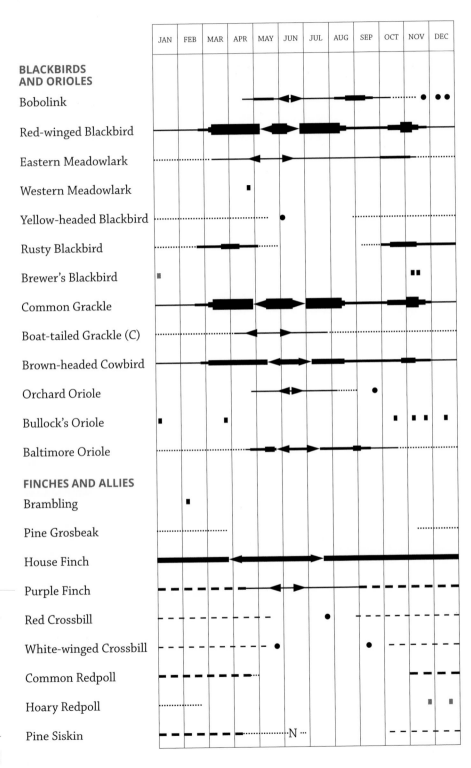

	JAN	FEB	MAR	APR	MAY	JUN	JUL	AUG	SEP	OCT	NOV	DEC

BLACKBIRDS AND ORIOLES

Bobolink

Red-winged Blackbird

Eastern Meadowlark

Western Meadowlark

Yellow-headed Blackbird

Rusty Blackbird

Brewer's Blackbird

Common Grackle

Boat-tailed Grackle (C)

Brown-headed Cowbird

Orchard Oriole

Bullock's Oriole

Baltimore Oriole

FINCHES AND ALLIES

Brambling

Pine Grosbeak

House Finch

Purple Finch

Red Crossbill

White-winged Crossbill

Common Redpoll

Hoary Redpoll

Pine Siskin

Species Status Bar Graphs

	JAN	FEB	MAR	APR	MAY	JUN	JUL	AUG	SEP	OCT	NOV	DEC
American Goldfinch												
Evening Grosbeak						N						
OLD WORLD SPARROWS												
House Sparrow												

APPENDIX B

Annotated Species List

In 2017, Connecticut's bird list stood at 439 species. The following accounts describe each species, its relative abundance, and its preferred habitat.

The information is based on bar graphs first produced by Greg Hanisek for the Connecticut Ornithological Association, which I have updated with eBird data and minor modifications from my own experiences. The order follows the American Ornithologists' Union's *Checklist of North American Birds*, seventh edition, 1998, and its supplements to the fifty-seventh, July 6, 2016, as published in *The Auk*, as well as the American Birding Association's Checklist.

■ Status of Abundance Terms

Abundant: The most common species. One hundred or more can be found daily in proper habitat, or more than one thousand daily at key migratory sites; present in extensive breeding habitat. Examples: American Robin during breeding season; Semipalmated Sandpiper along coast from late July to late August; winter crow roosts; migrating Broad-winged Hawks in September.

Common: Widespread and easily found, with visits to appropriate habitat yielding dozens of individuals. Extensive searches of prime habitat or visits to key migratory sites may produce more than one hundred individuals. Examples: Black-bellied Plover at coastal locations in May or from mid-July to mid-September; Red-eyed Vireo in deciduous forest during breeding season.

Fairly Common: Moderate numbers found on most trips to suitable habitat. Many of the regularly occurring species fit within this category during at least a portion of the year. Examples: Hairy Woodpecker throughout the year; Scarlet Tanager from May to early July.

Uncommon: Modest numbers occur annually. Limited numbers may be found by active birders in the proper season, but species can easily be missed on any given day; without effort, it could be missed for the season. Examples: Philadelphia Vireo from late August to mid-September; Mourning Warbler from mid-May to early June.

Rare: Very few found annually or, in the case of rare breeders, in very limited locations. Note that a species may be rare in one season, but not in another. Examples: Greater White-fronted Goose throughout the period of its occurrence, from mid-October to mid-April; Blue-headed Vireo in December; American Golden-Plover in spring; Least Bittern or Common Gallinule (Moorhen) as a breeding species.

Very Rare: Species that occur less than annually, with limited numbers of documented records. Note that sightings can be years apart and yet still show seasonal patterns of occurrence. Example: Most of the more than a dozen White-faced Ibis records are from April or May. The terms "accidental" and "vagrant" also have been used to describe birds in this category, but these evoke a misleading sense of randomness. A combination of luck and skill is required to find a species listed in this category.

Irruptive: These species stage incursions into Connecticut that can vary greatly from year to year. Red-breasted Nuthatch and Pine Siskin may appear in large numbers some years, while predators such as Snowy Owl or Northern Shrike typically irrupt in smaller numbers.

■ Species List

Common names marked with an asterisk (*) are rare in Connecticut; the Avian Records Committee of Connecticut (ARCC) requests details. Names marked with two asterisks (**) are rare or potential nesters; ARCC requests breeding records. Names marked with the pound sign (#) are rare as well as rare or potential nesters; ARCC requests details for either instance. Names followed by (I) indicate introduced species (not native to Connecticut); (S) indicates sight records only. Common names enclosed in "quotation marks" are identifiable forms, now considered subspecies, reviewed by the ARCC.

Fulvous Whistling-Duck* *Dendrocygna bicolor*: Very rare visitor from the south.

Pink-footed Goose* *Anser brachyrhynchus*: Very rare late winter and early spring. Sightings in Northeast are on the increase. Associates with Canada Goose and other geese.

Greater White-fronted Goose *Anser albifrons*: Rare but increasing migrant and winter visitor; occurs with flocks of Canada Goose. Most records are of the darker-bellied, orange-billed Greenland race, *A. a. flavirostris*, but the Canadian race, *A. a frontalis*, is possible.

Greylag Goose* *Anser anser*: Very rare.

Snow Goose *Chen caerulescens*: Fairly common migrant in flocks passing overhead, especially from October to November and from March to April. A few winter, usually with Canada Geese in fields. White morphs far outnumber blue.

Ross's Goose* *Chen rossii*: Very rare. Found with Canada or Snow Geese.

Brant *Branta bernicla*: Common to abundant migrant and winter visitor from October to May. Feeds on aquatic marine vegetation and grazes grass in estuaries, inlets, bays, and on nearby lawns. Rare inland with Canada Geese. A few occasionally summer on the coast. The rare subspecies "Black" Brant (*Branta bernicla nigricans*) has occurred.

Barnacle Goose *Branta leucopsis*: Rare but nearly annual winter visitor. Occurs with Canada Goose and other geese in open fields and waterways.

Cackling Goose *Branta hutchinsii*: Recorded annually in small numbers. At least two races, *B. h. hutchinsii* (Richardson's Goose) and *B. h. taverneri*, are known to occur. Found on ponds, lakes, rivers, agricultural fields, and lawns, usually with Canada Geese.

Canada Goose *Branta canadensis*: Common year-round resident, abundant when augmented by arctic migrants from March to April and October to November. Winter populations may include Lesser Canada Goose, *B. c. parvipes*. Found on open lawns, farm fields, golf courses, coastal estuaries, and inland waterways.

Mute Swan (I) *Cygnus olor*: Common (declining) from fall to spring, and fairly common in summer when pairs disperse to smaller bodies of water mainly along the coast. Coastal Connecticut is the epicenter for Mute Swan distribution in the United States.

Trumpeter Swan* *Cygnus buccinator*: Very rare in estuaries and freshwater lakes and rivers.

Tundra Swan *Cygnus columbianus*: Rare visitor from fall through spring to inland lakes, rivers, and tidal estuaries. Occasionally seen flying over during migration.

Wood Duck *Aix sponsa*: Fairly common to common migrant, especially in March and from July to September. Sometimes overwinters locally in small numbers. Fairly common nesting species on densely vegetated ponds, lake edges, backwater river eddies, and freshwater marshes and swamps.

Gadwall *Anas strepera*: Fairly common fall migrant and coastal wintering species, common in spring, especially March. Uncommon inland in winter. Very local nesting species in tidal marshes, brackish estuaries, and small coastal ponds, and possibly very rarely in inland freshwater marshes or swamps.

Eurasian Wigeon *Anas penelope*: Rare visitor most often found on the coast from fall through spring, with American Wigeon and Gadwall.

American Wigeon *Anas americana*: Fairly common to common spring migrant, and fairly common fall migrant and wintering species. Occasionally one summers, typically along the coast. Usually found along the coast in fresh and tidal marshes, especially in winter, and on inland lakes, ponds, and rivers.

American Black Duck *Anas rubripes*: Common coastal migrant and wintering species. In summer, an uncommon breeding species in freshwater and brackish habitats, especially coastal marshes; inland nesting occurs in freshwater marshes, densely forested swamps, and beaver ponds, mainly in central and western Connecticut.

Mallard *Anas platyrhynchus*: This introduced species from the west is an abundant migrant and wintering species throughout Connecticut, nearly anywhere there is water. In summer, this common breeding species is found in almost any freshwater or brackish environment.

Blue-winged Teal** *Anas discors*: Uncommon spring and fall migrant; fairly common in September; rare in winter; very rare and local breeder in larger coastal and inland marshes.

Cinnamon Teal *Anas cyanoptera*: Very rare in coastal marshes.

Northern Shoveler *Anas clypeata*: Uncommon fall and spring migrant and local wintering species in coastal estuaries and marshes, and inland marshes, lakes, and ponds.

Northern Pintail *Anas acuta*: Uncommon to fairly common fall and spring migrant and local wintering species in coastal estuaries and marshes, and inland marshes, lakes, and ponds. Occasionally seen in flooded agricultural fields, often with other dabbling ducks.

Green-winged Teal** *Anas crecca*: As a migrant, common to fairly common in fall, and common to abundant in spring in coastal estuaries, brackish and freshwater marshes, inland ponds, and lakes; a very rare and local breeder in coastal marshes and inland swamps. A few of the Eurasian form, *A. c. crecca*, occur annually; most in March or April.

Canvasback *Aythya valisineria*: Uncommon migrant and wintering diving duck of coastal bays, estuaries, impoundments, and inlets, occasionally seen on larger rivers, and inland on lakes and reservoirs.

Redhead *Aythya americana*: Rare from fall through spring, seen most often in March, usually with Scaup and Canvasback. A few are found in the large coastal scaup rafts or along the coast in winter.

Ring-necked Duck *Aythya collaris*: Fairly common migrant from late October through November and late February through late April, but common in March. Mostly found on freshwater ponds, lakes, reservoirs, and rivers.

Tufted Duck* *Aythya fuligula*: This Eurasian species is very rare, occurring only from January to April and in November. Found in association with other Aythya species, especially scaup, in coastal bays, inlets, estuaries, and freshwater lakes and rivers.

Greater Scaup *Aythya marila*: Arrives in October, a common migrant and wintering species from mid-November through mid-April in Long Island Sound and on inland lakes, ponds, and rivers. Rafts of thousands occur in the sound, with impressive morning and evening flights offshore.

Lesser Scaup *Aythya affinis*: Uncommon to fairly common migrant and wintering species, most often found on coastal and inland ponds, lakes, and rivers. Some winter among the coastal rafts of Greater Scaup; look for their shorter wing stripe in flight.

King Eider *Somateria spectabilis*: Rare but regular visitor along the coast, mid-November to mid-May, often found near rocky shorelines.

Common Eider** *Somateria mollissima*: Rare to uncommon but regular along the coast mid-September to mid-June, with a few seen in summer, especially in eastern Connecticut. Breeds in nearby New York and Rhode Island.

Harlequin Duck *Histrionicus histrionicus*: Rare and irregular visitor from late October to May along rocky shorelines. Both males and females are seen, usually as lone individuals.

Surf Scoter *Melanitta perspicillata*: Abundant in late October; fairly common to common migrant and winter visitor; and rare summer visitor. Flocks pass through Long Island Sound to and from their breeding grounds to offshore wintering grounds south of Cape Cod, Massachusetts. Overland migrants, they are sometimes found on inland reservoirs and large lakes in fall and spring, often after a storm.

White-winged Scoter *Melanitta fusca*: The largest and second most commonly encountered of the three species of scoter, especially in the west end of the sound from mid-March to May and in late October. Rarely, individuals occur in summer.

Black Scoter *Melanitta americana*: The smallest and least common scoter in Connecticut. Fairly common from mid-October to late November and from March through May, but rare in winter and very rare in summer. Often found in association with other scoters. Flocks sometimes drop into inland lakes during migration.

Long-tailed Duck *Clangula hyemalis*: Common to abundant as an offshore migrant in March and early April; otherwise a fairly common to uncommon migrant and wintering species, mainly in western Connecticut, and a very rare migrant on inland reservoirs and lakes.

Bufflehead *Bucephala albeola*: Found in both fresh and salt water. Fairly common to locally common migrant and winter visitor in coastal inlets, bays, open marshes, and inland lakes, ponds, and rivers.

Common Goldeneye *Bucephala clangula*: Common migrant and winter resident along the coast, offshore, in bays, inlets, and river mouths, and on larger inland rivers and lakes. This diving duck is generally seen in tight flocks, often feeding off rocky shorelines.

Barrow's Goldeneye *Buchephala islandica*: Rare but regular; most often found November through mid-April among flocks of Common Goldeneye. Females in our waters usually have all, or nearly all, orange bills. Common × Barrow's hybrids have occurred in Connecticut.

Hooded Merganser *Lophodytes cucullatus*: Year-round resident; fairly common to common migrant in March and from October to November; and fairly common in winter on fresh or brackish water on the coast or larger rivers. Uncommon and very local cavity-nesting breeder in secluded wooded swamps, beaver ponds with open water, mostly in the northwest hills and lower Connecticut River.

Common Merganser *Mergus merganser*: Fairly common to abundant (March and early December) migrant and uncommon to locally common winter visitor, mainly on larger freshwater rivers, ponds, and lakes. Will go to brackish estuaries in winter when freshwater freezes. An uncommon and local cavity-nesting species found mostly along the upper Farmington and

Housatonic Rivers in the north-central and northwest sections of Connecticut.

Red-breasted Merganser *Mergus serrator*: Common migrant and winter visitor from October to April offshore, and in coastal bays, inlets, and estuaries. Rarely seen inland, on large lakes, reservoirs, and large rivers. A few usually summer on the coast.

Ruddy Duck *Oxyura jamaicensis*: Uncommon to fairly common migrant, October to mid-May; locally common late November to December, mainly on large inland lakes and ponds, but frequents both fresh and saltwater environments. Small numbers winter on coast.

Northern Bobwhite *Colinus virginianus*: Extirpated from Connecticut.

Ring-necked Pheasant**(I) *Phasianus colchicus*: Found on agricultural areas and fields where they are stocked for hunting. Decreasing statewide.

Ruffed Grouse *Bonasa umbellus*: Uncommon; found in mature woodlands, often on hillsides.

Wild Turkey *Meleagris gallopavo*: An adaptable species of varied habitats. Often found in forested edge of agricultural areas and in woodlands. Seen now in residential areas; found statewide and increasing.

Red-throated Loon *Gavia stellata*: Occurs mid-September to mid-April; common widespread migrant along coast from late October to November and mid-March to mid-April; fairly common in winter; rare on inland lakes.

Pacific Loon* *Gavia arctica*: Very rare; in same habitats as Common Loon.

Common Loon *Gavia immer*: Uncommon to fairly common migrant and winter visitor mid-September to mid-April; common late April to mid-May, mainly in coastal waters, on large inland reservoirs, and lakes; non-breeders rarely seen coastally in summer; recently recorded as breeding in the state.

Pied-billed Grebe *Podilymbus podiceps*: Occurs year-round; endangered, secretive but vocal breeder in ponds and wetlands with extensive emergent vegetation; fairly common migrant mid-October to November and late March into early May in similar habitat; uncommon in winter in coastal estuaries and marshes.

Horned Grebe *Podiceps auritus*: Fairly common migrant and winter visitor from mid-October through April; common in November and late March to late April in coastal bays, inlets, and offshore; rare inland.

Red-necked Grebe *Podiceps grisegena*: Uncommon migrant mid-October to mid-December and mid-February to mid-May, especially along rocky coastlines and flying offshore; rare in winter, occasionally on larger inland lakes.

Eared Grebe* *Podiceps nigricollis*: Rare but regular, with individuals occurring every few years. Possible from September to mid-April in sheltered coastal inlets, bays, and inland lakes.

Western Grebe* *Aechmophorus occidentalis*: Very rare usually in inlets and bays.

Northern Fulmar* *Fulmarus glacialis*: Very rare in Long Island Sound, mostly storm-driven.

Black-capped Petrel* *Pterodroma hasitata*: Very rare in Long Island Sound, mostly storm-driven.

Cory's Shearwater* *Calonectris diomedea*: Rare to very rare in Long Island Sound, mostly storm driven. Try an August ferry ride from New London.

Great Shearwater* *Puffinus gravis*: Very rare in Long Island Sound, mostly storm-driven.

Sooty Shearwater* *Puffinus griseus*: Very rare in Long Island Sound, mostly storm-driven.

Manx Shearwater*(S) *Puffinus puffinus*: Very rare in Long Island Sound, mostly storm-driven. Seen spring through early autumn.

Audubon's Shearwater*(S) *Puffinus lherminieri*: Very rare, storm-driven. Have been found on inland reservoirs.

Wilson's Storm-Petrel* *Oceanites oceanicus*: Uncommon visitor to Long Island Sound from mid-May to mid-September; most numerous in mid-summer.

White-faced Storm-Petrel* *Pelagodroma marina*: Very rare, first continental U.S. record is from Milford Point.

Leach's Storm-Petrel* *Oceanodroma leucorhoa*: Very rare in Long Island Sound, usually storm-driven.

White-tailed Tropicbird* *Phaethon lepturus*: Very rare; storm-driven.

Wood Stork* *Mycteria americana*: Very rare in summer.

Magnificent Frigatebird* *Fregata magnificens*: Very rare in Long Island Sound and inland along major rivers.

Brown Booby* *Sula leucogaster*: Very rare in Long Island Sound.

Northern Gannet *Morus bassanus*: Occurs September to December and March to May along entire coast; common in November; rare in winter.

Double-crested Cormorant *Phalacrocorax auritus*: Widespread common nester on offshore islands; common to abundant (late September) migrant along coast, lakes, and inland waterways; winters locally in small but increasing numbers along coast and larger rivers.

Great Cormorant *Phalacrocorax carbo*: Fairly common to common from October through April; rare May and September; replaces Double-crested Cormorant in same locations.

Anhinga*(S) *Anhinga anhinga*: Very rare June and September migrant at ponds and over hawk-watch stations.

American White Pelican *Pelecanus erythrorhynchos*: Rare but fairly regular visitor occurring most years, usually along the coast or major rivers; also over hawk-watch stations.

Brown Pelican* *Pelecanus occidentalis*: Very rare coastal visitor. Not seen annually.

American Bittern *Botaurus lentiginosus*: State-endangered migratory breeder, encountered more often in coastal marshes, October to April; rare breeder in larger inland marshes with cattail and bulrush.

Least Bittern *Ixobrychus exilis*: State-threatened, widely scattered and secretive migratory breeder, found mid-April to mid-September, in brackish and freshwater cattail and reed-cattail marshes.

Great Blue Heron *Ardea herodias*: Fairly common to common (late September to October and April into May) migratory resident of inland and coastal wetlands; uncommon breeder; nests communally mainly in interior wooded swamps, often in coastal estuaries in winter.

Great Egret *Ardea alba*: Uncommon to locally fairly common migratory nester mid-March to late October in coastal and occasionally inland marshes and wetlands. State-threatened breeder on islands. Rare in winter along coast.

Snowy Egret *Egretta thula*: Uncommon to locally common migratory breeder, found mid-March to late October in coastal marshes; very rare inland. State-threatened breeder on islands; rare into December in coastal marshes.

Little Blue Heron *Egretta caerulea*: Rare breeder on offshore islands; uncommon migrant; found April to late September, rarely into winter. Feeds in saltmarshes; occasionally disperses inland in late summer.

Tricolored Heron** *Egretta tricolor*: Rare migrant mid-March to December; very rare and sporadic nester on offshore islands; feeds in saltmarshes.

Cattle Egret** *Bubulcus ibis*: Rare, decreasing migrant April to late November in coastal pastures, lawns, and wet meadows. Often associates with livestock. Once bred here.

Green Heron *Butorides virescens*: Fairly common statewide late April to October; breeds in wooded edges of swamps, rivers, and ponds, often with dense emergent vegetation, on offshore islands, and in some coastal marshes.

Black-crowned Night-Heron *Nycticorax nycticorax*: Fairly common to locally common March to October; rare and local through winter. Breeds colonially on islands, and in isolated woodlots adjacent to fresh and brackish marshes, mainly along the coast.

Yellow-crowned Night-Heron *Nycticorax violacea*: Uncommon to locally fairly common migratory breeder. Small colonies nest in isolated trees within a few miles of the coast, often in residential neighborhoods, and in heron rookeries offshore.

White Ibis* *Eudocimus albus*: Very rare in coastal marshes and inland ponds; often alone, not with other ibis.

Glossy Ibis *Plegadis falcinellus*: Uncommon local breeder in offshore island heron rookeries; fairly common migrant. Found late March into October. Feeds in coastal marshes. Rare inland.

White-faced Ibis# *Plegadis chihi*: Rare, but annual; usually seen in April or May in coastal marshes with Glossy Ibis. May summer in Glossy Ibis colonies. Hybrid × Glossy have occurred.

Black Vulture *Caragyps atratus*: Uncommon but increasing southern species. Rare and local breeder. Favors traprock and other ridges.

Turkey Vulture *Cathartes aura*: Common migrant and summer resident; fairly common to local in winter; increasing throughout New England. Seen soaring over ridges, forests, and open areas. Roosts communally on natural and man-made structures in towns, and on ridgelines.

Osprey *Pandion haliaetus*: Fairly common (spring) to common migrant (fall), and local breeder along the coast and inland on larger bodies of water. Nests in most coastal reserves, especially along central and eastern coast.

Swallow-tailed Kite *Elanoides forficatus*: Very rare spring migrant, usually seen overhead.

White-tailed Kite* *Elanus leucurus*: Very rare.

Golden Eagle *Aquila chrysaetos*: Rare but regular migrant, and winter visitor to the lower Connecticut River and large reservoirs and rivers, often in association with Bald Eagle. A few winter along the lower Connecticut River. Seen occasionally inland.

Mississippi Kite *Ictinia mississippiensis*: Rare migrant throughout Connecticut, and very rare local inland breeder.

Northern Harrier** *Circus cyaneus*: Uncommon (spring) to fairly common (fall) migrant, especially along the coast and over open inland areas, including large freshwater marshes, farm fields, and meadows. An endangered very local breeder, in open salt or freshwater marshes, coastal dunes, extensive pastures, and grasslands; few pairs remain.

Sharp-shinned Hawk *Accipiter striatus*: Fairly common (spring), common (fall) to abundant (September to October) migrant, especially along the coast. Endangered very local nester. Most often nests in the western and eastern highlands in conifers near an opening, usually within extensive woodlands. Uncommon in winter; found near feeders.

Cooper's Hawk *Accipiter cooperii*: Fairly common and increasing spring and fall migrant, common in mid-September to mid-October, especially along the coast. An uncommon but increasing nesting species, adapting to residential situations. Nests in coniferous and deciduous stands, near fields, wetlands, or clearings; does not need mature woodlands.

Northern Goshawk** *Accipiter gentiles*: Rare resident and uncommon migrant. Tends to breed on isolated hillsides, near wetlands, within extensive woodlands free from human disturbance. Concentrated in the maturing forests of the northwest and northeast highlands. Irruptive in winter but generally remains uncommon and local. Most conspicuous while courting in spring.

Bald Eagle** *Haliaeetus leucocephalus*: Fairly common migrant, locally common wintering species, and uncommon but increasing breeder, in coastal marshes, and on large inland reservoirs and rivers. Concentrations of seventy or more gather on the lower Connecticut River in midwinter.

Red-shouldered Hawk *Buteo lineatus*: Uncommon migrant, and locally common and increasing wetland resident with a patchwork distribution within Connecticut. Found most commonly in the central coast lowlands, and western and eastern interior. Often sits low in trees.

Broad-winged Hawk *Buteo platypterus*: Uncommon to locally common summer resident of larger tracts of mixed woods, deciduous forest, and isolated woodlots. Often nests in a tree crotch, adjacent to paths or roads and near wetlands. Avoids developed areas. Most common in eastern and western interior and highlands. A common spring and abundant fall migrant at inland hawk watches but strays to the coast.

Swainson's Hawk* *Buteo swainsoni*: Very rare spring, and rare fall migrant, with individuals seen inland, but more often along the coast.

Zone-tailed Hawk* *Buteo albonotatus*: Very rare fall migrant.

Red-tailed Hawk *Buteo jamaicensis*: Uncommon to locally common breeder, and common migrant and winter resident throughout Connecticut. A perch-hunting generalist found in many wooded habitats often adjacent to open fields; also hunts by roadsides.

Rough-legged Hawk *Buteo lagopus*: Rare but irruptive fall and early spring migrant. In winter, can be locally common in coastal and inland marshes, farmland, and open country. Perches horizontally, often on small trees, and hovers while hunting.

Yellow Rail* *Coturnicops noveboracensis*: Very rare migrant and winter visitor. Secretive denizen of short-grass marshes; extremely difficult to find. (Don't hold your breath; try Texas.)

Black Rail# *Laterallus jamaicensis*: Very rare migrant and breeder, in coastal and inland marshes, with most sightings from May to July. Extremely difficult to find. Decreasing across its range. Listening for calls on still, moonless nights offers the best chance of detecting them.

Corn Crake* *Crex crex*: Very rare visitor from Europe. No modern records.

Clapper Rail *Rallus longirostris*: Uncommon to fairly common nesting species in coastal salt and brackish marshes; rare and local in winter in coastal marshes. Hybridizes with King Rail.

King Rail** *Rallus elegans*: Rare nesting species and migrant in larger inland freshwater and coastal brackish marshes. May linger into early winter. Hybridizes with Clapper Rail.

Virginia Rail *Rallus limicola*: Our most common freshwater nesting and migrant rail, usually in marshes with emergent vegetation, some cattail, and sedges; less common in coastal marshes; rare in winter. Difficult to view, but vocal after dark.

Sora *Porzana carolina*: A very secretive, uncommon to locally fairly common migrant and nesting species, mainly in freshwater marshes with cattail and swamps, mostly in western and central Connecticut.

Purple Gallinule* *Porphyrio martinica*: Very rare, with recent sightings concentrated between April and August. Try ponds with lush emergent vegetation.

Common Gallinule (Moorhen)** *Gallinula galeata*: Very rare breeder; locally uncommon and decreasing migrant on inland fresh and coastal marshes, and ponds with lush emergent vegetation.

American Coot *Fulica americana*: Generally an uncommon migrant and winter visitor on inland lakes, ponds, larger rivers, and coastal marshes, estuaries, and harbors. Locally common November and December. Very rare in summer.

Sandhill Crane[**] *Grus grus*: Rare. Can occur any month in open farm fields, pastures, or coastal marshes; seen occasionally as a migrant in fall. Potential nester; breeds in Massachusetts.

Black-necked Stilt[*] *Himantopus mexicanus*: Very rare but consistent migrant (May and June) in coastal habitats.

American Avocet *Recurvirostra americana*: Rare, nearly annual, mainly summer and fall migrant at coastal sites.

American Oystercatcher *Haematopus paliatus*: Uncommon to locally fairly common (August and September) migrant breeder, nesting locally on open pebbly coastal sandbars.

Black-bellied Plover *Charadrius squatarola*: Fairly common (spring) to locally common (July through September) migrant on coastal marshes, beaches, and mudflats. Rare in winter. Visits rain pools on coastal lawns and inland agricultural fields.

American Golden-Plover *Charadrius dominica*: Rare in spring; uncommon fall migrant (July and October to November), in same areas at Black-bellied Plover. Found regularly on airports and flooded or plowed fields.

Snowy Plover[*] *Charadrius alexandrinus*: Very rare, in coastal areas.

Wilson's Plover[*] *Charadrius wilsonia*: Very rare, in coastal areas with other plovers.

Semipalmated Plover *Charadrius semipalmatus*: Common to locally abundant migrant in May and from July to September. Rare in winter. Found on beaches, marshes, and mudflats, and on inland airports and plowed fields.

Piping Plover *Charadrius melodus*: Endangered, rare to locally uncommon migrant; breeds on sandy beaches with limited human disturbance, mid-March to mid-November.

Killdeer *Charadrius vociferus*: Fairly common (spring) to common (August to October) migrant; variable in winter. Found on coastal rocky and sandy beaches and mudflats; inland on plowed fields, playing fields, and airports. A widespread fairly common breeder on coastal and inland open grassy upland areas with bare, gravelly patches.

Spotted Sandpiper *Actitis macularius*: Fairly common widespread breeder and migrant mid-April to September; rarely lingers into December, mainly along inland rivers, ponds, and lakeshores. Nests in upland adjacent to wetlands. Found coastally on mudflats and shorelines in migration.

Solitary Sandpiper *Tringa solitaria*: Uncommon to locally common migrant in inland marshes, vegetated swamps, edges of streams, rivers, ponds, and rarely coastal impoundments.

Spotted Redshank* *Tringa erythropus*: Very rare; coastal mudflats.

Greater Yellowlegs *Tringa melanoleuca*: Uncommon to common (April) migrant in coastal wetlands and inland ponds, lakes, rain pools, and marshes. A few remain on the coast in winter.

Willet *Tringa semipalmata*: Uncommon to fairly common and local breeder, and migrant in larger coastal wetlands.

Lesser Yellowlegs *Tringa flavipes*: Uncommon to fairly common migrant in coastal wetlands and inland ponds, lakes, rain pools, and marshes.

Upland Sandpiper** *Bartramia longicauda*: Rare and decreasing breeding migrant in large open grassy areas. A prairie-dependent species, its strongholds are at airports and military bases.

Whimbrel *Numenius phaeopus*: Uncommon spring and fall migrant mainly in coastal marshes, estuaries, fields, lawns, rain pools, and airports.

Long-billed Curlew* *Numenius phaeopus*: Very rare; same habitats as Upland Sandpiper.

Black-tailed Godwit* *Limosa limosa*: Very rare; coastal marshes, estuaries, rain pools.

Hudsonian Godwit *Limosa haemastica*: Rare fall migrant from late July to mid-November in coastal marshes, estuaries, airports, and rain pools.

Bar-tailed Godwit* *Limosa lapponica*: Very rare; coastal marshes, estuaries, rain pools.

Marbled Godwit *Limosa fedoa*: Rare migrant May to June and August to October in coastal marshes, mudflats, and airport rain pools.

Ruddy Turnstone *Arenaria interpres*: Uncommon fall, and fairly common spring migrant on coastal mudflats, beaches, and rocky shores; uncommon on rocky coasts, harbors, and marinas in winter.

Red Knot *Calidris canutus*: Uncommon and decreasing migrant in coastal wetlands; rare in winter.

Ruff* *Philomachus pugnax*: Rare migrant; there are scattered records from coastal wetlands, March to September.

Sharp-tailed Sandpiper* *Calidris acuminata*: Very rare; occurs with Pectoral Sandpiper.

Stilt Sandpiper *Calidris himantopus*: Rare spring, and uncommon and local fall (July to September) migrant, in coastal marshes, mudflats, and rain pools. Often found with dowitchers.

Curlew Sandpiper* *Calidris ferruginea*: Very rare. Records are concentrated from May to July and in October, in coastal wetlands. Associates with similar Dunlin.

Red-necked Stint* *Calidris ruficollis*: Very rare; coastal sandbars, marshes, estuaries, mudflats with other peeps.

Sanderling *Calidris alba*: Common migrant, and uncommon wintering species. Found on sandy beaches and mudflats, and on rock jetties in winter.

Dunlin *Calidris alpina*: Fairly common coastal migrant and wintering species, except in May, when it is common along tidal mudflats, beaches, and sandbars.

Purple Sandpiper *Calidris maritima*: Uncommon to fairly common (May) coastal migrant, and winter visitor to rocky shores, breakwaters, and jetties.

Baird's Sandpiper *Calidris bairdii*: Rare coastal and very rare inland migrant (July to October). Shows preference for grassy edges of shore-grass wetlands, lawns, and airport rain pools, tidal (marsh) impoundments, and mudflats.

Little Stint* *Calidris minuta*: Very rare; coastal sandbars, marshes, estuaries, mudflats.

Least Sandpiper *Calidris minutilla*: Common spring and fall migrant in coastal wetlands. Prefers marshes and grassy edges. The most common "peep" of any size at inland wetlands.

White-rumped Sandpiper *Calidris fuscicolli*: Uncommon to locally fairly common (May) coastal migrant of tidal marshes, beaches, and mudflats. Will visit rain pools on lawns. Found inland on rare occasion.

Buff-breasted Sandpiper *Tryngites subruficollis*: Rare but regular migrant late July to October on open lawns.

Pectoral Sandpiper *Calidris melanotos*: Uncommon in spring, and locally fairly common in September, in coastal and inland marshes, agricultural areas, wet fields, lawns, and airport rain pools.

Semipalmated Sandpiper *Calidris pusilla*: An abundant migrant in coastal wetlands and beaches; less common inland on the shores of ponds, rivers, marshes, and lakes.

Western Sandpiper *Calidris mauri*: Rare spring and uncommon fall migrant found coastally among flocks of other "peeps."

Short-billed Dowitcher *Limnodromus griseus*: Fairly common to locally common (August to September) migrant in coastal wetlands, beaches, and mudflats.

Long-billed Dowitcher *Limnodromus scolopaceus*: Rare to locally uncommon (September to November) fall migrant. Very rare in winter and spring in coastal wetlands, beaches, and mudflats.

Wilson's Snipe *Callinago delicata*: Fairly common fall (September and October) to locally abundant (early April) migrant, and uncommon and local winter resident in inland marshes, seeps, shallow streams, and coastal wetlands.

American Woodcock *Scolopax minor*: Fairly common to locally common (March) migrant and breeder; rare in winter. Found in inland wet meadow and field edges, sedge marshes, very early forest, and coastal wetlands.

Wilson's Phalarope *Phalaropus tricolor*: Rare but regular coastal migrant from May to June and August to September in fresh and brackish impoundments, tidal and rain pools, mudflats, and marshes.

Red-necked Phalarope* *Phalaropus lobatus*: Very rare, most often after severe storms drop them from their overland migrations in August and May into coastal wetlands, inland ponds, reservoirs, and lakes.

Red Phalarope* *Phalaropus lobatus*: Rare May to June and August to October, often after severe weather, in coastal wetlands, inland ponds, reservoirs, and lakes.

Pomarine Jaeger*(S) *Stercorarius pomarinus*: Very rare coastal migrant offshore and over beaches.

Parasitic Jaeger* *Stercorarius parasiticus*: Rare but regular migrant August to November offshore in association with feeding gull flocks and over beaches.

Long-tailed Jaeger* *Stercorarius longicaudus*: Very rare August to September migrant, usually seen in association with major weather events; mostly coastal.

Dovekie* *Alle alle*: Rare and irregular visitor mid-November to mid-March, mainly coastal and storm-driven, usually along rocky or sandy shores; can be stranded inland.

Common Murre* *Uria aalge*: Very rare; coastal, most seen on Long Island Sound ferry crossings.

Thick-billed Murre* *Uria lomvia*: Very rare; coastal estuaries, inlets, and bays, sometimes around docks. Also seen from ferries.

Razorbill* *Uria torda*: Rare but increasing. The most likely alcid in Connecticut waters. Can be local and uncommon after storms, usually along rocky shores, harbors, and inlets.

Black Guillemot* *Cepphus grille*: Very rare; coastal, usually along rocky shores.

Atlantic Puffin* *Fratercula arctica*: Very rare; mainly occurs after storms coastally, and occasionally inland; October to December.

Black-legged Kittiwake* *Rissa brevirostris*: Rare but regular, late October to early April, often storm-driven and found offshore, and in larger river mouths and bays. Seen on winter ferry crossings.

Ivory Gull* *Pagophila eburnea*: Very rare.

Sabine's Gull* *Xema sabini*: Very rare.

Bonaparte's Gull *Larus philadelphia*: Fairly common fall through spring; abundant (March to April) coastal and offshore migrant in bays, estuaries, and open water.

Black-headed Gull *Larus ridibundus*: Uncommon to rare but regular coastal migrant and winter visitor, found on lawns with flocks of Ring-billed Gull and Bonaparte's Gull, especially March to April and November to December.

Little Gull *Larus minutus*: Uncommon to very rare but regular coastal migrant and winter visitor. Most likely in flocks of Bonaparte's Gull in March and April in bays, inlets, and estuary mouths. Very rare in summer and fall.

Ross's Gull* *Rhodostethia rosea*: Very rare, coastal inlets, river mouths; most likely with flocks of Bonaparte's Gull.

Laughing Gull *Larus atricilla*: Uncommon in spring. Common summer nonbreeding visitor to mudflats, sandbars, coastal parking lots, and offshore with other gulls. Will feed on swarming wasps.

Franklin's Gull* *Larus pipixcan*: Very rare; scattered coastal records from June through November.

Mew Gull* *Larus canus*: Very rare to rare, increasing. Mainly coastal, a few inland records, November to March in gull flocks. Three subspecies have occurred; mostly European *L. c. canus*, also *L. c. kamtschatschensis* and *L. c. brachyrhynchus*.

Ring-billed Gull *Larus delawarensis*: Common year-round nonbreeding resident and migrant. Abundant from fall through spring; fairly common in summer. Found on beaches, mudflats, offshore, inland waterways, farm fields and ball fields, and fast-food parking lots. Will hawk flying insects.

Herring Gull *Larus argentatus*: Common year-round resident and migrant. Abundant from fall through spring; fairly common in summer. Found on beaches, mudflats, offshore, inland waterways, farm fields and ball fields, fast-food parking lots, and common on landfills. Fairly common breeder on offshore islands.

"Thayer's" Gull* *Larus glaucoides thayerii*: Very rare winter visitor from the west, mostly recorded on landfills and coast. Now considered a subspecies of Iceland Gull.

Iceland Gull *Larus glaucoides*: Rare to uncommon but regular from October to May with other gulls along the coast and on larger inland rivers, lakes, ponds, agricultural fields, and landfills.

Lesser Black-backed Gull *Larus fuscus*: Rare to uncommon but regular from October to May with other gulls along the coast and on larger inland rivers, lakes, ponds, agricultural fields, and active landfills. Also a rare summer visitor.

Slaty-backed Gull* *Larus schistisagus*: Very rare; all records from landfills.

Glaucous Gull *Larus hyperboreus*: Rare but regular and local from November to May with other gulls along the coast and on larger inland rivers, lakes, agricultural fields, and active landfills.

Great Black-backed Gull *Larus marinus*: Common coastal migrant and winter visitor; less common inland on larger waterways, lakes, ponds, and landfills; uncommon offshore island breeder. Widespread.

Sooty Tern* *Onychoprion fuscatus*: Very rare; storm-driven.

Bridled Tern* *Onychoprion anaethetus*: Very rare; all records from Falkner Island.

Least Tern *Sterna antillarum*: State-threatened, fairly common to locally common coastal migrant and breeder on mainland sandy beaches.

Gull-billed Tern* *Gelochelidon nilotica*: Very rare; coastal marshes and estuaries.

Caspian Tern *Hydroprogne aspia*: Rare but regular coastal migrant April to November on beaches and mudflats.

Black Tern *Chlidonias niger*: Rare to uncommon migrant May to October in coastal marshes, inlets, bays, and infrequently on inland lakes and ponds.

Roseate Tern *Sterna dougallii*: Federally endangered, uncommon coastal spring and fall migrant and declining breeder on offshore islands (Falkner Island). Fairly common post-breeding, in August, when it stages with other terns on beaches, mudflats, and inshore islands. Often feeds offshore.

Common Tern *Sterna hirundo*: State species of special concern; common spring migrant and breeder on Falkner Island, Guilford, and scattered inshore islands along the coast. Common to abundant August to September when staging on beaches and mudflats.

Arctic Tern* *Sterna paradisaea*: Very rare along the coast.

Forster's Tern *Sterna forsteri*: Rare spring, summer, and late fall into December. Uncommon late July to November. Fairly common in October. Regular coastal migrant in staging tern flocks on beaches and offshore; occasionally ventures to inland lakes, and up large rivers after storms.

Royal Tern *Thalasseus maximus*: Rare but regular coastal migrant June to November.

Sandwich Tern* *Thalasseus sandvicensis*: Rare coastal migrant on mudflats and beaches.

Black Skimmer** *Rhynchops niger*: Uncommon and very local migrant and sporadic breeder from mid-April to October on sandy beaches; often associates with Least Tern.

Rock Pigeon (I) *Columb livia*: Common introduced breeding resident of residential, industrial, and agricultural areas. Local in unpopulated areas.

Band-tailed Pigeon* (S) *Patagioenas fasciata*: Very rare.

Eurasian Collared-Dove# *Streptopedia decaocto*: Rare. Sightings increasing in the east.

Common Ground-Dove* *Columbina passerina*: Very rare.

White-winged Dove* *Zenaida asiatica*: Very rare; most records are at feeders.

Mourning Dove *Zenaida macroura*: Common breeding resident and migrant of residential, agricultural, and open forested areas; most plentiful in March and October migration.

Yellow-billed Cuckoo* *Coccyzus americanus*: Uncommon migrant breeder from May to mid-September; rare into October in open woodlands and especially brushy edges near water.

Black-billed Cuckoo *Coccyzus erythropthalmus*: Uncommon migrant breeder from May to mid-September; rare into October in mature woodlands, woodland edges, often near water. Populations fluctuate with caterpillar abundance; difficult to find unless vocalizing.

Barn Owl** *Tyto alba*: State-endangered, widespread but very rare and local resident migrant. Breeds near large open marshes, farm fields, and landfills; feeds especially on nocturnal rodents.

Eastern Screech-Owl *Megascops asio*: A fairly common widespread resident of suburban and urban neighborhoods, parks, woodlots, orchards, and wooded swamps where nest cavities are available.

Great Horned Owl *Bubo virginianus*: Fairly common, widespread adaptable resident and migrant; nests in conifers, preferring large, dry, upland woodlots adjacent to expansive open areas; also found in suburban and urban parks.

Snowy Owl *Bubo scandiacus*: Rare, irruptive winter visitor from November into April, mainly on coastal dunes, beaches, marshes, and islands, and occasionally inland farms.

Northern Hawk Owl* *Surnia ulula*: Very rare, with records spanning September to January. No recent records.

Burrowing Owl* *Athene cunicularia*: Very rare. Airports and coastal beaches.

Barred Owl *Strix varia*: Fairly common widespread resident; nests in mature woodlands, including hemlock ravines, near wetlands.

Great Gray Owl* *Strix nebulosa*: Very rare winter visitor from the north in open inland and coastal areas; records concentrated in January and February into March.

Long-eared Owl** *Asio otus*: State-endangered nester in conifers adjacent to open fields and farmland. Rare to uncommon migrant from October to mid-May; local winter visitor. Roosts communally in winter, mainly in coastal conifer stands.

Short-eared Owl** *Asio flammeus*: Rare to uncommon local migrant and winter visitor to larger inland meadows and farm fields, coastal marshes and dunes. Seen late September to mid-May. Once bred here.

Boreal Owl* *Aegolius funereus*: Very rare; inland and coastal cedar groves.

Northern Saw-whet Owl** *Aegolius acadicus*: Rare to uncommon, very local resident breeder mainly in highlands, in bogs and hillsides near wooded swamps; uncommon to fairly common from mid-October through November inland; coastal migrant; winter visitor to red cedar and mixed conifer groves, mainly along the coast.

Common Nighthawk** *Chordeiles minor*: Uncommon to fairly common and widespread daytime migrant mid-May to mid-June. Fairly common to common, especially along coast, mid-August to mid-September. Rare to very rare into November. Hawks insects over waterways, open areas, and cities. A very rare urban breeder, nesting on gravel rooftops in some larger cities.

Chuck-wills-widow* *Antrostomus carolinensis*: Rare spring visitor May into June, often along the coast; vocal at dawn and dusk.

Eastern Whip-poor-will *Antrostomus vociferus*: Uncommon migrant from mid-April through May, and late August through September; rare into October. Widespread but very local breeder in regenerating woodland clearings and young scrubby forest patches with dry soils and open canopy.

Chimney Swift *Chaetura pelagica*: Fairly common migrant and locally common summer breeder. Found mid-April to mid-September; less common through October. Often in towns and cities where unused chimneys are available.

Ruby-throated Hummingbird *Archilochus colubris*: Uncommon to fairly common ubiquitous migrant and breeder late April through September; rare into November; common late August and September coastally. Breeding concentrated in northwest highland's overgrown forest clearings, open woodland edges, power cuts, and rural gardens.

Black-chinned Hummingbird* *Archilochus alexandri*. Very rare; at feeders and gardens.

Rufous Hummingbird *Selasphorus rufus*: Rare annual migrant and winter visitor, mainly at feeders from mid-July to January. Most have been female or immature types. Care should be taken to separate from very rare Allan's Hummingbird, which have occurred in the east.

Calliope Hummingbird* *Stellula calliope*: Very rare; recorded at feeders from October to January; sightings increasing in the Northeast.

Broad-billed Hummingbird* *Cynandthus latirostris*: Very rare; at feeders.

Belted Kingfisher *Ceryle alcyon*: Fairly common resident migrant of wetlands; uncommon in winter where open water is available; breeds in burrows along inland and coastal waterways, ponds, lakes, and marshes.

Red-headed Woodpecker** *Melanerpes erythrocephalus*: Rare year-round, except uncommon regular migrant mid-September to mid-October, mainly along coast; sporadic very rare breeder at inland wooded swamps and open oak-hickory woodlands.

Red-bellied Woodpecker *Melanerpes carolinus*: Fairly common and increasing resident of suburban and rural open deciduous woodland, floodplains, and near feeders.

Yellow-bellied Sapsucker *Sphyrapicus varius*: Year-round resident migrant; fairly common mid-April to late October; uncommon otherwise. Northern highland breeder extending its range south; winters in sheltered riparian areas and orchards. Responds to Barred Owl call.

Downy Woodpecker *Picoides pubescens*: Common resident in any wooded habitat throughout the state; visits marshes in winter; visits feeders.

Hairy Woodpecker *Picoides villosus*: Widespread, fairly common, more local than Downy Woodpecker. Requires large trees in mixed and wet woodlands, riparian floodplain forest, and suburban woodlots; will shift to residential feeders in winter.

Black-backed Woodpecker* *Picoides arcticus*: Very rare irruptive species September to May, especially October and November.

Northern Flicker *Colaptes auratus*: Fairly common to common migrant late September to late August; widespread resident breeder, uncommon to fairly common in winter. An ant specialist, it is especially common in rural areas and on lawns, as well as forested areas. Eats fruit in winter.

Pileated Woodpecker *Dryocopus pileatus*: Uncommon resident and local denizen of deep mature forest, increasingly common in suburban areas with larger woodlots.

American Kestrel** *Falco sparverius*: Rare and rapidly declining nesting species of farmland, grassland, and open areas where cavities are available for nesting. Fairly common (spring) to common (fall) migrant, especially along the coast.

Merlin** *Falco columbarius*: Uncommon to fairly common migrant and rare wintering species. Mainly coastal in migration. Now breeding in New England; a potential nesting species.

Gyrfalcon* *Falco rusticolus*: Very rare arctic migrant and winter visitor; has occurred over inland farmland, coastal marshes, and offshore.

Peregrine Falcon *Falco peregrinus*: Federally endangered but increasing. Uncommon (spring) and fairly common (fall) migrant. Very rare and local breeder on cliffs, bridges, skyscrapers, and other man-made structures.

Monk Parakeet (I) *Myiopsitta monachus*: Established introduced resident, fairly common along coast in residential neighborhoods; often in pines; rare inland along major rivers, and on the eastern coast.

Olive-sided Flycatcher** *Contopus cooperi*: Very rare and sporadic breeder in northwest highlands. Uncommon migrant from mid-May into June and early August to late September; rare into October. Seen most often atop dead snags in wooded swamps.

Eastern Wood-Pewee *Contopus virens*: Fairly common migrant May to early June and August to early October. Widespread breeder in mature woodlands with forest gaps and areas of open canopy.

Yellow-bellied Flycatcher *Empidonax flaviventris*: Uncommon migrant from mid-May to mid-June and mid-August to late September in open mixed or coniferous woodlands. Call similar to Least Flycatcher.

Acadian Flycatcher *Empidonax virescens*: Uncommon migrant and local breeder mid-May to September in open woodlands often with conifers and a dense canopy, near water, especially streams, often near a clearing.

Alder Flycatcher *Empidonax alnorum*: Uncommon migratory breeder mid-May to mid-September, difficult to identify off breeding grounds, best told by buzzy "fee-bee-o" song. Breeds mainly in northwest highlands in wet areas with small trees and shrubs, near open water, and bogs.

Willow Flycatcher *Empidonax traillii*: Uncommon to fairly common widespread migratory breeder mid-May to early September, difficult to identify off breeding grounds, best told by "fitz-bew" song. Found in coastal and inland wet or dry brushy areas.

Least Flycatcher *Empidonax minimus*: Uncommon to locally fairly common migratory breeder late April to late September; rare into October. Widespread migrant; breeds at higher elevations, generally not along coast. Found in mixed woodlands with understory of shrubs and herbaceous plants near water, but often drier habitat than for Willow and Alder Flycatchers.

Pacific-slope or "Western" Flycatcher* *Empidonax difficilis or E. difficilis/ occidentalis*: Very rare; inland field edges.

Eastern Phoebe *Sayornis phoebe*: Arrives early March. Common migrant late March to April and late September to October; decreasingly common into November. Rare and local in winter. Fairly common breeder in open woodlands and parks, on bridges, and other man-made structures near water; needs ledge or overhang for nest.

Say's Phoebe* *Sayornis saya*: Very rare; fall along field edges.

Ash-throated Flycatcher* *Myiarchus cinerascens*: Very rare; late fall along field edges.

Great Crested Flycatcher *Myiarchus crinitus*: Fairly common migrant and widespread cavity-nesting species in mixed and deciduous woodlands and suburban parks.

Tropical Kingbird* *Tyrannus melancholicus*: Very rare; fall.

Western Kingbird *Tyrannus verticalis*: Rare but regular fall migrant, usually in open fields along coast, September into December; very rare in spring.

Eastern Kingbird *Tyrannus tyrannus*: Uncommon to common (late August) migrant and widespread breeder. Found late April into October (rare) in open areas, often near water, along rivers, woodland, marsh edges, and farmland.

Gray Kingbird* *Tyrannus dominicensis*: Very rare; fall.

Scissor-tailed Flycatcher* *Tyrannus forficata*: Very rare from April to July and October, mostly coastal open fields, on phone wires, and at airports.

Fork-tailed Flycatcher* *Tyrannus savanna*: Very rare on airports and open fields.

Loggerhead Shrike* *Lanius ludovicianus*: Very rare visitor March to May and September to October, in open grass, farmlands, and airports. Once bred here.

Northern Shrike *Lanius excubitor*: Rare to locally uncommon irruptive winter visitor from the north. Found on open farmland, pastures, and shrubby fields, especially with barbed wire or thorn bushes, usually from December to March.

White-eyed Vireo *Vireo griseus*: Uncommon and local nesting species and rare coastal migrant, most numerous in east, southeast, and western edge of Connecticut. Breeds in power-line cuts, brushy thickets, and field edges.

Bell's Vireo* *Vireo bellii*: Very rare; fall.

Yellow-throated Vireo *Vireo flavifrons*: Fairly common migrant breeder late April to September along rivers and in deciduous woodlands near water; nearly absent as a breeder from Connecticut River Valley and coast.

Blue-headed Vireo *Vireo solitarus*: Found early April into December (rare); uncommon to fairly common (late April and October) migrant in mixed woodlands. Uncommon highland breeder in northern deciduous-coniferous woods. Singing is sporadic by late May.

Warbling Vireo *Vireo gilvus*: Fairly common to locally common migrant breeder in open areas with trees, usually near water, late April to October.

Philadelphia Vireo *Vireo philadelphicus*: Rare migrant mid-May to early June; uncommon late August into October. Found in mixed woodlands.

Red-eyed Vireo *Vireo olivaceus*: Common widespread migrant breeder of mixed and deciduous woods late April (uncommon) to November (rare).

Blue Jay *Cyanocitta cristata*: Common widespread resident in most forested habitats, including urban neighborhoods; secretive while breeding; abundant migrant mid-September to mid-October, staging impressive coastal flights.

Eurasian Jackdaw* *Corvus monedula*: Very rare; found with other corvids.

American Crow *Corvus brachyrhynchos*: Widespread common to locally abundant resident in most habitats; forms huge communal winter roosts.

Fish Crow *Corvus ossifragus*: Uncommon to locally common resident along coast, expanding inland along larger rivers Roosts with American Crows.

Common Raven *Corvus corax*: Uncommon local resident expanding its range along traprock ridges and hilltops throughout Connecticut.

Horned Lark** *Eremophila alpestris*: Very rare breeder restricted to airports and a few coastal and agricultural sites. Uncommon to locally fairly common migrant and winter visitor to farmland, coastal dunes, grassy fields, gravel parking lots.

Northern Rough-winged Swallow *Stelgidopteryx serripennis*: Fairly common statewide migrant and nesting species from April into September near water. Breeds along waterways in holes, drainpipes, crevices, riverbanks, often near bridges or old bridge foundations, and coastal retaining walls.

Purple Martin *Progne subis*: Uncommon open-area migrant and local breeder at nest boxes in farmland, coastal marshes, often near water, late April into September. May stage in groups near breeding sites in fall.

Brown-chested Martin* (S) *Progne tapera*: Very rare.

Tree Swallow *Tachycineta bicolor*: Arrives early March. Widespread common migrant breeder mid-March into October; rare into December. Nests in tree cavities and nest boxes near water. Abundant mid-August to mid-September, gathering along coast; lower Connecticut River roost of 300,000 or more.

Bank Swallow *Riparia riparia*: Uncommon to locally fairly common widespread migrant over open areas, saltmarshes, ponds, lakes, and waterways mid-April to late September; migrates over coastal marshes mid-July and August; nests very locally in steep river, sand, and gravel banks, and sand quarries statewide.

Barn Swallow *Hirundo rustica*: Arrives mid-March; common migrant and statewide breeder mid-April to October; rare into November. Found in open habitats, farm fields, salt and freshwater marshes, and rivers; nests on buildings and other manmade structures.

Cliff Swallow *Petrochelidon pyrrhonota*: Uncommon scattered migrant and local breeder mid-April to October. Breeding concentrated in western Connecticut; absent from central and southeastern Connecticut. Usually under bridges, on dams or barns near open fields or water; seen coastally in fall.

Cave Swallow *Petrochelidon fulva*: Rare but regular coastal migrant in November; may linger into December; expect after winds turn northerly following several days of southerly winds.

Black-capped Chickadee *Parus atricapillus*: Widespread common statewide resident and migrant in mixed forest types, forest edges, urban and suburban parks, neighborhoods, and feeders.

Boreal Chickadee* *Parus hudsonicus*: Very rare, irregular November migrant and winter visitor, usually along coast in conifer stands and tree farms.

Tufted Titmouse *Parus bicolor*: Common widespread woodland and neighborhood resident and migrant; also visits feeders.

Red-breasted Nuthatch *Sitta canadensis*: Rare to locally uncommon highland breeder in pine stands and mixed conifer forest; irruptive migrant and winter visitor, especially along coast in fall, late August through April. Can be common some years.

White-breasted Nuthatch *Sitta carolinensis*: Fairly common widespread cavity-nesting resident in mixed and deciduous woodlands, riparian forest, and suburban neighborhoods; visits feeders.

Brown Creeper *Certhia americana*: Fairly common migrant April and mid-October to mid-November; uncommon, widespread mainly highland resident. Nests under loose bark in coniferous and mixed pine-hardwood forests, and especially wooded swamps with dead trees. Local in winter; some move to lowlands.

House Wren *Troglodytes aedon*: Fairly common to common migrant and summer resident April to October; rare into December. Found in woodland edges, orchards, old fields, gardens, residential neighborhoods, and parks.

Winter Wren *Troglodytes troglodytes*: Uncommon in migration early April and October to early November. Uncommon and local breeder, mainly in highlands, in blow-down areas in hemlock ravines and densely shaded conifer-hardwood forests, often near water. A few winter in protected wet pockets, freshwater marshes, beaver swamps, and parks.

Sedge Wren# *Cistothorus platensis*: Rare migrant May through October in brush dumps, coastal waste areas, and marsh edges, usually in fall; very rare and irregular breeder in wet meadows and agricultural field edges.

Marsh Wren *Cistothorus palustris*: Uncommon migrant and breeding species mid-April to October; rare in winter. Mainly in coastal brackish tidal marshes and some inland marshes.

Carolina Wren *Thryothorus ludovicianus*: Fairly common resident of edge habitat, thickets, brushy woods, and neighborhoods; visits feeders. Highest distribution in southern half of Connecticut; expanding into highlands; severe winters cause range contraction.

Blue-gray Gnatcatcher *Polioptila caerulea*: Uncommon migratory breeder mid-April into October. Often associated with oaks in open mixed woodlands, floodplain forest, old fields, forest, river, and pond edges.

Golden-crowned Kinglet* *Regulus satrapa*: Common April and October migrant, and uncommon winter resident, in conifer and mixed woodlands. Rare to uncommon, very local breeder in isolated highland spruce stands within mixed forest, often along roadsides.

Ruby-crowned Kinglet *Regulus calendula*: Common widespread migrant late March to April and in October; uncommon into December; rare mid-winter. Found in mixed and open deciduous forests, and conifer stands.

Northern Wheatear* *Oenanthe oenanthe*: Rare but fairly regular fall visitor mid-September to October; very rare in May. Usually found in open coastal areas; occasionally inland.

Eastern Bluebird *Sialia sialis*: Fairly common to common migrant in October and November. Cavity-nesting resident in open meadows, fields, beaver swamps, woodland edges, and neighborhoods with shrubs and cavities or nest boxes available. Fairly common but local in winter.

Mountain Bluebird* *Sialia currucoides*: Very rare; found in November and December near cedar groves, often with other fruit-eaters.

Townsend's Solitaire* *Myadestes townsendii*: Very rare winter visitor, November to January, often in cedar groves with other fruit-eaters.

Veery *Catharus fuscenscens*: A fairly common migratory breeder in forests and swamps with dense thickets late April through August; common in September.

Gray-cheeked Thrush *Catharus minimus*: Rare migrant May and September to October in deep shaded woods, mixed woods, and woodland edges; often feeds on paths.

Bicknell's Thrush *Catharus bicknelli*: Difficult to identify off breeding grounds, but banding records indicate rare migrant, May and September to October.

Swainson's Thrush** *Catharus ustulatus*: Uncommon migrant May and September into October in broad range of wooded habitats, often on forest paths; potential very rare breeder in mixed white pine-hemlock forests of western highlands.

Hermit Thrush *Catharus guttatus*: Uncommon resident migrant; breeds in mid to upper elevations, open dry forested hillsides, forest edges, often near white pine or hemlock groves, expanding; in migration, mid-April and October; local in winter, often in lowland forest and wet thickets.

Wood Thrush *Hylocichla mustelina*: Fairly common migratory breeder late April to September; rare into October; found in mixed wetter forest types with thicket cover, often near streams and other wetlands, also suburban parks.

Fieldfare* *Turdus pilaris*: Very rare.

American Robin *Turdus migratorius*: Widespread abundant migratory resident March through August and mid-October to mid-November; fairly common otherwise; annual winter numbers vary dramatically depending on fruit availability.

Varied Thrush* *Ioxoreus naevius*: Very rare winter visitor November to March at feeders.

Gray Catbird *Dumetella carolinensis*: Fairly common in open woodlands, wetland edges, parks, thickets, and suburban neighborhoods with shrubs from late April to mid-October; uncommon in winter in lowland thickets and wetlands.

Brown Thrasher *Taxostoma rufum*: Uncommon migratory resident mid-April to early November; rare and local in winter; found in old fields, farm and woodland edges; secretive outside breeding season; decreasing.

Northern Mockingbird *Mimus polyglottos*: Fairly common widespread resident of landscaped neighborhoods, farm and woodland edges, old fields, parks, and rose thickets.

European Starling (I) *Sturnus vulgarus*: Abundant in all suburban, urban, and rural areas. Large flocks gather fall through spring to feed on fruit, and where there is grain and livestock.

American Pipit *Anthus rubescens*: Uncommon to fairly common migrant April to May and September to January, heard overhead at coastal hawk watches, and visits inland and coastal farms, dunes, airports, and open lake edges; rare and local in winter, mostly on farmland and coastal dunes.

Bohemian Waxwing* *Bombycilla garrulus*: Very rare irruptive winter visitor from the north; found on crabapple and other fruit trees and berry bushes, usually in the northern half of the state, often with Cedar Waxwing.

Cedar Waxwing *Bombycilla cedrorum*: Fairly common year-round resident, and common flocking migrant mid-September to mid-November, especially along coast; breeds along river, lake, and woodland edges, beaver swamps, and orchards. Prefers cherry and apple blossoms in spring, and areas with cedars and berries in winter.

Lapland Longspur *Calcarius lapponicus*: Rare to uncommon visitor late October to April to coastal dunes, grasslands, beaches, farm fields, and lawns, with Snow Bunting and Horned Lark.

Chestnut-collared Longspur* *Calcarius ornatus*: Very rare, on coastal grasslands and inland ball fields.

Smith's Longspur* *Calcarius pictus*: Very rare, on coastal grasslands.

Snow Bunting *Plectrophenax nivalis*: Uncommon flocking visitor to coastal dunes, beaches, lawns, airport grasslands, gravel parking lots; less common on inland farms; late October to April.

Ovenbird *Seiurus aurocapilla*: Common widespread migratory breeder late April to mid-August; less common in fall; rare in winter in mixed deciduous forest.

Worm-eating Warbler *Helmitheros vermivorum*: Uncommon widespread but local migratory breeder on dry hillsides and steep talus slopes in open deciduous forest.

Louisiana Waterthrush *Parkesia motacilla*: Widespread fairly common migratory breeder early April to August in open woodlands along smaller moving streams and pond edges; uses similar habitat in migration but uncommon along coast.

Northern Waterthrush *Parkesia noveboracensis*: Widespread fairly common (spring) and uncommon (fall) migratory breeder mainly of highland wooded swamps with standing water, spruce bogs, and sluggish woodland streams, April to September; found in more diverse wetlands in migration.

Golden-winged Warbler** *Vermivora chrysoptera*: Rare, local, and declining migratory breeder seldom seen in migration May to October in early successional habitat, and old fields with scattered bushes and trees near forest. May be extirpated now as a breeder.

Blue-winged Warbler *Vermivora cyanoptera*: Fairly common widespread migratory breeder in old fields, power-line cuts, shrubby forest clearings, and forest and wetland edges; nests close to ground.

Black-and-white Warbler *Mniotilta varia*: Widespread fairly common to common (late April to May) migratory breeder April to October in deciduous or mixed coniferous-deciduous woodlands with an understory, often of laurel; forages on tree trunks; nests on ground.

Prothonotary Warbler** *Protonotaria citrea*: Very rare in fall; rare but overshoots regularly from the south, mid-April to July, especially April and May in wooded swamps, lowland river-edge forest, and woodland edge near water; very rare breeder.

Tennessee Warbler *Oreothlypis peregrina*: Uncommon but regular widespread treetop migrant in mixed woodlands, May and mid-August to mid-September.

Orange-crowned Warbler *Oreothlypis celata*: Rare to uncommon but regular October to November; rare winter and spring visitor; in thickets and woodland edges, mainly along coast.

Nashville Warbler** *Oreothlypis ruficapilla*: Rare to uncommon migrant and local, mainly highland, breeder mid-April to July and mid-August to mid-September; rare into January. Found in overgrown pastures, old fields, and woodland edges, usually associated with young evergreens.

Connecticut Warbler *Oporornis agilis*: Rare, regular but secretive late August to October migrant in thickets, wetland scrub, beaver swamps, and woodland edges.

MacGillivray's Warbler*(S) *Geothlypis tolmiei*: Very rare, in wetland edges with dense cover.

Mourning Warbler** *Geothlypis philadelphia*: Uncommon but regular migrant May into June and mid-August to October in thickets, woodland and wetland edges, forest clearcuts with shrubbery; singing males are rare into summer. Potential very rare breeder.

Kentucky Warbler** *Geothlypis formosa*: Rare to uncommon in May; rare in fall and as a scattered very rare and local breeder in woodlands with dense understory throughout.

Common Yellowthroat *Geothlypis trichas*: Most common breeding warbler; found in dense shrubby tangles with interspersed herbaceous plants, edge habitat, especially along wetlands and watercourses.

Hooded Warbler *Setophaga citrina*: Uncommon local breeder, either on wooded hillsides with dense understory or in lowland forest, often in barberry thickets, concentrated in the central and eastern coast spreading into northwest highlands; uncommon but rarely encountered in migration.

American Redstart *Setophaga ruticilla*: Common and ubiquitous migratory breeder late April through October in most wooded and shrubby habitats; most common in wet forests with dense mid-story saplings.

Cape May Warbler *Setophaga tigrina*: Rare to uncommon upper canopy migrant May and mid-August to September; rare to December; often in isolated spruces in parks, yards, mixed woodlands, spruce groves, and woodland edges.

Cerulean Warbler *Setophaga cerulea*: Uncommon and local migratory breeder; found at river's edge of large unbroken tracts of forested hillside (at least one thousand acres), often in tall silver maples or sycamores; rarely seen in migration.

Northern Parula *Setophaga americana*: Fairly common widespread migrant and very rare breeder in riparian forest, wetter woodlands, and wooded swamps.

Magnolia Warbler *Setophaga magnolia*: Fairly common migrant May and mid-August to October; uncommon western highland breeder in younger open forest; usually in spruce or pines, black spruce bogs, spruce plantations.

Bay-breasted Warbler *Setophaga castanea*: Uncommon May and late August to October migrant; usually in stands of conifers in open mixed forest.

Blackburnian Warbler *Setophaga fusca*: Fairly common May and mid-August to mid-September treetop migrant, often in conifers in mixed woods. Uncommon to locally common breeder in tall dense pine and hemlock stands in western and eastern highlands.

Yellow Warbler *Setophaga petechia*: Common widespread migratory breeder April to September in brushy thickets of river-edge forest, wetland edges, moist power-line cut segments, and open woodland.

Chestnut-sided Warbler *Setophaga pensylvanica*: Uncommon to common migratory forest and field edge breeder, in overgrown pastures and forest clearings, on drier sites than Yellow Warbler; widespread but sparse on southwest coast and in central valley.

Blackpoll Warbler *Setophaga striata*: Fairly common to common migrant May to early June and late August to November in open deciduous and mixed woodlands, often in conifers.

Black-throated Blue Warbler *Setophaga caerulescens*: Widespread and fairly common in migration mid-April to May and mid-August to September. Highland hillside nester in larger tracts of mature mixed open forest with dense shrubby undergrowth, often in mountain laurel.

Palm Warbler *Setophaga palmarum*: Fairly common April into May and mid-September into November in dunes and coastal scrub, grassy fields, wetland and pond edges and thickets, in understory of open wet deciduous forest; both races common in early October, rare and local in winter.

Pine Warbler *Setophaga pinus*: Fairly common to locally common migratory breeder usually in pines or pine stands within mixed woodlands; scattered and local statewide.

Yellow-rumped Warbler *Setophaga coronata*: Common widespread migrant mid-April and May, abundant mid-September to October, in mixed woods; fairly common winter visitor, especially in coastal bayberry thickets; uncommon breeder in mature hemlock and white pine woodlands and edges at higher elevations. The "Audubon's" race is a rare fall visitor.

Yellow-throated Warbler** *Setophaga dominica*: Rare but annual southern visitor mid-April to mid-July at scattered locations; associated with sycamores along rivers, sometimes in pines; very rare in winter at feeders. Has attempted to breed here.

Prairie Warbler *Setophaga discolor*: Uncommon to locally fairly common nesting migrant of open brushy habitats, power-line cuts, overgrown regenerating fields, especially with cedars, traprock ridges.

Black-throated Gray Warbler* *Setophaga nigrescens*: Very rare but regular October to November and May, vagrant in coastal cedar groves and mixed woods.

Hermit Warbler*(S) *Setophaga occidentalis*: Very rare.

Black-throated Green Warbler *Setophaga virens*: Mid-April to November; fairly common to common late September to early October; widespread migratory breeder; rare into December. Breeds mainly in hemlock forest and ravines, scattered statewide, but concentrated in highlands.

Canada Warbler *Cardellina canadensis*: Uncommon to fairly common migratory breeder of wet shaded woodlands, especially in highlands, with dense understory of mountain laurel near water; in brushy wetland edges during migration.

Wilson's Warbler *Cardellina pusilla*: Uncommon migrant late April to May and late August to October; rare into December; found in brushy thickets of lowland wetlands, forest edges, and vine tangles, especially in winter.

Yellow-breasted Chat *Icteria virens*: Rare to uncommon migrant mid-April to May and mid-August to January, and very rare resident breeder in southeastern Connecticut, in dense vine tangles and thickets in overgrown pastures, field and forest edges, and power-line cuts. A few linger through winter. Very secretive.

Grasshopper Sparrow *Ammodramus savannarum*: State-endangered and declining migratory grassland breeder at airports and large open fields.

Henslow's Sparrow* *Ammodramus henslowii*: Very rare November migrant in wet meadows and field edges. Once bred here.

Le Conte's Sparrow* *Ammodramus leconteii*: Very rare October through December in wet meadows, community gardens and coastal marshes.

Nelson's Sparrow *Ammodramus nelsoni*: Status uncertain because of confusion with the very similar Saltmarsh Sparrow. Considered uncommon May into June and October to mid-November in coastal marshes.

Saltmarsh Sparrow *Ammodramus caudactutus*: State species of special concern. Locally fairly common breeder in coastal short-grass (*Spartina patens*) and fairly common migrant in saltmarshes May to mid-November; rare into winter. Connecticut is epicenter of their world distribution.

Seaside Sparrow *Ammodramus maritimus*: State species of special concern. Uncommon migratory breeder in coastal tall-grass (*Spartina alterniflora*) tidal marshes May through September; rare into December.

American Tree Sparrow *Spizelloides arborea*: Fairly common migrant and winter visitor late October to mid-April, in edges of shrubby fields, pastures, wet woodlands, and marshes.

Chipping Sparrow *Spizella passerina*: Widespread common migratory breeder mid-April to November; rare and local in winter; in areas with short grass and trees, residential neighborhoods, parks, open upland forest.

Clay-colored Sparrow** *Spizella pallida*: Rare but regular migrant and winter visitor September to mid-February, usually in coastal fields, brush dumps, and waste areas, with gatherings of sparrows; has attempted to nest April to June in weedy inland fields.

Field Sparrow *Spizella pusilla*: Migratory breeder, fairly common March to early April and mid-October to mid-November; uncommon in winter and summer; found in weedy or shrubby fields, power-line cuts, and forest edges.

Lark Sparrow *Chondestes grammacus*: Rare migrant September to October and April to May, and very rare winter visitor, in coastal brush dumps, meadows, and waste areas.

Lark Bunting* *Calamospiza melanocorys*: Very rare in open fields.

Fox Sparrow *Passerella iliaca*: Widespread, fairly common migrant March into April and mid-October into December, in overgrown pastures, brushy edges of farm fields and open forest, hedgerows; uncommon winter visitor in sheltered cedar groves, wet areas, and at feeders.

Dark-eyed Junco *Junco hyemalis*: Resident migratory breeder, fairly common to common, widespread, September to mid-April; very rare, local highland breeder. Lawns, open woodlands, forest and field edges, gardens, and feeders.

White-crowned Sparrow *Zonotichia leucophrys*: Uncommon to fairly common migrant October and late April to May, and winter visitor to hedgerow thickets, brushy pastures, farm field and forest edges; often winters in rose thickets.

Golden-crowned Sparrow*(S) *Zonotichia atricapalla*: Very rare in field edges with other sparrows.

Harris's Sparrow* *Zonotichia querula*: Very rare at feeders, community gardens, field edges, and brush dumps.

White-throated Sparrow *Zonotichia leucophrys*: Resident migratory breeder common late September through May, abundant in October, uncommon June to August. Can appear in any habitat; visits feeders; mainly a highland breeder in semi-open woodland with brushy thickets, sometimes on hillsides above swamps.

Vesper Sparrow *Pooecetes gramineus*: Rare to uncommon migrant April and October to November, and winter and summer visitor on agricultural land, weedy fields, coastal brush dumps, and meadows. Has bred here.

Savannah Sparrow *Passerculus sandwichensis*: Uncommon local breeder in scattered grasslands and agricultural areas. Common migrant September to October and fairly common April in farm and weedy fields, community gardens, and marsh edges. Uncommon in winter; a few of the pale "Ipswich" subspecies winter locally on coastal dunes.

Song Sparrow *Melospiza melodia*: Common widespread migratory resident of thickets, shrubby pastures, hedgerows, freshwater wetland edges, and power-line cuts.

Lincoln's Sparrow *Melospiza lincolnii*: Uncommon to fairly common mid-May and late September into November, secretive migrant of wet meadows, beaver swamps, shrubby wetland, and field edges.

Swamp Sparrow *Melospiza georgiana*: Fairly common breeder and spring migrant; common October to early November; uncommon and local in winter. Found mainly in freshwater wetlands.

Green-tailed Towhee* *Pipilo chlorurus*: Very rare at feeders.

Spotted Towhee* *Pipilo maculatus*: Very rare in coastal brushy and residential areas.

Eastern Towhee *Pipilo erythrophthalmus*: Uncommon to common migrant October in field, woodland, and wetland edge thickets; breeds in dry upland habitat with dense cover of blueberry, huckleberry, and other shrubs.

Summer Tanager *Piranga rubra*: Rare but regular spring migrant in riparian woodlands, mid-April into June.

Scarlet Tanager *Piranga olivacea*: Fairly common to common, widespread migrant; breeds in larger forest tracts; often nests in conifers. Absent in winter.

Western Tanager* *Piranga ludoviciana*: Very rare visitor October through March, usually at feeders or in orchards.

Northern Cardinal *Cardinalis cardinalis*: Common, widespread resident of thickets bordering woodlands, meadows, open woods, parks, neighborhoods and gardens; visits feeders.

Rose-breasted Grosbeak *Pheucticus ludovicianus*: Fairly common, widespread migratory breeder late April to October in mixed and deciduous woodlands, old pasture and forest clearing edges, and red maple swamps.

Black-headed Grosbeak* *Pheucticus melanocephalus*: Very rare, mainly at feeders.

Blue Grosbeak** *Passerina caerulea*: Rare but annual migrant September to October and mid-April to July, at coastal brush piles and weedy fields; feeds on burdock. Has attempted to breed here.

Lazuli Bunting* *Passerina amoena*: Very rare.

Indigo Bunting *Passerina cyanea*: Arrives in April. Fairly common to common migratory breeder late August to mid-September, less common into December. Found in power-line cuts, abandoned pastures, field edges, traprock ridgetops, and with sparrows in gardens, brush piles, farm and weedy fields in migration.

Painted Bunting* *Passerina ciris*: Very rare April to May and October at feeding stations, brushy areas, and tree farms.

Dickcissel *Spiza americana*: Rare but regular migrant in spring, very rare sporadic nester, most common in September and October in grassy fields and brush dumps, especially along coast.

Bobolink *Dolichonyx oryzivorus*: Uncommon local breeder in grassy fields, but fairly common to common migrant (mid-August to mid-September), found late April to October in weedy and grassy fields.

Red-winged Blackbird *Agelaius phoeniceus*: Locally abundant, widespread resident migratory breeder in coastal and freshwater marshes and wetlands; uncommon in winter, but large local winter roosts form sometimes; migrants return in February.

Western Meadowlark* *Sturnella neglecta*: Very rare in coastal meadows and marshes with other meadowlarks.

Eastern Meadowlark *Sturnella magna*: Resident, uncommon, and declining local migratory breeder in larger grassy fields and alfalfa meadows; spring migrants arrive in March; most common in fall (October to early November) in grassy farmland, meadows, pastures, and coastal marshes. Rare and local in winter.

Yellow-headed Blackbird *Xanthocephalus xanthocephalus*: Rare migrant September through April, usually with other blackbirds in cattail and coastal marshes, and farm fields.

Rusty Blackbird *Euphagus carolinus*: Uncommon and declining migrant October into November and mid-March to April; rare to local in winter; in wooded swamps and wetland edges.

Brewer's Blackbird*(S) *Eupahgus cyanochephalus*: Very rare in (horse) farm pastures.

Common Grackle *Quiscalus quiscula*: Abundant breeder March to mid-August. Large migrant flocks form early November; migrants return late February. Uncommon through winter. Found on open woodlands, often near water.

Boat-tailed Grackle*(S) *Quiscalus major*: Small resident breeding populations at Stratford marshes, Clinton and Madison marshes, Hammonasset; occasionally seen at Milford Point and Sherwood Island; very rare elsewhere.

Brown-headed Cowbird *Molothrus ater*: Fairly common to common widespread migratory breeder late February through November. Uncommon and local in winter. Found in riparian forest, parkland, open woods, neighborhoods, farms, and wetlands; visits feeders.

Orchard Oriole *Icterus spurius*: Uncommon migratory breeder late April to mid-August in semi-open areas with trees, pastures, orchards, field edges, usually near water; expanding inland, especially along major rivers.

Bullock's Oriole* *Icterus bullockii*: Rare, scattered records from October to May. Found at bird feeders, in forest and edge. Wintering orioles should be studied carefully to rule out this species.

Baltimore Oriole *Icterus galbula*: Fairly common widespread nesting species late April to October, common during late August migration. A few usually overwinter. Found in floodplain forest, often in cottonwoods and willows, semi-open woodlands along roadways, fields, lawns, and wetland edges.

Brambling* *Fringilla montifringilla*: Very rare at feeders.

Pine Grosbeak *Pinicolla enucleator*: Rare irruptive winter visitor mid-November to late March, most often in highlands; may be locally common in flight years. Visits crabapple and other fruiting trees, conifers, and birch.

House Finch *Carpodacus mexicanus*: Common widespread resident in neighborhoods, parks, open space, river-edge forest, semi-open woodlots, pastures, orchards, and feeders.

Purple Finch *Carpodacus purpureus*: Uncommon resident highland breeder, uncommon to common irruptive migrant mid-April to mid-May and mid-September to early December. Numbers vary in winter.

Red Crossbill** *Loxia curvirostra*: Irruptive; numbers vary annually from none to many. Widespread, in pines, but most common along coast in migration October to mid-May; visits feeders; sporadic highland nester after flight years.

White-winged Crossbill** *Loxia leucoptera*: Irruptive; numbers vary annually from none to many. Widespread, in spruce and hemlocks; most common along coast in migration October to mid-April; visits feeders; sporadic highland nester after flight years. Less common than Red Crossbill.

Common Redpoll *Acanthis flammea*: Irruptive but fairly regular flocking migrant November into April, often in birches, weedy fields, coastal brush dumps; visits feeders.

Hoary Redpoll* *Acanthis hornemanni*: Rare, irregular winter visitor usually found with Common Redpoll at feeders.

Pine Siskin** *Spinus pinus*: Rare, scattered, sporadic breeder; irruptive flocking migrant and winter visitor to conifer and birch stands, weedy fields, woodland edge, residential feeders. In fall, coastal migration sites most reliable.

American Goldfinch *Spinus tristis*: Fairly common to common migratory resident breeder into November in residential neighborhoods, weedy field and marsh edges, river-edge forest with catkins, and feeders. Late summer breeder. Winter numbers vary with food availability.

Evening Grosbeak** *Coccothraustes vespertinus*: Rare and declining coastal migrant October to May, and winter visitor; has nested in mixed deciduous and deciduous-coniferous forest; visits box elder, ornamental plantings, and bird feeders in winter, mainly in highlands.

House Sparrow (I) *Passer domesticus*: Widespread common resident in urban and suburban neighborhoods, in association with people, often near fast-food restaurants.

APPENDIX C

Species by Habitat

This section is a concise guide to the representative species of the more common habitats in Connecticut. It lists predominantly breeding birds; migrants are included where they occur typically, with the common name <u>underlined</u>.

Habitats are defined in a broad sense and may include several microhabitats under one heading. On the ground, habitats tend to blend with and overlap one another. Correspondingly, many bird species may occur in several habitats; for this reason, some species are included on more than one list.

■ Ubiquitous Species

Widespread and common species found in a variety of habitats.

Aquatic: Canada Goose, Mute Swan, Mallard, Double-crested Cormorant.

Land: Wild Turkey, Turkey Vulture, Red-tailed Hawk, Cooper's Hawk, Ring-billed Gull, Rock Pigeon, Mourning Dove, Downy Woodpecker, Red-bellied Woodpecker, Blue Jay, American Crow, Black-capped Chickadee, Tufted Titmouse, White-breasted Nuthatch, Carolina Wren, American Robin, European Starling, Song Sparrow, Northern Cardinal, Common Grackle, Brown-headed Cowbird, American Goldfinch, House Finch, House Sparrow.

■ Developed Areas

Birds of urban (and suburban) neighborhoods, city greenways and small open spaces, landscaped commercial and industrial areas.

Widespread or Common: Mallard, Ring-billed Gull, Rock Pigeon, Monk Parakeet (coastal), Chimney Swift, Red-bellied Woodpecker, Downy Woodpecker, Northern Flicker, European Starling, American Crow, Tufted Titmouse, Black-capped Chickadee, White-breasted Nuthatch, House Wren, Carolina Wren, American Robin, Northern Mockingbird, European Starling, Dark-eyed Junco, <u>White-throated Sparrow</u>, Song Sparrow, Northern

Cardinal, Common Grackle, Brown-headed Cowbird, House Finch, House Sparrow.

Local or Uncommon: Cooper's Hawk, Barn Owl, Common Nighthawk, Peregrine Falcon, Fish Crow.

■ Suburban Areas

Older residential neighborhoods, gardens, and orchards.

Widespread or Common: Urban species (see above), Red-tailed Hawk, Eastern Screech-Owl, Cedar Waxwing, Wood Thrush, Chipping Sparrow, Baltimore Oriole.

Local or Uncommon: Red-shouldered Hawk, Ruby-throated Hummingbird, Hairy Woodpecker, Great Crested Flycatcher, Eastern Kingbird, Common Raven, Eastern Bluebird, Rose-breasted Grosbeak, Indigo Bunting, Orchard Oriole.

■ Landfills

Widespread or Common: Canada Goose, Mallard, Turkey Vulture, Red-tailed Hawk, Killdeer; Ring-billed, Herring, and Great Black-backed Gulls; Rock Pigeon, Mourning Dove, Northern Flicker, European Starling, American Crow, Fish Crow, Barn Swallow, Cedar Waxwing, Red-winged Blackbird, Brown-headed Cowbird, Northern Cardinal, House Finch, House Sparrow

Local or Uncommon: Snow Geese, Black Vulture, Northern Harrier, Peregrine Falcon; Iceland, Lesser Black-backed, and Glaucous Gulls, and other rare gulls; Barn Owl, Short-eared Owl, Common Raven, Horned Lark, Savannah Sparrow, Snow Bunting

■ Upland Deciduous and Mixed Woods

Roughly 60 percent of Connecticut is forested, much of it deciduous, with oaks, hickories, and maples predominating. Many tree species are widespread, thriving in varied conditions, but oaks and hickories tolerate drier sites, while maples—along with ash, beech, elm, and other species—abound in wetter areas. The northern third of Connecticut has broad regions with mixed deciduous and coniferous forest (mixed forest), which become increasingly coniferous at higher elevations and as you travel north. Tree species vary slightly between specific forest types, but there is broad overlap. **Note:** The occurrence of some of bird species is dependent upon the presence and composition of an understory.

Widespread or Common: Cooper's Hawk, Great Horned Owl, Downy and Hairy Woodpeckers, Eastern Wood-Pewee, Great Crested Flycatcher, Blue Jay, American Crow, Red-eyed Vireo, Black-capped Chickadee, Tufted Titmouse, White-breasted Nuthatch, Veery, Wood Thrush, Black-throated Blue and Black-and-white Warblers, Ovenbird, American Redstart, Scarlet Tanager (mature forest), Rose-breasted Grosbeak, Eastern Towhee.

Local or Uncommon (concentrated in highlands): Broad-winged Hawk, Ruffed Grouse, Yellow-bellied Sapsucker, Pileated Woodpecker, Common Raven (cliffs), Least Flycatcher, Brown Creeper, Winter Wren (blow-downs), Hermit Thrush, Blue-headed Vireo, Worm-eating Warbler (talus slopes), White-throated Sparrow.

■ Conifer Forests

Native and plantation pines, spruce and hemlock stands, hemlock ravines, red and white cedar groves, and black spruce bogs. **Note:** The bird species listed here may occur in all or only one of these forest types (specifics noted in parentheses).

Widespread or Common: Great Horned Owl (upland), Barred Owl (lowland), Black-throated Green Warbler, Blackburnian Warbler, Pine Warbler, Scarlet Tanager.

Local or Uncommon: Sharp-shinned Hawk, Northern Goshawk, Long-eared Owl, Northern Saw-whet Owl, Red-breasted Nuthatch, Winter Wren, Golden-crowned Kinglet, Hermit Thrush, Swainson's Thrush, Nashville Warbler (small pines), Magnolia Warbler (spruce stands), Yellow-rumped Warbler, Cape May Warbler (in single spruce), Bay-Breasted Warbler, Northern Waterthrush (bogs), Purple Finch, Red and White-winged Crossbills, Pine Siskin, Evening Grosbeak.

■ Lowland Deciduous and Riparian Forest

Mixed forests comprised of water-tolerant, often shallow-rooted tree species, especially red and silver maple, sycamore, cottonwood, willow, and elm.

Widespread or Common: Wood Duck, Red-shouldered Hawk, Barred Owl, Eastern Screech-Owl, Belted Kingfisher, Red-bellied Woodpecker, Least Flycatcher, Eastern Phoebe, Eastern Kingbird, Yellow-throated and Warbling Vireos; Northern Rough-winged, Bank, and Cliff Swallows; Carolina Wren, Veery, Wood Thrush, Gray Catbird, Yellow Warbler, American Redstart, Louisiana Waterthrush, Northern Waterthrush, Common Yellowthroat, Rose-breasted Grosbeak, Common Grackle, Baltimore Oriole, House Finch.

Local or Uncommon: Hooded Merganser, Common Merganser, Hairy Woodpecker, Acadian Flycatcher, Prothonotary Warbler (rare), Cerulean Warbler (large tracts), Canada Warbler (laurel thickets), Hooded Warbler (laurel and barberry thickets), Summer Tanager (rare).

■ Forest Edge

The boundary area between woodlands and adjacent habitats (often includes thickets); can be within or at the periphery of a forest tract. Edges, because they join two habitats, are generally rich in bird life, harboring species from each.

Widespread or Common: Mourning Dove, Eastern Screech-Owl, Red-bellied Woodpecker, Least Flycatcher, Eastern Bluebird, Chestnut-sided Warbler, Yellow Warbler, Common Yellowthroat, Song Sparrow, Northern Cardinal, Brown-headed Cowbird, migrant warblers, sparrows, finches, and flycatchers.

Local or Uncommon: American Kestrel, American Woodcock, Ruby-throated Hummingbird, Brown Thrasher, White-eyed Vireo, Kentucky Warbler.

■ Thickets and Old Fields

Brushy habitat, including power-line cuts, old fields, early successional forest, and rose, dogwood, and other thickets.

Widespread or Common: Gray Catbird, Northern Mockingbird; Blue-winged, Chestnut-sided, and Prairie Warblers; Common Yellowthroat, Field Sparrow, Northern Cardinal, Indigo Bunting.

Local or Uncommon: American Woodcock, Eastern Whip-poor-will (successional habitat), Ruby-throated Hummingbird, Brown Thrasher, White-eyed Vireo, Golden-winged Warbler, Nashville Warbler, Mourning Warbler, Yellow-breasted Chat, Rose-breasted Grosbeak, Eastern Towhee.

▪ Fields and Meadows

Open lands, including remnant prairie, pastures, wet and dry meadows, cropland, lawns, hayfields, grassy airport strips, community gardens, and cemeteries. Without fire, flooding, or human manipulation, most fields eventually revert to forest.

Widespread or Common: Killdeer, Mourning Dove, Warbling Vireo (wet meadow edges), Barn and Bank Swallows, Chipping Sparrow, migrant sparrows, American Goldfinch, Common Grackle.

Local or Uncommon: Ring-necked Pheasant, Northern Harrier, Rough-legged Hawk, American Kestrel, American Golden-Plover, Upland Sandpiper, Buff-breasted Sandpiper, Northern Shrike, Horned Lark, Purple Martin, Cliff Swallow; Savannah, Grasshopper, and Field Sparrows; Bobolink, Eastern Meadowlark.

▪ Inland Wetlands

Wooded Swamps

Includes beaver ponds, and ponds with dense aquatic vegetation. Cavity nesters often use dead trees within wooded swamps. The species listed may be in all or only one of these wetlands.

Widespread or Common: Wood Duck, Great Blue and Green Herons, Spotted Sandpiper, Wilson's Snipe, Belted Kingfisher, woodpeckers, Black-billed Cuckoo, Eastern Kingbird, Tree and Northern Rough-winged Swallows, Eastern Bluebird, Cedar Waxwing, American Redstart, Common Yellowthroat, Swamp Sparrow, Red-winged Blackbird, Common Grackle.

Local or Uncommon: Hooded Merganser, Pied-billed Grebe, American and Least Bitterns, Sora, Virginia Rail, Common Gallinule, Solitary Sandpiper, Olive-sided Flycatcher, Brown Creeper, Red-headed Woodpecker (rare), Northern Parula, Prothonotary Warbler (rare), Rusty Blackbird.

Black Spruce Bogs

Very local wetlands, mainly within forests in the highlands.

Widespread or Common: Brown Creeper, Yellow-rumped Warbler, Canada Warbler (laurel thickets), Northern Waterthrush, Purple Finch.

Local or Uncommon: Northern Saw-whet Owl, Yellow-bellied Flycatcher, Rusty Blackbird.

Freshwater Marshes

Includes areas with extensive cattails and tussock sedge, often at the periphery of a pond or lake.

Widespread or Common: Canada Goose, Wood Duck, Great Blue and Green Herons, Sora, Virginia Rail, Solitary Sandpiper, Spotted Sandpiper, Wilson's Snipe, Belted Kingfisher, Black-billed Cuckoo, Eastern Kingbird, Tree and Rough-winged Swallows, Marsh Wren, Eastern Bluebird, Cedar Waxwing, American Redstart, Common Yellowthroat, Red-winged Blackbird, Common Grackle, Swamp Sparrow.

Local or Uncommon: Hooded Merganser, Pied-billed Grebe, American and Least Bitterns, King Rail, Alder and Willow Flycatchers.

▪ Ponds and Lakes

Includes reservoirs, ponds, lakes, and their edges.

Widespread or Common: Mute Swan; diving and dabbling ducks, including American Wigeon, Ring-necked Duck, Hooded Merganser, Common Merganser, Ruddy Duck, Double-crested Cormorant, Great Blue and Green Herons, Solitary Sandpiper, Spotted Sandpiper, Belted Kingfisher, Tree Swallow, migrant swallows, Red-winged Blackbird, Common Grackle.

Local or Uncommon: Blue-winged Teal, Northern Pintail, Lesser Scaup, Common Loon, American Coot.

▪ Coastal Habitats

Sandy Beaches, Dunes, and Mudflats

Widespread or Common: American Black Duck, Sanderling, most shorebirds, Laughing and Bonaparte's Gulls, Common Tern, migrating terns, American Crow, Fish Crow, European Starling, Palm Warbler, House Sparrow.

Local or Uncommon: Gadwall, Piping Plover, American Oystercatcher, Least Tern, Black Skimmer, Short-eared and Snowy Owls, Horned Lark, Ipswich Savannah Sparrow, American Pipit.

Rocky Shoreline and Gravel Beaches

Includes rock jetties and seawalls.

Widespread or Common: Black-bellied and Semipalmated Plovers, Ruddy Turnstone, Double-crested Cormorant, Great Cormorant, Herring and Great Black-backed Gulls.

Local or Uncommon: Purple Sandpiper, Snowy Owl.

Tidal Saltmarshes and Estuaries

Includes *Spartina* and *Phragmites* marshes, brackish river mouths, and coastal ponds (often concealed within the marsh).

Widespread or Common: Mute Swan, American Black Duck, Mallard, Green-winged Teal, Double-crested Cormorant, Great Blue Heron, Black-crowned Night-Heron, Clapper Rail, most shorebirds, Common Tern, Osprey, Tree Swallow, Marsh Wren, Saltmarsh (Sharp-tailed) Sparrow.

Local or Uncommon: Gadwall, Canvasback, Willet, Spotted Sandpiper, Great and Snowy Egrets, Yellow-crowned Night-Heron, Glossy Ibis, Least Tern, Bald Eagle, Northern Harrier, Rough-legged Hawk, Peregrine Falcon, Short-eared and Snowy Owls, Purple Martin, Nelson's (Sharp-tailed) Sparrow, Seaside Sparrow, Eastern Meadowlark, Boat-tailed Grackle.

Long Island Sound

Includes coastal and offshore waters.

Widespread or Common: Brant; sea ducks, including Greater Scaup, scoters, Long-tailed Duck, Bufflehead, Common Goldeneye, and Red-breasted Merganser; Common and Red-throated Loons, Horned Grebe, Double-crested Cormorant, Great Cormorant, Bonaparte's Gull.

Local or Uncommon: Common Eider, Red-necked Grebe, Northern Gannet, Wilson's Storm-Petrel, Razorbill.

Offshore Islands

Many waterbirds seek the relative safety of isolated rocky islands as nesting sites. Some of these islands also have trees.

Widespread or Common: Great and Snowy Egrets, Black-crowned Night-Heron, American Oystercatcher, Spotted Sandpiper, Herring and Great-black-backed Gulls, Common Tern, Double-crested Cormorant.

Local or Uncommon: Little Blue Heron, Tricolored Heron, Glossy Ibis, Yellow-crowned Night-Heron; Roseate Tern.

Checklist of the Birds of Connecticut

This list includes the 439 bird species recorded in Connecticut and accepted by the Avian Records Committee of Connecticut (ARCC). The names and sequences of species follow the American Ornithologists' Union's *Checklist of the Birds of North America* (seventh edition, 1998, and its supplements to the fifty-seventh, July 6, 2016).

Common names marked with an asterisk (*) are rare in Connecticut; the ARCC requests details. Names followed by (I) indicate introduced species (not native to Connecticut); (S) indicates sight records only; (Xr) indicates that the species has been extirpated in the state; (E) signifies an extinct bird.

Ducks, Geese, and Swans
Fulvous Whistling-Duck*
Pink-footed Goose*
Greater White-fronted Goose
Greylag Goose*
Snow Goose
Ross's Goose*
Brant
Barnacle Goose
Cackling Goose
Canada Goose
Mute Swan (I)
Trumpeter Swan*
Tundra Swan
Wood Duck
Gadwall
Eurasian Wigeon
American Wigeon
American Black Duck
Mallard
Blue-winged Teal
Cinnamon Teal*
Northern Shoveler
Northern Pintail

Green-winged Teal
Canvasback
Redhead
Ring-necked Duck
Tufted Duck*
Greater Scaup
Lesser Scaup
King Eider
Common Eider
Harlequin Duck
Surf Scoter
White-winged Scoter
Black Scoter
Long-tailed Duck
Bufflehead
Common Goldeneye
Barrow's Goldeneye
Hooded Merganser
Common Merganser
Red-breasted Merganser
Ruddy Duck

New World Quail
Northern Bobwhite (Xr)

Partridges, Grouse, Turkeys
Ring-necked Pheasant (I)
Ruffed Grouse
Wild Turkey

Loons
Red-throated Loon
Pacific Loon*
Common Loon

Grebes
Pied-billed Grebe
Horned Grebe
Red-necked Grebe
Eared Grebe*
Western Grebe*

Shearwaters and Petrels
Northern Fulmar*
Black-capped Petrel*
Cory's Shearwater*
Great Shearwater*
Sooty Shearwater* (S)
Manx Shearwater*
Audubon's Shearwater* (S)

Storm-Petrels
Wilson's Storm-Petrel
White-faced Storm-Petrel*
Leach's Storm-Petrel*
Band-rumped Storm-Petrel*

Tropicbirds
White-tailed Tropicbird*

Storks
Wood Stork*

Frigatebirds
Magnificent Frigatebird*

Gannets
Brown Booby*
Northern Gannet

Cormorants
Double-crested Cormorant
Great Cormorant

Darters
Anhinga*

Pelicans
American White Pelican
Brown Pelican*

Bitterns and Herons
American Bittern
Least Bittern
Great Blue Heron
Great Egret
Snowy Egret
Little Blue Heron
Tricolored Heron
Cattle Egret
Green Heron
Black-crowned Night-Heron
Yellow-crowned Night-Heron

Ibises
White Ibis*
Glossy Ibis
White-faced Ibis*

New World Vultures
Black Vulture
Turkey Vulture

Ospreys
Osprey

Hawks, Kites, and Eagles
White-tailed Kite*
Swallow-tailed Kite
Mississippi Kite
Golden Eagle
Northern Harrier
Sharp-shinned Hawk

Cooper's Hawk
Northern Goshawk
Bald Eagle
Red-shouldered Hawk
Broad-winged Hawk
Swainson's Hawk
Zone-tailed Hawk*
Red-tailed Hawk
Rough-legged Hawk

Rails, Gallinules, and Coots
Yellow Rail*
Black Rail*
Corn Crake*
King Rail
Clapper Rail
Virginia Rail
Sora
Purple Gallinule*
Common Gallinule
American Coot

Cranes
Sandhill Crane

Stilts and Avocets
Black-necked Stilt*
American Avocet

Oystercatchers
American Oystercatcher

Lapwings and Plovers
Black-bellied Plover
American Golden-Plover
Northern Lapwing*
Snowy Plover*
Wilson's Plover*
Semipalmated Plover
Piping Plover
Killdeer

Sandpipers and Phalaropes
Spotted Sandpiper
Solitary Sandpiper
Spotted Redshank*
Greater Yellowlegs
Willet
Lesser Yellowlegs
Upland Sandpiper
Whimbrel
Long-billed Curlew*
Black-tailed Godwit*
Hudsonian Godwit
Bar-tailed Godwit*
Marbled Godwit
Ruddy Turnstone
Red Knot
Ruff*
Sharp-tailed Sandpiper*
Stilt Sandpiper
Curlew Sandpiper*
Red-necked Stint*
Sanderling
Dunlin
Purple Sandpiper
Baird's Sandpiper
Little Stint* (S)
Least Sandpiper
White-rumped Sandpiper
Buff-breasted Sandpiper
Pectoral Sandpiper
Semipalmated Sandpiper
Western Sandpiper
Short-billed Dowitcher
Long-billed Dowitcher
Wilson's Snipe
American Woodcock
Wilson's Phalarope
Red-necked Phalarope
Red Phalarope*

Skuas and Jaegers
Pomarine Jaeger* (S)
Parasitic Jaeger
Long-tailed Jaeger*

Auks, Murres, and Puffins
Dovekie*
Common Murre*
Thick-billed Murre*
Razorbill
Black Guillemot*
Atlantic Puffin*

Gulls, Terns, and Skimmers
Black-legged Kittiwake*
Ivory Gull*
Sabine's Gull*
Bonaparte's Gull
Black-headed Gull
Little Gull
Ross's Gull*
Laughing Gull
Franklin's Gull*
Mew Gull*
Ring-billed Gull
California Gull*
Herring Gull
Iceland Gull
Lesser Black-backed Gull
Slaty-backed Gull*
Glaucous Gull
Great Black-backed Gull
Sooty Tern*
Bridled Tern*
Least Tern
Gull-billed Tern*
Caspian Tern
Black Tern
Roseate Tern
Common Tern
Arctic Tern*
Forster's Tern

Royal Tern
Sandwich Tern*
Black Skimmer

Pigeons and Doves
Rock Pigeon (I)
Band-tailed Pigeon* (S)
Eurasian Collared-Dove*
Common Ground-Dove*
White-winged Dove*
Mourning Dove

Cuckoos
Yellow-billed Cuckoo
Black-billed Cuckoo

Barn Owls
Barn Owl

Typical Owls
Eastern Screech-Owl
Great Horned Owl
Snowy Owl
Northern Hawk Owl*
Burrowing Owl*
Barred Owl
Great Gray Owl*
Long-eared Owl
Short-eared Owl
Boreal Owl*
Northern Saw-whet Owl

Goatsuckers
Common Nighthawk
Chuck-will's-widow*
Eastern Whip-poor-will

Swifts
Chimney Swift

Hummingbirds
Ruby-throated Hummingbird
Black-chinned Hummingbird*

Rufous Hummingbird
Calliope Hummingbird*
Broad-billed Hummingbird*

Kingfishers
Belted Kingfisher

Woodpeckers
Red-headed Woodpecker
Red-bellied Woodpecker
Yellow-bellied Sapsucker
Downy Woodpecker
Hairy Woodpecker
Black-backed Woodpecker*
Northern Flicker
Pileated Woodpecker

Caracaras and Falcons
American Kestrel
Merlin
Gyrfalcon*
Peregrine Falcon

Parrots
Monk Parakeet (I)

Tyrant Flycatchers
Olive-sided Flycatcher
Eastern Wood-Pewee
Yellow-bellied Flycatcher
Acadian Flycatcher
Alder Flycatcher
Willow Flycatcher
Least Flycatcher
Pacific-slope Flycatcher*
Eastern Phoebe
Say's Phoebe*
Ash-throated Flycatcher*
Great Crested Flycatcher
Tropical Kingbird*
Western Kingbird
Eastern Kingbird
Gray Kingbird*

Scissor-tailed Flycatcher*
Fork-tailed Flycatcher*

Shrikes
Loggerhead Shrike*
Northern Shrike

Vireos
White-eyed Vireo
Bell's Vireo*
Yellow-throated Vireo
Blue-headed Vireo
Warbling Vireo
Philadelphia Vireo
Red-eyed Vireo

Crows and Jays
Blue Jay
Eurasian Jackdaw*
American Crow
Fish Crow
Common Raven

Larks
Horned Lark

Swallows
Northern Rough-winged Swallow
Purple Martin
Brown-chested Martin* (S)
Tree Swallow
Bank Swallow
Barn Swallow
Cliff Swallow
Cave Swallow

Chickadees and Titmice

Black-capped Chickadee
Boreal Chickadee*
Tufted Titmouse

Nuthatches
Red-breasted Nuthatch

White-breasted Nuthatch

Creepers
Brown Creeper

Wrens
House Wren
Winter Wren
Sedge Wren
Marsh Wren
Carolina Wren

Gnatcatchers
Blue-gray Gnatcatcher

Kinglets
Golden-crowned Kinglet
Ruby-crowned Kinglet

Old World Flycatchers
Northern Wheatear*

Thrushes
Eastern Bluebird
Mountain Bluebird*
Townsend's Solitaire*
Veery
Gray-cheeked Thrush
Bicknell's Thrush
Swainson's Thrush
Hermit Thrush
Wood Thrush
Fieldfare*
American Robin
Varied Thrush*

Mockingbirds and Thrashers
Gray Catbird
Brown Thrasher
Northern Mockingbird

Starlings
European Starling (I)

Wagtails and Pipits
American Pipit
Sprague's Pipit*

Waxwings
Bohemian Waxwing*
Cedar Waxwing

Longspurs and Snow Buntings
Lapland Longspur
Chestnut-collared Longspur*
Smith's Longspur*
Snow Bunting

Wood-Warblers
Ovenbird
Worm-eating Warbler
Louisiana Waterthrush
Northern Waterthrush
Golden-winged Warbler
Blue-winged Warbler
Black-and-white Warbler
Prothonotary Warbler
Tennessee Warbler
Orange-crowned Warbler
Nashville Warbler
Connecticut Warbler
MacGillivray's Warbler* (S)
Mourning Warbler
Kentucky Warbler
Common Yellowthroat
Hooded Warbler
American Redstart
Cape May Warbler
Cerulean Warbler
Northern Parula
Magnolia Warbler
Bay-breasted Warbler
Blackburnian Warbler
Yellow Warbler
Chestnut-sided Warbler
Blackpoll Warbler

Black-throated Blue Warbler
Palm Warbler
Pine Warbler
Yellow-rumped Warbler
Yellow-throated Warbler
Prairie Warbler
Black-throated Gray Warbler*
Hermit Warbler*
Black-throated Green Warbler
Canada Warbler
Wilson's Warbler
Yellow-breasted Chat

Towhees and Sparrows

Grasshopper Sparrow
Henslow's Sparrow*
Le Conte's Sparrow*
Nelson's Sparrow
Saltmarsh Sparrow
Seaside Sparrow
American Tree Sparrow
Chipping Sparrow
Clay-colored Sparrow
Field Sparrow
Lark Sparrow
Lark Bunting*
Fox Sparrow
Dark-eyed Junco
White-crowned Sparrow
Golden-crowned Sparrow* (S)
Harris's Sparrow*
White-throated Sparrow
Vesper Sparrow
Savannah Sparrow
Song Sparrow
Lincoln's Sparrow
Swamp Sparrow
Green-tailed Towhee*
Spotted Towhee*
Eastern Towhee

Cardinals and Tanagers

Summer Tanager
Scarlet Tanager
Western Tanager*
Northern Cardinal
Rose-breasted Grosbeak
Black-headed Grosbeak*
Blue Grosbeak
Lazuli Bunting*
Indigo Bunting
Painted Bunting*
Dickcissel

Blackbirds and Orioles

Bobolink
Red-winged Blackbird
Eastern Meadowlark
Western Meadowlark*
Yellow-headed Blackbird
Rusty Blackbird
Brewer's Blackbird* (S)
Common Grackle
Boat-tailed Grackle
Brown-headed Cowbird
Orchard Oriole
Bullock's Oriole*
Baltimore Oriole

Finches and Allies

Brambling*
Pine Grosbeak
House Finch
Purple Finch
Red Crossbill
White-winged Crossbill
Common Redpoll
Hoary Redpoll*
Pine Siskin
American Goldfinch
Evening Grosbeak

Old World Sparrows
House Sparrow (I)

Extinct or Extirpated (six species)
Labrador Duck (E)
Gray Partridge (E)

Eskimo Curlew (E)
Greater Prairie-Chicken (Heath Hen subspecies; E)
Passenger Pigeon (E)
Northern Bobwhite (native populations; Xr)

APPENDIX E

Connecticut Rare Species Review List

What is the Avian Records Committee of Connecticut (ARCC) and what does it do? The ARCC consists of twelve members who serve three-year terms. The committee maintains the official list of bird species acceptably documented as occurring, or having occurred, in Connecticut. It also maintains and publishes a review list of species of rare annual occurrence, rare historical occurrence, or no previously documented occurrence in Connecticut. Most species on this list average fewer than five occurrences annually, but some species that are difficult to identify are included even if they occur more frequently. The committee reviews submitted reports and votes either to accept or not to accept them to the official state list of birds. For details on the ARCC and on submitting a report, visit www.ctbirding.org.

The following list of Connecticut's review species provides the number of records since 1965, the months of occurrence, and the first and last years of occurrence. Numbers (in parentheses) after a date indicate the number of sightings for that year. Entries marked with a single asterisk (*) have historical records that predate 1965 and are not included in the total. Entries marked with three asterisks (***) include all historical records. Common names enclosed in "quotation marks" are identifiable forms, now considered subspecies, reviewed by the ARCC.

If you sight any of these species or subspecies, the ARCC requests that any documentation be submitted to the secretary: Greg Hanisek, 175 Circuit Avenue, Waterbury, CT 06708; ctgregh@gmail.com.

Species	Records	Month(s)	Year(s) of Occurrence
Fulvous Whistling Duck	1	May	1987
Pink-footed Goose	10	Dec–May	1998–2017
Greylag Goose	1	Mar	2009
Ross's Goose	7	Sep/Dec–Jan	2006–2017
"Black" Brant	4	Jan–Apr	2009–2017
Trumpeter Swan	1	Nov–Mar	2014
Cinnamon Teal	1	Nov	1994

Species	Records	Month(s)	Year(s) of Occurrence
Tufted Duck*	9	Jan–Apr/Nov	1992–2017
Pacific Loon	6	Oct–Jan/May	1992–2017
Eared Grebe	13	Dec–Feb/Sep–Oct	1987–2017
Western Grebe*	5	Nov–Jan/Mar/Oct	1973–2016
Northern Fulmar*	3	Sep–Oct/Dec	1998–2009
Black-capped Petrel	1	Oct	1938
Cory's Shearwater	10+	Jul–Aug/Oct	1976–2017
Great Shearwater*	6	Jun–Jul/Nov	1973–2017
Sooty Shearwater	2	Jul	1996, 2004
Manx Shearwater	4	May–Jun	1980–2011
Audubon's Shearwater	1	May	1977
White-faced Storm-Petrel	1	Aug	1976
Leach's Storm-Petrel*	3	Aug–Nov	1976–2012 (7)
Band-rumped Storm-Petrel	1	Aug	2011
White-tailed Tropicbird	1	Aug	2011
Wood Stork***	5	Jun–Jul	1949–1999
Magnificent Frigatebird* [1]	4	Jul–Sep	1979–2016
Brown Booby	1	May	2013
Anhinga	5	Apr/Jun/Aug–Sep	1996–2011
Brown Pelican	9+	Jun–Nov	1902–2012
White Ibis	11+	May–Sep/Dec–Jan	1980–2016
White-faced Ibis	15	Apr–May/Jul–Sep	1995–2017
Swallow-tailed Kite	9	Apr–Jun	1989–2016
White-tailed Kite	1	Aug–Oct	2010
Mississippi Kite*	7+	May–Sep	1995–2017
Zone-tailed Hawk	1	Sep	2015
Yellow Rail	5	Sep–Dec	2004–2013
Black Rail	6	May–Oct	1983–1997
Corn Crake	2	Oct	1887, 1943
Purple Gallinule*	7	Apr–Dec	1977–2015
Black-necked Stilt	7	May–Jun/Aug–Sep	2003–2013
Northern Lapwing	1	Nov	2010
Snowy Plover	1	Oct	2004

Species	Records	Month(s)	Year(s) of Occurrence
Wilson's Plover*	2	Apr–Jun/Sep	1989, 2007
Spotted Redshank	1	Nov	1969
Long-billed Curlew	2	Jul	1968, 1995
Black-tailed Godwit	1	Apr	2001
Bar-tailed Godwit	1	Apr	2001
Ruff	10	Mar–Aug	1976–2016 (3)
Sharp-tailed Sandpiper	3	May/Aug/Oct	1977–1999
Curlew Sandpiper	9	May–Oct	1965–2012
Red-necked Stint	3	Jul	2000 (2), 2006
Little Stint	1	Aug	2005
Red Phalarope	11	May/Jul–Nov	1981–2012
Pomarine Jaeger	4	May/Aug–Oct	1985–2015
Long-tailed Jaeger*	5	Aug–Sep	1979–2014
Dovekie*	5	Oct–Mar	1990–2012
Common Murre	8+	Dec–Feb	2011–2017
Thick-billed Murre	10+	Jan–Feb/May/Oct	1973–2015
Black Guillemot*	3	Dec–Apr	1980–2017
Atlantic Puffin***	3	Oct/Nov/Dec	1947–1968
Black-legged Kittiwake	15	Sep–Oct/Dec–Feb	2010–2016
Ivory Gull	1	Jan	1986
Sabine's Gull	2	Sep	1995, 2017
Ross's Gull	1	Apr	1984
Franklin's Gull	6	Jun/Aug–Nov	1971–2015
Mew Gull	8	Nov–Apr	1973–2016 (2)
California Gull	2	Mar/Sep	2016
"Thayer's" Gull	9	Dec–Feb/Apr	1988–2016
Slaty-backed Gull	2	Nov/Feb	2008, 2009
Sooty Tern*	4+	Apr/Jul	1996–2011
Bridled Tern*	2	Jun/Aug	1992, 2017
Gull-billed Tern	10	Jun/Oct	1985–2017
Arctic Tern	4	May/Jul–Aug	1977–2014
Sandwich Tern	7	Jul–Sep	1991–2012
Band-tailed Pigeon	2	Nov–Dec	1982, 1985

Species	Records	Month(s)	Year(s) of Occurrence
Eurasian Collared-Dove	3	May–Jun	2004, 2008,11
Common Ground-Dove	1	Oct	2007
White-winged Dove	10	May/Jul/Sep–Feb	1973–2016
Northern Hawk Owl***	5	Sep–Jan	Old Records
Burrowing Owl	3	May/Dec	1979,80, 2015
Great Gray Owl*	2	Jan–Mar	1996
Boreal Owl	2	Nov–Jan	1992, 1996
Chuck-will's-widow	7	Apr–Jun	1982–2012
Black-chinned Hummingbird	1	Oct–Nov	2013
Broad-billed Hummingbird	1	Aug	2008
Calliope Hummingbird	5	Oct–Jan	2006–2015
Black-backed Woodpecker*	12+	Sep–May	1956–61
Gyrfalcon	4	Dec–Apr	1988–2006
Pacific-Slope Flycatcher [2]	2	Dec	2007, 2015
Say's Phoebe	3	Oct–Dec	1916, 2012, 16
Ash-throated Flycatcher	6	Nov–Dec	1992–2016
Tropical Kingbird	1	Nov	1990
Gray Kingbird	2	Oct/Nov	1974, 1992
Scissor-tailed Flycatcher*	9	Apr–Jul/Oct–Nov	1983–2010
Fork-tailed Flycatcher	5	Jul–Aug/Oct–Dec	2000–2014
Loggerhead Shrike*	6	Mar–May/Sep–Oct	1986–2006
Bell's Vireo	2	Oct–Nov	1991, 2016
Eurasian Jackdaw	1	Mar	1988
Brown-chested Martin	1	Jul	2006
Boreal Chickadee*	6	Oct–Nov/Jan–Feb	1976–2001
Northern Wheatear*	20+	May/Sep–Oct	1990–2011
Mountain Bluebird	3	Dec–Feb	1994–95, 2010
Townsend's Solitaire	7	Nov–Mar	1983–2016
Fieldfare***	1	Apr	1887
Varied Thrush*	7	Sep/Nov/Jan–Mar	1986–2013
Sprague's Pipit	1	Oct	2016
Bohemian Waxwing	9+	Oct–Apr	1994–2008
Chestnut-collared Longspur	3	May–Jun/Aug	1968–2000

Species	Records	Month(s)	Year(s) of Occurrence
Smith's Longspur	4	Mar/May	1968–2015
MacGillivray's Warbler	2	Dec–Jan	2001, 2002
"Audubon's" Warbler*	3+	Nov	2012 (3–4)
Black-throated Gray Warbler*	8	May/Oct–Jan	1991–2016
Hermit Warbler	2	May/Dec–Jan	1977, 2016
Green-tailed Towhee	2	Feb/Apr	1983,199
Spotted Towhee	1	Dec–Feb	2005–2006
Lark Bunting	2	Oct/May	1978–2008
Henslow's Sparrow*	3	Apr–May/Sep–Dec	1991–2005
Le Conte's Sparrow	7	Oct–Dec/Apr	1987–88, 2012
Harris's Sparrow	3	Nov–Dec	1986–2007
Golden-crowned Sparrow	2	Oct/Dec	1991, 1998
Western Tanager*	15+	Oct–Apr	1984–2016
Black-headed Grosbeak*	4	Nov–Apr	1980–2016
Lazuli Bunting	1	Jan–Feb	2007
Painted Bunting	13	Mar–May/Sep–Jan	1982–2016
Western Meadowlark	1	Apr	2009
Brewer's Blackbird	3	Nov–Dec	1990–2002
Bullock's Oriole	6	Oct–May	1977–2013
Brambling	1	Jan–Mar	2000
Hoary Redpoll*	13+	Nov–Mar	1977–2013

[1] Includes records for Frigatebird species.

[2] Includes a record for "Western Flycatcher" (Pacific-slope or Cordilleran).

APPENDIX F

Birding Resources

■ The Connecticut Audubon Society Centers

The Connecticut Audubon Society State Headquarters
2325 Burr Street
Fairfield, CT 06824
203-259-6305
www.ctaudubon.org

The Connecticut Audubon Society Center at Fairfield
2325 Burr Street
Fairfield, CT 06824
203-259-6305, ext. 109
www.ctaudubon.org/visit/fairfield.htm
e-mail: fairfield@ctaudubon.org

The Connecticut Audubon Society Birdcraft Museum in Fairfield
314 Unquowa Road
Fairfield, CT 06824
203-259-0416
www.ctaudubon.org/visit/birdcraft.htm
e-mail: birdcraft@ctaudubon.org

The Connecticut Audubon Society Coastal Center at Milford Point
1 Milford Point Road
Milford, CT 06460
203-878-7440
www.ctaudubon.org/visit/milford.htm
e-mail: milford@ctaudubon.org

The Connecticut Audubon Society Center at Glastonbury
1361 Main Street
Glastonbury, CT 06033
860-633-8402
www.ctaudubon.org/visit/glastonbury.htm
e-mail: glastonbury@ctaudubon.org

The Connecticut Audubon Society Center at Pomfret

189 Pomfret Street
Pomfret Center, CT 06259
860-928-4948
www.ctaudubon.org/visit/pomfret.htm
e-mail: pomfret@ctaudubon.org

The Connecticut Audubon Society Center at Trail Wood

The Edwin Way Teale Memorial Sanctuary
93 Kenyon Road
Hampton, CT 06247
860-928-4948
www.ctaudubon.org/visit/trailwood.htm

National Audubon Society Centers

Audubon Center at Bent of the River

185 East Flat Hill Road
Southbury, CT 06488
203-264-5098
http://bentoftheriver.audubon.org
e-mail: bentoftheriver@audubon.org

Audubon Center of Greenwich

613 Riversville Road
Greenwich, CT 06831
203-869-5272
http://greenwich.audubon.org
e-mail: greenwich_center@audubon.org

Audubon Guilford Salt Meadows Sanctuary

330 Mulberry Point Road
Guilford, CT 06437
203-458-9981
http://www.audubon.org/local/sanctuary/guilford/index.html

Audubon Miles Wildlife Sanctuary

99 West Cornwall Road
Sharon, CT 06069
860-364-0048
http://ct.audubon.org/Centers_Sanctuaries.html

Sharon Audubon Center

325 Cornwall Bridge Road
Sharon, CT 06069

860-364-0520
http://sharon.audubon.org

■ National Audubon Society Local Chapters

Housatonic Audubon Society
P.O. Box 211
Sharon, CT 06069

Litchfield Hills Audubon Society
P.O. Box 861
Litchfield, CT 06759
www.lhasct.org
e-mail: webmaster@lhasct.org

Mattabeseck Audubon Society
27 Washington Street
Middletown, CT 06457
www.audubon-mas.org
e-mail: mattabeseck@mac.com

Menunkatuck Audubon Society
P.O. Box 214
Guilford, CT 06437
www.menunkatuck.org

Naugatuck Valley Audubon Society
P.O. Box 371
Derby, CT 06418
http://naugatuckvalleyaudubon.org

New Canaan Audubon Society
P.O. Box 241
New Canaan, CT 06840

Potapaug Audubon Society
P.O. Box 591
Old Lyme, CT 06371
www.potapaugaudubon.org
e-mail: potapaugaudubon@gmail.com

Quinnipiac Valley Audubon Society
Riverbound Farm
c/o 107 Green Road
Meriden, CT 06450

Birding Resources

■ Bird Clubs and Societies

Connecticut Ornithological Association (COA)
314 Unquowa Road
Fairfield, CT 06824
www.ctbirding.org (bird lists, photos, and rare records)
www.ctbirding.org/resources/ (useful links to Connecticut bird-related resources)
http://lists.ctbirding.org/mailman/listinfo/ctbirds_lists.ctbirding.org (online forum and listserv about bird sightings in Connecticut)

Hartford Audubon Society
P.O. Box 270207
West Hartford, CT 06127
860-282-BIRD (2473)
www.hartfordaudubon.org
e-mail: hartfordaudubon@yahoo.com

Natchaug Ornithological Society
P.O. Box 192
Mansfield Center, CT 06250
www.nosbird.org

New Haven Bird Club
P.O. Box 9004
New Haven, CT 06532
www.newhavenbirdclub.org
e-mail: ask-us@newhavenbirdclub.org

Western Connecticut Bird Club
44 Church Street
Woodbury, CT 06798
203-263-2502

■ Other Nature Organizations

Connecticut Butterfly Association
P.O. Box 9004
New Haven, CT 06532
www.ctbutterfly.org
e-mail: ask-us@ctbutterfly.org

Wyndham Land Trust
11 Town House Drive
Pomfret Center, CT 06259
www.wyndhamlandtrust.org
e-mail: info@wyndhamlandtrust.org

Naromi Land Trust
P.O. Box 265
Sherman, CT 06784
860-354-0260
e-mail: office@naromi.org

Land Trust Alliance
(for a full listing of Connecticut's numerous land trusts)
1660 L Street, NW, Suite 1100
Washington, DC 20036
202-638-4725
www.landtrustalliance.org
e-mail: info@lta.org

The Nature Conservancy, Connecticut Chapter
55 High Street
Middletown, CT 06457
860-344-0716
www.nature.org
e-mail: ct@tnc.org

Stewart B. McKinney National Wildlife Refuge
U.S. Fish and Wildlife Service
733 Old Clinton Road
Westbrook, CT 06498
860-399-2513
www.fws.gov/northeast/ct/sbm.htm
e-mail: R5RW_SBMNWR@fws.gov

■ Seal and Whale Strandings

Report sick or injured seals to park rangers, the Maritime Aquarium in Norwalk, or Mystic Aquarium in Mystic.

■ Rare Bird Alerts and Bird Forums

ABA.org
The American Birding Association's online resource for birders. See Birding News for rare bird alerts.

Daily Connecticut Rare Bird Report
To receive reports of rare and uncommon bird sightings, http://lists.ctbird-ing.org/mailman/listinfo/ctdailyreport_lists.ctbirding.org
To submit a sighting for inclusion in the report,
e-mail: CTBirdReport@ftml.net

COA Webpage and Avian Records Committee of Connecticut
http://www.ctbirding.org/ARCC.htm
To submit a report of a rare sighting,
e-mail: ctgregh@gmail.com or jaybrd49@aol.com

E-bird.org
The Cornell Lab of Ornithology's online global resource tool for birders.

■ Birding Tours

Connecticut Audubon Society EcoTravel Office
(includes eagle and swallow cruises)
35 Pratt Street, Suite 201
Essex, CT 06426
860-767-0660
For trip information and reservations: 800-996-8747
http://ecotravel.ctaudubon.org
e-mail: ecotravel@ctaudubon.org

RiverQuest
Connecticut River Expeditions
(eagle, swallow, and other bird cruises)
P.O. Box 496
Essex, CT 06426
860-662-0577
http://www.ctriverexpeditions.org
e-mail: captainmark@yuknat.com

Sunrise Birding
P.O. Box 274
Cos Cob, CT 06807
203-453-6724
www.sunrisebirding.com
e-mail: gina@sunrisebirding.com

■ Birding Stores

The Audubon Shop
907 Boston Post Road
Madison, CT 06443
203-245-9056 or 888-505-9056
www.theaudubonshop.com
e-mail: postmaster@theaudubonshop.com

The Fat Robin
3000 Whitney Ave
Hamden, CT 06518
203-248-7068 or 866-FAT-ROBIN (866-328-7624)
www.fatrobin.com
e-mail: e-mail@fatrobin.com

American Birding Association. http://www.aba.org.

American Birds: A Seasonal Journal of the Birds of the Americas. New York: National Audubon Society, 1970–1988.

American Ornithologists' Union Checklist Committee. *Checklist of North American Birds.* 6th ed. Lawrence, KS: American Ornithologist's Union, 1998.

———. "Fifty-seventh Supplement to the American Ornithologists' Union Checklist of North American Birds." *The Auk* 133 (2016): 544–560.

Askins, R. A. *Restoring North America's Birds: Lessons from Landscape Ecology.* 2nd ed. New Haven: Yale University Press, 2002.

Clark, G. A., Jr., *Birds of Storrs, Connecticut and Vicinity*, 3rd ed. Portland, CT: Nathaug Ornithological Society and Joshua's Tract Conservation and Historic Trust, 1999.

Connecticut Ornithological Association. http://www.ctbirding.org.

Connecticut Warbler: A Journal of Connecticut Ornithology 1–36 (1981–2016). Fairfield: The Connecticut Ornithological Association.

Cornell Lab of Ornithology and National Audubon Society. http://www.eBird.org.

Department of Environmental Protection. *The Atlas of Breeding Birds of Connecticut*, by L. R. Bevier. Bulletin 113. Hartford, CT: State Geological and Natural History Survey of Connecticut, 1994.

Department of Environmental Protection. *The Face of Connecticut: People, Geology, and the Land*, by M. C. Bell. Bulletin 110. Hartford, CT: State Geological and Natural History Survey of Connecticut, 1985.

Devine, B., and D. G. Smith. *Connecticut Birding Guide.* Dexter, MI: Thomson-Shore, Inc., 1996.

Fry, A. J. *Bird Walks in Rhode Island: Exploring the Ocean State's Best Sanctuaries.* Woodstock, VT: Backcountry Publications, 1992.

Kemper, J. *Birding Northern California.* A Falcon Guide. Guilford, CT: The Globe Pequot Press, 2001.

Lynch, P. J. *A Field Guide to Long Island Sound.* New Haven: Yale University Press, 2017.

Mackenzie, L. *The Birds of Guilford, Connecticut*. New Haven: Peabody Museum, Yale University, 1961.

Masterson, E. A. *Birdwatching in New Hampshire*. Hanover, NH: University Press of New England, 2013.

Merriam, C. H. "A Review of the Birds of Connecticut." Transactions of the Connecticut Academy 4 (1877). New Haven: The Connecticut Academy.

Petersen, W. R., and W. R. Meservey. *Massachusetts Breeding Bird Atlas*. Natural History of New England Series. Lincoln, MA: Massachusetts Audubon Society, 2003.

Pranty, B. *A Birder's Guide to Florida*. Colorado Springs: American Birding Association, 1996.

Proctor, N. S. *25 Birding Areas in Connecticut*. Chester, CT: Pequot Press, 1978.

Sage, J. H., L. B. Bishop, and W. P. Bliss. *The Birds of Connecticut*. Bulletin 20. Hartford, CT: State Geological and Natural History Survey, 1913.

Sibley, D. A. *The Sibley Guide to Birds*, 2nd ed. New York: Alfred A. Knopf, 2014.

Stejskal, D., and G. H. Rosenburg. *Finding Birds in Southeast Arizona*, 8th ed. Tucson: Tucson Audubon Society, 2011.

Viet, R. R., and W. R. Petersen. *Birds of Massachusetts*. Natural History of New England Series. Lincoln, MA: Massachusetts Audubon Society, 1993.

Yrizarry, John Cameron. *Observing Birds in the New Haven Region*. New Haven, CT: New Haven Bird Club, 1956.

Zeranski, J. D., and T. R. Baptist. *Connecticut Birds*. Hanover, NH: University Press of New England, 1990.

INDEX

Bird species

The bold page numbers refer to the species account.

INDEX

471

348, 362, 363, 365, 369, 371, 374, 378, 392, **424**, 445, 452
  Yellow-bellied 47, 67, 84, 141, 147, 150, 161, 166, 205, 234, 259, 288, 392, **424**, 445, 452
Frigatebird, Magnificent 9, 383, **409**, 449, 457
Fulmar, Northern 340, 382, **409**, 449, 457

G

Gadwall 12, 13, 34, 35, 41, 43, 47, 57, 60, 74, 76, 82, 86, 87, 88, 89, 93, 94, 95, 97, 146, 164, 169, 172, 173, 174, 178, 195, 197, 200, 205, 207, 212, 243, 261, 267, 275, 280, 310, 311, 314, 317, 319, 326, 347, 353, 371, 380, **405**, 446, 448
Gallinule (Moorhen), Common 84, 88, 99, 122, 141, 146, 148, 212, 280, 296, 300, 403, **413**, 444, 450
Gallinule, Purple 280, 385, **413**, 450, 457
Gannet, Northern 6, 19, 29, 33, 35, 45, 47, 50, 57, 72, 75, 79, 82, 84, 90, 93, 166, 183, 251, 257, 263, 264, 315, 316, 322, 324, 329, 331, 332, 333, 334, 339, 383, **409**, 446, 449
Gnatcatcher, Blue-gray 22, 27, 36, 47, 62, 65, 66, 67, 102, 116, 120, 135, 140, 153, 159, 199, 210, 217, 220, 234, 297, 303, 305, 341, 348, 350, 357, 360, 362, 365, 372, 376, 395, **428**, 453
Godwit
  Bar-tailed 387, **415**, 450, 458
  Black-tailed 167, 326, 387, **415**, 450, 458
  Hudsonian 50, 52, 89, 98, 166, 193, 259, 260, 346, 387, **415**, 450
  Marbled 52, 89, 166, 193, 248, 249, 387, **415**, 450
Goldeneye
  Barrow's 33, 35, 51, 53, 56, 79, 81, 151, 171, 183, 236, 251, 253, 269, 271, 272, 313, 381, **407**, 448
  Barrow's × Common 79
  Common 16, 19, 29, 33, 35, 47, 53, 60, 74, 81, 84, 90, 151, 166, 171, 176, 183, 188, 195, 213, 236, 251, 257, 263, 267, 269, 288, 308, 311, 313, 317, 322, 327, 329, 331, 332, 340, 341, 381, **407**, 446, 448
Golden-Plover, American 50, 61, 86, 89, 93, 166, 193, 240, 259, 262, 265, 282, 288, 290, 386, 403, **414**, 444, 450
Goldfinch, American 7, 12, 36, 41, 44, 47, 48, 52, 63, 84, 101, 119, 125, 131, 132, 135, 138, 140, 149, 161, 177, 199, 210, 214, 217, 223, 257, 267, 286, 295, 312, 325, 355, 401, **439**, 440, 444, 454
Goose
  Barnacle 6, 60, 70, 269, 273, 274, 299, 305, 350, 380, **404**, 448

Cackling 6, 50, 60, 70, 75, 205, 269, 273, 274, 299, 305, 348, 350, 380, **404**, 448
  Canada 6, 41, 43, 50, 58, 60, 70, 74, 75, 97, 137, 146, 151, 156, 199, 209, 210, 213, 217, 233, 269, 274, 293, 295, 308, 311, 322, 327, 350, 354, 371, 380, 403, **404**, 440, 441, 445, 448
  Greater White-fronted 6, 50, 60, 70, 153, 156, 269, 273, 274, 295, 299, 305, 344, 348, 350, 371, 380, 403, **404**, 448
  Greylag 6, 305, 306, 380, **404**, 448, 456
  Lesser Canada **404**
  Pink-footed 6, 14, 58, 269, 273, 274, 278, 299, 350, 380, **403**, 448, 456
  Ross's 6, 50, 56, 60, 75, 273, 274, 350, 380, **404**, 448, 456
  Snow 24, 25, 47, 50, 60, 70, 75, 151, 156, 212, 213, 233, 269, 274, 275, 295, 299, 305, 327, 328, 348, 350, 371, 380, **404**, 441, 448
Goshawk, Northern 7, 24, 25, 62, 64, 71, 102, 106, 114, 116, 121, 131, 135, 138, 140, 149, 150, 227, 234, 257, 262, 268, 308, 360, 361, 362, 385, **412**, 442, 450
Grackle
  Boat-tailed 1, 47, 51, 82, 86, 88, 90, 96, 164, 167, 235, 255, 257, 266, 400, **438**, 446, 454
  Common 4, 25, 34, 36, 38, 41, 47, 50, 54, 84, 101, 103, 135, 140, 146, 167, 188, 199, 210, 214, 219, 220, 233, 239, 257, 277, 286, 302, 358, 400, **438**, 440, 441, 443, 444, 445, 454
Grebe
  Eared 19, 51, 151, 236, 264, 327, 382, **409**, 449, 457
  Horned 3, 6, 12, 14, 16, 19, 29, 33, 35, 47, 54, 56, 74, 75, 76, 84, 141, 144, 151, 166, 178, 183, 188, 191, 197, 228, 236, 251, 257, 263, 315, 316, 322, 327, 329, 331, 332, 334, 339, 340, 341, 344, 382, **408**, 446, 449
  Pied-billed 12, 14, 42, 43, 74, 76, 88, 94, 95, 98, 114, 141, 144, 146, 148, 151, 174, 176, 184, 185, 200, 212, 257, 261, 280, 293, 296, 297, 308, 365, 382, **408**, 444, 445, 449
  Red-necked 3, 6, 12, 14, 16, 19, 29, 33, 35, 47, 51, 54, 56, 75, 76, 84, 141, 144, 151, 164, 183, 185, 191, 197, 236, 244, 251, 259, 264, 269, 271, 315, 316, 319, 322, 324, 327, 329, 331, 332, 334, 339, 340, 382, **408**, 446, 449
  Western 382, **409**, 449, 457
Grosbeak
  Black-headed 399, **436**, 454, 460

N

Nighthawk, Common 24, 25, 34, 42, 54, 63, 66, 103, 110, 141, 191, 199, 203, 212, 219, 222, 227, 232, 266, 275, 281, 293, 297, 301, 302, 355, 376, 391, **422**, 441, 451

Night-Heron
  Black-Crowned 12, 16, 29, 32, 36, 38, 44, 47, 51, 54, 60, 74, 80, 84, 85, 94, 95, 153, 156, 166, 170, 174, 176, 178, 181, 183, 185, 188, 199, 204, 207, 217, 221, 227, 228, 235, 240, 241, 245, 253, 257, 296, 317, 334, 339, 341, 384, **411**, 446, 447, 449
  Yellow-Crowned 32, 45, 51, 55, 57, 80, 82, 85, 86, 90, 94, 98, 164, 169, 170, 178, 181, 183, 185, 188, 235, 251, 253, 384, **411**, 446, 447, 449

Nuthatch
  Red-breasted 6, 22, 24, 37, 45, 63, 103, 111, 114, 120, 121, 127, 130, 132, 135, 140, 144, 145, 150, 174, 217, 227, 234, 237, 257, 263, 308, 360, 363, 365, 394, 403, **427**, 442, 452
  White-breasted 6, 7, 26, 36, 41, 44, 47, 50, 62, 64, 84, 120, 125, 131, 132, 135, 140, 144, 145, 185, 210, 214, 217, 227, 234, 257, 271, 312, 345, 348, 357, 360, 394, **427**, 440, 442, 453

O

Oriole
  Baltimore 12, 14, 16, 27, 28, 32, 36, 38, 39, 41, 44, 47, 50, 51, 52, 55, 61, 63, 65, 66, 67, 69, 71, 74, 84, 103, 106, 111, 116, 125, 135, 140, 143, 144, 145, 147, 149, 159, 161, 166, 167, 168, 174, 176, 182, 185, 188, 192, 199, 205, 206, 210, 214, 219, 220, 221, 225, 227, 228, 235, 237, 241, 245, 248, 257, 267, 278, 279, 285, 286, 290, 293, 296, 297, 301, 303, 305, 325, 355, 358, 360, 369, 400, **438**, 441, 443, 454
  Bullock's 400, **438**, 454, 460
  Orchard 12, 16, 18, 22, 27, 28, 29, 32, 36, 39, 40, 41, 44, 45, 51, 52, 55, 61, 69, 71, 72, 80, 82, 96, 98, 102, 106, 111, 112, 114, 140, 156, 159, 161, 164, 167, 168, 174, 176, 178, 182, 188, 214, 217, 225, 227, 238, 241, 245, 248, 251, 253, 257, 275, 278, 286, 293, 295, 296, 297, 322, 325, 341, 347, 365, 369, 371, 373, 376, 378, 400, **438**, 441, 454

Osprey 5, 12, 18, 24, 25, 34, 38, 42, 45, 54, 55, 58, 62, 72, 75, 77, 80, 82, 89, 102, 106, 125, 153, 166, 168, 170, 172, 174, 176, 178, 180, 183, 188, 190, 195, 199, 208, 217, 219, 228, 231, 238, 240, 241, 245, 247, 249, 253, 255, 257, 262, 286, 293, 297, 303, 305, 308, 315, 316, 317, 319, 320, 322, 324, 326, 328, 329, 331, 334, 339, 341, 343, 346, 347, 354, 355, 359, 376, 384, **411**, 446, 449

Ovenbird 22, 27, 63, 64, 66, 70, 102, 111, 116, 118, 121, 135, 140, 144, 145, 150, 159, 237, 285, 334, 341, 347, 350, 357, 360, 367, 376, 396, **430**, 442, 453

Owl
  Barn 32, 85, 235, 390, **421**, 441, 451
  Barred 22, 28, 62, 64, 65, 70, 80, 102, 114, 120, 127, 135, 138, 139, 140, 142, 159, 162, 235, 267, 286, 297, 301, 348, 356, 359, 360, 365, 372, 390, **421**, 423, 442, 443, 451
  Boreal 391, **421**, 451, 459
  Burrowing 18, 390, **421**, 451, 459
  Great Gray 390, **421**, 451, 459
  Great Horned 16, 22, 28, 36, 41, 47, 48, 80, 102, 114, 127, 135, 138, 140, 150, 153, 159, 183, 209, 217, 220, 235, 245, 249, 267, 275, 278, 286, 297, 301, 345, 348, 356, 359, 360, 365, 371, 390, **421**, 442, 451
  Long-eared 80, 178, 180, 181, 235, 365, 391, **421**, 442, 451
  Northern Hawk 390, **421**, 451, 459
  Northern Saw-whet 24, 27, 62, 114, 159, 267, 345, 356, 365, 391, **421**, 442, 445, 451
  Short-eared 25, 47, 84, 87, 90, 91, 93, 156, 158, 164, 168, 178, 180, 181, 195, 209, 259, 260, 288, 292, 320, 341, 345, 391, **421**, 441, 446, 451
  Snowy 7, 45, 61, 72, 79, 82, 87, 93, 164, 168, 169, 178, 180, 195, 209, 228, 253, 255, 257, 261, 320, 341, 353, 390, 403, **421**, 446, 451

Oystercatcher, American xiii, 16, 18, 29, 33, 45, 57, 74, 82, 95, 164, 172, 178, 181, 182, 188, 190, 228, 236, 251, 253, 254, 257, 264, 315, 320, 329, 331, 339, 340, 341, 344, 386, **414**, 446, 447, 450

P

Parakeet, Monk 2, 29, 35, 45, 50, 60, 61, 72, 77, 82, 95, 98, 164, 167, 169, 183, 188, 192, 195, 196, 199, 205, 208, 217, 251, 253, 392, **424**, 440, 452

Partridge, Gray 455

Parula, Northern 22, 36, 102, 113, 117, 150, 159, 163, 185, 221, 350, 357, 360, 367, 397, **432**, 444, 453

Swallow

Bank 25, 44, 63, 70, 82, 99, 100, 103, 111,
114, 122, 126, 140, 146, 153, 169, 174,
177, 178, 191, 206, 214, 222, 275, 279,
286, 290, 308, 341, 348, 365, 376, 394,
427, 443, 444, 452

Barn 12, 18, 25, 36, 41, 43, 47, 62, 74, 84, 99,
100, 102, 105, 112, 122, 123, 125, 135,
140, 143, 146, 153, 156, 158, 169, 177,
185, 186, 188, 191, 196, 199, 206, 210,
214, 216, 217, 220, 221, 227, 228, 241,
245, 257, 261, 279, 285, 286, 290, 297,
299, 317, 319, 334, 348, 354, 360, 363,
371, 374, 394, **427**, 441, 444, 452

Cave 5, 35, 54, 57, 74, 87, 90, 153, 161, 180,
191, 233, 237, 238, 239, 259, 261, 394,
427, 452

Cliff 25, 36, 44, 62, 70, 71, 87, 99, 100, 102,
105, 116, 146, 153, 156, 158, 169, 177,
191, 206, 214, 216, 275, 279, 290, 394,
427, 443, 444, 452

Northern Rough-Winged 12, 18, 22, 25, 36,
41, 43, 62, 72, 84, 87, 99, 100, 102, 105,
112, 116, 122, 140, 146, 153, 159, 169,
174, 176, 177, 178, 184, 185, 188, 196,
199, 203, 206, 210, 214, 216, 217, 221,
228, 237, 241, 245, 275, 279, 281, 286,
290, 297, 299, 303, 317, 319, 339, 348,
360, 363, 365, 376, 394, **426**, 443, 444,
445, 452

Tree 3, 5, 12, 18, 22, 25, 27, 28, 36, 39, 41,
43, 47, 55, 62, 66, 74, 84, 87, 99, 100, 102,
105, 106, 112, 122, 124, 125, 126, 135,
139, 140, 145, 146, 147, 148, 153, 156,
158, 168, 169, 171, 177, 185, 188, 191,
199, 206, 210, 214, 217, 220, 221, 227,
228, 237, 241, 245, 257, 261, 279, 286,
290, 297, 299, 300, 317, 319, 334, 348,
355, 358, 360, 370, 371, 374, 394, **426**,
444, 445, 446, 452

Swan

Mute 12, 16, 41, 43, 45, 72, 82, 88, 95, 96, 97,
140, 146, 151, 164, 169, 178, 183, 188, 195,
199, 210, 213, 217, 228, 241, 257, 261, 275,
280, 293, 295, 308, 317, 322, 329, 331, 339,
341, 380, **404**, 440, 445, 446, 448

Trumpeter 97, 195, 210, 212, 213, 380, **404**,
448, 456

Tundra 35, 97, 151, 195, 213, 261, 295, 313,
353, 380, **404**, 448

Swift, Chimney 25, 41, 62, 74, 84, 99, 100, 102,
105, 140, 156, 158, 174, 177, 183, 199, 210,
217, 221, 228, 241, 245, 269, 275, 281, 293,
297, 355, 391, **422**, 440, 451

T

Tanager

Scarlet 22, 28, 36, 40, 42, 62, 64, 66, 67, 70,
99, 101, 102, 108, 112, 116, 118, 120,
121, 124, 135, 139, 140, 145, 150, 153,
159, 162, 177, 185, 200, 212, 217, 223,
224, 225, 267, 334, 336, 341, 347, 350,
356, 357, 358, 360, 361, 367, 372, 374,
375, 376, 378, 399, 402, **436**, 442, 454

Summer 3, 38, 39, 40, 203, 227, 399, **436**,
443, 454

Western 399, **436**, 454, 460

Teal

Blue-winged 35, 41, 42, 43, 55, 72, 80, 87, 88,
97, 146, 148, 151, 166, 169, 170, 213, 243,
261, 275, 278, 280, 295, 296, 319, 341,
353, 365, 370, 371, 380, **405**, 445, 448

Cinnamon 380, **405**, 448, 456

Green-winged 27, 35, 38, 41, 43, 47, 57, 60,
72, 87, 88, 94, 97, 146, 151, 166, 169, 170,
172, 200, 207, 212, 213, 243, 250, 261,
278, 280, 295, 299, 305, 310, 311, 314,
317, 319, 326, 341, 353, 365, 370, 371,
376, 381, **406**, 446, 448

Green-winged ("Eurasian") 166, 169, **406**

Tern

Arctic 172, 190, 390, **420**, 451, 458

Black 81, 84, 97, 144, 151, 166, 172, 188, 194,
214, 340, 389, **420**, 451

Bridled 9, 389, **419**, 451, 458

Caspian 72, 81, 166, 172, 194, 251, 253, 262,
268, 389, **419**, 451

Common 14, 18, 29, 33, 47, 58, 72, 75, 77, 81,
82, 91, 164, 172, 178, 181, 188, 190, 192,
193, 194, 195, 196, 228, 241, 244, 245,
251, 253, 257, 264, 316, 320, 322, 325,
326, 329, 334, 339, 340, 341, 344, 353,
389, **420**, 445, 446, 447, 451

Forster's 72, 75, 84, 97, 151, 166, 172, 188,
194, 262, 267, 316, 327, 334, 340, 341,
344, 390, **420**, 451

Gull-billed 92, 172, 389, **419**, 451, 458

Least 18, 29, 45, 72, 75, 82, 85, 91, 164, 172,
178, 181, 183, 188, 190, 192, 193, 195,
196, 208, 228, 241, 244, 249, 251, 257,
264, 316, 320, 322, 325, 326, 329, 334,
339, 340, 341, 344, 346, 389, **419**, 420,
446, 451

Roseate 81, 84, 91, 166, 172, 188, 194, 251,
253, 257, 264, 322, 325, 326, 327, 329,
331, 339, 340, 389, **420**, 447, 451

Royal 166, 172, 194, 251, 253, 262, 268, 316,
390, **420**, 451

Sandwich 9, 92, 172, 190, 390, **420**, 451, 458

Sooty 9, 172, 389, **419**, 451, 458

199, 206, 210, 214, 216, 225, 286, 292, 296, 301, 302, 308, 311, 312, 332, 355, 365, 384, **411**, 440, 441, 449

W

Place names

Page numbers in bold refer to the start of a chapter
or a site within a chapter.

Garnet Books

Titles with asterisks (*) are also in the Driftless Connecticut Series

*Garnet Poems: An Anthology of Connecticut Poetry Since 1776**
Dennis Barone, editor

*The Connecticut Prison Association and the Search for Reformative Justice**
Gordon Bates

Food for the Dead: On the Trail of New England's Vampires
Michael E. Bell

*The Case of the Piglet's Paternity: Trials from the New Haven Colony, 1639–1663**
Jon C. Blue

Early Connecticut Silver, 1700–1840
Peter Bohan and Philip Hammerslough

The Connecticut River: A Photographic Journey through the Heart of New England
Al Braden

Tempest-Tossed: The Spirit of Isabella Beecher Hooker
Susan Campbell

*Connecticut's Fife & Drum Tradition**
James Clark

Sunken Garden Poetry, 1992–2011
Brad Davis, editor

*Rare Light: J. Alden Weir in Windham, Connecticut, 1882–1919**
Anne E. Dawson, editor

The Old Leather Man: Historical Accounts of a Connecticut and New York Legend
Dan W. DeLuca, editor

*Post Roads & Iron Horses: Transportation in Connecticut from Colonial Times to the Age of Steam**
Richard DeLuca

*The Log Books: Connecticut's Slave Trade and Human Memory**
Anne Farrow

*Birding in Connecticut**
Frank Gallo

Dr. Mel's Connecticut Climate Book
Dr. Mel Goldstein

Hidden in Plain Sight: A Deep Traveler Explores Connecticut
David K. Leff

Maple Sugaring: Keeping It Real in New England
David K. Leff

*Becoming Tom Thumb: Charles Stratton, P. T. Barnum, and the Dawn of American Celebrity**
Eric D. Lehman

*Homegrown Terror: Benedict Arnold and the Burning of New London**
Eric D. Lehman

*The Traprock Landscapes of New England**
Peter M. LeTourneau and Robert Pagini

Westover School: Giving Girls a Place of Their Own
Laurie Lisle

*Heroes for All Time: Connecticut's Civil War Soldiers Tell Their Stories**
Dione Longley and Buck Zaidel

*Along the Valley Line: A History of the Connecticut Valley Railroad**
Max R. Miller

*Crowbar Governor: The Life and Times of Morgan Gardner Bulkeley**
Kevin Murphy

Fly Fishing in Connecticut: A Guide for Beginners
Kevin Murphy

Water for Hartford: The Story of the Hartford Water Works and the Metropolitan District Commission
Kevin Murphy

African American Connecticut Explored
Elizabeth J. Normen, editor

Henry Austin: In Every Variety of Architectural Style
James F. O'Gorman

Breakfast at O'Rourke's: New Cuisine from a Classic American Diner
Brian O'Rourke

*Ella Grasso: Connecticut's Pioneering Governor**
Jon E. Purmont

*The British Raid on Essex: The Forgotten Battle of the War of 1812**
Jerry Roberts

Making Freedom: The Extraordinary Life of Venture Smith
Chandler B. Saint and George Krimsky

Welcome to Wesleyan: Campus Buildings
Leslie Starr

Barns of Connecticut
Markham Starr

*Gervase Wheeler: A British Architect in America, 1847–1860**
Renée Tribert and James F. O'Gorman

Connecticut in the American Civil War: Slavery, Sacrifice, and Survival
Matthew Warshauer

*Inside Connecticut and the Civil War: One State's Struggles**
Matthew Warshauer, editor

Prudence Crandall's Legacy: The Fight for Equality in the 1830s, Dred Scott, *and* Brown v. Board of Education*
Donald E. Williams Jr.

*Riverview Hospital for Children and Youth: A Culture of Promise**
Richard Wiseman

Stories in Stone: How Geology Influenced Connecticut History and Culture
Jelle Zeilinga de Boer

*New Haven's Sentinels: The Art and Science of East Rock and West Rock**
Jelle Zeilinga de Boer and John Wareham

About the Author

Frank Gallo is a leading expert on where to find birds in Connecticut. Through his birding tours, lectures, and classes he has inspired countless birders to discover and appreciate the region's rich bird life.

Frank leads tours for Sunrise Birding, an international bird tour company. He worked for the Connecticut Audubon Society from 2005 to 2017 as senior naturalist and director of the Connecticut Audubon Coastal Center at Milford Point. Previously, he served at the New Canaan Nature Center, and before that with the New Haven Parks Department. He is a past president of the New Haven Bird Club, a current member of the Connecticut Avian Rare Records Committee, and a federally licensed master bird bander.

He has led birding expeditions throughout North America and abroad, including New Zealand, South Africa, Central and South America, Trinidad and Tobago, and Spain.

Frank is the author of two highly successful children's nature books, *Bird Calls* and *Night Sounds*, and is a published freelance photographer. He holds a bachelor's degree in biology with a specialization in ornithology from Southern Connecticut State University.

About the Driftless Connecticut Series

The Driftless Connecticut Series is a publication award program established in 2010 to recognize excellent books with a Connecticut focus or written by a Connecticut author. To be eligible, the book must have a Connecticut topic or setting or an author must have been born in Connecticut or have been a legal resident of Connecticut for at least three years.

The Driftless Connecticut Series is funded by the Beatrice Fox Auerbach Foundation Fund at the Hartford Foundation for Public Giving. For more information and a complete list of books in the Driftless Connecticut Series, please visit us online at http://www.wesleyan.edu/wespress/driftless.

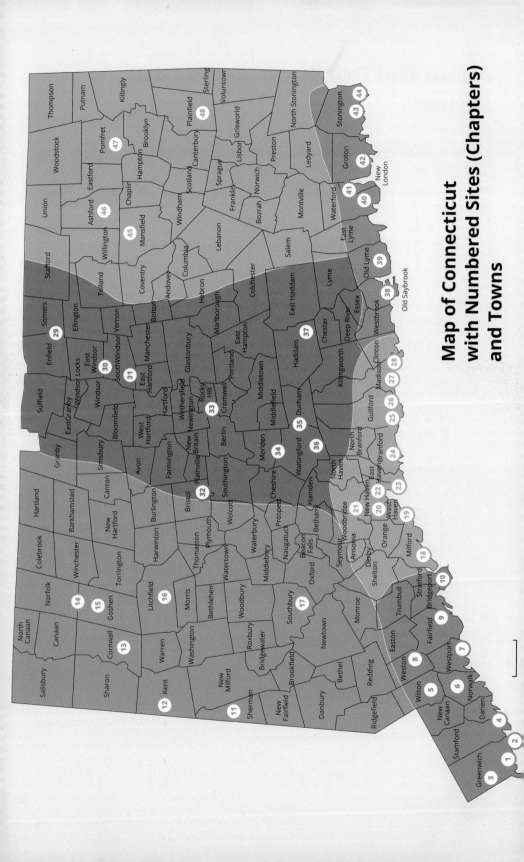

Map of Connecticut
with Numbered Sites (Chapters)
and Towns